OXFORD
UNIVERSITY PRESS

ASPIRE
SUCCEED
PROGRESS

Cambridge International AS & A Level

Complete Economics

Second Edition

Terry Cook
Clive Riches
Richard Taylor
Reema Shah
Chloe Tan

OXFORD
UNIVERSITY PRESS

OXFORD

UNIVERSITY PRESS

Great Clarendon Street, Oxford, OX2 6DP, United Kingdom

Oxford University Press is a department of the University of Oxford. It furthers the University's objective of excellence in research, scholarship, and education by publishing worldwide. Oxford is a registered trade mark of Oxford University Press in the UK and in certain other countries

First published in 2021

British Library Cataloguing in Publication Data
Data available

9781382023030

3 5 7 9 10 8 6 4

Paper used in the production of this book is a natural, recyclable product made from wood grown in sustainable forests. The manufacturing process conforms to the environmental regulations of the country of origin.

Printed in China by Shanghai Offset Printing Products Ltd

Acknowledgements

The publisher and authors would like to thank the following for permission to use photographs and other copyright material:

Cover: loveguli/Getty Images.

Photos: p10: David Warren/Alamy Stock Photo; **p13:** Andrii Yalanskyi/Shutterstock; p14(t): junrong/Shutterstock; p14(b): Bogdan VASILESCU/Shutterstock; p15(l): David M. Benett/Getty Images; p15(r): Bloomberg/Getty Images; **p16:** ESB Professional/Shutterstock; **p18:** Tayvay/Shutterstock; **p20:** Richard Thornton/Shutterstock; **p23:** Myroslava Bozhko/Shutterstock; **p24:** Anthony Asael/Art in All of Us/Getty Images; p25(t): c sa bum/Shutterstock; p25(b): RedTC/Shutterstock; **p29:** Hung Chung Chih/Shutterstock; **p31:** Joseph Sohm/Shutterstock; p32(t): Thomas Cockrem/Alamy Stock Photo; p32(b): Sappasit/Shutterstock; **p33:** Jeremy Horner/Alamy Stock Photo; **p65:** Owen Franken/Getty Images; **p66:** urosr/Shutterstock; **p70:** RHJPhtotoandilustration/Shutterstock; p71(l): Peter Burana/Shutterstock; p71(r): JUNG YEON-JE/AFP via Getty Images; **p75:** Worawee Meepian/Shutterstock; **p80:** Paul Prescott/Shutterstock; **p82:** Christopher Pillitz/Getty Images; **p83:** Suzuki Kaku/Alamy Stock Photo; **p90:** tenkl/Shutterstock; **p91:** Lakeview Images/Shutterstock; **p92:** XiXinXing/Shutterstock; **p132:** Classic Image/Alamy Stock Photo; **p142:** John Carnemolla/Corbis via Getty Images; **p153:** ER Productions Limited/Getty Images; p166(t): Simon Dack/Alamy Stock Photo; p166(b): paul kennedy/Alamy Stock Photo; p170(l): INTERFOTO/Alamy Stock Photo; p170(r): Kirill Neiezhmakov/Shutterstock; **p171:** CHIH YUAN Ronnie Wu/Alamy Stock Photo; **p175:** LADO/Shutterstock; **p177:** Dmitry Chulov/Shutterstock; **p179:** CPYstudio/Shutterstock; **p181:** Nick Poon/Shutterstock; **p183:** Joe Ravi/Shutterstock; **p191:** AliveGK/Shutterstock; **p206:** Degtyaryov Andrey/Shutterstock; **p210:** Fesus Robert/Shutterstock; **p211:** BOB STRONG/Staff/Getty Images; **p214:** FOTOGRIN/Shutterstock; **p218:** Owaki/Kulla/Getty Images; **p219:** nvxstudios/Shutterstock; **p221:** InnaFelker/Shutterstock; **p225:** Follow Focus/Shutterstock; **p234:** Kaspars Grinvalds/Shutterstock; **p236:** Makistock/Shutterstock; **p242:** mapman/Shutterstock; p244(l): littlewormy/Shutterstock; p244(r): Krunja/Shutterstock; p245(t): KishoreJ/Shutterstock; p245(b): Kevin Hellon/Shutterstock; p246(t): Claudio Divizia/Shutterstock; p246(b): DrPhee Jummy/Shutterstock; **p248:** Wirestock Creators/Shutterstock; **p249:** REUTERS/Alamy Stock Photo; **p250:** Mike Goldwater/Alamy Stock Photo; p252(t): Tea Talk/Shutterstock; p252(b): Peter Cook-VIEW/Alamy Stock Photo; **p254:** Eric Broder Van Dyke/Shutterstock; p258(t): Calin Stan/Shutterstock; p258(b): De Visu/Shutterstock; **p260:** XiXinXing/Shutterstock; p261(t): elina/Shutterstock; p261(b): robertharding/Alamy Stock Photo; **p278:** Jamie Lamor Thompson/Shutterstock; p287(tl): Pojana Jermsawat/Shutterstock; p287(bl): Sapsiwai/Shutterstock; p287(tr): Leonid Andronov/Shutterstock; p287(br): tcharts/Shutterstock; **p290:** Bettmann/Contributor/Getty Images; **p307:** Aman Ahmed Khan/Shutterstock; **p311:** Leonid Andronov/Shutterstock; **p313:** Robert Clay/Alamy Stock Photo; **p302:** Office for National Statistics. Contains public sector information licensed under the Open Government Licence v3.0; **p323:** Georgios Kollidas/Alamy Stock Photo; **p325:** Abaca Press/Alamy Stock Photo; **p326:** leungchopan/Shutterstock; **p337:** Dinodia Photos/Alamy Stock Photo; **p345:** Feifei Cui-Paoluzzo/Getty Images.

Artwork by Q2A Media Services Pvt. Ltd, Integra Software Services, and Oxford University Press.

The authors and publisher are grateful for permission to reprint extracts from the following copyright material:

p. 24 table based on data from/adapted from The World Factbook; p. 136 table based on data from/adapted from OECD (2021), Terms of trade (indicator). doi: 10.1787/7722246c-en (Accessed on 05/05/2021); p. 146 table based on data of Office for National Statistics. Contains public sector information licensed under the Open Government Licence v3.0; p. 302 figure based on data of Office for National Statistics. Contains public sector information licensed under the Open Government Licence v3.0; p. 330 table based on data of Office for National Statistics. Contains public sector information licensed under the Open Government Licence v3.0; p. 335 text based on data from/adapted from Exchange Rate Regimes in an Increasingly Integrated World Economy, June 2006. Reproduced with permission from International Monetary Fund; p. 340 table based on data from/adapted from http://hdr.undp.org/en/content/latest-human-development-index-ranking. ©United Nations; p. 341 table based on data from/adapted from Multidimensional Poverty Index 2020. ©United Nations; p. 341 text from Multidimensional Poverty Index, Case Study (Tamang Nepal). ©Oxford Poverty & Human Development Initiative (OPHI). Reproduced with permission of OPHI; p. 342 table based on data from/adapted from World Bank. Under CC BY-4.0; p. 343 table based on data from/adapted from https://data.worldbank.org/indicator/SP.DYN.IMRT.IN. Under CC BY-4.0; p. 344 table based on data from/adapted from https://databank.worldbank.org/indicator/NY.GDP.MKTP.KD.ZG/1ff4a498/Popular-Indicators. ©The World Bank Group; p. 344 Table based on data from/adapted from https://databank.worldbank.org/indicator/NY.GDP.MKTP.KD.ZG/1ff4a498/Popular-Indicators. Under CC BY-4.0; p. 346 text based on data from/adapted from Urban populace to increase to 38.2% by 2036 by Kumar Vikram, published in The New Indian Express; p. 346 table based on data from/adapted from The World Factbook; p. 347 table based on data from/adapted from https://data.worldbank.org/indicator/SL.AGR.EMPL.ZS. Under CC BY-4.0.

Every effort has been made to contact copyright holders of material reproduced in this book. Any omissions will be rectified in subsequent printings if notice is given to the publisher.

Contents

Introduction

What is Economics?

There are many different definitions of Economics, but one of the best known is by Lionel Robbins (1898–1994) who stated that "Economics is the science which studies human behaviour as a relationship between ends and scarce means which have alternative uses".

This definition stresses three important elements of the subject:

- First, it can be regarded as a science.
- Second, it is concerned with the concept of scarcity, both in terms of the possible consequences of scarcity and as ways in which it might be possible to try to deal with the problem of scarcity.
- Third, there are alternative ways in which scarce resources can be allocated, suggesting that choices will need to be made about how to utilise them in the most effective way.

The aims of the Cambridge 9708 syllabus

This book has been written specifically to meet the requirements of AS Level and A Level Economics for Cambridge. The Cambridge International AS and A Level syllabus has a number of distinct aims. These are to enable students to:

- know and understand the terminology, concepts, theories and principles of Economics
- express ideas in writing and using statistics and diagrams, or other methods, where appropriate
- develop the habit of using works of reference as sources of information specific to Economics
- read critically to gain information about the changes in the wider economic and social environment
- appreciate the methods of study that economists use, and the most effective ways economic information may be analysed, correlated, discussed, evaluated and presented
- develop an interest in, and enthusiasm for, Economics that could lead to further study.

The content of the Cambridge 9708 syllabus

The Cambridge syllabus is divided into six topic areas:

1 Basic economic ideas and resource allocation

2 The price system and the microeconomy

3 Government microeconomic intervention

4 The macroeconomy

5 Government macroeconomic intervention

6 International economic issues

Each of the eleven chapters in this book will focus on a particular curriculum topic area at either AS or A Level. Occasionally, A Level content is introduced in passing in AS Level chapters to help you contextualise the AS Level content you are learning. Remember that AS + A = A Level.

How to use this book

This book is designed to cover information in a clear way that is easy to access. Its features include:

- **Learning objectives** to help you identify the main topics you will be covering in each chapter.
- **Key terms** and their definitions, which are identified throughout the book and also feature in a glossary.
- **Case studies** which identify up-to-date examples of Economics from around the world. These also contain questions or activities to help you develop your understanding.
- **Getting it right** to help you identify common errors or misconceptions in examinations.
- **Progress questions** which help you to remember what you have been learning in each chapter.
- **Activities** which help you to look at the economic environment, often in your area or country. Many of these activities can be done individually, in pairs or in groups.
- **Links** to other chapters and content areas of the syllabus.
- **Key concepts** at the end of each chapter, which show how the key concepts from the syllabus are covered in each chapter (see key concepts section below).
- **Progress check** at the end of each chapter, to summarise what you should be able to do after completing the chapter.
- **Exam-style questions** to help you to reinforce what you have learnt in the chapter and to give you practice of the type of questions you can expect in an examination, although remember that there is no substitute for looking at questions from past papers.

The key concepts of the Cambridge 9708 syllabus

In addition to the six topic areas of the syllabus, there are also a number of key concepts. The seven key concepts are essential ideas, theories, principles or mental tools that will help you to develop a deeper overall understanding of the subject of Economics and make you better able to understand the links between the different topics in the syllabus.

The key concepts which run through the study of Economics are described below. These key concepts will be referred to throughout the course and can be used as helpful tools when considering both familiar and unfamiliar issues and contexts in Economics.

The key concepts of the Cambridge 9708 syllabus ▼

Key concept	Description
Scarcity and choice	The fundamental problem in Economics is that resources are scarce and wants are unlimited, so there is always a choice required between competing uses for the resources and an opportunity cost in making this choice.
The margin and decision-making	In economic theory, decision-making by consumers, firms and governments is based on choices at the margin, for example, firms will produce up to the point where the revenue generated by an extra unit of output is equal to the cost of producing it. However, economic decision-making can be based on facts, theory, effectiveness, priorities/objectives and values/ethical judgements.
Equilibrium and disequilibrium	Individual markets and the economy as a whole are always moving into and out of equilibrium, constantly altering the allocation of resources.
Time	Economic conditions change in different time periods, such as the short run and the long run. Individuals, firms, markets and governments are able to respond to these changes in different ways depending on the time frame. Some economic decisions have a time frame element, for example, trading off a cost in the present for a benefit in the future.
Efficiency and inefficiency	Individual markets and the economy as a whole can be both efficient and inefficient in different ways when using scarce resources.
The role of government and the issues of equality and equity	There is a trade-off between, on one side, freedom for firms and individuals in unregulated markets and, on the other side, greater social equality and equity through government regulation of individuals and markets.
Progress and development	Economics studies how societies can progress in measurable money terms and develop in a wider, more normative, sense regarding living standards, inclusivity and sustainability.

1 Basic economic ideas and resource allocation

In this chapter you will develop your knowledge and understanding of:

- scarcity, choice and opportunity cost
- economic methodology
- factors of production
- resource allocation in different economic systems
- production possibility curves
- classification of goods and services.

1.1 Scarcity, choice and opportunity cost

1.1.1 *The fundamental economic problem of scarcity*

The fundamental economic problem, which underlies all that is in this book, is that there are scarce resources to satisfy the unlimited needs and wants of people.

The resources are finite and yet the wants and needs of people are infinite. This is why scarcity is at the heart of Economics. Skilled labour could be regarded as a scarce resource; there may be some unemployment in all economies, but highly skilled labour is always scarce in terms of the potential demand for it. If there was not a condition of scarcity, there would be no need to consider the different ways in which resources could be allocated. This is one of the key concepts on the Economics course.

Getting it right

Do not confuse the existence of the economic problem, which underlies economics in all countries, with the existence of particular economic problems in specific countries, such as in relation to a high rate of inflation or a low rate of economic growth.

Key terms

Economic problem: the situation of the relative scarcity of resources in relation to the unlimited needs and wants of people.
Needs: the demand for something that is essential, such as food or shelter.
Wants: the demand for something that is less important than the demand for a need, such as a new car, and which is not necessarily achieved by a consumer.
Scarcity: a condition where there are insufficient resources to satisfy all the needs and wants of people.

Activity

Scarcity

Working in groups, discuss which economic resources or factors of production are particularly scarce in your own country or in your region of the world.

The existence of needs and wants has already been referred to, but it is very important to distinguish between these two terms. A need is something of vital importance that is demanded, such as a need for food, shelter or clothing. A want is something of less crucial importance that is demanded, such as a new television or a new car.

Key term

Choice: the need to make decisions about the possible alternative uses of scarce resources, given the existence of limited resources and unlimited needs and wants.

1.1.2 *The need to make choices at all levels*

As a result of the economic problem, and particularly the existence of the condition of scarcity, decisions need to be made about the allocation of these scarce resources, i.e. a choice will need to be made between alternative possible uses of the scarce resources.

Such choices will need to be made in relation to the variety of economic agents in an economy, such as:

- individuals
- firms
- governments.

Given the existence of limited resources and unlimited wants and needs, a choice is inevitable. This is why choice is one of the key concepts on the Economics course.

1.1.3 *The nature and definition of opportunity cost*

The concept of opportunity cost arises from the need to make choices that have already been referred to in section 1.1.2. It enables the true cost of any choice that has to be made to be assessed. Opportunity cost is defined as the next best alternative that is foregone as a result of making a choice, i.e. when a decision is taken to produce one product with a given combination of resources, it is very clear what other products *cannot* be produced with those scarce resources. The concept can apply to both production decisions and consumption decisions.

Link

Given the nature of the economic problem, the concept of opportunity cost can be related to many aspects of Economics. For example, it is an important element in the theory of comparative advantage, see Chapter 6, section 6.1.1.

Key term

Opportunity cost: the cost of something in relation to a foregone opportunity, i.e. it indicates the benefits that could have been obtained by choosing the next best alternative.

Activity

Your own opportunity cost

1. You have to think about what you are going to do in a two-hour period of time this evening. Decide what you are going to do in that time and then make a list of the other things you could have done in that time. Rank these in descending order of importance. The one that is at the top of the list of other possibilities is the opportunity cost of doing what you are going to do in the time, i.e. it is the *next best* alternative that you have decided to forego.
2. You have a certain amount of money that somebody has given you. Decide what you are going to do with that sum of money and then make a list of the other things that you could have bought with that money. Rank these in descending order of importance. The one that is at the top of the list of other things that you might have bought with the money is the opportunity cost of your decision to buy whatever you have decided to purchase, i.e. it is the *next best* alternative that you have decided to forego.

Case Study

Opportunity cost

Governments in every country in the world need to take important economic decisions in terms of how they allocate scarce resources. A government will have a certain amount of money to spend on a variety of different areas and these could include education, health care, police, defence and national security, transport and infrastructure.

All of these areas of economic activity need vast amounts of money to be spent on them, but a country will only be able to budget for a certain amount of money to finance public expenditure. A government will therefore need to take a number of difficult economic decisions, such as how much will be spent on health care and how much on education.

For example, the UK government has decided to spend a great deal of money (the cost has been estimated at over US$100 billion) on the building of a new, high-speed rail service, HS2, between London and Birmingham. This will then be continued on to Manchester and Leeds in the future. It is scheduled to be open in phases between 2028 and 2040. This will substantially reduce the journey time between these cities, but if money is spent on this project, there is an opportunity cost in that the money cannot be spent on something else.

1 Explain how the decisions faced by governments indicate the concept of opportunity cost.
2 Discuss the implications of the UK government deciding to spend money on a high-speed rail link between London, Birmingham, Manchester and Leeds on other possible areas of public expenditure.

Progress question

1 Explain what is meant by opportunity cost.

1.1.4 *The basic questions of resource allocation*

The key elements of the economic problem, scarcity and choice, have already been referred to in sections 1.1.1 and 1.1.2 of this chapter, and it is now necessary to focus on the three basic questions of resource allocation that need to be asked in every economy:

- **What goods to produce**: it is important to consider in every economy what is going to be produced and how much will be produced; there is therefore a process of selection involved in terms of what products will be produced in an economy.
- **How to produce the goods**: the production process involves the combination of four factors of production, land, labour, capital and enterprise (see section 1.3.1) and it is necessary to consider how these four factors will be coordinated to produce what is required in an economy, i.e. which methods of production will be used.
- **For whom to produce the goods**: the key feature of the economic problem is that it is impossible to satisfy all the wants and needs of all the people in a country in the same period of time; it is therefore necessary to consider who is going to receive what, i.e. decisions need to be taken in terms of priorities in the process of distribution.

The answers to these three basic questions determine how limited resources with alternative possible uses will be allocated in an economy with unlimited needs and wants to achieve certain objectives.

Link

Resource allocation in different economic systems is explained in section 1.4 of this chapter.

1.2 Economic methodology

1.2.1 *Economics as a social science*

The definition of Economics by Lionel Robbins, in the introduction of this book, refers to Economics as a science. This may appear a somewhat odd statement to make because economic behaviour clearly cannot be confined to a laboratory.

It is possible, however, to formulate laws of behaviour in Economics which can predict likely behaviour in given social situations and within certain parameters. Economics is social in that it studies different aspects of human behaviour and, in particular, the choices that humans need to make. For example, economists state that evidence from a demand schedule shows there is a law of demand that indicates the level of demand will go up when the price of a product is reduced and will go down when the price of a product is increased, i.e. the level of demand for a product is inversely related to its price. Economists do not state that this law will operate in *every* situation, but that it will operate in the vast majority of situations. It is for such reasons that it is possible to describe Economics as a social science. It is a science in the sense that it uses a number of theories and facts capable of making verifiable predictions and it is social in that it relates to the behaviour of human beings.

Link

The law of demand is covered in detail in Chapter 2, section 2.1.

Getting it right

Economics can be regarded as a social science because it uses scientific methods to establish theories that help to explain the behaviour patterns of individuals, groups and organisations in societies.

1.2.2 *Positive and normative statements*

Positive statements

A positive statement is one which is based on factual evidence, i.e. it will be objective rather than subjective. An emphasis on positive, rather than normative, statements reflects a broadly scientific approach to the study of Economics where facts can be discovered as a basis for producing theories of behaviour. This approach stresses the importance of the construction of appropriate models of behaviour in an attempt to predict future developments with a reasonable degree of accuracy.

Normative statements

In contrast to a positive statement that is based on factual evidence, a normative statement is one which involves making a value judgement, i.e. an opinion that is based upon a belief rather than on factual evidence. This is usually referred to as a normative statement because the person expressing the judgement has based it on particular norms or values, i.e. it will be subjective rather than objective.

Key terms

Positive statement: a statement that is based on factual evidence.

Normative statement: a statement that is based upon beliefs rather than factual evidence.

Value judgement: a judgement that is a reflection of particular values or beliefs.

Activity

Positive or normative?

Read the following statements and decide whether they are examples of positive or normative statements.

1. A government should intervene as much as possible in an economy.
2. A price index is used to measure the rate of inflation in a country.
3. A government ought to impose controls on all imports.
4. A national rail system ought to be controlled by the state.
5. Gross domestic product is the value of all that has been produced in an economy over a given period of time.
6. The external value of the country's currency should have been lowered last year.
7. More money should be spent on education than on health care.
8. Income tax is a direct tax.

Getting it right

Learners sometimes confuse normative and positive statements and the terms "subjective" and "objective". Make sure that you clearly understand the distinction between facts and value judgements and can demonstrate this.

1.2.3 *The meaning of the term "ceteris paribus"*

One of the problems in regarding Economics as a science is that it would in practice be difficult to isolate certain behaviour from other possible influences. For example, in the case of the law of demand already referred to in section 1.2.1, it may be the case that there is a close correlation between changes in the price of a product and changes in the level of demand for the product, but there may well be other possible influences on the level of demand for the product other than changes in its price, such as changes in the incomes of people, changes in the prices of other products or the impact of an advertising campaign.

Economists, in dealing with this problem, isolate other possible influences so that it is possible to derive the law of demand. This gives rise to the idea of *ceteris paribus*. This Latin phrase translates as "all other things being equal". This means that to make it possible to derive economic laws or models of behaviour, certain variables should be isolated so that the link between them can be identified without other factors impacting on the relationship.

It has already been stated that it would be impossible to study economic behaviour in a laboratory, but the existence of *ceteris paribus* enables such behaviour to be studied with an element of control, similar to what happens with scientific experiments in a laboratory.

Key terms

Ceteris paribus: literally "all other things being equal", i.e. the other factors which could influence a relationship between two variables are assumed to remain constant.

Economic law: an underlying principle in Economics that can be observed to operate on a regular basis.

Getting it right

The concept of *ceteris paribus* is extremely important in the study of Economics, especially in relation to the claim that it can adopt a scientific approach to study. Make sure that you fully grasp what the term means and that you can explain it.

Progress question

2 Can Economics be regarded as a science?

1.2.4 *The importance of the time period*

It is important to distinguish between three different time periods:

- The short run: this refers to a time period in which only some variables may change, i.e. some factors of production will be fixed and some will be variable.
- The long run: this refers to a period of time when all factors of production may change.
- The very long run: this is a time period when it is possible for supply to change as a result of technical progress. In the other two time periods, technical progress is said to be held constant.

Key terms

Short run: a period of time in which at least one factor of production is fixed in supply, and output can only be increased by using more of the variable factors.
Long run: a period of time when all factors are variable and output can be increased by using more of all factors.
Very long run: a period of time when technical progress is taking place, affecting the ability of firms to supply. In the other two time periods, the technical progress is held constant.

Progress question

3 Distinguish between the short run, the long run, and the very long run.

1.3 The factors of production

1.3.1 *The nature and definition of the factors of production*

It has already been stressed that economic resources are scarce in relation to the infinite needs and wants of people in an economy. It is now necessary to establish exactly what is meant by economic resources. Economic resources can be divided into four factors of production.

Key terms

Resources: the inputs used to produce goods and services.
Land: the factor of production that is concerned with the natural resources of an economy, such as farmland or mineral deposits.
Labour: the factor of production that is concerned with the workforce of an economy in terms of both the physical and mental effort involved in production.

Farming is an example of the factor of production, land ▲

Land

Land can also be referred to as the natural resources of an economy. It includes all that is on the surface of the earth, including forests, lakes and rivers. It also includes the mineral deposits of a country, such as coal or oil. It is sometimes referred to as the gifts of nature.

Labour

This factor refers to the labour force of an economy, including both the physical and mental aspects of work. It therefore includes not only physical output but also the skills, knowledge and abilities (sometimes referred to as the intellectual capital) of the workforce. This factor is sometimes referred to as human capital and the size of it in any economy will depend on such influences as population size, the working age (i.e. the difference between the age at which people in a country can leave education and the age at which they retire) and the level of education and training of the workforce. It is important to note that the term "labour" includes not only those who are actually working in an economy, but also the potential workforce.

Health workers are an example of the factor of production, labour ▲

Key term

Capital: the factor of production that relates to the human-made aids to production.

Getting it right

The term "capital", used in this sense as a factor of production, can often be confused with the capital or money that is used to purchase the aids to production. It is important that you understand this difference in meaning.

Capital

Capital can be referred to as the human-made aids to production, such as tools, machinery and equipment. It can also refer to buildings, such as factories. A distinction is sometimes made between fixed capital, such as machinery, and working capital, such as stocks of raw materials.

Capital can be used to refer to human-made aids to production and also to buildings ▲

Key terms

Enterprise: the factor of production that takes a risk in organising the other three factors of production.

Entrepreneur: the individual who takes the risk of organising the other three factors of production.

Enterprise

Enterprise refers to the role of the entrepreneur in combining, organising and coordinating the other three factors of production to enable production to take place and, in doing so, takes a risk. This element of risk-taking is fundamental to the factor and distinguishes the entrepreneur from other workers. Enterprise is responsible for organising the other factors of production to promote efficiency and an increase in output.

Two entrepreneurs: James Dyson and Lakshmi Mittal ▲

Activity

Entrepreneurs

Select an entrepreneur, preferably from your own country or region of the world, and research what he or she has achieved and the skills used. You can then give a presentation to the class on what you have discovered about this person.

1.3.2 *The difference between human capital and physical capital*

It is important to understand the difference between the following two forms of capital:

- Human capital: this refers to the human aspect of production, i.e. the talent, knowledge, abilities, training, education and skills of the labour force.
- Physical capital: this refers to the non-human resources used in the production of goods and services, e.g. the tools, equipment, plant, buildings and machinery.

Key terms

Human capital: the human aspect of production, including the talent, knowledge, abilities, training, education and skills of a labour force.

Physical capital: the non-human resources used in production, including tools, equipment, buildings and machinery.

1.3.3 *The rewards to the factors of production*

The nature and definition of the four factors of production have already been covered in section 1.3.1. It is now necessary to focus on the rewards to the different factors, as indicated below:

- **land:** the reward to land is rent
- **labour:** the reward to labour is wages and salaries
- **capital:** the reward to capital is interest
- **enterprise:** the reward to enterprise is profit

1.3.4 *Division of labour and specialisation*

Specialisation

Specialisation can apply to an individual person, a particular firm, a specific district or region or, at the national level, a whole country. It refers to the concentration on the provision of particular goods and services rather than other products. Specialisation allows, and indeed encourages, individuals, firms, regions or whole countries to concentrate on what they are best at producing; as a result of this specialisation, the production of such products will be increased.

Key term

Specialisation: the process by which individuals, firms, regions and whole economies concentrate on producing those products in which they have an advantage.

Activity

Specialisation

As an individual or in pairs, list as many examples of specialisation as you can in your own country. These can be by individuals, firms, districts, regions or the whole country.

Link

The concept of specialisation is very important in international trade, especially in relation to the concept of comparative advantage. See Chapter 6, section 6.1.1.

Key term

Division of labour: the process whereby workers specialise in, or concentrate on, particular tasks.

The division of labour

One particular form of specialisation is the application of the principle to the work of particular individuals. Division of labour is the specialisation of economic activity by product or process.

A famous example of this was included in the book *An Inquiry into the Nature and Causes of the Wealth of Nations*, by the Scottish economist Adam Smith (1723–1790) in 1776. In this book, he applied the principle of the division of labour to production in a factory.

Case Study

Adam Smith

Adam Smith applied the concept of the division of labour to the production of pins in a factory. He argued that the production of pins could be broken down into 18 specific operations. If each worker concentrated on just one of these operations, rather than attempting to work on every one of the operations, production would rise significantly. Smith calculated that each worker would be able to produce about 5,000 pins per day, a significant increase on the number that could be produced if each worker performed all 18 of the operations which he estimated might be only 20 pins a day.

In his book, *An Inquiry into the Nature and Causes of the Wealth of Nations*, Smith wrote: "The greatest improvement in the productive powers of labour, and the greater part of the skill, dexterity and judgement with which it is anywhere directed, or applied, seem to have been the effects of the division of labour".

He went on: "One man draws out the wire, another straights it, a third cuts it, a fourth points it, a fifth grinds it at the top for receiving the head; to make the head requires two or three distinct operations; to put it on, is a peculiar business, to whiten the pins is another; it is even a trade by itself to put them into the paper".

1 Find out about a firm in your country that uses a production system based on the principle of division of labour.

The advantages and disadvantages of division of labour

It has already been stated that one advantage of division of labour is that it enables production or output to be increased. It does, however, have a number of potential disadvantages. Table 1.1 indicates some of the various advantages and disadvantages of the division of labour.

Table 1.1 The advantages and disadvantages of the division of labour

Advantages of the division of labour	Disadvantages of the division of labour
Saving of time: it can take a lot of time moving from one task to another in the production process. Division of labour helps to reduce this wastage of time and so can contribute to a reduction in costs.	**Dependency on others:** specialisation, through the division of labour, means that the process of production is divided into separate tasks, but there is a potential danger of one group of workers being held back by another group at a different part of the production process.
Application of technology is made easier: division of labour involves workers becoming specialists in particular tasks and this will make it easier to apply technology, such as machinery, to specific tasks.	**Dependency on technology:** although technology can be used to support workers, and enhance their skills, there is always the danger that the technology takes over and this may cause workers to become disaffected.
Increase in skill: division of labour enables workers to concentrate on particular tasks and this will enable the worker to become very skilled in these specific tasks. Repeated practice in the task will enhance efficiency and by concentrating on what they do best, workers will become highly motivated.	**Frustration, boredom and alienation:** by its very nature, division of labour involves workers in repetitive tasks and this may lead to a reduction in levels of motivation (some firms get round this by giving workers some degree of variety in what they do rather than getting them to do the same thing every day). If levels of motivation are reduced, this is likely to have a negative effect on the productivity of a worker.
Increased productivity: division of labour enables workers to specialise in particular tasks and, as a consequence, productivity, or the output per worker per time period, is likely to increase. If output is increased, this will lead to an improvement in the standards of living of economies.	**Over-concentration on particular skills:** division of labour is based on the idea that workers concentrate on using particular skills, but there is a danger that this focus on certain skills could be at the expense of other useful skills that are not being encouraged.
The potential to earn higher earnings: an individual worker who is highly skilled and well motivated is in a better position to try to secure higher earnings (this will, of course, depend on a number of other factors, such as the profitability of the firm).	**Unemployment:** specialisation, through division of labour, is useful as long as there is a demand for the particular skills of workers, but there is a danger that if the demand for such skills decreases, some workers may find themselves unemployed. This would be less of a problem if the workers soon found alternative employment (this would be frictional unemployment), but if the demand for such skills applies to a whole industry, it may be very difficult for the workers to find alternative employment (this would be structural unemployment).

Getting it right

There are both advantages and disadvantages of the division of labour and you should be prepared to answer a question on the topic from both points of view. It would also be helpful to consider the advantages and disadvantages from the perspective of the worker, the firm and the national economy.

Link

See Chapter 4, section 4.5.3 on the different types of unemployment.

Progress question

4 Discuss the advantages and disadvantages of division of labour to (a) an individual worker, (b) an individual firm and (c) the whole economy.

1.3.5 *The role of the entrepreneur in contemporary economies*

Enterprise plays a very significant role in a modern economy. It has already been pointed out in section 1.3.1 that there are two aspects of the entrepreneur's role in contemporary economies:

- the organisation of the other factors of production of land, labour and capital
- the risk taking that arises from the situation of uncertainty that will be associated with any initiative that they take

Case Study

The entrepreneur

Lakshmi Matel is an Indian entrepreneur who founded the Mittal Steel company in India. This is now part of Arcelor Mittal, a multinational company established in 2006. The company has steadily expanded and it now produces in 18 countries worldwide. It has become a truly global steel company and produces about 10 per cent of the world's steel. It is by far the world's largest steel company, employing 191,000 workers in 2020.

Mittal is the chief executive officer of the company and owns about 40 per cent of the shares in the company. He is regularly included in the list of the richest 100 people in the world.

He opened his first steel plant in India in 1976 at the age of 26. He was awarded the Entrepreneur of the Year Award by the *Wall Street Journal* in 2004, and in 2008 he received a Lifetime Achievement Award from *Forbes* magazine.

1 Discuss the role of Lakshmi Mittal in starting and expanding this business.

Table 1.2 indicates the extent of entrepreneurial activity in ten countries. It shows the percentage of the adult population in each country who have started a new business.

Table 1.2 Top ten countries for entrepreneurial activity in 2020 ▼

Country	Percentage
Nigeria	39.9
Zambia	39.9
Senegal	38.6
Namibia	33.3
Ecuador	32.7
Uganda	30.4
Cameroon	30.1
Botswana	29.0
Burkina Faso	28.3
Angola	28.2

Case Study

Entrepreneurship in Nigeria

Entrepreneurial activities are relatively strong in Nigeria. There are non-profit organisations, such as the Fate Foundation, that are dedicated to the promotion of entrepreneurship. The Fate Foundation was established in 2000 to harness the strong entrepreneurial culture of Nigerians and to provide the knowledge and support required to fully explore their innovative potential.

In particular, there has been a recognition of the critical role of technology and there have been many start-up internet cafés. The majority of entrepreneurs are operating in Lagos, the former capital of the country. Entrepreneurial activity has played an important role in the economy of Nigeria, with SMEs (small and medium-sized enterprises) accounting for 48 per cent of GDP and providing 84 per cent of employment.

1 Discuss the contribution that entrepreneurs can make to an economy, such as that of Nigeria.

> **Activity**
>
> **Contributing to economic development**
>
> Research an entrepreneur in your own country and explain how this person has contributed to the economic development of your country. You can use the same entrepreneur that you used in the previous activity or choose a different one.

1.4 Resource allocation in different economic systems

1.4.1 and 1.4.2 *Decision-making and resource allocation in market, planned and mixed economies*

The three basic questions of resource allocation (what to produce, how to produce and for whom to produce) have already been covered in section 1.1.4. They can be answered in different ways, depending on the type of economic system in existence in a country. There are three main types of economic system in existence in the world and they each use different allocative mechanisms to decide on how the scarce resources should be used:

- market economies
- planned economies
- mixed economies

> **Key terms**
>
> **Economic system**: the way in which a particular country attempts to answer the basic economic problem.
>
> **Allocative mechanism**: the method by which scarce economic resources are allocated between alternative uses.

Decision-making and resource allocation in market economies

This type of economic system (also known as a free enterprise economy) is characterised by a very low level of state or government intervention in the economy. In theory, there will be no state intervention and everything will be controlled by the private sector. However, in reality, there are no countries in the world without some form of state intervention. The USA is sometimes regarded as a good example of a market economy, but even in that country the government will intervene in a number of ways. For example, the rail system Amtrak is state-owned.

> **Key terms**
>
> **Market**: a means of bringing together buyers and sellers to exchange products. A market can exist in a physical sense, but it can also be used to refer to an exchange of goods and services through the internet or by telephone.
>
> **Market economy**: also known as a market system, this is the type of economic system where decisions about the allocation of resources are taken in the private sector by producers and consumers.

Case Study

Amtrak

In many economies, there has been a move away from passenger rail transport being organised in the public sector towards a greater role for the private sector, a process generally known as privatisation.

In the USA, however, there has been an opposite trend. Rail passenger transport had generally been provided by private sector firms, but by the 1960s these firms found themselves in severe financial difficulties. In 1970, the Rail Passenger Service Act was passed and on 1 May 1971 the intercity rail operator Amtrak came into existence (the name Amtrak comes from the words "America" and "track").

Today, it employs more than 20,000 people and operates more than 300 medium and long distance passenger trains daily on 44 routes on 21,400 miles of track connecting more than 500 destinations in 46 US states and three Canadian provinces. In 2019, it had 31.7 million passengers.

1 Discuss the advantages and disadvantages of a national government operating a rail passenger service.

In market economies:

- decisions are made by individual sellers and buyers who can generally be expected to act in their own self-interest
- the producers' main aim is to maximise their profits
- the consumers' main aim is to maximise their satisfaction or utility, giving rise to the idea of consumer sovereignty
- the allocation of resources is determined by the market forces of demand and supply through what Adam Smith termed the "invisible hand" of the price mechanism
- there is no, or certainly very little, state or government intervention.

Key term

Price mechanism: the process by which changes in price (resulting from changes in demand and/or supply) bring about changes in the allocation of resources in a market economy.

Table 1.3 shows the advantages and disadvantages of this type of economic system.

Table 1.3 The advantages and disadvantages of market economies ▼

Advantages of market economies	Disadvantages of market economies
Resources are allocated through market forces and the operation of the price mechanism; there is therefore no need for state or government intervention in the economy, and the state can then concentrate on areas such as international diplomacy.	Some goods, called public goods, would not be provided in a market economy. Examples of these would include the provision of police and defence forces.
In a market economy, the key objective of producers is profit maximisation and the profit motive can give an incentive to sellers; they will be encouraged to be more innovative and cost-effective than might otherwise have been the case.	Some goods, called merit goods, would be under-produced and under-consumed in a market economy. Examples of these would include the provision of education and heath services.
If firms can be more cost-effective in such an economy, this should lead to lower prices for consumers. Consumers would also be likely to benefit from more choice.	Some goods, called demerit goods, would be over-produced and over-consumed in a market economy. Examples of these would include the production and consumption of alcohol (in some countries) and tobacco.
The market economy, based on the idea of free enterprise, will maximise both producer surplus and consumer surplus.	There could be negative externalities in a market economy. Examples of these would include noise and visual pollution.

Link

Public, merit and demerit goods are explained more fully in section 1.6 of this chapter. Externalities will be explained more fully in Chapter 7, section 7.4.

Decision-making and resource allocation in planned economies

This type of economic system is characterised by a very high level of state or government intervention in the economy. In theory, there will be no private sector involvement and everything will be controlled by the public sector. However, in reality there are no countries in the world without some form of private sector involvement. North Korea is sometimes regarded as the country that comes nearest to this type of economic system.

In planned economies:

- economic decisions are primarily made by the state or government through some form of central planning agency, rather than through the operation of market forces
- the state or government will own all, or certainly most, of the economic resources
- the prices are generally determined by the state rather than the price mechanism
- the key aim of production is the maximisation of social welfare rather than profit.

Key term

Planned economy: the type of economic system, also known as a command economy, where decisions about the allocation of resources are taken by the state or by government agencies.

Table 1.4 shows the advantages and disadvantages of this type of economic system.

Table 1.4 The advantages and disadvantages of planned or command economies ▼

Advantages of planned economies	Disadvantages of planned economies
The state or government controls all, or at least most, of the economic resources and so economic decisions can be taken in the interests of the whole society. For example, it might be the policy of such a government to bring about a more equitable distribution of income and wealth in the society.	The economic system tends to be very bureaucratic because the government intervenes in so many areas. This can contribute to the system being very inflexible and unresponsive to changes in consumer demand.
The state or government can decide which goods are going to be produced and to whom they are going to be supplied. For example, it could decide to ban the production of products which it believes are against the public interest.	There is less of an incentive for firms to be innovative. The profit motive is not as important as in a market economy and, as a result, the variety of goods on offer is often rather restricted and sometimes the products are of poor quality.
Prices are more likely to be kept under control and there is likely to be a lower rate of unemployment than in a market economy.	The majority of firms will be state owned and the lack of competition means that there is often a high level of inefficiency and a low level of productivity.

Key term

Mixed economy: the type of economic system where decisions about the allocation of resources are taken in both the private sector and the public sector.

Getting it right

Mixed economies are not static, i.e. the extent of the mixture changes over the years. Sometimes there is a trend towards more state intervention and sometimes a trend in the other direction. In 2008–2009, a number of financial institutions in different countries experienced difficulties and many of these were supported by the governments of such countries, indicating a trend towards more state intervention in the economy. The total amount spent by governments in various countries to support financial institutions in difficulties and to prevent a "global financial meltdown" was US$1.6 trillion.

Decision-making and resource allocation in mixed economies

It should be clear that while both market and planned economies have a number of advantages, they also have considerable disadvantages. It is for this reason that the majority of economic systems in the world today are mixed economies, i.e. they combine elements of both a market economy and a planned economy. Both the private sector and the public sector are involved in the taking of economic decisions. The broad idea is that such an economy will maximise the advantages of both market and planned economies and minimise the disadvantages.

In mixed economies:

- ownership of the economy's resources is divided between the public sector and the private sector
- the private sector will be influenced by self-interest, with producers aiming to maximise profits and consumers aiming to maximise their welfare, whereas the public sector will have broader, community aims relating to the public interest
- there will (possibly) be competition within the private sector, whereas the public sector will intervene through such measures as taxation and regulation
- the allocation of resources in the private sector will be determined through the price mechanism, whereas in the public sector decisions will be taken by the government, with prices either free at the point of use or in the form of certain charges.

Progress question

5 To what extent do you think that a government should intervene if a firm in its country was facing financial difficulties and needed state support to avoid collapsing?

Case Study

Mauritius

Mauritius is a relatively small island in the Indian Ocean with a population of 1.3 million people. Many important economic decisions are taken by both producers and consumers and in many ways it can be seen as an example of a market economy.

The government of Mauritius, however, has been prepared to intervene in the economy. For example, it has developed a strategy to encourage the economic development of the country. Sugar cane is grown on about 90 per cent of the cultivated land area, accounting for 15 per cent of export earnings, and the government has provided financial support to increase the area of fertile soil for growing the cane.

Another example of intervention is the decision of the government to put a maximum limit on water use at certain times of the year when there is a water shortage.

1 Research your own country and find out the extent to which the government intervenes in the economy.

Issues of transition when central planning in an economy is reduced

In a number of countries, there has been a move away from planned economies towards economies with a greater role for the market. This has particularly been the case in the former communist countries of Eastern Europe and it has also been a feature of economic developments in the People's Republic of China. The World Bank, an international organisation which aims to support developing economies, has encouraged such economic changes.

Key term

Transitional economy: an economy that is in the process of changing from a planned economy to more of a mixed economy where market forces have greater importance.

A transitional economy is one which is in the process of changing from a planned economy towards a more market-focused economy, but there have been problems associated with this process of transition. These are shown in Table 1.5.

Table 1.5 The issues of transition

Inflation	Planned economies tended to keep prices relatively low, but when the economy allowed a greater role for market forces, the state could no longer control prices in the way that it previously did. One possible effect of this is that the rate of inflation in a transitional economy could be higher than that experienced in a planned economy, although of course it is possible that the general level of prices in such an economy could fall, a situation known as deflation. Either way, a government will have less control than used to be the case in a planned economy.
Industrial unrest	Trade unions had largely limited powers in a planned economy, but once state control was reduced, the trade unions demanded wage rises to match the increases in prices and these demands were backed up by strike action. There is therefore the possibility of more working days being lost in a transitional economy than in a planned economy as a result of this industrial action.
International trade	The various planned economies had been in a trading bloc, but as they moved towards market economies they needed to establish new trading relationships with other countries. Transitional economies have a greater degree of freedom in terms of which countries they trade with, but this could possibly cause problems, such as an imbalance between exports and imports, leading to a deficit in the current account of the balance of payments.
Employment	In many of the former planned economies, there have been changes in the employment structure, such as a move from the secondary to the tertiary sector. Many workers were unable to move from one form of employment to another and so the rate of unemployment in many of the countries increased significantly, leading to a fall in incomes. The rate of unemployment in planned economies tended to be very low, but the rate is likely to be much higher in a transitional economy.

Continued . . .

Output	When the economies had a great deal of state intervention, many firms were supported by the government, but when a greater degree of market forces were introduced, a number of these firms were unable to survive. There was therefore a consequent fall in output. The level of output in a transitional economy will depend on the demand for the various products and so it is quite possible that a number of firms will fail to survive.
Reduction in welfare services	The planned economies had generally had a good level of welfare provision, such as in education, housing and health care, but as the economies moved towards a larger role for the market, some groups of people found that there was a fall in the quality of their standard of living.
Markets	When these countries had planned economies, the vast majority of decisions were taken by the state. Once the role of the state was reduced, and greater market forces introduced, it was recognised that specialised markets and services needed to be significantly improved, such as in banking and legal services. In many of the transitional economies, the quality of banking and legal services is still relatively poor.

Case Study

Change in Eastern Europe and China

In Russia and eastern Europe, at the end of the 1980s and the beginning of the 1990s, communism collapsed and the economic systems have gone through a process of transition away from a planned economy towards more of a market economy. There was less state intervention and control and more economic decisions were taken by producers and consumers. In some of these countries, such as Poland and Hungary, the move towards a greater role for market forces has led to greater efficiency and there have been significant increases in income and output. In other countries, however, such as Bulgaria and Ukraine, the process of transition has been more painful; the rate of unemployment, for example, is now significantly higher than it was at the end of the 1980s.

China has also experienced significant change since the late 1990s. It remains a communist country, in which the state still plays an important role, but there has been a process of transition allowing market forces to have a greater influence on economic decisions. The annual rate of economic growth has averaged 9.3 per cent in the period between 1989 and 2019.

Entrepreneurs have been encouraged to set up businesses and there has been much investment in the economy, both from Chinese and foreign investors. The high rate of economic growth, however, has been associated with environmental concerns and there has also been a worry that the high rate of growth could lead to increases in the rate of inflation.

China overtook Japan in 2011 as the world's second largest economy by Gross Domestic Product (US$bn). The GDP figures for the world's ten biggest economies today are given below:

1	United States	$18,037
2	China	$11,226
3	Japan	$ 4,382
4	Germany	$ 3,365
5	United Kingdom	$ 2,836
6	France	$ 2,420
7	India	$ 2,088
8	Italy	$ 1,826
9	Brazil	$ 1,801
10	Canada	$ 1,553

Source: *The Economist*

1 Discuss the possible advantages and disadvantages of an economy moving away from a planned structure towards more of a market economy.

Key term

Production possibility curve: a curve that joins together the different combinations of products that can be produced in an economy over a particular period of time given the existing resources and level of technology available. It can also be called a production possibility frontier or a production possibility boundary.

1.5 Production possibility curves

1.5.1 *The nature and meaning of a production possibility curve (PPC)*

A production possibility curve (PPC) (it can also be called a production possibility frontier or a production possibility boundary) can be used to illustrate the idea of choice and the concept of opportunity cost. A PPC shows the maximum possible output or production that can be achieved in an economy given the use of a particular combination of resources and technology in a given time period.

Getting it right

You may be asked in a multiple-choice question to indicate that you understand the output that must be given up of one type of product, as a result of increasing the output of another.

If an economy is operating on its PPC, in order to increase the output of one type of product, it will be necessary to reduce the output of the other. The two axes of the diagram can be labelled as two different types of product and then a decision to move from one point on the PPC to another can be shown in terms of the changes in output of the two products.

Figure 1.1 shows the opportunity cost of moving from one point on a PPC to another.

Getting it right

Make sure that you do not label the axes Price and Quantity. They need to be labelled in terms of two different types of product, such as agricultural output and industrial output or consumer goods and capital goods.

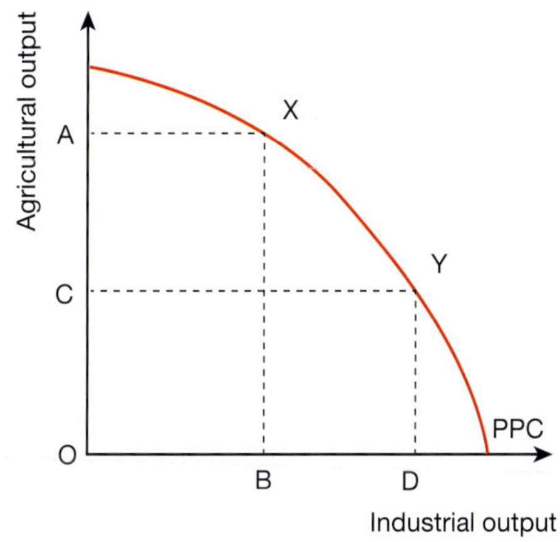

Figure 1.1 Opportunity cost and the production possibility curve ▲

An example of agricultural output ▲

An example of industrial output ▲

At point X, the economy is producing a combination of OA (in a graph, an O, or a zero, indicates the origin) agricultural output and OB industrial output. If there is a movement down the PPC from point X to point Y, the new combination of production would be OC agricultural output and OD industrial output. In other words, as a result of this movement along the PPC, there has been a reduction of agricultural output by AC and an increase of industrial output by BD. This clearly shows that the opportunity cost of the decision to increase industrial output by BD is a loss in agricultural output of AC. The diagram therefore shows what the next best alternative would have been.

Link

The production possibility curve (PPC) is a very useful concept in the analysis of productive efficiency, see Chapter 7 section 7.3.

The production possibility curve: microeconomics and macroeconomics

A production possibility curve can be used in relation to both microeconomics and macroeconomics.

- **Microeconomics**: microeconomics is the study of particular elements in an economy, such as the decisions of particular firms or individuals. It therefore focuses on the study of behaviour and decision making in relatively small economic units, such as individual consumers or particular firms. The essence of microeconomics is the study of individual markets within an economy. For example, within microeconomics, a PPC can be used to indicate the concept of opportunity cost or productive efficiency in a particular firm.
- **Macroeconomics**: macroeconomics is the study of elements that affect a whole economy, such as the rate of inflation, the level of unemployment, the rate of economic growth or the composition of a country's balance of payments. These areas of concern go beyond particular firms or individuals to the national, and indeed the international, economy. For example, within macroeconomics, a PPC can be used to show the extent of unemployment or the existence of economic growth in an economy.

Key terms

Microeconomics: that part of the subject of Economics that is concerned with the decisions of particular firms or individuals.

Macroeconomics: that part of the subject of Economics that is concerned with the whole economy.

Link

Unemployment is discussed in Chapter 4, section 4.5 and Chapter 9, section 9.3.

1.5.2 The shape of the PPC: constant and increasing opportunity costs

As has already been indicated, a PPC shows the maximum combination of goods and services which can be produced in a particular time period given the existing resources and level of technology.

It might be thought that it could be drawn as a straight line, rather than as a curve, but this would only be the case if there were constant returns as economic resources were transferred from the production of one type of product to another, i.e. the amount of production sacrificed by one product and gained by the other are the same or constant.

In reality, this is unlikely to happen because of the law of diminishing returns. This means that as extra units of a resource are used in production, they will lead to successively smaller increases in output. This is why a PPC is drawn the way it is. This can be seen in Figure 1.1. As resources are transferred from agricultural output to industrial output, the extra output of industrial production becomes successively smaller while the amount of agricultural production being sacrificed becomes successively larger. This is because not all factor inputs are equally suited to the production of different products.

Link

The law of diminishing returns is also covered in Chapter 7, section 7.5.1.

Key terms

The law of diminishing returns: as extra units of a resource, or input, are used in the production process, there will be increases in output, but there will be successively smaller increases in output as more inputs are added.

Increasing opportunity costs: this occurs when the extra production of one good involves ever-increasing sacrifices of another.

Constant and increasing opportunity costs

As has been explained above, a production possibility curve is not drawn as a straight line. This is because of the distinction between constant and increasing opportunity costs. At some point along the curve, it would be possible to move from one point on the curve to another with an equal sacrifice of resources. This would indicate constant opportunity costs.

However, as a position is reached that is closer to the end of the production possibility curve, this is no longer the case. Ever increasing amounts of one will need to be sacrificed to produce more of the other. The reason for this is that different factors of production have different qualities. If a country concentrates more on the production of one good, it has to use an increasing amount of resources that are less suitable. The use of an increasing number of factors that are increasingly less suitable will lead to an increase in the marginal cost of production.

Progress question

6 Explain why a production possibility curve is not usually drawn as a straight line.

1.5.3 *The causes and consequences of shifts in a PPC*

Figure 1.1 showed a movement from one point on a PPC to another, but it is also possible for there to be a shift of the whole PPC. This is shown in Figure 1.2, where there is a movement of the PPC to the right from PPC1 to PPC2. In this situation, an economy can produce more of both types of good.

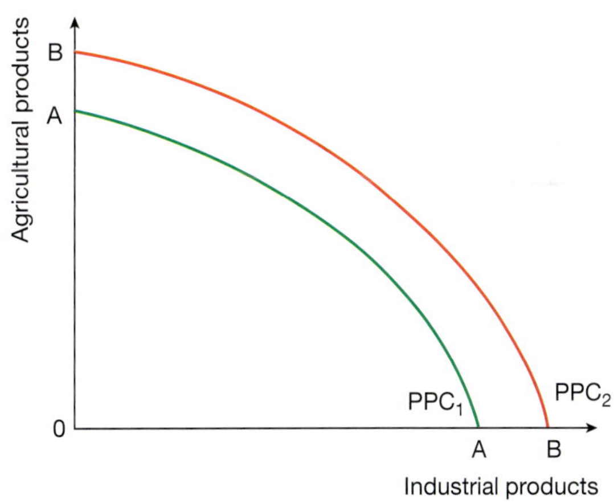

Figure 1.2 Capacity of an economy to produce agricultural and industrial products ▲

Table 1.6 indicates what can influence a shift of a PPC to the right.

Table 1.6 Causes of a shift of a PPC to the right ▼

Investment in improved technology	An improvement in technology could help to shift a country's PPC to the right. For example, if there was a move towards more intensive capital production, such as through making greater use of machinery, this should enable an economy to produce more. This improvement in technology should contribute to an increase in the productivity of labour. Such investment in capital equipment should increase an economy's future production potential or capacity.
Introduction of new resources	This could involve a new resource in terms of land, such as new mineral deposits. This would enhance the possibility of an economy to produce more.

Continued . . .

Increase in the supply of labour	An increase in the size of a country's population would affect labour. For example, if the birth rate of a country substantially increased and/or there was a substantial increase in net migration into a country, this would increase the potential quantity of labour available for employment.
Improvements in human capital	It is not simply the quantity of labour that is important, but also the quality of labour. The skills of the labour force can be improved through education and training. This is sometimes referred to as an increase in human capital and this can also lead to an increase in the rate of productivity.
Improved management of resources	Changes in the system of production can lead to greater output. For example, if there is a greater degree of division of labour in the production process, the level of productivity should be improved.
Encouragement of an enterprise culture	A government could encourage the development of an enterprise culture by providing support to new firms, such as through financial support and/or the provision of appropriate information.

Of course, it is always possible that the PPC of an economy could shift to the left rather than to the right; for example, if there was net migration out of a country, reducing the labour supply, or if there was a reduction in the money provided by a government for education and training initiatives, possibly reducing the quality of the future labour force.

Progress question

7 Discuss the extent to which a country is able to shift its production possibility curve to the right.

Key term

Economic growth: an increase in the productive potential or capacity of an economy. It is possible to distinguish between actual and potential growth in national output.

A shift of a PPC and economic growth

The shift of a country's PPC to the right, as shown in Figure 1.2, can be used to illustrate the concept of economic growth. The shift from PPC1 to PPC2 shows that more of both goods can be produced, i.e. the productive capacity or potential of an economy has been increased.

Link

The concept of economic growth is examined more fully in Chapter 4, section 4.4 and in Chapter 9, section 9.2.

1.5.4 *The significance of a position within a PPC*

It is important to understand the significance of a position within a PPC. As can be seen in Figure 1.1, a point on the PPC, such as point X or point Y, is where an economy is using its resources efficiently. Any point inside the PPC, however, is where an economy is using its resources inefficiently. At such a point inside the PPC, not all resources are being utilised and the output of both products is lower than it would be if all resources were being used.

1.6 The classification of goods and services

1.6.1 *The nature and definition of free goods and private goods (economic goods)*

Key term

Free good: a good which is not scarce and so therefore does not need a mechanism to allocate it. The demand for the free good is equal to the supply of it at zero price.

Free goods

A free good is one in which the situation of scarcity, referred to in section 1.1.1, does not apply. There is a sufficient quantity of it to

The existence of pollution will affect the quality of air in a community ▲

satisfy demand so that it is not necessary to involve an allocative mechanism. As free goods are not scarce, there is no cost involved in the consumption of them, unlike the consumption of a private or economic good. Examples include sunshine, air and sea water.

Of course, although air may be regarded as a good example of a free good, it may not necessarily be the case that fresh air is such a good example.

Progress question

8 Discuss to what extent fresh air is a free good or an economic good.

Getting it right

Do not confuse a free good, such as air, with a good or service that is provided free by a government. For example, in some countries a visit to a hospital may be free in the sense that a patient does not pay a fee directly to the hospital, but it is still an economic good because the resources involved have alternative uses.

Private goods

The condition of scarcity, discussed in section 1.1.1, relates to private or economic goods (in this sense, goods can refer to both goods and services). An economic good is defined as a private good which has the feature of relative scarcity.

A private good, or economic good, is a product which has two essential characteristics: it is both rival and excludable. Examples of a private good would include a bicycle, a car or an item of clothing.

Rival

A good that is said to be rival means that when one person consumes a product, it reduces the quantity available to others.

Excludable

A good that is said to be excludable means that a producer can exclude consumers from using a particular product by charging a price for the product.

Key terms

Private or economic good: a good that is relatively scarce and so will need to be allocated to a particular use in some way through an allocative mechanism.

Rival: a rival good is one where if one person consumes a good there is less available for others.

Excludable: a situation that exists when a price is charged for a good. It will be excluded from those who are unable and/or unwilling to pay this price.

Public good: a good which has the two characteristics of being "non-rival" and "non-excludable".

1.6.2 *The nature and definition of public goods*

A public good is the opposite of a private good. It also has two essential characteristics: non-rival and non-excludable. Examples of a public good would include:

- street lighting
- police and law and order
- the national defence of a country.

Non-rivalness or non-rival

Non-rivalness (or non-rival) means that if one person consumes a product, it does not reduce the extent of its availability to other people (the opposite of the case with a private good). As more people consume the product, it is impossible to stop all the other consumers from benefiting from it.

Non-excludability or non-excludable

Non-excludability means that if a public good is produced, it is *not* possible to exclude any person from its use (the opposite of the case with a private good), i.e. it is not possible to prevent other people from benefiting from the consumption of the good.

The free rider problem

As a result of the characteristic of non-excludability, the benefits gained from the production and consumption of public goods could not be limited to those who had paid for it if a price was charged for the product in a market, i.e. it would be impossible to exclude those who had not paid for the product. This is known as the free rider problem and it is a significant reason why a price cannot be charged for such a product.

Non-rejectability

Some economists have added a third characteristic of a public good to those of non-rivalness and non-excludability. This is the idea of non-rejectability, i.e. that certain public goods cannot be rejected. A police force would be an example of this; everybody in a society would benefit from the existence of a police force (except the criminals!) because it would help to deter crime. The armed forces of a country would be another such example as the existence of these would help to deter an attack on, or an invasion of, a country.

Key terms

Non-rivalness or non-rival: if one person consumes a product, it does not reduce the extent of its availability to other people.

Non-excludability or non-excludable: if a public good is produced, it is not possible to exclude any person from its use.

Free rider: a person who has no incentive to pay for the use of a public good because there can be consumption without any payment being made.

Non-rejectability: the idea that certain public goods can not be rejected, such as the police force or the armed forces of a country.

Link

Public goods and market failure are discussed in Chapter 3, section 3.1.1.

Progress question

9 Explain the difference between a private good and a public good.

Public goods and market failure

It should be clear that private goods can be provided through a market because a price is charged for their consumption. In the case of a public good, however, because of the characteristics of non-rivalness and non-excludability, it would not be possible to charge a price for it in a market and so it would not be produced in a market economy. This is why a country's police force and armed forces are usually provided by the state or government.

Activity

Private and public goods

Working in groups, think about the possible consequences of providing street lighting and a police force as a private, rather than as a public, good in an economy, i.e. by charging a market price for them.

Quasi-public goods

It is possible to distinguish between private goods and public goods, but some goods are somewhere in-between the characteristics of the two types of goods. These goods are called quasi-public goods (the word "quasi" meaning near or almost).

Activity

Quasi-public goods

Working in groups, think of three examples of quasi-public goods.

Case Study

Nairobi National Park

Nairobi National Park is a national park in Kenya. It was the first national park in Kenya, established in 1946. It is located about 7 kilometres (4 miles) outside Nairobi, the capital city of Kenya. It covers an area of 117.21 square kilometres or 28,963 acres.

A national park that is open to all, without the requirement for any payment for entry, would be non-excludable. Given its large size, a national park could also be seen as non-rival because there is enough space for everybody to enjoy the park.

On the other hand, a national park could be regarded as excludable if a payment was required to enter it. It could also be regarded as rival in that if too many people entered the park at the same time, space would become increasingly limited and this could adversely affect the enjoyment of the people visiting the national park.

1 Describe the characteristics of a private good and a public good.
2 To what extent do you think a national park, such as the one near Nairobi, is an example of a quasi-public good?

1.6.3 *The nature and definition of merit goods*

A merit good is a private good, with the characteristics of being rival and excludable, but if provided in a market economy, would be likely to be under-produced and under-consumed. The reason for this is because people may not be aware of the potential benefits of the product to themselves, or underestimate such benefits. Merit goods are therefore the outcome of imperfect information held by consumers. Examples of a merit good would include education, public libraries, health care and museums.

Activity

Museums

Working in pairs or groups, consider the possible advantages of being able to go to a museum, either for free or for a very low price, because of a government decision to use public money to make entry into museums either free or relatively cheap.

Key terms

Merit good: a product which would be under-produced and under-consumed in a market economy as a result of the imperfect information held by consumers.
Imperfect information: a situation in which people, including both producers and consumers, do not have the full information needed to make rational decisions, reducing the extent of efficiency.

Providing a merit good

Governments may decide to subsidise, or provide free at the point of use, a product such as education so that consumption is not limited to those who have the ability to pay for it. This will involve government expenditure.

Figure 1.3 shows how a merit good can be under-provided and under-consumed in a market.

In Figure 1.3, the original market equilibrium is a price of P2 and a quantity of Q2. This is determined by the intersection of the demand curve D1 and the supply curve S. In this situation, however, the consumers undervalue the potential benefits of the merit good, such as education. If the demand curve took into account this benefit, the demand curve would shift to the right and now be D2.

Getting it right

You need to demonstrate you understand that a merit good is an example of a private good, not a public good.

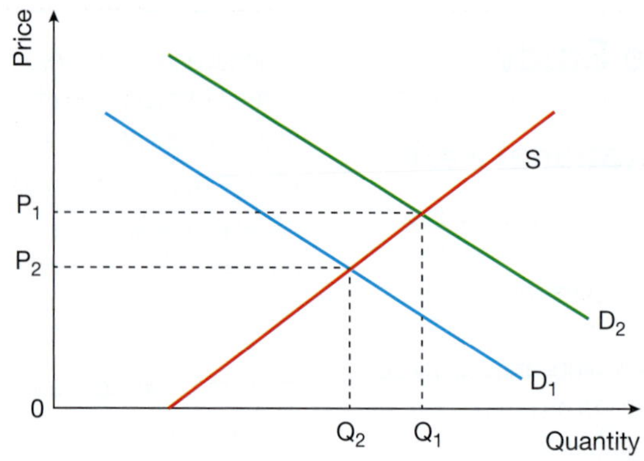

Figure 1.3 The under-production and under-consumption of a merit good in a market ▲

This equilibrium would involve a price of P1 and a quantity of Q1. Without this recognition of the benefits of a merit good, such as education, there would be both under-production and under-consumption of the good, shown in the diagram by the horizontal distance between Q1 and Q2. This is why governments intervene in many countries to encourage the consumption and the production of merit goods, such as education or health care.

Case Study

Education in Mauritius

After Mauritius became independent in 1968, the government announced that the quality of the education system was going to be one of its main objectives, recognising the importance of education to the development of the country.

There has been substantial investment in the education system by a succession of governments and progress in the education system has been very impressive. Education through the primary and secondary sectors has been free since 1976 and through the post-secondary level since 1988.

1 Discuss why governments in Mauritius have been so keen to allocate resources to education.

Case Study

Public libraries in The Maldives

At a lecture at a meeting of The Maldives Library Association on the importance of public libraries and the role that they can play in a democracy, it was stated that important aspects of a successful democracy, such as freedom of speech and the freedom to read, could be supported by public libraries.

It was also stated that an important aspect of democracy was that individuals should be allowed to achieve their fullest possible potential. In order to achieve this potential, individuals required knowledge and access to ideas. This is where public libraries could contribute to democracy in a country.

1 Explain why a public library can be regarded as an example of a merit good.

Case Study

Health care in Brunei

Brunei has been an independent country since 1984. It has the second highest Human Development Index in South East Asia, after Singapore, and is classified as a developed country. It is ranked sixth in the world by Gross Domestic Product per capita at purchasing power parity.

The country has developed a very good health care system, recognising the various benefits that this can bring. A comprehensive and efficient health care system is available to all and the Ministry of Health in Brunei ensures that the health care service is accessible and reliable. It also concentrates on the improvement of the standard of health care in the country.

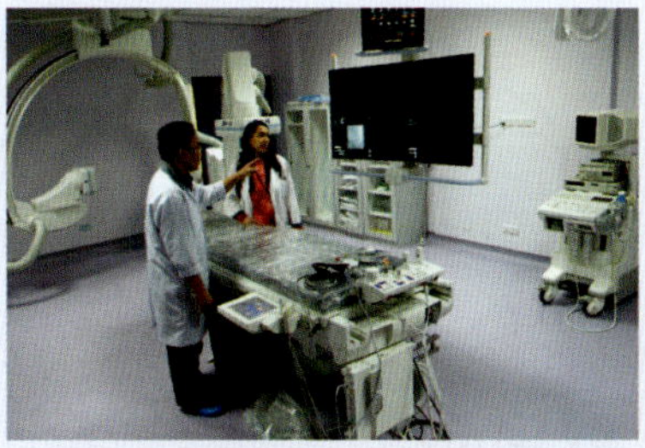

1 Explain why the Ministry of Health in Brunei is so keen to make a comprehensive and efficient health care system available to all.

Key term

Demerit good: a product which would be over-produced and over-consumed in a market economy as a result of the imperfect information held by consumers.

1.6.4 *The nature and definition of demerit goods*

A demerit good is the opposite of a merit good. It is a private good with the characteristics of being rival and excludable, but if provided in a market economy, would be likely to be over-produced and over-consumed. The reason for this is that individuals may not be aware of the potential damage to themselves of such over-consumption. A demerit good is therefore the outcome of imperfect information held by consumers. Examples of a demerit good would include such products as cigarettes and alcohol.

Governments may decide to discourage the consumption of such products, such as by putting a very large tax on them to make them much more expensive than would otherwise be the case, leading to a reduction in the demand for them. For example, if the demand for cigarettes and alcohol could be reduced, this would be good for the individuals concerned. The effect of such a tax would clearly depend on the price elasticity of demand for them. The demand for many of these products is likely to be quite price inelastic and so consumers may not be able to significantly reduce their consumption because of addiction to the product.

Figure 1.4 shows how a demerit good can be over-provided and over-consumed in a market.

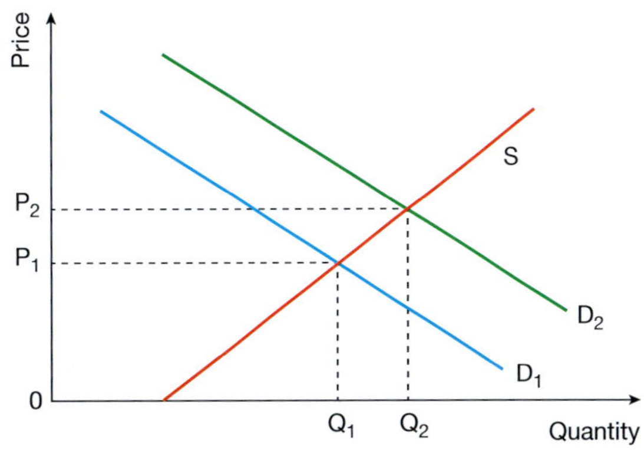

Figure 1.4 The over-production and over-consumption of a demerit good in a market ▲

The appropriate level of demand would be a price of P_1 and Q_1. This is where S is equal to D_1. Consumers, however, are likely to over-consume and producers to over-produce in a market economy and this is shown in the diagram by a price of P_2 and a quantity of Q_2. This is where S is equal to D_2.

Key terms

Information failure: a situation where people do not have the full information needed to make informed decisions about their behaviour.

Imperfection: a situation where a market does not behave as it is expected to, leading to a misallocation of resources.

Progress question

10 Explain what is meant by a demerit good.

Information failure

A key element in both merit and demerit goods is the existence of information failure. Consumers may under-consume merit goods, such as education or health care, because they do not have enough information about the potential benefits of the consumption of such goods.

Similarly, consumers may over-consume demerit goods, such as cigarettes or alcohol, because they do not have enough information about the potential dangers of the consumption of such goods.

This is why a government may decide to intervene in a market, either to encourage the consumption and production of merit goods or to discourage the production and consumption of demerit goods. This can be regarded as an imperfection of a market, especially in relation to having an understanding of the potential long-term benefits of the consumption of a merit good or of the potential long-term disadvantages of the consumption of a demerit good. Such an imperfection in a market means that a product will be produced and consumed, but not in the right quantities, i.e. the merit goods will be under-produced and under-consumed and the demerit goods will be over-produced and over-consumed. There is therefore a misallocation of resources in the market.

Getting it right

Make sure that you can clearly demonstrate an understanding of the link between information failure and the possible under-consumption of merit goods and over-consumption of demerit goods.

Key concepts

- **Scarcity and choice** are fundamental to the economic problem. Scarcity was discussed in section 1.1.1 and choice in sections 1.1.2 and 1.1.3 (in relation to the concept of opportunity cost).
- **The margin and decision-making** can be considered in the many decisions in Economics that are taken at the margin. Economists, when analysing decision making, will tend to concentrate on decisions that are taken at the margin. This is the point at which the last unit of a product is consumed or produced. The discussion of constant and increasing opportunity costs in section 1.5.2 pointed out that where increasing opportunity costs applied, the marginal cost of production, i.e. the additional cost of producing one more unit of a product, would increase.
- **Time** was the focus of section 1.2.4 when the importance of the three time periods of short run, long run and very long run were discussed.

Progress check

After completing this chapter you should be able to:

- understand the importance of scarcity, choice and opportunity cost in relation to the economic problem
- understand the key elements of economic methodology
- understand the different factors of production
- appreciate how decisions are made and how resources are allocated in different economic systems
- understand the importance of production possibility curves
- understand how goods and services can be classified.

Exam-style questions

Essay questions

1a Explain the role of the factor enterprise in a modern economy and consider its importance in relation to the other three factors of production. [8 marks]

b Assess whether Economics can be described as a science. [12 marks]

2a Explain the three basic questions of resource allocation that all economies face and consider which is the most significant. [8 marks]

b Assess whether a market economy can solve the economic problem more effectively than a planned economy. [12 marks]

3a Explain what is meant by the division of labour and consider the strength of the relationship between division of labour and productivity. [8 marks]

b Assess whether different time periods can have a significant effect on economic behaviour. [12 marks]

4a Explain what is shown by a production possibility curve and consider the importance of the distinction between a movement along, and a shift of, a production possibility curve. [8 marks]

b Assess which of the factors that could cause the shift of a production possibility curve to the left are likely to be the most important in an economy. [12 marks]

5a Explain, with the use of examples, the distinction between free goods and private goods and consider whether both require an allocative mechanism. [8 marks]

b Assess whether public goods can be provided in a market economy. [12 marks]

6a Explain what is meant by information failure and consider the extent to which it is a market imperfection. [8 marks]

b Assess the extent of the impact of information failure on the consumption of merit goods and demerit goods in an economy. [12 marks]

Multiple-choice questions

7 Which of the following could cause an outward shift of a production possibility curve? [1 mark]

A A reduction in unemployment
B A more efficient use of existing resources
C An improvement in the level of technology
D An increase in net migration out of a country

8 Which of the following is a positive statement? [1 mark]

A Trade unions should be encouraged in an economy.
B A government ought to discourage smoking in public places.
C The rate of inflation is measured through a prices index.
D Teachers ought to have significant increases in their salaries.

2 The price system and the microeconomy

In this chapter you will develop your knowledge and understanding of:

- demand and supply curves
- price elasticity, income elasticity and cross elasticity of demand
- price elasticity of supply
- the interaction of demand and supply
- consumer and producer surplus.

2.1 Demand and supply curves

2.1.1 *Effective demand*

An individual's demand for a good or service is the quantity they are willing and able to purchase over a range of prices over a period of time. It is important to distinguish an individual's demand for a product from the desire or need for a product. For example, an individual may desire a Ferrari motor car, but because they do not have the money to buy one, as far as economists are concerned, they do not have a demand for it. Economists often, therefore, refer to effective demand, which is the desire for a product backed up with the ability to pay for it.

Key terms

Effective demand: the quantity of a good or service an individual is willing and able to purchase over a range of prices over a period of time.

Law of demand: for most goods and services the quantity demanded varies inversely with its price.

Demand curve: a curve showing the relationship between the quantity of a product individuals are willing and able to buy over a range of prices over a period of time, on the assumption that all other factors affecting demand are held constant.

Getting it right

Make sure you understand the difference between the desire for a good or service and the *effective demand* for it.

2.1.2 *Individual and market demand and supply*

Demand

Individual demand

The relationship between individual demand and the price of a product

For most goods and services, but not all, the quantity demanded varies inversely with the price. This is sometimes referred to as the law of demand.

The relationship between demand and price is generally illustrated by either a demand schedule or a demand curve. The demand schedule (Table 2.1) and demand curve (Figure 2.1) show the quantity of rice demanded by an individual (Vikram) over a range of prices.

Table 2.1 Vikram's demand schedule for rice ▼

Price of rice per kilo (cents)	Quantity demanded (kilos per month)
5	60
10	50
15	40
20	30
25	20
30	10

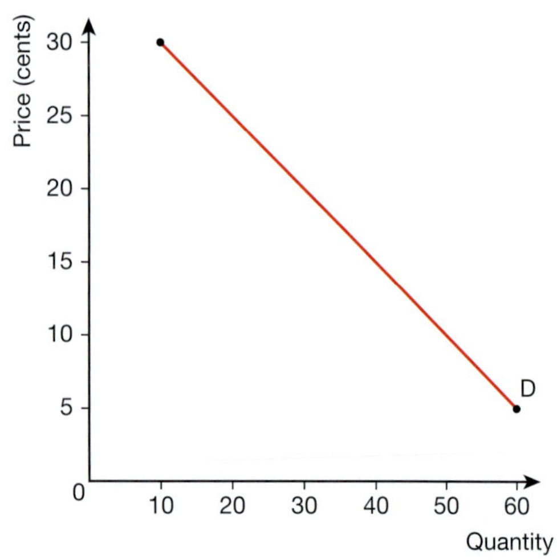

Figure 2.1 Vikram's demand curve for rice ▲

As can be seen from both the demand schedule and the demand curve, as the price of rice falls the demand rises and vice versa.

Link

See Chapter 1, section 1.2.3 for an explanation of *ceteris paribus*.

Key terms

Supply curve: a curve showing the relationship between the quantity of a product producers are willing and able to offer for sale over a range of prices over a period of time, on the assumption that all other factors affecting supply are held constant.

Market demand: the total demand for a particular product in the market.

Supply: the quantity of a good a producer is willing and able to offer for sale over a range of prices over a given period of time.

The demand curve is drawn on the assumption of *ceteris paribus*, that all other factors affecting Vikram's demand for rice remain unchanged. At this stage we only know how much rice Vikram is prepared to purchase at various prices. Until we combine the demand curve with a supply curve, we cannot say exactly how much will be purchased and at what price.

Market demand

The relationship between market demand and the price of a product

In addition to individuals' demand for a product, Economists are often interested in the total or market demand for a product. This is found simply by adding together the quantity demanded of each individual, in this case for Vikram, Hamza and Bella, at any given price. This is shown in the demand schedule (Table 2.2) and demand curve (Figure 2.2).

Table 2.2 The market demand schedule for rice ▼

Price of rice per kilo (cents)	Quantity demanded (kilos per month) Vikram	Quantity demanded (kilos per month) Hamza	Quantity demanded (kilos per month) Bella	Market demand (kilos per month)
5	60	40	30	130
10	50	35	25	110
15	40	30	20	90
20	30	25	15	70
25	20	20	10	50
30	10	15	5	30

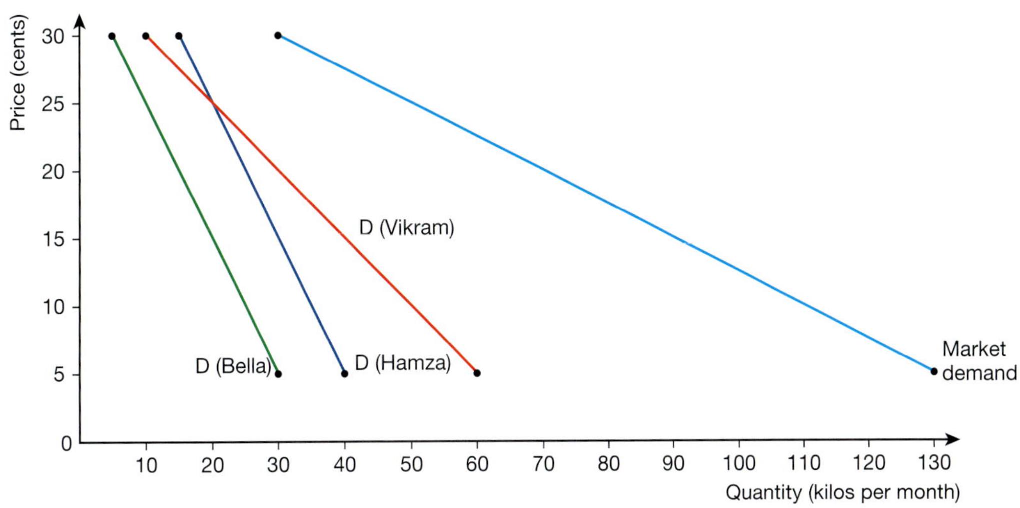

Figure 2.2 Market demand for rice ▲

Supply

In order to establish the equilibrium price for a product, we need to look at both the demand for and supply of it. The supply refers not simply to the quantity produced, but the quantity producers are prepared to offer for sale over a range of prices over a period of time.

Individual supply

The relationship between an individual producer's supply and the price of a product

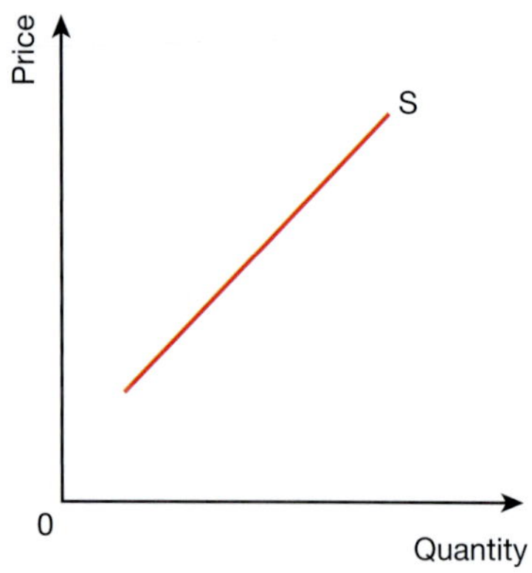

Figure 2.3 An individual producer's supply curve for rice ▲

In most cases as the price rises producers are willing to supply more because it is likely to be more profitable. It is also likely to be the case that costs of production will increase and so it will be necessary to increase price in order to maintain profit margins. The relationship between the supply of a product and its price is, as with demand, generally illustrated by either a schedule or a curve. Table 2.3 and Figure 2.3 show the supply schedule and supply curve for rice respectively.

Table 2.3 An individual producer's supply curve for rice ▼

Price of rice per kilo (cents)	Quantity supplied (kilos per month)
5	10
10	15
15	20
20	25
25	30
30	35

Key term

Law of supply: for most goods and services the quantity supplied will increase as price rises and decrease as price falls.

As can be seen from both the supply schedule and the supply curve, as the price of rice increases the supply increases and vice versa. This is known as the law of supply.

Like the demand curve, the supply curve is drawn on the assumption of *ceteris paribus*, that all other factors affecting the supply of rice remain unchanged. At this stage we only know how much rice the producer is prepared to purchase at various prices. Until we combine the supply curve with a demand curve we cannot say exactly how much will be supplied and at what price.

Market supply

The relationship between market supply and the price of a product

In order to establish the market supply we simply add together the quantity offered by each producer at each price. Table 2.4 and Figure 2.4 show the market supply schedule and market supply curve for rice respectively.

Table 2.4 Market supply of rice ▼

Price of rice per kilo (cents)	Quantity supplied (kilos per month) Producer A	Quantity supplied (kilos per month) Producer B	Quantity supplied (kilos per month) Producer C	Market supply (kilos per month)
5	10	5	15	30
10	15	25	20	60
15	20	45	25	90
20	25	65	30	120
25	30	85	35	150
30	35	105	40	180

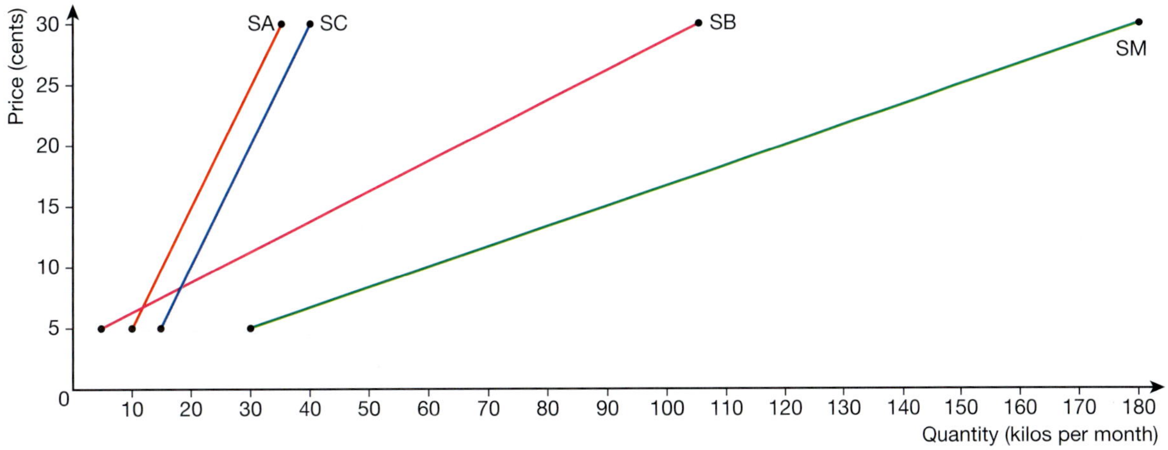

Figure 2.4 Market supply of rice ▲

2.1.3 *Determinants of demand*

Other influences on demand – the conditions of demand

There are a range of factors other than price which affect an individual's demand for a good or service. These conditions of demand affect how much an individual will demand at each price and, as we shall see later, will bring about a shift of the demand curve to the right or left.

Income

Here we need to distinguish between normal and inferior goods. A normal good is one for which the demand rises as income rises and falls as income falls. This applies to most goods and services. However, there are some exceptions to this. For example, during recessions as unemployment rises and consumers' incomes fall, many supermarkets find their sales of low price "value" own brands increase.

Key terms

Inferior good: a good whose demand falls as income rises and rises as income falls.
Normal good: a good whose demand rises as income rises and falls as income falls.
Substitutes: goods that are alternatives for one another.
Complements: goods that are consumed together.

The price of other goods

Many goods are related to one another as substitutes or complements. Coffee and tea are, for many people, substitutes for one another. The demand for coffee will vary directly with the price of tea. If the price of tea rises, individuals will reduce their demand for tea and switch to coffee. The demand for coffee will therefore increase. The opposite will happen if the price of tea falls.

Fuel is a complement to a motor car. Consequently the demand for fuel is likely to be inversely related to the price of cars. If there is a significant rise in the price of cars, it is likely that the demand will fall and consequently so will the demand for fuel.

Tastes

This relationship is relatively straightforward in that individuals are unlikely to buy goods they do not like. The more attractive individuals find a particular product, the greater their demand for it is likely to be. However, it is important to remember that our tastes and preferences can be swayed and influenced by intensive advertising and promotion campaigns.

Expectations of future prices

Some products are purchased because of their investment potential. Individuals may buy these products in the hope that their price will rise and they can be sold at a profit in the future. Examples of such products are houses, shares and antiques. If individuals believe the price of such goods is likely to rise in the future, this may lead to an increase in demand. Speculators hoarding sugar because they anticipated a rise in price following a poor crop yield is another example.

Size, age and gender distribution of the population

Generally the overall demand for most goods and services will rise and fall as the population rises and falls. Changes in the age and gender distribution of the population will influence the pattern of demand for particular goods and services, e.g. those purchased primarily by the young or elderly or by males or females.

Distribution of income

Generally if the income distribution in a country becomes more even, the demand for most normal goods increases. If the distribution becomes less even, the demand for basic necessities and luxury goods will be affected depending on the nature of the change in distribution. It is likely that the demand for both luxury and inferior goods would increase.

2.1.4 *Determinants of supply*

Other influences on supply – the conditions of supply

There are a range of factors other than price which affect an individual's supply for a good or service. These are collectively known as the conditions of supply and will bring about shifts of the whole supply curve.

Costs of production

Generally as the costs of production increase, supply falls. If the cost of land for growing rice rises or there is an increase in wages of farm workers, it means that producers are able to offer less for sale at each and every price.

Availability of resources

As more resources become available, it is likely that more will be offered for sale. If, for example, more land becomes available, then it will be possible for a farmer to grow more rice.

Climate

Clearly this factor will not affect all goods, but it is important in some, e.g. agriculture. Adverse weather conditions will obviously reduce the ability to produce and supply most crops. Weather conditions can also have an impact on the construction industry.

Technology

Technology can affect supply in a number of ways. It can lead to the creation of new products, e.g. laptops and mobile phones did not exist 60 years ago, or it can reduce costs of production enabling firms to produce more at each price. The introduction of new advanced machinery might significantly increase a farmer's ability to grow rice.

Government regulation

This looks mainly at health and safety, consumer protection, minimum standards legislation and employment legislation which affects employees' rights in such areas as equal pay and the minimum wage. These can all have an impact on a producer's costs and, therefore, the supply of a particular product.

Taxes and subsidies

Here we are looking at indirect taxes on expenditure such as Value Added Tax (VAT) and Goods and Services Tax (GST) which are initially paid by producers, but then may be passed on to consumers through higher prices. These taxes increase costs of production and, therefore, reduce supply. Subsidies, which are payments made by the government to producers, are designed to reduce firms' costs of production and enable them to supply more at lower prices.

Price of other goods the producer could supply

A farmer is in a position to grow a range of crops. If the farmer is currently concentrating on the production of wheat but the market price of barley rises significantly relative to wheat, making its production more profitable, then the farmer would switch to growing barley and the supply of wheat would fall. The supply of a product, therefore, varies inversely with the price of alternative products the firm could produce.

2.1.5 Causes of a shift in the demand curve (D)

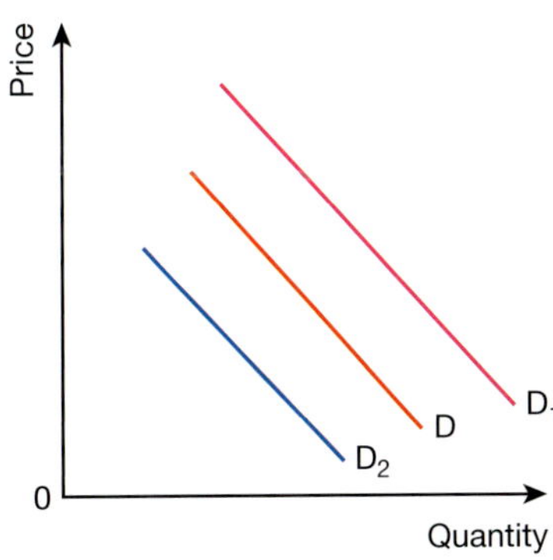

Figure 2.5 Shifts of the demand curve ▲

Shifts of the demand curve

If any of the conditions of demand described above change, then it means that individuals are able to purchase more or less at each and every price. This will cause the whole demand curve to shift. If the change enables individuals to buy more of the product, the demand curve will shift to the right (D to D_1) and if they are able to purchase less, it will shift the curve to the left (D to D_2) as illustrated in Figure 2.5.

Table 2.5 summarises the effect of changes in the conditions of demand on the demand curve for a product.

Table 2.5 The effect of changes in the conditions of demand on the demand curve for a product ▼

Shifts the demand curve to the right (an increase in demand)	Shifts the demand curve to the left (a decrease in demand)
A rise in income for a normal good	A fall in income for a normal good
A fall in income for an inferior good	A rise in income for an inferior good
A rise in the price of a substitute	A fall in the price of a substitute
A fall in the price of a complement	A rise in the price of a complement
A change in tastes in favour of a product	A change in tastes away from a product
The expectation of a future price rise	The expectation of a future price fall
An increase in population	A fall in population
A more even distribution of income	A less even distribution of income

Progress question

1 Using diagrams, explain the effect of each of the following on the demand curve for privately-owned housing in a particular area.

- **a** Rising unemployment in the area
- **b** A reduction in private rents in the area
- **c** A rise in mortgage interest rates
- **d** An increase in the number of single person households
- **e** Expectations of significant increases in house prices over the coming year

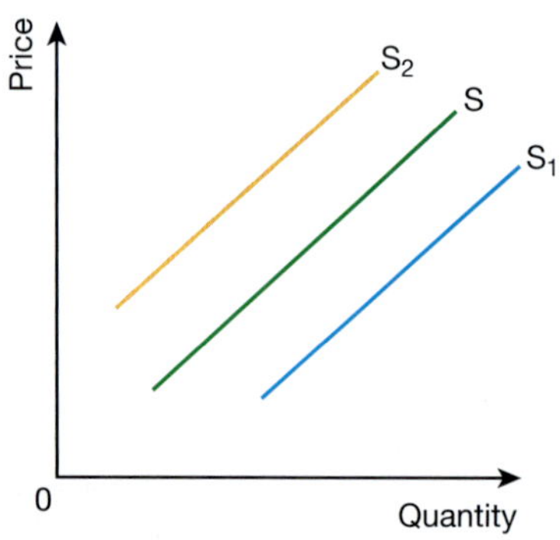

Figure 2.6 Shifts of the supply curve ▲

2.1.6 *Causes of a shift in the supply curve (S)*

Shifts of the supply curve

If any of the conditions of supply described above change, then it means that producers are now able to offer more or less for sale at each and every price. This will cause the whole supply curve to shift. If the change enables producers to offer more for sale, the supply curve will shift to the right (S to S_1) and if they are able to offer less for sale it will shift the curve to the left (S to S_2) as illustrated in Figure 2.6.

Table 2.6 summarises the effect of changes in the conditions of supply on the supply curve for a product.

Table 2.6 The effect of changes in the conditions of supply on the supply curve for a product ▼

Shifts the supply curve to the right (an increase in supply)	Shifts the supply curve to the left (a decrease in supply)
Reduced costs of production	Increased costs of production
More resources become available	Fewer resources become available
Improved climate conditions (mainly agriculture)	Worsening climate conditions (mainly agriculture)
Improvements in technology	Setbacks in technology
Changes in government regulations in an industry reducing costs or making it easier to supply	Changes in government regulations in an industry increasing costs or making it more difficult to supply
Fall in expenditure taxes or granting of a subsidy	Increase in expenditure taxes
Reduction in the price of an alternative product the firm could produce	Increase in the price of an alternative product the firm could produce

Progress question

2 Using diagrams, explain the effect of each of the following on the supply curve for privately-owned housing in a particular area.

- **a** A decrease in the productivity of building workers
- **b** An increase in wages in the building industry
- **c** The government relaxes planning restrictions on building in the area
- **d** A rise in VAT or sales tax on building materials
- **e** A subsidy to builders of low-cost housing for first-time buyers
- **f** A major supplier of bricks in the area goes bankrupt

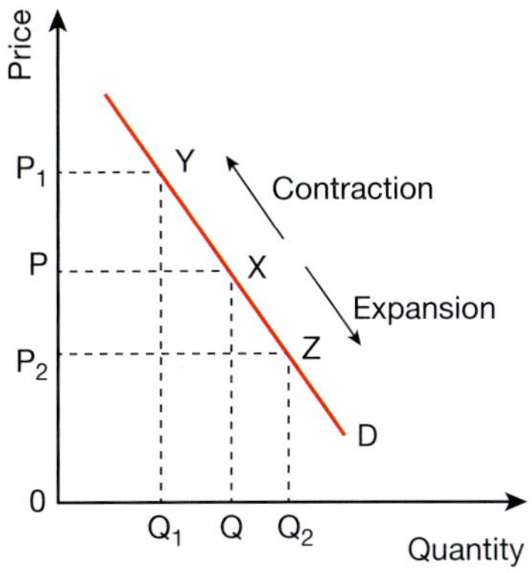

Figure 2.7 Changes in the quantity demanded resulting from price changes ▲

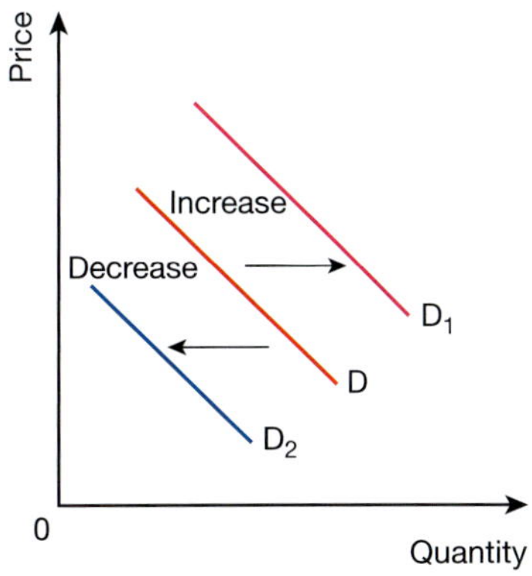

Figure 2.8 Changes in demand resulting from changes in the conditions of demand ▲

Getting it right

It is very important that you have a clear understanding of the distinction between movements along a demand curve (caused by price changes) and shifts of the whole demand curve (caused by a change in the conditions of demand).

2.1.7 *Distinction between the shift in the demand or supply curve and movements along these curves*

Movements along the demand curve versus shifts of the demand curve

It is important to distinguish clearly between movements along a demand curve and shifts of the whole curve.

A market demand curve shows the relationship between changes in price and changes in the quantity purchased and so if the price of a product increases it will simply mean a movement from one price quantity combination to another. In Figure 2.7 an increase in price from P to P_1 will result in a movement up along the demand curve from X to Y resulting in a fall in the quantity demanded from Q to Q_1. Correspondingly a decrease in price from P to P_2 will result in a movement down along the demand curve from X to Z resulting in an increase in the quantity demanded from Q to Q_2.

If, however, any of the factors other than price, i.e. the conditions of demand, change resulting in more or less being demanded at each and every price, then this will result in a shift in the whole curve; an increase in demand resulting in a shift of the curve to the right and a decrease a shift to the left. This is shown in Figure 2.8.

In order to distinguish between changes in demand resulting from movements along a demand curve from those resulting from shifts of the whole curve, we use the terminology shown in Table 2.7.

Table 2.7 Changes in demand ▼

Change in demand	Description
Increase in demand resulting from a rise in price (movement down along the demand curve)	Increase in the quantity demanded or expansion of demand
Decrease in demand resulting from a fall in price (movement up along the demand curve)	Decrease in the quantity demanded or contraction of demand
Increase in demand resulting from a shift of the demand curve to the right	Increase in demand
Decrease in demand resulting from a shift of the demand curve to the left	Decrease in demand

Activity

Demand curves

Using the figures in the table below, draw the demand curve for oil for a particular country.

Price per barrel ($)	80	90	100	110	120	130	140
Barrels consumed per day (millions)	20	18	16	14	12	10	8

Now the country's demand increases by 10 per cent at each price. Draw the new demand curve.

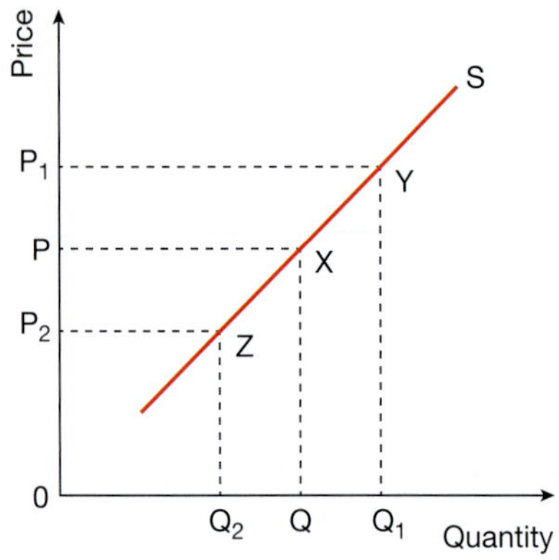

Figure 2.9 Changes in the quantity supplied resulting from price changes ▲

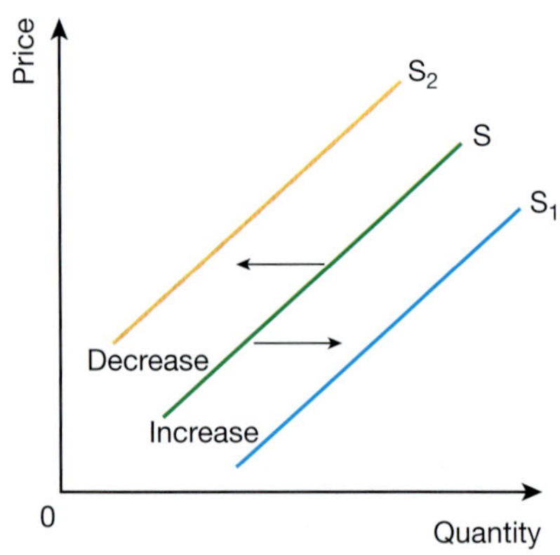

Figure 2.10 Changes in supply resulting from changes in the conditions of supply ▲

Movements along the supply curve versus shifts of the supply curve

Just as in the case of demand, it is important to distinguish between a movement along a particular supply curve and a shift of the whole curve. As the supply curve shows the relationship between the price of a good or service and the quantity supplied, a change in price will simply result in a movement along the curve. In Figure 2.9 the rise in price from P to P_1 results in a movement up along the supply curve from X to Y leading to an increase in the quantity supplied from Q to Q_1 and a fall in price from P to P_2 results in a movement down along the curve from X to Z leading to a reduction in the quantity supplied from Q to Q_2.

If, however, any of the factors other than price, i.e. the conditions of supply, change resulting in more or less being supplied at each and every price then this will result in a shift in the whole curve; an increase in supply resulting in a shift of the curve to the right and a decrease, resulting in a shift to the left. This is shown in Figure 2.10.

In order to distinguish between changes in supply resulting from movements along a supply curve and those resulting from shifts of the whole curve we use the terminology shown in Table 2.8 below.

Table 2.8 Changes in supply ▼

Change in supply	Description
Increase in supply resulting from a rise in price (movement up along the supply curve)	Increase in the quantity supplied or expansion of supply
Decrease in supply resulting from a fall in price (movement down along the supply curve)	Decrease in the quantity supplied or contraction of supply
Increase in supply resulting from a shift of the supply curve to the right	Increase in supply
Decrease in supply resulting from a shift of the supply curve to the left	Decrease in supply

Getting it right

It is very important that you have a clear understanding of the distinction between movements along a supply curve (caused by price changes) and shifts of the whole supply curve (caused by a change in the conditions of supply).

Activity

Supply curves

Using the figures in the table below, draw the supply curve for oil for a particular country.

Price per barrel (US $)	80	90	100	110	120	130	140
Barrels produced per day (millions)	10	15	20	25	30	35	40

Now as a result of an increase in demand the country's production of oil increases by 5 million barrels per day at each price. Draw the new supply curve.

2.2 Price elasticity, income elasticity and cross elasticity of demand

We have already seen that a change in the price of a product, which as we will see later will have been caused by a shift of the supply curve, will bring about a change in the quantity demanded. A rise

> **Key term**
>
> **Elasticity**: the responsiveness of demand or supply to a change in one of its determinants.

> **Key terms**
>
> **Price elasticity of demand**: the responsiveness of demand for a product to a change in its price.
>
> **Income elasticity of demand**: the responsiveness of demand for a product to a change in consumers' income.
>
> **Cross price elasticity of demand**: the responsiveness of the demand for one product to a change in the price of another.

in price will bring about a fall in the quantity demanded, and a fall in price will bring about an increase in the quantity demanded. We now need to look at the *extent* of these changes as well as the extent demand will change as a result of changes in income and the price of other goods (substitutes and complements). This involves us in looking at elasticity, which is a measure of the responsiveness of demand (and as we shall see later supply) to a change in a determinant variable.

2.2.1 Definition of price elasticity, income elasticity and cross elasticity of demand

We will be concerned with three types of elasticity, as listed below.

- Price elasticity of demand (PED) which measures the extent of the change in the quantity demanded of a product as a result of a change in its price.
- Income elasticity of demand (YED) which measures the extent of the change in the quantity demanded of a product as a result of a change in consumers' income.
- Cross price elasticity of demand or cross elasticity of demand (XED) which measures the extent of the change in the quantity demanded of a product as a result of a change in the price of other products.

2.2.2 Formulae for and calculation of price income and cross elasticity of demand

Price elasticity of demand

Figures 2.11 and 2.12 show the demand curves for two different products. In both cases the price has fallen by the same amount, but the rise in the quantity demanded is significantly different. The reason for this is clearly the fact that the two demand curves have different slopes, which, in turn, is due to the fact that the two products have a different price elasticity of demand (PED).

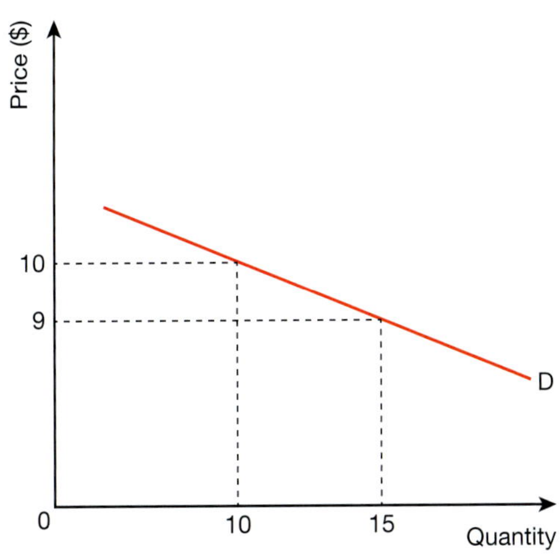

Figure 2.11 Demand curve for product A

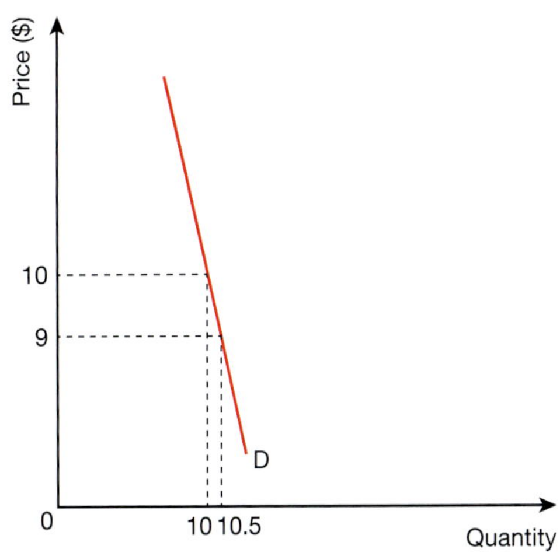

Figure 2.12 Demand curve for product B

Price elasticity of demand (PED) is a measure of the responsiveness of the quantity demanded of a product to a change in its price and as we can see from Figures 2.11 and 2.12 the quantity demanded of product A is significantly more responsive to a change in its price than product B. However, the term "more responsive" is rather vague and so economists attempt to be more precise by calculating the actual magnitude of the price elasticity of demand.

Calculation of the price elasticity of demand

The formula for the price elasticity of demand is:

$$\text{PED} = \frac{\text{the proportionate change in demand}}{\text{the proportionate change in price}}$$

$$\text{PED} = \frac{\text{new demand } (Q_1) - \text{Original demand } (Q)}{\text{original demand } (Q)}$$

$$\div \frac{\text{new price } (P_1) - \text{original price } (P)}{\text{original price } (P)}$$

If we now apply the formula to product A in Figure 2.11, then:

new demand (Q_1) = \$15

original demand (Q) = \$10

new price (P_1) = \$9

original price (P) = \$10

$$\text{PED} = \frac{Q_1 - Q}{Q} \div \frac{P_1 - P}{P} = \frac{15 - 10}{10} \div \frac{9 - 10}{10}$$

$$= \frac{1}{2} \div \frac{-1}{10} = \frac{1}{2} \times \frac{-10}{2} = -5$$

We could instead have used percentages in the calculation, in which case the formula is:

$$\text{PED} = \frac{\text{percentage change in demand}}{\text{percentage change in price}}$$

$$\text{PED} = \frac{\%\Delta Qd}{\%\Delta P}$$

In the case of product A this would now give us:

$$\text{PED} = \frac{50\%}{-10\%} = -5$$

Progress question

3 Calculate the price elasticity of demand for product B when price rises from \$9 to \$10 in Figure 2.12.

Calculation of the income elasticity of demand

The formula for the income elasticity of demand (YED) is:

$$YED = \frac{\text{the proportionate change in demand}}{\text{the proportionate change in income}}$$

$$YED = \frac{\text{new demand } (Q_1) - \text{original demand } (Q)}{\text{original demand } (Q)} \div \frac{\text{new income } (Y_1) - \text{original income } (Y)}{\text{original income } (Y)}$$

We could instead have used percentages in the calculation, in which case the formula is:

$$YED = \frac{\text{percentage change in demand}}{\text{percentage change in income}}$$

$$YED = \frac{\%\Delta Qd}{\%\Delta Y}$$

Calculation of the cross elasticity of demand

The formula for the cross elasticity of demand is:

$$XED = \frac{\text{the proportionate change in demand for product X}}{\text{the proportionate change in price of product Y}}$$

$$XED = \frac{\text{new demand X } (Q1_x) - \text{original demand X } (Q_x)}{\text{original demand X } (Q_x)} \div \frac{\text{new price Y } (P1_y) - \text{Original price Y } (P_y)}{\text{Original price Y } (P_y)}$$

We could instead have used percentages in the calculation, in which case the formula is:

$$XED = \frac{\text{percentage change in demand for product X}}{\text{percentage change in price of product Y}}$$

$$XED = \frac{\%\Delta Q_d \text{ good}_x}{\%\Delta P \text{ good}_y}$$

2.2.3 Significance of relative percentage changes, the size and sign of the coefficient

Price elasticity of demand

Interpreting the figure for the price elasticity of demand

We have calculated the price elasticity of demand for product A for a fall in price from \$10 to \$9 to be (–)5, but what does this figure actually mean?

Remember that we are interested in the extent to which the quantity demanded for a product changes. Because the quantity demanded of a product varies inversely with its price, the demand curve will have a negative slope which means that the numerical value of the price elasticity of demand will always be negative (–). However, we are only interested in whether the absolute value of the proportionate

Key terms

Elastic demand: the proportionate (percentage) change in demand is greater than the proportionate (percentage) change in price.

Inelastic demand: the proportionate (percentage) change in demand is less than the proportionate (percentage) change in price.

Getting it right

Although when interpreting the meaning of any value for the price elasticity of demand it is conventional to ignore the negative (minus) sign, it is essential that in any calculation made it is included.

or percentage change in demand is greater than, less than or equal to the proportionate or percentage change in price. Hence, although it is important that the negative sign is always included in any calculation, when we are interpreting any figure for the price elasticity of demand it is conventional to ignore this negative (–) sign so that the price elasticity of demand of –5 in this example means that the change in the quantity demanded is *five times* the change in price. As the answer is greater than 1, economists describe the demand for the product as elastic. If the answer had turned out to be less than 1, we would describe the demand for the product as being inelastic.

The numerical value for the price elasticity of demand can vary between zero and infinity. Table 2.9 summarises the meaning of particular values for the price elasticity of demand.

Table 2.9 Meaning of values for price elasticity of demand ▼

Value of PED	Terminology	Meaning
0	Perfectly inelastic demand	A change in price leaves the quantity demanded unchanged
< 1	Inelastic	Proportionate or percentage change in quantity demanded is less than the proportionate or percentage change in price
= 1	Unitary elasticity of demand	Proportionate or percentage change in quantity demanded is equal to the proportionate or percentage change in price
>1	Elastic	Proportionate or percentage change in quantity demanded is greater than the proportionate or percentage change in price
Infinity	Perfectly elastic demand	A tiny change in price brings about an infinite change in the quantity demanded

Income elasticity of demand

Interpreting the figure for the income elasticity of demand

Unlike price elasticity of demand, which is always negative, income elasticity of demand can be either positive or negative. Table 2.14 summarises the meaning of particular values for the income elasticity of demand

Table 2.10 Meaning of values for the income elasticity of demand ▼

Value of YED	Terminology	Meaning
> 1	Income elastic	Proportionate (or percentage) change in the quantity demanded greater than proportionate (or percentage) change in income
= 1	Unitary income elasticity	Proportionate (or percentage) change in the quantity demanded is equal to proportionate (or percentage) change in income
< 1	Income inelastic	Proportionate (or percentage) change in the quantity demanded less than proportionate (or percentage) change in income
0	Zero income elasticity	A change in income has no effect on demand
< 0	Negative income elasticity of demand	A change in income results in a change in demand in the opposite direction

Values above zero clearly indicate positive income elasticity, which means that changes in demand and changes in income move in the same direction, rising and falling together. This will be the case for normal goods. Inferior goods will have a negative income elasticity indicating that a rise in income will result in a fall in the demand for a product and vice versa.

Interpreting the figure for the cross elasticity of demand

When looking at cross elasticity of demand, economists are interested not only in its magnitude, but also whether the answer is positive or negative. If the answer is positive, it means that a given change in the price of one good has led to a corresponding change in the quantity demanded for another in the same direction. For example, an increase in the price of tea will lead to a reduction in the quantity of tea demanded and an increase in the quantity of coffee demanded. Products with a positive cross elasticity of demand are *substitutes* for one another. Products with a negative cross elasticity of demand are *complements* to one another; an increase in, say, the price of cars is likely to lead to a reduction in the quantity of cars demanded and a consequent reduction in the quantity of fuel demanded. The greater the magnitude of the value of the cross elasticity of demand for two products, the closer is their relationship as substitutes or complements.

2.2.4 Descriptions of elasticity values: perfectly elastic, (highly) elastic, unitary elasticity, (highly) inelastic, perfectly inelastic

Following the discussion of price elasticity of demand in section 2.2.3, we are now in a position to describe the different possible elasticity values.

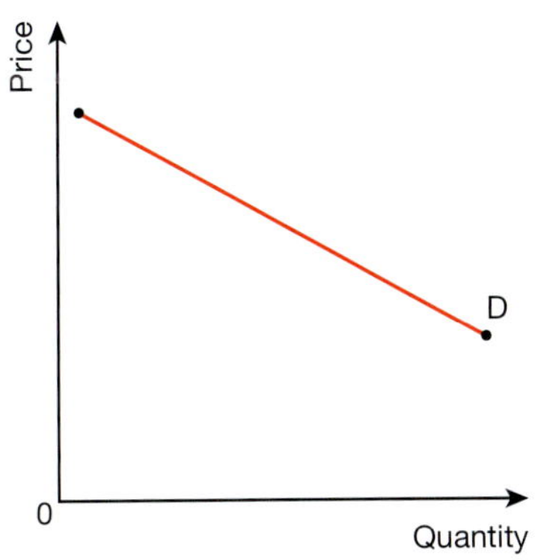

Figure 2.13 Elastic demand ▲

Elastic demand

Figure 2.13 illustrates elastic demand. In this case the proportionate or percentage change in demand is greater than the percentage change in price and the PED coefficient is greater than 1 (PED > 1). This is often the case for products consumers regard as luxuries such as expensive perfumes or toiletries. The higher the figure for the price elasticity of demand, the more price elastic is the demand for the product. Price elasticity of demand tends to be higher at high prices than low prices

Figure 2.14 Inelastic demand ▲

Inelastic demand

Figure 2.14 illustrates inelastic demand. In this case the proportionate or percentage change in demand is less than the percentage change in price and the PED coefficient is less than 1 (PED < 1). This is often the case for products consumers regard as necessities such as salt in India. The lower the figure for the price elasticity of demand, the more price inelastic is the demand for the product. Price elasticity of demand tends to be higher at high prices than low prices.

Link

For further discussion on the way in which price elasticity of demand varies along the length of a demand curve see section 2.2.5 in this chapter.

Perfectly elastic, perfectly inelastic and unitary elastic demand

In the case of the elastic and inelastic demand curves (Figures 2.13 and 2.14) the price elasticity of demand will vary along the length of the demand curve. However, there are three limiting cases illustrated in Figure 2.15 in which the price elasticity of demand is constant throughout the whole length of the curve.

- **Perfectly elastic** demand refers to a case in which even a tiny change in price brings about an infinite change in the quantity demanded so that the demand curve is a horizontal straight line.
- **Perfectly inelastic** demand refers to a case in which however great the change in price there is no change in the quantity demanded so that the demand curve is a vertical straight line.
- **Unitary elasticity** of demand at all prices means that the demand curve is a rectangular hyperbola, which means that any price/quantity combination will yield exactly the same total revenue.

Figure 2.15 Perfectly elastic demand, perfectly inelastic demand and unitary elasticity of demand ▶

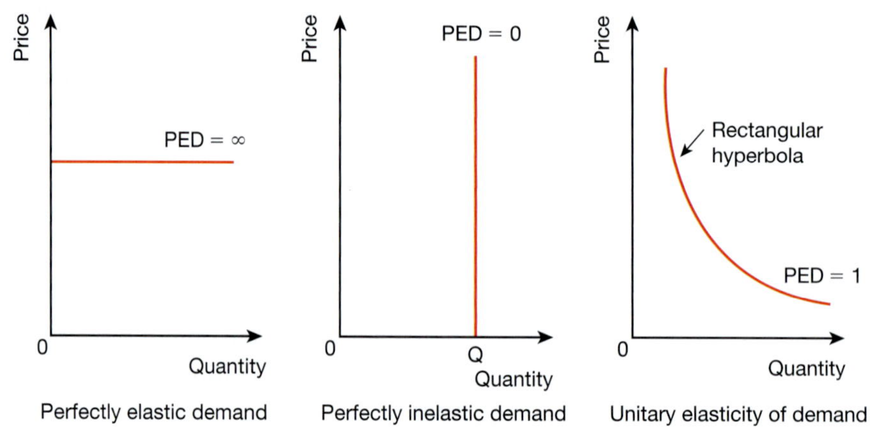

2.2.5 *Variation in price elasticity of demand along the length of a straight-line demand curve*

Point elasticity of demand

Up to now when looking at the price elasticity of demand we have been considering the value for a change in price. This is referred to as the arc price elasticity of demand. There are occasions, however, when economists are interested in the price elasticity of demand at a single price or point on the demand curve. This is known as point price elasticity of demand and is particularly useful when considering straight-line demand curves. This is illustrated in Figure 2.16 and Table 2.11.

Key terms

Arc price elasticity of demand: a measurement of the price elasticity of demand over a range of prices

Point price elasticity of demand: a measurement of the price elasticity of demand at a particular price

In order to calculate the point price elasticity of demand at any particular price we take the corresponding point on the demand curve, X, and then divide the distance XZ by the distance XY. Clearly, at the price corresponding to the midpoint of the demand curve, XZ = XY and, therefore, the price elasticity of demand is equal to unity. In this case this corresponds to a price of $5.50 and a quantity demanded of 11. At prices below the midpoint of $5.50, XZ is less than XY and so

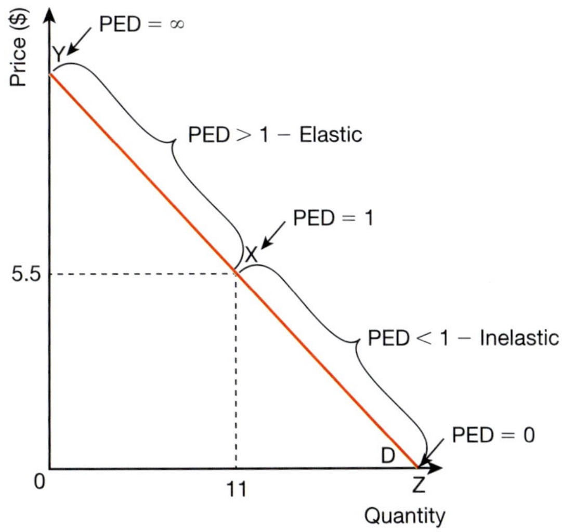

Figure 2.16 Demand curve for product ▲

Table 2.11 The demand schedule for a particular product ▼

Price ($)	Quantity demanded
1.00	20
2.00	18
3.00	16
4.00	14
5.00	12
5.50	11
6.00	10
7.00	8
8.00	6

the price elasticity of demand is less than 1 or inelastic. At point Z the price elasticity of demand is zero. At prices above $5.50, XY is greater than XZ and so the price elasticity of demand is greater than 1 or elastic. At point Y the price elasticity of demand is infinity.

From this discussion and that of arc elasticity, it is clear that for a product with a normal downward-sloping demand curve the price elasticity of demand will vary along the length of the curve. For this reason, it is not possible to say that the demand for a product is elastic or inelastic; we can only say that demand is elastic or inelastic at a particular point on the curve (at a particular price) or over a range of prices. It also means that price elasticity of demand can only be meaningfully measured for small price changes.

2.2.6 *Factors affecting demand*

Price elasticity of demand

Time

Generally the longer the time period being considered, the more elastic the demand for a particular product is likely to be. There are a number of reasons for this. Firstly, it may take time for individuals to become aware of price changes, particularly for products they may buy infrequently such as cookers or refrigerators. In addition, it may take time to research and discover suitable substitutes.

The number of substitutes

This leads us into another factor affecting the price elasticity of demand for a product – the number and closeness of any substitutes it has. A product such as a particular brand of chocolate bar will have a considerable number of close substitutes to which consumers could quickly switch if the price of this brand rose and so we would expect the demand for it to be relatively price elastic. If, on the other hand, a product has relatively few substitutes, we would expect the demand to be relatively price inelastic.

Linked to this factor is the number of uses to which a product may be put. Generally the more uses a product has, the more markets in which it can be sold and hence the more price elastic its demand is likely to be. Sugar, for example, has a range of possible domestic and business uses and so a change in price may have a significant impact on the overall market demand when prices change even though the effect in any individual market may be relatively small. Economists use the term "composite demand" to describe products that are demanded for more than one purpose.

The degree of necessity

The more essential an individual believes a product to be, the more inelastic the demand for it is likely to be. Generally, therefore, necessities have an inelastic demand and luxuries an elastic demand. We should be aware, however, that what one individual or group may deem a necessity, others may see as a luxury. For example, a family living in a remote rural area may believe it is a necessity to have two or even three cars to enable them all to get to work and engage in their leisure activities, whereas a similar family living in a town with good public transport facilities might see owning more than one car as a luxury.

Durability and perishability

Some products by their very nature are durable, such as televisions, cars and cookers, which means they are consumed over a long period of time. It is possible to postpone the purchase of these products and repair them when prices are high or rising and bring forward the purchase of replacements when prices are falling. The more durable a product is, the more price elastic the demand is likely to be. On the other hand, products such as batteries for digital cameras have a relatively short lifespan and have to be replaced immediately when worn out. Such products have a more inelastic demand.

Proportion of income taken by the product

Another important factor in determining price elasticity of demand is the proportion of an individual's income taken up by a product. A product will account for a significant proportion of a family budget if its price is high or it is consumed regularly in large quantities. In such cases a given percentage change in price will have a significant impact on the family's budget. Rice, for example, takes up a high proportion of family expenditure in some countries and so a given percentage change is likely to have a much greater impact on the quantity of it demanded than the same percentage change in the price of, say, salt which accounts for a much lower proportion of income.

Activity

Elastic or inelastic

Which of the following products would you expect to have an elastic demand and which an inelastic demand? In each case explain why demand might be price elastic or price inelastic.

1 Bread
2 Unleaded petrol
3 Exotic foreign holidays
4 Visits to the cinema
5 Mobile phones
6 Designer jeans

Income elasticity of demand

The major factor determining the income elasticity of demand (YED) of a product is the extent to which it is regarded as either a necessity or a luxury. Necessities are goods or services which are regarded by individuals as essential and which they will purchase irrespective of changes in their income. Examples might include food, utilities such as gas and water, vital medicines such as insulin for diabetics as well certain addictive or habit forming products such as cigarettes. Luxuries, on the other hand, tend to be expensive high quality products whose demand increases disproportionately as an individual's income increases and they have more money available for discretionary expenditure. Examples might include expensive perfumes, designer clothes and high quality accessories such as Hermès Birkin handbags. Luxuries will generally have substitutes, but these are regarded as less desirable.

It is important to acknowledge, however, that, as indicated earlier, the distinction between necessities and luxuries is not an absolute one as what one individual might regard as a necessity, another may regard as a luxury, e.g. the latest mobile phone. Even within product categories such as food individual products may be viewed differently by individuals.

At this point it might be useful to review our understanding of normal and inferior goods. Inferior goods generally have superior substitutes and the demand for them varies inversely with changes in an individual's income; increasing when incomes fall and decreasing when incomes rise.

Normal goods are those for which the demand varies directly with changes in an individual's income; increasing when incomes fall and vice versa.

Necessities are either inferior goods whose demand falls as income rises and as such have a negative income elasticity of demand (YED < 0) or normal goods in that the demand for them rises or falls by a smaller percentage than the percentage change in income. In this case the demand is income inelastic (YED < 1). For example, an individual or household on a very low income may satisfy its need for food by purchasing canned processed meat and vegetables and supermarket own brands, but as their income rises they are able to afford more nutritious fresh meat and vegetables and branded goods. Hence the demand for tinned food and supermarket own brands declines and the demand for fresh food and branded goods increases, but by a smaller proportion than the increase in income. Necessities occupy a lower proportion of household income as incomes rise. For luxuries the demand increases rapidly as income changes which means that they take up a higher proportion of household income as incomes increase. The percentage increase in demand for luxuries is greater than the percentage change in income. Demand is income elastic (YED > 1).

It is also important to note that the income elasticity of demand can be affected by how broadly or narrowly a product or product category is defined. Generally the broader the definition of a product, the more inelastic the demand is likely to be. For example, overall the income elasticity of demand for food is inelastic, but within this product grouping there are items which have an elastic demand with respect to income such as asparagus or exotic cheeses.

It is also important to remember that throughout this analysis we are assuming that the only variable affecting the demand for the product that is changing is household income and that all other determinants of demand are held constant.

Cross elasticity of demand

The major determinant of the cross elasticity of demand for a product is the closeness of its relationship to its complements and substitutes. As we have seen the cross elasticity of demand for complements is negative and that for substitutes is positive. In each case the higher the value of the cross elasticity coefficient, the greater the effect a change in the price of the complement or substitute will have on the demand of the product in question. We would expect, for example, the coefficient to be a high negative figure for the change in the demand for fuel as a result of a change in the price of cars, as they are clearly highly complementary products. Similarly we might expect the cross elasticity of demand for hairdressers to be a relatively low positive figure in a very large city where there are a very large number of competitors supplying a similar service.

One other possible value for the value of the coefficient of cross elasticity of demand for a product is zero (XED = 0). This would be the case for products that are independent of or unrelated to one another. We would not, for example, expect a change in the price of strawberries to have an effect on an individual's demand for coal. Having said this, however, for individuals with a finite limited income, particularly for those with a very low income, ultimately all products are substitutes for one another and so it is possible that a change in the price of one product might impact on the demand for a seemingly unrelated product.

As with income elasticity of demand, it is also important to remember that throughout this analysis we are assuming that the only variable affecting the demand for the product that is changing is household income and the price of complements or substitutes and that all other determinants of demand are held constant.

2.2.7 Relationship between price elasticity and total expenditure on a product

Price elasticity of demand is particularly useful to producers in deciding on their pricing strategies and for the government in deciding on the likely impact of decisions taken about the level of expenditure taxes on goods and services.

In order to explain this we need to first introduce the concepts of total expenditure and total revenue. These are mirror images of one another in that the total amount of money spent by consumers on a product must equal the total amount of money or revenue received by the firm selling the product. As we are mainly interested in the implications for firms, we will concentrate on total revenue (TR).

The total revenue (TR) received from the sale of a good or service is found by multiplying the price of the product by the quantity sold.

$$TR = P \times Q$$

Using the demand schedule in Table 2.11, we can now illustrate the relationship between changes in the price of the product, the total revenue and the price elasticity of demand. This is shown in Table 2.12.

Table 2.12 Price elasticity of demand and total revenue ▼

Price ($)	Quantity demanded	Total revenue	PED
1.00	20	20.00	Over this price range PED < 1
2.00	18	36.00	
3.00	16	48.00	
4.00	14	56.00	
5.00	12	60.00	
5.50	11	60.50	= 1
6.00	10	60.00	PED > 1
7.00	8	56.00	
8.00	6	48.00	
9.00	4	36.00	
10.00	2	20.00	

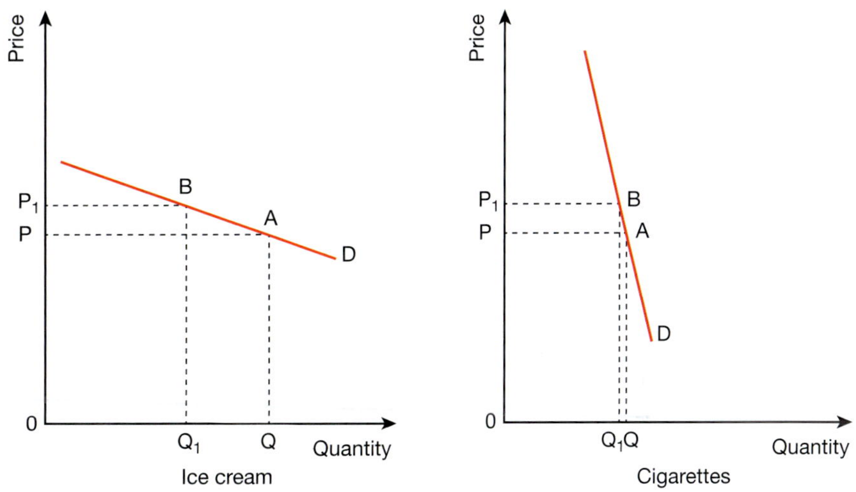

Figure 2.17 Demand curves for ice cream and cigarettes ▲

2.2.8 *Implications for decision-making of price income and cross elasticity of demand*

Implications of price elasticity of demand for firms

A knowledge of the price elasticity of demand for a firm's product will clearly influence its pricing strategy. It will aim to set a price of $5.50 because this will maximise the revenue from sales. If it is currently charging a price below this, then it knows that demand is price inelastic and so any increase in price will increase *total revenue*. If it is currently charging a price above $5.50, then demand is price elastic over this range and the firm knows that reducing price will increase total revenue.

The same point can be illustrated diagrammatically. Figure 2.17 shows the demand curves for a particular brand of ice cream and cigarettes. Ice cream is likely to have a relatively more elastic demand curve than cigarettes and hence the demand curve has a shallower slope. In both cases the initial price is P, giving a total revenue equal to the area of the rectangle equal to OPAQ. If both products have an equal percentage rise in price to P_1 then the total revenue becomes $OP_1B_1Q_1$.

Clearly the total revenue has fallen in the case of ice cream and risen in the case of cigarettes. A fall in price will have the opposite effect on total revenue in each case.

Implications of price elasticity of demand for governments

Price elasticity of demand and indirect taxes

The price elasticity of demand is also important for the government in deciding on which goods to impose indirect taxes.

Key term

Indirect tax: a tax on expenditure which is levied on the producer, but may then be passed on to consumers through an increase in price.

Indirect taxes on expenditure are either *ad valorem* or specific. An *ad valorem* (according to value) tax is a percentage tax such as VAT in the UK or state sales taxes in the USA or General Sales Tax (GST) in a number of other countries. A specific tax such as UK excise duty levies a fixed amount per unit of a particular product. Figure 2.18 illustrates the effect of a specific tax on ice cream and on cigarettes.

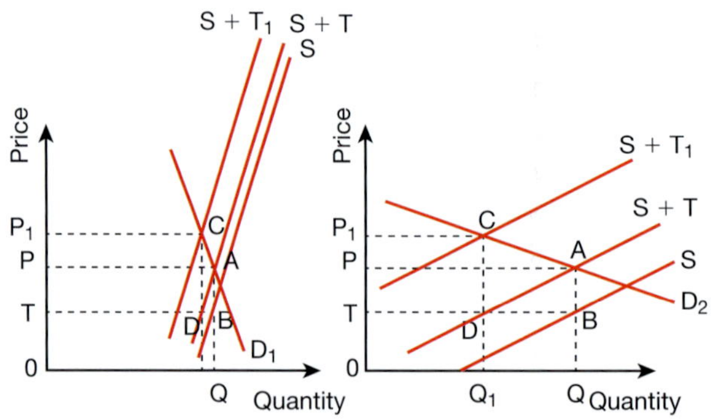

Figure 2.18 The effect of a specific tax on cigarettes and ice cream ▲

Figure 2.18 shows the demand curves for cigarettes (D_1) and ice cream (D_2). In each case the government initially imposes a specific tax of TP per unit on the product generating a tax revenue in each case of TPAB (= tax per unit × quantity sold). If the government now increases the tax to TP_1 per unit, the tax revenue is now TP_1CD in each case. It can clearly be seen that in the case of ice cream the tax revenue received by the government will fall as the increase in price has resulted in a more than proportionate decrease in the quantity demanded. In the case of cigarettes, however, the tax revenue has increased because the proportionate fall in the quantity demanded is less than the proportionate increase in price. This is the rationale behind governments imposing taxes on goods which have an inelastic demand such as fuel, tobacco and alcohol. However, governments need to be aware of the fact that some goods which have an inelastic demand are basic necessities, e.g. food, so that imposing taxes on them might cause hardship for those on low incomes.

Link

For more on indirect taxes see Chapter 8, section 8.1.1.

The price elasticity of demand along with the price elasticity of supply is also important in establishing how the burden of a given indirect tax is distributed between consumers and producers. We will consider this after we have discussed price elasticity of supply in the next section.

2.3 Price elasticity of supply

2.3.1 *Definition of price elasticity of supply (PES)*

Price elasticity of supply (PES)

Figure 2.19 shows the supply curves for X and Y. In each case an increase in demand has brought about the same percentage increase in price providing producers with an incentive to increase quantity supplied. However, it is clear that there has been a significantly greater increase in the supply of X compared to Y. As in the case of demand, the reason for this is the differences in the slopes of the two curves. This is determined by their different price elasticity of supply, which is the responsiveness of the quantity of a product supplied to a change in its price.

Key term

Price elasticity of supply: the responsiveness of the quantity supplied of a product to a change in price.

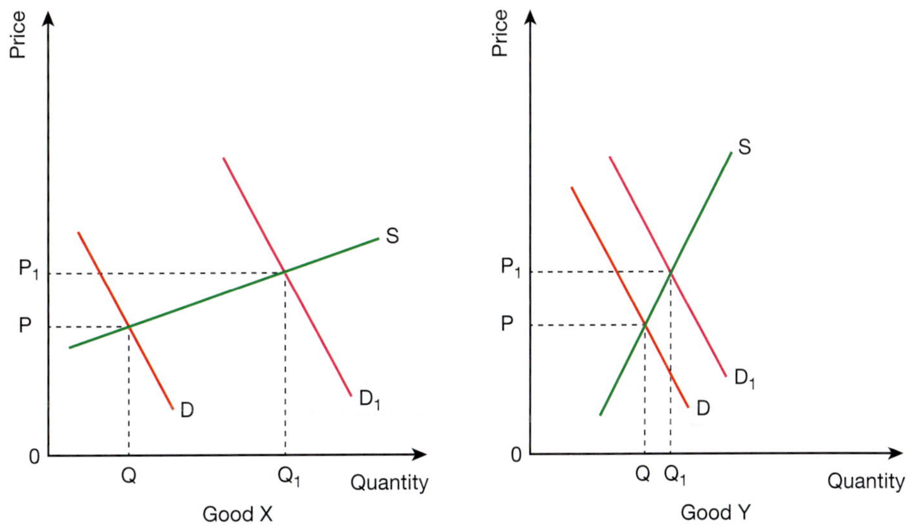

Figure 2.19 Price elasticity of supply ▲

2.3.2 *Formula for and calculation of price elasticity of supply*

Calculation of the price elasticity of supply

The formula for the price elasticity of supply is:

$$\text{PES} = \frac{\text{the proportionate change in supply}}{\text{the proportionate change in price}}$$

$$\text{PED} = \frac{\text{new supply } (Q_1) - \text{original supply} (Q)}{\text{original supply } (Q)} \div \frac{\text{new price } (P_1) - \text{original price } (P)}{\text{original price } (P)}$$

If instead we use percentages in the calculation, the formula is:

$$\text{PES} = \frac{\text{percentage change in supply}}{\text{percentage change in price}} = \frac{\%\Delta Qs}{\%\Delta P}$$

2.3.3 Significance of relative percentage changes, the size and sign of the coefficient of price elasticity of supply

Unlike demand, the price elasticity of supply for a product will always be positive. The price elasticity of supply will vary in magnitude at different prices along a normal upward-sloping supply curve. Table 2.13 provides a summary of the meaning and significance of the different possible values for the coefficient of price elasticity of supply.

Table 2.13 Meaning of values for the price elasticity of supply ▼

Value of PES	Terminology	Meaning
0	Perfectly inelastic supply	A change in price leaves quantity supplied unchanged
< 1	Inelastic	Proportionate or percentage change in quantity supplied is less than the proportionate or percentage change in price
= 1	Unitary elasticity of supply	Proportionate or percentage change in quantity supplied is equal to the proportionate or percentage change in price
>1	Elastic	Proportionate or percentage change in quantity supplied is greater than the proportionate or percentage change in price
Infinity	Perfectly elastic supply	A tiny change in price brings about an infinite change in the quantity supplied

Although the elasticity of supply will vary along the length of a normal upward-sloping supply curve, in parallel with demand, there are three possible limiting cases where the elasticity of supply is the same at all points on the curve. These cases are illustrated in Figure 2.20.

Figure 2.20 Perfectly elastic supply, perfectly inelastic supply and unitary elasticity of supply ▶

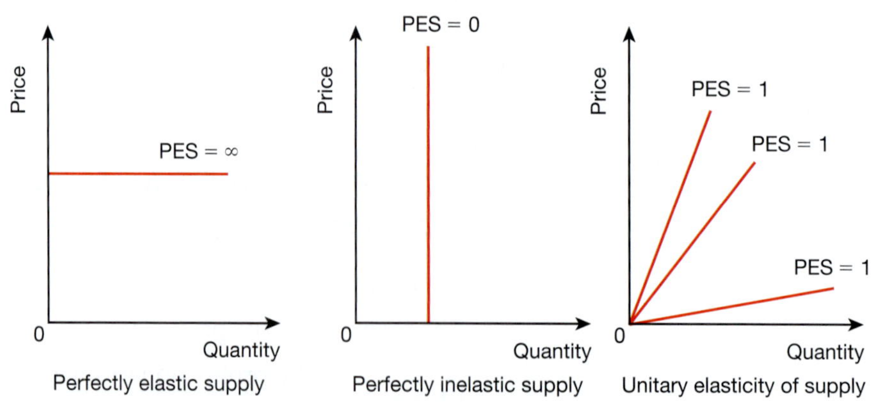

- **Perfectly elastic** supply refers to a case in which even a tiny change in price brings about an infinite change in the quantity supplied so that the supply curve is a horizontal straight line.
- **Perfectly inelastic supply** refers to a case in which however great the change in price, there is no change in the quantity demanded so that the supply curve is a vertical straight line.
- **Unitary elasticity of supply at all prices** is illustrated by any straight-line supply curve passing through the origin.

2.3.4 *Factors affecting price elasticity of supply*

> **Link**
>
> See section 2.3.5 in this chapter for more on the importance of elasticity of supply in relation to the speed with which firms are able to respond to changing market conditions.

Time

As with demand, time is an important factor determining the price elasticity of supply. Generally the longer the time period under consideration, the more elastic the supply will be. Because elasticity of supply can vary significantly over time, it cannot in fact be measured without specific reference to the time period involved. The importance of the time period involved is explored in greater depth in the next section when looking at the importance of elasticity of supply in relation to the speed with which firms are able to respond to changing market conditions.

Availability and nature of resources

Clearly the supply of a product will be more elastic if the resources required to produce it are plentifully available. The nature of the resources required is also important in that if highly specialised, expensive capital is needed or labour has to be highly qualified or requires long periods of training then supply is likely to be inelastic.

Extent of spare capacity in a firm

Supply is likely to be more elastic if a firm has spare capacity in terms of labour and capital. If all factors of production are being fully utilised, it will not be possible for a firm to increase production quickly in response to an increase in demand, and supply will be inelastic.

Availability of stocks

If a firm has stocks of goods available or stocks can be obtained very quickly then supply is likely to be relatively elastic. Clearly it is possible to store and stockpile some products more easily than others. Manufactured goods and those that can be processed or frozen can be stored relatively easily whereas perishable goods like fresh vegetables cannot.

> **Link**
>
> For more on ease of entry to and exit from markets see contestable markets in Chapter 7, section 7.6.4.

Number of firms in the market

The number of firms in a particular market is also an important factor. The greater the number of firms in a market, the more elastic the supply is likely to be. Linked to this is the ease of entry to and exit from the market with more firms being able to enter if start-up costs are low and there are no sunk costs.

Possibility of switching factors of production between alternative uses

The range of products produced by a firm and the ease with which it can switch capital and labour between them is another important factor. The greater the range of products and the more flexible are the resources, the more elastic supply is likely to be. For example, in a school or college, Economics teachers can switch quickly to teach Business Studies in response to a sudden change in demand.

> **Activity**
>
> **Elastic or inelastic**
>
> Which of the following would you expect to have an elastic supply and which an inelastic supply? In each case explain why supply might be elastic or inelastic.
>
> 1 Natural vanilla
> 2 Oil
> 3 Freshly cut flowers
> 4 Canned tomatoes
> 5 Houses
> 6 Vintage wine
> 7 Tickets for the Australian Open Tennis Final

The factors affecting the elasticity of supply are summarised in Table 2.14.

Table 2.14 Factors affecting the price elasticity of supply ▼

Factor affecting PES	Impact on PES
Time period	The longer the time period, the more elastic is supply
Availability of resources	The greater the number of resources and the less specialised they are, the more elastic is supply
Spare capacity	The existence of spare capacity will make supply more elastic
Stocks	Supply will be more elastic if stocks are available or can easily be obtained
Number of firms in the market	The greater the number of firms in the market, the more elastic is supply
Possibility of switching factors between uses	If factors can easily be switched between uses then supply will be more elastic

2.3.5 *Implications for speed and ease with which firms react to changed market conditions*

The value of the price elasticity of supply is an important factor in determining firms' ability to expand or reduce production in response to changing market conditions and the speed with which they are able to do so. In discussing this economists often distinguish between three time periods when considering the price elasticity of supply:

- **Immediate or market period:** in this period the quantity supplied is completely fixed. At this time, supply is perfectly inelastic.
- **Short period:** in this period one or more factors of production are fixed and the quantity supplied can only be increased by making greater use of the variable factors. Elasticity of supply will increase, but may still be relatively inelastic.
- **Long period:** in this period all factors of production are variable and the producer can increase the quantity supplied by increasing the scale of production. Supply is likely to be relatively elastic.

Take the case of fresh fish. If there is a sudden significant increase in the demand for fresh fish, it will not be possible for fish companies to increase the quantity supplied to the market in the immediate period and so the supply will be perfectly inelastic. However, the increase in demand is likely to provide an incentive for companies to increase the quantity supplied by using more variable factors – recruiting more workers and making greater use of existing ships, plant and equipment – thereby, making supply more elastic in the short run. At this stage, though, companies will not be able to produce more ships. If fishing companies believe that the increase in demand is likely to be permanent, they can, in the long run, increase the entire scale of production, not only utilising existing resources more fully, but building new ships and investing in new technology and training more workers. In the long run, therefore, supply becomes yet more elastic.

The impact and incidence of indirect taxes

Having considered both elasticity of demand and elasticity of supply, we are now in a position to apply these concepts to the way in which the burden of indirect taxes on expenditure is distributed between consumers and producers. In looking at this, economists refer to the impact and incidence of tax.

The impact of taxation refers to the individual or group who bears the initial burden of any tax, i.e. who actually pays the money to the tax-gathering authority. The incidence of taxation refers to who ultimately bears the burden of paying the tax. In the case of a direct tax, such as income tax in the UK, which is levied on a worker's weekly or monthly pay, the individual worker bears both the impact and incidence of the tax. The tax is paid directly by the individual to the revenue-collecting authority and the individual normally has no mechanism for passing the tax on to anyone else.

Key terms

Impact of a tax: where the initial burden of paying the tax falls.

Incidence of a tax: where the final burden of paying a tax falls.

Link

See Chapter 3, section 3.2.1, for more on the impact and incidence of taxes.

This is not, however, the case with indirect taxes on expenditure. Here, although the impact is borne by the producer who initially makes payment of the tax, the producer will then attempt to pass the tax on to consumers in an attempt to ensure they bear all or part of the incidence of the tax by raising the price of the product. The proportion of the incidence of the tax that the producer is able to pass on to the consumer will depend upon the extent to which the producer is able to raise the price and this, in turn, will depend upon the relative magnitudes of the elasticity of demand and elasticity of supply for the product. This is illustrated in Figure 2.21.

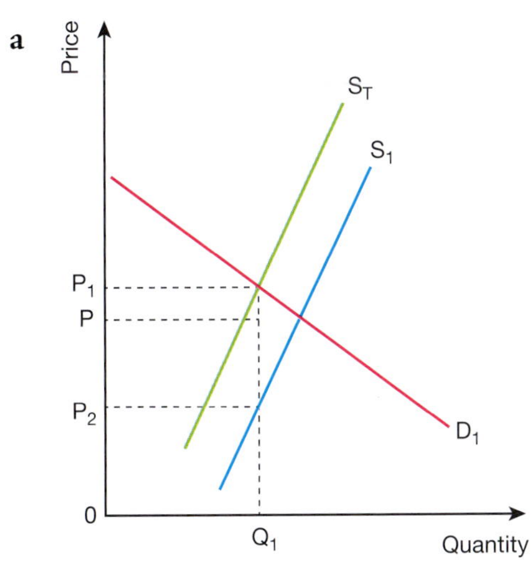

Figure 2.21a

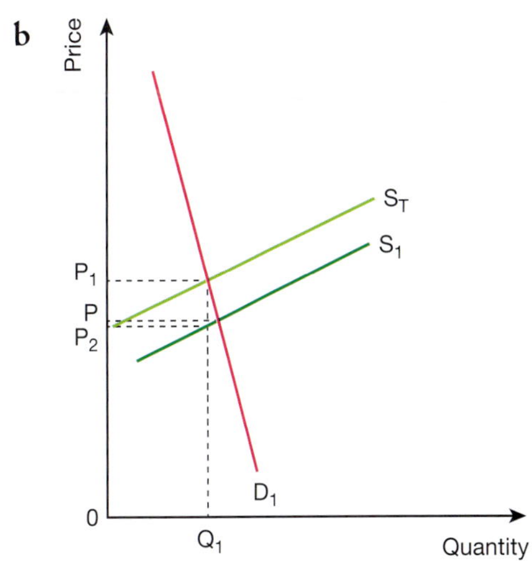

Figure 2.21b

Incidence of indirect taxation ▲

In both cases the initial demand and supply curves are D_1 and S_1 giving an initial equilibrium price, P. The government now imposes a specific tax on the product which shifts the supply curve upwards to the right to S_T, increasing the price to P_1. The amount of the tax per unit is given by the vertical distance between the two supply curves, i.e. P_2P_1.

The proportion of the incidence which is borne by the consumer is given by the increase in price – PP_1 and the proportion borne by the producer is the remainder of the tax – P_2P.

Where demand is elastic relative to supply as in Figure 2.21a, the majority of the incidence of the tax is borne by the producer because it is not possible to raise the price without a much greater proportionate change in demand. In Figure 2.21b, however, demand is relatively inelastic compared to supply, which means that the producer is in a strong position to increase the price of the product and so the consumer bears the majority of the incidence of the tax.

Progress question

4 How would the incidence of an indirect tax between producers and consumers have an effect in the following situations?

a Demand for the good is perfectly elastic or supply perfectly inelastic.

b Demand for the good is perfectly inelastic or supply perfectly elastic.

c The elasticity of demand for and elasticity of supply of the good are the same.

2.4 The interaction of demand and supply

2.4.1 *Definition of market equilibrium and disequilibrium*

In discussing the nature of market equilibrium, we begin by looking at the role of markets.

The role of markets

Markets are in equilibrium when the plans and decisions of buyers and sellers coincide and so there is no tendency for change to price or output. As we shall see, this will occur *ceteris paribus* at the price and output at which the quantity demanded by consumers is equal to the quantity supplied by producers. This is referred to as the equilibrium price or market clearing price.

Market equilibrium refers to the price and quantity demanded and supplied from which, once they have been achieved, there will be no tendency for change. As we shall see, this will be at the point where the quantity demanded of a product equals the quantity supplied. Market disequilibrium will occur if the price is set above or below this level because there will be pressure for the price to change. If price is set above the level at which the quantity demanded equals the quantity supplied, there will be surplus, which will exert downward pressure on price, and if price is set below this level, there will be a shortage in the market, which will exert upward pressure on the price.

Key terms

Equilibrium price: the market price from which there will be no tendency for change. This will be at the price where quantity demanded = quantity supplied.

Market equilibrium: the price from which there will be no tendency for change given existing conditions of demand and supply – the price at which demand equals supply. Also known simply as "equilibrium".

Market disequilibrium: a situation in which demand does not equal supply, in which case there will be a tendency for price to change – to rise if demand is greater than supply and to fall if supply is greater than demand. Also known simply as "disequilibrium".

The determination of the equilibrium market price

In order to establish the market equilibrium price for a particular good or service, in this case rice, we bring together the market demand and supply schedules and curves for rice considered earlier.

The equilibrium price and quantity demanded and supplied are given by the intersection of the demand and supply curve, in this case giving a price of 15 cents and an equilibrium quantity demanded and supplied of 90 kilos per month.

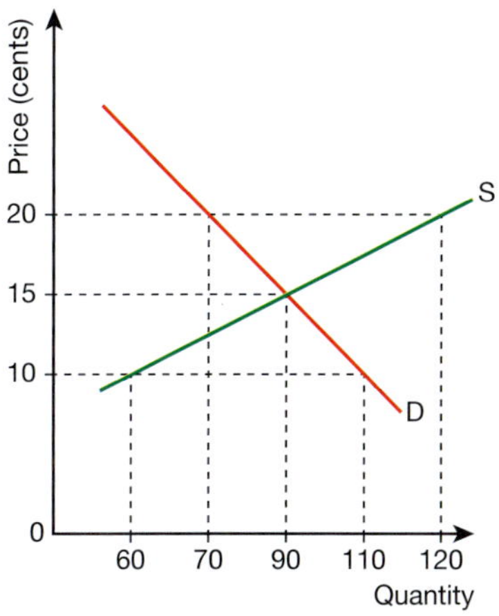

Figure 2.22 Market demand and supply curves for rice ▲

Getting it right

It is important to remember that the equilibrium price and quantity demanded and supplied cannot change unless there is a change in the conditions of demand and/or supply.

Table 2.15 Market demand and supply schedules for rice ▼

Price of rice per kilo (cents)	Market demand (kilos per month)	Market supply (kilos per month)
5	130	30
10	110	60
15	90	90
20	70	120
25	50	150
30	30	180

In order to see why this must be the equilibrium (the position from which there is no tendency for change), let us look at what happens if the price is above or below 15 cents.

If we assume that the price is above the equilibrium at, say, 20 cents, then the quantity supplied is 120 kilos, but consumers wish only to consume 70 kilos. There is a surplus or excess supply of 50 kilos. Producers will prefer to receive something for their rice rather than let it go to waste and so will begin to reduce the price. As this takes place, there will be a movement down along the supply curve as the quantity supplied falls, but at the same time the fact that the rice is now cheaper encourages some consumers into the market leading to an increase in the quantity demanded and a movement up along the demand curve. This process continues until there is no longer any surplus remaining, i.e. at the point where the demand and supply curves intersect.

No price above 15 cents can be an equilibrium because there will always be a surplus and, therefore, a tendency for the price to fall.

Similar logic applies if we look at any price below 15 cents, e.g. 10 cents. Here the quantity demanded exceeds the quantity supplied by 50 kilos. Competition for rice amongst consumers combined with producers seeing an opportunity to increase profits will result in the price beginning to rise. This rise in price will bring about a movement up along both the supply and demand curves as producers increase the quantity supplied and some consumers find they can no longer afford the rice, reducing the quantity demanded. Price will continue to rise until there is no longer any excess demand, i.e. where the demand and supply curves intersect.

No price below the point at which the quantity demanded equals the quantity supplied can be an equilibrium position because there will always be excess demand which will tend to drive up the price. Hence the equilibrium price and quantity demanded and supplied will be found at the point where the demand and supply curves intersect and there is no excess supply, which would tend to drive the price down, or excess demand, which would tend to drive the price up.

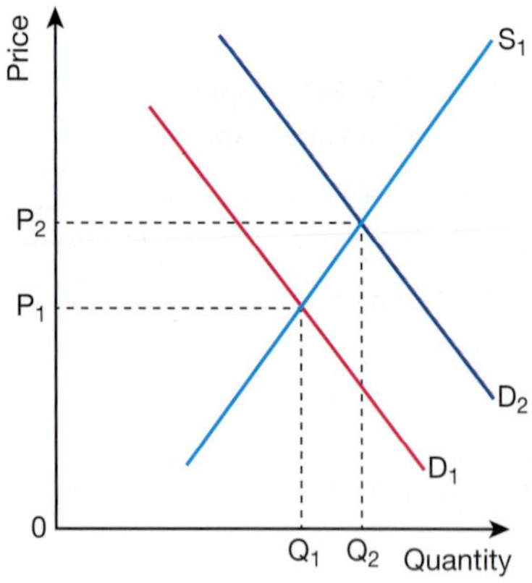

Figure 2.23 The effect of an increase in demand ▲

2.4.2 Effect of shifts in demand and supply curves on equilibrium price and quantity

The effect of shifts of the demand and supply curves on the equilibrium price and quantity demanded and supplied

An increase in demand

In Figure 2.23 the original demand curve for rice is D_1 and the supply curve is S_1 giving an equilibrium price of P_1 and quantity demanded and supplied of Q_1. If now the conditions of demand change, causing an increase in the demand for the good at each and every price, the demand curve will shift outwards to the right. This leads to a new equilibrium price of P_2. Supply expands along the existing supply curve leading to a new equilibrium quantity demanded and supplied of Q_2. Note that there is no need for a new supply curve because all that has changed for the producer is the price; the conditions of supply have not altered.

Getting it right

The effect of an increase in demand is to increase both the equilibrium price and quantity demanded and supplied.

A decrease in demand

In Figure 2.24 the original demand curve for rice is D_1 and the supply curve is S_1 giving an equilibrium price of P_1 and quantity demanded and supplied of Q_1. If now the conditions of demand change, causing a decrease in the demand for the good at each and every price, the demand curve will shift inwards to the left. This leads to a new equilibrium price of P_2. Supply contracts along the existing supply curve leading to a new equilibrium quantity demanded and supplied of Q_2. Note that there is no need for a new supply curve because all that has changed for the producer is the price; the conditions of supply have not altered.

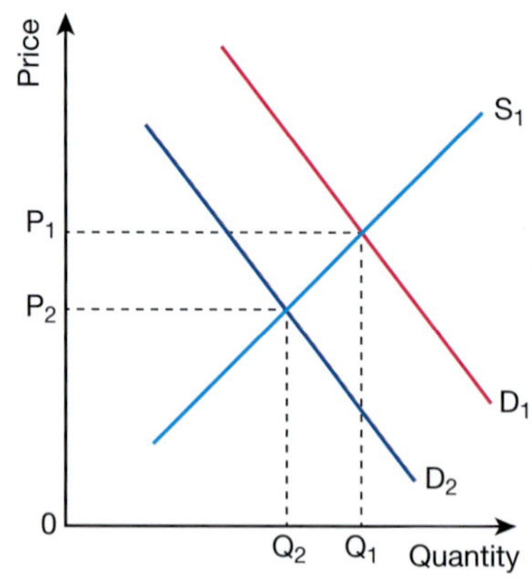

Figure 2.24 The effect of a decrease in demand ▲

Getting it right

The effect of a decrease in demand is to decrease both the equilibrium price and quantity demanded and supplied.

An increase in supply

In Figure 2.25 the original supply curve for rice is S_1 and the demand curve is D_1 giving an equilibrium price of P_1 and quantity demanded and supplied of Q_1. If now the conditions of supply change, causing an increase in the supply of the good at each and every price, the supply curve will shift outwards to the right. This leads to a new equilibrium price of P_2. Demand expands along the existing demand curve leading to a new equilibrium quantity demanded and supplied of Q_2. Note that there is no need for a new demand curve because all that has changed for consumers is the price; the conditions of demand have not altered.

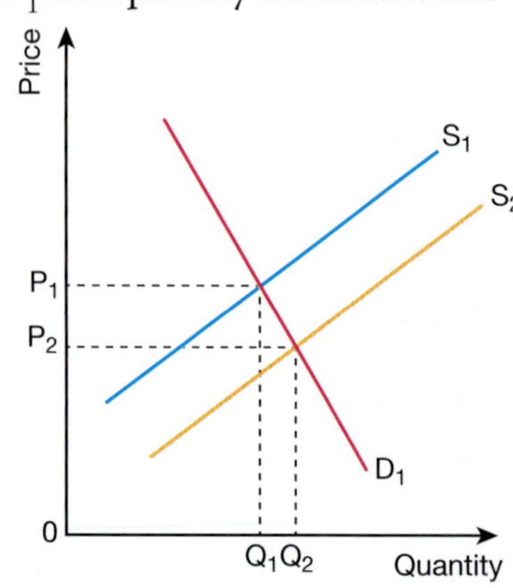

Figure 2.25 The effect of an increase in supply ▲

Getting it right

The effect of an increase in supply is to decrease the equilibrium price and increase quantity demanded and supplied.

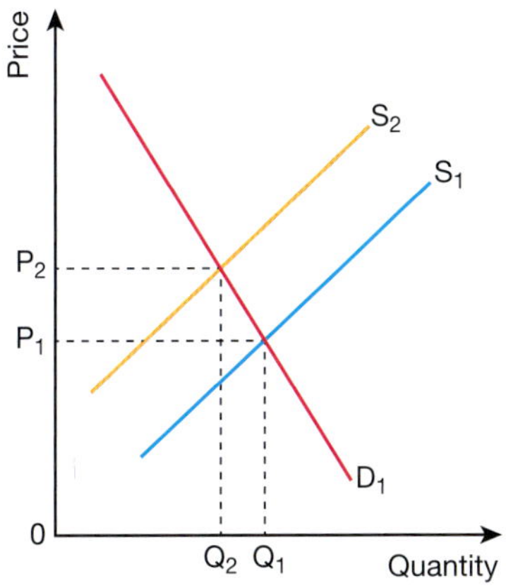

Figure 2.26 The effect of a decrease in supply ▲

A decrease in supply

In Figure 2.26 the original supply curve is S_1 and the demand curve is D_1 giving an equilibrium price of P_1 and quantity demanded and supplied of Q_1. If now the conditions of supply change, causing a decrease in the supply of the good at each and every price, the supply curve will shift inwards to the left. This leads to a new equilibrium price of P_2. Demand contracts along the existing demand curve leading to a new equilibrium quantity demanded and supplied of Q_2. Note that there is no need for a new demand curve because all that has changed for consumers is the price; the conditions of demand have not altered.

The effect of a decrease in supply is to increase the equilibrium price and decrease the quantity demanded and supplied.

Getting it right

The effect of a decrease in supply is to increase the equilibrium price and decrease the quantity demanded and supplied.

Case Study

Rollercoaster ride for vanilla in Madagascar

Vanilla is the second most expensive spice in the world after saffron. Why is the price so high? One reason is that it is in high demand as it is used in a number of products, most of which have an income elastic demand such as chocolate, cakes, ice cream and expensive perfumes. Also global demand has been increasing with the trend towards eating natural foods as opposed to synthetic alternatives. In 2015 Nestlé and Hershey announced plans to use only natural ingredients. On the supply side it is only grown in a few places around the world. Over 80 per cent of the world's supply is grown in Madagascar, with Mexico, Papua New Guinea, Indonesia and India being the other main suppliers. It is also very difficult to grow and extremely labour intensive. In Madagascar the orchid flowers which grow the vanilla beans have to be hand-pollinated by an experienced worker during a short flowering period. After this, the crop must be cured and dried before it is ready for export. The whole process takes a year.

Prices of Madagascan vanilla have fluctuated widely in recent years. At the beginning of 2012, the price of vanilla was $25 an ounce, but with the exception of Madagascar, producers saw poor harvests with Mexico's production falling by 90 per cent. Fears of a worldwide shortage and price rises fuelled large-scale speculative purchases (40 per cent of the world's supply) driving the price to $40 an ounce. Following this a combination of increasing demand and the island being ravaged by multiple storms such as Cyclone Enawo in 2017 drove the price of Gourmet Grade Madagascan Vanilla up to over $600 per kilo in 2018, more expensive than silver by weight. Since then prices have fallen and there is some evidence that the price in 2021 could be as much as 50 per cent lower than the 2018 high. There appear to be a number of reasons for this: firstly, lower overall demand for real vanilla as firms switch to using synthetic vanilla; secondly, recently other vanilla producing countries have produced larger crops. There are still 400 metric tonnes of the 2019 crop unsold and the 2020 crop in Madagascar is thought to be 25 per cent larger than that of 2019.

1 With the aid of demand and supply diagrams, explain the reasons for the changes in the price of vanilla over the period described in the extract.
2 With the aid of demand and supply diagrams, explain the likely impact of the changes in price of vanilla on the market for ice cream.
3 Explain the likely nature of the cross elasticity of demand between natural vanilla produced in Madagascar and synthetic vanilla and vanilla produced by alternative suppliers.
4 With the aid of demand and supply diagrams, explain how the changing price of natural vanilla produced might impact on the market for synthetic vanilla and the market for vanilla produced in other countries.

Progress question

5 The diagram below illustrates the market for petrol. D and S represent the initial demand and supply curves and the initial equilibrium price is X. What will the new equilibrium price be (A, B, C, D, E, F, G or H) if there is:
   - **a** a fall in the cost of refining petrol
   - **b** a fall in bus and train fares
   - **c** a fall in the price of crude oil and an increase in the price of cars
   - **d** a rise in household incomes
   - **e** a rise in the sales tax on petrol and a reduction in the sales tax on cars?

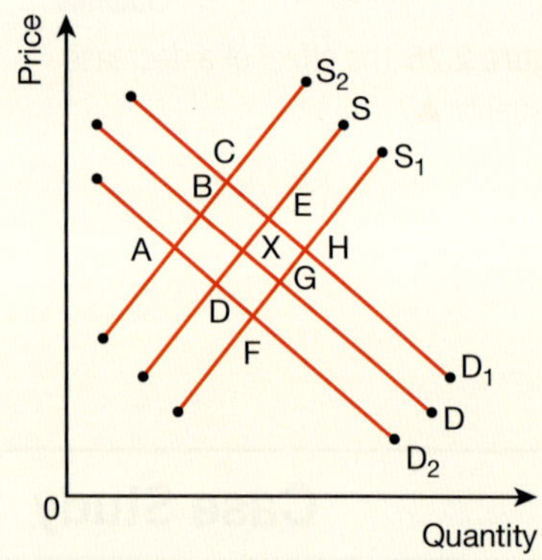

Case Study

UK market for lamb

The last decade has seen considerable volatility in the market for UK lamb. Lamb has always been priced at a premium relative to other meats such as beef and pork in the UK, but 2012 saw this premium increase significantly. In the year to March 2012 prices soared from an average of £7.33 per kilo to £8.51 per kilo leading to a decline in sales of 66,427 tonnes or 20 per cent. A number of factors accounted for this price rise, but chief amongst them according to EBLEX, the organisation for the English sheep and beef industry, was the change in farming practices in New Zealand, the source of much lamb sold in Britain. New Zealand farmers were switching from sheep to cattle farming, which was more profitable.

Following this surge, lamb prices fell with lamb trading at between £3.20 and £3.59 a kilo between 2013 and 2018. The past 2 years, however, have seen prices rise again. Exports of lamb from New Zealand have continued to fall, but this is not the only reason for the rise. Sales of UK-produced lamb are rising. There appear to be a number of reasons for this. Retailers have invested significantly in targeted marketing with the result that not only have sales increased amongst the traditional market of older consumers, but new customer groups are giving lamb a try with significant increases in sales to households with children and the under 45s. In addition, lamb is benefiting from the expanding takeaway business. Finally, although UK lamb is now more expensive, it is cheaper than European producers in Germany, France and Italy and as such remains relatively competitive in world markets. This may enable the industry to take advantage of expanding markets in the Far East and China where the demand is increasing to replace pork whose production has been badly hit by the African Swine Flu epidemic. In 2020, overall sales increased by 7.9 per cent and farmers' revenue increased.

Questions

1 Calculate the price elasticity of demand for lamb in 2012.
2 Given the price elasticity of demand for lamb, explain the likely impact on farmers' revenue of the surge in its price.
3 Explain the difference in price elasticity of demand in 2012 and 2020.
4 With the aid of demand and supply diagrams, explain the increase in the price of lamb in (i) 2012 and (ii) 2020.

2.4.3 *Relationships between different markets*

Joint demand (complements)

Key term

Joint or complementary demand: a situation in which two goods are normally demanded together.

If two or more products are commonly consumed together, such as cars and fuel or bread and butter, then an increase in demand for one will lead to an increase in the demand for the other. Such products are in joint or complementary demand. Hence, in Figure 2.27, an increase in the demand for cars has led to a shift in the demand curve for cars to the right, and an increase in price and quantity demanded and supplied. As a consequence, there will be an increase in the demand for fuel, shifting the demand curve for fuel to the right, and increasing its price and quantity demanded and supplied. The extent of the increases in price in each case will depend upon the elasticity of supply.

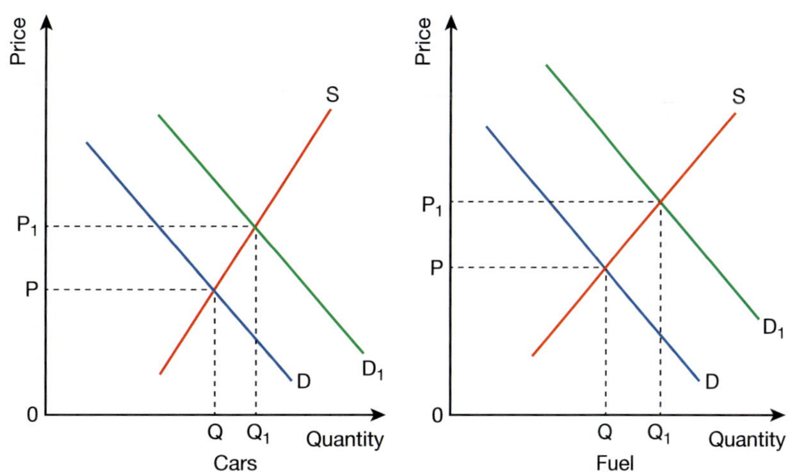

Figure 2.27 Joint demand ▲

Alternative demand (substitutes)

If two products are close substitutes for one another, in that they serve more or less the same purpose to consumers, then an increase in the demand for one will bring about a corresponding fall in the demand for the other. Examples include butter and margarine, fish and meat, tea and coffee and, in the market for factors of production , in some processes,

Key term

Alternative demand: a situation in which two goods are regarded as alternatives for one another.

machines and labour. These are examples of alternative demand. In Figure 2.28 an increase in the demand for product A shifts the demand curve to the right and leads to an increase in the price and the quantity demanded and supplied. This will have the effect of reducing the demand for product B, shifting the demand curve to the left and bringing about a reduction in the price and the quantity demanded and supplied. The extent of the rise in price and quantity demanded and supplied will depend on the price elasticity of supply (the slope of the supply curve).

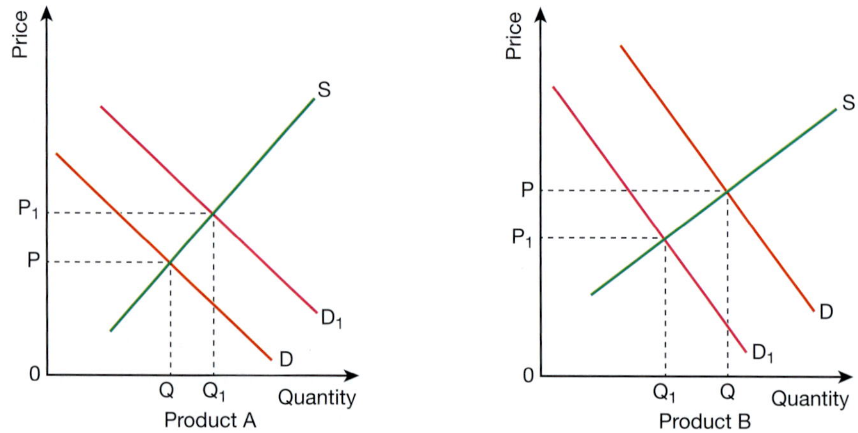

Figure 2.28 Alternative demand ▲

Key terms

Derived demand: a situation in which a product or service, such as labour, is not demanded for itself, but its demand is dependent on the demand for the product it helps to produce.

Derived demand

Factors of production such as labour are not demanded for themselves, but because they produce goods and services which people want. Hence the demand for labour is derived from the demand for the goods and services it provides. The demand for workers in a supermarket will, therefore, increase if the demand for the products sold by the supermarket increases. This is illustrated in Figure 2.29.

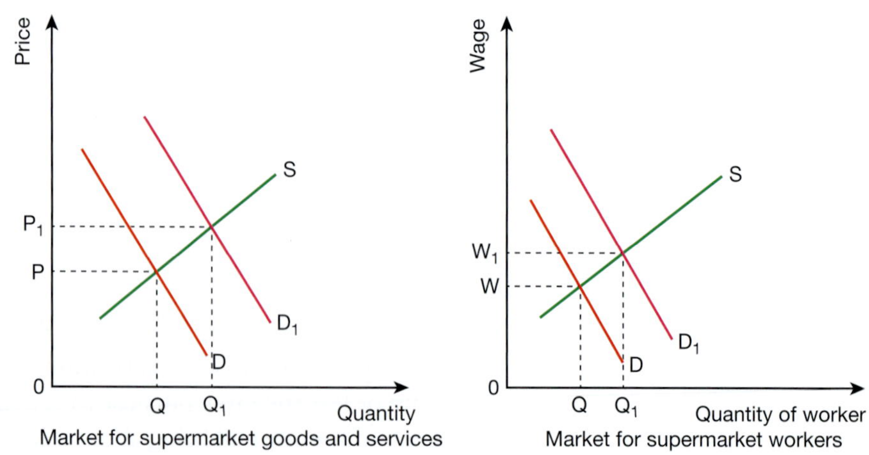

Figure 2.29 Derived demand ▲

Key terms

Composite demand: the situation in which a good is demanded for more than one purpose.

Joint supply: a situation where the production of one good automatically brings about an increase in the supply of another.

Composite demand

Products which can be used for more than one purpose are said to have a composite demand. Bricks, for example, can be used to build schools, office blocks, houses or a garden wall. Wheat can be used as animal feed or increasingly to produce bio fuels. An increase in the demand for wheat to produce bio fuels will shift the demand curve to the right and raise the price, but in the short run, at least, the supply of wheat for animal feed will be reduced, shifting the supply curve to the left and raising the price in this use. This is illustrated in Figure 2.30.

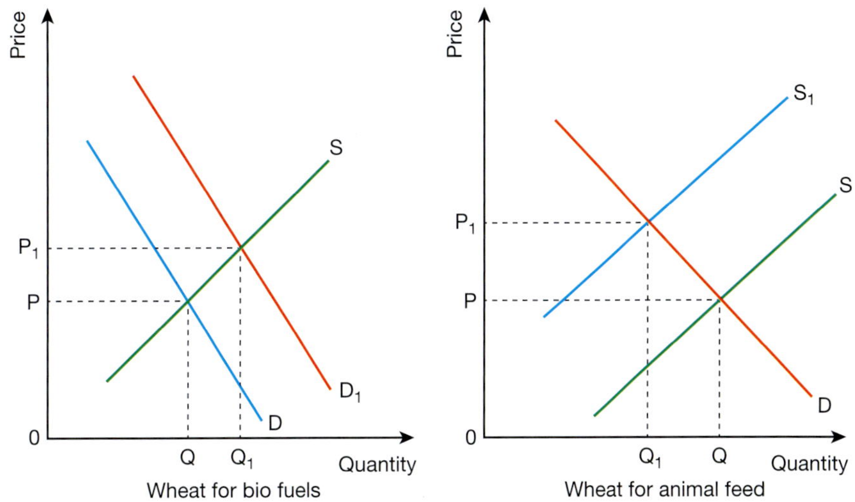

Figure 2.30 Composite demand ▲

Joint supply

Products such as beef and hides for making leather are in joint supply because an increase in the production of beef will lead to an increase in the supply of hides. In Figure 2.31, an increase in the demand for beef has shifted the demand curve for beef to the right raising production and its price, but at the same time it has resulted in an increase in the supply of hides with a consequent fall in the price.

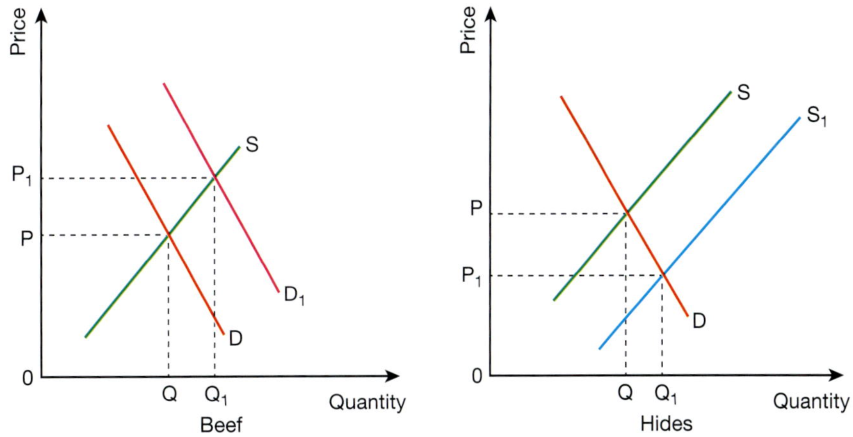

Figure 2.31 Joint supply ▲

Competitive supply

> **Key term**
> **Competitive supply**: an increase in the supply of one product will automatically lead to a reduction in the supply of another.

Given that the overall supply of land in a particular area is fixed, a decision to increase the quantity used for building houses will result in less being available for farming. In a fully employed economy, if more workers move into the tertiary sector, clearly fewer will be available for the primary and manufacturing sectors. These are examples of competitive supply where an increase in the production of one product reduces the supply of another. In Figure 2.32, an increase in the supply of houses has led to a reduction in the supply of agricultural products and an increase in their price.

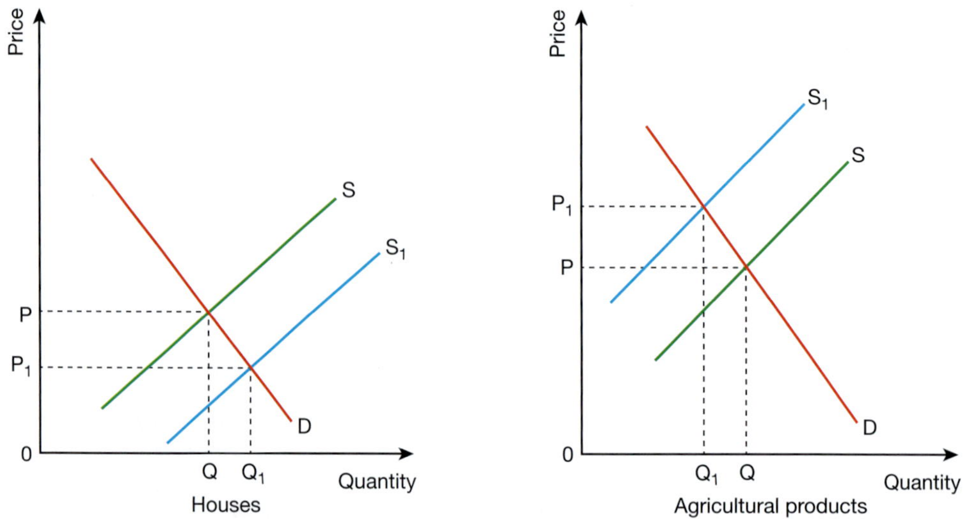

Figure 2.32 Competitive supply ▲

Case Study

Soaring price of rhodium

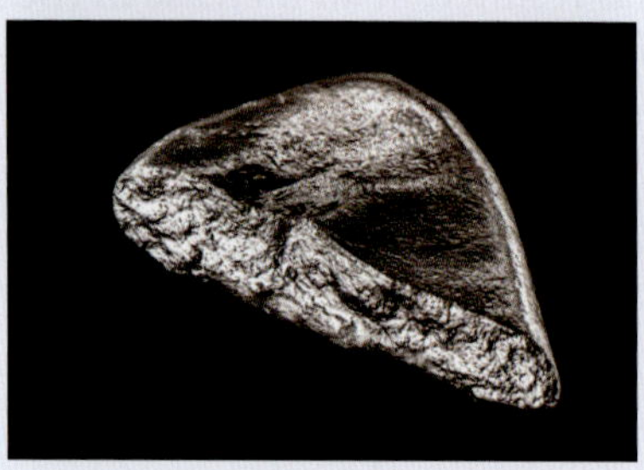

Rhodium is a silver white metallic element considered to be the rarest and most valuable precious metal in the world, largely because of its extreme rarity.

It is incredibly resistant to heat and so its main use is, alongside platinum and palladium, in cars to clean vehicle emissions. It is used in catalytic convertors which convert toxic gases in vehicle exhaust systems into less harmful substances.

As it is also quite brilliant and resistant to tarnishing, it is used as a finish for jewellery, searchlights and mirrors.

In the first three weeks of 2020, the price of rhodium soared 63 per cent to just under $10,000 an ounce. The reasons for this are a combination of very limited supply and surging demand.

80 per cent of all rhodium is mined in South Africa. Its rarity, together with a lack of capital investment, meant that only 792,000 ounces of rhodium were mined in 2019, a tiny fraction of the amount of gold extracted in the same period. Demand from carmakers is also predicted to continue to grow significantly as concerns about the environment and global warming are leading to ever more stringent emission control regulations around the world.

However, the long-term outlook for rhodium prices is uncertain in the light of the shift towards the development of electric cars as they do not use catalytic convertors.

1 What does the article suggest about the price elasticity of supply of rhodium?
2 Why might the demand for rhodium be regarded as an example of both "derived demand" and "composite demand"?
3 With the aid of a demand and supply diagram, explain an increase in the price of rhodium in the first three weeks of 2020.

2.4.4 Functions of price in resource allocation; rationing, signalling (transmission of preferences) and incentivising

The role of markets

As we saw in Chapter 1, the problem of scarcity means that societies have to make decisions about how to allocate resources within markets. In a free market economy these decisions are made through changes in prices. The role of a market is to provide a mechanism for bringing buyers and sellers together to establish a price for goods, services and factors of production. Markets can be located in a single physical place where buyers and sellers meet face to face such as a weekly fruit and vegetable market in a small town or village, Smithfield meat market in London or the Mercat de la Boqueria in Barcelona, or they can be global such as the foreign exchange market (FOREX) which encompasses virtually every financial institution in the world where the majority of trade is undertaken over the internet.

Key term

FOREX: a short way of stating foreign exchange market

Local fruit and vegetable market ▲

Dealing on the forex ▲

The functions of prices

Within any market, prices perform three basic functions:

- a signalling function indicating surpluses or shortages in the market
- a rationing function allocating resources among alternative uses
- an incentive function encouraging producers to supply more or less of a good or service

Let us take the example of the housing market in a particular area of a country. Assume that as a result of a significant influx of population into the area, the demand for houses increases. As supply cannot be increased immediately, the price of houses will rise signalling a shortage in the market. This rise in prices will mean that some individuals are no longer able to afford to purchase a house and so will ration or reduce their demand. The increase in prices of houses and the potential profits to be made will act as an incentive to building firms to increase the supply of houses, thereby removing the initial shortage. There will be similar changes in the market for factors of production, e.g. labour. In order to provide the increased supply of houses, building firms will need to employ more workers. This will increase the demand for labour, creating

> **Link**
> See Chapter 8, sections 8.3.7 and 8.3.8, for discussion of the determination of wages.

a shortage signalled by a rise in wages (the price of labour). The rise in wages will mean that some firms will no longer be able to afford to employ as many workers and will reduce (ration) the number they employ. The increase in wages will act as an incentive for existing building workers to move into the area and for more individuals to train to become building workers thereby removing the shortage of labour. Changes in prices have thus brought about a reallocation of resources in the product and factor markets.

> **Activity**
> **Operation of markets**
> In groups, explain how the signalling, rationing and incentive functions of prices would operate following a significant increase in the price of oil for a major oil importing country such as Japan.

2.5 Consumer and producer surplus

2.5.1 *Meaning and significance of consumer surplus*

Figure 2.33 shows the demand and supply curves for a product for an individual. At the equilibrium price of $6, four units are demanded and supplied. However, the section of the demand curve AB shows that the individual derives so much satisfaction from consuming the product that he or she would be prepared to pay a higher price in order to consume it. The difference between the price an individual is prepared to pay for the product and the price actually paid is known as consumer surplus and in this case amounts to $8 ($3.50 for the first unit + $2.50 for the second + $1.50 for the third + $0.50 for the fourth). The total consumer surplus is shown by the green shaded area PAB (the area under the demand curve at the equilibrium output – the total revenue from the sale of this output).

> **Key term**
> **Consumer surplus**: the difference between the maximum price an individual is prepared to pay for a good and the price actually paid.

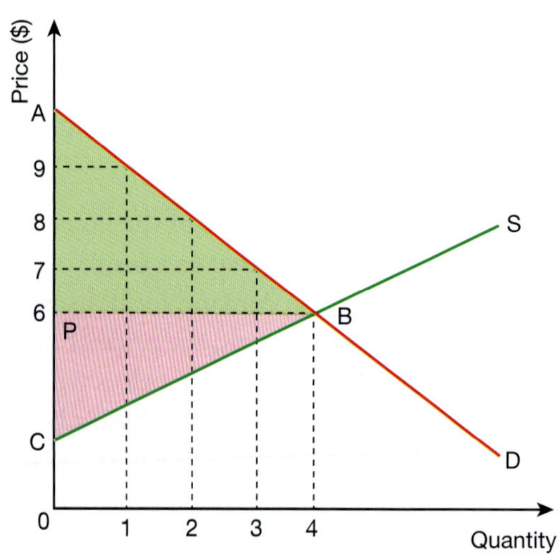

Figure 2.33 Consumer and producer surplus ▲

> **Progress question**
> 6 Why is it difficult to estimate the consumer surplus generated by online applications such as Google Search and Facebook?

Key term

Producer surplus: the difference between the minimum price a supplier is prepared to accept for a good and the price actually received.

2.5.2 Meaning and significance of producer surplus

The supply curve in Figure 2.33 indicates that the producer may also gain what is known as producer surplus. The producer would have been prepared to accept a lower price for the first three units than is actually received and this difference, producer surplus, is given by the pink shaded area CPB.

A market is said to be efficient when price and quantity demanded and supplied are set at a level at which consumer and producer surplus are at a maximum.

2.5.3 Causes of changes in consumer and producer surplus

Shifts of the demand and supply curves for a product will clearly have an impact on the amount of consumer and producer surplus. This is illustrated by Figures 2.34 and 2.35 below.

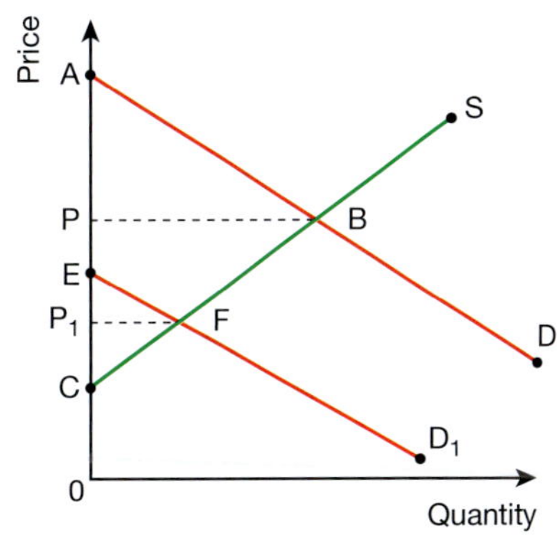

Figure 2.34 The effect of shifts of the demand curve on consumer and producer surplus ▲

In Figure 2.34 D and S are the original demand and supply curves. At the equilibrium price P, consumer surplus is equal to the triangle PAB and producer surplus to the triangle CPB. If now the demand falls at each and every price, the demand curve will shift to the left to D_1 and the equilibrium price falls to P_1. Now both consumer and producer surplus have fallen, consumer surplus to P_1EF and producer surplus to CP_1F. It is clear from this diagram that a decrease in demand will result in a fall in consumer and producer surplus and an increase in demand will cause both to rise.

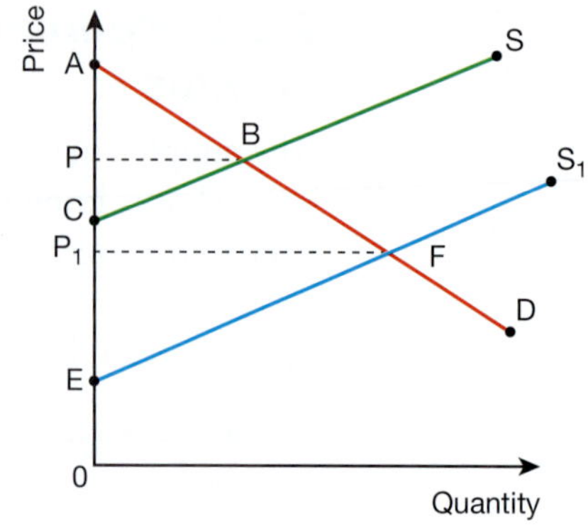

Figure 2.35 The effect of shifts of the supply curve on consumer and producer surplus ▲

Link

For a detailed discussion of the factors which might cause a shift in demand and supply curves, see section 2.4.2 in this chapter.

Link

Consumer and producer surplus are important concepts in the analysis of utility, monopoly and welfare and price discrimination. See Chapter 7 sections 7.1.1–7.1.5, 7.6.4 and 7.8.3

Progress question

7 Explain with the aid of a diagram (one in each case) the impact on consumer and producer surplus in relation to a particular product of:

a the demand for the product becoming more price elastic
b the supply of the product becoming more price elastic
c the demand curve for the product shifting to the right, supply remaining unchanged
d the supply curve shifting to the right, demand remaining unchanged.

Figure 2.35 shows the effect of changes in supply. D and S are the original demand and supply curves. Again at the equilibrium price P, the consumer surplus is PAB and the producer surplus is CPB. If now there is an increase in supply at each and every price the supply curve will shift to the right to S_1 and the equilibrium price will fall to P_1. At this price, both consumer and producer surplus have risen; consumer surplus to P_1AF and producer surplus to EP_1F. It is clear from the diagram that an increase in supply will bring about an increase in consumer and producer surplus and that a decrease in supply will cause both to fall.

2.5.4 Significance of price elasticity of demand and supply in determining the extent of these changes

The relative size of consumer and producer surplus at any given price will depend upon the slopes of the demand and supply curves which will in turn depend upon the price elasticities of demand and supply for the product. The more inelastic are the demand and supply curves at a particular equilibrium price, the higher the level of consumer and producer surplus and the greater, therefore, the extent of the change in size of consumer and producer surplus that will result from the shifts of the demand and supply curves described in the previous section.

If the price elasticity of demand for a product is zero (PED = 0), the demand curve will be perfectly inelastic and consumer surplus will be equal to infinity because a change in the price of the product will have no effect on the demand. If the demand for a product is perfectly elastic (PED = ∞), then consumer surplus will be zero because the price exactly matches what individuals are prepared to pay for it.

There are corresponding limiting cases for producer surplus. If the supply of the product is perfectly elastic (PES = ∞), then producer surplus is zero as producers are receiving the minimum price they are prepared to accept. If the price elasticity of supply is zero (PES = 0), then producer surplus will be infinite.

Case Study

Surge pricing

Surge or dynamic pricing involves companies making frequent price adjustments often on a minute-by-minute basis to match demand and supply particularly in markets subject to surges in demand at particular times. Such companies make use of modern technology to monitor surges in demand in real time and apply sophisticated algorithms to adjust prices to match supply with demand. Companies can link such pricing to what is known about individuals' income, location and past spending patterns. Modern technology also allows suppliers to monitor and match the prices of rivals.

Surge pricing extends across the economy. It is used by airlines, concert and event organisers, online ticketing agencies, hotel booking agencies such as Expedia and even motorway tolls. The Spanish company Cintra has opened several tolls in Texas which change prices every five minutes in an attempt to keep traffic flowing.

The advantages of surge pricing for companies are clear in that it enables them to smooth out demand and extract higher prices from richer customers. Perhaps the most famous and controversial user of surge pricing is Uber, the technology company which links independent cab drivers with customers through an app which enables customers to hail drivers from their smartphone. When demand rises rapidly, prices surge raising drivers' pay encouraging more to make themselves available. For example, on New Year's Eve in New York prices can surge to 7 or 8 times normal levels.

For this reason, surge pricing is regarded by many as unfair with some even equating it with price gouging. However, defenders of the practice argue that surge pricing is merely demonstrating the efficient working of the free market system, with the price mechanism performing the signalling, rationing and incentive functions in the market to efficiently align demand and supply. They also argue that both drivers and customers benefit.

Questions

1. Define (i) surge/dynamic pricing (ii) price gouging.
2. Explain how surge pricing exploits consumer surplus.
3. With the aid of a demand and supply diagram, explain how surge pricing matches demand and supply of goods and services.
4. Explain with reference to Uber how surge pricing illustrates the signalling, rationing and incentive functions of the price mechanism in the market for cabs.
5. Assess the advantages of surge pricing for (i) suppliers (ii) customers.

Key concepts

- **Scarcity and choice** is covered in the role of markets. Within markets, changes in price signal surpluses and shortages ration the available quantity of a good or service amongst consumers and provide incentives for producers to allocate scarce resources between competing uses.
- **Equilibrium and disequilibrium** is explicitly explored in the section on the determination of the equilibrium price and quantity demanded and supplied of a product. This shows that any movement away from this position will create a disequilibrium which will be detrimental as long as the conditions remain unchanged.
- **Time** is developed through the discussion of the nature and importance of price, income and cross-elasticities of demand and price elasticity of supply.
- **Efficiency and inefficiency** is explored when considering the significance of consumer and producer surplus.

Progress check

After completing this chapter you should be able to:

- explain the nature of effective demand
- explain individual and market demand and supply curves
- explain how the interaction of demand and supply bring about the equilibrium price and quantity demanded and supplied for a product
- explain how the equilibrium price and quantity demanded and supplied will be affected by shifts of the demand and supply curves
- explain the interaction of demand and supply and apply the analysis to real-world problems
- define, calculate and explain the factors affecting price, income and cross elasticity of demand and elasticity of supply and be able to apply these concepts to real-world problems
- understand the nature and functions of markets
- understand the role of prices in allocating resources
- explain the nature of consumer and producer surplus
- explain the causes of changes in consumer and producer surplus and the significance of price elasticity of demand and supply in determining the extent of these changes.

Exam-style questions

Essay questions

1a With the help of a formula, explain what is meant by the price elasticity of demand and consider which factors are most important in determining whether demand is likely to be price elastic or price inelastic. [8 Marks]

b Assess the importance of knowledge of the price elasticity of demand for its product, for a firm. [12 Marks]

2a With the help of diagrams, explain the difference between income and cross-price elasticity of demand and consider the factors which affect them. [8 Marks]

b Assess the importance, to a firm, of knowledge of the income and cross-price elasticities of demand for its products. [12 Marks]

3a With the aid of diagrams, explain and compare a movement along and a shift of the demand curve. [8 Marks]

b Assess the likely effects of a fall in interest rates on the market for privately-owned houses and rented accommodation. [12 Marks]

4a With the help of diagrams, explain and compare an increase in the quantity supplied and an increase in supply of a product. [8 Marks]

b Assess the likely effects of the provision of subsidies to manufacturers of electric cars on the markets for electric and petrol cars. [12 Marks]

5a With the help of a diagram, explain and compare consumer and producer surplus. [8 Marks]

b Assess the factors that might cause changes in consumer and producer surplus and the significance of price elasticity of demand and supply in determining the extent of these changes. [12 marks]

6a Explain what is meant by the price elasticity of supply and consider its significance for the speed and ease with which firms react to a change in demand. [8 Marks]

b Discuss the relative importance of the factors which explain the difference in the price elasticities of supply for fresh and tinned tomatoes. [12 Marks]

Multiple-choice questions

7 At a price of $50, a bookshop can sell 200 copies of a textbook each month. If it reduces the price to $45, it can increase its sales to 212. The price elasticity of demand for this textbook for a fall in price from $50 to $45 is: [1 mark]

A −0.42
B −1.67
C −0.60
D −2.40

8 Which of the following will cause a movement down along the demand curve for apples? [1 mark]

A A decrease in consumer incomes
B A major advertising campaign emphasising the health hazards of eating apples
C An increase in the demand for a substitute, oranges
D A fall in the wages of workers producing apples

3 Government microeconomic intervention

In this chapter you will develop your knowledge and understanding of:

- reasons for government intervention in markets
- methods and effects of government intervention in markets
- addressing income and wealth inequality.

3.1 Reasons for government intervention in markets

3.1.1 *Addressing the non-provision of public goods*

Public goods have already been covered in Chapter 1, section 1.6.2. It was made clear that it would not be possible to provide a public good, such as street lighting, police or national defence, through a market because it is not possible to prevent someone who had not paid for it from benefiting. It was pointed out that this gives rise to the free rider problem, due to the fact that public goods are non-rival, non-excludable and non-rejectable.

Therefore, if a public good cannot be provided through a market, because it is impossible to charge a price for the good or service, one reason for government intervention is to address this market failure of the non-provision of public goods by providing the good or service itself.

Link

Public goods are covered in Chapter 1, section 1.6.2.

Progress question

1 Explain why a public good cannot be provided through a market system.

3.1.2 *Addressing the under-consumption of merit goods and the over-consumption of demerit goods*

Merit goods

Merit goods have already been covered in Chapter 1, section 1.6.3. It was made clear that that merit goods, such as education and health care, would be under-consumed in a market as a result of the existence of imperfect information in the market. The problem is that there is information failure and people do not appreciate the value of a merit good.

Therefore, if a merit good is under-consumed, because of the existence of information failure, one reason for government intervention is to address this market failure by encouraging the consumption of merit goods, e.g. through government provision of subsidies.

Link

See Chapter 1, section 1.6.3, for more on merit goods.

Link

Subsidies are covered in section 3.2.2 of this chapter.

Demerit goods

Demerit goods have already been covered in Chapter 1, section 1.6.4. It was made clear that demerit goods, such as cigarettes and alcohol, would be over-consumed in a market as a result of the existence of imperfect information in the market. The problem is that there is information failure and people do not appreciate the potential harm that the consumption of such products can cause.

Link

Demerit goods are covered in of Chapter 1, section 1.6.4.

Therefore, if a demerit good is over-consumed, because of the existence of market failure, one reason for government intervention is to address this market failure by discouraging the consumption of demerit goods, e.g. through indirect taxes and/or minimum prices.

Progress question

2 Explain, with the use of examples, how the under-consumption of merit goods and the over-consumption of demerit goods can be explained by the existence of information failure.

3.1.3 *Controlling prices in markets*

Another reason for government intervention in markets is in relation to controlling prices. There are three possible situations that can bring this intervention about:

- **High prices:** the price of some essential goods, such as bread or rice, could rise so high that poorer sections of a community would be unable to afford them and this could have damaging effects on their health and standard of living. A government could therefore decide to intervene in a market through maximum price controls to prevent the price from rising above a certain level.
- **Low prices:** the price of some goods in a market could fall so low that certain producers could go out of business, e.g. a government might need to intervene in certain agricultural markets to help producers maintain their incomes. A government could also decide to intervene in a market for demerit goods, such as tobacco and alcohol, through minimum price controls to discourage consumption.
- **Unstable prices:** there is always a chance that, if left to market forces, prices will fluctuate widely in those markets where there may be great variations in supply over a period of time due to difficult weather conditions. This is especially the case with agricultural markets, where supply is relatively fixed in the short run, and in such a situation a government might need to intervene in the market, possibly through a buffer stock scheme.

Link

Price controls are also discussed in Chapter 8 section 8.1.1.

3.2 Methods and effects of government intervention in markets

3.2.1 *The impact and incidence of specific indirect taxes*

Key terms

Indirect tax: a tax levied on expenditure.

Specific tax: where a specific amount of money has to be paid in taxation.

One way in which a government can intervene in a market is through indirect taxation. An indirect tax is one which is levied when goods and services are bought. They are, therefore, taxes on expenditure. One of these is excise duties. This is a tax imposed on a product, such as petrol, alcohol or tobacco. An excise duty is usually a specific tax placed on a particular product, i.e. a specific amount is required to be paid.

Tax on petrol is a specific tax ▲

The effect of imposing a specific indirect tax in a market can be seen in Figure 3.1

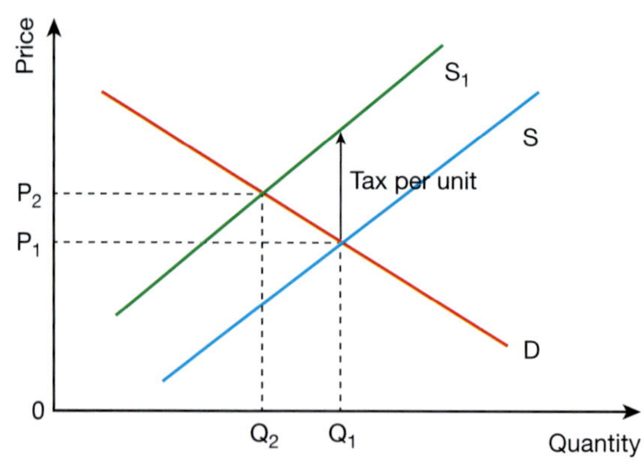

Figure 3.1 The effect of imposing a specific indirect tax in a market ▲

The market equilibrium would be price P_1 and quantity Q_1. At this point, the demand curve D intersects with the supply curve S. The imposition of a specific indirect tax will shift the supply curve to the left from S to S_1. The effect of the imposition of the indirect tax can be seen by the vertical distance between the two supply curves. The new equilibrium position, resulting from the imposition of the indirect tax, would now be a price of P_2 and a quantity of Q_2.

Link

Indirect taxes are also covered in Chapter 5, section 5.2.4 and Chapter 8, section 8.1.1.

Activity

Indirect taxes

Carry out research in your own country to discover the main examples of indirect taxes.

Discouraging the consumption of goods or services

Governments in many countries tax certain goods or services to deliberately try to discourage their consumption. The actual effect of any such government intervention may well be limited by the extent of the price elasticity of demand for such products. For example, the consumption of cigarettes and alcohol can be very addictive and so the imposition of taxes on such products may not change the level of demand for them by very much. It is for this reason that a government may decide to ban all alcohol or cigarette advertising or to make the drinking of alcohol or the smoking of cigarettes illegal.

Case Study

South Africa is planning to ban all alcohol advertising

One product that many governments try to reduce the consumption of is alcohol. Alcohol consumption in South Africa is high by comparison with other countries. For example, the World Health Organisation has produced figures which show that per person, alcohol consumption in South Africa is twice as high as that in either France or the United States of America.

The government in South Africa has estimated that about 75 per cent of knife murders and 40 per cent of gun murders are committed by people under the influence of alcohol. It also estimates that about 50 per cent of the 14,000 road deaths in the country a year are due to the influence of alcohol.

The South African government, therefore, is planning to introduce a ban on all alcohol advertising in the country.

1 Discuss whether a ban on alcohol advertising would be likely to have an impact on the demand for the product.

Key terms

Impact of a tax: this refers to the person or company on which a tax is levied.

Incidence of a tax: this refers to the eventual distribution of the burden of a tax.

Impact and incidence

It is important to distinguish between the impact and the incidence of taxes. The impact of a tax refers to the person or company on which a tax is levied, i.e. someone will be legally responsible for handing over the levy to the tax authorities.

The incidence of a tax, however, refers to the eventual burden of a tax. For example, a tax on a retailer, or at least part of the tax, could be passed on to the consumer. With a specific sales tax, the incidence will depend on the elasticity of the demand and supply curves. The more inelastic is the demand, and the more elastic is the supply, the greater will be the burden on the consumer.

Progress question

3 Distinguish between the impact and the incidence of a tax.

Key term

Subsidies: an amount of money paid by a government to a producer so that the price to the consumer will be lower than it otherwise would have been.

3.2.2 The impact and incidence of subsidies

Whereas a tax is imposed to discourage consumption and production, a subsidy is used to encourage consumption and production.

The effect of imposing a subsidy in a market can be seen in Figure 3.2.

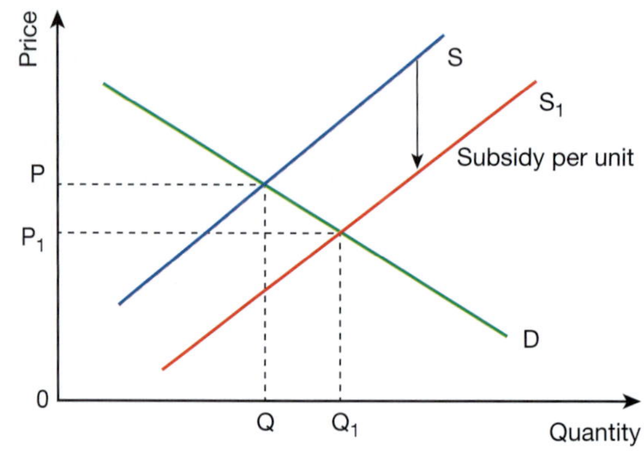

Figure 3.2 The effect of providing a subsidy in a market ▲

The market equilibrium would be price P and quantity Q. At this point, the demand curve D intersects with the supply curve S. If a government decides to subsidise the production of a product, the supply will shift to the right, from S to S_1. The subsidy can be seen by the vertical distance between the two supply curves. The new equilibrium position in the market will be price P_1 and quantity Q_1. It is clear that there is a greater quantity in the market at a lower price.

Case Study

Electricity subsidies in Pakistan

In Pakistan, subsidies are provided to people to keep down the price of electricity so that all of the population, whether rich or poor, are able to benefit from the electricity.

One problem arising from the provision of the subsidies to people, however, is that they are expensive for the government to finance. Economists have pointed out that they contribute to large budget deficits.

A further problem is that the subsidies have led to an increase in the demand for electricity, so that the demand exceeds supply. One effect of this is that there are frequent electricity blackouts, some of which can last as long as ten hours.

1 Discuss the advantages and disadvantages of a country, such as Pakistan, providing electricity subsidies to its population.

Progress question

4 Contrast the effect of a tax and a subsidy in a market.

Impact and incidence

The distinction between impact and incidence has already been referred to in relation to taxes, but impact and incidence can also be applied to subsidies. The different effects of a subsidy reflect differences in the demand for, and the supply of, a product. For example, if the demand for a product is elastic, the provision of a subsidy would lead to a relatively small reduction in price, but a relatively large increase in consumption.

If, on the other hand, the demand for a product is inelastic, the provision of a subsidy would lead to a relatively large reduction in price, but a relatively small increase in consumption. The incidence of a subsidy, therefore, clearly depends on the demand and supply conditions in a market for a particular product.

Link

Subsidies are also covered in Chapter 8, section 8.1.1.

3.2.3 *The direct provision of goods and services*

Another way in which a government can intervene in a market is through the direct provision of goods and services.

Key term

Direct provision of goods and services: this is where a government decides to provide particular goods and/or services itself.

Instead of intervening to discourage certain activities, such as through the use of indirect taxation, or to encourage other activities, such as through the use of subsidies, a government could decide to directly provide certain goods and services alongside the private sector. This is likely to be the case with certain merit goods, such as education and health care. In many countries, these services are provided through both the public and the private sectors.

However, it is necessary to consider the effect of the direct provision of goods and services on a market, particularly in terms of the reduced role of the private sector. Critics of such direct provision of goods and services argue that without the existence of competition, and without the drive of the profit motive, the provision of such goods and services may be less inefficient compared to the case of provision through competing firms in the private sector.

Case Study

Education in Botswana

Education in Botswana is provided in both the public sector and the private sector. The government is involved in the direct provision of education through the operation of public schools; about 90 per cent of children are educated in these schools. However, private schools also operate in Botswana and about 10 per cent of children are educated in these schools.

1 Explain why the government of Botswana provides education directly.

Link

The direct provision of goods and services is also discussed in Chapter 8, section 8.1.1.

Progress question

5 Explain why a government might decide to provide certain goods and services directly.

3.2.4 Maximum and minimum prices

Maximum prices

A government could intervene in a market by establishing a maximum price, but this would only be the case if the maximum price imposed is below what would normally be the equilibrium price in the market as determined by demand and supply. If the maximum price set was above the equilibrium price in a market, it would have no effect.

Key term

Maximum price: a situation where a maximum price or price ceiling is established in a market below what would have been the equilibrium price without government intervention.

The effect of establishing a maximum price control in a market can be seen in Figure 3.3.

Getting it right

Make sure you understand that if a maximum price was established in a market, this would need to be below what would normally be the equilibrium price.

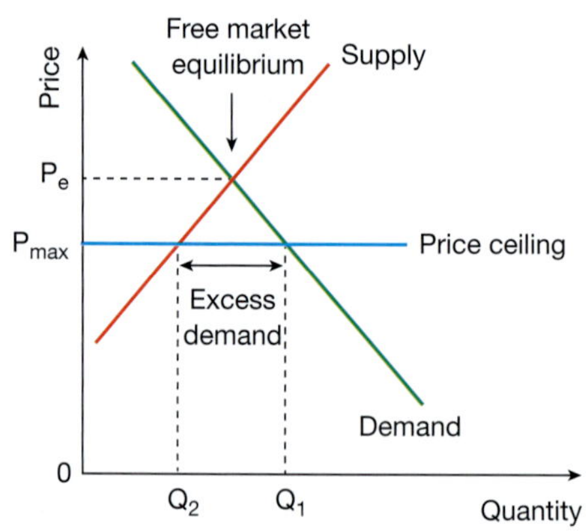

Figure 3.3 Maximum price control in a market ▲

The maximum price or price ceiling is established at P_{max}; this is the price ceiling and indicates that the price cannot go any higher than this. Without this government intervention, the equilibrium price in the market would have been P_e. At P_{max}, quantity Q_2 will be supplied, but the quantity demanded will be Q_1. There is therefore excess demand shown by the horizontal distance between Q_2 and Q_1. Without government intervention, the equilibrium price in the market would have gone up and the effect of this price rise, to P_e, would have been to eliminate the excess demand for the product. With the intervention of the government, this would not be allowed to happen and so the excess demand remains as a consequence of the maximum price imposed by the government.

Activity

Maximum price

Carry out research in your own country to find out if there are any examples of a maximum price in operation. Work in pairs or groups and find out how well it seems to be working in terms of its objectives.

There are clearly both advantages and disadvantages of a maximum price being imposed in a market by a government, as Table 3.1 indicates.

Table 3.1 The advantages and disadvantages of a maximum price control in a market ▼

Advantages of a maximum price control in a market	Disadvantages of a maximum price control in a market
The price of essential products, such as important items of food, can be limited, making such items more affordable to people.	The maximum price control will lead to excess demand in the market and this will create some form of queue or waiting list.
In the housing market, the rent of certain types of accommodation could be prevented from becoming too expensive.	The existence of a queue or waiting list may lead to bribery and corruption of those who are responsible for regulating the queue or waiting list.
In the transport market, fares could be restricted from going above a certain price.	It is possible that a secondary or informal market, or black market, may emerge where the supply is increased through illegal methods outside of the market. In such a situation, the price is likely to be well above the maximum price in the formal market.

Progress question

6 Discuss the advantages and disadvantages of using a maximum price control in a market.

Case Study

Maximum price control in India

In India, the government has established maximum prices of essential medicines since 2013. The National Pharmaceutical Pricing Authority (NPPA) establishes these prices and they are monitored by regulatory bodies.

This method of price control ensures that there is adequate availability of essential medicines at affordable prices for the public who would otherwise not be able to pay for the medicine. However, it is sometimes the case that the demand for these essential medicines at these prices is significantly more than the amount that can be supplied.

1 Discuss the arguments for and against a government establishing a maximum price for essential products, such as medicines.

Minimum prices

Key term

Minimum price: a situation where a minimum price or price floor is established in a market above what would have been the equilibrium price without government intervention.

As well as imposing maximum price controls in an economy, a government could also decide to impose a minimum price. Minimum prices work in the same way as price ceilings, but instead of having a maximum price, prices are not allowed to fall below a minimum price or price floor.

Such a situation can occur when a government intervenes in an agricultural market to ensure that the incomes of farmers do not fall below a certain level.

The effect of establishing a minimum price control in a market can be seen in Figure 3.4.

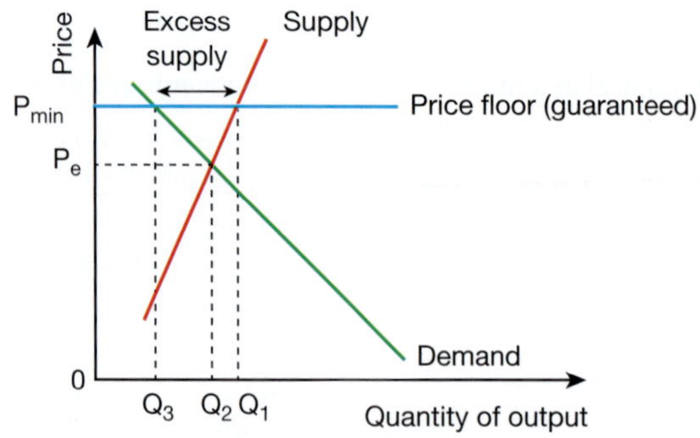

Figure 3.4 Minimum price control in a market

The normal equilibrium position, without government intervention, would be at P_e and Q_2 where demand is equal to supply. However, if a government decided to prevent the price falling below a particular level, indicated by P_{min}, then the price would not be allowed to fall beneath this. In such a situation, the supply would be Q_1 and the demand Q_3, creating an excess supply shown by the distance between Q_3 and Q_1. If the minimum price set was below the equilibrium price in a market, it would have no effect.

Case Study

Minimum price of alcohol in Scotland

In 2018, the government of Scotland introduced a law establishing a minimum unit price for alcohol. The minimum price of alcohol, or price floor, is 50 pence per unit. In taking this action, Scotland became the first country in the world to implement a minimum unit price for alcohol.

This law was introduced to make alcohol more expensive than it would otherwise be without any government intervention. The government argues that it would save lives, reduce hospital admissions and have positive effects across the whole public health system in Scotland and the whole society.

The impact of the law has been significant, with a 4 per cent to 5 per cent reduction in alcohol consumption in Scotland since 2018.

1 Discuss the arguments for and against a government establishing a minimum price for a demerit good, such as alcohol.

3.2.5 *Buffer stock schemes*

Price stabilisation

Price stabilisation refers to a situation where action needs to be taken by a government when there are wide fluctuations in price, largely as a result of unplanned fluctuations in supply. This is a particular feature of agricultural markets where supply is affected by a variety of factors beyond control, such as bad weather, natural disasters and the effects of pests.

Key term

Buffer stock: an amount of a commodity that is held to limit the range of price fluctuations in a market.

Buffer stocks

One way that a government could intervene in such a situation is through the establishment of a buffer stock. A buffer stock is where a reserve of a commodity is kept in order to stabilise prices in a market, so that the prices fluctuate within a given price range. When a surplus of a commodity is produced, the product is bought, adding to the buffer stock. When there is a shortage of the product, stocks can be run down.

The effect of creating a buffer stock in a market can be seen in Figure 3.5.

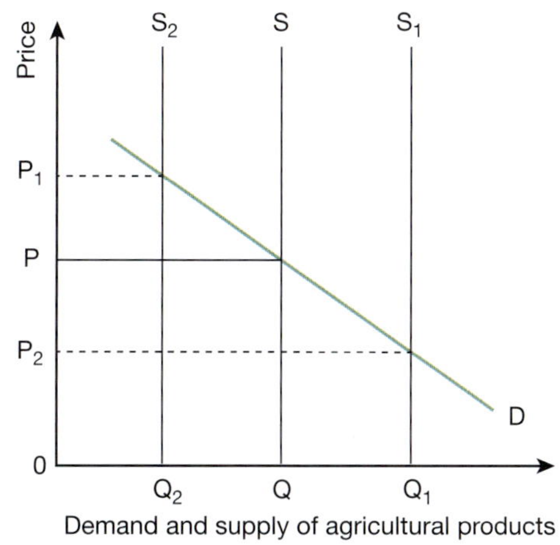

Figure 3.5 The use of a buffer stock in an agricultural market

The supply of an agricultural product in any one year will be perfectly inelastic. The supply in three years is shown by the supply curves S, S_1 and S_2. The government, in operating a buffer stock scheme, will want to maintain a price of P and a quantity of Q in the market.

In the year shown by the supply curve S_1, the equilibrium quantity would have been Q_1 and the equilibrium price would have been P_2. In this situation, the government would buy the extra output shown by the horizontal distance between Q and Q_1 and store it. This would keep the price at P.

In the year shown by the supply curve S_2, the equilibrium quantity would have been Q_2 and the equilibrium price would have been P_1. In this situation, the government would sell the extra output shown by the horizontal distance between Q and Q_2. This would keep the price at P.

Advantages and disadvantages of buffer stock schemes

There are clearly both advantages and disadvantages of a government operating a buffer stock scheme in a market, as Table 3.2 indicates.

Table 3.2 The advantages and disadvantages of a buffer stock scheme

The advantages of a buffer stock scheme	The disadvantages of a buffer stock scheme
It overcomes the problem of wide fluctuations in prices from one year to another.	It may not be easy for the government to establish what the equilibrium price in the commodity market should be. The producers will want the highest possible price to be maintained in the market whereas the consumers will want the lowest possible price to be maintained.
If prices can be stabilised through a buffer stock scheme, there will also be more stability in the incomes that producers, such as farmers, receive.	The cost of operating the buffer stock scheme will need to be paid by somebody. There may be different views about this. For example, the government may decide to pay for the scheme or it may want the producers to contribute to the cost.
This stability in incomes will encourage producers to make long-term plans.	There may be problems if there is a succession of good harvests. For example, it may be difficult to store it all and there may also be concerns about the perishability of the stock. On the other hand, if there is a succession of poor harvests, it may not be possible to store enough supplies.

Progress question

7 Discuss the advantages and disadvantages of using a buffer stock scheme to bring about greater price stability in a market.

3.2.6 *The provision of information*

Market failure can be caused by imperfect information. A government could therefore decide to intervene in a market to increase the availability of information in order to try to influence economic behaviour.

It is assumed that consumers will always aim to maximise their utility or satisfaction, but this objective will only be achieved if they have all the necessary information. If this is not the case, it is unlikely that they will make rational decisions.

Information failure is a major cause of market failure and so a government will need to take measures to improve both the accuracy and the availability of information that consumers need. For example, a government could make people as well informed as possible about the potential advantages of merit goods, such as education and health care. It could also make people as well informed as possible about the potential disadvantages of demerit goods, such as alcohol and tobacco. A particular example of such an approach in relation to the consumption of demerit goods is 'nudge' theory.

Link

Provision of information and nudge theory are also covered in Chapter 8, section 8.1.1.

3.3 Addressing income and wealth inequality

3.3.1 *The difference between income as a flow concept and wealth as a stock concept*

There are clear differences between income and wealth. One of the most important is the idea of income as a flow concept and wealth as a stock concept.

Key terms

Income: money received, especially on a regular basis.

Wealth: all possessions that have a monetary or exchange value.

Income is a flow of money that goes to factors of production, including the following:

- **Wages** and **salaries:** these are paid to people as a reward for the work they have carried out.
- **Benefits:** income can be received by people in the form of various benefits, such as a state pension or a tax credit.
- **Profits:** this is income that flows to businesses.
- **Dividends:** this is the income that is distributed to the shareholders of a business.
- **Rental income:** this is a flow of income to people who own, and rent or lease out, property.
- **Interest:** this is paid to people who hold money in interest paying accounts with financial institutions.

Wealth is a stock of money or assets, including the following:

- **Savings:** these are held in various forms of accounts with financial institutions.
- **Shares:** ownership of shares issued by limited companies.
- **Property:** ownership of property.
- **Bonds:** money held in bonds.
- **Pension schemes:** wealth held in occupational pension schemes and life assurance schemes.

Progress question

8 Distinguish, with the use of examples, between income and wealth.

3.3.2 *Measuring income and wealth inequality*

A number of policies can be used with the objective of bringing about a redistribution of income and wealth in an economy. These will be covered in section 3.3.4. However, it is necessary to consider how that distribution can be measured.

The Gini coefficient

Key term

Gini coefficient: a statistical measure of the degree of inequality of income in an economy. The lower the figure, the more equal is the distribution of income.

A Gini coefficient is a way of measuring the extent of inequality in the distribution of income in an economy. It is measured by the ratio of the area between the diagonal line of total equality and the Lorenz curve to the total area under the diagonal line (the Lorenz curve will be discussed in Chapter 11, section 11.4.2). The bigger this area, the more unequal is the distribution of income.

Table 3.3 shows the 10 countries in 2020 with the highest Gini coefficient and the 10 countries with the lowest Gini coefficient. The higher the value, the less equally income in the country is distributed. The lower the value, the more equally income is distributed.

Table 3.3 Examples of Gini coefficient data

Country	Gini Coefficient
HIGHEST GINI COEFFICIENT	
South Africa	0.630
Namibia	0.610
Botswana	0.605
Zambia	0.571
Central African Republic	0.562
Lesotho	0.542
Mozambique	0.540
Swaziland	0.515
Brazil	0.513
Colombia	0.508

Continued . . .

LOWEST GINI COEFFICIENT	
Azerbaijan	0.166
Ukraine	0.250
Slovenia	0.254
Iceland	0.256
Czech Republic	0.259
Moldova	0.263
Slovakia	0.265
Kyrgyzstan	0.268
Kazakhstan	0.269
Belarus	0.270

Case Study

Gini coefficient in Azerbaijan and South Africa

The Gini coefficient measures the extent to which a country's distribution of income deviates from a perfectly equal distribution. The Gini coefficient was developed by the Italian statistician Corrado Gini in 1912 and is today the most commonly used measurement of income or wealth inequality in a country

The Gini coefficient for a country ranges between 0 and 1 where 0 is complete equality and 1 is complete inequality. In 2020, the country with the lowest Gini coefficient was Azerbaijan, with a coefficient of 0.166. The country with the highest Gini coefficient was the Republic of South Africa, with a coefficient of 0.630

1 Explain what is meant by a Gini coefficient and what it is used to show.

Link

Calculation of the Gini coefficient and Lorenz curve analysis are covered in Chapter 11, section 11.4.2.

3.3.3 *Economic reasons for inequality of income and wealth*

There are a number of different possible economic reasons for the inequality of income and wealth, including the following:

- **employment:** a major cause of income equality is the ability of people to obtain well-paid employment. When there is an increase in unemployment in an economy, there will be fewer people receiving wages and salaries and more people receiving benefits. When there is a decrease in full-time employment and an increase in part-time employment, income inequality will increase because pay is usually lower in part-time than in full-time employment
- **government policy:** for many workers, a weak economic situation could have given rise to a "wage freeze" or to lower-than-inflation wage rises as a result of government policy to reduce the rate of inflation. This is particularly true of workers in the public sector who may have experienced a fall in their real standard of living where wage increases have been less than price increases
- **taxation:** a government may decide to raise the level of taxation in order to increase public revenue. It might also make tax more

regressive where proportionally more tax is taken from people on lower incomes than those on higher incomes

- **distribution of wealth:** people who already hold wealth are able to invest which creates new wealth, i.e. the existing concentration of wealth makes inequality a vicious cycle

3.3.4 *Policies to redistribute income and wealth*

Minimum wage

A government could decide to establish a minimum wage rather than allow wages to be determined by demand and supply factors in particular markets. The actual wage paid to workers may sometimes depend on their age.

However, one problem with a minimum wage is that it could lead to income becoming more unequal because some employers may not be able, or willing, to pay all its workers the minimum wage and so some of them will become unemployed and be forced to live on benefits.

Link

Minimum wages are also discussed in Chapter 8, section 8.3.8.

Case Study

Minimum wage in New Zealand

The adult minimum wage in New Zealand applies to all employees aged 18 and over, who are full-time, part-time, fixed-term, casual, working from home, and paid by wages, salary, commission or piece rates (there are some exceptions).

The minimum wage applies to all hours worked. There is no minimum hours requirement.

The minimum wage rate is set by the New Zealand government and is reviewed each year. It was increased from NZ$17.70 to NZ$18.90 an hour from 1 April 2020. It will be NZ$20.00 from 1 April 2021. There are two lower minimum wage rates for those workers starting out (aged 16 or 17) and for those workers in training schemes.

1 Discuss the arguments for and against a government establishing a minimum wage to redistribute income and wealth.

Progress question

9 Discuss the advantages and disadvantages of a minimum wage as a way of bringing about greater income equality in an economy.

Key term

Transfer payment: a payment made to an individual by a government that is not a reward for any productive effort.

Transfer payments

A government could decide to intervene in a market through the provision of transfer payments. This is where revenue received from taxation is used to provide financial support to people, such as in the form of pensions and social security payments. A transfer payment is usually paid to an individual by a government. It does not involve any productive effort, i.e. it is not a reward for any output produced. Transfer payments can be a very useful way to bring about a redistribution of income.

Activities

Transfer payments

Carry out research in your own country to discover examples of transfer payments.

Getting it right

It is important in the examination that you do not confuse transfer payments with transfer earnings.

The effect of transfer payments on the market

Transfer payments can be given out in various forms of income support to support those who are less well off. These payments can be in the form of pensions and social security payments. One type of transfer payment is unemployment benefit, which is money paid out to those who are unable to find employment. It has been argued by some economists that these payments are too high; it may have a distorting effect on the labour market, making some people unwilling to make themselves available for employment.

Case Study

Unemployment benefits in the USA

In the USA, unemployment benefits – or unemployment compensation, as it is more usually called – are paid to workers who have become unemployed through no fault of their own. This is an example of a transfer payment and is usually paid by the state government.

This social welfare benefit is only paid for a certain period of time, usually six months. Once that period of time has elapsed, the unemployed worker will no longer receive this benefit.

1 Discuss the advantages and disadvantages of a country, such as the USA, providing unemployment benefit to its population for a limited period of time.

Activity

Income tax

Carry out research in your own country to discover what the rates of income tax are. This will enable you to judge how progressive income tax is in your country.

Progressive income taxes, inheritance and capital taxes

Income taxes

A government could address income inequality through the use of progressive taxes. Many economies make use of progressive taxation to achieve a more equitable distribution of income.

It is important to understand what is meant by a progressive tax. Such a tax will not only take more from a person as their income rises, but a higher proportion of that income, i.e. there is an increase in the marginal rate of taxation. For example, income tax might start at 20 per cent and then increase to 30 per cent, 40 per cent and 50 per cent as income levels rise.

Getting it right

In the examination, make sure you can demonstrate to the examiner that you understand that a progressive system of taxation does not simply mean that a person pays more tax as they earn more, but that they pay an increasing proportion of their income as tax.

Key term

Progressive tax: where the proportion of income paid in tax increases as income increases.

Case Study

Personal Income Tax in the Republic of Ireland

In the Republic of Ireland, income tax is charged as a percentage of your income. There are two tax rates in Ireland. The first part of a person's income, up to a certain amount (up to €35,300 for a single person with no dependent children), is taxed at 20 per cent; this is known as the standard rate of income tax.

The remainder of a person's income, i.e. all income above €35,300, is taxed at 40 per cent; this is known as the higher rate of income tax.

Personal income tax in the Republic of Ireland is therefore an example of a progressive tax because it not only takes more from a person as their income rises, but it takes a higher proportion of that income as the rate changes from 20 per cent to 40 per cent. The top 23 per cent of earners paid 77 per cent of the government revenue received from income tax, whereas the bottom 77 per cent of earners paid only 23 per cent of the government revenue received from income tax.

1 Discuss the advantages and disadvantages of a progressive income tax system.

Link

Progressive taxes, along with regressive and proportional taxes, are discussed in Chapter 5, section 5.2.4.

Activity

Average and marginal rates of taxation

A person earns US$1,000 a month. The person is allowed a personal allowance of US$200 a month on which no tax is paid. The person then pays a tax rate of 10 per cent on the next US$300 earned, a tax rate of 20 per cent on the next US$300 earned and a tax rate of 30 per cent on the last US$200 earned.
Calculate (i) the tax that the person pays in the month, (ii) the average rate of taxation and (iii) the marginal rate of taxation.

Inheritance and capital taxes

A government may also decide to intervene in an economy to try to bring about a more equitable distribution of wealth, as well as income. Examples of taxes that can achieve this objective include inheritance taxes and capital taxes, such as a capital gains tax.

Key terms

Inheritance tax: a tax which is paid on the money, property and possessions of someone who has died.
Capital gains tax: a tax which is paid on the surplus obtained from the sale of an asset for more than was originally paid for it.

State provision of essential goods and services

State provision of essential goods and services helps to redistribute income and wealth because the money to pay for the provision of the essential goods and services comes from the money received from taxation. This helps to lesson inequality because the money received by the government pays for the goods and services the less well off are not able to afford. State provision of health care is an example of this.

In the case of public goods, such as street lighting, police and national defence, it has already been made clear in section 3.1.1 that a state would need to provide these services because they would otherwise not be provided at all.

Link

State provision of essential goods and services is also covered, under nationalisation, in Chapter 8, section 8.1.1.

Key concepts

- **The margin and decision-making:** this concept can be seen when applying the concept of the margin to taxation, such as in relation to the progressive nature of income tax where a person's marginal tax rate is more than their average tax rate.
- **Efficiency and inefficiency:** the over-consumption of demerit goods and the under-consumption of merit goods in markets are examples of an inefficient allocation of resources resulting from information failure. Government intervention to encourage the consumption of more merit goods and fewer demerit goods will help to make the allocation of resources more efficient.
- **The role of government and the issues of equality and equity:** this concept can be seen in terms of government policies to reduce income and wealth inequality, such as through the use of progressive income taxes to bring about a greater degree of equity in the distribution of income and wealth in an economy. Subsidies could also be used to keep down the price of essential products in an economy, making such products more affordable to the less well off.

Progress check

After completing this chapter you should be able to:

- understand the reasons for government intervention in markets
- understand the methods and effects of government intervention in markets
- understand how a government could address income and wealth inequality.

Exam-style questions

Essay questions

1a With the help of a demand and supply diagram, explain the effects on consumers and producers when a government introduces an indirect tax on a good and consider the distinction between the impact and the incidence of such a tax. [8 marks]

b Assess whether government intervention will always improve the operation of a market. [12 marks]

2a With the help of a demand and supply diagram, explain how a subsidy to producers of fuel will affect producers and consumers and consider the impact of such a subsidy on the government. [8 marks]

b Assess the extent to which a minimum wage would address income inequality in a country. [12 marks]

3a Explain why cigarettes are regarded as an example of a demerit good and consider whether taxation is likely to have a significant influence on the demand for them. [8 marks]

b Assess the possible economic consequences of imposing a ban on smoking cigarettes. [12 marks]

4a Explain what is meant by a public good and consider why they are not provided through a market.

b Assess whether it is possible for a government to significantly address the under-consumption of a merit good. [12 marks]

5a Explain what is meant by a buffer stock scheme and consider how easy it is to operate. [8 marks]

b Assess whether certain goods and services may be provided more efficiently by a government directly rather than through a market. [12 marks]

6a With the use of examples, explain the difference between income and wealth and consider whether both are flow concepts. [8 marks]

b Assess whether consumers would always benefit from the introduction of a maximum price on a product. [12 marks]

Multiple-choice questions

7 What effect will a minimum price have on a market? [1 mark]

A A minimum price will be above the equilibrium price in a market.
B A minimum price will be equal to the equilibrium price in a market.
C A minimum price will be below the equilibrium price in a market.
D A minimum price will be likely to create a situation of excess demand.

8 An income tax will usually be an example of a: [1 mark]

A proportional tax
B regressive tax
C progressive tax
D flat tax

4 The macroeconomy

In this chapter you will develop your knowledge and understanding of:

- national income statistics
- the circular flow of income
- aggregate demand (AD) and aggregate supply (AS) analysis
- economic growth
- unemployment
- inflation (price stability).

4.1 National income statistics

4.1.1 *Meaning of national income*

National income is *either* the total value of a country's final output of all goods and services produced in a year *or* the total value added of a country's production of all goods and services, both taking into account net property income from abroad and depreciation. What is important is not counting the same good twice. In the production, for example, of a car many parts are produced by different firms and then brought together to make the car. Using the first definition, the total value is the value of the car as a whole. The tyre production is not counted separately as the tyres are part of the car's value.

Key terms

National income: the total value added in the production of goods and services in a country plus net property income from abroad in a year minus depreciation in a year.

Net property income from abroad: consists of the inflow of interest, profits and dividends into a country minus the outflow.

Depreciation: a figure used to measure the fall in value of the capital stock of a country. It is sometimes referred to as capital consumption.

4.1.2 *Measurement of national income*

GDP, GNI and NNI

National income can be measured in a variety of different ways using expenditure, income or output data. As with national income, gross domestic product (GDP) can be measured either in terms of the value of all final goods and services produced or in terms of the value added in the production process. The key point is that both of these prevent double counting from taking place, i.e. counting the same output twice.

GDP deals with the output side of the economy. Gross national income (GNI) and Net national income (NNI), however, are concerned with the sum of all income earned by residents of the country. The difference between GNI and NNI is shown below:

GNI – depreciation = NNI

All three are often stated as per capita, for example GDP per capita is:

$$\text{GDP per capita} = \frac{\text{GDP}}{\text{population}}$$

Key terms

Gross domestic property (GDP): the total value added in the production of goods and services in a country in a year.

Gross national income (GNI): the total incomes received by a country's residents in a year.

Net national income (NNI): GNI minus the depreciation of fixed capital assets (dwellings, buildings, machinery, transport equipment and physical infrastructure) through wear and tear and obsolescence.

Key terms

Market prices: a measure of value in terms of actual market prices at which the goods are sold. It includes taxes, but excludes subsidies.

Basic prices: the amount the producer receives from the purchaser per unit of goods or service produced, less the taxes on the products and plus any subsidies on the products.

Link

For information on how to convert gross to net for national income figures, including depreciation, see section 4.1.4 of this chapter.

4.1.3 *Adjustment of measures from market prices and basic prices*

GDP and GNP figures can be shown as either market prices or basic prices. Market price is the gross value of goods and services produced by an economy in a year including all taxes but excluding any subsidies. The basic price, however, excludes taxes, but includes subsidies. It also excludes transport costs if these are invoiced separately. The difference can be stated as:

GDP at basic prices =
GDP at market prices – minus taxes + subsidies on products

4.1.4 *Adjustment of measures from gross values to net values*

The difference between gross and net measurements, such as GDP and net domestic product, is depreciation.

GDP – depreciation = net domestic product

GNI – depreciation = net national income

Depreciation consists of the loss in value of a country's capital assets including housing, vehicles, machinery, etc. The depreciation is known as capital consumption.

4.2 Introduction to the circular flow of income

4.2.1 *The circular flow of income in a closed economy and an open economy*

Key terms

Circular flow of income: shows how money circulates in an economy between households, firms and government.

Closed economy: an economy without exports or imports consisting solely of consumption, investment and government expenditure.

Open economy: an economy in which there are exports and imports.

The circular flow of income is a way of showing that money flows between households, or individuals, firms and government in an economy. If there is no foreign trade then this is called a closed economy. With foreign trade it becomes an open economy.

Table 4.1 Components of different types of economies ▼

Components	Type of economy
Y = C + S	simple, closed economy
Y = C + I	closed free market economy
Y = C + I + G	closed mixed economy
Y = C + I + G + (X–M)	open economy

The circular flow of income refers to the idea that money is provided to the factors of production in exchange for their services. In turn the owners of these factors then spend the money on the goods and services which are provided. In other words, the flow of money is like a circle. In Figure 4.1 households supply labour and in return receive income. They spend this, consumption, and get in return goods and services.

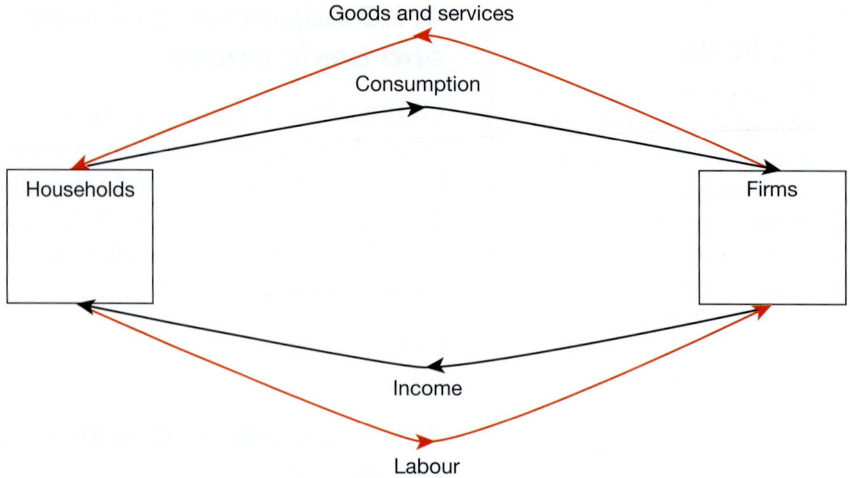

Figure 4.1 The circular flow of income in a closed economy without government ▲

In an open economy we would need to show money from exports coming into the system and money for imports leaving the system.

If we introduced the government, then part of each flow would need to go to and from the government. Households would supply labour to the government as well as firms and, in return, gain income. Similarly, some consumption would go to the government and some goods and services would flow to households.

Progress question

1 Explain what is meant by the circular flow of income.

4.2.2 *Injections and withdrawals*

In the real world this circular flow is affected by injections and withdrawals of money into the system. Some people save and this is a withdrawal or leakage from the system, reducing the circular flow. This is the same with taxes and imports where the money flows out to other economies. Equally, more money can be injected into the system through investment by firms, government expenditure and exports where money flows in from other economies.

This can be summarised as follows:

injections = investment + government expenditure + exports:
J = I + G + X
i.e. money coming into the circular flow from outside the system.

leakages = savings + taxes + imports: W= S + T + M
i.e. money that leaves the system.

Each of the leakages is an opposite to one of the injections:

Savings to investment; taxes to government expenditure; and imports to exports.

Key terms

Injection: money from outside the circular flow that increases the value of GDP.
Saving: that part of a household's current income which is not consumed.
Leakage: income received by households, firms or governments that is not passed on in the circular flow and thus reduces the value of GDP.

Link

For more information on investment, government expenditure, exports and imports see section 4.3 of this chapter.

Getting it right

Do not confuse investment done by firms, which is an injection, with savings done by individuals, which is a withdrawal.

Activity

Injections and withdrawals

Try to find out the values of the main injections and withdrawals in your country.

4.2.3 *Equilibrium and disequilibrium*

The economy is in equilibrium when J = W. This is not the same as full employment equilibrium, which is where resources are fully employed and the price level is not increasing, whereas J = W says nothing about the level of employment or the rate of inflation. The economy can be in equilibrium with millions of people unemployed or, equally, where prices are rapidly rising. Equally, the economy is in disequilibrium when J is greater than W or W is greater than J. In the first case, J > W, the economy is increasing in size. Where W > J then the economy is shrinking in size.

Key terms

Equilibrium: where the economy is neither growing nor shrinking: J = W.
Disequilibrium: where the economy is either growing in size, J > W, or shrinking in size, W > J.

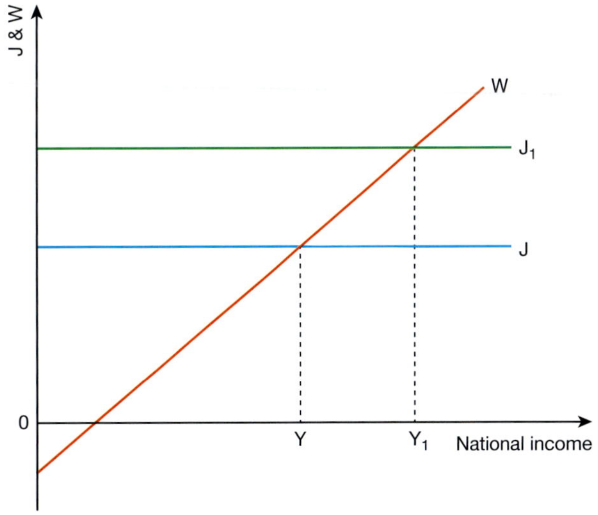

Figure 4.2 Injections and withdrawals ▲

Link

For more on injections and withdrawals and equilibrium national income, see section 4.3 of this chapter.

Figure 4.2 shows that national income is determined by the intersection of J and W, i.e. J = W.

4.3 AD and AS analysis

4.3.1 Definition of aggregate demand (AD)

Aggregate demand (AD) is the total amount of goods and services demanded or total expenditure on goods and services in an economy.

4.3.2 Components of aggregate demand and their meanings

AD consists of consumption, investment, government expenditure and net exports, which is exports – imports. This can be written as:
AD = C + I + G + (X – M)

Consumption is done by households/individuals. It consists of that part of their income spent on goods and services. Buying a bicycle or going to a restaurant for a meal are both examples of consumption.

Investment is usually done by firms. It consists of spending on an asset or capital good for future use. A firm building a new factory or offices or installing a new computer system are all examples of investment.

Government expenditure consists of all government consumption, investment and transfer payments. It includes spending on pay for government employees, education and health services and infrastructure.

Exports are the sale of goods and services to foreign countries or people living abroad. Exports bring money into a country and are an injection.

Imports are the purchase of goods and services from abroad. Imports take money away from a country and are a leakage.

4.3.3 Determinants of aggregate demand

The four main determinants of aggregate demand are:

- changes in interest rates affecting C and I. If interest rates fall then firms are more likely to invest leading to an increase in AD
- changes in income and wealth. If consumers' incomes rise then they are likely to spend more thus increasing AD
- changes in inflation expectations. If inflation is expected to increase then people are likely to spend now thus increasing AD
- currency exchange rate changes. If the value of your currency rises then imports will increase because they are cheaper, but exports will fall because they cost more in terms of the other currency.

Key terms

Aggregate demand: total amount of goods and services demanded or total expenditure on goods and services in an economy.
Consumption: that part of a household's current income which is spent on goods and services.
Investment: the expenditure on capital goods or assets, not for current consumption but for future consumption. It broadly refers to spending now on an asset that should generate an income at some point in the future.
Government expenditure: government expenditure consists of all government consumption, investment, and transfer payments.
Exports: the sale of goods and services abroad. Exports bring money into the country.
Imports: the purchase of goods and services from abroad. Imports take money away from a country.

4.3.4 *Shape of the aggregate demand curve*

Figure 4.3 shows that the AD curve slopes downwards so that if inflation rises (P_1 to P_2) real output falls (Y_1 to Y_2). This downward slope is due to rising price levels causing:

- nominal interest rates to rise leading to a fall in demand for goods and services (fall in C)
- reduction in the purchasing power of cash held as wealth (fall in C and I)
- domestic goods to be more expensive leading to a fall in exports and an increase in imports (fall in X–M).

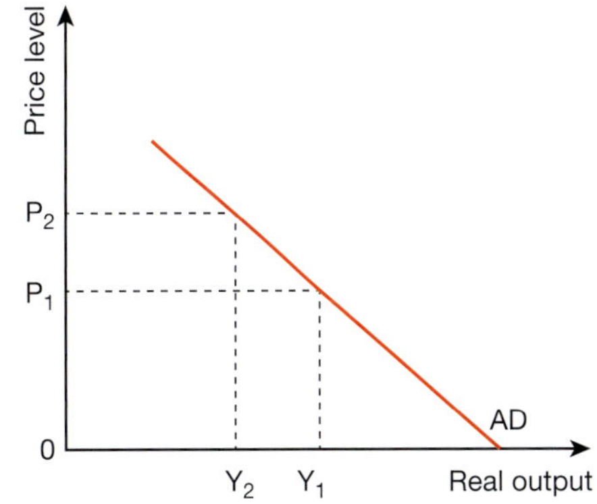

Figure 4.3 The aggregate demand curve ▲

4.3.5 *Causes of a shift in the AD curve*

A change in any one of C + I + G + (X–M) will lead to a shift in the curve. If any one of them increases then the curve will shift outwards, as seen in Fig. 4.4, from AD_1 to AD_2. This leads to the equilibrium level of output and the price level both rising.

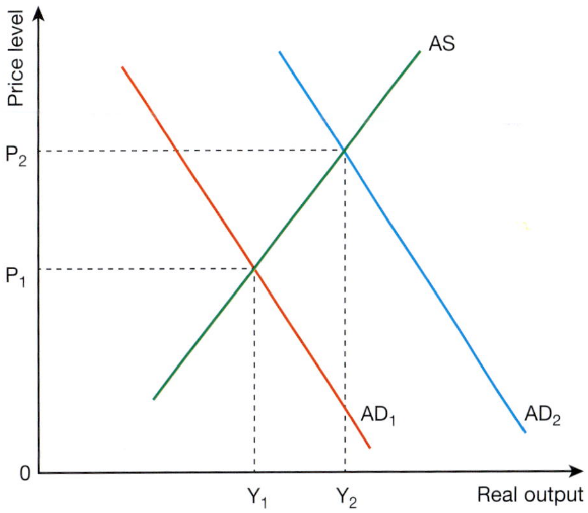

Figure 4.4 A shift of the AD curve ▲

> **Key term**
>
> **Aggregate supply**: the total value of goods and services produced in the economy.

4.3.6 *Definition of aggregate supply*

Aggregate supply (AS) is the total production of goods and services in an economy.

4.3.7 Determinants of aggregate supply

While there is a whole list of possible determinants, some important ones are:

- production costs including wages. If wages increase leading to a rise in production costs then AS is likely to be reduced
- technological innovations. These may increase the productivity of labour and capital leading to an increase in AS
- producer taxes and subsidies. Taxes have a negative effect, while subsidies have a positive effect, on AS
- quality of labour and capital. An improvement in the education of the workforce is likely to increase productivity and thus AS.

Key term

Productivity: the quantity of goods and services produced per unit of input per period of time.

4.3.8 Shape of the aggregate supply curve in the short and long run

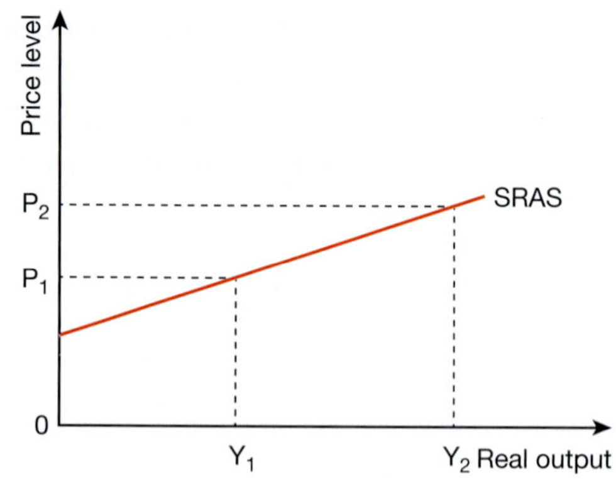

Figure 4.5 The short run aggregate supply curve ▲

Figure 4.5 shows that in the case of a short run AS curve as prices increase more will be supplied. This is because although production costs will rise, e.g. the need to pay workers overtime to produce more, the rise in prices will more than cover this. Indeed in some cases unemployment is so high that more can be produced without any increase in costs as there is considerable unused capacity so that the AS curve is completely horizontal. All of this depends on there being some excess capacity. Where there is excess capacity, the short run AS curve will look similar to that in Figure 4.6. The AS curve is initially horizontal, then curves upwards as full employment output is approached and then becomes a vertical line.

In the long run, when AS reaches full capacity, i.e. all resources are fully employed (full employment), there is no ability to increase output so that any increase in demand can only be met by a rise in prices. The long run aggregate supply (LRAS) curve can be shifted to the right, from LRAS to $LRAS_1$, by: improved education and training; increase in capital equipment; changes in technology; improved productivity;

etc. This shift will lead to an increase in output and employment and a fall in the price level. The LRAS can only be shifted if the productive capacity of the economy is increased. This is equivalent to shifting the production possibility curve to the right as seen in Figure 4.7.

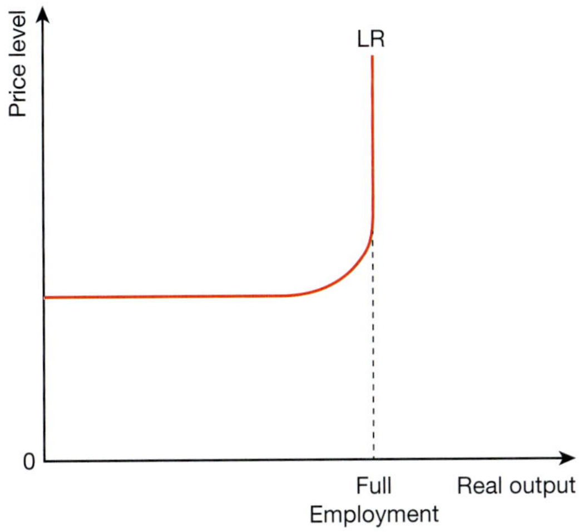

Figure 4.6 The aggregate supply curve ▲

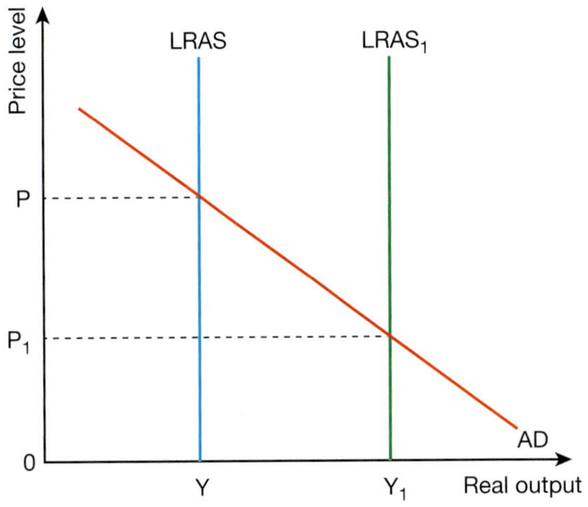

Figure 4.7 The long run aggregate supply curve ▲

The LRAS can be depicted, also, as shown in Figure 4.8.

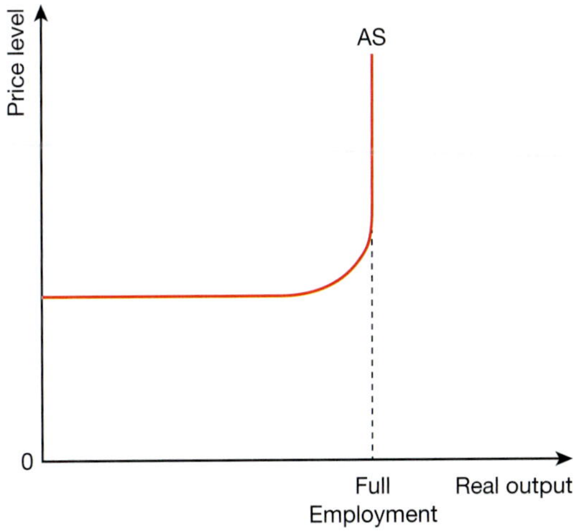

Figure 4.8 The long run aggregate supply curve ▲

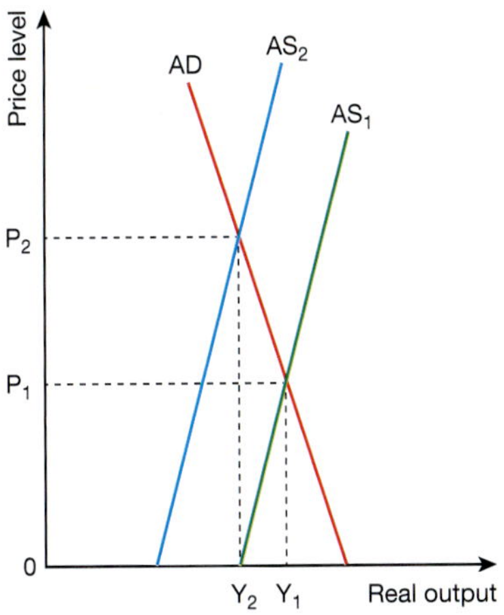

Figure 4.9 A movement along the AD curve/shift in AS ▲

4.3.9 Causes of a shift in the AS curve in the short run and in the long run

A shift in the short run aggregate supply curve (SRAS) from AS_1 to AS_2, in Fig. 4.9, could be due to increase in the costs of production or increase in indirect taxes leading to lower output and employment, Y_1 to Y_2, and higher price levels, P_1 to P_2. An increase in SRAS from AS_2 to AS_1 would lead to higher output and employment, Y_2 to Y_1, and a lower level of price increase, P_2 to P_1. This rightward shift could be caused by an increase in productivity or a fall in the price of inputs.

Link

For more on causes, see section 4.3.7 of this chapter.

Getting it right

Remember the price level shows the rate of inflation. A fall in the price level, therefore, is a fall in the rate of inflation *not* a fall in price.

Link

For more on the production possibility curve see Chapter 1, section 1.5.

Link

For more on shifts in and movement of demand and supply curves see Chapter 2, sections 2.1.5–2.1.7.

Activity

AD and AS

Try to find out the values of AD and AS for your country for the last five years. From this information what can you tell about the levels of employment and prices?

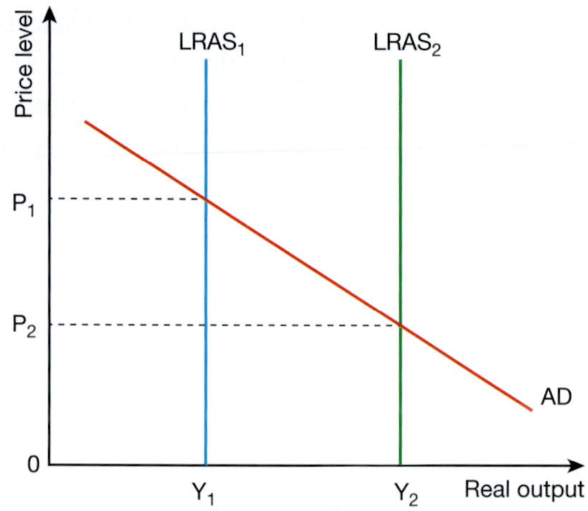

Figure 4.10 Increase in LRAS ▲

Figure 4.10 shows a shift in the long run aggregate supply (LRAS). A shift to the right from $LRAS_1$ to $LRAS_2$ would result from a change in the factors of production such as size of the workforce, size of capital stock, levels of education and labour productivity. An increase in labour productivity, for example, would mean that more could be produced with the same inputs so LRAS shifts to the right leading to an increase in output and employment, Y_1 to Y_2, and a fall in the price level, P_1 to P_2. On the other hand, destruction of capital, as in a war or a natural disaster, would shift the LRAS leftwards from $LRAS_2$ to $LRAS_1$ leading to a fall in output and employment, Y_2 to Y_1, and an increase in the price level, P_2 to P_1. Shifting the LRAS to the right is equivalent to shifting the production possibility curve outwards.

4.3.10 *Distinction between a movement along and a shift in AD and AS*

A shift of the AD curve is covered in section 4.3.5, while a shift in AS is covered in 4.3.9. In the case of a shift of the AD curve both output/employment and the price level move in the same direction as shown in Figure 4.4. With a shift of the AS curve, output/employment move in one direction and the price level in the opposite direction. Figure 4.9 shows that when AS falls from AS_1 to AS_2 there is a fall in output, but a rise in the price level.

A movement along the AD curve is caused by a shift in the AS curve as shown in Figure 4.9, whereas a movement along the AS curve is caused by a shift in the AD curve as shown in Figure 4.4.

4.3.11 *Establishment of equilibrium in the AD/AS model*

Equilibrium occurs where AD and AS intersect as shown in Figure 4.11 showing the equilibrium level of real output, and employment, and the equilibrium price level in the economy.

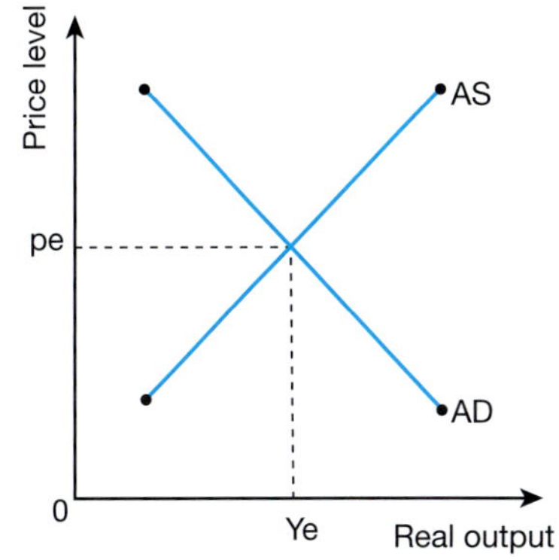

Figure 4.11 Equilibrium AD and AS ▲

This equilibrium level does not say anything about the size of real output or the levels of employment and prices. Equilibrium can occur when there is low employment/high unemployment and/or when price level is very high. All it says is that there is no increase or decrease in the economy.

4.3.12 *Effects of shifts in the AD/AS curves*

If AD shifts outwards from AD to AD_1 then real output and employment both increase to Y_1 and P_1 respectively. If AS increases from AS to AS_1 then real output and employment both increase to Y_2, but the price level falls to P_2.

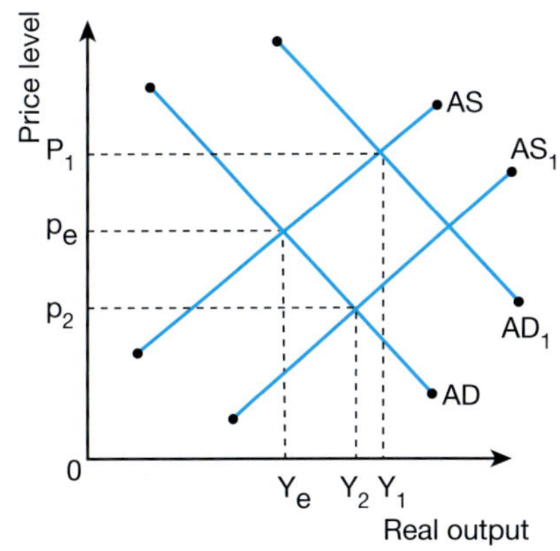

Figure 4.12 Shifts of AD and AS and the effects on output, employment and prices ▲

Link

Shifts in AD and AS are explained more in section 4.3.10.

Activity

Output, prices and employment

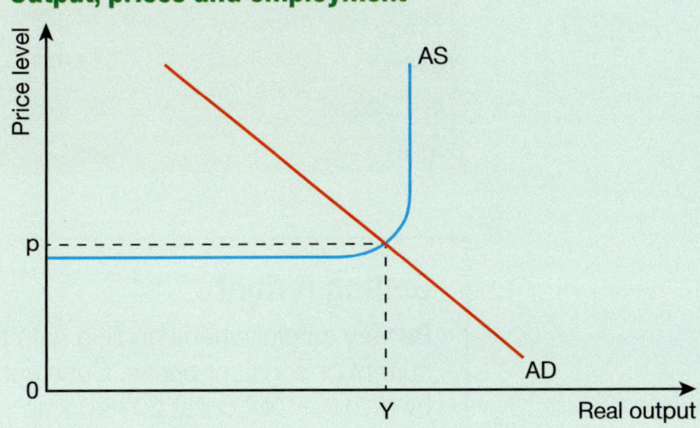

1. Copy the diagram.
2. Draw a new AD line to the right of AD and label AD_1.
3. Draw AD_2 to the right of AD_1.
4. Draw AD3 and AD4 to the left of AD.
5. For each of the shifts in AD state what has happened to output, employment and prices.

Link

For more information on GDP and GNP see section 4.1.2.

4.4 Economic growth

4.4.1 *Meaning of economic growth*

Economic growth is an increase in the real output of an economy. For real growth to occur it needs to be greater than the increase in inflation. Economic growth can be measured either in terms of GDP or GNP, but is usually referred to as a change in real GDP.

4.4.2 *Measurement of economic growth*

The most widely used measurement of economic growth is GDP, although GNP is also used. It is measured as the percentage rate of increase in real GDP, allowing, therefore, for the effects of inflation. To allow comparison of economic growth either over time or between countries, it is often measured in terms of GDP per capita thus allowing for differing sizes of population.

4.4.3 *Distinction between growth in nominal GDP and real GDP*

Nominal GDP is the value of goods and services using current prices. Real GDP is nominal GDP adjusted for changes in inflation. It is sometimes referred to as GDP at constant prices. If inflation is positive, real GDP will be lower than nominal. If inflation is negative – deflation – then real GDP will be higher than nominal. To move from nominal to real GDP we use the GDP deflator which measures price changes from a base year. In Table 4.1, this is 2010.

Table 4.2 Nominal and real GDP rates in $ millions in 2019 ▼

Country	Nominal GDP	Real GDP
Argentina	445,445	437,813
Botswana	18,340	18,643
Canada	1,736,425	1,939,183
Denmark	350,104	382,978
India	2,818,929	2,940,156
Mauritius	14,048	13,786
New Zealand	206,928	191,728
Nigeria	448,120	477,161

Getting it right

Be very careful when handling data to make certain whether it is at current or constant prices. Constant prices will be indicated, for example, by "2018 =100" or "at 2018 prices".

Key terms

Economic growth: an increase in the production potential or real level of output of an economy. It is possible to distinguish between actual and potential growth in national output.

Real GDP: nominal GDP adjusted for changes in inflation, sometimes called GDP at constant prices.

Nominal GDP: total value of goods and services at current prices.

Getting it right

Remember that real GDP per capita is an average and not what everyone gets. This may disguise great wealth and poverty.

Activity

Nominal and real GDP

1. Using Table 4.2, which countries experienced positive inflation between 2010 and 2019?
2. Find out the nominal and real GDPs for your country. How do these compare with the country geographically (in the same continent) nearest to you from Table 4.2?

4.4.4 *Causes of economic growth*

Economic growth can be caused by either shifting the AD or AS curves outwards. This can be seen in Table 4.3.

Table 4.3 Causes of economic growth ▼

Demand side	Supply side
Government expenditure – leading to higher G	Increased investment
Tax cuts – leading to higher C and I	Improved technology
Depreciation of the currency – leading to more X and less M	Higher labour productivity, including education and training
Lower interest rates - leading to higher C and I	Larger workforce
Higher real wages – leading to more C	Discovery or development of natural resources

Many of the causes mentioned in Table 4.3 are closely related. Some of them are developed below, while others, such as depreciation, are explained elsewhere.

- Government expenditure is mainly in the form of investment in new or improved infrastructure such as roads and rail and power supplies. Improved transport allows goods and people to flow more freely and thus facilitates production.
- Lower tax rates allow individuals to spend more and firms to invest more, while lower interest rates have a similar effect.
- Higher real wages mean that individuals are better off and feel able to spend more on goods and services.
- Increased investment is the spending on capital goods including equipment and machinery. This is likely to increase output and also improve the quality thus leading to greater sales. It will also lead to greater labour productivity.
- Improved technology means that more can be produced with the same quantity of capital. This is likely to lead to greater labour productivity.
- Improved education and training affects both the quality and quantity of goods and services. Increasing education and training leads to a more literate and skilled workforce and thus greater labour productivity.
- Discovery/development of natural resources has stimulated growth in many countries e.g. oil for Saudi Arabia and Norway or copper in Zambia.

Link

For more information on devaluation see Chapter 6, section 6.4.3.

Getting it right

Opportunity cost is a useful concept when discussing the consequences of economic growth.

Progress question

2 Discuss the consequences of economic growth for your country.

Activity

Costs and benefits of growth

As a group, make a list of the consequences of economic growth for your country. If you have a large group it could be split into pairs or threes and then each group shares its information to enable a whole group list to be made. You might then want to discuss the extent to which economic growth is good for your country.

4.4.5 *Consequences of economic growth*

Traditionally economic growth has been looked on as an "economic good", but it is clear that this overlooks the considerable costs involved both in terms of human lives, culture and the environment. Table 4.4 shows some of the main consequences in terms of benefits and costs.

Table 4.4 Consequences of economic growth ▼

Benefits	Costs
Rise in the standard of living – leading to reduction of absolute poverty. In addition, there should be more consumer goods.	Environmental damage – resulting from more pollution from factories, cars etc. Damage to the landscape by extracting mineral resources and in terms of the depletion of non-renewable resources. Global warming is another factor here.
Improved education and health – literacy rates should rise while infant mortality and death rates should fall together with the number of people dying from disease.	Opportunity cost – if a country is on its production possibility frontier then more investment in capital goods can only happen if there are less consumer goods, i.e. current consumption will fall.
Increased tax revenue – to fund better infrastructure, schools, hospitals and to provide benefits for the poor etc. This increase in revenue will come from more output/higher incomes and profits rather than from higher taxes.	Unequal benefits – growth is likely to mean changes in economic structure and ways of production, leading to some people becoming unemployed while others gain from more work opportunities. Equally, growth may mean some workers suffer more stress in terms of both having to learn new skills, but also having to work longer hours etc.
Increase in business and consumer confidence – growth should encourage business to take a positive view of the economy and to want to invest, innovate and use new technology. Consumers will be more willing to spend and thus increase aggregate demand if they feel that the economy is doing well.	Lower quality of life – due to rapid urbanisation leading to poor housing and overcrowding together with greater stress, breakdown of family networks and inferior air quality. This may also involve an opportunity cost, e.g. more income, but a poorer quality of life.

Getting it right

Note that unemployment consists of those "willing and able", not just out of work.

Sustainable economic growth requires that resources are both used and conserved for future use.

Demand for natural resources is greater than the potential supply so if nothing is done they will no longer exist. This has led governments all over the world to think about how to manage use so as to support growth while, at the same time, conserving resources.

4.5 Unemployment

4.5.1 *Meaning of unemployment*

Unemployment means those people of working age who are actively seeking work at the current wage rate, but have been unable to do so. It does not include people who are pensioners, full-time students, or those who choose to stay at home, perhaps to look after children. These are regarded as inactive.

4.5.2 *Measures of unemployment*

One common way of looking at unemployment is to refer to the unemployment rate. This is the percentage of the working population who are unemployed. This can be measured by:

$$\text{unemployment rate} = \frac{\text{number of people out of work}}{\text{working population}} \times 100$$

Measuring unemployment seems easy at first: just count up all those who are unemployed. It is not, however, that simple. Firstly, there are different ways of measuring unemployment and these can vary between countries.

The International Labour Organization (ILO) uses the labour force survey and this is used for international comparisons. The UK also uses the claimant count, which relates to those registered as unemployed and claiming the jobseeker's allowance. Those people who are not eligible for this, or who have not registered, are not included. This results in the labour force survey giving a higher figure than the claimant count. The labour force survey, however, is subject to sampling errors and may not be entirely representative.

In addition to the possibility of different measures, there are a number of other problems:

- Inactive workers. Although some of these are genuinely not interested in work, e.g. those who have retired early, many would work if either their situation changed, e.g. mothers or fathers with young children, or if the wage rate was more attractive.
- Discouraged workers are those who are willing and able to work, but because they have had no success finding a job have given up actively seeking employment.
- Part-time workers. Many of these may be working part time because they wish to, e.g. mothers or fathers with children at school may want hours which fit with the school day. Others, however, may want to work full time. These are counted as employed, but could be seen as semi-unemployed.
- Unreported legal employment. Some workers may register as unemployed to collect state benefits, but in fact work, thus defrauding the state.
- Unreported illegal employment. The so-called "underground economy" consists of illegal activities, such as gambling, the sale of drugs and prostitution. People engaged in these illegal activities, however, are in employment but are registered as unemployed.

Key terms

Unemployment: those people of working age who are actively seeking work at the current wage rate.

Unemployment rate: the percentage of the working population who are unemployed.

Labour force survey: a survey of a sample of households, counting people as unemployed if they are actively seeking work, but do not have a job.

Claimant count: measures unemployment according to the number of people claiming unemployment benefits.

Sampling: when a proportion of the population is taken as representative of the whole. The figure for the total is based on the sample being accurate.

Progress question

3 Explain the problems involved in the measurement of the unemployment rate.

Activity

Measuring unemployment

1 Find out how your country measures unemployment

2 Does your country have any other difficulties in measuring unemployment?

4.5.3 Causes and types of unemployment

The causes of unemployment are something that different schools of economists have differing views about. Causes are not the same as types, see below, although they clearly overlap.

Classical economists maintain that unemployment is due to trade, or business, cycles which the market is capable of putting right. Monetarists maintain that external interference in the labour market causes supply to not equal demand. They would argue that factors such as minimum wage laws, restrictive union practices, taxes on companies, unemployment and other benefits, and regulations and red tape which detract from production and employment all prevent the market from clearing. Occupational or geographical immobility will have the same effect.

Keynesians emphasise the cyclical nature of unemployment and that lack of aggregate demand for goods and services reduces the demand for workers. This can best be corrected by government intervention to increase demand.

Marxists claim that it is in the interest of owners to have unemployment, the "reserve army of labour", as this keeps wages low thus reducing costs. Their solution is to abolish capitalism and replace it with socialism.

Table 4.5 The different types of unemployment ▼

Type of unemployment	Explanation
Cyclical or demand deficient or general	Caused by the trade cycle and occurs during the downswing of the cycle becoming severe during the recession. This is the classic Keynesian unemployment due to lack of aggregate demand in the economy as a whole.
Frictional	This is unemployment that cannot be removed. It consists of those who are moving from one job to another, but have not yet started this new work.
Seasonal	In some industries the demand for workers depends on the time of the year. This is especially the case in industries such as agriculture, building and tourism.
Structural	This is caused by a permanent fall in demand for the products of an industry. It is caused by either resources being exhausted or by a country losing its comparative advantage. It is often associated with rising labour costs causing labour-intensive industries to move to low-cost countries.
Technological	This is a form of structural unemployment caused by technology replacing labour.

Getting it right

Be careful that you really know the differences between the various types of unemployment. It is easy to confuse cyclical, frictional and structural.

Activity

Types of unemployment

Discuss as a group what you consider to be the main types of unemployment in your country. Place these in rank order of importance.

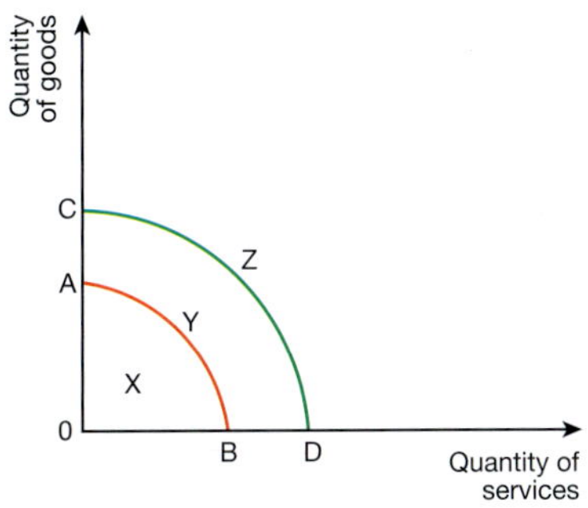

Figure 4.13 Actual and potential growth of an economy ▲

Key terms

NAIRU: the non-accelerating inflation rate of unemployment, i.e. the specific level of unemployment that exists in an economy that does not cause inflation to increase.

Hysteresis: the tendency for unemployment to lead to longer-term unemployment.

4.5.4 Consequences of unemployment

Unemployment leads both to a wastage of resources and to the opportunity cost of lost potential output. This can be seen in Figure 4.13 where the economy is operating at point X. It has both economic consequences for the economy and the individual as well as social consequences.

Economic consequences include the following:

- Labour resources are wasted not only because output is below what it could be, but also because the resources invested in education and training are not being utilised.
- Fall in living standards as unemployment means less income leading to lower consumption.
- Lower aggregate demand not only from those made unemployed, but also from those in employment deciding to save more, and consume less, in case they are made unemployed. This fall in consumption then leads to further unemployment and the development of a deflationary gap. The rise in savings can lead to a reverse multiplier effect.
- Rise in NAIRU as those made unemployed find that their skills become outdated so that it is harder to find work, leading to a lack of confidence and motivation and higher long run unemployment. This is sometimes called the hysteresis effect.
- In many countries governments provide unemployment benefits, so a rise in unemployment means more money is spent on these benefits. This increases the cost to the taxpayer of having to support these people when governments are receiving less revenue from both incomes and consumer expenditure. This can lead to a budget deficit.
- Regional problems, as unemployment is often concentrated in certain areas of a country. This can lead the younger and the more enterprising people in the area to move away, making it even more depressed and unlikely to attract new jobs.
- Income inequality can be widened as more people go into relative poverty.

Social consequences include the following:

- Health: in some countries the loss of income can make it more difficult to provide medical care, while in others financial worries can cause both mental and physical health problems and even higher suicide rates.
- Education: where education has to be paid for, families may be tempted to save money by withdrawing children from schools while at the same time sending them out to work to bring in more income.
- Family: the stress of unemployment can cause divorce and family break-ups if homelessness occurs. It can lead to higher crime rates as people are desperate to survive.

Case Study

Youth Unemployment in Tanzania

The population of Tanzania is increasing at over 3 per cent every year. One of the challenges this causes is youth unemployment. This is not a new problem, but one which has not been solved. The level of unemployment is at least 11.5 per cent, but some sources have it as high as 25 per cent. The problem is the way in which the information is collected and classified. Many of those who are unemployed are listed as self-employed or "entrepreneur".

Education provision has greatly improved and expanded in recent years, but many young people find that their skills are not required in the new jobs in mining and factories. This results in university graduates often taking more than five years to find suitable work. One reason for this is an information mismatch.

Among other consequences of this youth unemployment are: poor public health; low economic growth; emigration; and high crime rates.

1 Explain two causes of youth unemployment mentioned in the passage.
2 Explain how these causes could be prevented.
3 Explain how high youth unemployment could lead to low economic growth.
4 Discuss whether young people seeking employment abroad would be good for the Tanzanian economy.

4.6 Price stability

4.6.1 *Definition of inflation, deflation and disinflation*

Key terms

Inflation: a fall in the value of money shown by a persistent rise in the general price level. Alternatively, inflation is a persistent rise in the general price level leading to a fall in the value of money.
Deflation: a fall in the general price level.
Disinflation: when the general price level rises at a slower rate.

Inflation can be said to occur when prices rise and what you can buy with your money falls. This is known as money value. If, to start with, you had one unit of your currency and could buy five oranges with it, but then later found that you could only buy four oranges, you would be facing inflation. The purchasing power of the currency has fallen.

In general, inflation is when most prices rise so that the cost of living increases, i.e. it costs people more to buy the same goods and services. It is possible for some prices to fall even though prices in general have risen. The rate of inflation is the rate at which the general level of prices is rising over time and it is usually expressed as an annual rate.

Deflation is the opposite of inflation. It is when the general price level falls. In this case the rate of inflation is negative. Using the example of buying oranges in this case you would find that your money could now buy six oranges. The purchasing power of the currency has risen.

Disinflation is the slowing of the rate of inflation. The purchasing power of the currency is falling at a slower rate. It is often associated with periods of low inflation such as many countries had from 2018–20.

Getting it right

Be very careful not to confuse deflation and disinflation. Deflation gives a negative value for inflation e.g. –2 per cent, while disinflation is a fall in the rate of inflation e.g. from 5 per cent to 2 per cent.

Activities

Inflation

1. Compare the inflation rates of Greece, South Korea and Turkey. To which of these could you apply the terms: inflation; deflation; and disinflation?
2. Find out what the rate of inflation in your country was in 2020. How does it compare with the countries below?
3. What has happened to inflation in your country since 2020?

Inflation rates for December 2020

Country	Inflation %
Brazil	4.31
Chile	2.97
Greece	−2.32
India	5.28
Japan	−0.98
South Africa	3.18
South Korea	0.52
Turkey	14.60

Source: www.inflation.eu

4.6.2 *Measurement of changes in the price level*

Consumer price index

The UK and many other countries use the consumer price index (CPI). This is often referred to as the harmonised consumer prices index and is widely used for international comparisons. Other countries use the retail price index (RPI).

Price indices are usually a weighted average of prices for goods and services. To construct an index a base year is chosen and the average price level for that year given the value of 100. This allows price changes to be expressed as a percentage change. A weighted index is used because the weights express the relative importance of each item in the index. For example, a change in the price of food is likely to have more effect on household expenditure than a change in the price of cinema tickets. These indices are used to measure the rate of inflation.

This can be calculated by: $\frac{\text{index for Year 2}}{\text{index for Year 1}} \times 100$

The CPI is constructed by:

1. choosing a base year against which price changes are measured – this is given the value of 100
2. selecting the items bought by an average family, the basket of goods
3. giving each item a weight showing its relative importance in the average family budget

Key terms

Consumer price index: a measure of the weighted average of prices of a basket of goods and services purchased by households.

Base year: the year which is chosen as the point of reference for a comparison of prices in other years.

Weights: values given to items in an index to show their relative importance.

Household expenditure: the total expenditure by consumers resident in a country whether at home or abroad minus expenditure by visitors on goods and services.

4 obtaining new prices for each item from a wide variety of different sources across the country

5 taking this new price for each item and multiplying by its weight to give the weighted price relative

6 taking the sum of the weighted price relatives and dividing by the sum of the weights to give the change in price index.

Possible difficulties in measurement

There are a number of problems with these indices:

- The base year needs to be one in which there are not unusual fluctuations in prices, otherwise future calculations will be misleading.
- The basket of goods may not be representative of all groups (e.g. pensioners); different groups of people have different baskets of goods and services – they may, therefore, have a different cost of living.
- Unless the basket is regularly updated the goods and services included may not represent current expenditure patterns.
- Change in quality/type of good, e.g. mobile phones have many more features than they had ten years ago.
- The importance of goods and services may change, i.e. weights need to change.
- There are different measures, e.g. RPI and CPI.

Activity

Price index

1 Find out which goods and services are included in your country's consumer price index (or retail price index, if no CPI).

2 What goods and services would you and your friends have in a basket? How would this differ from that of your parents or grandparents?

Case Study

Consumer price index in Ghana

2010 = 100

Year	CPI
2015	176.0
2016	206.7
2017	232.3
2018	250.4
2019	268.4

1 By how much have prices increased between 2010 and 2019?

2 What has happened to prices in Ghana between the years:

a 2015 and 2016

b 2018 and 2019?

4.6.3 Distinction between money values (nominal) and real data

Prices, and other figures measured in money, can be quoted either as money data (money values), or nominal prices or as real data prices. The difference is that money wages, for example, are the actual wage that people get, while real wages represent what that money can buy. Real data is the money data adjusted for changes in the price level. If prices have risen by 5 per cent then a 6 per cent wage rise means that the real wage has gone up by 1 per cent, the difference between the wage rise and the rate of inflation.

This is an important distinction and you will meet it in many situations in economics, e.g. gross domestic product.

Key terms

Money data, money values, nominal prices: where figures are expressed in current prices.

Real data: where figures are adjusted for the change in the value of money (rate of inflation/price level).

Demand-pull inflation: occurs when the total (aggregate) demand in the economy exceeds the total (aggregate) supply.

Cost-push inflation: occurs when the cost of supplying goods and services is increased, causing a rise in the cost of final prices.

4.6.4 Causes of inflation: cost-push and demand-pull inflation

Many economists argue that inflation is the result of either an increase in total demand which pulls up prices (demand-pull inflation) or an increase in the costs of production which pushes prices up (cost-push inflation).

Demand-pull inflation usually happens when the economy is near its full employment level. In this situation resources are unable to supply sufficient goods (scarcity of resources) to meet demand. This results in prices being bid or forced upwards in order to bring aggregate supply and aggregate demand into equilibrium.

Cost-push inflation is caused by, three different factors.

- The most common factor today is the rise in the cost of raw materials forcing up the costs of production. This is seen, in particular, by the rise in the price of energy sources, especially oil. Many other raw materials, as they become scarcer relative to demand, have risen steeply in price.
- Where trade unions are powerful, they can push up wages in excess of productivity gains. This means that costs of production rise so that producers raise their prices so as to maintain profit levels. This was common in countries such as the UK in the 1960s and 1970s.
- Monopolies can raise prices due to the lack of competition. This is often linked to the rise in wages with producers using the wage rise to justify even higher price increases.

The latter two give rise to a wage–price spiral as rising wages push up prices leading to more wage demands.

Monetarists, such as Milton Friedman, have argued, however, that the sole cause of inflation is an excess in the money supply and the velocity of its circulation. This stems from the Quantity Theory of Money. They would maintain that demand-pull and cost-push are then a result of this. If governments, or central banks, increase the money in circulation by more than the increase in real output then the excess is "soaked up" by a rise in prices.

Link

The following are examined in more detail on the pages indicated:

Costs of production in Chapter 7, section 7.5.
Trade unions in Chapter 8, section 8.3.8.
Monopoly in Chapter 7, section 7.6.
Money supply and the quantity theory of money in Chapter 9, sections 9.4.2 and 9.4.3.

Getting it right

Where a question asks you to discuss whether something is the only cause, you are expected to look at other causes and then come to a conclusion.

4.6.5 *Consequences of inflation*

It is important to realise that inflation is the historical norm and that it is high levels of inflation that are potentially problematic. Deflation for any period of time leads to huge problems such as those which affected the world economy in the 1920s and 1930s. The questions are "what level of inflation is acceptable?" and "why are higher rates problematical?".

Many countries have now adopted policies requiring them to keep inflation at low levels. The Bank of England has a target of 2 per cent while the People's Bank of China has a target of 4 per cent. The target is never zero as a low positive one allows for greater flexibility such as allowing relative prices to adjust.

Getting it right

Remember that a lower rise in the price level just means that the rate of inflation has fallen, but is still positive.

Table 4.6 The types of consequences of inflation and their effects ▼

Income distribution problems	Borrowers gain because they are paying back less in terms of the value of money, but lenders and savers lose as their money becomes worth less. Those on fixed incomes lose as the income can buy less, but members of strong trade unions etc. can get wage increases in excess of inflation.
Labour market problems	If inflation is 5 per cent then workers will demand more than this to maintain their living standard. Employers faced with falling sales due to higher prices will not want to pay, leading potentially to strikes etc.
International competitiveness	Higher inflation causes goods and services to be expensive compared to other countries' goods. This results in less sales and exports being less than imports.
Unemployment	If sales fall, workers are likely to be made unemployed. This gives rise to stagflation.
Investment	Inflation creates uncertainty about the future which is likely to lead firms to invest less thus leading to lower future economic growth.
Unanticipated inflation	This is where the rate of inflation cannot be predicted. This is likely to lead to uncertainty. The opposite is anticipated inflation.
Shoe leather costs	If prices are rising then consumers and businesses will waste time trying to find the cheapest price.
Menu costs	If prices change frequently then the administrative costs for firms rise in having to adjust price lists etc. and to change vending machines.
Fiscal drag	As inflation rises people demand higher incomes. If tax thresholds do not change then people can be dragged into higher tax bands thus paying more tax.

Getting it right

Many countries now have inflation targets such as the Bank of England's 2 per cent.
Does your country's central bank have an inflation target? Make sure you know what it is.

Key concepts

- **Equilibrium and disequilibrium** can be seen with reference to AD and AS and the circular flow.
- **Time** can be seen in AD and AS, economic growth, unemployment and price stability.
- **Progress and development** can be seen in economic growth, unemployment and price stability.

Progress check

After completing this chapter you should be able to:

- define the meaning of national income and understand how to measure national income
- explain the difference between market prices and base prices
- explain the difference between gross values and net values
- understand the circular flow of income in both a closed and open economy including injections, leakages and equilibrium and disequilibrium
- define aggregate demand and aggregate supply
- describe the components of aggregate demand
- understand the determinants of aggregate demand and aggregate supply
- understand the shape of the aggregate demand curve
- understand the shape of the aggregate supply curve in both the short and long runs
- explain the causes of shifts in the aggregate demand and aggregate supply curves
- distinguish between a movement along and a shift of the aggregate demand and supply curves
- explain equilibrium aggregate demand and supply and the determination of the level of real output, the price level and employment
- explain the effects of the shifts in the aggregate demand and aggregate supply curves on the level of real output, the price level and employment
- define economic growth and how it is measured
- distinguish between nominal and real GDP
- explain the causes and consequences of economic growth

- define unemployment
- explain how unemployment is measured and some of the problems involved
- explain the causes and consequences of unemployment
- define inflation, deflation and disinflation
- explain how changes in the price level are measured and the difficulties in doing so
- distinguish between money values and real data
- explain the causes and consequences of inflation.

Exam-style questions

Essay questions

1a With the help of diagrams, explain and compare a movement along and a shift of the AD curve. [8 marks]
b Discuss whether an increase in AD will always lead to a rise in output and employment. [12 marks]
2a Explain the difference between growth in nominal and real GDP and consider the uses of both. [8 marks]
b Discuss whether the benefits of economic growth always outweigh the costs. [12 marks]
3a Explain how the consumer prices index is constructed and consider how useful it is as a measure of inflation. [8 marks]
b Discuss the view that inflation is always a major problem for an economy. [12 marks]
4a Explain the meaning of unemployment and compare the ways of measuring it. [8 marks]
b Discuss whether the consequences of cyclical unemployment result in greater problems for the economy than those of structural unemployment. [12 marks]
5a Explain how GNI at market prices can be adjusted to give NNI at basic prices and consider their uses. [8 marks]
b Discuss the view that improvements in education and training is the most important cause of economic growth. [12 marks]
6a With the help of diagrams, explain what is meant by equilibrium in the AD/AS model and comment on its usefulness. [8 marks]
b Discuss whether an increase in AD will always lead to economic growth. [12 marks]

Multiple choice questions

7 Which of the following is normally part of a country's GDP? [1 mark]
A Domestic services performed within a family
B Household savings
C Interest rates
D Investment spending by firms

8 The table shows the rate of inflation for a country for 2012–2016. [1 mark]

Year	Inflation rate %
2012	5
2013	4
2014	4
2015	2
2016	3

Which of the statements is correct?

A Prices fell from 2012 to 2015 and then increased.
B Prices rose throughout the period shown.
C Prices rose only in 2016.
D Prices were constant in 2013–2014.

5 Government macroeconomic intervention

In this chapter you will develop your knowledge and understanding of:

- government macroeconomic policy objectives
- fiscal policy
- monetary policy
- supply-side policy.

Link

See Chapter 4, sections 4.4–4.6, for more on inflation, unemployment and economic growth.

See Chapter 9, sections 9.2 and 9.3, for more on unemployment and economic growth.

See Chapter 10, section 10.1, for more on government macroeconomic objectives.

5.1 Government macroeconomic policy objectives

5.1.1 *Use of government policy to achieve macroeconomic objectives*

Although there is a range of economic policies that governments strive to achieve at this stage, this is confined to price stability, control of inflation, unemployment and economic growth.

Economic policy is the attempt by government to generate increases in economic welfare. Ever since the so-called "great depression" of the late 1920s and 1930s, economists have recognised that there is a role for government and monetary authorities in trying to ensure increased economic welfare by controlling inflation, unemployment and economic growth.

This control is through demand-side policies which affect AD. These are fiscal policy and monetary policy. Supply-side policies can also be used which affect AS.

Although inflation is seen as inevitable, and normal, all governments are concerned to try to achieve stable prices, or at least prices which only rise at a slow rate. If prices are continually rising at high rates then investors are reluctant to invest in new machinery, factories and products because they cannot calculate the outcome of their investments. Rising inflation leads to menu costs, such as sellers having to constantly revise their price lists. Similarly, those who are on fixed incomes, usually the economically inactive, such as those relying on state benefits, suffer as any increases lag well behind price rises.

In addition, inflation is likely to lead to other macroeconomic problems as indicated on pages 127–8.

Activity

Worst inflation rate in history

In 1946, inflation in Hungary reached a rate of 13 600 000 000 000 000 percent per month. Prices ended up doubling every 15 hours.
In 2008, prices in Zimbabwe doubled every 24.7 hours.
What has happened to inflation in your country in the last 10 years?

Activities

Fiscal year

Find out when your fiscal year runs from and to. Why were those dates chosen?

Governments aim to achieve full employment. It is difficult to know what this means as not only are there different definitions of full employment, but there is no agreement on what percentage of unemployment would indicate that full employment had been reached. All governments, however, aim for this objective (see the case study below).

Governments aim to achieve sustainable economic growth. High growth rates may be very good for developing countries, but if they are achieved by depletion and exhaustion of scarce natural resources or by creating too much pollution, leading to climate change, then the high rates will not be sustainable.

Case Study

Full employment in the UK

Speaking at a meeting near London in April 2014, George Osborne, Chancellor of the Exchequer, promised to restore the UK to full employment. He said that there was "no reason why Britain should not aim to have the highest employment rate of any of the world's leading economies". He went on to say "a modern approach to full employment means backing business. It means cutting the tax on jobs and reforming welfare".

The OECD states that Britain's employment rate for those aged 16–64 is 71 per cent, which is more than the USA, France and Italy, but lower than Germany, Canada and Japan. To overtake these three countries would involve creating one million more jobs.

1. What is meant by full employment?
2. Explain how "cutting the tax on jobs and reforming welfare" could lead to full employment.
3. Find out what your current employment rate for 16–64-year-olds is and compare it to two of the seven countries named in the text.
4. Discuss why a government might find it difficult to create a large number of new jobs.

Getting it right

Do not confuse the government's budget and the balance of payments (see Chapter 6). The budget is about internal finance and expenditure while the balance of payments deals with external finance.

5.2 Fiscal policy

5.2.1 *Meaning of government budget*

The government budget is an annual financial statement showing estimates of expected revenue and expenditure during a fiscal, or tax, year. In the UK the fiscal year is from 6 April to the following 5 April.

5.2.2 *Distinction between a government budget deficit and a government budget surplus*

The current budget deficit, or budget surplus, is the difference between the government's day-to-day expenditure and its (tax) revenue, that is, the difference between what it spends and what it receives.

If the government spends more than it receives then it would run a budget deficit. The opposite of this is that the government spends less than it receives, then it would run a budget surplus.

Key terms

Government budget: an annual financial statement showing estimates of expected revenue and expenditure during a fiscal year.
Budget deficit: when government spending is greater than tax revenue.
Budget surplus: when government spending is less than tax revenue.

Key term

National debt: the amount of money a government owes both domestically and abroad, which has accumulated over a number of years.

Activity

National Debt

Find out how the national debt of your country has changed in the last 10 years.

Discuss whether its size matters.

Getting it right

A common error is to confuse the national debt, which is related to the internal government, and the deficit on the balance of payments, which is external.

Key terms

Direct tax: a tax levied directly on incomes and wealth.

Progressive tax: where the proportion of income paid in tax increases as income increases.

Marginal rate of tax: the addition to tax paid out of an addition to income.

Link

Indirect tax is covered in Chapter 2, section 2.1.5 and in Chapter 3, section 3.2.1.

5.2.3 *Meaning and significance of the national debt*

The national debt is the net accumulation of the central government's annual budget deficits. It is the total amount of money that the central government owes its creditors.

If a government has a budget deficit then it needs to raise extra finance. It can raise finance either by printing more money or by borrowing. Printing money will reduce its value, leading to inflation.

Borrowing can be either short term or long term, and can be from domestic or foreign sources. The most common method is for the government to issue government bills (short term) or stock (long term).

Either of these, however, will result in an increase in the national debt. The size of the national debt only becomes important when a large proportion is owed abroad or if it looks as if it cannot be repaid. Otherwise a lot of the debt will be owed to a government's own citizens. This means that some of the tax collected from taxpayers will be paid back to those who hold short- or long-term government bills, that is, it is a circular flow of money within a closed economy. In 2019, the country with the highest national debt to GDP ratio was Japan at 237 per cent.

5.2.4 *Taxation*

Types of tax

The first way to look at type of tax is to distinguish between direct and indirect taxes.

A direct tax is one which is levied on the incomes of individuals and firms. They also include taxes on inherited wealth. Examples include income tax, corporation tax and inheritance tax.

An indirect tax is one which is levied when goods and services are bought. They are, therefore, taxes on expenditure. Examples include value added tax (VAT) and goods and services tax (GST).

Indirect taxes can take different forms. Firstly, there is excise duty, which is a tax imposed on a product, such as petrol, and is usually a specific amount placed on a product. Secondly, an *ad valorem* tax is one which places a percentage rate on a good or service, e.g. VAT might be set at 20 per cent.

Another way in which taxes can be grouped is progressive, regressive and proportional.

A progressive tax is one where as people's income rises a higher proportion of the increase is taken in tax. In this case, the marginal rate of tax (MRT) increases. In many countries, the proportion of income taken in tax rises when the income goes above certain levels or thresholds. For example, income tax might start at 20 per cent and then increase to 30 per cent, 40 per cent and 50 per cent as income levels rise.

Key terms

Regressive tax: where the proportion of income paid in tax falls as income increases.

Proportional tax: where the same proportion of income is paid in tax whatever the level of income.

Average rate of tax: the average percentage of total income that is paid in taxes.

Getting it right

You need to understand that:

1. a progressive tax does not just mean that a person pays more tax as their income increases, but an increasing proportion of their income.
2. with a regressive tax a person may pay more tax as income rises, but they pay a smaller proportion of their income.

Regressive taxes are the opposite of progressive. As people's income rises a lower proportion of the increase is taken in tax. In this case, the MRT falls. This will tend to apply to indirect taxes as the specific amount does not change nor does the fixed percentage of *ad valorem* taxes.

Finally, proportional taxes take the same proportion of a person's income whatever the level. These taxes have a constant MRT. In this situation, the marginal and the average rate of tax (ART) is the same.

The relationships of the three types to income are shown in Figure 5.1.

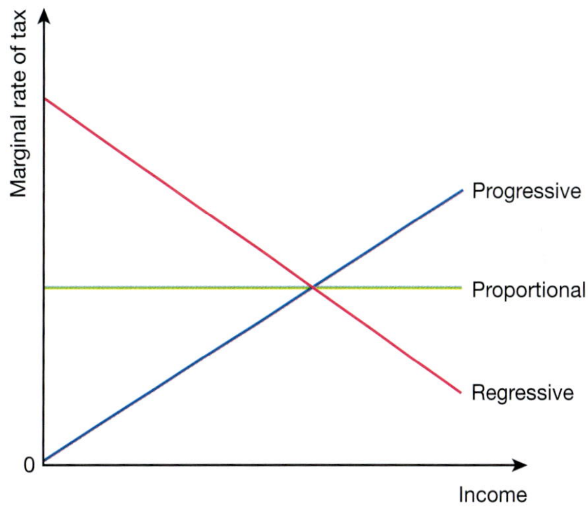

Figure 5.1 Progressive, proportional and regressive taxation ▲

Rates of tax

Average rates of taxation refer to the average percentage of total income which is paid in taxes. The average rate of tax can also be known as the effective rate of tax or the average propensity to pay tax. It can be calculated as:

$$\text{ART} = \frac{\text{total tax due}}{\text{total taxable income}}$$

Marginal rates of taxation refer to the proportion of an increase in income which is taken in tax. It can be calculated as:

$$\text{MRT} = \frac{\text{change in tax due}}{\text{change in taxable income}}$$

In a progressive tax system, such as income tax usually is, MRT will be greater than ART as income increases

Reasons for taxation

There are four main reasons for taxation:

- To raise revenue to help finance government spending. It is important to note that in most countries taxation is not the only way in which this is done because governments may need to spend now while taxes come in across the year.

Link

For market failure see Chapter 3, section 3.1 and Chapter 8, section 8.1.
For distribution of income and wealth see Chapter 3, section 3.3.

- To manage aggregate demand. Taxation is one way in which a government can try to meet its economic objectives.
- To change the distribution of income and wealth. Taxes such as income tax are deliberately designed in many countries to take money from the better off and give it to those who do not have enough.
- To manage market failure and environmental targets. Taxes are one way in which market failures, such as pollution, can be reduced.

Progress question

1 Discuss the reasons why your government raises taxes.

Activity

Taxation

If you have a number of people in your group, the following activities could be divided between them. They could then report back on their findings.
Research examples of progressive and regressive taxes in your country. Also, look for any research examples of proportional taxes.

1 Explain the marginal rate of tax in relationship to direct taxes in your country
2 Give examples for the four reasons for taxation in your country.
3 Do you think there are any other reasons for taxation?

5.2.5 *Government spending*

Types of spending: capital (investment) and current

Capital expenditure, or gross fixed capital formation, are the terms used for government investment. This is spending by the government on goods and services intended to create future benefits, such as:

- infrastructure investment in transport, such as road building
- health and education, such as new hospitals or schools or sewage systems
- research spending, such as defence, space or vaccinations.

Key terms

Capital expenditure: spending by the government on goods and services intended to create future benefits.

Current expenditure: government consumption expenditure on goods and services for current use to directly satisfy the individual or collective needs of members of the community.

Current expenditure is government consumption expenditure on goods and services for current use to directly satisfy the individual or collective needs of members of the community. This can include the wages of public sector employees, road maintenance, etc.

Reasons for government spending

Governments spend money for many different reasons including to:

- supply goods and services that the private sector would fail to do, such as public goods, including defence; merit goods such as hospitals and schools; and welfare payments and benefits, including unemployment and disability benefit
- achieve supply-side improvements in the macro economy, such as spending on education and training to improve labour productivity
- reduce the effects of negative externalities, such as pollution

Link

For public and merit goods see Chapter 1, sections 1.6.2 and 1.6.3.
For supply-side policies see section 5.4 of this chapter.
For negative externalities see Chapter 7, section 7.4.
For income and equality see Chapter 3, section 3.3.
For aggregate demand see Chapter 4, section 4.3.

Key terms

Fiscal policy: the use of government revenue and expenditure to control the economy.
Expansionary fiscal policy: the use of fiscal policy to enable the economy to grow.
Contractionary fiscal policy: the use of fiscal policy to reduce the size of the economy.

Link

AD and AS analysis is explained in Chapter 4, section 4.3.

- subsidise industries which may need financial support, and which is not available from the private sector. An example of this in many countries is agriculture
- help redistribute income and achieve more equity
- inject extra spending into the macro-economy, to help achieve increases in aggregate demand and economic activity.

5.2.6 Distinction between expansionary and contractionary fiscal policy

Fiscal policy is the use of government revenue and expenditure to control the economy. This includes government borrowing. Expansionary fiscal policy involves increasing aggregate demand resulting in economic growth, more employment, but also higher inflation and possibly a deficit in the balance of payments. In general, expansionary fiscal policy would result in a budget deficit. The opposite is contractionary (sometimes called deflationary) fiscal policy where government revenue is increased, often leading to a budget surplus, leading to lower inflation, higher unemployment and lower economic growth.

Fiscal policy can also be used as a supply-side measure. This is covered under supply-side policies later on this chapter.

5.2.7 AD/AS analysis of the impact of expansionary and contractionary fiscal policy on the equilibrium national income and the level of real output, the price level and employment

Figure 5.2 shows the effects of expansionary fiscal policy. An increase in government expenditure (G) or cut in tax rates (T) will lead to an increase in AD from AD to AD_1. This has resulted in a rise in the equilibrium national income from PY to P_1Y_1 and a rise in real output and employment from Y to Y_1 and in the price level from P to P_1.

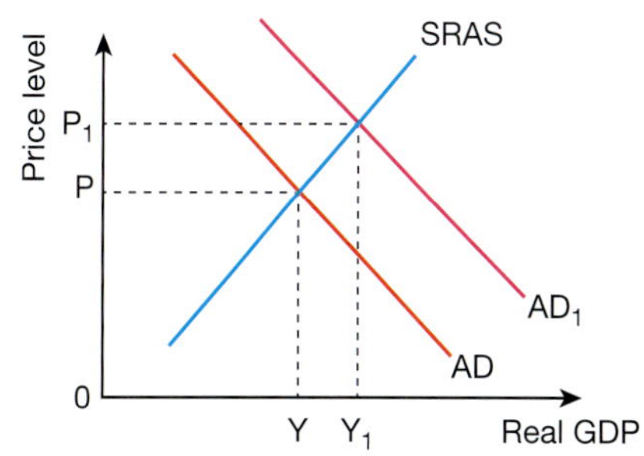

Figure 5.2 Expansionary fiscal policy ▲

The opposite effects for Contractionary fiscal policy can be observed in Figure 5.3. Here the equilibrium national income falls from PY to P_1Y_1 and output and employment fall from Y to Y_1 and the price level falls from P to P_1.

- there are different measures, e.g. RPI and CPI.

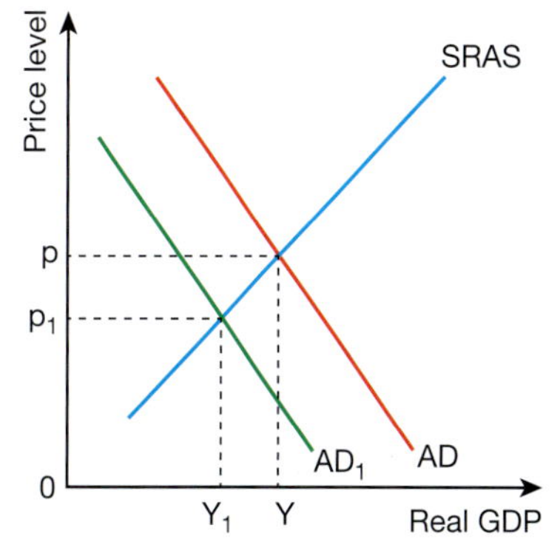

Figure 5.3 Contractionary fiscal policy ▲

Case Study

Fiscal policy in the Philippines

The Philippines' government has tried to support its economy and the very poor during 2020, but the shrinking growth and government revenues, which very largely rely on personal and income taxes, have led to an estimated fall in GDP of 9 per cent. It has also led to a large budget deficit.

Parliament has approved a record $94 billion budget for 2021, part of which will be used to buy COVID-19 vaccines as the government aims to immunize a third of its 108 million population and regain some resemblance of normality.

1 Explain why the Philippines had a large budget deficit in 2020.
2 Explain whether expenditure on vaccines would be classified as capital or current expenditure.
3 Discuss the extent to which fiscal policy could be used to stimulate renewed economic growth.

5.3 Monetary policy

5.3.1 *Definition of monetary policy*

Monetary policy is a demand-side economic policy. It is usually controlled by the central bank. It involves the management of money supply and the rate of interest.

Monetary policy has consisted of:

- targeting the money supply
- controlling interest rates
- maintaining the exchange rate.

5.3.2 *Tools of monetary policy: interest rates, money supply and credit regulations*

Interest rates are the cost of borrowing money and the return on lending money. In the last twenty to thirty years, many governments have stopped directing the central bank as to the rate of interest to set and has given it independence as in, for example, Australia, the UK and South Africa. All other banks in the economy then set their rates with reference to the base rate. In Singapore, however, interest rates are solely determined by the individual banks.

Central banks raise or lower interest rates to ensure that they meet by the inflation target set by the central bank and to ensure liquidity in the economy.

Link

For more on interest rates and money supply, see Chapter 9, section 9.4. For more on exchange rates, see Chapter 6, section 6.4.

Link

For interest rates and factors of production, see Chapter 1.

Key terms

Monetary policy: the use of the rate of interest or money supply or credit regulations to control the economy.
Interest rates: the cost of borrowing money and the return on lending money. Interest rate policy is the use of interest rates to influence demand by both consumers and businesses.

Link

For more on quantitative easing, see Chapter 9, section 9.4.

Key terms

Money supply: the total amount of money in an economy. This can be taken as notes, coins and easily accessible accounts, e.g. current accounts.

Credit regulations: the use of qualitative control measures by the central bank to regulate the consumer credit on certain products which are affected by inflation or deflation.

Activity

Tools of monetary policy

If you have enough people in your group you could split into three sub-groups and tackle one of the following questions each and then report back to the whole group.

1. What is the current interest rate in your country? How has it changed over the last three years?
2. What is counted as being part of money supply in your country? Does the central bank try to control it? If so, how?
3. What is meant by credit regulation in your country? How is it operated?

Table 5.1 Selected central bank inflation targets for 2021

Country	Inflation target %
Columbia	3±1
Ghana	8±2
Japan	2
Malawi	5
Sri Lanka	4–6
UK	2

Money supply is the total amount of money in an economy. This can be taken as notes, coins and easily accessible accounts, e.g. current accounts. Controlling the money supply has proved to be very difficult and has been largely abandoned in favour of interest rates, although money supply is still measured as one aspect to consider when deciding policy.

In recent years many central banks have used quantitative easing as a means of increasing the money supply.

Credit regulations are qualitative control measures used by the central bank to regulate the consumer credit on a certain products which are affected by inflation or deflation. They make borrowing and spending money, therefore, more difficult, in case of inflation, or easier, in the case of deflation.

5.3.3 *Distinction between expansionary and contractionary monetary policy*

The central bank of a country can adopt an expansionary or contractionary monetary policy. An expansionary monetary policy is focused on expanding, or increasing, the money supply in an economy. On the other hand, a contractionary monetary policy is focused on decreasing the money supply in the economy. The central bank uses its monetary policy tools to increase or decrease the money supply.

5.3.4 *AD/AS analysis of the impact of expansionary and contractionary monetary policy on the equilibrium national income and the level of real output, the price level and employment*

An expansionary monetary policy, such as a cut in interest rates, means that the AD curve shifts to the right, from AD to AD_1 in Figure 5.4. This will result in a rise in real GDP and employment from Y to Y_1 and an increase in the price level from P to P_1.

A contractionary monetary policy, such as a rise in interest rates, results in the opposite effects. This means that the AD curve shifts to the left, from AD to AD_1 in Figure 5.5. This will result in a fall in real GDP and employment from Y to Y_1 and a fall in the price level from P to P_1.

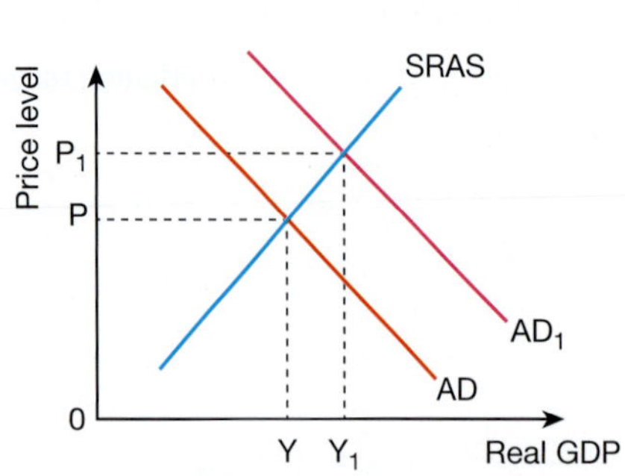

Figure 5.4 Expansionary monetary policy▲

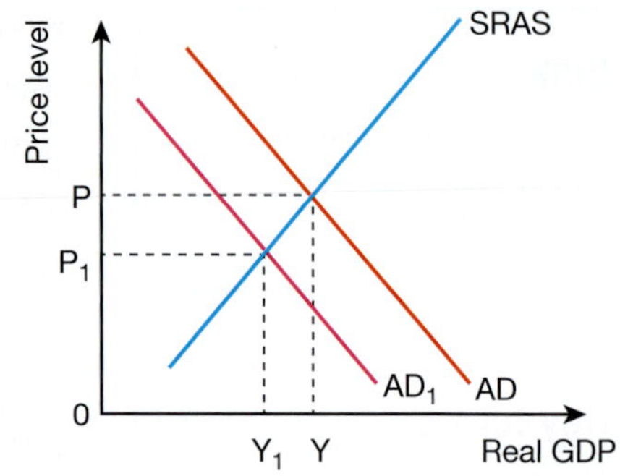

Figure 5.5 Contractionary monetary policy▲

> **Progress question**
>
> 2 Explain the difference between expansionary and contractionary monetary policies.

5.4 Supply-side policy

5.4.1 *Meaning of supply-side policy, in terms of its effect on LRAS curves*

Supply-side policies are aimed at affecting the aggregate supply as can be seen in Figure 5.6. The aim is to shift the long run supply curve to the right, LRAS to $LRAS_1$, leading to an increase in real growth and thus employment, while, at the same time, resulting in a fall in the price level.

> **Key term**
>
> **Supply-side policy**: any policy that helps to improve a country's productive potential.

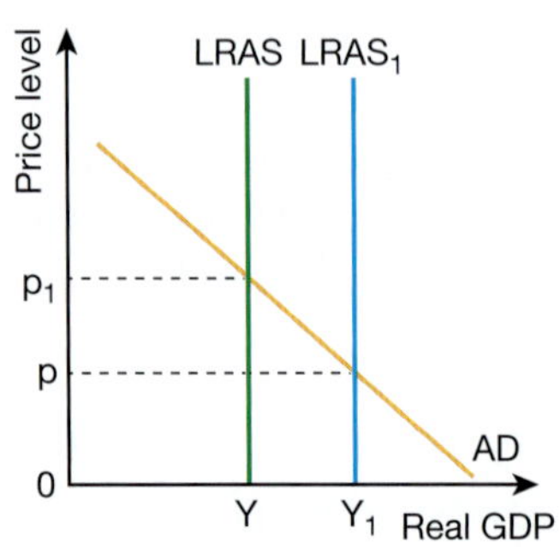

Figure 5.6 Supply-side policy▲

5.4.2 *Objectives of supply-side policy: increasing productivity and productive capacity*

Supply-side policies are largely aimed at improving productivity and productive capacity. As can be seen from this, they are essentially microeconomic measures used to influence the macro-economy.

Productivity is the quantity of goods and services produced per unit of input. By increasing productivity, therefore, the real output of the economy can be increased so that AS has shifted outwards without any increase in the price level.

Increasing productive capacity means increasing the potential output of an economy. In Figure 5.7 it is shifting the production possibility curve outwards from AB to CD.

> **Link**
>
> For more on productivity, see Chapter 4, section 4.3.7.
> For more on production possibility curves, see Chapter 1, section 1.5.

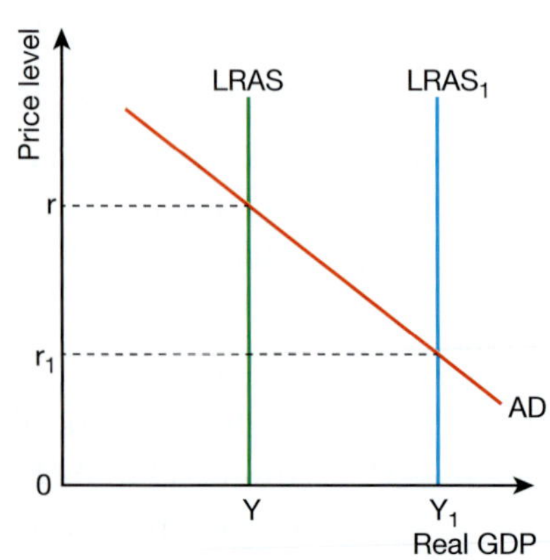

Figure 5.7 Increase in potential capacity▲

5.4.3 *Tools of supply-side policy*

These policies are often grouped under two headings: labour market measures and product market measures.

Labour market measures

- Ensuring that trade unions do not restrict the working of the labour market by making it more rigid. This has been controversial as it is difficult to decide between protecting the rights of workers and freeing up the market so it responds to the needs of the economy.
- Education and training. Government spending on education and training improves workers' human capital. They become better quality workers. Their productivity improves and so the LRAS curve shifts to the right.
- Tax and benefits. It is argued that high rates of direct tax act as a disincentive to people to work and firms to make profits. Lower rates would encourage more people to work, especially if these were linked to lower unemployment benefits thus providing a real incentive to find jobs. Equally, lower taxes on firms would lead to them trying to be more efficient as they now keep more of their profits and use these for investment. This idea is associated with Arthur Laffer. Lower income tax will act as an incentive for unemployed workers to join the labour market, or for existing workers to work harder. Lower corporation tax provides an incentive for entrepreneurs to start and so increase national output.
- Local versus national pay agreements. National pay rates often fail to reflect differences within a country of the supply and demand for labour thus preventing people in areas of high supply from finding work.

Link

For more on the Laffer curve, see Chapter 10, section 10.3.1.

Product market policies

- Privatisation and deregulation are ways of introducing competition into the market thus increasing efficiency and greater productivity.
- Government may help to improve supply-side performance by giving assistance to firms to encourage them to use new technology and innovate. This can be done through grants or through the tax system. This will also encourage a more entrepreneurial culture. Governments can also improve infrastructure so people and goods can move faster and more easily.
- Reduction in bureaucratic systems which hinders the ability of businesses to either establish themselves or to make changes. This "red tape" hinders enterprise.

Link

For more on privatisation and deregulation, see Chapter 8, section 8.1.

Activity

Tools of supply-side policy

Find out what supply-side policies the government of your country uses.

Case Study

Supply-side policies and India

In many ways India has been an economic success. Thanks to an entrepreneurial attitude, industry has grown and Bengaluru has established itself as a world leader in IT. In addition, agricultural productivity has steadily improved. All of this has led to rapid economic growth.

Some economists consider that the increase could be even greater if the infrastructure was better. Overall, supply constraints not only hinder growth, but also increase inflation. In addition, whereas the low wage costs have been a benefit for India, the increasing skills shortage means that wages will rise making it less attractive for foreign investment. The shortage of places at universities means that many Indian students have to seek places abroad from which they may not return to work in India.

Recently, the government has enacted supply-side policies which will be beneficial in the long run by raising India's potential output. These may not do anything, however, to reverse the slowdown in the economy.

1. Explain two ways in which India has achieved economic success.
2. Explain how improving the infrastructure could lead to greater economic growth.
3. Discuss which policy would be best at reversing 'the slowdown in the Indian economy'.

5.4.4 *AD/AS analysis of the impact of supply-side policy*

The outcome of supply-side policies will depend on the shape of the AS curve and whether only these policies are considered or whether AD is also changing. In Figure 5.8 the effect of say better education and training shifts the AS curve from AS to AS_1 leading to an increase in equilibrium national income, real output and employment from Y to Y_1. At the same time the price level falls from P to P_1.

Figure 5.9 shows the effects of an interaction between changes in AD and AS. The economy is originally in equilibrium at PY where AD = AS. If AD increases then equilibrium national income, output and employment all increase to Y_1, but the price level rises to P_1. If, however, at the same time supply-side policies have been put in place then the AS curve shifts to AS_1 reinforcing the effects on equilibrium national income, output and employment as they increase further to Y_2, but maintaining price stability at P.

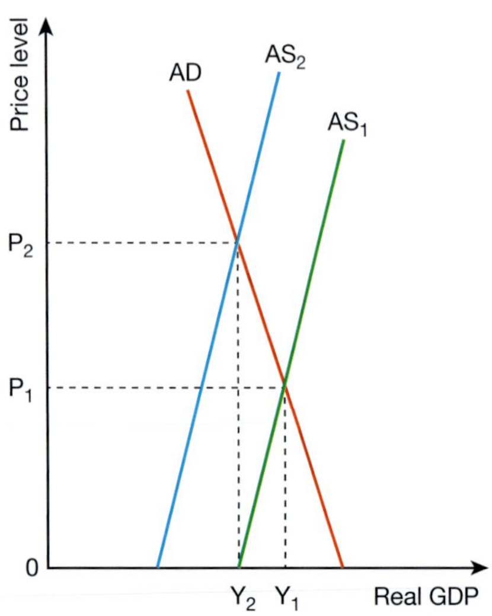

Figure 5.8 Effect of supply-side policies▲

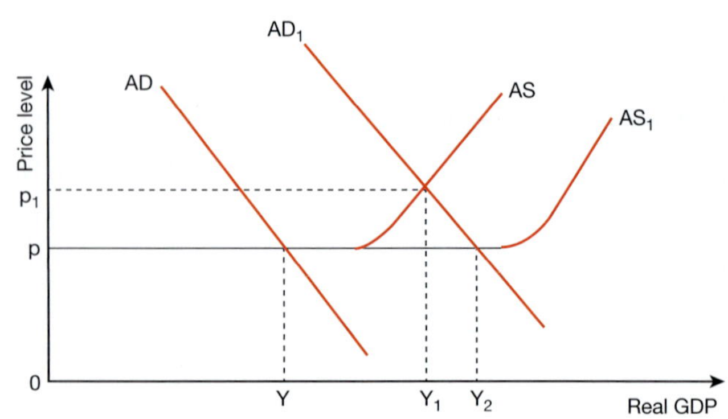

Figure 5.9 Operation of supply-side policy with demand-side policies▲

Key concepts

- **Margin and decision making** can be seen throughout this chapter.
- **Equilibrium and disequilibrium** can be seen throughout this chapter.
- **Progress and development** can be seen briefly, especially in government objectives, taxation and supply-side policies.

Progress check

After completing this chapter you should be able to:

- explain government macroeconomic objectives
- explain and distinguish between fiscal, monetary and supply-side policies
- use AD and AS analysis to explain the effects of fiscal, monetary and supply-side policies.

Exam-style questions

Essay questions

1a Explain what is meant by monetary policy and consider the differences between monetary and fiscal policy. [8 marks]

b Discuss what effects reducing the rate of interest might have on equilibrium national income. [12 marks]

2a Explain the difference between government capital and current spending and consider the reasons for government spending. [8 marks]

b Discuss the likely effects of an expansionary fiscal policy on the economy. [12 marks]

3a Explain the reasons for governments using taxation and consider their importance. [8 marks]

b Discuss whether the size of the national debt is important. [12 marks]

4a With the help of a diagram, explain what is meant by supply-side policies and compare the usefulness of labour market policies with product market policies. [8 marks]

b Discuss what effects government assistance to firms, to allow them to use new technology, might have on equilibrium national income, real output, employment and the price level. [12 marks]

5a Explain two reasons for government expenditure and consider their importance for the economy. [8 marks]

b Discuss whether a fall in government expenditure will always result in a lower price level. [12 marks]

6a Explain and compare two ways in which supply-side policies could increase productivity. [8 marks]

b Discuss whether supply-side policies are more effective than demand side policies in achieving increasing real output and employment. [12 marks]

Multiple-choice questions

7 Which of the following changes in AD and AS will **most** likely lead to a fall in the price level? [1 mark]

A aggregate demand and supply both increase
B aggregate demand stays constant and productivity increases
C aggregate supply falls while aggregate demand remains constant
D aggregate supply remains constant and aggregate demand increases

8 Which of the following is an example of supply-side policy? [1 mark]

A increasing expenditure on defence
B lowering the rate of price level increases
C raising the rate of interest
D reducing direct taxes on workers

6 International economic issues

In this chapter you will develop your knowledge and understanding of:

- the reasons for international trade
- protectionism
- current account of the balance of payments
- exchange rates
- policies to correct imbalances in the current account of the balance of payments.

6.1 The reasons for international trade

6.1.1 *Distinction between absolute and comparative advantage*

Absolute advantage occurs when one country, with the same amount of resources, can produce more of a good than another country.

The principle of comparative advantage was originally developed by David Ricardo in his book *On the Principles of Political Economy and Taxation* (1817), which demonstrates that it is possible for all countries to benefit from trade even in a situation in which one of the countries involved is more efficient at producing all products, i.e. has an absolute advantage in the production of all goods.

David Ricardo ▲

Key terms

Absolute advantage: the ability to produce more of a product than another country that has the same amount of resources can produce.

Comparative advantage: the ability to produce a product at a lower opportunity cost.

Link

See Chapter 1, section 1.3.4, to review your understanding of specialisation.

6.1.2 *Benefits of specialisation and free trade (trade liberalisation), including the trading possibility curve*

The benefits of specialisation and free trade can be shown by using absolute and comparative advantages examples.

In the case of absolute advantage, the amount of each good that each country, Japan and Sweden, is able to produce with the same quantity of resources is shown in Table 6.1.

If we assume that only one person is available and that person shares their time and other resources equally between cars and toys then we could represent absolute advantage as shown in Table 6.1.

Table 6.1 Output, example 1 ▼

Country	Cars	Toys
Sweden	2	8
Japan	8	2

Getting it right

In an exam, keep it simple by using numbers which are easy to manipulate. Remember this is an economics exam not a maths one so there is no credit for complicated examples, but only for correct ones.

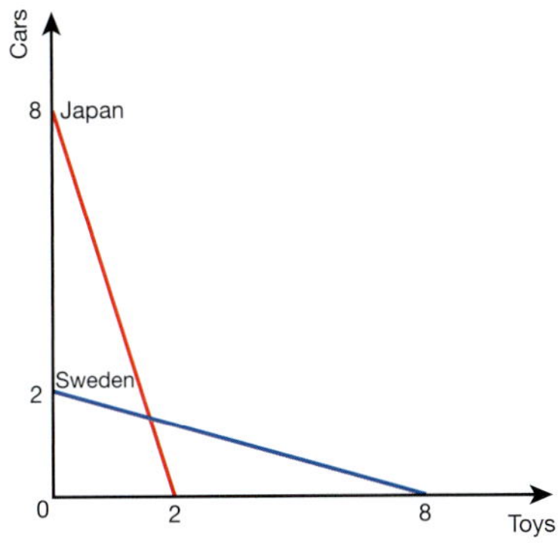

Figure 6.1 Trading possibility curves for Sweden and Japan showing absolute advantage ▲

Link

See Chapter 1, section 1.5, to review your understanding of production possibility curves.

In this situation the terms of trade are Sweden 1 : 4 and Japan 4 : 1. These production possibilities are shown in Figure 6.1.

It is clear that Sweden can produce more toys than Japan and Japan more cars. Sweden has, therefore, an absolute advantage in toys, while Japan has an absolute advantage in cars. In order to increase total output both countries should specialise in the good in which they have the absolute advantage.

Assuming that the output above represents what one person can produce in a day, then the person in Sweden will now only produce toys and the one in Japan only cars. The result is shown in Table 6.2.

Table 6.2 Output, example 2 ▼

Country	Cars	Toys
Sweden	0	16
Japan	16	0

The two countries can now trade so long as they stay within their terms of trade (1 : 4; 4 : 1).

A possible exchange rate favourable to both is 1 : 1. If Sweden gives up six toys it will get back six cars resulting in the situation below.

Table 6.3 Output, example 3 ▼

Country	Cars	Toys
Sweden	6	10
Japan	10	6

As can be seen, Sweden has gained four cars and two toys, while Japan has gained two cars and four toys. The result of specialisation and trade is that both countries have more cars and toys than they did previously.

Looking at comparative advantage, Indonesia can produce more cars and more toys so it has an absolute advantage in both as shown in Table 6.4. The opportunity cost of production in the two countries is quite different. The trading situation is shown in Figure 6.2.

Link

See Chapter 1, section 1.3.3, to review your understanding of opportunity cost.

Table 6.4 Output, example 1 ▼

Country	Cars	Toys
Indonesia	10	50
Botswana	8	8
Total output	18	58

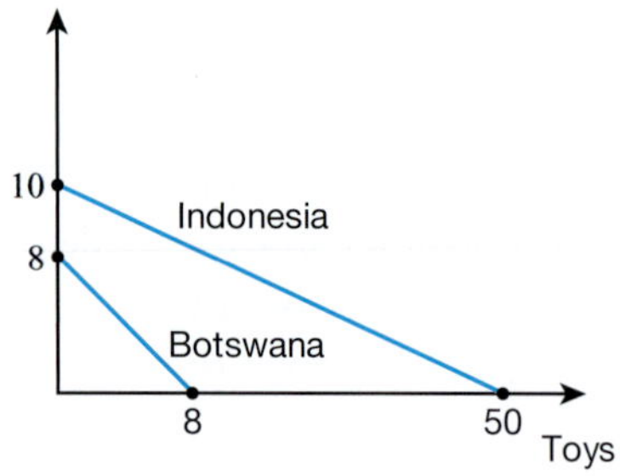

Figure 6.2 Trading possibility curves for Botswana and Indonesia showing comparative advantage ▲

In Indonesia five toys have to be given up to obtain one car (10 : 50 = 1 : 5), while in Botswana only one toy needs to be given up to get a car (8 : 8 = 1 : 1). The opportunity cost of a car is lower in Botswana than Indonesia. In this case Botswana has a comparative advantage in the production of cars, while Indonesia has the advantage in toys: Botswana gives up one car for one toy, but Indonesia only gives up one-fifth of a car for a toy.

A country has a comparative advantage in the production of a product if it has a lower opportunity cost ratio than other countries in its production.

As Indonesia had an absolute production advantage in both, it will need to continue to produce both, but will move 50 per cent of the resources used on cars into producing toys. Botswana, however, will specialise just in cars.

Table 6.5 Output, example 2 ▼

Country	Cars	Toys
Indonesia	5	75
Botswana	16	0
Total output	21	75

As can be seen, output of cars has increased by 3 while output of toys has risen by 17. The countries could then trade at a ratio somewhere between their two opportunity costs. If we assume that they choose 1 : 3 then the final outcome could be as in Table 6.6 with both countries having more cars and toys.

It is important to note that specialisation and trade will only take place if the opportunity cost ratios are different as otherwise no advantage would be gained.

Table 6.6 Output, example 3 ▼

Country	Cars	Toys
Indonesia	11	57
Botswana	10	18
Total output	21	75

Progress question

1 Explain why trade between two countries on the basis of comparative advantage will only be beneficial if the opportunity cost ratios for two goods are different in the two countries.

Activity

Absolute and comparative advantage

Indonesia, using all its resources to the full, can produce 2000 metric tonnes of rubber or 1200 metric tonnes of rice.

Thailand, using all its resources to the full, can produce 1400 metric tonnes of rubber or 1000 metric tonnes of rice.

1. Draw the production possibility curves for rubber and rice for Indonesia and Thailand.
2. Identify which country has an absolute advantage in the production of rubber and which in rice.
3. Identify which country has a comparative advantage in the production of rubber and which in rice.
4. Choose an appropriate exchange rate for the two commodities and demonstrate that both Indonesia and Thailand can benefit from specialisation and trade in accordance with the principle of comparative advantage.

Link

See Chapter 7, sections 7.5.5–7.5.7, to review your understanding of economies of scale.

Link

Exports and imports are defined in Chapter 4, section 4.2.

Key term

Terms of trade: the ratio of a country's export prices to import prices.

Activity

Terms of trade

Assume that between 2019 and 2020 Country A's index of exports prices fell from 100 to 95 while its index of import prices rose from 100 to 110. At the same time Country B's index of export prices rose from 100 to 110 while its index of import prices also rose from 100 to 105.

1. Calculate the terms of trade for both countries for 2020.

Overall free trade should provide lower prices and greater choice of goods for consumers, and allows firms to benefit from economies of scale and increased exports. This explains why countries, by specialising in goods and services where they have a lower opportunity cost, can all gain an increase in economic welfare.

6.1.3 *Exports, imports and the terms of trade*

Exports are the sale of goods and services abroad, while imports are the purchase of goods and services from abroad.

The terms of trade of a country are defined as the ratio of its export prices to import prices.

Measurement of the terms of trade

The terms of trade are calculated as follows:

$$\text{terms of trade} = \frac{\text{index of export prices}}{\text{index of import prices}} \times 100$$

An increase in the index indicates that more imports can be purchased with a given quantity of exports and so the *terms of trade* are said to have improved or to have become more favourable. Conversely, a reduction in the index indicates that fewer imports than previously can be purchased with a given quantity of exports and so the terms of trade are said to have deteriorated or worsened.

Causes of changes in the terms of trade

The terms of trade of any country will change over the years as can be seen in Table 6.7.

Table 6.7 Terms of trade for selected countries 2016–19 (2015 = 100) ▼

Country	2016	2017	2018	2019
Canada	98.89	102.49	103.25	103.13
France	100.99	99.68	98.56	99.36
Germany	101.76	100.88	100.06	100.93
Italy	103.25	101.72	101.16	101.83
Japan	105.45	101.12	97.00	98.08
Russia	84.07	94.22	108.04	105.34
South Africa	101.71	106.28	103.52	106.25
United Kingdom	100.21	99.09	99.69	99.64

Source: OECD

Key term

Globalisation: the expansion of world trade in goods and services, together with capital flows, leading to greater international interdependence.

Major factors in recent years affecting the terms of trade have been globalisation and economic development. The fall in the price of manufactured goods due to globalisation has tended to cause the terms of trade of countries such as France to worsen. The increased demand for natural resources, however, have pushed up prices thus benefiting the terms of trade of exporting countries such as Canada and South Africa.

Activity

Terms of trade

1. Find out what has happened to your country's terms of trade in the last five years.
2. Compare this information to one or more of the countries in Table 6.7
3. Try to suggest reasons for the changes you identify.

You may find www.data.worldbank.org a useful source of information

Table 6.8 Some factors affecting the terms of trade ▼

Factors influencing the terms of trade	Explanation
Price elasticity of demand	If a country's exports become more inelastic than its imports then the terms of trade will move in its favour as its exports' prices will be higher than its imports prices.
Economic development	If this causes an increase in demand for imports then the terms of trade will worsen. On the other hand, if there is an increase in supply of import substitutes or more goods for export then the terms of trade will move favourably.
Exchange rate	If the exchange rate depreciates or devalues then the terms of trade will worsen as export prices have fallen and import prices have risen.
Protectionist measures e.g. tariffs	If protectionist measures are taken then import prices are likely to fall leading to an improvement in the terms of trade.
Population growth	A rapidly growing population will demand more goods and thus imports leading to a worsening in the terms of trade.
Competition	If a country has a monopoly in the production of a good then it can raise prices causing an improvement in its terms of trade
Globalisation	This has increased competition leading prices of some countries exports to fall, worsening the terms of trade. For other countries the ability to gain trade has resulted in more exports and an improvement in the terms of trade

Getting it right

Make sure that you can explain the factors that affect a country's terms of trade and that you can explain the difference between an improvement and a deterioration in a country's terms of trade.

Progress question

2 Explain the importance of its terms of trade for a country.

Impact of changes in the terms of trade

The impact of changes in the terms of trade on a nation's economy will depend on the price elasticities of demand for imports and exports. If, for example, a nation's terms of trade improve because export prices have risen and import prices have fallen and the price elasticities of demand for both exports and imports are greater than unity (price elastic) then the total income from exports will fall because there has been a more than proportionate fall in the demand for them and the total expenditure on imports will rise because there has been a more than proportionate increase in the demand for them. The effect will be a worsening of the country's trade balance and possible adverse effects on unemployment. If, however the elasticities of demand for imports and exports are less than unity (inelastic), the improvement in the terms of trade will result in an improvement in the country's trade balance.

Changes in the terms of trade will have a significant impact on an economy. For example, many developing countries are very dependent on exports of primary products. The fall in the prices of such products means that these countries have a deterioration in their terms of trade. They are earning less from the same volume of exports and this means that they cannot afford to import as much. As a result their standard of living will fall.

A country, however, facing an improvement in the terms of trade is likely to see an improvement in its standard of living.

Another impact depends on how competitive a country's prices are. If the terms of trade have improved, then this means that export prices have increased more than import prices. This may indicate a fall in competitiveness leading to a fall in export demand. How much export demand falls will depend on the price elasticity of demand for exports. This may adversely affect the balance of payments. The opposite will be true of a deterioration in the terms of trade.

6.1.4 *Limitations of the theories of absolute and comparative advantage*

While both absolute and comparative advantages are useful in showing how free trade can benefit countries, a number of not very realistic assumptions have been made:

- there are only two commodities (in section 6.1.2 above, toys and cars)
- perfect competition in factor and product markets
- no transport costs
- no capital movements which would affect the exchange rate
- production is subject to constant returns to scale which means that all units are produced at the same cost
- no restrictions on trade

In addition, as Table 6.9 shows there are a number of economic limitations.

Table 6.9 Some of the limitations of absolute and comparative advantage ▼

Limitation	Explanation
Transport costs	These can reduce the advantages although sending goods in bulk has led to very low charges.
Protectionism	The use of import barriers such as tariffs can raise prices and thus reduce advantages.
Exchange rates	These can change for reasons not related to trade and thus affect price advantages.
Imperfect competition	This may lead to prices being different to opportunity cost ratios. Imperfect competition may also lead to the exploitation of economies of scale which may adjust to what comparative advantage theory suggests should happen.
Factors of production	Firstly, labour may not easily move from production of one product to another. Secondly, it ignores all non-labour costs involved in production.
Dynamic versus static	Comparative advantage theory is a static theory and does not take account of some of the more that the real economic world is dynamic and changes all the time.

Link

Exchange rates are covered in section 6.4 of this chapter.

6.2 Protectionism

6.2.1 *Meaning of protectionism in the context of international trade*

Protectionism is the opposite to free trade. It comes about because countries fear that without trade barriers their industries may not be able to compete with those of other countries.

Key terms

Protectionism: an action designed to reduce international trade.

Tariff: a tax on a product imported into a country. Tariffs can be either specific or *ad valorem*.

6.2.2 *Different tools of protection and their impact*

Tariffs

A tariff is a tax on a particular product as it is imported. They can be either specific or *ad valorem*.

Link

For more on specific and *ad valorem* taxes, see Chapter 5, section 5.2.4.

For more on price elasticity of demand, see Chapter 2, section 2.2.

In either case the effect is to shift the supply curve for the imported product to the left raising the price and reducing the quantity demanded of the imported product. The extent of the fall in the quantity demanded will depend upon the price elasticity of demand for the product. This increase in price clearly enables the domestic industry that was previously unable to compete with the foreign imports to increase its sales. However, the tariff has a significant impact on consumer welfare.

The effects of a specific tax on an imported good are shown in Figure 6.3 with domestic output increasing from Q_1 to Q_2 and imports declining from Q_1Q_4 to Q_2Q_3, but demand falling from Q_4 to Q_3. This leads to a rise in price P_2 to P_1 where supply (S_w + tariff) is equal to D.

Link

For trade diversion, see Chapter 11, section 11.6.3.

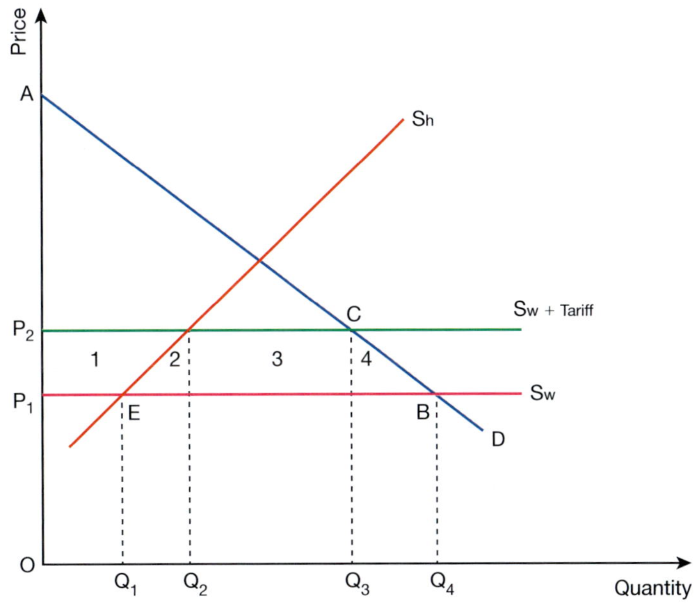

Figure 6.3 Effects of a tariff ▶

The other effects of the tariff are summarised below.

Domestic production

The quantity of the product produced domestically has increased from Q_1 to Q_2. Previously no more than Q_1 could be supplied by domestic producers because their marginal costs of production, represented by the domestic supply curve (S_h), exceeded the world price. The tariff has allowed domestic production to rise to Q_2

Imports

The tariff has resulted in the quantity of imports into the country being reduced from Q_1Q_4 to Q_2Q_3.

Consumer surplus

One of the most important welfare effects concerns the impact of the tariff on consumer surplus. Before the tariff was imposed, the consumer surplus was represented by the area P_1 AB. After the imposition of the tariff the consumer surplus has fallen to P_2AC, a loss of P_2CBP_1 or the areas 1 + 2 + 3 + 4. Some of this has been lost to producers in the form of increased producer surplus and some to the government as revenue from the tariff.

Producer surplus

Originally the producer surplus equalled P_1 E Q_1 O. The effect of the tariff is to increase it by areas 1 and 2. This was previously part of consumer surplus and so the tariff has resulted in welfare redistribution from consumers to producers.

Link

See Chapter 2, section 2.5, to refresh your memory about consumer and producer surplus.

Revenue effect

The tariff will generate revenue for the government equal to the amount of the tariff per unit multiplied by the quantity of imports. This gives the area 3 which was previously part of the consumer surplus. Again, welfare has been redistributed away from consumers, in this case to the government.

Import quota

A second common method of protection is an import quota which is a limit to the quantity imported. The limit can be in terms of an actual number or percentage share of the market. For example, the USA currently imposes a quota on the import of sugar. Quotas normally involve the issuing of licences to companies allowing them to import the product up to a particular limit.

Like tariffs, quotas, involve society, particularly consumers, in a welfare loss but arguably quotas may involve a greater overall welfare loss to society than tariffs because they generate no tax revenue for the government.

As can be seen in Figure 6.4, the imposition of a quota raises the price from P to P_1 and reduces quantity from Q_1 to Q_2 again reducing consumer surplus.

Key terms

Import quota: a legal limit on the quantity of a product that can be imported into a country.

Export subsidy: money given to an exporter so the price of the product can be reduced to make it more competitive on world markets.

Embargo: a complete ban on products from a particular country.

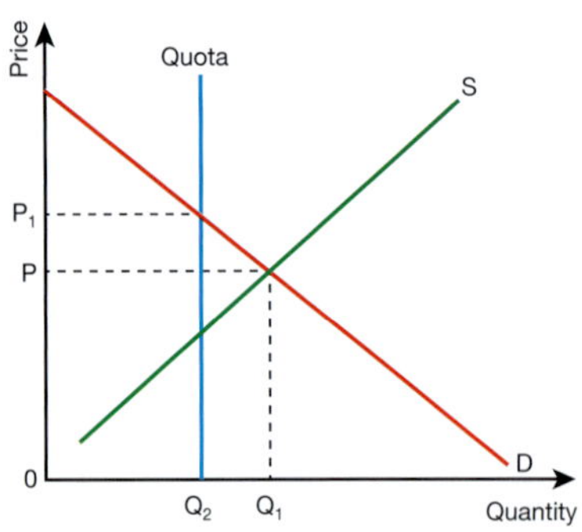

Figure 6.4 The effects of a quota ▲

Export subsidy

An export subsidy allows businesses whose price would be too high abroad to sell in foreign countries at the world price thus increasing their competitiveness. Although this will increase sales and thus output and employment, it may also increase inefficient allocation of resources. The government could have used the money to focus on goods in which the country had potential comparative advantage. In this case long-term economic growth may be reduced.

Embargoes

Embargoes involve a complete ban on the import of a particular product. Such bans are normally imposed for political reasons involving disputes between nations or during times of war. Many countries placed embargoes on Syria as a result of the recent civil war. There may also be embargoes on products that are deemed to be dangerous or harmful such as drugs. The longest standing embargo is that of the USA on foreign trade with Cuba.

Excessive administrative burdens ("red tape")

Countries may seek to limit the quantity of imports of particular products into a country by imposing excessive administrative burdens, so-called "red tape", for importers to go through. These may include having to meet country specific health or production standards, detailed documentation or having to bring all imported products through only one entry point, procedures and documentation processes. The impact is to benefit domestic producers but to reduce consumer welfare as foreign products are no longer available or only in small quantities thus reducing competition.

Key term

Excessive administrative burdens: excessive "red tape" imposed on importers to make importing more difficult.

6.2.3 *Arguments for and against protectionism*

A number of arguments to justify the imposition of protectionist policies have been put forward, not all of which can be justified on purely economic grounds.

> **Key terms**
>
> **Infant industry**: an industry which is expected to have a comparative advantage, but at the moment is small and unable to compete with established industries elsewhere in the world.
>
> **Sunrise industry**: new or relatively new industries which are rapidly growing and are believed to have the potential to be a market leader in the future.

Infant industry

The infant industries argument is usually seen as the strongest case for protectionist measures. An infant industry is one which is expected to have a comparative advantage in production in the future, but at present is too small and lacks the economies of scale to enable it to compete with well-established firms in the market. A similar case can be made for sunrise industries.

Protection is designed to enable the infant industry to establish its comparative advantage and compete in its own right. Consumers will experience higher prices in the short run, but lower prices in the future. This particular argument has been used by a number of developing countries.

The major issues with this particular argument are first of all accurately identifying infant and sunrise industries and secondly establishing when they are able to compete without protection.

This argument is often linked with that of diversification. If a country is highly specialised in the production of a single good such as a primary product, then it is highly susceptible to fluctuations in the demand and price of this product. Protection can be used as a way of diversifying the economy to reduce dependence on a single product. It may also be suggested as part of a balanced growth strategy. This idea is often put forward by developing countries to justify trade barriers.

Again, however, it is difficult to justify on purely economic grounds. It goes against the principle of comparative advantage and, in addition, there are other ways of achieving diversification; for example, the use of subsidies.

Case Study

Food processing in India – a sunrise industry

India is one of the world's leading food producers, producing over 600 million tonnes of grain each year. It is the largest producer of cereal in the world, the second largest producer of fruit and vegetables and is the second largest exporter of rice.

However, despite this food processing in India is relatively small with only 2 per cent of fruit and vegetables and 15 per cent of milk being processed domestically.

Food processing is regarded as a "sunrise" industry for India with great potential to generate economic growth with consequent implications for employment, export earnings and the attraction of foreign direct investment (FDI).

1 Explain what is meant by a "sunrise" industry.
2 Discuss the advantages and disadvantages for India and for the rest of the world of the Indian government deciding to use tariff barriers to enable it to develop its sunrise food processing industry.

Unfair competition

Unfair competition has been another particularly popular argument put forward to justify imposing protectionist policies against products imported from countries with vast supplies of low cost labour. These low labour costs mean that these countries such as China and India and others in Asia can sell at prices with which industrial countries cannot compete. Such arguments can appear even more compelling if it can be proved that the low wages of labour are the result of exploitation of labour.

This argument, however, cannot really be justified. The principle of comparative advantage shows that countries benefit from trade when differences in opportunity cost exist, whatever the reason for them. Consequently industrial nations should not be attempting to compete in these areas. Rather they should be specialising in products in which they have a comparative advantage.

In addition, labour costs are not the only factor in determining the selling price. It is possible, therefore, that products manufactured by relatively high cost labour, but using high quality capital and sophisticated mass production methods, might be able to produce at competitive prices.

People queue for work during the Great Depression ▲

Retaliation claims that a country is justified in employing tariffs and other restrictions on trade in order to retaliate against the protectionist policies of other countries. Although it is possible that the threat of retaliation might discourage another nation from imposing a tariff in the first place, actually imposing retaliatory tariffs cannot be justified. If countries continually raise tariffs in retaliation against one another, the ultimate effect will be a significant reduction in world trade and a consequent reduction in consumer welfare in all countries. In 1930, the USA's decision to increase tariffs on some 20,000 imported products led to retaliation from her major trading nations which significantly reduced the volume of world trade and was probably instrumental in prolonging the Great Depression.

Employment

The idea here is that protecting home industries from foreign imports will enable domestic industries to compete and, therefore, preserve or increase employment in the country. This is sometimes used alongside either the infant industry or sunrise industry arguments.

This, however, does not stand up to close scrutiny from an economics perspective. Instead, one should ask why these home industries cannot compete in the first place. If it is because they have higher costs than overseas producers and, therefore, lack comparative advantage, then they should not be competing in these markets, but in those where they have a comparative advantage.

There are also other ways of dealing with the problem of unemployment such as monetary, fiscal and supply side policies.

Link

See Chapter 5 and Chapter 10, section 10.3, for more detail on the relevant monetary, fiscal and supply side policies.

Sunset industries

Sunset industries are those long established industries which are declining due to losing their comparative advantage. Often, factors of production are immobile and so cannot shift quickly to other expanding areas.

Key term

Sunset industries: industries which have lost their comparative advantage.

Whilst there might be a case for temporary protection for a short transitional period of time to enable factors to move into other areas and prevent significant structural unemployment, there is no case for long-term protection as this will be supporting inefficiency and reducing consumer welfare.

Key term

Dumping: the sale of a product in a foreign market at a price below its marginal cost of production.

Link

See Chapter 7, section 7.8.3, for a discussion of price discrimination under monopoly. See Chapter 7, section 7.8.4, for a discussion of predatory pricing.

Getting it right

Make sure that you can clearly explain which arguments for protection can be justified on economic grounds and which cannot.

Dumping

Dumping refers to the practice whereby a product is sold in a foreign market at a price below its marginal cost of production and below the price received by producers in the importing country. Economists often distinguish between *persistent* and *predatory* dumping.

Persistent dumping may continue indefinitely as a result of the exporting firm being a monopoly, able to practice price discrimination by exploiting different elasticities of demand in the home and overseas markets.

Although it may not always be easy to distinguish in reality between the two, persistent dumping may reflect the fact that the exporting country has a comparative advantage in the production of the product in question and as such it is difficult to justify protection on economic grounds as it provides consumers in the importing country with consistently lower prices and welfare gains.

Predatory dumping is undertaken with the specific intention of destroying foreign competition and normally involves predatory pricing. Although consumers in the importing country may experience temporary benefits, the destruction of the domestic industry and the consequent loss of competition may mean that in the long term consumers may suffer as a result of the creation of an overseas monopoly. In these circumstances protection against dumping is generally regarded as being justified.

6.3 Current account of the balance of payments

6.3.1 *Components of the current account of the balance of payments*

Case Study

India imposes anti-dumping duty on 99 products

To protect domestic producers from cheap imports, India imposed anti-dumping duty on 99 Chinese products on 28 January 2019 including chemicals and petrochemicals, fibres and yarn, machinery items, pharmaceutical, rubber and steel items.

The duty tries to ensure fair trade practices and creates a level-playing field for domestic producers with regard to foreign producers and exporters.

This follows a report in 2018 which expressed worry about India's widening trade deficit with China. In the period April to December 2018 imports from China were $53.87 billion as against $76.38 billion in 2017.

1. Explain what is meant by dumping.
2. Explain why India imposed anti-dumping duties
3. With the aid of a diagram, discuss the effects of governments imposing such duties.

The current account of the balance of payments comprises trade in goods, trade in services, primary income and secondary income.

Trade in goods is sometimes referred to as visible trade and is the difference between exports and imports of goods.

This trade in goods consists of exports and imports of goods such as oil, agricultural products, computers, white goods and clothing. Historically, the UK has run a substantial and increasing deficit on its visible balance (income from merchandise exports less than the amount spent on merchandise imports) in contrast to countries such as China and Germany who run a substantial surplus (income from merchandise exports greater than money spent on merchandise imports) on this section of the accounts.

Key terms

Current account: a record of transactions in terms of trade in goods, services and primary and secondary income.
Trade in goods: the export and import of goods.
Trade in services: the export and import of services.
Primary income: the income from interest, profits, dividends generated from foreign investment and also i.e. payments from people living and working overseas.
Secondary income: the transfer of money, which is not investment, without receiving anything directly in return.
Deficit (in the current account): this is where payments made by a country exceed payments received by a country.
Surplus: this is where payments received by a country exceed payments made by a country.

Link

For definitions of exports and imports see Chapter 4, section 4.2.

Trade in services is sometimes referred to as invisible trade and is the difference between exports and imports of services. It is not possible to see these literally going into or out of a country. They consist of items such as international tourism, travel, financial services and insurance. The Rio de Janeiro Summer 2016 Olympic Games brought thousands of tourists to Brazil. In order to pay for goods and services whilst in Brazil, these overseas tourists had to change their own currency into Brazilian reals, bringing money into Brazil. This expenditure by overseas tourists represents an invisible export for Brazil.

If on the other hand a UK producer uses a foreign shipping company to transport its goods, this would represent an invisible import for the UK because it is taking money out of the UK.

The UK trade in services is in surplus, but it is not sufficient to offset the deficit on the trade in goods.

The visible and invisible balance together are sometimes called the balance of trade.

Primary income is the net flow of profits, interest and dividends from investments in other countries and net remittance flows (money sent home) from migrant workers. Qatar, for instance, owns buildings

Activity

Current account

Try to find out:

1. the main types of goods and services your country exports and imports
2. whether your country receives primary income and, if so, from what, and whether foreign countries, firms or individuals own income earning assets in your country
3. whether your country makes any payments to international organisations.

Key terms

Balance of the current account: this is the difference between money flowing in to the country from trade in goods and services and primary and secondary income and money flowing out.

Imbalance in the current account: this is where there is either a deficit, a negative figure, or a surplus, a positive figure.

such as Canary Wharf and The Shard in London from which it receives income. Indian workers in Dubai send money home to their families in India.

Secondary income refers to transfers of money where an economy receives no direct benefit, such as a good or service, in return. Some examples include overseas aid, military grants and payments to international organisations.

The balance of the current account is the difference between all the inflows of money from trade in goods and services and the primary and secondary income and the outflows. This is likely to give rise to imbalances in the current account where either more money has gone out than has come in, a deficit, or more money has flowed in than has flowed out, a surplus. This can be seen for Malaysia in Figure 6.5.

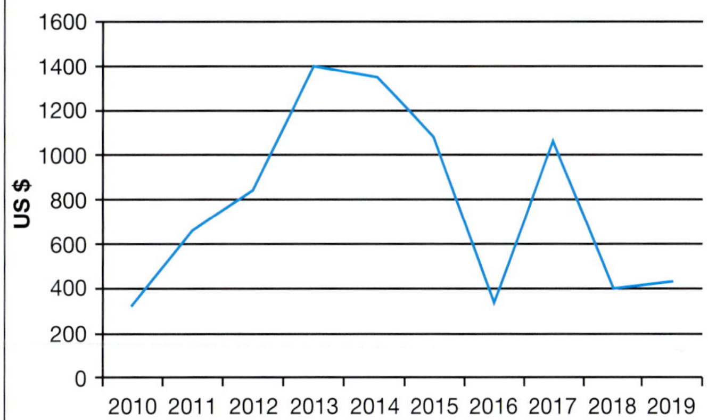

Figure 6.5 Malaysia's current account surplus 2010–2019 ▲

6.3.2 Calculation of balance of trade in goods, balance of trade in services, balance of trade in goods and services, and the current account balance (CAB)

Table 6.10 shows the UK's current account for 2019. For each balance, all the export values are added to give the total credits. Then the same is done for the imports to give total debits. The debits are then subtracted from the credits, for example:

Balance of trade in goods (£m):

Credits 373,149

Debits 504,029

Balance−130, 880

The balance of trade in services is calculated in a similar manner. To get the balance of trade in goods and services, the two previous balances are added.

Finally, the current account balance adds in the net figures for both primary and secondary income.

Table 6.10 Summary of UK current account of the balance of payments for 2019 ▼

All figures in £ million

Category	Credits	Debits	Balance
Trade in goods	373,149	504,029	−130,880
Trade in services	317,674	217,296	100,378
Balance of trade in goods and services	690,823	721,325	−30,502
Primary income	207,497	244,810	−37,313
Secondary income	18,040	45,535	−27,495
Total current account	708,863	1,011,670	−302, 807

Source: ONS

Activity

Current account figures

Try to access the current account figures for your country and draw up a current account balance like the one in Table 6.10.

6.3.3 Causes of imbalances in the current account of the balance of payments

Reasons for an imbalance, in these examples a deficit, include the following:

- An imbalance is likely to occur when there is limited domestic production so that a country relies on imports, or because of high standards of living residents demand a wider range of goods. It may be the case that the terms of trade are unfavourable so that developing countries, in particular, find that they need to export more and more goods just to maintain the same export revenue. This would lead to a deficit. A surplus could arise because a country has a reputation for excellence in particular areas of production, e.g. Germany for engineering products or because of cheap labour leading to lower prices, e.g. China.
- Countries may lack competitiveness due to an overvalued currency (e.g. Portugal and Greece as members of the euro could not devalue in the period 2008–2011) and/or the rate of inflation may be greater than that of their competitors so that exports fall but imports rise. Equally, China not only had cheap labour, but also an undervalued currency allowing it to undercut other producers.
- Economic growth requires the import of capital goods, leading to a persistent deficit. It may also lead to consumers being better off and thus demanding more imports.
- If inflation rises faster than a country's main competitors, then it will make exports less competitive and imports more competitive. This will lead to deterioration in the current account. However, inflation may also lead to a depreciation in the currency to offset this decline in competitiveness.
- A deficit is likely to occur when there is lack of confidence in an economy. This may be because of economic factors such as persistent

Activity

Causes of imbalances

Individually, or in groups, investigate the causes of imbalances in your country's current account.

Link

Terms of trade are covered in section 6.1 of this chapter. For more on economic growth, see Chapter 4, section 4.4. For government deficit, see Chapter 5, section 5.2.2.

current account deficits or large increases in the government deficit. Equally, investors may fear political change or lack of a stable government. The opposite will be true for a country with a surplus.

- If a country's main trading partners experience negative economic growth, then they will buy less of its exports, worsening the current account. The opposite will be true if the main trading partners are growing rapidly.

> **Link**
>
> For government policies, see Chapter 5.
> Protectionism is covered in section 6.2 of this chapter.

6.3.4 *Consequences of imbalances in the current account of the balance of payments*

The consequences for the domestic economy include the following:

- The government may need to tighten fiscal and monetary policies to reduce domestic demand and to introduce supply-side policies to improve productive capability.
- Consumers will have less access to imported goods as the government imposes protectionist policies.
- There will be a fall in foreign investment as confidence declines. This is likely to result in lower economic growth, higher unemployment, etc.

> **Link**
>
> Both Marshall–Lerner and the J-curve are covered in Chapter 11, section 11.2.5.

> **Activity**
>
> **Consequences of imbalances**
>
> Individually, or in groups, investigate the consequences of imbalances in your country's current account.

The consequences for the external economy include:

- Governments will be under pressure to introduce or increase protectionist measures.
- Devaluation of the exchange rate so that the currency becomes worth less than it was. This will lead to higher import prices and lower export prices. Whether this works may depend on Marshall–Lerner and the extent of the J-curve. Devaluation may lead, however, to further loss of confidence.

As can be seen, the domestic and external consequences of a negative disequilibrium are closely connected.

6.4 Exchange rates

6.4.1 *Definition of exchange rate*

An exchange rate is the price of one currency expressed in terms of another currency, or against a basket of other currencies.

> **Key terms**
>
> **Exchange rate**: the price of one currency expressed in terms of another currency.
> **Floating exchange rate**: where the value of a country's currency is determined solely by market forces.

6.4.2 *Determination of a floating exchange rate*

A floating exchange rate is where a government allows the external value of its currency to be determined by the market forces of supply and demand. This can be seen in Figures 6.6 and 6.7.

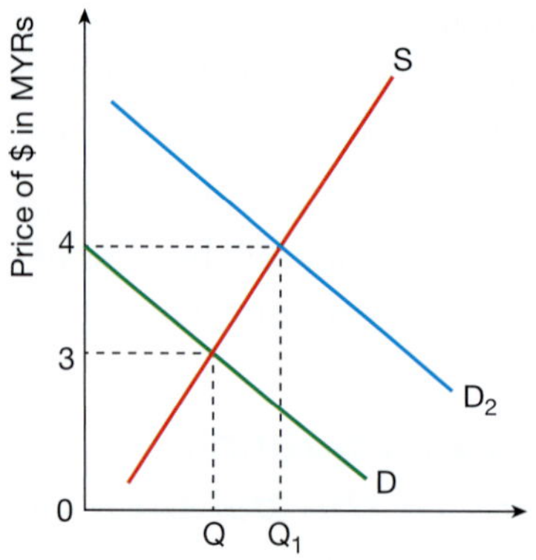

Figure 6.6 Demand and supply of US $ in Malaysian Ringgits ▲

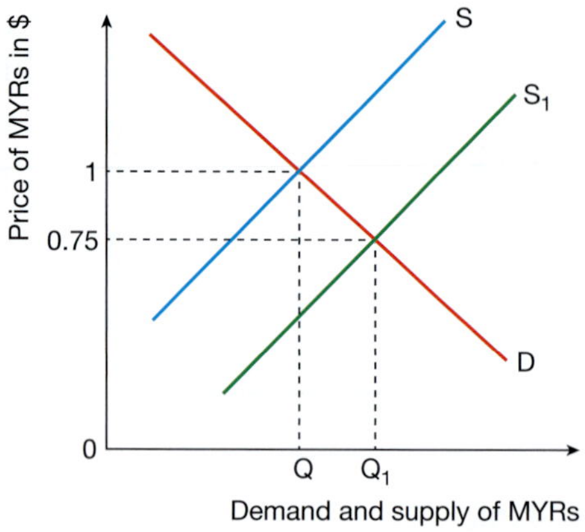

Figure 6.7 Demand and supply of MYRs ▲

The equilibrium price of the US dollar in terms the Malaysian ringgit is $1 to MYR_3. If the demand for dollars increases, the demand curve shifts to the right D to D_1 and the price of the dollar rises from MYR_3 to MYR_4. It has appreciated in terms of the ringgit while the latter has depreciated in terms of the dollar. Figure 6.7 shows the effects on the ringgit. To buy more dollars, more ringgits have to be supplied causing the price to fall from $1 to $0.75.

Key terms

Appreciation: when a floating exchange rate increases in value.

Depreciation: when a floating exchange rate decreases in value.

6.4.3 Distinction between depreciation and appreciation of a floating exchange rate

An appreciation of a floating exchange rate takes place when it increases in value compared to another currency. This can be seen in Figure 6.6.

A depreciation of a floating exchange rate takes place when it decreases in value compared to another currency. This can be seen in Figure 6.7.

Activity

Value of your country's exchange rate

Find out what has happened to the value of your country's exchange rate over the last two years. Try to discover what factors have affected its value.

6.4.4 Causes of changes in a floating exchange rate: demand and supply of the currency

Factors that cause the value of an exchange rate to change can include:

- Balance of payments disequilibrium. If a country runs a deficit then it is supplying more of its currency leading to a fall in its price. If it continues then foreign money will start to leave so it does not lose value. This again increases the supply of the currency.
- High inflation. A country with an inflation rate higher than that of other countries will find that people lose confidence in holding its currency so they sell the currency thereby increasing supply on the market lowering the price.
- Interest rates. International money seeks the highest return. If a country raises its rate of interest, this will attract inflows of money. Non-residents will need to buy the currency thus increasing the exchange rate.

Key term

Speculation: where one or people gamble on a currency rising, by buying, or falling, by selling a floating exchange rate increases in value.

- Foreign direct investment. Inflows of money to build factories etc will increase the exchange rate as this requires the purchase of the domestic currency.
- Speculation. If people expect the exchange rate of a country to fall, or rise, they will either sell, or buy, the currency to make a profit by buying it back at a lower price, or selling it at a higher price.

6.4.5 *AD/AS analysis of the impact of exchange rate changes on the domestic economy's equilibrium national income and the level of real output, the price level and employment*

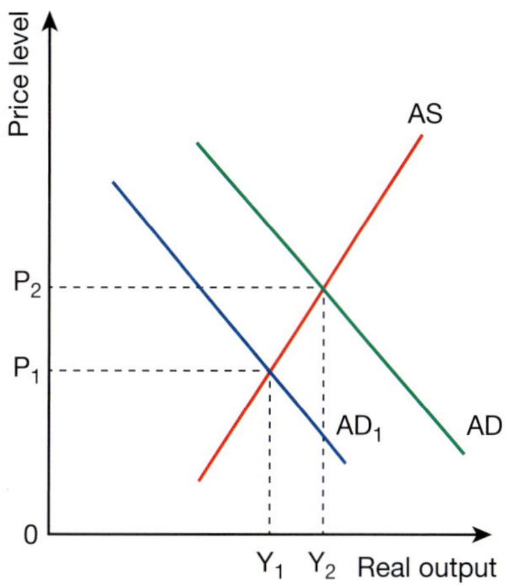

Figure 6.8 AD/AS analysis to show the effect of an appreciation ▲

The impact of exchange rate changes on the equilibrium national income, level of real output, employment and prices will depend on the price elasticities of demand for its exports and imports. This is called the Marshall–Lerner condition. If a country's exchange rate rises so that exports are more expensive and imports are cheaper then, if Marshall–Lerner holds, the volume and value of exports will fall while the volume and value of imports will rise. This means that AD falls to AD_1 at Y_1 and fewer people are employed as seen in Figure 6.8.

An appreciation is likely, therefore, to lead to a fall in equilibrium national income, real output, employment and the price level.

Conversely, a depreciation should lead to an increase in equilibrium national income, real output, employment and the price level. This is because exports are now cheaper and imports dearer. Demand for domestic goods will rise so more output is produced requiring more people to be employed. More output will require more raw materials thus putting upward pressure on the price level. This can be seen in Figure 6.9.

Getting it right

Make sure you are absolutely clear as to the effects of appreciation and depreciation on the exchange rate and on AD and AS.

6.5 Policies to correct imbalances in the current account of the balance of payments

6.5.1 *Government policy objective of stability of the current account*

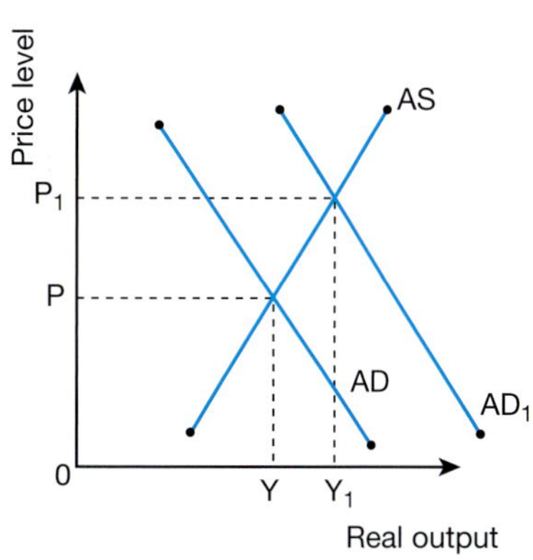

Figure 6.9 AD/AS analysis to show the effect of a depreciation ▲

The ideal situation would be for the current account to be in equilibrium i.e. the inflows of money equal the outflows across the account. In reality governments, especially those with deficits, try to keep the level of the imbalance steady and to not increase it as a ratio of GDP. If there is a persistent deficit then a country could face severe economic and financial problems such as depreciating exchange rate, inability to pay its debts and in extreme circumstances bankruptcy.

Equally, a continual positive balance is problematical because it causes difficulties for trading partners, especially if they are in a monetary union and cannot depreciate the exchange rate. A number of countries within the Eurozone have faced this with Germany being in credit and, for example, Greece in debt.

Link

Monetary union is covered in Chapter 11, section 11.6.2.

Progress question

3 Explain the effect of Country A selling off its supply of Country B's currency on the real output, employment and price level of Country B.

Link

For fiscal, monetary and supply-side policies, see Chapter 5.
For protectionism, see section 6.2 of this chapter.

Activity

Balance of payments

Look at the current account of the balance of payments for your country and one other for the last ten years

1 Over the ten years have they achieved a surplus, a deficit or nearly equilibrium? Compare their achievements.
2 Have either country achieved stability in their current account?

6.5.2 Effect of fiscal, monetary, supply-side and protectionist policies on the current account

The effects of the three policies are shown in Table 6.11 below.

Table 6.11 Effect of policies on the current account

Policy	Method	Outcome	Effect on the current account (CA)
Fiscal	Increase tax (T) and cut G	Demand falls along with output and employment and the price level.	Imports should fall so the CA should improve. Exports should rise if prices become more competitive. However, if output and employment fall, it is possible that there could be less exports and there is no guarantee on competitiveness.
	Cut T and increase G	Demand increases along with output and employment.	Imports are likely to rise, while exports may be diverted for home use. Price level may rise to make exports less competitive. CA deteriorates.
Monetary	Rise in interest rate	This is very similar to increase T and cut G. In this case consumption (C) falls and savings (S) rises.	Imports are likely to fall as demand falls. The problem is that higher interest rates may attract "hot money" leading to a rise in the value of the external currency making exports fall and imports cheaper.
	Fall in interest rate	C increase and S falls.	Imports rise so the CA deteriorates.
Supply-side	Two policies are: T incentives for more investment and for research and development	This is intended to create better and new products to try to gain competitive advantage.	This is likely to take time and there is no guarantee of success. If it does succeed then there should be more exports and an improvement in the CA.
	More and better education and training	Training to improve the skills of the workforce. Education so that the quality of all school leavers improves.	Again training takes time. There is no guarantee that skills will still be relevant, while education takes a very long time.
Protectionist	Impose tariffs, quotas, etc	Prices of imports will rise leading to a fall in imports, while with quotas home-produced products will replace the imports.	In theory they should reduce imports and improve the CA. The problem is that increasing tariffs etc is against World Trade Organisation (WTO) rules.
	Excessive administrative burdens	Imports are more difficult due to red tape etc.	These are likely to lead to retaliation though, for example, health measures etc are more difficult to prove as discriminating against countries.

Link

For fiscal, monetary and supply-side policies, see Chapter 5.
For protectionism, see section 6.2 of this chapter.

Key terms

Hot money: short-term capital flows in the foreign exchange market due to changes in interest rates.

World Trade Organization (WTO): the international organisation which establishes, monitors and reinforces the rules of trade between nations.

Case Study

Trade wars

The European Union (EU) and the USA have been in a long-running argument over government subsidies for their passenger aircraft manufacturing industries.

In 2019 the WTO ruled that the EU had failed to retract billions of dollars in illegitimate state aid to aerospace giant Airbus. In retaliation, the USA imposed $7.5bn of tariffs on goods coming from the EU.

Following more tariff threats from the USA in 2020, the EU threatened to hit back with their own duties, which if approved by the WTO on the grounds that the USA has illegally subsidized its own aerospace giant, Boeing, could be worth as much as $11.2bn.

1. Explain what is meant by a tariff.
2. Analyse the effect of imposing a tariff on imports.
3. Discuss whether tariffs would be the best way to settle this dispute.

Key concepts

- **Margin and decision making** can be seen in terms of trade and absolute and comparative advantage.
- **Equilibrium and disequilibrium** can be seen in the current account, exchange rates and application of government policies.
- **Time** can be seen throughout this chapter.
- **Progress and development** can be seen with reference to free trade and protection and absolute and comparative advantage.

Progress check

After completing this chapter you should be able to:

- explain the reasons for international trade
- define protectionism and explain the different tools of protection and their impact
- explain the components of the current account of the balance of payments
- calculate the balances involved in the current account
- explain the causes and consequences of imbalances in the current account
- define and explain exchange rates
- use AD and AS analysis to explain the impact of exchange rate changes on equilibrium national income, real output, employment and the price level.

Exam-style questions

Essay questions

1a Explain what is meant by protectionism and consider the effects of tariffs and import quotas on the imports of a country. [8 marks]

b Discuss whether protection is the best way of dealing with a current account deficit. [12 marks]

2a Explain what is meant by an imbalance in the current account of a nation's balance of payments and consider the causes of imbalances. [8 marks]

b Discuss the extent to which a country should be concerned about a significant increase in the size of its deficit on the current account of the balance of payments. [12 marks]

3a With the help of a diagram, explain how the value of a floating exchange rate is determined and consider the causes of changes in the value. [8 marks]

b Evaluate the likely economic consequences of a substantial depreciation in a nation's exchange rate. [12 marks]

4a Explain what is meant by absolute advantage and compare absolute with comparative advantage. [8 marks]

b Evaluate the usefulness of comparative advantage in deciding which goods and services a country should supply. [12 marks]

5a Explain and compare two consequences of imbalances in the current account of the balance of payments. [8 marks]

b Evaluate the effectiveness of fiscal policy in correcting an imbalance in the current account of the balance of payments. [12 marks]

6a With the help of a diagram, explain what is meant by an appreciation of an exchange rate and consider the impacts of an appreciation on a country's real output, employment and price levels. [8 marks]

b Discuss the effects of an appreciation on the economic growth of the country. [12 marks]

Multiple-choice questions

7 Which of the following is likely to lead to an improvement in a country's terms of trade? [1 mark]

A There is a rise in the value of the country's exchange rate.
B The average price of imports rises and the average price of exports falls.
C The average price of exports falls more rapidly than the average price of imports.
D The country decides to lower its tariff barriers.

8 Which of the following are components of the current account of the balance of payments? [1 mark]

A Trade in goods, trade in services, primary income, secondary income
B Trade in goods, trade in services, trade in investments, financial exchanges
C Trade in goods, capital and financial movements, transfer payments, membership of international organisations
D Trade in goods, primary income, secondary income, exchange rate costs

7 The price system and the microeconomy

In this chapter you will develop your knowledge and understanding of:

- utility
- indifference curves and budget lines
- efficiency and market failure
- private costs and benefits, externalities and social costs and benefits
- types of cost, revenue and profit, short and long run production
- different market structures
- growth and survival of firms
- differing objectives and policies of firms.

7.1 Utility

7.1.1 *Definition and calculation of total utility and marginal utility*

We saw in Chapter 2 that the individual and market demand curves for a product normally slope downwards from left to right, indicating that as the price falls the quantity demanded increases and vice versa. We will now look in more detail at why this is the case using marginal utility theory.

In order to develop this theory we need to introduce three important concepts: utility, total utility and marginal utility. By utility we simply mean the satisfaction that an individual obtains from the consumption of a product at a particular moment in time. It is important to note that utility does not imply usefulness, in that products which are bad for us such as cigarettes may still yield satisfaction. It is also important to emphasise the time aspect of utility. An individual who has just played a strenuous game of tennis in hot weather will be likely to gain far more utility from a bottle of cold orange juice than another who may simply have been sitting watching and may, therefore, derive little or no satisfaction from the drink.

How much satisfaction? ▲

Key terms

Utility: the satisfaction gained from a product.
Total utility: the satisfaction gained from the consumption of all units of a product over a particular time period.
Marginal utility: the satisfaction gained from the last unit of a product consumed over a particular time period.

Clearly utility is subjective and very difficult to measure. However, economists use the term "utils" to describe units of satisfaction, and in practice, as we shall see later, it is not necessary for the development of the theory for us to be able to give an absolute value to a unit of satisfaction.

If we return to the individual who has just played a strenuous game of tennis, it is quite likely that it will be necessary for them to consume a number of drinks to fully quench their thirst. Table 7.1 shows the amount of total and marginal utility an individual gains from consuming each of six drinks. The overall satisfaction that they obtain from consuming all six drinks is known as the total utility. The satisfaction obtained from the last unit consumed – the sixth – is known as the marginal utility.

Table 7.1 and Figure 7.1 illustrate the relationship between total and marginal utility.

Table 7.1 Total and marginal utility ▼

Quantity of drinks consumed	Total utility (TU) utils	Marginal utility (MU) utils
0	0	–
1	40	40
2	65	25
3	85	20
4	100	15
5	108	8
6	102	−6

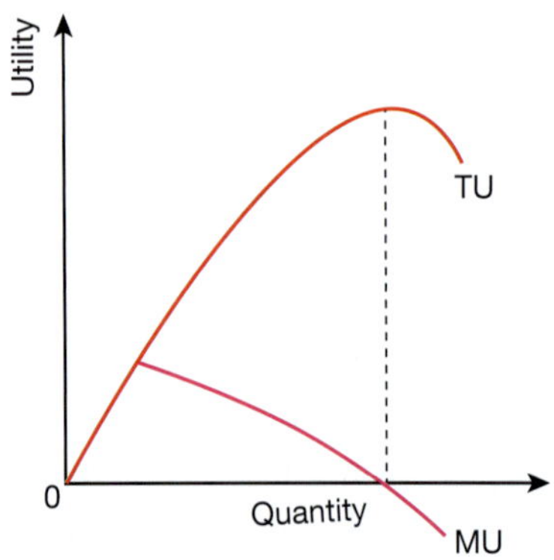

Figure 7.1 Total and marginal utility ▲

As shown in Table 7.1 total utility increases as more drinks are consumed up to five drinks, but at a decreasing rate, i.e. the marginal utility from consuming an additional drink is decreasing. Figure 7.1 shows the relationship between total and marginal utility graphically. As can be seen from the diagram, at the point at which total utility is at a maximum, the marginal utility is equal to zero and when total utility begins to decline, marginal utility becomes negative.

Getting it right

Make sure you clearly understand the distinction between total and marginal utility.

Progress question

1 Complete the following table:

Quantity	1	2	3	4	5	6	7	8
Total utility	100	190	250				360	
Marginal utility				50	40	10	7	3

7.1.2 *Diminishing marginal utility*

In taking the analysis further, if we look again at Table 7.1, it is clear that the amount of additional utility (marginal utility) the tennis player gains from each additional drink declines. The utility from the first drink following the tennis match is extremely high as the individual is extremely thirsty. A second drink may also be welcomed, but is unlikely to generate as much satisfaction as the first. The same is true of each subsequent drink, in that whilst each may add to the individual's overall satisfaction, the amount of additional utility added is likely to be less. This is known as the law of diminishing marginal utility. The individual having fully quenched their thirst by the fifth drink may find that further drinks actually reduce the overall level of satisfaction so that total utility declines and marginal utility becomes negative.

Key term

Law of diminishing marginal utility: as the quantity consumed of a product by an individual increases, the additional satisfaction gained from each unit (marginal utility) will eventually decline.

7.1.3 Equi-marginal principle

Key term

Equi-marginal principle: this states that a rational individual wishing to maximise total utility will allocate their expenditure amongst different products so as to ensure that the satisfaction (utility) gained from the last unit of money spent on each product is the same, i.e. MUx/Px = MUy/Py.

The analysis so far has been of the impact of a change in price on one product. However, a rise in the price of one good will affect the amount of income left over to purchase all other products and will, therefore, have an impact on the consumer's demand for its substitutes and complements.

We can use marginal utility theory to explain the way in which a rational consumer will allocate their expenditure across all products. This is explained by the equi-marginal principle.

This maintains that a rational consumer wishing to maximise utility will allocate expenditure in such a way that the amount of satisfaction (utility) gained from the last unit of money (Great British pound, Hong Kong dollar, euro or rupee) spent on each product consumed is the same.

Mathematically this can be written for two products as:

$$\frac{MUx}{Px} = \frac{MUy}{Py}$$

where:

MUx = marginal utility of product X

MUy = marginal utility of product Y

Px = price of product X

Py = price of product Y

If now the price of product X falls, the equality above becomes:

$$\frac{MUx}{Px} > \frac{MUy}{Py}$$

This means that the extra satisfaction gained from the last unit of money spent on product X gives greater satisfaction than that spent on Y. A rational consumer will, therefore, increase consumption of X. Because of the law of diminishing marginal utility this will have the effect of decreasing the marginal utility of X. The individual will continue increasing purchases of X until the equality is restored.

Hence, as the price of a product falls, the quantity of it demanded increases and vice versa.

7.1.4 Derivation of an individual demand schedule

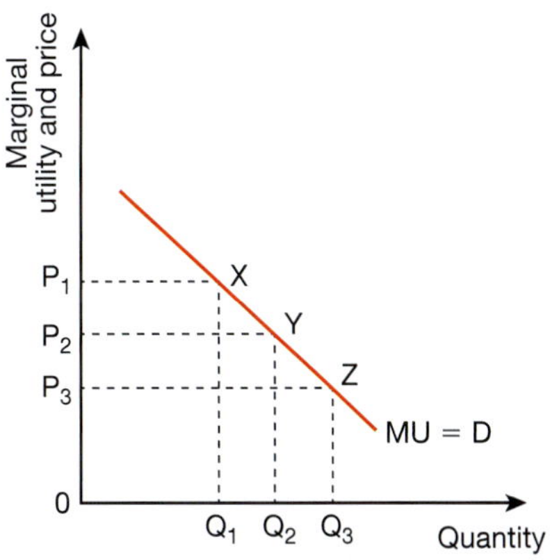

Figure 7.2 Individual marginal utility and demand curve ▲

We are now in a position to derive the demand curve for a product. In order to do so, we assume that the marginal utility of a product can be measured by the amount of money (the price) the individual is prepared to pay for it. In this case an individual's demand curve for a product will be the same as their marginal utility curve as shown in Figure 7.2.

A rational individual will wish to maximise their total utility from the consumption of a product and so will not purchase a product if the marginal utility obtained from it is perceived to be less than the price.

Consequently, an individual will consume a product up to the point where the price equals the marginal utility.

In Figure 7.2 if the price is at P_1, the individual will purchase quantity Q_1, corresponding to point X on the marginal utility curve because the extra satisfaction gained exactly equals the price paid. If now the price falls to P_2 and then P_3, the individual will increase purchases of the product to Q_2 and Q_3 corresponding to points Y and Z on the marginal utility curve. Clearly points X, Y and Z relate the quantity demanded by the individual and the price of the product and so are points on the individual's demand curve. Hence, as long as the individual continues to purchase up to the point where P = MU, the individual's demand curve will be the same as the marginal utility curve.

Getting it right

Consumers will purchase a product up to the point where P = MU.

Getting it right

The demand curve for an individual for a product is the individual's MU curve.

7.1.5 Limitations of marginal utility theory and its assumptions of rational behaviour

There are a number of limitations of marginal utility theory, particularly in relation to the law of diminishing marginal utility:

- Unit of measurement: As has already been indicated, it is difficult to find an appropriate unit of measurement of utility.
- Habit and impulse: Some purchases may be habit forming or made on impulse with the consumer not really considering the marginal utility.
- Enjoyment may increase as consumption increases: In some cases, the amount of satisfaction gained from additional units of consumption of a product might increase as the number consumed increases. This may well be the case with collectors. A collector wishing to have the largest collection in the world of Beatles memorabilia will obtain greater satisfaction from each additional item purchased and may be prepared to pay increasingly higher prices to obtain them.
- Quality and consistency of successive units of a good consumed: We are assuming throughout that all units of a product consumed are identical. If the quality of successive chocolate bars is not the same, then the amount of satisfaction obtained from additional bars may be more or less than previous ones.
- Other things remain constant: The theory assumes that all other factors affecting individuals' satisfaction remain the same. However, over time, there may be changes in income and the quality of other products as well as the development of new products and changes in individuals' tastes and attitudes, all of which may have an impact on consumers' satisfaction.
- Having said all this, proponents of marginal utility theory argue that at any moment in time, once a particular pattern of expenditure has been established, the law of diminishing marginal utility is valid.

Link

A developing branch of Economics "Behavioural Economics" attempts to address some of these concerns, see section 7.2.4 in this chapter.

7.2 Indifference curves and budget lines

7.2.1 *Meaning of an indifference curve and a budget line*

Indifference curves

An alternative explanation of consumer behaviour which attempts to overcome some of the difficulties involved with marginal utility theory is that of indifference curve analysis.

Key term

Indifference curve analysis: a theory of consumer behaviour based on the analysis of individuals' preferences.

Indifference curve analysis is based on the assumption that although it is not possible to measure exactly how much satisfaction (utility) an individual obtains from a product or combination of products, it is possible to conclude whether an individual obtains more or less satisfaction from one product than another or one combination of products as opposed to another.

Indifference curve analysis argues that the behaviour of rational consumers in their expenditure decisions can be used to establish a scale of preferences. If a ticket for a soccer match has the same price as one for a rugby match and the individual chooses to go to the soccer match it is reasonable to assume that the individual prefers to go to the soccer match rather than the rugby match. The analysis goes on to argue that it is possible to identify different combinations of two goods between which an individual has no preference at all, i.e. the individual is indifferent as to which of the combinations they consume. Table 7.2 shows an individual's indifference set for apples and pears. The individual is willing to accept any of the combinations.

Table 7.2 An individual's indifference set for apples and pears ▼

Apples	Pears
40	1
30	2
22	3
17	4
13	5
11	6
10	7

From this indifference set it is possible to construct an indifference curve which shows all possible combinations of apples and pears between which the consumer will be indifferent. This is shown in Figure 7.3.

Key term

Indifference curve: a curve showing all possible combinations of two products between which an individual consumer is indifferent.

Although we have assumed that there is only one indifference curve for each person, in fact there will be an infinite number, each one associated with a particular level of total utility. These indifference curves make up an indifference map such as the one illustrated in Figure 7.4.

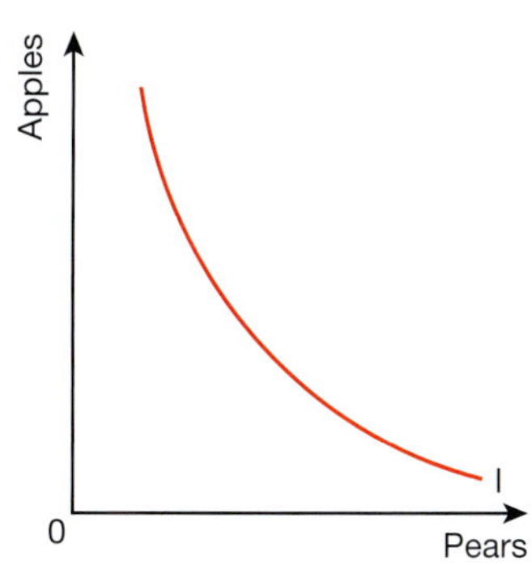

Figure 7.3 Indifference curve ▲

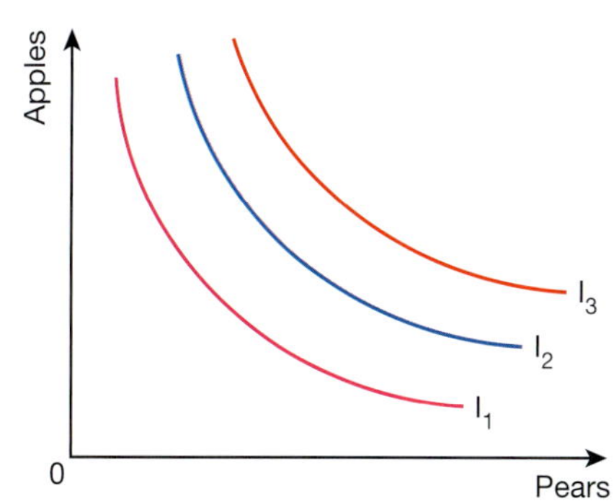

Figure 7.4 Indifference map ▲

Indifference curves further from the origin represent higher levels of total utility as they permit individuals to have increased quantities of at least one of the two goods, apples and pears.

Key terms

Marginal rate of substitution: the quantity of one good an individual is prepared to give up in order to obtain an additional unit of another while leaving the individual at the same level of utility.

Diminishing marginal rate of substitution: as more and more units of one good, A, are obtained, an individual will be prepared to give up fewer and fewer units of another, B, in order to obtain an additional unit of A.

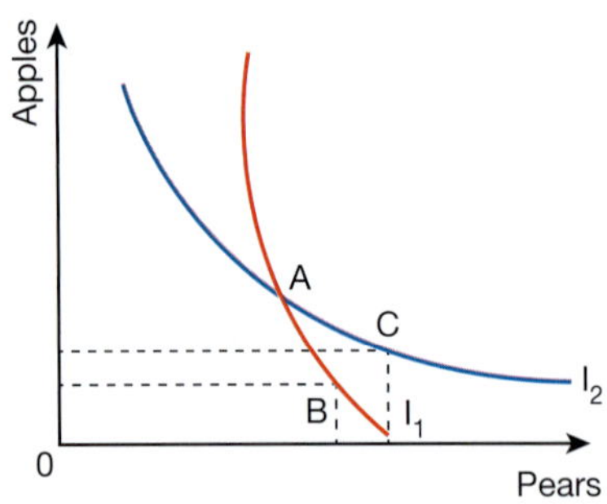

Figure 7.5 Indifference curves cannot intersect ▲

Key term

Budget lines: show all possible combinations of two products that an individual is able to purchase with a given level of income.

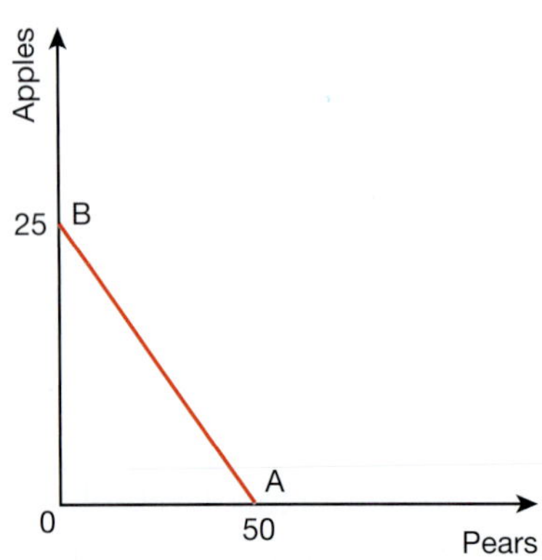

Figure 7.6 Budget line ▲

Properties of indifference curves

For rational consumers indifference curves have the following properties.

Indifference curves slope downwards from left to right and are convex to the origin. The slope of the indifference curve indicates the marginal rate of substitution, in this case of apples for pears. It shows the number of apples an individual is prepared to give up in order to obtain an additional pear while remaining at the same level of total utility. The indifference curve becomes shallower as we move down the curve from left to right, reflecting the individual's diminishing marginal rate of substitution of one good for another. As an individual obtains more and more of one good, pears, they will be prepared to sacrifice fewer and fewer units of the other, apples, in order to obtain another pear. As Table 7.2 shows, when an individual has only 1 pear, they will be prepared to give up 10 apples in order to obtain a second, but once the individual has 5 pears they will be prepared to sacrifice only 2 apples in order to obtain an additional pear.

Indifference curves can never intersect one another. Figure 7.5 explains this.

Points A and B represent two combinations which must give an individual equal satisfaction since they are on the same indifference curve. Similarly, points A and C represent combinations that give the same satisfaction since they are on the same, albeit, different indifference curve. If combinations A and B and A and C give the same levels of satisfaction, then logically combinations B and C must also give the same satisfaction. However, this is not possible as inspection of the diagram shows that point C gives the individual more of both goods and must, therefore, give greater satisfaction than the combination at point B. Hence indifference curves cannot intersect.

Budget lines

Another aspect of the analysis of consumers' expenditure is the budget line. Budget lines show the combinations of two goods that an individual is able to consume at particular prices with a given level of income.

Figure 7.6 shows an individual's budget line for two products, apples and pears. Let us assume that the individual has an income of \$100 to spend and that the price of apples is \$4 per kilo and pears \$2 per kilo. If all the income is spent on apples, then it is possible to buy 25 kilos, but no pears. If all the income is spent on pears, then it is possible to buy a maximum of 50 kilos of pears, but no apples. The budget line is AB. Any combination of apples and pears inside or on the budget line can be consumed, but the individual cannot consume beyond it.

7.2.2 Causes of a shift in the budget line

Budget line and changes in income

Changes in an individual's income will clearly mean that more or less can be consumed of each product. If we assume that the individual's income increases to \$200, then it is now possible for the individual to

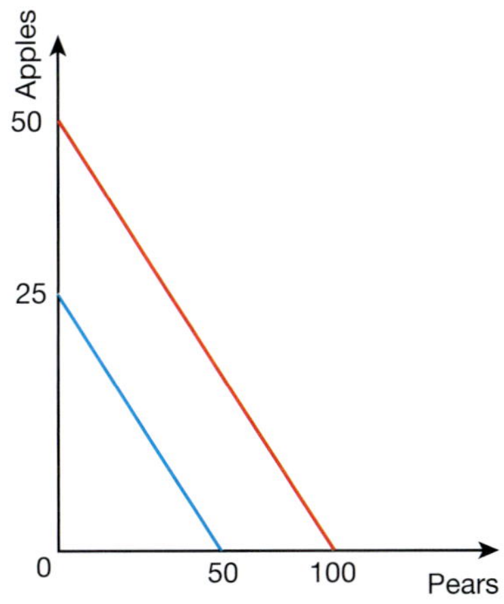

Figure 7.7 Effect on the budget line of a change in income

be able to buy 50 kilos of apples or 100 kilos of pears, which will shift the budget line upwards to the right parallel to the original budget line as indicated in Figure 7.7. Similarly, any reduction in the individual's income will shift the budget line inwards towards the origin.

Budget line and changes in price

If the price of one of the products changes, the slope of the budget line will alter. If we assume that the price of apples now falls to $2 per kilo with the price of pears remaining the same, then it will now be possible to purchase a maximum of 50 kilos of apples rather than the 25 kilos previously. The maximum possible amount of pears than can be purchased remains the same. The budget line now pivots outwards at point A and becomes AC. If the price of apples rises, the budget line would pivot inwards (Figure 7.8).

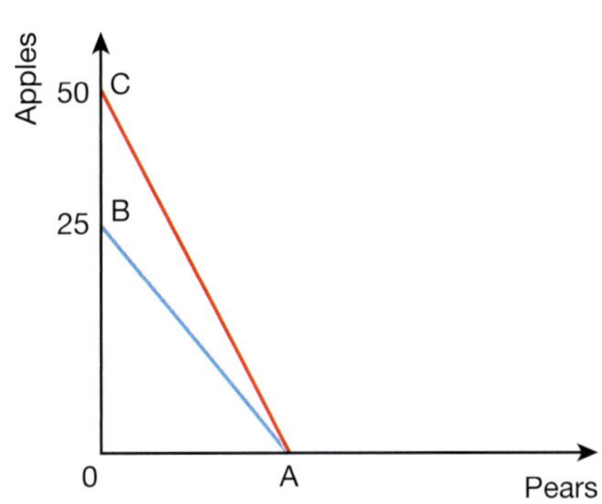

Figure 7.8 Effect on the budget line of a change in price

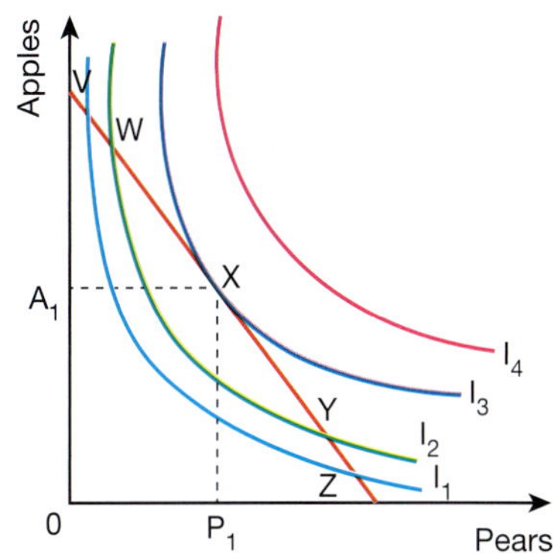

Figure 7.9 Optimum consumption point for an individual

Activities

Budget lines

1. Draw a diagram to illustrate the original budget line with a consumer income of $100 and the price of apples and pears $4 and $2 respectively.
2. Show what happens to the budget line if the price of pears (a) rises to $5 (b) falls to $1.

7.2.3 Income, substitution and price effects for normal, inferior and Giffen goods

The optimum consumption point

We are now in a position to bring together the analysis of indifference curves and budget lines to explain how much of the two goods, apples and pears, will be consumed by a rational consumer. This is illustrated in Figure 7.9.

Rational individuals will wish to allocate their expenditure between apples and pears so as to maximise their total utility, which means they will wish to achieve the highest indifference curve their income will permit. This is at point X in Figure 7.9 where the individual's budget line is tangential to the highest attainable indifference curve. The individual will consume A_1 apples and P_1 pears. Points V, W, Y and Z are attainable, but they are on lower indifference curves and are, therefore, associated with lower levels of satisfaction.

Getting it right

Make sure that you remember that the optimum consumption point for a rational consumer is at the point where their budget line is tangential to the highest attainable indifference curve.

The impact of changes in income and price on an individual's optimum consumption point

The effect of changes in income

The effect of increases and decreases in income are illustrated in Figure 7.10.

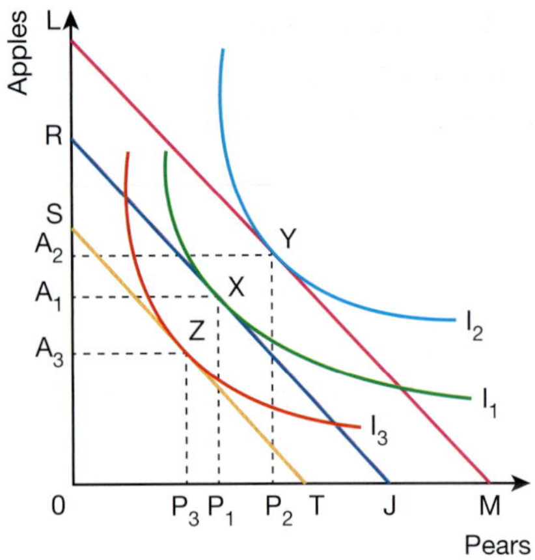

Figure 7.10 The effect of changes in income on the optimum consumption point ▲

> **Link**
>
> To refresh your memory on the distinction between normal and inferior goods see Chapter 2, section 2.1.3.

> **Key terms**
>
> **Giffen good**: a good the demand for which increases when its price increases and falls when its price falls.
>
> **Substitution effect**: the change in the quantity demanded of a good as a result of a change in its relative price.
>
> **Income effect**: the change in the quantity demanded of a good as a result of the fact that a change in its price has brought about a change in the consumer's real income.
>
> **Price effect**: in indifference curve analysis, the sum of the substitution and income effects showing the effect of a change in price on the quantity demanded.

The initial indifference curve is I_1 and the initial budget line is RJ. The individual's optimum consumption point is at X with A1 apples and P_1 pears being consumed. If the consumer's income now increases, the budget line shifts outwards to the right parallel to the original. The new budget line is LM. The individual is now able to consume more of all goods. The new optimum consumption point is at Y and the quantities of apples and pears consumed have increased to A_2 P_2. If instead the individual's income falls, the budget line will shift inwards to the left of the original to ST. The new optimum consumption point will be at Z with the individual now consuming only A_3 apples and P_3 pears.

The effect of changes in price

The effect of a price change on the quantity of a normal, inferior and Giffen good is shown in Figures 7.11, 7.12 and 7.13 respectively.

In each case the quantity of good A consumed is indicated on the Y axis and the quantity of good B consumed is shown on the X axis. The initial optimum consumption point is at X where the budget line RJ is tangential to the indifference curve I1. If we now assume that the price of B falls, an individual is now able to buy more of B but the same quantity of A and so the budget line pivots about point R and becomes RT. In each of the three figures the new optimum consumption point is at Y where RT is tangential to the new indifference curve I_2. In the case of both the normal and inferior goods, the quantity of B consumed has increased, but in the case of the Giffen good it has fallen. There are two major influences that determine whether individuals increase or decrease their consumption of a good when its price changes – the substitution effect and the income effect – and we need to understand the nature of these in relation to the fall in the price of B.

Income and substitution effects

A price effect involves both income and substitution effects. If the price of a product falls, it means that it is now cheaper relative to other products and the consumer is likely to purchase more of it. The fact that the consumer is likely to substitute purchases of products whose price has fallen for other relatively more expensive products is known as the substitution effect. The substitution effect always leads to an increase in the consumption of the good whose relative price has fallen.

The fall in price will also mean that the consumer's real income has effectively risen so that more of all products, including the one whose price has fallen, can now be purchased. This is known as the income effect. Whether this leads to more, less or the same amount of the product whose price has fallen being purchased depends upon the nature of the product. If the product is a normal good, then the income effect will operate so as to increase consumption of the product whose price has fallen, but if it is an inferior good then more of perceived superior products will be purchased and the income effect will lead to less of the product being purchased. Nevertheless, in the case of an inferior good, the substitution effect will be greater than the income effect and, so, overall the fall in price will lead to an increase in the quantity consumed of the good whose price has fallen. In the case of Giffen goods, however, the income effect will exceed the substitution effect and the fall in the price of the good will lead to less being consumed.

Normal, inferior and Giffen goods

It is possible to illustrate the substitution and income effects of the fall in the price of a good diagrammatically. This is shown in Figures 7.11, 7.12 and 7.13 for normal, inferior and Giffen goods respectively for the fall in the price of good B. As described above, the effect of the fall in price will, in each case, move the consumer from point X (consuming A_1, B_1) to point Y (consuming A_2, B_2). We begin by identifying the substitution effect. In order to do this we need to remove the income effect which is achieved by drawing in a new budget line, SV, parallel to the new budget line (RT), but tangential to the original indifference curve (I_1). This leaves the individual on the original indifference curve and shows how much of B would have been purchased had their real income not been increased. The movement from X to Z represents the substitution effect. The rest of the movement from X to Y is, therefore, the income effect.

It can be seen, therefore, that when the price of B is reduced the change in the quantity demanded, resulting from the substitution effect, is the movement from B_1 to B_3 and that resulting from the income effect by the movement from B_3 to B_2.

In the case of a normal good (Figure 7.11) the income and substitution effects of the price fall have worked in the same direction in order to bring about an increase in the quantity of B demanded.

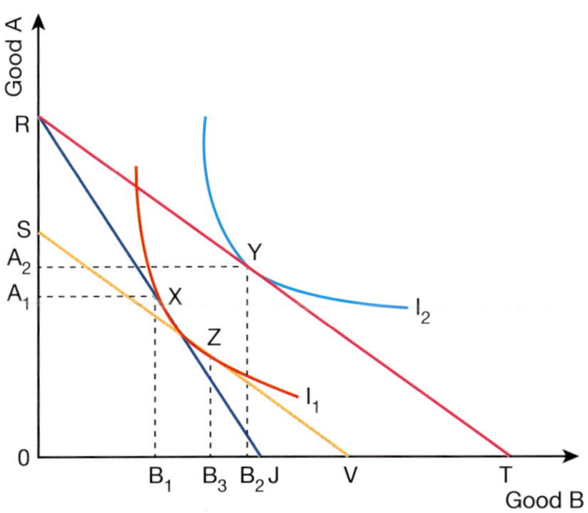

Figure 7.11 Income and substitution effects for a fall in price – normal good ▲

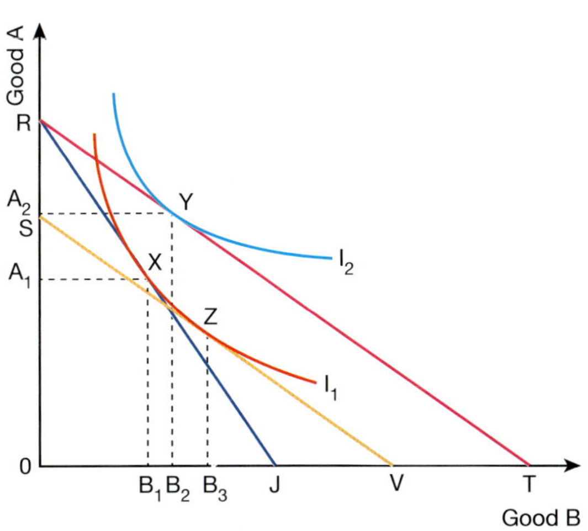

Figure 7.12 Income and substitution effects for a fall in price – inferior good ▲

Figure 7.12 illustrates the situation for an inferior good. An inferior good is one for which the quantity demanded will fall as consumers' income rises. In this case the substitution and income effects move in opposite directions. The substitution effect increases the quantity demanded from B_1 to B_3, but the negative income effect moderates the increase to some extent and will reduce the consumption of B from B_3 to B_2. Notice, however, that even though the substitution and income effects move in opposite directions, the final effect of the price reduction of good B is to increase the quantity of it which is demanded.

The final case illustrated in Figure 7.13 is that of a Giffen good. Giffen goods are generally regarded as goods of low quality which are important elements in the expenditure of those on low incomes. A good example is a basic food such as rice, which forms a significant part of the diet of the poor in many countries. The argument, not accepted by all economists, is that when the price of rice falls sufficiently individuals' real income will rise to an extent that they

Getting it right

Make sure you remember that in each of the three diagrams illustrating the income and substitution effects of a price fall, the movement from B_1 to B_3 represents the substitution effect and the movement from B_3 to B_2 represents the income effect.

will be able to afford more attractive substitutes such as fresh fruit or vegetables to make up their diet and as a result they will actually purchase less rice even though its price has fallen. In this case, the negative income effect (B_3 to B_2) completely outweighs the substitution effect (B_1 to B_3).

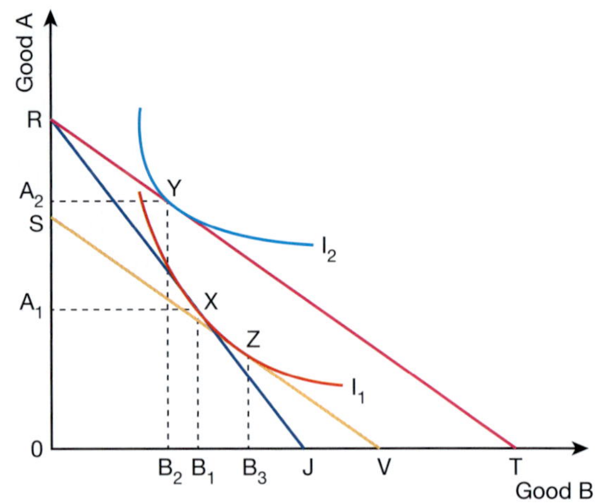

Figure 7.13 Income and substitution effects for a fall in price – Giffen good ▶

Getting it right

Make sure you have a clear understanding of the substitution and income effects of price changes.

Table 7.3 Summary of income and substitution effects of price changes ▼

Price change	Type of good	Substitution and income effect	Change in demand
Fall	Normal	Substitution and income effects both act in the same direction	Rise
Fall	Inferior	Substitution effect increasing demand is greater than the income effect reducing demand	Rise
Fall	Giffen	Income effect reducing demand is greater than the substitution effect increasing demand	Fall
Rise	Normal	Substitution and income effects both act in the same direction	Fall
Rise	Inferior	Substitution effect reducing demand is greater than the income effect increasing demand	Fall
Rise	Giffen	Income effect increasing demand is greater than the substitution effect reducing demand	Rise

Activity

Income and substitution effects

Draw diagrams to illustrate the income and substitution effects for a rise in the price of (a) a normal good (b) an inferior good (c) a Giffen good.

7.2.4 *Limitations of the model of indifference curves*

Although indifference curve analysis gets round the problem of measuring utility, when analysing consumer behaviour it has certain limitations.

To begin with, there is the issue of whether individuals can realistically be expected to be able to identify imaginary combinations of two goods which will give equal amounts of satisfaction and then compare them with other combinations of the same two goods which give more or less satisfaction, which is what is necessary to create an indifference map. It is also the case that indifference curves are drawn on the basis of an individual's perception of the amount of utility that will be obtained from commodities, which might differ significantly from the satisfaction that is obtained when they are actually consumed. Moreover, indifference curve analysis is unable to explain purchases of goods such as cars or computers or other consumer durables which are purchased infrequently with no consistent trade off against another product. Such goods may also only be purchased once. Finally, consumers may not act rationally when planning their expenditure. This latter point leads us into a developing branch of economic analysis known as behavioural economics.

Key term

Rational behaviour: the assumption made in Economics that individuals and firms take into account the marginal costs and benefits in making decisions in order to achieve the optimum outcome (maximisation of total utility).

Behavioural economics

A major assumption underpinning both marginal utility theory and indifference curve analysis is that consumers always act rationally. In the sense that economists use the term, rational behaviour in mainstream Economics means that:

- individuals act solely to maximise their own personal utility (satisfaction)
- individuals are in possession of or have access to all the information they need at low or zero cost
- consumer decisions are based upon a careful comparison of the costs and benefits in order to achieve the optimum final outcome
- once behaviour has been optimised, decision-making is based on changes at the margin
- individuals' preferences and attitude to risk are fixed.

In the real world, however, it is clear that individual behaviour may be irrational from the point of view of traditional economic models. For example, in financial crises and stock market crashes over the past century, investors and financial institutions appear to have repeated the mistakes of the past. At the individual level, why do individuals keep substantial surplus funds in current accounts or underperforming savings accounts when other accounts paying higher rates of interest are readily available? Why is it that many individuals automatically renew their annual car insurance with their existing company when identical cover can be obtained elsewhere at a lower price?

Key term

Behavioural Economics: the branch of Economics that attempts to explain the decisions and choices individuals make in practice particularly when they are opposed to those predicted by traditional economic theory.

Behavioural economics is a rapidly developing branch of Economics which attempts to explain such apparently "irrational" behaviour. Relying on empirical evidence and experiments, behavioural economics incorporates findings and insights from other disciplines such as sociology, social anthropology and particularly psychology to try to explain how individuals actually behave.

The pioneering study in behavioural economics is "Prospect Theory: An Analysis of Decision Under Risk" (1979) by Daniel Kahneman and Amos Tversky.

Prospect theory attempts to explain how people choose between alternatives involving risk where the probability of each outcome is known. It argues that rather than attempting to achieve optimal outcomes as traditional economic theory suggests, individuals actually make decisions based on the potential gains and losses that may arise.

Kahneman, Tversky and other behavioural economists identify a number of key elements in explaining individuals' apparently irrational behaviour.

Bounded rationality and heuristics

Let us return to our earlier example of irrational behaviour – an individual automatically renewing their annual car insurance with the existing provider. There is obviously an enormous quantity of information available which would enable the individual to make a rational decision as to whether this is in fact the best decision. There are many insurance companies from which to buy, each with their own publicity, website and telephone centres, as well as many comparison sites. However, for a variety of reasons individuals may not be able to use this information effectively to arrive at an optimum outcome. To begin with, the timescale may be short and accessing the quantity of available information may take many hours and possibly even involve some financial cost. The individual may feel that the opportunity cost in terms of the time taken in sifting through the information and inputting the same personal information possibly many times may not be worth any potential savings. They might simply find the enormous volume of information overwhelming – too much to absorb within the available timescale. The individual's ability to act in a rational manner is, therefore, restricted; in the language of behavioural economics it is "bounded". In the case of making other decisions, it could be the lack of sufficient information or the fact that there may be more than one possible solution that means a consumer may experience what Herbert Simon (1978) termed bounded rationality. As a result, individuals may engage in satisficing rather than optimising behaviour in their decision-making.

Key term

Bounded rationality: the idea that individuals' ability to make rational decisions is limited by the quantity of information available and their ability to absorb and interpret it within the timescale available.

Link

See section 7.8.2 in this chapter for more on satisficing behaviour.

Heuristics

In such cases, behavioural economists argue that individuals resort to heuristics, which are simplifying strategies or mental shortcuts to arriving at solutions.

Key term

Heuristics: rules of thumb or mental shortcuts made by individuals to speed up the decision-making process.

They argue that empirical evidence and experiment identify many such heuristics including the following:

- Anchoring: the tendency to rely on the first piece of information obtained (the anchor) when considering a decision.
- Availability: basing decisions on the easiest piece of information to recall. The way and order in which information is presented to an individual will be important here.
- Representativeness: basing decisions on past experience or assumptions. This can lead to stereotyping. An example of the representativeness heuristic would be to argue that simply because we have only met low-income individuals from a particular region

that all people from that region must be poor. This particular example illustrates that although the use of these heuristics (rules of thumb) may speed up decisions, it can also lead to individuals making mistakes or irrational decisions.

Framing

> **Key term**
>
> **Framing**: the way in which an issue or choice is presented (framed) which may affect the decision made by an individual.

Another feature of individual decision-making appears to be what behavioural economists refer to as framing. The way in which an issue, question or choice is presented or framed. There is evidence that the same information presented in different ways may lead to a different decision being made. For example, an individual may be more likely to buy an expensive pair of designer shoes if they are advertised as reduced from $400 to $300 rather than simply being priced at $300. Retailers can obviously use this knowledge in advertising and marketing their products.

Other aspects of behavioural economics

In addition to the ideas of bounded rationality, heuristics and framing, the experiments of behavioural economists have identified a range of other insights which challenge the views of traditional economic models of consumer decision-making and may help explain apparently irrational behaviour. These include the following:

- The endowment effect. This refers to the fact that individuals appear to be reluctant to give up goods which they own (their endowment) and as a result often demand much more to give up a product (their willingness to accept) than they would be prepared to pay for it (their willingness to pay). This appears to apply even to relatively mundane goods, e.g. coffee mugs. Some experiments have demonstrated that individuals require twice the amount to part with their endowment than they would have been prepared to pay for it in the first place. This endowment effect appears not to be associated with the value, characteristics or attraction of the product, but more the distress of losing it. Behavioural economists refer to this as loss aversion.
- Loss aversion. There is considerable evidence that individuals appear to give much greater weight in their decision-making to the possibility of losses than the possibility of gains even when the probabilities of either occurring are the same.
- Reference points. This refers to the apparent tendency for individuals to base decisions on the estimated gains and losses from a particular reference point (their position now) rather than looking at the overall picture. This may lead them to break down or compartmentalise the process of making a decision into a number of individual smaller decisions.
- Certainty versus uncertainty. This appears to be linked with loss aversion. Experiments suggest that individuals prefer outcomes that are certain, or perceived to be certain, to those which are uncertain

Too much choice? ▲

Conspicuous consumption ▲

even where the probability was high that the uncertain event would generate a significantly greater gain or benefit. This might explain why individuals might prefer the guarantee of a low return on an investment to a much larger gain from an alternative if there was even a low probability of this leading to a loss.

- Over-confidence and over-optimism. It seems from empirical studies by behavioural economists that individuals when looking to the future tend to be over-confident and over-optimistic about potential gains. This might be a factor in explaining speculative bubbles.
- Too much choice? Traditional economic theory argues that competition-creating choice is always a good thing. However, there is evidence that given too much choice individuals fail to make any decision at all.
- Herd instinct and competition. In making consumption decisions, individuals are often swayed by the desire to keep up with their peers or friends and as a result purchase products simply because others are doing so. It is also possible that individuals might exhibit competitive behaviour purchasing goods which are perceived to be luxuries, superior to those purchased by friends and peers and, therefore, conferring social status.

Behavioural economists argue that all this research indicates that, counter to traditional Economics, individuals' preferences and attitudes to possible gains or losses are not fixed. They may vary over time and according to the perceived uncertainty, risk and amount of money involved. This clearly undermines the assumptions underpinning traditional indifference curve analysis. Indeed one empirical study made in 1990 indicated the possibility of indifference curves intersecting.

Implications for policy

Behavioural economists argue that their findings can have important implications for government policy. Richard Thaler and Cass Sunstein in "Nudge: Improving Decisions About Health, Wealth and Welfare" (2008) suggest that insights from behavioural economics can be used by governments and others to persuade or "nudge" people into making decisions which are beneficial for them or in their best interests. For example, they suggest that individuals will be more likely to adopt energy conservation methods in their homes if the government advertises them as leading to a saving of $X per year rather than stating that they will lose (the same) $X per year if they do not adopt them – an example of "framing".

Another example is to make "opting in" rather than "opting out" the default position for schemes regarded as beneficial for individuals. For example, there is evidence that workers in a company are more likely to participate in a pension scheme if they are automatically enrolled and required to "opt out" if they do not wish to be a member than if they need to make a conscious decision to join or "opt in".

Link

Nudge theory is also discussed in Chapter 8, section 8.1.1.

Progress question

2 Explain two ways in which a government might use insights from behavioural economics to "nudge" individuals to take more exercise to improve their health.

Overview of behavioural economics

Through experiments, empirical analysis and taking insights from psychology, behavioural economics attempts to find patterns and common themes in apparently irrational behaviour which can be incorporated into economic models of consumer behaviour and decision-making. Supporters argue that behavioural economics improves economists' ability to deal with actual economic life and the way individuals behave in reality. Ignoring behavioural aspects of decision-making they believe may lead to errors in prediction in traditional economic models. In particular it is important to take into account, for example, endowment effects and the fact that some choices involve one or more goods or services with which individuals may be unfamiliar with the consequence that meaningful preferences will only be established after choices have been made.

Activities

Behavioural economics and decision-making

In groups of four or five:

1. Identify four individual decisions or purchases made in the last week which might be regarded as irrational.
2. Produce a presentation to the rest of the group explaining the extent to which theses irrational decisions or purchases might be explained by behavioural economics.

Criticisms of behavioural economics

Not all economists, however, agree. They argue that the conclusions of behavioural economists tend to be based on experiments involving college students who may not be representative of actual consumers, investors, business owners or entrepreneurs and, therefore, raises the issue of whether they will respond in the same way.

These experiments also, in the main, involve hypothetical options often requiring decisions about preferences which have not yet been made. In some cases the experiments require individuals to make choices or decisions in relation to very large issues which may be well outside their experience. It is argued that individuals' preferences might alter if the choices or decisions were not hypothetical and were more closely linked to their own experience. The same applies to experiments requiring decisions to be made where there is a risk of financial loss. Would individuals make the same decision if an actual loss was possible rather than a hypothetical one?

Another criticism centres on the fact that behavioural economists tend to ignore the fact that if an experiment was repeated or individuals came up against a particular set of circumstances, they might learn from past errors and, therefore, not repeat past mistakes.

Finally, with a few possible exceptions, e.g. the endowment effect and loss aversion, heuristics or rules of thumb for decision-making seem to be specific to particular choices or decisions, which makes it difficult to generalise about them and also makes it more difficult to make predictions based on them.

7.3 Efficiency and market failure

7.3.1 *Definitions of productive efficiency and allocative efficiency*

Economic efficiency refers to a situation where scarce resources are used in the "best" or most effective possible way to achieve the maximum output possible.

Key term

Economic efficiency: the optimal use of scarce inputs to produce the largest possible output.

Link

Efficiency is generally concerned with how well resources are used to produce an output. It would be useful to look back at the discussion of the three fundamental questions in Chapter 1, section 1.1.4.

Key terms

Optimality or optimum: the best situation that can be attained in particular circumstances.

Productive efficiency: the most efficient use of scarce resources whereby the maximum output is produced with the minimum of resources.

Allocative efficiency: the quantity of output produced with scarce resources that leads to the best satisfaction for consumers.

Link

See the discussion of scarcity in Chapter 1, section 1.1.1.

Link

See the discussion of utility in section 7.1.1 in this chapter.

Key term

Technical efficiency: the situation in which a firm produces the maximum output technologically possible from a given quantity of factor inputs.

Another way of describing efficiency is in relation to the concept of optimality, or optimum which can be defined as the best situation or outcome possible in a particular situation. It is a very important concept in Economics given the existence of scarcity that underpins the basic economic problem.

Productive and allocative efficiency

Economic efficiency, or an optimal allocation of scarce resources, can only exist when there is **both** productive efficiency and allocative efficiency.

Productive efficiency

Productive efficiency occurs when products are made with the least possible use of scarce resources.

Allocative efficiency

Whereas the concept of productive efficiency places the emphasis on production at the lowest possible cost, allocative efficiency emphasises that it is necessary that the right products be produced in an economy. This is related to the satisfaction or utility that consumers get from the consumption of particular products.

7.3.2 Conditions for productive efficiency and allocative efficiency

Productive efficiency

Productive efficiency in a firm

This can be shown in Figure 7.14 which illustrates the average total cost curves of a firm because productive efficiency will occur when products are produced at the lowest possible cost of production.

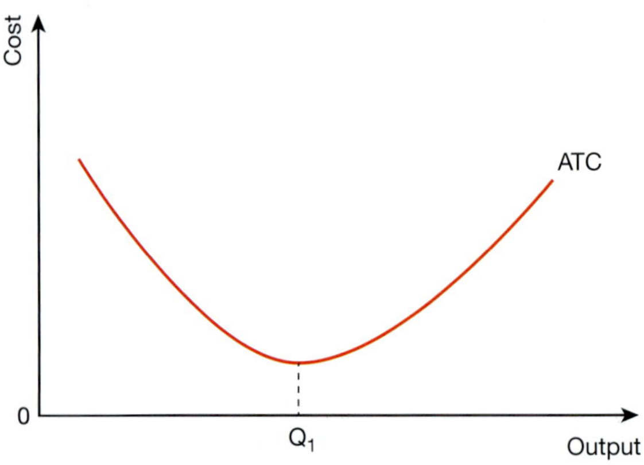

Figure 7.14 Productive efficiency in a firm ▲

Productive efficiency for a firm occurs where the firm's output is produced at the minimum point of the average total cost curve; in Figure 7.14, this is an output of Q_1. There are actually two elements to this situation. Firstly, a firm may have a number of average total cost curves; productive efficiency takes place on the lowest possible average total cost curve. Secondly, production needs to be at the lowest point on the lowest average total cost curve (as shown in Figure 7.14). This second element is known as technical efficiency.

Getting it right

Productive efficiency refers to a situation in which a given output is produced using the least cost combination of factors of production.

Link

The production possibility curve was introduced in Chapter 1, section 1.5.1. The concept of productive efficiency can also be seen in section 7.6.4 in this chapter in relation the characteristics of different market structures.

Link

The concept of allocative efficiency can be seen in 7.6.4 in this chapter, when comparing monopoly and perfect competition.

Getting it right

Make sure you understand that a production possibility curve is usually used to illustrate the concept of productive efficiency, although if consumer preferences are known it could be used to show the concept of allocative efficiency.

Key term

Pareto optimality: the situation that exists when it is not possible to make one person better off without making someone else worse off as a result of the reallocation of resources.

Productive efficiency in an economy

Productive efficiency can also be shown in relation to a whole economy rather than just a particular firm.

The production possibility curve can be used to show the existence of productive efficiency in an economy. Figure 7.15 assumes that there is a two-product economy where scarce resources are allocated to the production of either good A, shown on the horizontal axis, or to good B, shown on the vertical axis. The production possibility curve shows the possible combinations of production of these two goods. Point X, inside the production possibility curve, indicates that there are unused resources in the economy that could be used to produce either good A, good B or a combination of the two goods. Any point along the production possibility curve, however, such as point Y, indicates that all possible resources are being used to produce a particular combination of the two goods, i.e. productive efficiency is being maximised.

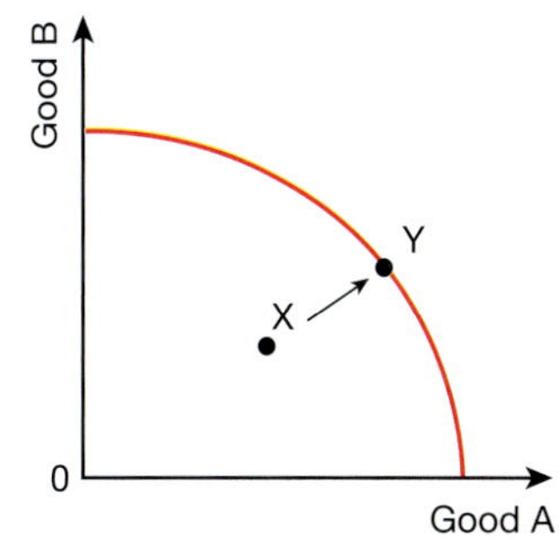

Figure 7.15 Productive efficiency in an economy ▲

Allocative efficiency

Allocative efficiency is best shown in terms of the relationship between the marginal cost of production and the price of a product. The marginal cost of production refers to the cost of producing one more product; when this is equal to the price charged for the product, allocative efficiency is said to exist. The explanation for this is that the value put on the resources by the producer is exactly equal to the value put on the product produced by the resources by the consumer. If any more or any less was produced, price and marginal cost would no longer be in equilibrium.

It has already been explained that a production possibility curve can be used to illustrate the concept of productive efficiency in an economy (see Figure 7.15). A production possibility curve can also be used to show the concept of allocative efficiency, but only if the particular preferences of consumers are known. Any point along the production possibility frontier could possibly show the existence of allocative efficiency; the exact point on the curve would depend on the particular preferences of consumers.

For allocative efficiency to exist throughout an economy, this must operate in all markets in the economy.

7.3.3 *Pareto optimality*

One particular type of optimality is associated with the Italian economist Vilfredo Pareto (1848–1923). Pareto optimality (or Pareto efficiency) refers to a situation where it is not possible to reallocate scarce resources to make someone better off without making someone else worse off. For this situation to be achieved, there needs to be *both* productive and allocative efficiency. This optimal allocation of resources means that inputs into the production process are used in the most efficient way (productive efficiency) and that the output produced yields the maximum possible utility or satisfaction to consumers (allocative efficiency).

Pareto first put forward this condition in 1909. If an allocation of resources is Pareto inefficient, this means that it would be possible to make at least one person better off without making anybody worse off.

7.3.4 *Definition of dynamic efficiency*

Dynamic efficiency results from improvements in technical or productive efficiency over a period of time. For example, new products may appear in markets as a result of research and development, invention and innovation. It is important to understand the difference between invention and innovation; innovation is the practical application of inventions to general products that can be sold in the market place. Innovation is the hardest part of technical progress, i.e. transforming a good idea into something that is successful in that it is workable and profitable.

Getting it right

Make sure you understand the difference between invention and innovation. Invention is when somebody comes up with an original idea or concept, whereas innovation is when that idea or concept is translated into a viable undertaking that can supply customers with products that they want to buy, at a profit.

Vilfredo Pareto ▲

Case Study

Innovation in the United Arab Emirates

The United Arab Emirates has a very strong record in relation to innovation. It has produced a UAE National Innovation Strategy and a 50 Year Innovation Challenge. Some of its key achievements in innovation include the following:

- development of education and the introduction of computers and smart devices in schools
- expansion of the number of higher education institutions
- establishment of a number of complexes, research institutions and technical institutes to promote research
- establishment of Masdar City in Abu Dhabi
- establishment of Dubai Science Park
- establishment of Mohammed bin Rashid Solar Park
- establishment of the Arab Institution for Science and Technology in Sharjah
- establishment of the Technology and Innovation Center in Ras Al Khaimah.

Innovation is a key part of the pillar "United in Knowledge" of Vision 2021 which focuses on building an innovative and competitive economy. According to the 2020 Annual Global Innovation Index, the UAE is the most innovative country in the Arab world. The aim is for the UAE to rank among the top ten countries in the Global Innovation Index. For the UAE government, innovation is indispensable to keep pace with technological advancements.

The Dubai Science Park was established in 2005 to support innovation by helping businesses utilise cutting-edge technology and knowledge to foster growth in human, plant, material, environmental and energy sciences. It is a holistic science-focused business community, home to more than 350 businesses employing over 3,600 people.

1 Discuss how innovation can play a key part in promoting dynamic efficiency in the UAE.

Key term

Dynamic efficiency: the greater efficiency that results from improvements in technical or productive efficiency over a period of time.

New methods of production could also be introduced, incorporating the latest technology in order to increase productivity. There could also be the introduction of radically different methods of management, resulting from investment in human capital.

Both productive and allocative efficiency can be regarded as examples of static efficiency, i.e. they are concerned with the allocation of scarce resources at a particular moment in time. Dynamic efficiency, in contrast, is concerned with the allocation of scarce resources over a period of time.

Progress question

3 Explain the difference between invention and innovation.

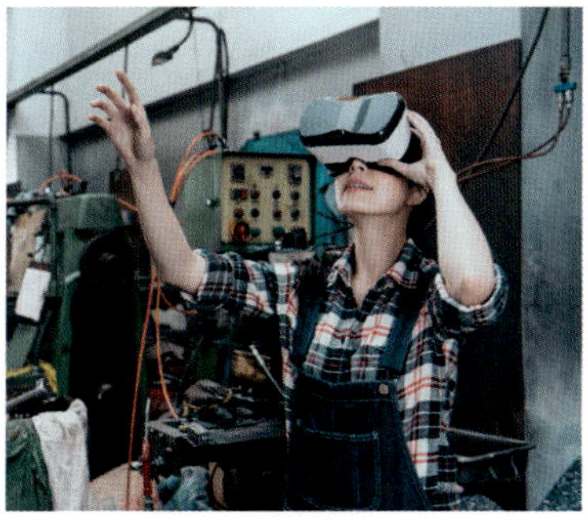

Advances in technology can bring about dynamic efficiency. ▲

Progress question

4 Discuss how (i) new methods of production and (ii) new methods of management might lead to the more efficient use of resources in an economy.

Case Study

The allocation of resources

Some countries are more likely to be dynamic, such as in relation to the impact of technological change, than others and so it might be expected that the use of scarce resources would become more efficient in such countries over a period of time. The following tables give some indication of which countries these might be.

The Global Innovation Index

This index measures the use of new technology in economies. It averages countries' capacity for innovation (inputs) and success in innovation (outputs), based on 80 indicators. The higher the number, the greater the application of new technology in a particular economy. A figure of 50.0 or more is seen as very good. The table shows the top ten countries in 2020.

Country	Innovation Index
Switzerland	67.2
Sweden	63.7
United States of America	61.7
Netherlands	61.4
United Kingdom	61.3
Finland	59.8
Denmark	58.4
Singapore	58.4
Germany	58.2
Israel	57.4

The Technological Readiness Index

This index measures the ability of economies to adopt new technology. In this case, a figure of 6.00 or more is considered to be very good. The table shows the top ten countries in 2020.

Country	Technological Readiness Index
Sweden	6.12
Luxembourg	6.11
Iceland	5.99

Netherlands	5.99
Hong Kong	5.96
Denmark	5.62
Switzerland	5.60
United Kingdom	5.58
Norway	5.56
Germany	5.36

Total expenditure on research and development (% of GDP)

The table shows the top ten countries in 2020.

Country	% of GDP
South Korea	4.55
Israel	4.54
Switzerland	3.37
Sweden	3.33
Taiwan	3.30
Japan	3.21
Austria	3.16
Denmark	3.06
Germany	3.02
United States of America	2.79

1 Discuss how research and development and technological change could be used to improve the efficiency of the allocation of resources in an economy.

7.3.5 *Definition of market failure*

Market failure can be defined as a market imperfection which produces a sub-optimal allocation of scarce resources which is not as efficient as it might otherwise have been. It therefore occurs when there is an inefficient allocation of resources in a market economy.

Activity

Dynamic efficiency

Use the internet to discover how the Innovation Index and the Technology Readiness Index are compiled.

7.3.6 *Reasons for market failure*

Public goods, merit goods, demerit goods and information failure have already been covered in Chapter 1. There are other examples of market failure, such as the existence of imperfect competition, which will be covered in section 7.6 of this chapter, inequality in the distribution of income and wealth, which will be covered in Chapter 8, and government failure, which will be covered in Chapters 8 and 10.

It will therefore be useful at this point to provide a summary of the main reasons for market failure.

Table 7.4 The reasons for market failure ▼

Type of market failure	Explanation
Public goods	These are goods which would not be provided in a market economy because it would be impossible to charge a price for them because of the "free rider" problem.
Merit goods	These are goods or services which are regarded as being socially desirable and which would be under-consumed and under-produced in a market economy.
Demerit goods	These are goods which are regarded as being socially undesirable and which would be over-consumed and over-produced in a market economy.
Information failure	This is where there is a lack of full information and so the allocation of resources is less efficient than it would otherwise be. This information failure is a major reason why consumers make the wrong decisions in relation to the consumption of merit and demerit goods.
Government failure	A government can attempt to intervene in a market economy to try to overcome the existence of a market failure, but there is the possibility that such intervention might create further distortions in the market.
Externalities	Externalities are costs or benefits which can affect third parties and are sometimes referred to as "spill-over" effects. There can be both positive and negative externalities and these can be related to both production and consumption.
Imperfect competition	There are different forms of imperfect competition that can exist in an economy and one of these would be the existence of a monopoly where one firm controls a market. If a firm has monopoly power in a market, it will operate very differently from a firm in perfect competition. For example, the price is likely to be higher and the output lower than would be the case in perfect competition. Also, abnormal or supernormal profits can exist in the long run as well as the short run.
Inequality in the distribution of income and wealth	A market economy may lead to a very unequal distribution of income and wealth, and this will have the effect of giving some people more influence than others in the economy.
Price instability	Price acts as a signal in a market economy and it has sometimes been described as an 'invisible hand', responsible for the allocation and reallocation of resources in an economy. However, in some situations, there can be a great deal of price instability in a market economy where prices can change quite rapidly in a relatively short period of time. This can, for example, be a feature of agricultural markets.
Factor immobility	The factors of production should be able to move easily from one sector to another in a market economy, but this is not always the case because of the existence of geographical and occupational immobility of labour.
Asymmetric information	Not all parties will have the same knowledge and one party could exploit this advantage.
Moral hazard	A person or organisation may be more likely to take a risk in the knowledge that someone else will bear the cost of that risk.

7.4 Private costs and benefits, externalities and social costs and benefits

7.4.1 *Definition and calculation of social costs as the sum of private costs and external costs*

A social cost is defined as the sum of private costs and external costs. Private costs refer to those costs that are incurred by a firm in the process of production, excluding any external costs. They can also be called internal costs and could include such costs as wages and salaries, component parts and raw materials and interest payments. They also refer to the costs to a consumer of buying a product. External costs refer to those costs which come about as the result of any activities which are not paid for by the firm or the consumer carrying out the activity.

When all of the internal and external costs of production are added together, this represents the total costs to society of that production and these total costs are therefore known as social costs.

Key terms

Social cost: the total cost of producing a product which takes into account the private costs to the firm and any external costs to society resulting from that production.

Private cost: the internal cost to a firm of producing a product, such as the cost of wages and salaries, or the cost of a product to a consumer.

External cost: a cost which arises from any activity which is not paid for by the firm or the consumer carrying out the activity.

7.4.2 Definition and calculation of social benefits as the sum of private benefits and external benefits

A social benefit is defined as the sum of private benefits and external benefits. Private benefits refer to those benefits that are gained by a firm in the process of production, and include such benefits as the revenue and profit received from sales of a product. They also refer to the benefits to a consumer of buying a product, such as the satisfaction gained. External benefits refer to those benefits to a third-party that come about as the result of any activities carried out by a firm or a consumer.

Getting it right

Make sure that you do not confuse external costs and social costs. External costs are only one part of social costs, along with private costs.

Getting it right

Make sure that you do not confuse external benefits and social benefits. External benefits are only one part of social benefits, along with private benefits.

Key terms

Social benefit: the total benefit of producing a product which takes into account the private benefits to the firm and any external benefits to society resulting from that production.
Private benefit: the satisfaction or utility obtained by an individual when consuming a product, or the benefit to a firm of producing a product.
External benefit: a benefit to a third-party which arises from an activity carried out by a firm or a consumer.

When all of the internal and external benefits of production are added together, this represents the total benefit to society of that production and these total benefits are therefore known as social benefits.

Progress question

5 Explain the difference between external costs and benefits and social costs and benefits.

7.4.3 Definition of positive externality and negative externality

An externality can be either a cost or a benefit of production or consumption which has effects that are not paid for by either the producer or the consumer. They are called external costs or external benefits because they are have spill-over or third party effects. A third party refers to someone who is not directly involved, but who will be affected by the actions of others.

- Positive externality: The external benefits of production or consumption, i.e. the benefits to a third party not involved in the production or consumption of a product, are referred to as positive externalities.
- Negative externality: The external costs of production or consumption, i.e. the costs imposed on a third party not involved in the production or consumption of a product, can be referred to as negative externalities.

Key terms

Externality: an action that results in either external benefits or external costs in relation to either production or consumption.
Positive externalities: a third-party effect resulting from production or consumption that creates a benefit to society which is not paid for by either the producer or the consumer.
Negative externalities: a third-party effect resulting from production or consumption that imposes a cost on the society which is not paid for by either the producer or the consumer.

7.4.4 Positive and negative externalities of both consumption and production

Table 7.5 gives some examples of different types of externality.

> **Getting it right**
> Remember that an externality can refer to either production or consumption costs or benefits or to both.

Table 7.5. External costs and benefits of production and consumption

Type of externality	Example
External cost of production	A firm dumps waste into a river, causing pollution and killing the fish
External benefit of production	A firm trains its workers, some of whom go on to work somewhere else and this reduces the costs of training for this other firm
External cost of consumption	A person driving a motor vehicle produces car exhaust fumes and this increases the level of pollution
External benefit of consumption	Well maintained gardens can help to improve the environment of a particular neighbourhood

Externalities and market failure

Externalities have already been explained in terms of third-party effects from the production or consumption of products for which no payment is made. This is why they can be regarded as an example of market failure, because the price mechanism does not take into account the wider costs and benefits to the whole society as a result of the production or consumption that has taken place. In essence, the market fails to produce an allocation of scarce resources that is efficient.

Negative externalities and market failure

The existence of negative externalities in production or consumption creates a separation or divergence between the private costs and the social costs. In this situation, social costs are greater than private costs.

Case Study

Rising consumption of meat

Across the world many governments are becoming increasingly concerned about the quantity of red meat being consumed by their populations. Worldwide the consumption of red meat has been increasing by about 3 per cent a year since 1960. Most of this growth is in poorer countries where people buy more meat as their income rises, but consumption is also growing in rich countries albeit at a slower rate. The UK and USA have seen a 10 per cent increase in consumption since 1970 and China, already the world's largest consumer of pork, has seen its imports of beef soar by 4000 per cent in the past decade.

Whilst red meat is an effective source of protein, important nutrients and calories, high levels of consumption of red meat are associated with a number of health, environmental and ethical issues. Health issues include increased risk of obesity, high blood pressure, type 2 diabetes and certain types of cancer. As a result, the World Cancer Research Fund suggests eating fewer than 500 grams per week and minimising the intake of processed meats such as bacon and salami.

In terms of the environment, increased consumption of red meats, particularly beef, impacts on global warming and Latin American forests as cattle farming leads to the emission of greenhouse gases and land clearance.

There are also ethical issues involved in the way in which animals are kept and slaughtered.

1. With the aid of a diagram, use the information in the extract and your own knowledge and research to assess the private, external and social costs and benefits of high levels of red meat consumption.
2. Explain how a government might use insights from behavioural economics and nudge theory to devise policies to influence the consumption of red meat.

This can be seen in Figure 7.16. This shows demand and supply in a market, but it takes into account that decisions are generally said to be taken "at the margin". The marginal cost or marginal benefit refers to the additional cost or benefit as a result of producing or consuming one more unit.

It has already been stated that social costs are equal to the sum of private costs and external costs, but if the concept of marginal analysis is introduced, this can be rewritten as marginal social cost = marginal private cost + marginal external cost.

Key terms

The margin: the point at which the last unit of a product is produced or consumed.

Marginal social cost: the addition of marginal private cost and marginal external cost.

Getting it right

You need to be careful you do not suggest that the pollution will no longer exist in such a situation. You need to emphasise, however, that the market has taken such external costs into account.

The equilibrium position in the market is where the demand curve D (representing marginal social benefit) crosses the supply curve S_1 (representing marginal private cost), producing a price of P_1 and a quantity of Q_1. However, if the production has involved an element of pollution, this equilibrium will not indicate the true cost of the resources used. If negative externalities exist, these need to be shown in a separate supply curve, S_2. This supply curve takes into account the external costs to society, i.e. the marginal social cost. The supply curve S_2 represents the addition of marginal private cost and marginal external cost. The new equilibrium position is now with a higher price of P_2 and a lower quantity of Q_2. The external costs have now been taken into account and this new equilibrium is therefore the socially efficient equilibrium. The pollution has not been eliminated, but it has been reduced and included in the equilibrium market price.

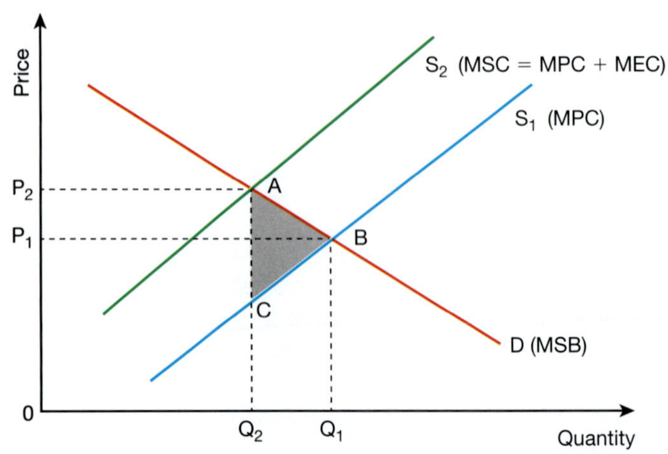

Figure 7.16 Negative externalities ▲

Case Study

Pollution from a factory in Bangladesh

An example of a negative externality is pollution from a factory in Dhaka, the capital city of Bangladesh. In the course of the production process, the factory gives off smoke which can be seen, and smelled, by all of the people in the neighbourhood. This pollution will make the neighbourhood a dirtier place to live in and some people with breathing problems may be particularly badly affected. The factory itself is likely to be an eyesore and there will certainly be greater traffic congestion with lorries going to and from the factory.

The owners of the factory will take into account the private costs of production, such as the wages and salaries that are paid to the workforce, but will not take into account the cost to the community. This external cost will have a spill-over effect on third parties, i.e. people in the neighbourhood who have not been directly responsible for the pollution.

1 Describe what is meant by a spill-over or third-party effect on a community.
2 Explain, with the aid of a diagram, how the amount of pollution in the community, caused by the factory, could be reduced.

Positive externalities and market failure

The concept of externalities does not apply only to negative externalities. It can also apply to positive externalities, production or consumption which create a divergence between private and social benefits. In this situation, social benefits are greater than private benefits.

Key term

Marginal social benefit: the addition of marginal private benefit and marginal external benefit.

This can be seen in Figure 7.17. The importance of decisions taken "at the margin" has already been stressed. Marginal social benefit can therefore be expressed as equal to marginal private benefit + marginal external benefit.

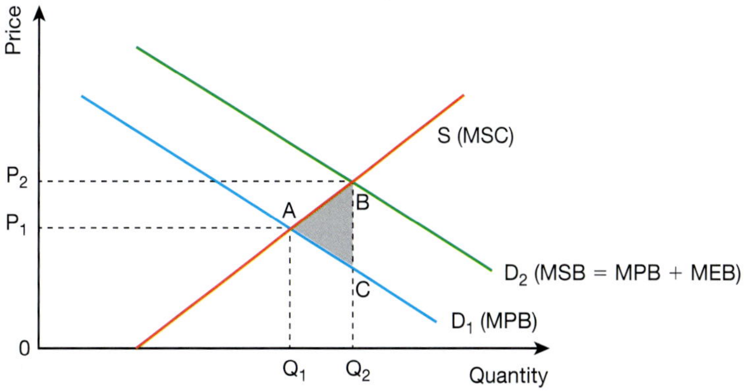

Figure 7.17 Positive externality ▲

The equilibrium position in the market is where the demand curve D_1 (representing marginal private benefit) crosses the supply curve S (representing marginal social cost), producing a price of P_1 and an output of Q_1. However, if all the benefits to society were taken into account, and not just the private ones, the demand curve would shift to the right with D_2 representing the marginal social benefit, consisting of both marginal private benefit and marginal external benefit. In a free market, there would under-production and under-consumption; if the positive externalities were taken into account, however, there would be a socially optimal equilibrium with a price of P_2 and a quantity of Q_2.

7.4.5 Deadweight welfare losses arising from positive and negative externalities

Deadweight loss is a measure of lost efficiency when the socially optimal quantity of a product is not produced. Non-optimal production can be caused by a positive or a negative externality. Externalities bring about a deadweight loss as a result of the differences between marginal social cost or benefit and marginal private cost or benefit.

Key term

Deadweight loss: the loss of economic efficiency that occurs when the socially optimal quantity of a product is not produced.

The deadweight or welfare loss is the decreased economic well-being caused by the existence of negative externalities. It represents a reduction in consumer surplus and producer surplus when output is restricted to less than the optimum level. It is shown by the shaded triangle ABC in Figure 7.16.

Link

For a discussion of deadweight loss under monopoly see below in this chapter.

There can also be a welfare gain in relation to positive externalities. It is shown by the shaded triangle in Figure 7.17.

7.4.6 Asymmetric information and moral hazard

Asymmetric information

Akerlof's Lemons

The 2001 Nobel Prize in Economics was awarded jointly to three American Economists – George Akerlof, Michael Spence and Joseph Stiglitz – "for their analyses of markets with asymmetric information".

Asymmetric information is a form of market failure that exists when one economic agent has more information than another enabling them to use that information advantage to exploit the other agent.

Key term

Asymmetric information: a situation where there is an unequal knowledge between economic agents involved in a transaction with the result that there is an advantage given to the party with the extra knowledge.

The single most important study of the nature and impact of asymmetric information was George Akerlof's 1970 paper "The Market for Lemons" in which he argued that in a market in which asymmetric information means that a seller has more information than the buyer regarding the quality of a product, this can cause the whole market to collapse or reduce it to an "adverse selection" of low quality products. Akerlof demonstrated this with reference to the second-hand car market in the United States.

In his study, Akerlof divided the second hand car market between high quality reliable cars which he referred to as "peaches" and poor quality unreliable cars as "lemons". To develop his argument, let us assume that

Akerlof's Lemons ▲

in a particular second-hand market peaches are valued at $20,000 and lemons at $10,000. In a market in which both buyers and sellers had perfect information, peaches would sell for $20,000 and lemons for $10,000. However, in this case the dealer/seller knows the quality of the cars and so which is a peach and which is a lemon. The buyer on the other hand is not an expert and does not know which is which. Asymmetric information exists, therefore, in that the dealer is in possession of information that the buyer has not and can potentially benefit from this.

This leads to market failure. Take first the position of the buyers. They will not be prepared to pay more than they believe the car is worth. They know peaches are worth $20,000 and lemons $10,000, but do not know which is which and so to mitigate against the risk are likely to offer a price between $10,000 and $20,000. If they believe there is a 50/50 chance of the car being a lemon then they are likely to offer a maximum of $15,000.

Looking at the position from the perspective of the dealer they will only be prepared to sell the low quality lemon and the high quality peach will not be offered for sale. Buyers will be faced with what Akerlof described as "adverse selection" in that the only cars available are of low quality as the only dealers prepared to accept $15,000 are selling lemons.

As high quality peaches are removed from the market, the value of the remaining low quality cars falls and buyers will now be prepared to pay less than $15,000 for cars. It is possible that once potential buyers realise only lemons are for sale, they may not wish to purchase them and so the whole market might collapse.

Asymmetric information has, therefore, resulted in market failure in the form of "adverse selection" and the potential collapse of the market.

However, in many countries throughout the world there are flourishing markets in which buyers can purchase reliable second-hand vehicles. The reason for this is that under certain conditions well informed economic agents (in this case car dealers) can improve their market outcome by signalling to poorly informed economic agents (in this case car buyers) information about the quality of their products.

Signalling

Michael Spence concentrated on asymmetric information in the jobs market. In particular he looked at how applicants for jobs might indicate (signal) to potential employers their talent, abilities and willingness to work hard and job suitability compared to other applicants by obtaining expensive high-level qualifications. This signalling of quality can equally be applied to the second-hand car market where dealers can signal the quality of used cars by offering guarantees, service histories of the cars and extended warranties.

Screening

Joseph Stiglitz looked at another way of dealing with the problem of asymmetric information particularly in the insurance market where companies do not have information about the potential risk positions of clients. Up to now we have been concerned with situations in which the seller has more information than the buyer, but in most insurance markets it is the other way round. For example, buyers of car insurance know more about their driving habits (careful or reckless) than insurers and similarly purchasers of health insurance know more than insurers about their lifestyle and underlying health conditions.

Stiglitz, in his 1976 paper, showed that insurers can give potential clients incentives to declare information on their individual risk situations through "screening". This normally involves insurance companies providing a range of different policies for its customers designed to distinguish between different risk categories of policyholders. These policies usually require completion of questionnaires relating to an individual's driving history or health conditions and companies invite customers to choose between alternative policies offering lower premiums in exchange for higher excesses/deductibles. In this way, low risk customers can identify themselves by being prepared to accept higher excesses/deductibles as they are less likely to make claims.

Key term

Moral hazard: a situation in which an individual or organisation takes a decision about how much risk to take in the knowledge that someone else will bear the cost of that risk.

Link

See section 7.3.3 in this chapter for more on the optimum resource allocation.

Moral hazard

Moral hazard occurs when someone increases their exposure to risk when insured because a person is more likely to take risks when someone else bears the cost of those risks. An individual or organisation, therefore, has an incentive to change their behaviour. For example, if a government promises to support businesses that are losing money, it can encourage those businesses to take greater risks than would otherwise have been the case. Just as asymmetric information can lead to market failure by creating adverse selection and the possible collapse of a market, moral hazard can create market failure through the principal-agent problem. This is explained more fully in the context of differing objectives of shareholders/owners and managers in section 7.7.5 of this chapter, but essentially refers to a situation in which one individual or group of owners (principals) of an asset hires an agent and gives them the ability to control and make decisions in relation to that asset, but retains ownership and responsibility for any costs or losses that are incurred. The problem arises if there is a conflict of interests or priorities between the principal and the agent such that the principals' interests are not met.

The principal-agent problem can arise in many situations. Take the example of an individual taking their car to a garage to fix a fault. The individual will not have as much knowledge as the garage and will not know whether all the repairs charged for were actually necessary or whether the parts supplied were the recommended or sub-standard ones. Similarly employers will not be able to monitor their employees at all times to know whether they are actually working particularly if the employees are working from home. The solution to these problems is to try to develop a system of rewards which encourages the objectives of agents to align with those of the principal.

7.4.7 The use of costs and benefits in analysing decisions

One of the problems with external costs and benefits is that they can be very difficult to measure with any degree of accuracy. For example, it might be the case that a factory causes pollution in a neighbourhood, but how do you actually put a price or value on such pollution? Of course, there may be ways of putting a figure on the consequences of pollution, such as the fall in value of properties nearby. It would be much more difficult, however, to put a monetary figure on a person who was finding it more difficult to breathe, although if the person had to take a number of days off work as a result of the breathing problems, it would be possible to calculate the wages lost as a result of the absence of work.

Key term

Cost-benefit analysis: a method used to evaluate large-scale investment projects which takes into account all possible costs and benefits.

One method which economists have used to aid the decision-making process when externalities are involved is cost-benefit analysis. It is an attempt to quantify the externalities that can exist in a neighbourhood. It could be used, for example, to analyse the wider impact of a particular investment project taking into account all of the costs and benefits involved, not just private ones. The advantage of cost-benefit analysis is that it can be used to calculate and compare the costs and benefits of an investment project to determine whether it is a sound and worthwhile decision. As a result of this, it is possible to discover if the benefits outweigh the costs and, if so, by how much.

Case Study

The Hong Kong-Zhuhai-Macau Bridge

The Hong Kong-Zhuhai-Macau Bridge is an example of a major infrastructure project that used cost-benefit analysis before a decision was taken to go ahead with the building of the bridge. It consists of a series of bridges and tunnels that will connect Hong Kong, Macau and Zhuhai, three major cities situated on the Pearl River Delta in southern China. The link is 55 km (34 miles) in length. It is the first major combined bridge and tunnel sea crossing project to be undertaken in China and is the longest sea crossing in the world. It cost US$18.8 billion to build, significantly more than the original estimated cost of US$10.7 billion. Construction began in 2009 and the bridge opened in 2018.

1 Justify, with reasons, why you would or would not support the building of this bridge.

Activity

Cost-benefit analysis

In groups of 3 or 4:

1 Identify an example of a major project in your country that was the subject of a cost-benefit analysis.
2 Identify the main private and external benefits and costs involved.
3 Evaluate the final decision.

The stages of a cost-benefit analysis

Table 7.6 shows the four main stages that are usually involved in a cost-benefit analysis of an investment project.

Table 7.6 The four stages of a cost-benefit analysis ▼

1 The identification of all the relevant costs and benefits involved in the project	This first stage of the process involves identifying all relevant costs and benefits, i.e. the private costs, the private benefits, the external costs and the external benefits.
2 The decision about the monetary value of all of the relevant costs and benefits involved in the project	The second stage of the process involves putting a monetary value on all of these costs and benefits, including those where a market price can be established and those where a market price is not easily established, such as placing a value on time.

3 The forecasting of the future costs and benefits involved in the project	The third stage of the process involves forecasting the future costs and benefits of an investment project into the future; this forecasting will be based on estimates of future costs and benefits.
4 The interpretation of the results of the cost-benefit analysis so that an appropriate decision can be taken	The fourth stage of the process involves the compilation of all of the data obtained as a result of the cost-benefit analysis and this can then be used to ensure that the decision-making process is an informed one.

The advantages and disadvantages of cost-benefit analysis

It should be clear, from what has been said, that the process of cost-benefit analysis has both advantages and disadvantages. These are shown in Table 7.7.

Table 7.7 The advantages and disadvantages of cost-benefit analysis ▼

The advantages of cost-benefit analysis	The disadvantages of cost-benefit analysis
It takes into account all of the various costs and benefits resulting from a proposed investment project.	It may be difficult to identify all of the relevant external costs and external benefits. For example, how wide will the spill-over or third-party effects be? It may therefore not be easy to decide on which costs and benefits to include in the analysis.
Many of the various costs and benefits will have market prices attached to them, making it relatively easy to calculate monetary values.	Some of the costs and benefits will not have market prices attached to them and this will make it much more difficult to calculate their monetary value. To overcome this problem, shadow prices can be used to estimate such values, but these shadow prices may be very difficult to estimate.
The process can analyse costs and benefits today, but also well into the future. This has the advantage that the cost-benefit analysis can take a long-term view of the possible consequences of an investment project.	The estimation of costs and benefits well into the future can be very difficult. There are forecasting techniques which can be used, but it is very difficult to estimate the costs and benefits of a project 10 or 15 years into the future. This raises the issue of the time value of money, i.e. where the value of the costs and benefits today will be different from their value in 10 or 15 years' time; this will therefore involve a process of discounting these future values.
All of the information obtained as a result of the cost-benefit analysis can be used to ensure that the correct decision is taken. It is therefore a very significant aid to the decision-making process.	Cost-benefit analysis is usually used to assess investment projects in the public sector and so even if the analysis suggests that an investment project would yield a net benefit to a community, there may be political reasons why it does not actually go ahead.
It provides a framework that is particularly useful for investment projects in the public sector. For example, it may be that as a result of the analysis, it is shown that the private costs are greater than the private benefits, but it may still go ahead if the total benefits of the project are greater than its total costs, taking all of the costs and benefits into account and not just the private ones. The analysis may therefore lead to a better allocation of resources in the economy.	It may be that if the external costs and benefits are taken into account, a decision to go ahead with a project may be taken, but this could involve public expenditure, the money for which will need to be obtained from somewhere.

Case Study

Bangalore (Bengaluru) Airport

Construction of the new airport at Bangalore, the third largest city in India, began in July 2005 and it was opened in May 2008. Its official name is Kempegowda International Airport. It is the third busiest airport in India, behind Delhi and Mumbai, and in 2019 it handled 33.3 million passengers. It has been built on 4,000 acres (1,600 hectares) about 40 kilometres (25 miles) from the centre of the city of Bangalore.

There are 29 international airlines and 6 domestic airlines operating out of the airport, connecting the city to over 50 destinations in India and the rest of the world.

Between the opening of the airport in 2008 and 2018, there was only one runway. However, it was always intended to build a second runway once this became necessary to deal with the number of passengers using the airport. A second runway has now been built and came into operation in December 2019.

It was also intended to eventually build a second terminal. The airport has operated with just one terminal since it opened, but this can only handle 20 million passengers annually. It has been expanded to handle an additional 5 million passengers annually, but a decision was taken in 2020 to begin construction of Terminal 2. The cost of building the new terminal is estimated to be US$430 million. The

first phase of this is expected to be ready by 2021.

1 Produce a cost-benefit analysis of the proposed second terminal at Bangalore Airport.
2 Justify, with reasons, why you would or would not support the building of this second terminal.

7.5 Types of cost, revenue and profit, short and long run production

Having looked at the basis of demand it is now necessary to look at the background to supply. The theory of the firm is concerned with the way in which firms in different market structures determine their price, output and competitive strategies.

The way in which firms go about making decisions on these issues depends upon the objectives of the firm and the market structure in which they operate. Although as we shall see later this may not always be the case, the traditional theory of the firm assumes that firms have one sole objective, which is profit maximisation.

We will begin by looking at costs.

> **Key term**
>
> **Profit maximisation**: a possible objective for a firm. In the traditional theory of the firm, this is assumed to be the sole objective and is at the output at which MC = MR.

7.5.1 *Short-run production function*

In analysing costs we need to see how production increases as factor inputs increase and make a distinction between the short run and the long run.

For example, if a supermarket receives a sudden increase in demand, it will be able to respond quickly, by perhaps increasing the number of staff or opening for more hours each day, but it will not, immediately, be able to build a new store. Hence, for a period of time, the supermarket will only be able to increase output by making use of additional variable factors. This period is known as the short run. Over a sufficiently long period, however, the supermarket will, if it believes the increase in demand to be permanent, be able to build a new store. This is the long run when all factors are variable and output can be increased by using any of them.

> **Key terms**
>
> **Short run**: that period of time in which at least one factor of production is fixed in supply and output can only be increased by using more of the variable factors.
>
> **Long run**: that period of time when all factors are variable and output can be increased by using more of all factors.

Key terms

Production function: the relationship between the quantity of inputs of factors of production and the resulting output.

Law of diminishing returns or law of variable proportions: as increasing quantities of a variable factor are added to fixed quantities of other factors, the return to the variable factor will eventually diminish.

Link

For more on law of diminishing returns see Chapter 1, section 1.3.1.

The relationship between the factor inputs required, in producing a product and the final output is known the production function.

Production and costs in the short run

Definition and calculation of total product, average product and marginal product; the law of diminishing returns (law of variable proportions)

The way output and hence costs vary in the short run is governed by the law of diminishing returns (also sometimes referred to as the law of variable proportions) which states that as increasing quantities of a variable factor are added to fixed quantities of other factors, the return to the variable factor will eventually diminish. This is illustrated by Table 7.8 and Figure 7.18.

Number of workers	Total physical product of rice (TPP)	Average physical product (APP) of rice TPP/No. of workers	Marginal physical product (MPP) of rice ΔTPP/ΔNo. of workers
			8
1	8	8	
			20
2	28	14	
			23
3	51	17	
			29
4	80	20	
			40
5	120	24	
			24
6	144	24	
			10
7	154	22	
			6
8	160	20	
			2
9	162	16	
			−12
10	150	15	

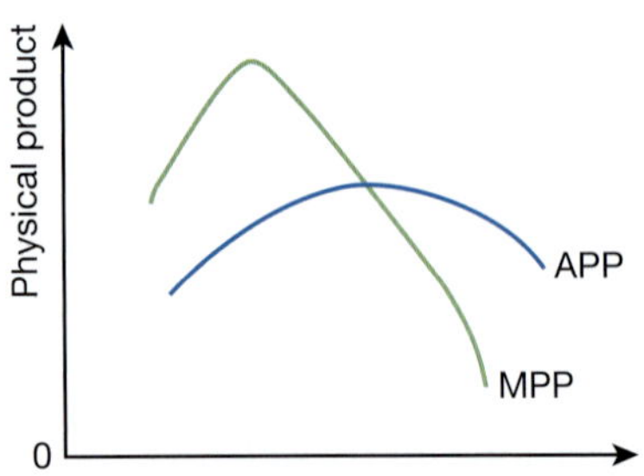

Figure 7.18 Average and marginal physical product ▲

The table shows how the production of rice varies as the number of workers employed increases. We assume that:

- the supply of other factors – land and capital – are fixed
- the state of technology is constant
- all workers are homogeneous – no worker is more or less efficient than any other.

As we can see from Table 7.8, as the number of workers increases, the total physical product (TPP) or total output increases until the ninth worker is employed. When the tenth is employed, TPP falls because there are too many workers being employed for the quantity of land and capital. The other two columns show the average physical product (APP) and the marginal physical product (MPP).

APP is the output per worker. APP = TP/quantity of labour

MPP is the increase in TPP as a result of employing one more worker. MPP = ΔTPP/Δ quantity of labour.

Table 7.8 shows that APP increases up to the employment of the sixth worker and then declines, while MPP increases up to the fifth worker and then declines. It can be seen, therefore, that both the APP and MPP eventually decline as more workers are employed with all other factors of production fixed. This is the law of diminishing returns.

The reason for this is that beyond a certain number of workers employed, they will begin to get in each other's way.

The relationship between average and marginal physical product is illustrated in Figure 7.18.

Key terms

Total physical product (TPP): the total output produced from a combination of fixed and variable factors.
Average physical product (APP): total physical product divided by the quantity of the variable factor (TPP/quantity of the variable factor).
Marginal physical product (MPP): the addition to total physical product resulting from the employment of an additional unit of the variable factor (ΔTPP/Δ quantity of the variable factor).

Getting it right

When drawing the APP and MPP curves, make sure the MPP and APP curves intersect at the maximum point of the APP curve.

7.5.2 Short-run cost function

We can now use the analysis of the short-run production function to show how a firm's costs will vary in the short run. The main cost concepts involved are illustrated in Table 7.9. In the short run some factors are fixed in supply. These will therefore be fixed costs that do not vary with output. The costs of the variable factor, labour in the example above will, however, rise with output; these are known as variable costs.

Key terms

Fixed costs: costs which do not vary with output.
Variable costs: costs which increase with output.

We assume that the fixed costs are \$500 and the variable costs are \$100 per worker. The TPP figures for column one are taken from Table 7.8.

Fixed costs are the costs of the fixed factor which do not vary with output. Interest on any loans a firm has taken out are an example of a fixed cost in that it will have to be paid whether or not anything is produced.

Variable costs are the costs of the variable factor, in this case labour, which will rise and fall with output. If there is no production, there will be no variable costs.

Total costs are equal to fixed costs + variable costs. This is shown in Figure 7.19.

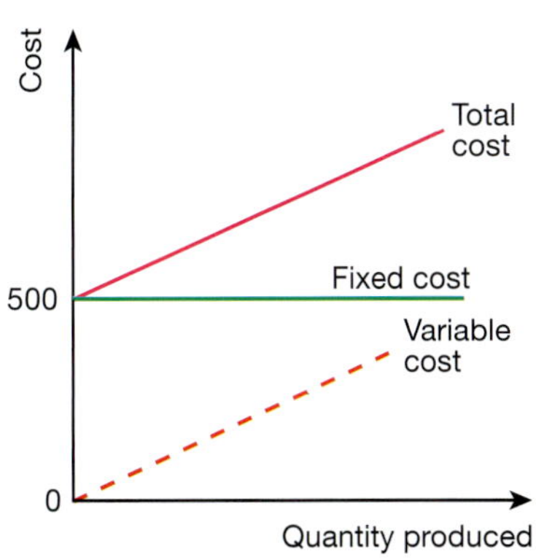

Figure 7.19 Quantity produced ▲

Average fixed costs (AFC) are the fixed costs per unit of output. AFC fall rapidly to begin with and then very slowly as the fixed costs are spread over a larger output. The shape of the curve is a rectangular hyperbola.

AFC = FC/Q

Average variable costs (AVC) are variable costs per unit of output. AVC fall to begin with as the optimum combination of factors of production is approached and then rise rapidly as diminishing returns set in giving a U-shaped curve.

AVC = VC/Q

Link

See section 7.3.3 in this chapter for more on the optimum resource allocation.

Key terms

Average fixed costs (AFC): Fixed costs per unit – AFC = FC/Q

Average variable costs (AVC): Variable costs per unit – AVC = VC/Q

Average costs: Costs per unit of production – AC = TC/Q or AFC + AVC

Marginal costs: the addition to total cost when output is increased by one additional unit – MC = ΔTC/ΔQs

Average costs are the cost per unit of production.

AC = TC/Q or AFC + AVC

Average total costs (ATC or AC) decline quickly over low ranges of output as AFC are falling rapidly and AVC are falling or rising only slowly, as diminishing returns set in. Over higher ranges of output AVC are rising rapidly and although AFC are still falling they are doing so very slowly and the fall is insufficient to offset the rising AVC. The result is that AC rise rapidly.

Marginal cost is the increase in total cost when output increases by a single unit. If output is increasing by more than one unit then

MC = ΔTC/ΔQ

The AVC, AFC, ATC and MC curves are illustrated below.

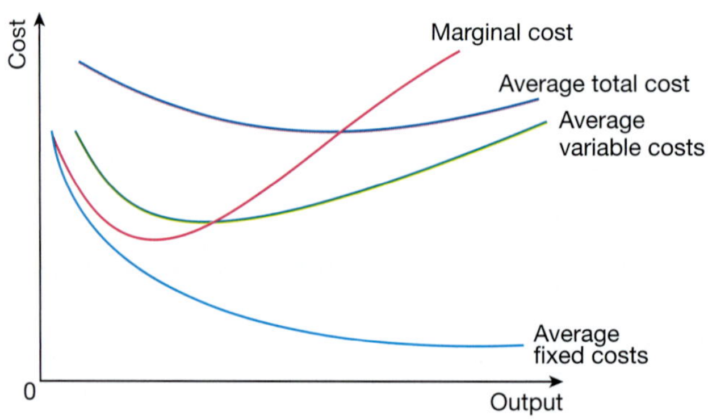

Figure 7.20. A firm's cost curves ▲

Table 7.9 summarises these costs for a typical firm.

Table 7.9 A firm's costs ▼

Column 1 (Q)	Column 2	Column 3	Column 4 (FC + VC)	Column 5 (FC/Q)	Column 6 (VC/Q)	Column 7 (TC/Q) or AFC + AVC	Column 8 ΔTC/ΔQ
TPP (Q)	Fixed costs (FC)	Variable costs (VC)	Total cost (TC)	Average fixed costs (AFC)	Average variable costs (AVC)	Average costs (AC)	Marginal cost (MC)
8	500	100	600	62.5	12.5	75	
							5
28	500	200	700	17.9	7.1	25	
							7.7
51	500	300	800	9.8	5.9	15.7	
							3.4
80	500	400	900	6.25	5	11.25	
							2.5
120	500	500	1000	4.2	4.1	8.3	
							4.2
144	500	600	1100	3.8	4.2	7.6	
							10
154	500	700	1200	3.2	4.5	7.7	
							16.7
160	500	800	1300	3.1	5	8.1	
							50
162	500	900	1400	3	5.6	8.6	

Getting it right

When drawing the average variable cost, average cost and MC curves make sure the marginal cost curve intersects with the average variable and average cost curves at their minimum points.

Progress question

6 Complete the table below.

Output	TC	FC	VC	AFC	AVC	AC	MC
0	110						
1	170						
2	220						
3	260						
4						80	
5						84	
6	560						
7							220

Key terms

Increasing returns to scale: a situation in which a given increase in the quantity of factor inputs leads to a greater proportionate increase in output.

Decreasing returns to scale: a situation in which a given increase in the quantity of factor inputs leads to a smaller proportionate increase in output.

Constant returns to scale: a situation in which a given increase in the quantity of factor inputs leads to an equal proportionate increase in output.

Long run average cost (LRAC) curve: a curve which shows how costs per unit (average costs) change as output changes in the period when the supply of all factors of production can be increased.

Short run average cost (SRAC) curve: a curve which shows how costs per unit (average costs) change as output changes in the period when at least one factor of production is fixed in supply.

7.5.3 *Long-run production function*

No fixed factors of production

The short-run production function and corresponding short-run costs are based on the fact that there is at least one fixed factor. In the long run, all factors are variable and so it is possible for the firm to increase output by increasing all factors by the same amount or in proportion. This means that the firm is able to increase the scale of production.

In the long run, when all factors are variable, firms will be able to produce a given output with any combination of factors. Given the assumption that firms' only objective is to maximise profits, they will try to produce their chosen output by employing factors of production in the combination that minimises their costs of production.

Returns to scale

If, as a firm increases its scale of production by increasing all factors of production by the same percentage, output increases by a greater percentage, e.g. if factor inputs increase by 10 per cent and output increases by 15 per cent, then the firm is said to be experiencing increasing returns to scale. If on the other hand output increases by a smaller percentage then the firm is said to be experiencing decreasing returns to scale. Finally, if output increases by the same percentage as the increase in factor inputs, then the firm will be experiencing constant returns to scale.

7.5.4 *Long-run cost function*

SRAC and LRAC

We can now move on to look at costs in the long run. As we have seen, in the long run all factors are variable and, as a consequence, as a firm expands, it is able to increase the quantity of factors that were previously fixed in supply. This means that the long run average cost (LRAC) curve will be a combination of a series of short run average cost (SRAC) curves as shown in Figure 7.21.

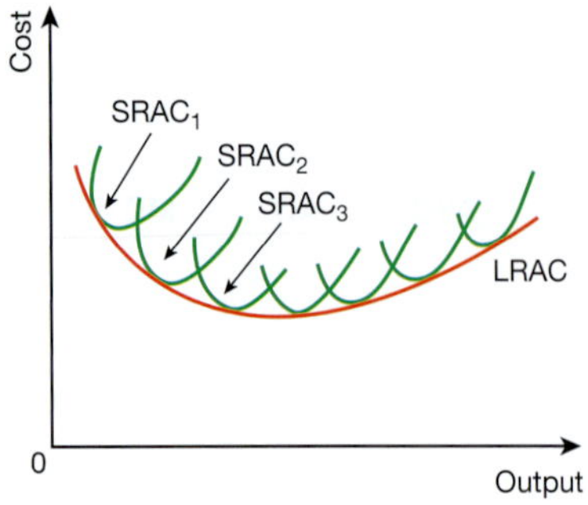

Figure 7.21 LRAC envelope curve ▲

If we take the case of a car assembly plant operating with just one production line (the fixed factor) it will be producing on SRAC1. As it expands its output by introducing new production lines in the long run it will move to a new SRAC curve. With two production lines it will be operating on SRAC2, with three production lines SRAC3 and so on. The long run average cost (LRAC) curve joins all the points, giving the lowest cost of producing a given output. As there are, in the long run, a potentially infinite number of SRAC curves close together, the LRAC is drawn as a smooth envelope curve.

> **Key terms**
>
> **Economies of scale**: reductions in LRAC as the scale of production increases.
>
> **Diseconomies of scale**: increases in LRAC as the scale of production increases.

7.5.5 *Relationship between economies of scale and decreasing average costs*

What determines the shape of the LRAC curve?

As Figures 7.22 to 7.23 show, the LRAC curve could take a number of shapes. Declining long run average costs are the result of economies of scale and increasing long run average costs result from diseconomies of scale.

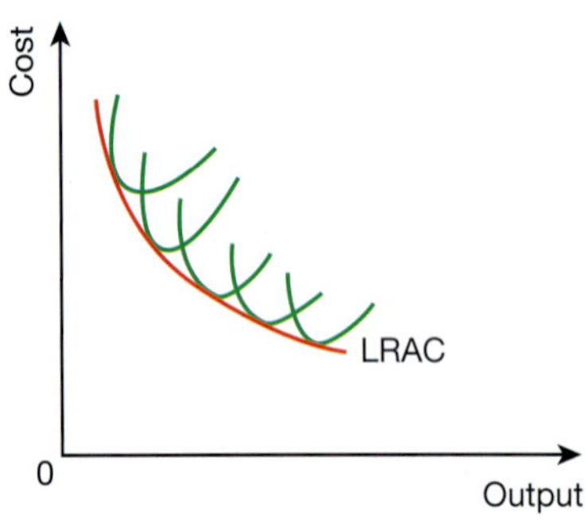

Figure 7.22 Falling LRAC curve ▲

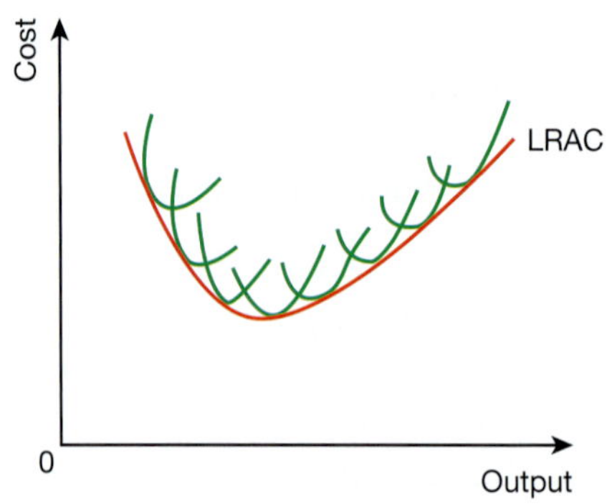

Figure 7.23 U-shaped LRAC curve ▲

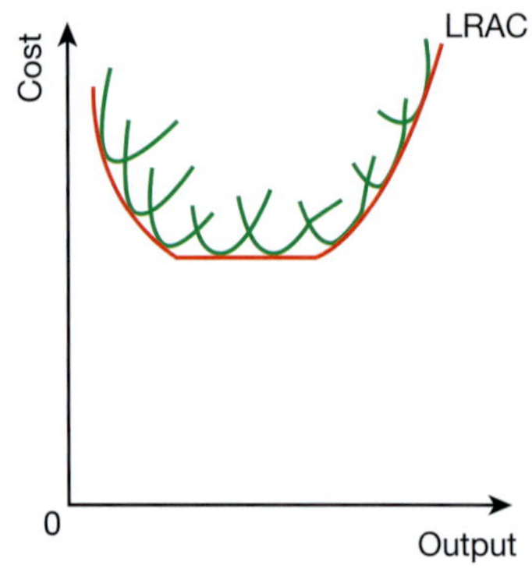

Figure 7.24 Falling, constant and rising LRAC curve ▲

> **Key terms**
>
> **Internal economies of scale**: reductions in LRAC as a result of the firm itself increasing the scale of production.
>
> **External economies of scale**: reductions in LRAC from a firm as a result of the industry growing in size.

7.5.6 *Internal and external economies of scale*

Economies of scale

Economies of scale can be internal economies of scale, resulting from an increase in the scale of production of an individual firm leading to a movement down along its LRAC curve as output increases, or external economies of scale resulting from the growth and interrelationship of all firms in the industry. External economies of scale are available to all firms in the industry, large or small, and therefore bring about a lowering of the entire LRAC curve of the firm.

Internal economies of scale

The following are a number of possible economies of scale that might be available to a firm.

Key terms

Technical economies: reductions in LRAC as a result of the improvements and innovations in the production process as the firm increases the scale of production.

Economies of increased dimensions: reductions in LRAC which arise as a result of increasing the size of a container. Increasing the surface area will lead to a greater increase in volume, thereby reducing unit costs.

Technical economies

Technical economies can take a number of forms.

- Economies of increased dimensions. Economies of increased dimensions are linked to the mathematical relationship between the surface area of a container and its volume. The cost of producing a container is normally linked to its surface area. Doubling the length of each of the sides of a cubic container will increase its surface area, and therefore the costs by four times. However, the volume of the container has increased by eight times, thus halving the unit costs of carrying say, oil, compared to the original container. This is the reason for shipping firms building larger and larger supertankers.
- Division of labour. Large organisations are able to practise division of labour and mass production which small firms cannot. As we saw in Chapter 1, dividing the production process into a number of smaller tasks, each performed by a single individual, will increase the output from a given number of workers, thereby reducing average costs.
- Large capital equipment. Large-scale companies producing very high output can afford to buy large specialist equipment to reduce unit costs which would be uneconomic for a small firm because the high cost involved would be spread over too low an output.
- Research and development. Large organisations may be able to fund their own research and development departments to develop cost-saving processes and innovations. This is particularly important in industries such as pharmaceuticals.

Key terms

Financial economies of scale: reductions in LRAC resulting from the fact that large firms have access to a wider range of sources of finance and on more preferential terms than small firms because they are seen as a lower risk.

Shares: a unit of ownership in a private or public limited company.

Financial economies

Financial economies of scale result from the fact that larger organisations are able to access greater amounts of funds from a wider range of sources and on better terms than small firms. Plcs have access to the stock market and can raise finance through the issue of shares. Large firms are often seen by banks as less risky than small ones and as a result they are able to borrow money at lower rates of interest.

Marketing economies

Large organisations are often able to obtain discounts on products as a result of buying in large bulk. Large supermarket chains, such as Tesco and Walmart, are able to obtain goods from suppliers at significantly lower prices per unit than a small local store. In addition, such organisations can spread their marketing budget over a larger output and range of products. Large firms may even have their own distribution channels and transport.

Managerial economies

Large organisations, particularly private and public limited companies, are likely to be able to afford to employ highly qualified specialist staff. They may even be able to afford their own departments in areas such as exporting, marketing, human resources and administration. Although these may be expensive, they are likely to increase productivity and output significantly and so bring down unit costs.

Key terms

Risk-bearing economies of scale: as a firm grows in size it is able to move into other product areas and markets which reduces the risks associated with a decline in any one of them.

Diversification: the process in which a firm moves into a number of different product areas, usually to reduce risk or as a mechanism for growth.

Risk-bearing economies

As a firm grows in size, it may be able to obtain risk-bearing economies of scale by diversifying into other related or non-related areas to reduce the risks associated in operating in a single market. Large supermarket chains, such as Tesco, not only provide groceries and food, which was their original market, but have now diversified significantly into areas such as clothing, banking, insurance and the sale of fuel. This means that should one market collapse, they will be able to fall back on others. Large tobacco producers are another example of diversification to reduce risk.

Economies of scope

This refers to reductions in average costs as a result of a firm producing two or more products. They derive from the fact that advertising and distribution costs can be spread across a range of products. It may be possible to reduce unit costs by transporting a range of products to a given destination rather than just one product. Common raw materials can be used across brands as with Volkswagen using common parts across its VW, Audi and Skoda ranges. It may also be that synergies are created in that a range of products may be seen by consumers as more desirable than a single product.

Getting it right

Remember that all firms are able to gain external economies of scale and not just large ones.

External economies of scale

External economies of scale are available to all firms in an industry regardless of their size as the industry as a whole grows and develops. If an industry becomes concentrated in a particular area, it may benefit from improved transport links and infrastructure. Ancillary industries may develop to provide supplies of components. Specialist labour with specific skills may become available and colleges and universities in the area may develop courses specifically linked to the industry. All of these developments are likely to increase the productivity of all firms and reduce their average costs.

7.5.7 Internal and external diseconomies of scale

Diseconomies of scale

- Internal diseconomies: Diseconomies of scale refer to increases in LRAC as a firm increases its scale of production. They can be internal, affecting a single firm as it grows, or external, affecting all firms in the industry irrespective of their size. Examples of internal diseconomies of scale include managerial diseconomies and alienation of workers. As the firm increases in size, the complexity of the organisation may increase and managers may find it more difficult to effectively co-ordinate production and monitor performance. Communication may become more difficult, time-consuming and costly.

  In extremely large organisations, workers may experience alienation, feeling that they are merely "a small cog in a large wheel". Their tasks are likely to be repetitive and they may regard them as boring. They may feel unimportant and distanced from management and any involvement in decision-making. As a result, they may lack motivation and consequently productivity suffers, leading to falling productivity and rising unit costs. There is also some evidence that larger organisations suffer more from labour disputes. It is also the fact that in large complex organisations labour disputes amongst a few key workers can cause all production to be disrupted.

- External diseconomies: these refer to increases in LRAC as the size of the industry increases. They are outside the control of the individual firm. As the industry grows, particularly if it is highly localised, it can create external costs, in terms of pollution problems, which may impact local residents and employees. The growth of the industry may also place a strain on the local services and infrastructure which increase firms' costs. Transport costs may increase as a result of increased congestion in an area. Growth of an industry may also increase the demand for scarce resources, such as raw materials and skilled labour, driving up prices and wages. All of these factors can increase an individual firm's costs. A good example of the impact of external diseconomies of scale is in the financial sector. Many financial firms wish to set up in major financial capitals such as London, New York and Tokyo in order to benefit from existing infrastructure and expertise, but as a consequence can face extremely high rental costs, arising from competition for a limited number of premises, in such areas.

Case Study

Increasing size of supertankers

April 2020 saw the Hyundi Merchant Marine Corporation (HMMC) launch the world's largest container ship, the HMM Algeciras. It is longer than 4 rugby pitches is 61 metres wide and 14 stories high.

This is just one of an increasing number of ultra-large containerships being built. HMMC has 69 supertankers in its fleet, but is dwarfed by Maersk Lines who have over 700.

These ships are designed to operate on the world's most important and lucrative sea route from Asia to Europe, bringing low-cost goods from South Korea, Malaysia and China to European shops.

Given that these supertankers can cost a up to $200 million each (the HMM Algeciras cost $140 million), why are shipping companies building such gigantic ships?

The answer is economies of scale. To make it viable for shippers and retailers to transport goods halfway round the world, huge numbers of containers must be transported at one time enabling European retailers to buy in bulk from low-cost suppliers. Fully laden these ships are capable of carrying nearly 24,000 containers, the equivalent of the amount that could be carried by a freight train 44 miles long.

Another factor is the price of oil. Oil makes up a large percentage of the cost of operating these ships and its rising cost means that shipping lines need to find ways of reducing the unit costs of carrying each container.

These supertankers incorporate the latest technology so not only are the engines incredibly fuel efficient, but the sophisticated computer technology

means that they are capable of operating with a crew of just 13.

All this makes it possible for TVs made in China to be sold at a competitive price in the UK.

1 Explain the economies of scale available to shipping lines and retailers identified in the extract.
2 Explain any other economies of scale that might be available to large shipping lines and retailers.
3 Are there any diseconomies of scale that might result from using such huge supertankers?

Key terms

Total revenue: the aggregate amount received by a firm from the sale of its products. TR = P × Q

Average revenue: revenue per unit sold. AR = TR/Q = P × Q/Q = P

7.5.8 Definition and calculation of revenue: total, average and marginal revenue (TR, AR, MR)

In order to find a firm's profit maximising price and output, we need to look at both costs and revenue. There are three revenue concepts that are important.

- Total revenue is the revenue received from the sale of a product. As we have seen, TR = P × Q
- Average revenue is the revenue per unit. This is calculated by AR = TR/Q

  As TR = P × Q, then AR = P × Q/Q
  Therefore, at any given output AR = Price.

Because AR = P, it follows that the demand curve facing a firm, which shows how much will be purchased at any given price, must be the same as its average revenue curve which shows the relationship between average revenue and sales.

- Marginal revenue is the addition to total revenue when sales increase by an additional unit and is calculated by MR = ΔTR/ΔQ

Key term

Marginal revenue: the addition to total revenue when output/sales are increased by an additional unit.

Total, average and marginal revenue curves

The shape of the firm's revenue curves depends on whether it is a price taker that charges the same price for all units sold or a price maker that has to reduce the price in order to sell more units. As we shall see later, whether a firm is a price taker or price maker depends upon the market structure in which it operates.

Revenue curves for a price taking firm

Total, average and marginal revenue for a price taking firm are given in Table 7.10 below. We assume all units are sold for $10. It can be clearly seen that in these circumstances AR = MR.

Table 7.10 Total, average and marginal revenue for a price taker ▼

Output	Price	Total revenue	Average revenue	Marginal revenue
1	10	10	10	10
2	10	20	10	10
3	10	30	10	10
4	10	40	10	10
5	10	50	10	10

Revenue curves for a price making firm

Table 7.11 shows the total, average and marginal revenue for a price making firm on the assumption that the price of all units is reduced by $1 each time the firm wishes to sell additional units.

Table 7.11 Total, average and marginal revenue for a price maker ▼

Output	Price	Total revenue	Average revenue	Marginal revenue
1	10	10	10	10
2	9	18	9	8
3	8	24	8	6
4	7	28	7	4
5	6	30	6	2
6	5	30	5	0
7	4	28	4	-2

Here, both average revenue and marginal revenue fall continuously and, because in order to sell an additional unit the price of all units has to be reduced, marginal revenue is always below average revenue and falls at twice the rate of average revenue.

Total, average and marginal revenue curves for price taking and price making firms are illustrated in Figures 7.25 and 7.26.

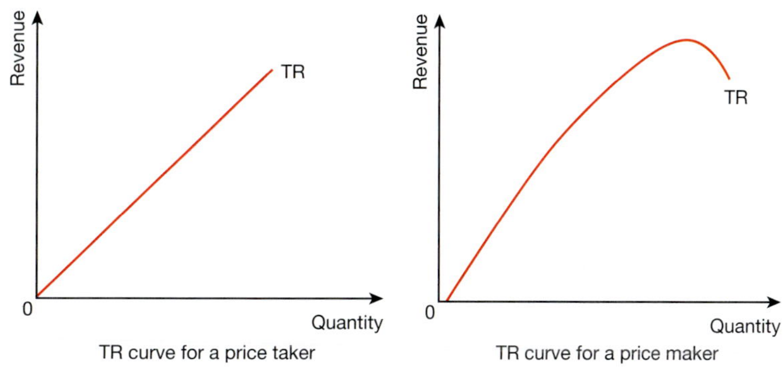

Figure 7.25 Total revenue curves for a price taker and price maker ▲

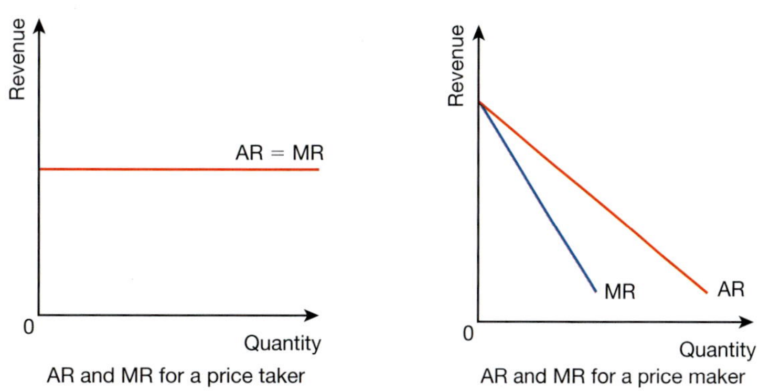

Figure 7.26 Average and marginal revenue curves for a price taker and price maker ▲

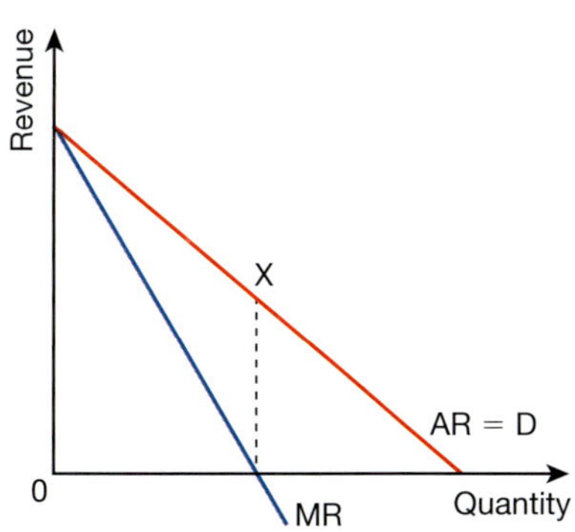

Figure 7.27 Relationship between price elasticity of demand, average, marginal and total revenue for a downward-sloping demand curve ▲

Relationship between price elasticity of demand, average, marginal and total revenue for a downward-sloping demand curve

The relationship between price elasticity of demand, average, marginal and total revenue for a downward-sloping demand curve is shown in Figure 7.27.

As the graph shows, the marginal revenue curve falls at twice the rate of the demand (average revenue) curve. The point where the MR curve crosses the horizontal axis corresponds to the midpoint of the D (AR)

Link

For more on point elasticity of demand see Chapter 2, section 2.2.5.

curve, designated X. As we saw from our study of point elasticity of demand in Chapter 2, at the midpoint of a straight-line demand curve, the price elasticity of demand is unity (PED = −1). Total revenue for a firm is maximised at the point where the price elasticity of demand is unity. It follows, therefore, that:

where MR = 0, the PED = −1 and total revenue is at a maximum.

7.5.9 Definition of normal, subnormal and supernormal profit

Getting it right

Make sure you have a clear understanding of the difference between economists' and accountants' views of profit.

Profit maximisation

Having looked at the way in which costs and revenue vary as output and price change we are now in a position to bring together the various cost and revenue concepts in order to find a firm's profit maximising output and price together with the level of profit made in a particular market structure. This is known as the profit-maximising equilibrium position for a firm. This is the price and output from which, once it is achieved, there will be no tendency for change for the firm.

In order to explain this further, we first need to understand exactly what economists mean by profit. The economists' definition of profit differs from that of accountants. Accountants' definition of profit is the difference between revenue and expenses, costs and taxes. Accountants also have a different definition of revenue from economists in that they include not only income from the sale of goods and services, but also any earnings from interest, dividends and rents.

For the economist, profit is the difference between total revenue (TR) and total cost (TC).

As we have seen, total revenue is the amount received by producers from the sale of their products.

Total cost is made up of all the payments made to the factors of production, i.e.:

- rent, which is the payment for land
- wages, which are the payment for labour
- interest, which is the payment for capital
- profit, which is the reward to the entrepreneur for organising and taking the risks associated with production.

This immediately poses an issue. Clearly profit cannot, at the same time, be the difference between total revenue and total cost and an element of total costs, unless we are referring to different types of profit. This is, in fact, the case. Economists distinguish between three types of profit – normal profit, subnormal profit and supernormal or abnormal profit.

Key terms

Normal profit: the amount of profit that can be made in the next most profitable enterprise. It is the opportunity cost to an entrepreneur of being in a particular line of business and is included in a firm's costs of production.

Subnormal profit: profit less than normal profit.

Supernormal or abnormal profit: any profit in excess of normal profit.

Normal profit refers to the minimum payment required to keep an entrepreneur in a particular line of business. If this amount is not made the entrepreneur will leave the industry for the next most profitable business venture, and so in this sense normal profit represents the opportunity cost of a particular line of business – the amount that can be earned in the next most profitable enterprise. Normal profit is regarded as a cost of production because, if this is not earned, the entrepreneur will leave the industry. It is, therefore, included in the firm's AC curve. Normal profit is not a specific sum of money; it will differ from entrepreneur to entrepreneur and may vary over time as market conditions change.

- Subnormal profit is a situation in which a firm is making less than normal profit.
- Supernormal profit is any profit in excess of normal profit.

7.5.10 *Calculation of supernormal and subnormal profit*

As normal profit is regarded by economists as a cost of production, then a firm will be earning normal profit at the price and output at which TR = TC. At this point, the price per unit will be equal to the average cost of production, i.e. P = AC.

It follows, therefore, that if a firm is making supernormal profit then total revenue will exceed total cost (TR > TC) and price per unit will be greater than average costs of production (P > AC).

Similarly if a firm is experiencing subnormal profits then total revenue earned will be insufficient to cover total costs and price per unit will be less than average costs of production. The firm may be covering the costs of the other factors of production (land, labour and capital), but entrepreneurs believe the level of profit is insufficient to make it worth continuing in this particular enterprise. Whether the business will close immediately or remain in business for a short period is discussed in detail later in this chapter in the section on shut down points in the discussion of perfect competition

Getting it right

Make sure you have a clear understanding of the difference between normal and supernormal (abnormal profit).

Table 7.12 Summary of profit ▼

Total revenue > Total cost	Firm is making supernormal profit
Total revenue = Total cost	Firm is making normal profit
Total revenue < Total cost	Firm is making less than normal profit and could be making a loss

Profit maximisation using total cost and revenue curves

If we now bring the cost and revenue concepts together, we are in a position to find a firm's profit maximising output and go on to establish the price charged and the amount of profit obtained. As we have seen, Profit is TR – TC and so the profit maximising output is at the point where there is the greatest difference between TR and TC. This is illustrated in Figure 7.28.

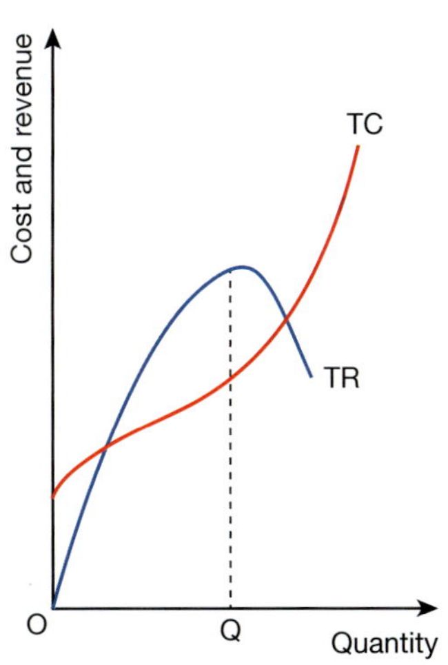

Figure 7.28 Profit maximisation using total revenue and total cost curves ▲

The disadvantage of using total cost and total revenue curves is that it is not straightforward to identify the profit maximising price. As a result it is more common to analyse profit maximisation by looking at average and marginal cost and revenue.

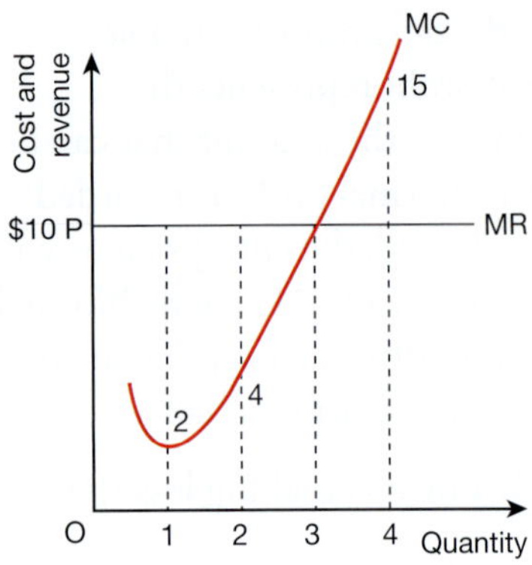

Figure 7.29 Profit maximising output (MC = MR) ▲

Profit maximisation using marginal and average cost and revenue curves

Profit maximising output

The profit maximising output is found at the point where marginal cost = marginal revenue (MC = MR). This is shown in Figure 7.29.

When MR > MC, it is advantageous for the firm to increase output as each unit produced and sold brings in more revenue than it costs to produce and hence adds to overall profit. In Figure 7.29 the first unit adds $10 to revenue, but only $2 to costs, adding $8 to profits. Producing the second unit adds another $10 to revenue and only $4 to costs and so total profits are increased by a further $6. The third unit adds the same amount to revenue as costs, but if the firm produces a fourth unit, costs increase by $15 and revenue by only $10, therefore reducing profits by $5. Clearly it will not pay the profit maximising firm to produce this unit or any other where MR < MC. Consequently the firm will maximise profit at the output where MR = MC.

Getting it right

The profit maximising firm will always produce the output at which MC = MR.
Price at this output is given by AR.
Profit per unit at this output is given by AR – AC.
Total profit at this output is given by TR (the area of the rectangle under the AR curve) – TC (the area of the rectangle under the AC curve).

Profit maximising price and profit level

To obtain the price charged by the firm and the level of profit made at the profit maximising output, we need to look at the firm's average revenue and average cost curves. These are shown in Figure 7.30.

If the profit maximising output is at Q, then the price will be given by the AR curve, i.e. P (remember that price = AR at any given level of output). Profit is given by TR – TC at this output. We can calculate the total revenue by multiplying the price by the quantity sold, which gives the area OPAQ. The total cost at this output is given by multiplying the average cost per unit by the output, which gives the area OCBQ. The difference, the area CPAB, is the level of profit. Since TR > TC, the firm in this case is making supernormal profit.

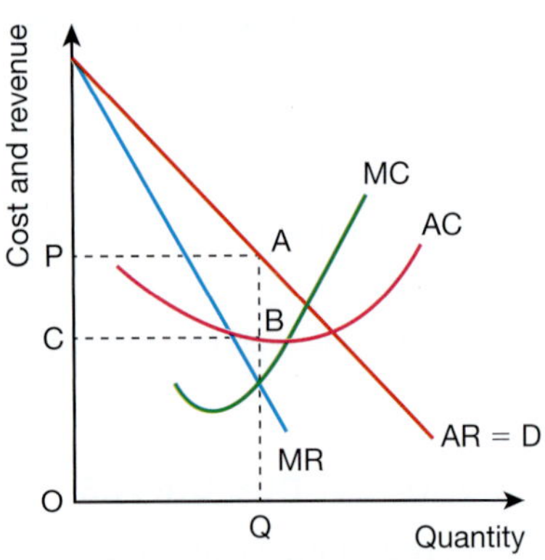

Figure 7.30 Profit maximising price and level of profit ▲

7.6 Different market structures

7.6.1 *Perfect competition and imperfect competition: monopoly, monopolistic competition, oligopoly, natural monopoly*

We are now in a position to apply the analysis of profit maximisation to the operation and performance of firms in different market structures experiencing markedly different competitive environments. The main types of market structure are:

- perfect competition
- monopoly and natural monopoly
- monopolistic competition
- oligopoly.

> **Key term**
>
> **Imperfect competition**: market structures in which individual firms have the ability to influence price – monopoly, monopolistic competition and oligopoly.

Monopoly and natural monopoly, monopolistic competition and oligopoly are collectively referred to as imperfect competition.

A crucial difference between perfect and imperfect competition is that in perfect markets firms have no control over the market price (they are price takers), whereas in imperfectly competitive markets firms have at least some control over the market price (they are price makers). The reasons for this and the implications for the price, output and profits of firms are explained in the sections below.

> **Activity**
>
> **Market structure**
>
> Identify an example of each of the four forms of market structure in your country.

7.6.2 Structure of the listed markets as explained by numbers of buyers and sellers, product differentiation, degree of freedom of entry and availability of information

Perfect competition

In their purist form perfectly competitive markets exist nowhere in the world although there are markets which approximate to them, particularly those for agricultural products produced worldwide as well as the Forex market and the market for stocks and shares.

> **Key term**
>
> **Perfect competition**: an "ideal type" market structure in which there are infinite numbers of producers each producing a homogeneous product, freedom of entry to and exit from the market by firms, an infinite number of consumers each of whom are indifferent between suppliers and perfect knowledge within the market, all of which means that all firms within the market are price takers, unable to influence the price of the product by their own actions.

The benefit to economists of studying perfect markets is that they provide us with an "ideal type" model which can be compared with actual real-world firms in terms of their behaviour and performance.

Characteristics of perfect competition

- infinite numbers of small producers
- all firms produce a homogeneous (identical product) product
- infinite numbers of consumers
- consumers are indifferent as to which firm they buy from – no brand or company loyalty
- perfect knowledge throughout the market; all decisions made by producers or consumers are instantaneously known to all in the market
- freedom (zero) cost entry to and exit from the market
- perfectly elastic supply of all factors of production

The implication of these characteristics is that all firms in the industry are price takers. The price will be determined in the market through the interaction of demand and supply for the product and each individual firm will have to charge this price. No individual firm by its own actions is able to influence the price.

Take the example of a firm that attempted to increase its profits by raising its price. Instantaneously all consumers in the market would know about it because of the assumption of perfect knowledge, and because consumers are indifferent as to the producer, they will shift their demand to other suppliers. These suppliers will be able to obtain the factors of production to meet this increase in demand. The consequence is that the firm which raised its price will go out of business.

Figure 7.31 shows the relationship between the setting of the market price for a product and that charged by an individual firm. The demand curve for the industry will be downward sloping, but since all firms will have to sell all units of output at the same price, the demand curve will be perfectly elastic (a horizontal straight line) at the market price and AR(P) = MR at all levels of output.

The diagram for the industry indicates that both consumer and producer surplus are at a maximum which means the industry is allocatively efficient.

Progress question

7 Given the characteristics of a perfectly competitive market listed above, explain why an individual firm would not reduce its price in a perfectly competitive market.

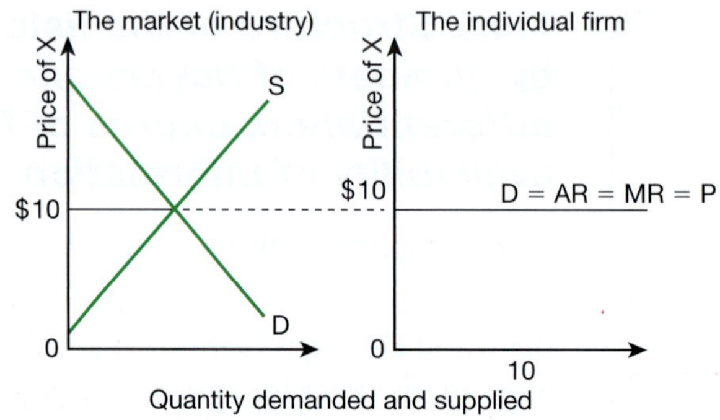

Figure 7.31 Industry and firm in perfect competition ▲

Characteristics of monopoly and natural monopoly

The opposite extreme to perfect competition in terms of competitiveness is monopoly, which is a situation in which one firm dominates the market. This market structure is an example of imperfect competition.

Monopolies are able to exist because of barriers to entry which prevent new firms from entering an industry to compete. The nature and importance of these barriers to entry are discussed in the sections below.

A natural monopoly is a specific example of a monopoly market which exists in a situation in which high start-up costs or extensive economies of scale means that the most efficient way of providing the product is through a single monopoly firm.

Key terms

Monopoly: sole supplier of a product.

Natural monopoly: an industry or service which is most efficient when run as a monopoly because the average costs would be higher if the market was shared between more than one supplier.

Monopolistic competition: a market with many firms producing similar but differentiated products.

Product differentiation: the process of creating real or perceived differences between products.

Monopolistic competition

Monopolistic competition is a market in which there are a very large number of firms producing products that are similar, but differentiated in some way from one another so that they are not perfect substitutes, such as the quality of service provided by hairdressers competing with one another in a major city.

The main characteristics of monopolistic competition are:

- very large numbers of firms
- very large numbers of consumers
- product differentiation
- freedom (zero cost) of entry to and exit from the market.

Oligopoly

An oligopoly is a market in which a few large firms control the majority of the market. A fundamental characteristic of such markets is that firms operate in an environment of uncertainty and mutual interdependence. Unlike firms in perfect or monopolistic competition, oligopolistic firms must take into account the impact their individual pricing decisions and competition strategies are likely to have on their competitors and the way in which these competitors might react.

Oligopoly markets may be national or, as in the case of the Organisation of Petroleum Exporting Countries (OPEC), international and may produce homogeneous or virtually identical products or, as in most cases, differentiated products. As we shall see later, competition between oligopolistic firms tends to be non-price in nature.

> **Key terms**
>
> **Oligopoly**: a market dominated by a few firms which are mutually interdependent.
>
> **Mutual interdependence**: a characteristic of oligopolistic markets in which each firm is aware that any action it takes will have an impact on other firms and as a consequence will have to take this into account when making any decisions.

7.6.3 Barriers to entry and exit

Barriers to entry refers to any factors that restrict new firms from entering a particular market. They are present to a greater or lesser extent in monopoly, monopolistic competition and oligopoly. The existence of such barriers gives incumbent firms in the market some ability to fix prices.

> **Key term**
>
> **Barriers to entry**: obstacles which prevent new firms entering a particular industry.

Barriers to entry

There are a number of barriers to entry, including the following.

Legal barriers

Legal monopolies protect an organisation by law. In many countries, public utilities such as water, postal services and nationalised industries are given monopoly status by the government.

Copyright and patents can also be included under this heading. Copyrights guarantee sole rights to producers over new inventions, processes, music and intellectual property rights for a period of time preventing others from exploiting them. An example is Microsoft in the area of computer operating systems and software. Patents are also particularly important in the pharmaceutical industry.

Cost barriers

Cost barriers. The existence of high start-up costs and economies of scale can act as barriers to the entry of new firms. If a great deal of capital investment is required to enter a particular market in order to achieve the minimum efficient level of scale, then it will be very difficult for new firms to enter the industry. The problem will be compounded if these costs are likely to be sunk costs in the future. This would mean that the initial high costs could not be recouped if the firm was forced to exit the market. These potentially high exit costs would make new firms even less likely to enter the market.

It is also possible that firms already in a market may be experiencing significant economies of scale which enable them to produce at low unit costs. New firms will not immediately be able to benefit from these economies of scale and so existing firms may be able to charge low prices with which new entrants could not compete.

Market barriers

Market barriers. Brand loyalty may sustain a monopoly, if not create one. If a brand becomes identified with a product, such as Coca-Cola with cola drinks and Kellogg's with cornflakes, then this may create a loyalty to the product which creates some monopoly power.

Physical barriers

Physical barriers. These are commonly linked to the control of sources of supply. Control of a substantial proportion of the supply of a raw material can enable a firm to acquire monopoly power in a market. For example, the Potash Corporation of Saskatchewan controls some 20 per cent of the world's potash supplies. OPEC is another example in the oil industry.

Link

See section 7.7.3 in this chapter for more on external growth of firms through takeovers and mergers

Other barriers

Other possible barriers to entry include:

- Mergers and takeovers. A firm can obtain a monopoly in an area by taking over other companies in the industry.
- Location. Small shops and post offices can have a localised monopoly in a small village.
- Networking barriers. Some products are valued highly by consumers because they are widely used by a very large number of other individuals. Such network effects mean that an individual purchaser gains increased benefit from the fact that there are multiple users of the product. Examples of significant networking effects include on-line shopping sites such as eBay and social media sites such as Facebook. Where incumbent firms in a market have strong network effects then it places them at an advantage in the market and it may be difficult for new firms to enter.
- Switching cost barriers. In some cases consumers may be reluctant switch to a new product or provider of a service because of the high monetary and non-monetary costs of doing so. For example, an individual may not wish to switch to an alternative printer, even if it is initially cheaper, if the associated cost of repeat purchases of compatible printer cartridges is much higher. Similarly individuals may be discouraged from switching to an alternative telephone, internet or utility provider because of the financial costs of purchasing new equipment together with the time taken in searching for a new supplier as well as the risk of loss of service during the transfer process. Such switching costs are emphasised by incumbent firms in the market. The reluctance of consumers to switch to alternative products or service providers clearly gives existing firms an advantage and may deter new entrants into the market.
- Aggressive pricing strategies. An established monopolist or large oligopoly firm in a market may embark on a price war or adopt strategies such as limit pricing and predatory pricing which involve setting prices at very low levels in order to deter new entrants. These low prices may mean that the firm may not maximise profits and may even incur subnormal profits or losses in the short run.

Link

For a detailed consideration of limit and predatory pricing see discussion of contestable markets in section 7.6.4 and section 7.8.4 in this chapter on other pricing policies.

Activity

Barriers to entry

Identify an example of a monopoly, monopolistically competitive firm and oligopolistic firm operating in your region or country and in each case identify the barriers to entry into their particular market which enable them to maintain their position and influence the price of their product.

Key term

Barriers to exit: obstacles which make it difficult or expensive for a firm to leave an industry.

Link

For more on barriers to exit see discussion of contestable markets in section 7.6.4 in this chapter.

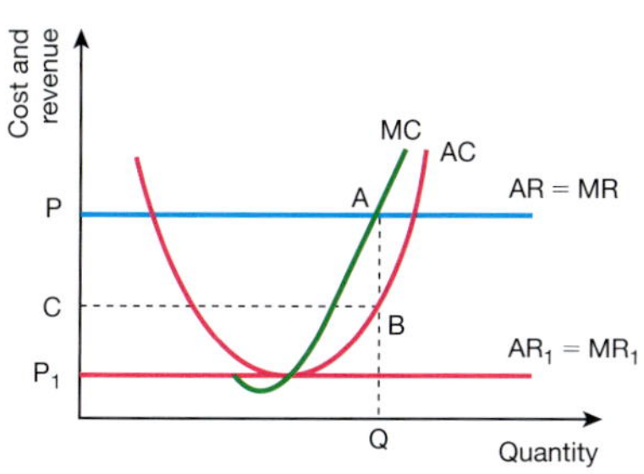

Figure 7.32 Short-run supernormal profits and market adjustment ▲

Barriers to exit

In some markets barriers to exit may be as important as barriers to entry and may in fact actually act as a barrier to entry into a market in the first place. Examples include the market for public utilities and privatised railway franchises which in some countries are regulated by governments and required to provide guaranteed service obligations such as the need to operate services on unprofitable routes. Such requirements increase firms' operating costs and at the same time make it difficult to leave the market and may discourage them from entering the market. The possibility of incurring potentially high sunk costs which cannot be recouped such as advertising or the purchase of expensive industry specific capital costs may also deter firms from entering a market.

7.6.4 *Performance of firms in different market structures*

Performance of firms in perfect competition: short- and long-run equilibrium

In the short run it is possible for a perfectly competitive firm to experience supernormal profits or less than normal profits.

Figure 7.32 illustrates a firm in perfect competition making supernormal profits in the short run. The market price has been established at P, which means that firms are making supernormal profit equal to CPAB. As a result, new firms will be attracted into the industry, shifting the industry supply curve to the right and reducing the market price. This shifts the horizontal D (AR) = MR curve for the individual firm downwards. This process continues until there are no longer any supernormal profits to be earned to attract new firms. This will occur at the point when price has fallen to P_1 with the new D (AR_1) = MR_1 curve tangential to the minimum point of the AC curve and firms making normal profits.

Figure 7.33 shows a firm in the opposite situation making a loss equal to PABC because at the point where MC = MR, AC > AR. Firms in this position will ultimately leave the industry and the industry supply curve will shift to the left driving up the market price. This process will continue until the price has risen to a level where AR is just equal to AC and the firm is making normal profits.

It is clear therefore that while it is possible for firms in perfect competition to earn supernormal profits or make losses in the short run, the only long-run equilibrium for the firm and industry occurs at the point where all firms are making normal profits as illustrated in Figure 7.34.

As we can see, at the profit maximising equilibrium:
MC = MR = AR (P) = AC

The fact that P = MC and P = Minimum AC means that the firm is both allocatively and productively efficient.

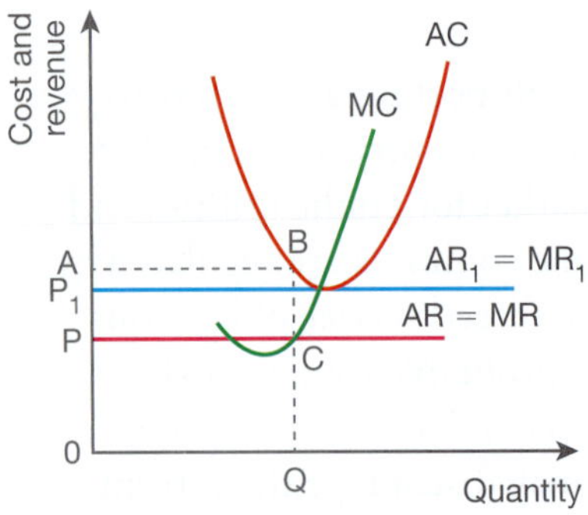

Figure 7.33 Less than normal profits in the short run and market adjustment ▲

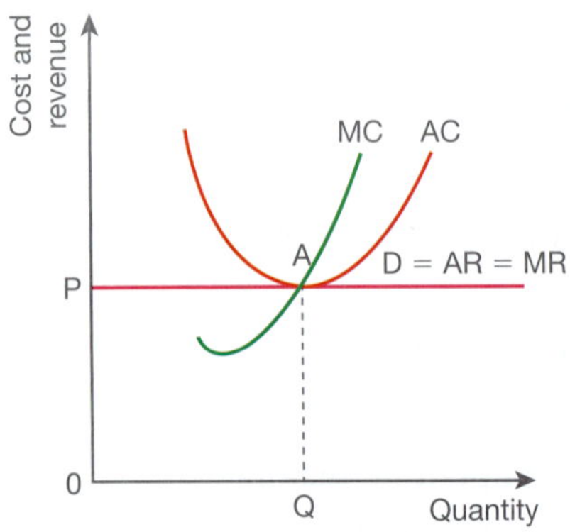

Figure 7.34 Long-run equilibrium for a firm in perfect competition ▲

> **Key terms**
>
> **Long-run equilibrium for the firm in perfect competition:** MC = MR = AC = AR. Firms are both productively efficient, P = minimum AC, and allocatively efficient, P = MC.
>
> **Long-run equilibrium for the industry in perfect competition:** there is no tendency for the number of firms in the industry to change.

Supply curve for the firm in perfect competition

It is possible to derive a unique supply curve for a firm in perfect competition. As we saw in Chapter 2, a supply curve shows how much a producer is prepared to offer for sale over a range of prices over a period of time. Figure 7.35 derives the supply curve for the firm in perfect competition. If the price is P the firm will maximise profits where MC = MR at point X and supply output Q. If the price rises to P_1 the firm will again produce where MC = MR, point Y and supply output Q. If price rises to P_2 the firm will produce at point Z and supply Q2.

Because the profit maximising firm will always produce the output at which MC = MR and all firms in perfect competition are price takers so that Price = MR, all the points X, Y and Z lie on the firm's MC curve.

In perfect competition, therefore, the firm's supply curve is its MC curve.

Shut down points for the firm

There are certain prices, however, at which the firm will not produce at all. As we saw above, if a firm is making losses it will eventually have to leave the industry and consequently it will be supplying nothing. The question is, how quickly will the firm leave the industry?

The following numerical example will illustrate this.

Take a firm currently producing 100 units.

At this output TR = \$1000 and TC = \$1200 made up of \$800 in FC and \$400 VC. AR = TR/Q = \$1000/100 = \$10 and AC = TC/Q = \$1200/100 = 12. AFC = \$8 and AVC = \$4.

In the long run, this firm must cover all its costs and since it is making an overall loss of \$200, in the long run it must close down. In order to cover its TC the firm must set a price (AR) which at least covers AC. Hence, in the long run, a firm can only stay in business and supply a product if price is at least equal to its AC. This means that the firm will have to shut down in the long run if price falls below minimum AC.

The long run shut down point for a firm occurs at the point where P = minimum AC.

This means that the long run supply curve for the perfectly competitive firm is only that part of the MC curve above minimum AC. This is shown by LY in Figure 7.35.

Should this firm close down immediately?

If it does, its TR will clearly be 0. However, in the short run the firm will still have to cover its FC of \$800. This means that it will have TR = 0 and TC = \$800. It will make a greater loss (\$800) by shutting down immediately than by staying in business until it can exit the industry with no FC to pay. However, if in this case the TC of \$1200 was made up of FC of \$1100 and VC of \$100, the firm should close down immediately because by staying in business losses are increased to \$900. As long as the firm is covering its VC, it should stay in business because it will have a surplus of TR over VC which can contribute to the payment of the FC and, therefore, reduce losses. Clearly the shutdown point in the short run occurs where the firm is just covering its VC and the loss is the same whether it continues to produce or leaves the industry immediately. The lowest price at which a firm can produce in the short run is that equal to minimum AVC.

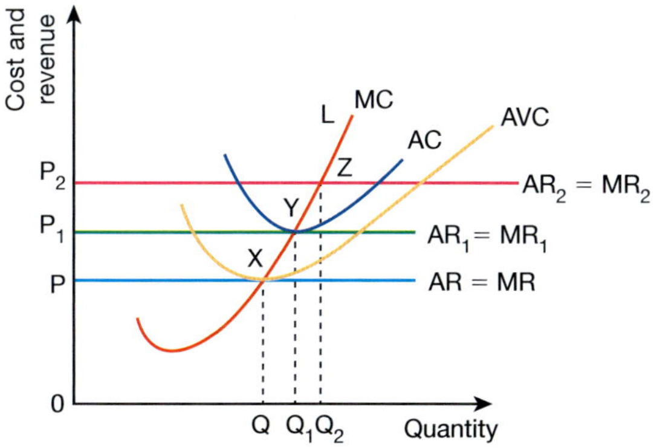

Figure 7.35 Supply curve for a firm in perfect competition ▲

The short run shutdown point for a firm occurs at the point where P = minimum AVC.

This means that the short run supply curve for the perfectly competitive firm is only that part of the MC curve above minimum AVC. This is shown by LX in Figure 7.35.

Equilibrium price and output in monopoly

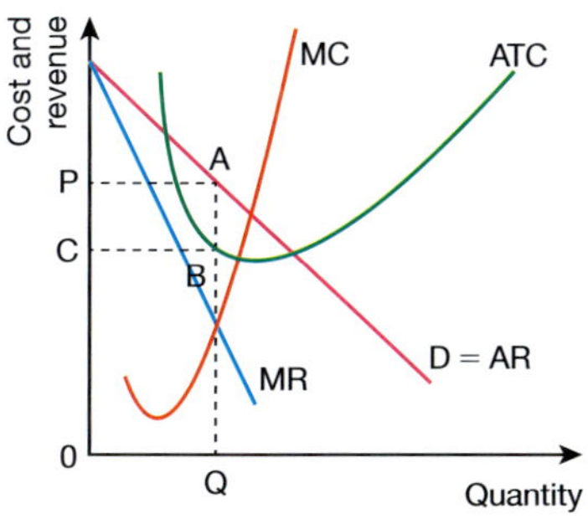

Figure 7.36 Equilibrium price and quantity for a profit maximising firm in monopoly ▲

As the monopolist is a price maker it will face downward-sloping demand (AR) and MR curves. These, combined with the AC and MC curves, give the profit maximising position shown in Figure 7.36.

The profit maximising output is at Q where MC = MR; the price at this output is given by the AR curve and the firm is making supernormal profit. Unlike perfect competition, new firms cannot enter the industry to take advantage of these supernormal profits and thus the monopoly is able to make supernormal profits in the long run.

Natural monopoly

The role of economies of scale in the creation of monopolies has already been indicated. Economies of scale are particularly important in the analysis of natural monopolies. A natural monopoly exists in situations where it would be inefficient and a wasteful duplication of resources for there to be more than one firm operating in the market. Examples include: public utilities such as water, gas and electricity, or railways where having different firms duplicating the required infrastructure to the same area or over the same routes would clearly be wasting scarce resources. Natural monopolies typically have very high start-up costs and because they experience economies of scale over most of their production, the minimum efficient scale of production is only achieved at an extremely high level of output.

> **Key term**
>
> **Minimum efficient scale of production**: the level of output at which lowest LRAC begin.

The LRAC curve for a natural monopolist is, therefore, downward sloping throughout its length which means that the associated LRMC curve is always below it as shown in Figure 7.37. The profit maximising monopolist will wish to produce at Q where MC = MR, but this output will not enable the full benefits of the economies of scale to be obtained.

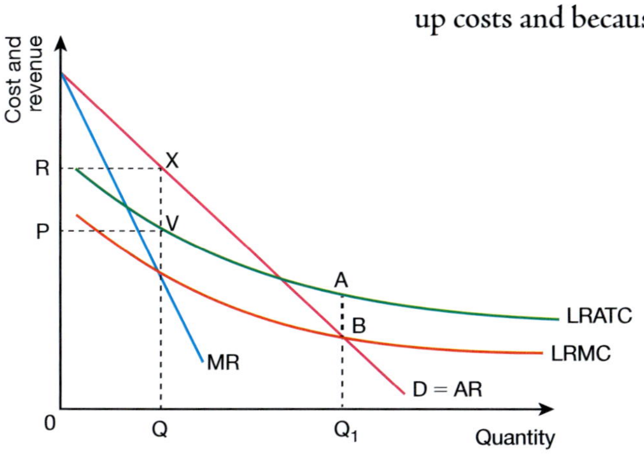

Figure 7.37 Natural monopoly ▲

The allocatively efficient position occurs where Price = MC which occurs at an output of Q_1 with a price equal to B. However, at this point price is below LRAC and so the firm would be operating at a loss. Therefore, if the government deems the service to be sufficiently important to be provided at this price it must take it into state ownership or provide a subsidy.

Price discrimination

Key term

Price discrimination: the practice of selling the same product at different prices in different markets

It is possible for firms with significant market power, particularly monopolists, to practise what is known as price discrimination. Referring to Figure 7.36 above, it can be seen that at the profit maximising price is at P. However, the demand (AR) curve indicates that a number of consumers would be prepared to pay a higher price. As we saw in Chapter 2, the difference between what an individual is prepared to pay for a product and the amount they actually pay is known as consumer surplus.

Link

See Chapter 2, section 2.5.1, for a detailed discussion of consumer surplus.

If a monopoly can separate out some or all of these individuals and charge them the price they are prepared to pay it, will clearly increase profits. Charging individuals different prices in different markets, when this is not based on cost differences, is known as price discrimination. Most firms with some form of market power are able to exercise price discrimination provided certain conditions are met. The different types of price discrimination, conditions necessary for them to be effective for firms and an evaluation of their welfare effects are discussed in detail later in this chapter.

Link

For detailed analysis of price discrimination see section 7.8.3 in this chapter.

Monopoly and perfect competition compared

Price and output

It is often argued that a monopoly will charge a higher price and produce a lower output than is the case under perfect competition. Figure 7.38 analyses the issues.

The perfectly competitive industry will produce QC at price PC, which is the point where price equals marginal cost. If the industry is now taken over by a single firm so as to become a monopoly then AR is no longer equal to MR and we need to draw in a new MR curve below the AR curve. The monopolist will now equate MR with MC to give an output of QM and a price PM. This has resulted in a reduction in output and an increase in price.

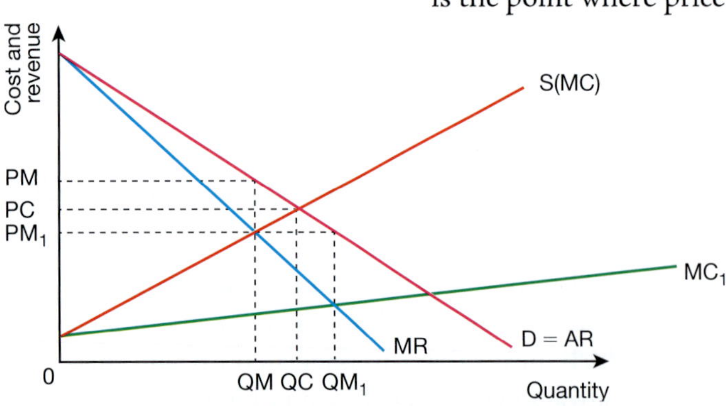

Figure 7.38 Price and output under perfect competition and monopoly ▲

However, this assumes that when the perfectly competitive industry becomes a monopoly the cost curves remain the same. It is probable, though, that the monopoly will now be able to enjoy economies of scale, which will reduce costs. If this is the case, it is possible that the MC curve will fall sufficiently (shown by MC_1) to intersect with the MR curve to give a higher output and lower price than in the perfectly competitive situation. This is shown by output QM_1 and price PM_1.

Efficiency and X-inefficiency in the short- and long-run

Efficiency

Efficiency is the optimum use of resources and it is useful at this point to remind ourselves of the various types of efficiency.

Static efficiency is concerned with efficiency at a moment in time and incorporates productive and allocative efficiency.

Productive efficiency is achieved when Price = minimum AC.

Allocative efficiency is achieved when Price = MC. At this point consumer and producer surplus are at a maximum.

Technical efficiency and X-inefficiency

Technical efficiency is achieved when a firm produces the maximum possible output with given resources utilising the best available technology. Economists use the term X-inefficiency to describe the situation where technical efficiency is not present within a firm. This is often linked to the concept of organisational slack.

Dynamic efficiency refers to efficiency over time resulting from innovation and the development of new products.

Looking back at Figures 7.34 and 7.36 showing the long-run equilibrium positions of firms in perfect competition and monopoly, we can see that the perfectly competitive firm is both productively and allocatively efficient, while the monopoly firm is both productively and allocatively inefficient.

The analysis of allocative efficiency in perfect competition and monopoly is developed in Figure 7.39.

Under perfect competition the price will be PC and the output QC. The total consumer surplus is given by the areas 1 + 2 + 3 + 4 + 5 and producer surplus by 6 + 7 + 8. Consumer and producer surplus are both at a maximum and so the industry is allocatively efficient. Consumer welfare is maximised. When the industry becomes a monopoly the output falls to QM and price rises to PM. Consumer surplus has been reduced to areas 1 + 2 and producer surplus has increased to 3 + 4 + 6 + 7. Not only has there been a redistribution of welfare away from consumers to producers, but there has been an overall loss of welfare of 5 (lost consumer surplus) + 8 (lost producer surplus). This is known as a *deadweight loss* in that it is completely lost to society. The area 5 + 8 is known as a *welfare loss triangle*.

Although the monopoly is neither allocatively or productively efficient, as we saw in Figure 7.38, it is possible for the monopoly to be more dynamically efficient than a perfectly competitive industry if it experiences economies of scale and uses its supernormal profits for research and development and the introduction of new products.

Key term

X-inefficiency: the inefficiency that can occur in a monopoly when production is not at the lowest point on the average total cost curve. It is where production takes place at a cost above the average and marginal cost curve due to a lack of strong competition in an industry and to organisational slack in a firm.

Link

For further analysis of the concept of organisational slack see section 7.8.2 in this chapter.

Link

For more on the various types of efficiency see sections 7.3.1–7.3.4 in this chapter.

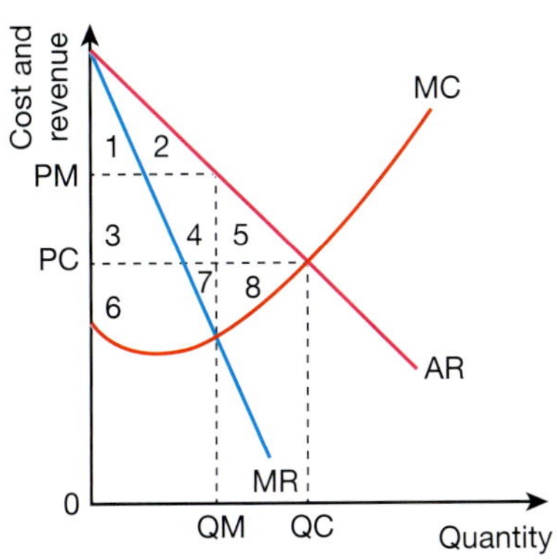

Figure 7.39 Allocative efficiency in perfect competition and monopoly ▲

It is also the case, as we shall see later in this chapter, that some monopolies operate in markets which are contestable, which means that the behaviour of firms is closer to the competitive than monopoly models discussed.

Variety and innovation

It is sometimes argued that because a monopoly is the sole producer of a product with no competition there is no incentive to increase the variety of products, to innovate or undertake investment into the development of new processes and products.

The A380 Airbus ▲

However, an alternative argument is that the security from competition enjoyed by monopolies together with their supernormal profits means that they are prepared to take the risks and incur often massive costs associated with developing new products and innovations because they know their market will still be there even if they fail. Firms in competitive markets may not be prepared to take the risks associated with such developments because of the risk of losing market share.

Examples of firms with some degree of market power that support this view include: Microsoft which continues to develop new versions of its Windows operating system and Office software; and the European airline corporation Airbus which invested $16 billion in the production of the A380, the world's largest passenger airliner, in an attempt to challenge Boeing's monopoly of the large airline market.

Link

For an evaluation of the welfare effects price discrimination see section 7.8.3 in this chapter.

Price discrimination

As indicated earlier in this section, monopolies are in a position to practise price discrimination. The issues surrounding price discrimination and the public interest are discussed in section 7.8.3 of this chapter.

Link

The characteristics of monopolistic competition have been identified in section 7.6.2 in this chapter.

Performance of firms in monopolistic competition – short- and long-run equilibrium

As the name suggests, this form of competition has elements of both monopoly and perfect competition. Examples of monopolistic competition include hairdressers, solicitors, restaurants and garages.

The crucial difference between monopolistic and perfect competition is the fact that there is product differentiation; individual firms are producing similar but not identical products. An example would be hairdressers in a particular locality that offer essentially the same service, but may provide a different range or quality of service. Product differentiation may simply be in packaging. Hence an individual firm will have a monopoly of its own product although the product may have a great many similar substitutes. This means that consumers may have some degree of loyalty to a particular firm or brand. For example, a family may always have their cars serviced at a particular garage because it has provided a reliable, quality service over a number of years.

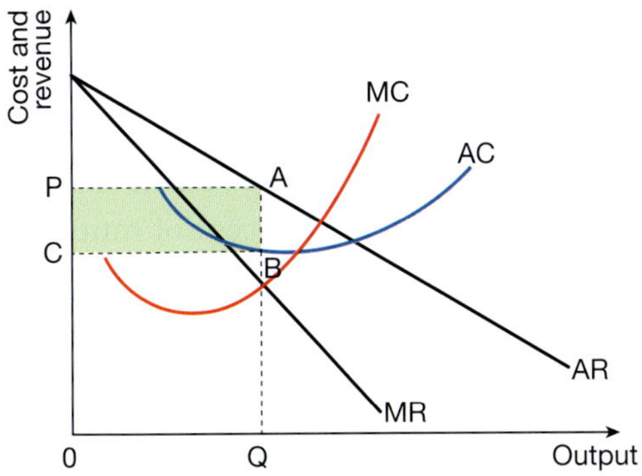

Figure 7.40 The short-run equilibrium for a firm in monopolistic competition ▲

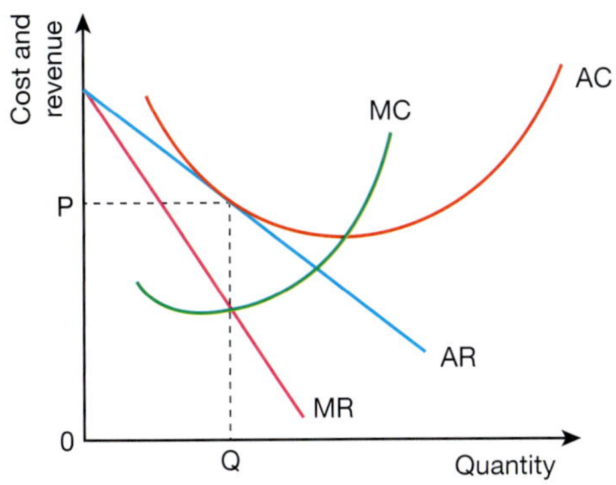

Figure 7.41 Long-run equilibrium for a firm in monopolistic competition ▲

This all means that the demand curve facing an individual firm in an industry will be downward sloping. If the garage mentioned above raises its price, it will lose some market share, but not all, as some people remain loyal because of the quality of service. If the garage reduces its price then it is likely to attract more customers, but not the whole market because some consumers will remain loyal to other garages.

At the same time, however, the demand curve will be relatively elastic because the nature of monopolistic competition is that there are many other firms providing similar substitutes.

In Figure 7.40 the profit maximising output is at Q where MC = MR, the price is P and the shaded area represents the firm's supernormal profit. Apart from the fact that the demand curve is significantly more elastic, the diagram is the same as that for monopoly. The difference, however, is that this is only a short-run equilibrium for the monopolistically competitive firm.

The supernormal profits will attract new firms into the industry. Assuming that the total demand for the product remains the same, this increase in the number of firms will mean that the demand for any single firm's product will fall. As a result the individual firm's AR and MR curves will move inwards towards the origin until there are no further supernormal profits to attract new firms into the industry. This will occur when the AC curve is tangential to the downward-sloping AR curve. This is illustrated in Figure 7.41.

The final position has all firms charging the same price and so competition tends to be non-price, for example advertising, promotion, range and quality of service and after-sales service.

Activity

Monopolistic competition

Identify three firms in your area that operate in a monopolistically competitive market and explain the non-price methods they use to compete with their rivals.

Advantages and disadvantages of monopolistic competition

The advantages and disadvantages of monopolistic competition are summarised in Table 7.13.

Table 7.13 Advantages and disadvantages of monopolistic competition ▼

Advantages	Disadvantages
Wide variety of differentiated products	Price higher and output lower than in perfect competition
Prices likely to be lower and output higher than under monopoly	Price > MC – Allocatively inefficient
High levels of competition encourage firms to keep costs down	Price > minimum AC – Productively inefficient This also means firms have excess capacity. Because there is a large number of firms producing very similar products, they are not producing at their maximum capacity (the minimum point on the AC curve). Consumers pay for this through higher prices
High levels of competition encourage firms to provide high-quality products	Non-price competition may be wasteful in terms of resources, e.g. advertising campaigns creating minor differences between products

Performance of firms in oligopoly

In terms of value of output, oligopolies are the dominant form of market structure worldwide. An oligopoly is a market dominated by a few large firms each producing a large number of brands. Few in this sense is not an absolute number, but is linked to the concept of mutual interdependence. The number of firms in the industry is sufficiently low for each seller to have to take into account the actions and reactions from others in the market to any strategic decisions it might take. A few firms operating in a market will know that their prices and competition strategies are interrelated. If firm A is considering reducing its prices or increasing its advertising budget in order to increase its market share, it will know that other firms in the market are unlikely to take no action in response. Firm A is aware of this and needs to take the likely responses of its competitors into account in formulating its decision.

Oligopolistic markets are also characterised by high barriers to entry similar to those which exist in monopoly discussed earlier in this chapter.

The mutual interdependence and consequent uncertainty caused by having to take into account the possible behaviour of rivals in oligopolistic markets means that, unlike the other types of market structure considered earlier in this chapter (perfect competition, monopoly and monopolistic competition), there is no single model of the equilibrium for a firm in oligopoly.

Link

For more on barriers to entry see section 7.6.3 in this chapter.

This will depend upon how firms respond to the actions or anticipated actions of rivals and may change for a particular market over time.

Within oligopolistic markets there is a constant tension within an individual firm as to whether to collude with its rivals or compete with them. Collusion brings security and a guarantee of some market share, but is unlikely to enable an individual firm to maximise its profits.

Competition with other firms might bring about increased profits but there is the risk of retaliation from other firms which might lead to a price war and eventual bankruptcy for the firm.

Analysis of the behaviour of firms in oligopolistic markets, therefore, needs to look at both collusive and non-collusive models.

Collusion and the prisoner's dilemma in oligopolistic markets, including a two-player pay off matrix

Collusive oligopolies

Cartels

This section should be read in conjunction with section 7.7.4.

Collusion can take two forms – formal and informal. Formal collusion involves the creation of a cartel, which is an agreement between firms to fix price and output of a product and may also involve common marketing strategies. The most famous cartel in the world is OPEC in the oil industry.

Key term

Cartel: a formal agreement between firms to collude, usually to fix prices and output.

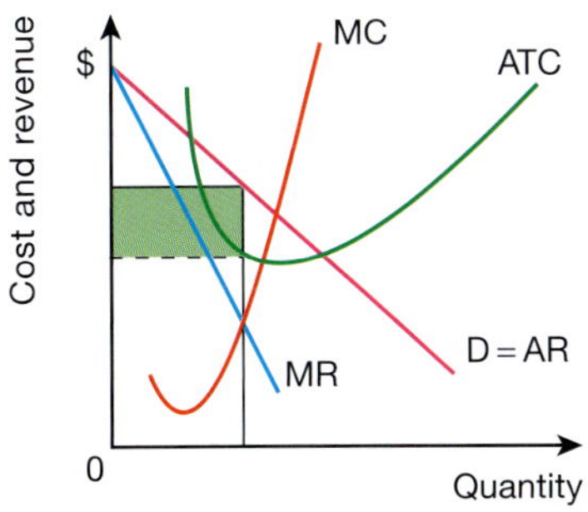

Figure 7.42 Joint profit maximisation ▲

In most countries, cartels are illegal. A cartel may either operate as a multi-firm monopoly or set output quotas for individual members.

If it operates as a multi-firm monopoly it will seek to maximise the joint profits of the cartel. This is illustrated in Figure 7.42. The cartel will equate the overall MC of the members with the market MR curve to determine the profit maximising price and output. Competition among the members is then likely to be non-price as in monopolistic competition.

The problem with this is that whilst the overall profit is maximised at this price, individual firms have different cost structures and so not all firms will be maximising their own profits and this can cause constant tension within the cartel. Firms within the cartel, particularly those with low costs relative to the other members, have an incentive to break ranks and increase their own output and sell at a lower price than that which maximises joint profits in order to increase their own profits.

Link

For a discussion of the conditions for an effective cartel and the consequences of a cartel see section 7.7.4 in this chapter.

From the point of view of the consumer, the price is likely to be high because it will be set at a level which enables all firms, including the least efficient, to make a profit. They may, however, be beneficial if the cartel's supernormal profits are used to provide improved products.

An alternative to joint profit maximisation is for the cartel to set quotas as to the amount each member can produce and sell. The problem for the cartel here is to decide on a "fair" quota for individual companies.

As indicated above, there are a number of tensions within cartels which can threaten their stability and effectiveness and so for a cartel to operate successfully certain conditions must be met. These conditions are discussed in section 7.7.4.

Key term

Price leadership: a situation in an oligopoly where one firm sets or changes its prices and others follow.

Game theory: the analysis of strategies and decision-making by rational players in any activity or situation in which those involved know their decision will have an impact on other players and the way these other players are expected to react will affect the original decision made.

Informal agreements

Informal agreements normally involve some form of price leadership or tacit collusion.

Price leadership occurs when a well-established leading firm in a market has sufficient market power to effectively determine the price of a particular product. When this firm changes its price, other firms follow this lead.

Tacit collusion occurs when it is recognised in the market that firms will follow certain established guidelines such as average cost plus or average variable cost plus pricing strategies. This tacit collusion may also extend to adopting common conventions in relation to advertising and marketing.

Link

For a detailed discussion of price leadership see section 7.8.4 in this chapter.

Game theory

Developed by John Von Neumann and Oscar Morgenstern in 1944, game theory involves the analysis of the strategies adopted by rational players (individuals, groups, firms or even nations) in situations when each player must make decisions in the knowledge that the final outcome (payoff) will depend on the reactions of other players and where the first player knows the other is thinking in the same way. Game theory has been applied to an enormous range of activities and aspects of human behaviour including wars, chess, driving, choosing a marital partner and selling a house. It has applications across a range of disciplines including both the physical and social sciences.

Game theory ▶

> **Key terms**
>
> **Zero-sum game**: a game of pure conflict in which one player's gain will equal the other player's loss.
>
> **Prisoner's dilemma**: in game theory, a competitive situation in which attempts by two or more firms, individuals or groups to find the best strategy for themselves by acting independently results in a worse final outcome than if they had colluded or worked co-operatively.

All games, however, have the common features that they are played out in an environment of uncertainty, interdependence and often conflicts of interest amongst the players.

Here we concentrate on relatively straightforward two-player zero-sum games where one player's gain must equal the other player's loss.

The prisoner's dilemma in oligopolistic markets and the two-player matrix

The most famous and often quoted example of game theory strategy is the prisoner's dilemma. In this example, two individuals, Adam and Ben, have been arrested on suspicion of having committed a very serious crime, which carries a maximum prison sentence of ten years.

Adam and Ben are being detained in separate parts of the prison and have no way of communicating with one another.

The chief of police meets with each in turn and speaks to them in the same way:

"I have sufficient evidence to send both of you to prison for three years if neither of you confesses. However, if you alone are prepared to confess to the crime you will receive a light sentence of one year and your partner will receive a prison sentence of ten years.

If both of you confess, you will both receive a sentence of five years".

What should Adam and Ben do? What is the best strategy for each in these circumstances?

> **Key term**
>
> **Two-player pay-off matrix**: in game theory, a table showing the outcomes (pay-offs) for two players of their respective strategies or decisions.

The possible strategies for each are indicated in the two-player pay-off matrix in Figure 7.43 below.

		ADAM	
		NOT CONFESS	CONFESS
BEN	NOT CONFESS	A Adam 3 Years Ben 3 Years	B Adam 1 Year Ben 10 Years
	CONFESS	C Adam 10 Years Ben 1 Year	D Adam 5 Years Ben 5 Years

Figure 7.43 The prisoner's dilemma ▶

Let us begin with Adam. He will reason as follows.

It is best that I confess because in the best case scenario I will receive a light sentence of one year if Ben does not confess and in the worst case scenario I will receive a sentence of five years rather than ten years in prison if Ben also confesses.

Ben will follow the same path of reasoning and also conclude that the best strategy is to confess.

The final result is that both Adam and Ben will confess and receive a sentence of five years each as illustrated in quadrant D of the matrix.

Clearly this is not the best outcome (pay-off) for Adam and Ben. The best outcome would be for them to co-operate or collude and both agree to not confess as illustrated in quadrant A, which would give them a lighter sentence of three years. However, in the absence of any ability to communicate with one another this is unlikely, and even if they could communicate with one another they would each have to trust in the other's willingness to stick to the deal.

John Nash ▲

Game theory and oligopoly

The application of game theory to the behaviour of firms in oligopolistic markets is most closely associated with the work of the Nobel Prize winner in Economics for 1994, John Nash.

Let us take the example of a duopoly in the low-cost airline market. In this case two firms, Batflight and Swing Airlines, are the players; the game takes place in the market and the pay-off is the expected final profit for each firm resulting from their respective strategies.

Currently both airlines are charging the same fare, \$100 return on a particular route. We assume that they are not prepared to co-operate with one another and are independently considering the impact on their profits if they reduce fares on the route to $90.

In deciding whether to leave fares at $100 or lower them to $90, each airline will need to take into account the likely response of the other airline to the decision it makes. The pay-off matrix below (Figure 7.44) shows the profits made (in $ millions) by the two firms as a result of leaving fares at $100 and reducing them to $90.

Current profits for each firm are indicated in quadrant A.

If we begin with Batflight and assume that it decides to adopt a conservative approach, anticipating that whatever strategy Batflight chooses, Swing will adopt a counter strategy which is best for itself but worst for Batflight, then under these circumstances Batflight should reduce its fares.

		Batflight	
		Keep fares at $100	Reduce fares to $90
Swing Airlines	Keep fares at $100	A Batflight $30m Swing $30m	B Batflight $35m Swing $15m
	Reduce fares to $90	C Batflight $15m Swing $35m	D Batflight $20m Swing $20m

Figure 7.44 Pay-off matrix for Batflight and Swing ▶

Maximin strategy

The reason is this. If Batflight reduces its fares to $90 and Swing leaves its fares unchanged then Batflight's profits will rise to $35 million as shown in quadrant B. If on the other hand Swing responds by reducing its fare to $90 also, then the worst that can happen to Batflight's profits is that they will be reduced to $20 million, which is obviously better than the reduction in profits to $15 million if Batflight had left its fares at $100. This particular conservative strategy is referred to as the maximin strategy.

Maximax strategy

An alternative approach that Batflight might take is a more optimistic, if riskier, strategy known as the maximax strategy which assumes that Swing will respond to any move by Batflight which leads to the most advantageous outcome in terms of profits for Batflight. In this case Batflight would assume that Swing would leave its price unchanged whatever move Batflight made.

However, this maximax strategy would still give the same result. It is still best for Batflight to reduce its fares to $90 as this would result in the position shown in quadrant B with Batflight's profits rising to $35 million.

Key terms

Maximin strategy: in game theory, a conservative strategy chosen by a player which provides the best of the worst possible outcomes of a decision.

Maximax strategy: in game theory, a strategy chosen by a player which provides the best of the best possible outcomes of a decision.

> **Key term**
> **Dominant strategy**: in game theory, a strategy which leads to the best outcome for a player irrespective of the strategy adopted by other players.

> **Key term**
> **Nash equilibrium**: in game theory, a solution in a non-co-operative situation in which each firm's best strategy is to maintain its present behaviour given the present behaviour of other firms in the market.

> **Link**
> For more on collusion see earlier in this section and in section 7.7.4 in this chapter.

As with the prisoner's dilemma example, the other player in this game, Swing, is faced with the same choice of strategies as Batflight and so if it plays the game rationally it will come to the same conclusion and will decide its best strategy is to reduce its fares whatever Batflight chooses to do.

Dominant strategy

Whether the players adopt the maximin or maximax strategies, the result is the same – both should reduce their fares and so reducing fares is a dominant strategy in that it is the best one for each player irrespective of that adopted by the other.

Nash equilibrium

The final position in this game is shown in quadrant D with both airlines reducing their fares and achieving profits of $20 million. This position is known as a Nash equilibrium in that it is the best for each airline given the circumstances in which each finds itself, taking into account the likely decisions of the other, and as such neither airline will have any incentive to change its strategy unless the other does.

It is important to note that while this final position represents equilibrium by acting independently in a non-co-operative fashion, the airlines have failed to achieve the best possible outcome for themselves. This is shown in quadrant A with both firms leaving their fares at $100 and making profits of $30 million.

Collusion

However, if, as is likely in reality, this is not a single-move game but one which is repeated over time, it is likely that the airlines will come to realise that their mutual interests are best served by co-operating or colluding either tacitly or through a formal cartel.

However, as the pay-off matrix shows, there may still be incentives for one of the players to cheat and undercut the other in order to increase its own profits.

For collusion to be effective, therefore, there must be clear punishments or penalties for cheating that can be imposed for this together with a willingness and ability to implement them. For example, one reason for the OPEC cartel members maintaining their quotas once they have been agreed is that all members are aware that Saudi Arabia is in a position to flood the market with oil thereby significantly reducing its price which would penalise all members. Saudi Arabia actually took this action in 2020.

One strategy which may prove effective in ensuring collusion in repetitive games is a "tit for tat" strategy. In this strategy a firm co-operates in the first round of moves, but makes it clear that it will only maintain this stance if all the other firms continue to co-operate. If other firms cheat then in the next round of moves the first firm will mimic the actions of the other firms in the previous round and cheat. This immediately punishes the cheats and ensures there are no long-term gains from cheating. This strategy has the advantage of providing a clear punishment without undermining the collusive agreement because the firm will only cheat if others do.

Game theory in oligopolistic markets conclusion

In this section we have only looked at two-player, single-move (non-repetitive), zero-sum games, but it is clear even from this that game theory provides a useful framework for analysing the behaviour of firms in oligopolistic markets.

In the real world, however, games are far more complicated. Not only do most oligopolistic markets comprise more than two firms, but the firms within the market have more than a single strategy available to them to influence their profits. Within the low-cost airline market in our example the firms not only have the option of changing their fares; there are also a number of non-price strategies they could adopt in addition or instead of changing prices, such as higher baggage allowances, speedy check-in and on-board services such as free meals, films or extra leg-room.

It is also the case that not all games are zero sum, involving total conflict in that one player's gain is the other player's loss. In reality, games and strategies may involve mutual if not always equally distributed gain. For example, in our airline example it might be that at the same time as Batflight and Swing are planning their price strategies the size of the market is expanding and as a result there may be opportunities for both airlines to benefit. More complex game theory models have the scope to incorporate all of these additional complications.

However, it is important to remember that game theory assumes that all players act rationally in the economic sense when planning their strategies and executing their decisions and as we have seen in our earlier discussion of behavioural economics this may not always be the case.

Non-collusive oligopolies

In this situation individual firms set their price and output independently, but clearly they have to be aware of the responses of others. The result tends to be long periods of price stability with non-price competition being the norm, although occasional price wars break out as in the UK food retail market in 2017 and the low cost airline market in 2019.

Case Study

Price wars

The recent price war in the oil market clearly illustrates the way in which the effects of price wars can extend far beyond those immediately involved.

Between March and May 2020, Saudi Arabia and Russia were involved in an all-out price war following Russia's failure to agree to a reduction in production. Saudi Arabia immediately embarked on a price war by flooding the market with oil. Oil prices plummeted by over 50 per cent to below $23 a barrel. This had an immediate global impact.

Both Saudi Arabia and Russia would seem to be in relatively strong positions

to withstand the effects of the price fall. Whilst Saudi Arabia needs a price in excess of $80 for its budget to break even, which is important given its drive to diversify its economy away from overdependence on oil revenues, it has very low operating costs (around $3.20 per barrel) as well as 50 years' worth of oil reserves and Russia is able to break even at $42 and has over $500bn in foreign reserves.

However, in the event neither country was immune from the fall out. Saudi Arabia was forced to cut its capital expenditure budget by $10 bn and Russia saw the ruble fall 30 per cent in the first quarter and expected to run a budget deficit for the year. Other members of OPEC and US shale producers were in a much more precarious position. Many oil exporting countries need much higher prices to break even and risked having to cancel government infrastructure projects.

Even though the price war was short lived, it had a global impact. Stock markets fell with energy companies seeing millions wiped off their share values and given that oil is priced in dollars, there were even implications for exchange rates. Investment in oil exploration, production and refining projects was put at risk. Oil importers such as Japan clearly stood to benefit from the fall in price, but the extent to which the Japanese economy and Japanese households benefited depended on how the windfall was spent.

1 With reference to the examples in the extract and your own knowledge and research evaluate the impact of price wars on (i) the participants (ii) consumers (iii) employees and (iv) the wider domestic and world economy.

Key term

Kinked demand curve: in a non-collusive oligopoly an individual firm will believe that rivals will not follow any price rise that it makes, but will follow any price reductions meaning that the demand curve it faces will be price elastic for a price rise and price inelastic for a price fall and will, therefore, be kinked at the current price.

The kinked demand curve

One model of the behaviour of oligopolistic firms in non-collusive situations is given by the kinked demand curve developed independently by Paul M Sweezey in America and Hall and Hitch in the UK in 1939.

The kinked demand curve for an individual firm in an oligopoly is shown in Figure 7.45. The firm is initially operating at an output of Q with price equal to P. The firm is contemplating its future pricing strategy.

It would seem reasonable for the firm to assume, based on past experience, that if it reduces its price its rivals will do so also, so that the firm is unlikely to gain significantly from the move. For this reason the firm is likely to perceive its demand (AR) curve to be relatively inelastic. The demand curve D_1 illustrates this.

However, the firm is likely to believe that if it decides to increase its price, its rivals are unlikely to follow suit, hoping by leaving their prices unchanged to increase their market share. Hence for a price rise the firm believes that it is likely to lose a significant amount of sales and in this case is likely to perceive its demand curve to be relatively elastic. This is illustrated by D_2. The overall demand curve that the firm perceives it is facing is a composite of the two demand curves. The overall demand curve is YXZ. The demand curve has a kink in it at point X.

As a result of this the price is likely to remain stable at P because the firm will reason that reducing the price will result in limited gains and might even provoke a price war which it could lose, and raising price will result in a substantial loss of market share.

The kinked demand curve can also be used to explain price stability in oligopolistic markets even in the face of rising costs. This is shown in Figure 7.46.

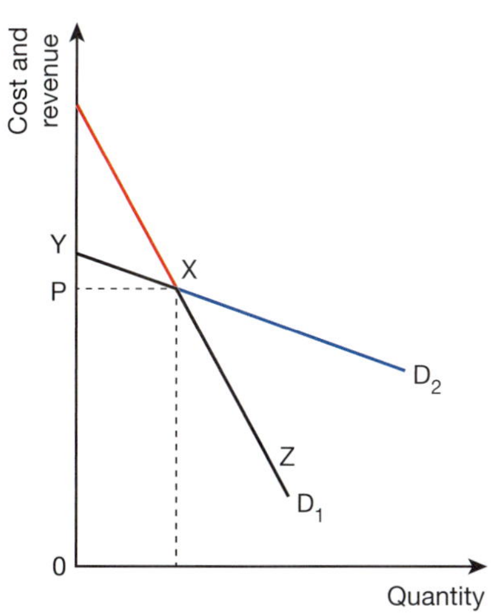

Figure 7.45 Kinked demand curve ▲

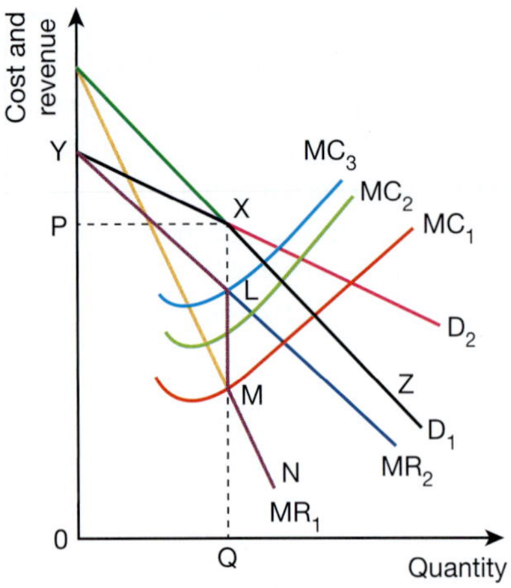

Figure 7.46 Kinked demand curve and rising costs ▲

In order to explain this we need to first of all draw in the MR curve associated with the kinked demand curve. We have established earlier that the MR curve for a price making firm will always be below the AR curve and will fall at twice the rate. Clearly it is not possible for a single continuous MR curve to fall at twice the rate of the kinked AR curve. Hence the MR has a discontinuity in it, LM, at output Q.

Up to output Q the demand (AR) curve is YX and so the MR curve associated with it is YL. Beyond output Q the demand (AR) curve becomes XZ and so the MR curve associated with this is MN. The MR curve, therefore, has a step or discontinuity in it at output Q equal to LM. The overall MR curve is YLMN.

We know that the profit maximising firm will always produce the output at which MC = MR, hence if the MC curve rises within the discontinuity LM, the profit maximising output and associated price will remain unchanged at Q and P respectively. Only if the MC curve rises to intersect with the MR curve at a point above L will the profit maximising price and output change.

Criticisms of the kinked demand curve

Almost immediately the kinked demand curve model attracted criticism, mainly in that it fails to explain how the firm determines the original price and output and also that it assumes firms in oligopolies always operate in the same predictable ways over time. In addition it does not take into account the fact that there is much non-price competition in oligopolistic markets.

Contestable market features and implications

Contestable market theory was developed by William Baumol in 1982 to explain why in some monopoly or oligopolistic markets, firms may operate in a competitive manner which will enable consumers to obtain the benefits of economies of scale and lower prices as well as reducing the welfare losses associated with markets dominated by a few firms. The equilibrium position for a firm in a contestable market will be closer to that predicted by perfect competition than monopoly or oligopoly.

In the theory of contestable markets, it is not the number of firms in the industry, the actual level of competition, which is important in determining the behaviour of firms within it, but the threat of potential competition from new firms possibly entering the industry.

Activity

Market structures compared

Construct a table comparing the following characteristics of the four market structures in perfect competition, monopolistic competition, oligopoly and monopoly:

- number of firms
- entry to industry
- type of product
- pricing policy
- profit levels
- non-price competition
- productive efficiency
- allocative efficiency
- technical efficiency and X-efficiency and X-inefficiency
- slope of the demand curve and relationship between AR and MR.

Provide an example of each.

Key terms

Non-price competition: alternatives to price reductions as methods used by firms to increase market share, e.g. advertising, after-sales service.

Contestable market: a market or markets in which there is the threat of potential competition in the future, in which case, even though an existing firm may currently have a monopoly position, it may decide to act more like a perfectly competitive firm (in terms of price and output strategy) in order to deter such competition. The lower the entry and exit costs, the more contestable the market.

Key term

Limit pricing: a strategy adopted by a monopoly or oligopoly of setting prices below that which will maximise profits in order to deter new entrants.

If an incumbent firm in a monopoly or oligopoly market believes that by fixing high prices and earning supernormal profits there is the possibility that this will attract new firms into the industry who might take over the market, then it might set prices equal to or relatively close to average costs to prevent this from happening. This strategy, of setting a price below that which will maximise a firm's profits in order to deter new entrants into the market, is known as limit pricing.

Clearly the extent to which a market is contestable will depend upon how easy it is for new firms to enter the industry and so an absence of barriers to entry or low barriers to entry are crucial in determining this. It is also important for any prospective new entrant that the product is standardised and that they have access to the same technology as established firms.

There must also be no collusion between existing firms.

Barriers to exit

However, it is not only the ease of entering the market that is important. Any prospective new entrant needs to plan for the eventuality that its attempt to enter a particular market may fail and that it will be forced out of the industry by the existing firms. The costs for the firm if it has to exit the market, therefore, need to be considered. Sunk costs are those costs which cannot be recovered if a firm goes out of business and may act as a barrier to exit. If entering the market involves the purchase of expensive capital equipment which could not be diverted to other uses or sold if the firm goes bankrupt, then this expenditure represents a sunk cost. If the risk of potential sunk costs is perceived by the firm as great, this is likely to deter it from entering the market.

Link

See section 7.8.4 in this chapter for a detailed discussion of limit pricing.

Hence the lower the perceived risk of high sunk costs, the more contestable the market is likely to be.

A characteristic of contestable markets is "hit and run" competition. If an incumbent firm in the industry raises its price significantly above AC in order to increase profits to earn supernormal profits, the absence of barriers to entry will attract new firms into the industry who will remain, offering lower prices as long as there are profits to be made. When the incumbent firm reduces its price, the new entrants leave. In order to avoid the possibility of hit and run competition, the existing firm in the industry will have to keep prices close to AC.

It is important to remember that it is the threat of competition not the actual competition that forces firms to be productively efficient.

Contestable market theory has been used by some governments as an argument for reducing regulatory and legal barriers to entry to some industries in order to increase competition.

Case Study

Taxis – a contestable market

Is the market for taxis a contestable market?

In theory, yes this should be the case. Costs of entry to the market should be low, all that is needed is a car, and there are rarely any large-scale incumbents in a particular area.

However, completely unregulated markets can cause problems, in terms of congestion, exploitation of consumers, and health and safety issues.

In response to this, many countries have introduced licensing systems to regulate quality and ensure fair pricing.

To operate a taxi in Rome or Mumbai, drivers are required to live in the geographical area.

London taxi drivers must pass a test to be licensed, but this can take up to four years to complete.

In Tehran, any private car can pick up passengers.

In New York, a medallion system operates which imposes a cost for a permit for a company to run taxis in the city within certain laid down rules. If drivers break these rules, they are banned and the medallion is suspended.

However, so lucrative is the market that medallions have been known to sell for $1 million.

1 To what extent can the taxi markets in these examples be regarded as contestable?

Key terms

Merger: the process by which two independent firms come together to form a new company. This will normally involve one company taking over the other through the purchase of shares.

Predatory pricing: a firm setting extremely low prices, often below average costs of production, in order to force competitors out of the market and enable a firm to exploit increased monopoly power in the market by raising prices in the future.

The extent to which contestable markets can be applied to the real world is questioned by some economists. It is unlikely that a market will be free from sunk costs. Any new firm entering a market is likely to have to undertake extensive advertising and promotion costs at the outset, which will be irretrievable. It is also likely that there will be some barriers to entry, either innocent in the form of economies of scale for existing firms, or ones deliberately created by incumbents such as mergers and takeovers, limit and predatory pricing.

Price and non-price competition

Now that we have analysed the behaviour and performance of firms in different market structures, we are in a position to summarise the extent to which price and non-price competition exists between firms in each case.

Price competition

The most obvious type of price competition involves a firm undercutting its competitors in order to increase its share of the market. This can take a number of forms from all out price wars to more limited promotions such as sales like "Black Friday", discounts for bulk/multiple purchases, supermarket loss leaders and 3 for 2 or "buy one get one free" offers. However, reducing prices below those of competitors is not the only form of price competition. It is important that a product is priced appropriately for the desired market. For example, a firm wishing to compete in the luxury markets for perfume or accessories would be unlikely to charge a very low price for its products compared to its competitors, fearing that customers would regard them as of inferior quality. In fact, some products sometimes known as goods of ostentation may be purchased because their prices are high largely because possession of them is seen by some as a sign of status. Also firms which produce a range of similar products, e.g. confectionary, will want to ensure products, particularly new lines, are priced appropriately in relation to one another.

In perfect competition there is no price competition. Firms are price takers producing a homogeneous product. The price of the product is determined in the market by demand and supply and no individual firm can, by its own actions, influence the price. They are, however, able to sell all they wish at the ruling price.

In all other market structures, monopoly, monopolistic competition and oligopoly, firms face a downward sloping demand curve and hence have some control over price. In these markets, firms are price makers. In these circumstances, firms set prices and sales are determined by demand. Changes in market conditions are indicated by changes in sales which may or may not lead firms to change prices. Although on occasions firms in imperfect markets adopt particular pricing strategies for tactical reasons, including limit or predatory pricing designed to deter potential entrants or eliminate existing competitors, or price discrimination to take advantage of different price elasticities of demand in different market segments, in the main imperfectly competitive markets exhibit considerable price stability. There are clear reasons for this. Frequent price changes can be very costly administratively, particularly for large multi-product firms who may produce hundreds if not thousands of different products and price cuts will inevitably reduce profits.

As a result of this, firms in imperfectly competitive markets make extensive use of non-price competition.

Non-price competition

Non-price competition involves a range of techniques designed to differentiate a firm's products from those of its competitors.

Such competition will not be seen in perfectly competitive markets because, as indicated earlier, perfectly competitive firms produce a homogeneous product and can sell all they wish at the ruling price. As such, they have no need to undertake promotional activities. Similarly, a pure monopolist will not need to use non-price competition as by definition it has no competitors.

However, there is extensive use of non-price competition in both monopolistic competition and by firms in oligopolistic markets. The object is to increase overall demand in the industry, attract customers from competitors and hopefully make the demand for the firm's product more price inelastic.

Non-price competition can take many forms including the following:

Advertising – creating a difference ▲

- Advertising. This is possibly the most important and effective form of non-price competition in that it is the way in which firms communicate to customers the features which differentiate and make their products and services more attractive than those of their competitors. In 2019, companies worldwide spent over $550 bn on advertising, with the majority of growth being in internet advertising. This figure is anticipated to rise to over $620 bn by 2024. Amazon alone spent $11 bn on advertising in 2019.

- Packaging which is convenient, attractive and in different forms and sizes. For example many soft drinks come in bottles, cans and cartons and in different quantities to suit the requirements of different customers.
- A range of purchasing options to meet different customer needs such as in store, on-line and "click and collect".
- Loyalty schemes designed to ensure repeat purchases. For example Tesco and American Express have reward cards which can be used in store or to purchase gifts.
- Free upgrades or extras. These are often offered by airline, hotels and package holiday companies.
- Differences in quality or design. These may enable a firm to gain a reputation for high quality and innovation which may enable it to establish a brand monopoly in the market.
- Range of models aimed at different segments in the market. This is common amongst car manufacturers.
- After sales service, such as technical support, guarantees or extended warranties.
- Free delivery on products over a certain price or purchases over a particular value.

There are many more examples.

Activity

Types of competition between firms

In groups of 3, 4 or 5 identify three firms (one small, one medium and one large multinational company) operating in your region or country and produce a presentation explaining the ways in which they each compete with their rivals and evaluating which competition techniques or strategies are most effective. Each group should choose a different group of three companies

7.6.5 Definition and calculation of concentration ratios

The extent to which a particular market might be regarded as an oligopoly is often measured through concentration ratios. The most commonly used are the four-, five- or eight-firm concentration ratios which measure the proportion or percentage of the market's output provided by the largest four, five or eight firms.

Table 7.14 identifies the ten markets with the largest five-firm concentration ratios in the UK.

Table 7.14 UK concentration ratios ▼

Industry	Five-firm concentration ratio (%)
Sugar	99
Tobacco products	99
Oils and fats	88
Gas distribution	82
Confectionary	81
Man-made fibres	79
Coal extraction	79
Weapons and ammunition	77
Soft drinks and mineral waters	75
Pesticides	75

Case Study

Concentration, monopoly and competition in the USA

In the past few years, increasing concern has been expressed in the USA over the extent of concentration of monopoly power in the hands of a few large corporations. What some call the concentration crisis extends across many sectors of the economy. Apple has 62 per cent of the market share of handsets in the US. American Express, Mastercard and Visa control 95 per cent of the credit card market. Google 60 per cent of the browser market and three firms 78 per cent of the telecom market. Elsewhere, two companies, Fresenius Medical Care and Da Vita, control 92 per cent of the $24 billion dialysis industry. Some argue such levels of concentration is one reason for high healthcare costs even impacting on those with insurance through higher premiums.

Concentration extends throughout the economy. In the washer and dryer manufacturing and baby formula markets, three firms control respectively 100 per cent and 80 per cent of the market, and airlines where the four firm concentration ratio is over 76 per cent with higher levels of concentration on individual routes.

Critics argue that such high levels of concentration reduce competition, squeeze suppliers, cause workers' wages to stagnate, harm small businesses and drive up prices for consumers.

Defenders, however, argue that this view is too simplistic and that these large monopoly corporations are efficient and innovative and often pass these gains on to consumers.

1 With particular reference to the examples given in the extract, evaluate the advantages and disadvantages of high concentration levels in markets to (i) the firms themselves (ii) the firms' suppliers (iii) employees of the firms (iv) small businesses (v) consumers of the final product.

Small vs. large enterprises ▲

7.7 Growth and survival of firms

7.7.1 *Reasons for different sizes of firms*

Regionally, nationally and internationally firms vary significantly in size from huge multinational corporations such as Apple, Amazon, Walmart and Royal Dutch Shell to tiny enterprises such as a local village shop or market stall owned and run by one person or a single household.

An important issue in looking at the size of firms is the way in which the size of a business is actually measured. A number of measures is possible, but it is important to note that different measures may give different results, particularly in ranking the size of very large multinational companies. One common measure used in many countries is the numbers employed by firms. In the UK, for example, the Office for National Statistics (ONS) classifies firms as small (0–49 employees), medium sized (50–249 employees) and large enterprises (250+) employees. This measure has the advantage of making national and international comparisons relatively straightforward, but will clearly rank firms in labour-intensive markets, such as the retail grocery trade, as larger than firms using more capital intensive methods of production.

Other measures used include market capitalisation (share values), annual revenue, profits and asset values, but here again the measures yield different results.

For example, in 2020, in terms of market capitalisation, the technology giant Apple, at $1.9bn was the world's largest corporation. However, in terms of revenue Walmart at over $500bn, from its 11,000 stores in 27 countries, was the largest. Forbes uses a composite measure of sales, profits, assets and market capitalisation and has the Industrial and Commercial Bank of China (ICBC) as the largest with revenue of $177bn, profits of $45bn, assets of $4.3bn and a market value of $242bn. Clearly, in terms of ranking the size of the very largest multinational corporations, the method of measurement used is important.

There are many reasons for differences in the size of firms, some of which we have already touched on.

They include the following:

- Type of business organisation/nature of ownership: state-owned enterprises, multinational corporations and public limited companies (Plcs) tend to operate on a much larger scale than other types of organisation, such as sole traders or partnerships.
- Size of profits: some firms, particularly as they grow larger, may see an increase in profits which can be reinvested back into the company to finance R & D, new and better capital equipment and further expansion.
- Access to finance: some firms may have greater access to different sources of finance than others. State-owned enterprises may receive funding from the government while public limited companies can issue shares and often find it relatively easy to obtain loans from banks and other financial institutions. Sole traders and other small and medium-sized enterprises have more limited sources of finance.
- Government assistance: some enterprises may receive subsidies, tax relief or other forms of financial assistance from government.
- Size of the market: if the size of the market for a particular product is large and/or expanding rapidly, there is clearly scope for a firm to expand and increase its scale of operation. Similarly, relatively small or specialist markets may offer much less scope for firms to grow in size.
- Mergers and takeovers: firms may grow larger by merging with or taking over other firms. Mergers and takeovers are discussed in detail in sections 7.7.2 and 7.7.3 below.
- Motives and aspirations of owners and managers: some owners/managers may wish for their company to remain small. Some of the possible reasons for this and the survival of small firms are discussed later in this chapter. At the same time, some managers and entrepreneurs may regard expansion and growth of the firm as an objective in its own right as an alternative to profit maximisation.
- Economies and diseconomies of scale: economies and diseconomies of scale have been discussed in detail in sections 7.5.5–7.5.7 later in this chapter. In summary, economies of scale provide benefits to firms as they increase their scale of production in terms of reductions in long run average costs and, therefore, profits and as such encourage firms to grow in size. If a firm grows too large, however, it may risk incurring diseconomies of scale and this may inhibit the desire for growth in size.

- Time in the market: it takes time for firms to grow. Firms that have been in the market will have had more time to generate profits to expand and to achieve and benefit from economies of scale.

7.7.2 Internal growth of firms: organic growth and diversification

As we have seen in this chapter, there can be considerable advantages to growing in size, particularly in terms of economies of scale, and for some managerial theorists this can be regarded as a key objective of managers. A firm may grow in two ways: internal or organic growth or external growth.

Key term

Internal or organic growth: increase in the size of a company through increasing sales and innovation.

Internal or organic growth is the result of increasing sales, which can either be through selling within an expanding market or increasing existing market share through advertising, promotion or price competition.

However sales are increased, it will be necessary for the firm to grow in size, to increase its productive capacity. In order to increase productive capacity, investment will be required. It is likely that a mixture of innovation, invention and the introduction of new products will be crucial to internal growth.

Internal growth is usually financed through retained profits, borrowing or the issue of shares.

7.7.3 External growth of firms – integration (mergers and takeovers)

Methods of and reasons for integration

Key terms

External growth: growth through takeovers and mergers.

Integration: the merger of two firms; this can be horizontal, vertical, conglomerate or lateral.

Horizontal integration: mergers of firms at the same stage of production or producing the same product.

Vertical integration: mergers of firms at different stages in the production process.

External growth is achieved by firms merging or taking over another firm. It is possible to identify four types of merger or integration.

- Horizontal integration involves firms at the same stage in the production process or producing the same product merging together. An example of this is the takeover by Virgin Active, a health club company, of Esporta Gyms for £77.6 million. This acquisition meant that Virgin Active almost doubled its size, enabling it to increase its market share, increase its range of geographical outlets and reap economies of scale. Lloyds TSB's takeover of HBOS gave it an increased share of the UK mortgage market and a branch network in Scotland.
- Vertical integration involves the merger of firms at different stages in the production process. Vertical integration can either be backward towards earlier stages in the supply chain or forward to later stages in the supply chain. A wine merchant buying a vineyard would be an example of backward vertical integration to ensure a source of supply, while the same company purchasing a wine shop or wine bar to ensure an outlet for their product would be an example of forward integration. Vertical integration is common in the oil industry where companies such as Shell and BP are involved in every step in the production, processing and distribution through the process

of acquiring oil wells, refineries and outlets for their products. In addition to providing guaranteed sources of supply of raw materials and outlets for their final products, which gives a firm some control over both production costs and selling prices, vertical integration is a way for a firm to establish monopoly power in an industry. Of course such monopoly power may have adverse consequences for consumers. The major disadvantage for the firm is that such mergers may be expensive.

- Conglomerate integration occurs when a firm takes over or merges with other companies in completely unrelated fields. These were common in the US in the 1960s, but are relatively uncommon today. Motives for such mergers include managerial ambition, a desire to expand without contravening any national monopoly legislation, diversification to reduce risk, and the possible benefits that can be derived from shared research and development. Like vertical integration, however, conglomerate mergers can be costly.
- Lateral integration occurs when a firm merges with another in a similar field. An example might be a hotel chain taking over a chain of restaurants.

Key terms

Conglomerate integration: mergers of firms producing unrelated products.

Lateral integration: mergers of firms producing similar products.

Consequences of integration

It is not possible to come to a definitive conclusion as to whether integration through mergers and acquisitions are in the public interest; a judgement needs to be made on a case by case basis. Some relevant issues are identified below

Advantages and disadvantages of integration

The advantages of integration include:

- Economies of scale. Firms may be able to benefit from a range of internal economies of scale, particularly from horizontal mergers which enable them to reduce average costs (AC) as the scale of the organisation increases. This might also enable the firm to reduce prices, thereby benefiting customers.
- Rationalisation. Integration may enable the firms involved to rationalise common functions, reducing wasteful duplication and removing unprofitable elements of the organisation. Advertising and marketing costs could also be consolidated and reduced. This would reduce costs and give the firm scope to reduce prices.
- Vertical integration might also benefit consumers by reducing the number firms involved in the supply chain. If a product goes through a number of stages in its supply chain and each stage is initially supplied by an independent firm, then each will apply its own individual profit mark-up. Following vertical integration, these separate mark-ups can be eliminated and so prices may fall. For example, if a holiday package tour company owns its own hire cars and hotels, it will not have to pay profits to the hire car companies and hotels, reducing its costs and potentially its prices.

Activity

Integration

1 Identify one example of each type of integration in your own country.
2 Construct a table that summarises the advantages and disadvantages to the firm of the different types of integration.

- Firms are able to share ideas, information and expertise so that the market failure associated with asymmetric information may be reduced.
- The integrated firms may have more access to funds and, therefore, be able to undertake R & D projects which might result in innovation, new techniques of production, improved quality of products and possibly new products.

The disadvantages of integration include:

- The main disadvantages of integration through mergers and acquisitions are associated with reduced competition, putting the integrated firm in a position to exploit its monopoly power in the market in terms, for example, of increasing price and restriction of output.
- Integration may make formal collusion and the formation of cartels more likely.
- Integration may lead to reduced choice. This may be a particular issue with horizontal integration where the firms sell similar goods or services and there is limited product differentiation such as mergers of insurance companies or grocery supermarkets.
- Particularly in the case of vertical integration, potential new entrants may be denied access to sources of supply or sales outlets for their products. This may deter new entrants and make the market less contestable.
- Rationalisation may lead to unemployment. Two large firms merging may only need one payroll or Human Resources department.
- The integrated firms may experience diseconomies of scale, particularly managerial and those linked to the alienation of workers.
- The integrated firm may be able to exert monopsony power over its suppliers pushing down their prices and profits to reduce its own costs and/or over its employees keeping down their wages.

Survival of the small business ▲

Survival of small firms

Despite the fact that there are many advantages that accrue to a firm as a result of growth in size, in most countries there are significant numbers of small firms particularly in areas such as farming, car repair, hairdressing and local food stores. Some of the main reasons for the survival of the small firm are summarised below:

- low start-up costs in many areas
- an individual's desire to be their own boss
- the market for the product may be small or highly localised, e.g. a village store
- small firms may have close contact with their customers and be able to react quickly and flexibly to changes in demand
- large-scale production requires the product to be of a standard design. If the market is for a very high-quality product of individual or customised design then a small firm may be better placed to provide, for example, customised jewellery

- small firms may be able to survive by supplying component parts to large organisations
- a small firm may be on its way to being very large, e.g. Google started off as a small company
- a government may provide financial support for small firms in some countries

7.7.4 *Cartels*

Cartels have already been discussed briefly in section 7.6.3 of this chapter when looking at the behaviour and performance of firms in collusive oligopolies. Here we take the analysis further to consider in detail the conditions necessary for a cartel to operate effectively and successfully in the interests of its members.

As we have seen, cartels are agreements between firms and, in the case of OPEC countries, to fix the price and output of a product often setting quotas for individual members. They may also exchange information and have advertising and marketing agreements. Cartels are illegal in most countries and as such their existence and activities are often difficult to detect.

Conditions for an effective cartel

There are a number of conditions necessary for a cartel to operate successfully. These include the following:

- A limited number of firms in the industry, all of whom are members
- Very high concentration ratios. Studies suggest that two-thirds of cartels are in industries with a four firm concentration ratio in excess of 75 per cent
- Control over the source of supply. For example, it has been estimated that OPEC control 50 per cent of global oil supplies and 90 per cent of proven oil reserves
- An ability on the part of the members to control price and restrict output
- Similar cost structures for all firms. If one or more companies has significantly lower costs than the others they may have an incentive to increase their output and reduce price in order to increase their profits
- High barriers to entry to prevent new firms entering the industry
- All firms obey the rules of the cartel and there are measures in place to ensure compliance with the rules possibly involving sanctions
- A stable market – cartel agreements are likely to be vulnerable in times of recession when total demand in the economy is falling. This is a particular problem if the product is one with a high-income elasticity of demand
- The firms' produce very similar or identical products which inspire little consumer loyalty, such as industrial components. This tends to make agreements on price easier to establish.

Another factor that may impact on the stability of a cartel agreement is increased scrutiny by competition and anti-trust regulators across the world who are developing increasingly sophisticated techniques to monitor pricing arrangements to detect evidence of price fixing and other anti-competitive practices. On top of this, regulators the powers regulators have to impose penalties on firms and individuals found to have been guilty of being involved in cartel arrangements have increased significantly.

The effect of this may be to create tensions within the cartel, particularly if one or more of the members believe there is the likelihood of their activities being investigated. In such cases one firm may have the incentive to break ranks and reveal the activities of the cartel in the hope of being dealt with more leniently. This was the case with the European Competition Commission investigation into a truck-makers cartel. Ultimately the Commission issued fines totalling €3.8 bn, but one of the cartel members MAN was exempt from any penalty as it was the first to admit the collusion.

Consequences of a cartel

As the objectives of cartels are to increase members profits and reduce competition, the consequences of their activities is largely detrimental to the interests of consumers.

These include the following:

- Price agreements: as we saw when looking at the behaviour and performance of firms in collusive oligopolies firms may adopt a strategy of joint profit maximisation, which involves fixing the price of a product so as to maximise the joint profits of the members. Since individual firms will have different cost structures, the price will be at a level which enables all members of the cartel to make a profit and as such will inevitably be higher than in a competitive market. These price agreements may be "horizontal" (amongst competitors in a market) or "vertical" (involving a manufacturer and its suppliers and/or its outlets). One estimate has indicated that the excess charges resulting from price fixing agreements for poor countries is as much the amount they receive in foreign aid. Price fixing amongst members may extend to agreements on promotions or discounts. One final benefit for members of these price fixing agreements is that they eliminate or at least substantially reduce the risk of punishing price wars.
- Restriction of supply: in order to manipulate the price, it is often necessary to restrict the supply of the product. For example, in May 2020 the 23 members of the OPEC + alliance agreed to cut oil production by 9.7 million barrels per day in order to support the price.
- Division of the market: the members may agree to divide the market between themselves, possibly on the basis of location or market segment. The firms may agree not to compete in certain markets, thereby effectively creating monopolies in these areas.

- Agreements on tendering: this can take a number of forms, but is designed to ensure that a particular member of the cartel wins a contract. Firms may agree not to submit a bid, guaranteeing the only bidder will win the contract. The firms not bidding may benefit from being subcontracted to complete part of the project. Alternatively, firms may ensure one firm wins a contract by submitting intentionally uncompetitive bids or ones that knowingly contain unacceptable conditions. Firms may even have agreements to rotate who the successful bidder will be in successive contracts ensuring that all members of the cartel eventually get a share of the profits. Whatever the form of rigged bidding process, the result is the same: the issuer of the contract pays a higher price than if the auction was genuinely competitive with consequences for consumers and, in the case of government contracts, taxpayers.
- Reduced incentives to innovate: protected by what is effectively monopoly power, firms may not have the incentive to innovate to increase efficiency and reduce costs. However, in the absence of price competition, firms may wish to undertake R & D in order to improve their products and attract customers.
- Monopsony power: the cartel members may collectively exercise monopsonistic power, dictating prices and conditions favourable to themselves to their suppliers.

Case Study

Cartels

The past few year has seen a number of high profile investigations and prosecutions by competition and anti-trust regulators across the world into price fixing and other anti-competitive practices by cartels whose members include a number of world famous multinational companies. The following examples give an indication of the extent of cartel activity, its nature and implications.

The German competition authority has imposed €90.5 million in fines on Lidl, Edeko, Metro and Netto for a range of vertical price agreements with suppliers of beer, confectionary and coffee products. Leading brands involved included Becks, Haribo and Melitta.

One of the most far reaching investigations was the agreement by a number of leading banks including Barclays, Deutsche Bank, JP Morgan Chase and the Citi Group involving the manipulation of LIBOR (London Interbank Offered Rate), falsely inflating or deflating the rate in order to profit from their own trades. LIBOR is basically the rate at which banks lend to one another and its importance lies in the fact that it has a major influence on the rates banks charge their customers and the fact that it is an indication of the liquidity of the financial system. Manipulation of LIBOR, therefore, had global implications in that it is the benchmark rate to set the interest rate on $800 trillion worth of financial instruments worldwide from loans to multinational companies and complex interest rate derivatives to mortgages and student loans. Many of these may have been priced incorrectly as a result of the LIBOR manipulation. The LIBOR manipulation also impacted on foreign exchange contracts. Worldwide fines of $9 billion were awarded.

In other cases the Mexican anti-trust regulator uncovered schemes involving six companies to rig the bidding for contracts to provide insulin and other health supplies to the health service. In any given tender, each company, apart from the pre-determined winner, would offer prices within 1.5 per cent of one another with the winner offering slightly less. The companies agreed to rotate the successful firm in successive auctions. It has been estimated that this cartel agreement cost the Mexican taxpayer $46 million.

Whilst competition authorities worldwide are increasingly investigating the activities of possible cartels, there is concern that the process can take years and in some cases the penalties, although increasing, may not be a sufficient deterrent.

1 With reference to the examples in the extract, evaluate the impact of the activities of cartels on (i) the cartel members (ii) consumers and (iii) the national and international economy.

7.7.5 Principal-agent problem arising from differing objectives of shareholders/managers and owners

Up to now our analysis of the performance and behaviour of firms has assumed that shareholders/owners and managers share the same objectives and goals for the firm. However, particularly in large corporations this may not be the case and we shall now move on to look at why this may not be the case and what the implications of this might be for the behaviour of firms.

It is often argued that within large public limited companies there is a divorce of ownership from control, which is a result of what economists refer to as the principal–agent problem. The owners of the company, the principal, are the shareholders, but because they do not have the skills, specialist knowledge or expertise to effectively run the organisation they normally appoint managers (agents) to run the company and exercise day-to-day control. This principal–agent relationship is thus characterised by asymmetric information in that the agent knows more about the business than the principal.

> **Key terms**
>
> **Divorce of ownership from control**: the fact that a public limited company is owned by one group (shareholders) and controlled and run by another (managers).
>
> **Principal–agent problem**: in large public limited companies the divorce of ownership and control may mean that principals (shareholders) may have different objectives from the agents (managers) and principals cannot guarantee that their agents will operate in the principals' best interests.

This may lead to a divorce of ownership and control which could produce a situation in which managers/agents pursue their own goals and objectives which may not be entirely consistent with or in some cases opposed to the interests of the shareholders/principal.

Shareholders will wish to make the maximum income possible from their investments and so they will wish the firm to maximise profits.

However, managers may have different objectives. It is assumed that managers will wish to gain the maximum satisfaction or utility from their work. This may be derived in a number of ways, e.g. salary, power, prestige, size of the organisation, growth of the organisation, perks and fringe benefits, discretionary expenditure, etc.

There are a number of alternative theories that attempt to take into account these possible objectives of managers.

Although profit maximisation may not be the primary objective of managers, they cannot ignore profit entirely. If profits are too low, managers may be replaced at the company's AGM. It is also possible that if profits are too low, shareholders may sell their shares, depressing the share price, which might possibly lead to a hostile takeover bid which would also threaten the managers' positions. As a result, purely to ensure their own survival, managers are likely to ensure that a minimum acceptable level of profit for shareholders is achieved before pursuing their own aims. This is known as "profit satisficing".

In addition, many firms adopt share and profit sharing schemes for managers, which will increase the incentive for them to pursue profit as one of their objectives.

7.8 Differing objectives and policies of firms

7.8.1 *Traditional profit-maximising objective of firm*

The traditional theory of the firm assumes firms have one single objective: profit maximisation. However, with developments such as the growth of modern public limited companies, particularly multinational companies with large numbers of stakeholders, economists have called this assumption into question.

It is now recognised that not only may large corporations find it difficult to maximise profits even if they wished to, but they may pursue other goals instead of or in addition to profit maximisation.

We will look at these issues and some of the alternative theories that have been put forward concerning the objectives of firms.

Difficulties in maximising profits

The traditional theory of the firm is that the firm will maximise profit at the output where MC = MR. Price will be determined by AR at this output and the level of profit, normal, subnormal or supernormal given by the difference between TR and TC at this output. This presupposes, however, that the firm can actually calculate its MR and MC. In order to calculate the MR curve, the firm needs to be able to accurately estimate the position and elasticity of its demand (AR) curve, which is extremely difficult. Calculating MC accurately poses similar difficulties. There is also the issue of whether firms should use short run or long run marginal costs. All these difficulties are compounded in extremely large multinational companies producing an extremely wide range of products.

There is some evidence to indicate that rather than using MC and MR to fix price and output, firms adopt more simple strategies such as applying a percentage mark up to average costs. This is known as cost plus pricing.

7.8.2 *An understanding of other objectives of firms*

Differing objectives of the firm

Survival

Perhaps the overriding objective of the firm, certainly in the short run, is simply survival in the market. This is particularly true in the start-up and early stages in the life of an enterprise or during periods of crisis or extreme market volatility, for example, a nationwide or international recession or supply-side shock causing a major decline in demand. During such periods, firms may discard other objectives and instead put in place strategies to ensure their long-term survival.

> **Key term**
>
> **Survival**: an overarching objective of firms, particularly in the early stages of their growth and development.

Profit-satisficing

Profit-satisficing as an objective is linked to a number of organisational theories of the firm which were developed in the late 1950s and 1960s, particularly as a result of work by Herbert Simon and Cyert and March.

> **Activity**
> **Stakeholders**
> 1 Identify a large public limited company in your country, identify the main stakeholders it has and explain what their primary interests are likely to be.
> 2 Explain how these interests might conflict with one another and how this might affect the firm's behaviour.

These theories recognise that modern organisations have a range of internal and external stakeholders including managers, workers, trade unions and customers. These stakeholders are likely to have a range of different interests which may differ over time and at times may conflict with one another. For example, customers will wish for quality products at low prices while shareholders may wish for high profits. Managers will thus have to prioritise objectives at any one time. It is likely that the final result will involve bargaining among the stakeholders with the final outcome depending on relative bargaining strengths of those involved.

> **Key term**
> **Satisficing**: a situation in which a firm aims for a minimum level of attainment of a number of objectives.

One feature of these theories is the prediction that firms will practise satisficing behaviour, aiming for a minimum level of attainment of a number of objectives in order to keep as many stakeholders as possible happy. The firm is thus seen to be pursuing multiple goals rather than a single objective as in the traditional theory of the firm. The importance of particular objectives may change over time in the light of market conditions and relative bargaining strengths.

Organisational theories also predict that organisations are likely to experience organisational slack associated with inducements provided to ensure certain stakeholders' agreement, which will raise the firm's costs.

Sales and sales revenue maximisation

> **Key term**
> **Sales revenue maximisation**: an alternative theory of the objectives of a firm which assumes that managers aim to maximise sales revenue as opposed to that of the traditional theory which assumes firms aim to maximise profit. Also known as "sales maximisation".

This theory of the objectives of firms was first developed by William Baumol and argues that managers wish to maximise their salary and perks. There is some evidence to suggest that managers' pay and conditions are linked to the size of the company, which is in turn linked to the sales revenue of the firm rather than profits. If the sole aim of the firm was sales revenue maximisation, then the firm would produce the output at which MR = 0 and price elasticity of demand = 1. Price would be given by AR at this output. The output will be higher and the price lower than the profit maximising position. In reality the managers are likely to ensure that at least a satisfactory profit is made to please shareholders, which means that the firm is likely to maximise revenue subject to a minimum profit constraint. This would take the price and output closer to the profit maximising position.

The issue for managers in this model is identifying the minimum acceptable level of profit.

7.8.3 Price discrimination – first, second and third degree

We have already seen earlier in this chapter that monopolies and firms in oligopolistic markets are able to practise price discrimination (selling the same product in different markets at different prices) enabling them to increase their revenue and possibly profits above the level that would be achieved if the entire output of the product was sold at the same price. In order for a firm to effectively and successfully practise price discrimination, certain conditions must be met. These conditions, together with an example of their application to the railway industry, are summarised in Table 7.15 below.

Table 7.15 Conditions for price discrimination ▼

Condition	Application
The firm must exercise some monopoly power in the market.	In the UK, train operating companies are granted franchises for a period of time during which they have a monopoly over particular routes.
It must be possible to separate the markets.	Markets are separated in a number of ways according to: • age of customer – cheaper tickets for children • status – student discounts • time of travel – fares lower at weekends, middle of the day.
It must not be possible to buy in one market and resell in another. This is called arbitrage.	Ticket barriers/guards ensure individuals only travel with the correct ticket.
Price elasticities of demand must be different in the markets.	Peak-time business travellers have a more inelastic demand than off-peak leisure travellers, enabling them to be charged a higher price.

Types of price discrimination

Economists identify three types of price discrimination.

First-degree price discrimination occurs when the monopolist is able to charge each individual consumer the maximum amount they are prepared to pay for a product. Individuals with spare tickets for major sell-out concerts and sports events will try to bargain with potential buyers to try to estimate the maximum they are prepared to pay. If first-degree price discrimination is successful, the whole consumer surplus will be eliminated. First-degree price discrimination is illustrated in Figure 7.47. If all four units of the product are sold at the same price, the firm's TR = $40. If all units of the product are sold at the same price, this will be $10 where demand equals supply. If each unit is sold at the maximum possible price, the TR = $70.

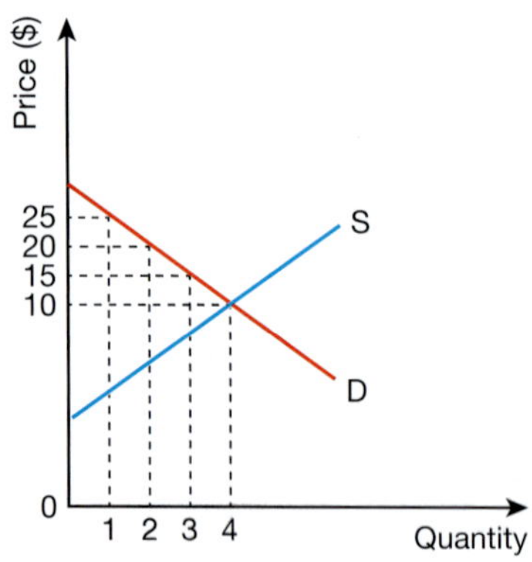

Figure 7.47 First-degree price discrimination ▲

> **Key terms**
>
> **First-degree price discrimination**: the practice of charging each consumer the maximum they are prepared to pay.
>
> **Second-degree price discrimination**: the practice of charging consumers different prices for successive blocks of consumption.

Second-degree price discrimination is common in markets for public utilities such as electricity where different prices are charged for successive blocks of consumption. Electricity companies typically charge higher prices for the first block of units sold and then lower prices for the rest.

Second-degree price discrimination is shown in Figure 7.48.

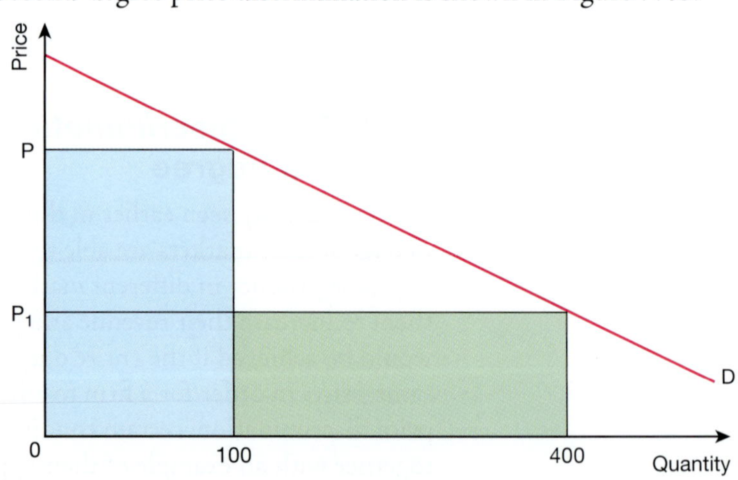

Figure 7.48 Second-degree price discrimination ▲

> **Key term**
>
> **Third-degree price discrimination**: the practice of charging different consumers different prices for the same product.

Third-degree price discrimination refers to the selling of the same product in different markets to different consumers at different prices. Examples include: different fares on public transport for individuals of different ages or different prices for products in domestic and foreign markets.

Figure 7.49 illustrates the way in which output and price are determined under third-degree price discrimination. If there is no price discrimination, the price charged will be P in the combined market and the profit is shown by the shaded area. If price discrimination takes place, the firm will equate the overall MC with the MR in the individual markets and charge a price of P_1 in the foreign market and P_2 in the domestic market. The price will be highest in the domestic market as demand is more inelastic because there are likely to be fewer substitutes. The combined total of the profits made in the domestic and foreign markets will exceed the profit made if the same price had been charged for all sales.

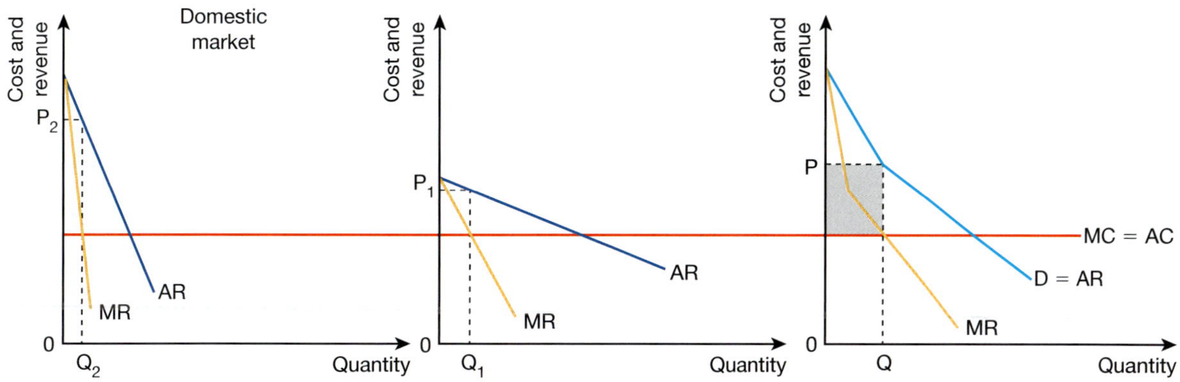

Figure 7.49 Third-degree price discrimination ▲

> **Activity**
>
> **Price discrimination**
>
> Identify two examples of firms operating each of the three types of price discrimination in your own country. Are these examples in the public interest?

Issues surrounding price discrimination

It is not possible to make a definitive judgement as to whether price discrimination is in the public interest. Table 7.16 identifies some of the issues.

Table 7.16 Price discrimination ▼

Producers benefit from higher revenue and profits
Welfare loss for individuals as consumer surplus is removed
Some individuals now paying a higher price for the product
Some individuals pay a lower price than previously
Some low income earners may now be able to afford a product that was previously out of their reach
Profits earned by companies may be used to finance R&D which may ultimately benefit consumers in terms of new or better-quality products
Charging some individuals higher prices might enable organisations to provide equipment which benefits all consumers. For example, charging high fees to private patients for operations may enable hospitals to purchase equipment which will benefit non-paying patients

Case Study

Price discrimination and the internet

The development of the internet has made it easier for individuals to compare prices in order to search for the best deal and so, in line with economic theory, as more perfect information becomes available, price discrimination by firms should become more difficult.

But is this actually the case? There is evidence that the internet actually makes it easier for firms to engage in price discrimination. For example, airline websites can now differentiate fares by date of booking and times of flights. It is not possible to buy such a ticket in one market and resell in another because government security measures mean that a passenger's name must match that on the ticket.

Currently, a number of retail outlets, including booksellers, charge different prices for the same product depending on whether it is purchased in one of their stores or via the internet.

1 Explain the conditions necessary for firms to successfully practise price discrimination.

2 Using the information in the case study and your own research, evaluate the extent to which the development of the internet might make price discrimination by firms more likely.

7.8.4 *Other pricing policies*

Limit pricing

Limit pricing, as discussed in section 7.6.4 when looking at contestable markets, is a strategy used by a firm usually operating in a market with relatively low barriers to entry to deter new firms from entering the market. The Organisation for Economic and Commercial Development (OECD) defines limit pricing as "pricing by incumbent firms to deter or inhibit entry or the expansion of fringe firms. The limit price is set below the short-run profit maximising price, but above the competitive level". Limit pricing means that the incumbent firm(s) sacrifice current profits in order to retain monopoly power and ensure future profits. Limit pricing is designed to indicate to potential new entrants that demand in the market is relatively low and/or that the incumbent firm is prepared to act aggressively to retain its market share.

Limit pricing is most likely to be effective when:

- there is incomplete information possessed by the potential entrant about the level of demand in the market and/or the cost structure of the incumbent firm
- the incumbent firm is able to make a reasonable estimate of the average costs (AC) of the potential entrant
- the incumbent firm has been established in the market for a sufficiently long period of time to have reaped the benefits of significant economies of scale and can therefore be reasonably confident of having lower costs than the potential entrant.

Given these conditions, the incumbent firm can be reasonably confident of being able to set a price which will be below the AC of possible new competitors, but sufficiently high to enable it to still make a profit.

Advantages and disadvantages of limit pricing

From the perspective of the firm(s) already in the market, the clear advantage of a successful limit pricing strategy is to deter new entrants and ensure the retention of their monopoly power along with the advantages that it brings, particularly in terms of the ability to fix price or output and make supernormal profits. However, there is some uncertainty as to whether a limit pricing strategy is in fact superior to one in which prices and, therefore, profits are maintained at the existing level, but decline as new firms enter. It is also the case that the limit pricing strategy may not work if the potential entrants believe that if the incumbent firm is prepared to accept lower profits it may be worthwhile if they have sufficient funds or exit costs are low. Another possible advantage to the incumbent firm is that limit pricing may reduce the risk of investigation by government or competition regulators.

The advantage of limit pricing for consumers is the possibility of lower prices in the short run. In the long run, however, once the incumbent firm has established its monopoly position, it is likely that prices will rise again to previous levels.

Predatory pricing

Unlike limit pricing, which is designed to deter new entrants into a market, predatory pricing is a strategy of setting very low prices (possibly even below marginal costs of production) in order primarily to drive existing competitors out of the market, although it will also deter potential new entrants. The predatory firm will make losses in the short run, but once it has successfully driven out existing competition it can raise prices to gain greater profits.

Predatory pricing is defined by the OECD as price set below average variable costs ($P < AVC$). As we saw when discussing the shut-down points for a firm, although a firm will have to shut down in the long run if it cannot cover all its costs, i.e. $P < AC$, it may be able to stay in business in the short run if it can cover its variable costs, i.e. $P > AVC$ because under these circumstances shutting down immediately will incur greater losses than continuing in business. Hence, if a firm continues to trade even though $P < AVC$, this is an indication of predatory pricing.

The advantages and disadvantages of predatory pricing to firms and consumers are the same as discussed in relation to limit pricing above. The firm embarking on predatory pricing will sacrifice short-term profits in return for a hoped-for increase in monopoly power and higher long-term profits. The predatory pricing strategy may also be costly to the predator as the targeted competitors may not easily be driven out of the market and the firm may find it difficult to recoup initial losses. Ultimately it could be that all firms in the market lose.

As with limit pricing, consumers may benefit from reduced prices in the short run, but face the possible disadvantages associated with the predatory firm consolidating its monopoly position in the long run.

Predatory pricing is a tactic adopted by some supermarkets to attract customers ▲

Some supermarkets adopt predatory pricing on a partial scale through the practice of offering customers occasional loss leaders. This involves selling some products at a heavily discounted price in order to attract customers into a store in the hope they will buy other products as well. The supermarket is able to do this because it makes a profit on other lines. Overall, therefore, the company remains profitable.

In most countries both limit and predatory pricing are regarded as anti-competitive strategies and as such are illegal.

Price leadership

Price leadership is a feature of oligopolistic markets with high barriers to entry where one of a small number of firms has sufficient power in a particular market to essentially be able to set a price which others in the market will feel obliged to follow in order to not lose market share. Price leadership is most likely to be effective in markets in which there is a high, stable and inelastic demand and in which firms produce similar products.

There are three common models:

- Dominant firm model. This normally involves firms following the lead of a firm which has a dominant position in the market in terms of its output and market share. Other firms will be likely to keep to the agreement for fear that if they do not, their existence could be threatened by an aggressive pricing strategy by the dominant firm. Saudi Arabia, for example, is a dominant player in OPEC.
- Barometric price leadership. This involves leadership by a firm that has consistently been seen to judge market conditions accurately over time and is, therefore, seen as a good "barometer" of market trends.
- Parallel pricing. This involves firms in the industry making the same price changes at any given time. In this case it is possible that different firms may act as the price leader on different occasions.

> **Link**
> For a detailed discussion of all aspects of price elasticity of demand see Chapter 2, sections 2.2.1–2.2.8.

7.8.5 Relationship between price elasticity of demand and a firm's revenue

At this point it would be useful to recap on the relevant key concepts.

> **Link**
> For a detailed discussion of TR, AR and MR and TR, AR and MR curves see section 7.5.8 in this chapter.

Price elasticity of demand

Price elasticity of demand was discussed extensively in sections 2.2.1–2.2.8 in Chapter 2.

Price elasticity of demand refers to the responsiveness of the quantity demanded of a product to a change in price and the formula is:

PED = proportionate (percentage) change in quantity demanded/ proportionate (percentage) change in price

> **Link**
> See Figure 2.16 and Tables 2.11 and 2.12 in Chapter 2.

If the proportionate (percentage) change in quantity demanded is greater than the proportionate change in price (PED > 1) then demand is said to be elastic.

If the proportionate (percentage) change in quantity demanded is less than the proportionate change in price (PED < 1) then demand is said to be inelastic.

If the proportionate (percentage) change in quantity demanded is equal to the proportionate change in price (PED = 1) then demand is said to have unitary elasticity.

Firms revenue

The important concepts here are total revenue (TR), average revenue (AR) and marginal revenue (MR). These were discussed in detail in section 7.5.8 earlier in this chapter.

TR is the total receipts from a firm's sales – the price of the good multiplied by the quantity sold: TR = P – Q

AR is TR/Q; since TR = P – Q then AR = P – Q/Q = P. Hence at any given output AR = P and the demand curve facing a firm is its AR curve.

MR is the addition to a firm's TR resulting from the sale of an additional unit of its product and is calculated by $\Delta TR/\Delta Q$.

Relationship between price elasticity of demand and a firm's revenue in a normal downward sloping demand curve

This has already been introduced and discussed in some detail in section 2.2.5 when looking at the variation in price elasticity of demand along the length of a straight-line demand curve and in the forthcoming discussion it is important to refer to Figure 2.16 and Tables 2.11 and 2.12 on pages xx respectively of Chapter 2.

From these we can see that at the price which corresponds to the midpoint of the demand (AR) curve, $5.50, the price elasticity of demand is equal to unity (PED = 1) and at this point total revenue (TR) is at a maximum. For prices above this, demand becomes increasingly price elastic (PED >1) and is equal to infinity (PED = ∞) at point Y where the demand curve meets the vertical price axis. Over this range it is clear that price rises will reduce the firm's TR and price reductions increase it.

At prices below that at which the price elasticity of demand is unity, the demand curve becomes increasingly price inelastic (PED < 1) becoming equal to zero (PED = 0) at a price of zero. Over this range, price rises will increase the firm's TR and price reductions decrease it.

We can now introduce the marginal revenue (MR) curve. As the demand (AR) curve is downward sloping, it means that the firm is operating in an imperfect market such as monopoly and as such has

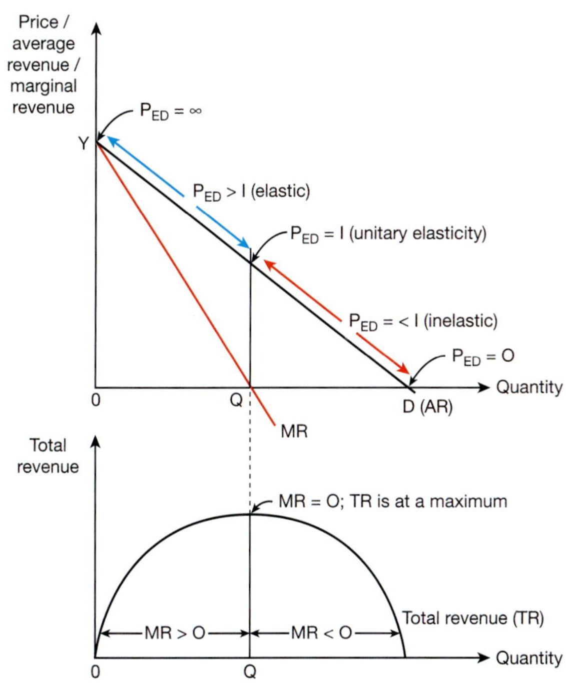

Figure 7.50 The relationship between price elasticity of demand and total, average and marginal revenue (TR, AR, MR) ▲

Link

The reason why the MR curve falls at twice the rate of the AR curve for a downward sloping demand curve is explained in section 7.5.8 in this chapter.

Getting it right

It is important to remember that at the price and output at which PED = 1, MR = 0 and TR is at a maximum.

some control over the price of its product. In these circumstances, as explained in section 7.5.8, the MR curve will fall at twice the rate of the AR curve as shown in the top diagram of Figure 7.50.

This means that the MR curve will intersect the horizontal quantity axis at the midpoint between the origin and the point at which the AR curve meets the quantity axis, i.e. at Q. This point is vertically below the mid-point of the demand curve at which price the price elasticity of demand is unity and TR is at a maximum. Hence, as shown in the diagram, MR is positive over the elastic part of the demand curve, negative over the inelastic part of the demand curve and zero at the price at which the price elasticity of demand is unity. All this is illustrated in Figure 7.50 below.

We can use the relationships discussed above to explain why a profit maximising monopolist will never produce at any point on its demand curve where demand is inelastic.

The profit maximising monopolist will produce at the point at which MC = MR. At an output of Q, MR is zero and beyond Q, MR is negative. Since MC will always be positive, it is impossible for MC and MR to be equal at an output of Q or more and so a profit maximising will never produce on the inelastic part of the demand curve.

Relationship between price elasticity of demand and a firm's revenue in a kinked demand curve

The relationship between, price elasticity of demand, TR, AR and MR in relation to the kinked demand curve has been discussed in some depth in section 7.6.4 when looking at the kinked demand curve model as an explanation of the behaviour and performance of firms in non-collusive oligopolies.

Firms in such markets operate in an environment of risk and uncertainty which means that when considering any changes to the prices of their product(s) they need to factor in and take account of the anticipated reaction of rival competitors. It is important at this point to refer to Figures 7.45 and 7.46. Figure 7.45 shows that at the profit maximising price and output, the firm's demand (AR) curve will be kinked because the firm will believe that whilst competitors might match or exceed any price reduction so as not to lose their market share it makes, they will almost certainly not match any price increase hoping to seize some of the firm's market share for themselves. The firm will, therefore, perceive its demand (AR) curve to be relatively inelastic for price reductions and elastic for price increases. In this case, price rises would increase TR and price falls decrease it for the firm over the inelastic section of the demand curve and vice versa for the elastic part of the curve.

The logical solution for the firm, therefore, is to keep price unchanged.

Figure 7.46 introduces the MR curve. As the demand (AR) curve is kinked, the corresponding MR curve will have a vertical discontinuity at the current price. This means that if a firm's costs increase or

Link

See section 7.6.4 in this chapter for a detailed discussion of the kinked demand curve model.

decrease, but the MC curve remains within this discontinuity, then the equilibrium price and quantity will remain unchanged.

As with the case of a normal downward sloping demand curve at the point at which MR = 0, price elasticity of demand will be equal to unity and TR will be at a maximum. For the same reasons as in monopoly firms, profit maximising facing a kinked demand curve will only produce on the relatively elastic part of the demand curve.

Key concepts

- **Scarcity and choice** is considered in the sections in this chapter on marginal utility theory and indifference curve analysis which explain how individuals allocate their limited income so as to maximise their satisfaction. In addition the section on market structures explains how firms in different competitive situations allocate their scarce resources in making price and output decisions.
- **The margin and decision-making** runs throughout the chapter, but is particularly evident in the sections on consumer decision-making behaviour and the price and output decisions of profit maximising firms in different market structures.
- **Equilibrium and disequilibrium** is explored at various points, particularly when looking at the way in which firms arrive at the profit maximising price and output position in different market structures.
- **Time** as a concept is addressed here when looking at firms, fixed and variable costs and the way in which a firm's costs vary with output in the short and long run together with the analysis of firms' short and long run profit maximising price and output.
- **Efficiency and inefficiency** is an underlying theme The different types of efficiency (allocative, productive, static, dynamic and Pareto) and inefficiency (X-inefficiency including organisational slack) are explicitly defined and explained and their importance discussed.

Progress check

After completing this chapter you should be able to:

- understand marginal utility theory and how it can be used to explain the downward-sloping demand curve
- explain indifference curves and budget lines together with the income and substitution effects of price changes for normal, inferior and Giffen goods
- explain the limitations of marginal utility theory and indifference curve analysis as explanations of consumer behaviour
- explain "rational behaviour"
- explain the contribution of behavioural economics to the study of decision-making
- understand what is meant by an efficient or optimum allocation of resources
- understand what is meant by allocative and productive efficiency and the differences between them
- understand the nature of dynamic and Pareto efficiency
- understand what is meant by an inefficient allocation of resources
- explain what is meant by market failure and the reasons it might occur
- understand the nature of and reasons for positive and negative externalities in both production and consumption
- understand that social costs are the sum of private and external costs and that social benefits are the sum of private and external benefits

- analyse and evaluate the role of cost-benefit analysis in relation to decision making
- explain how production in the short run is determined by the law of diminishing returns and in the long run by economies and diseconomies of scale
- explain the link between production in the short and long run and short- and long-run costs
- understand the importance of profit as an objective in the traditional theory of the firm
- explain the main features of the main forms of market structure
- explain the relationship between elasticity of demand, marginal, average and total revenue for a downward-sloping demand curve
- explain, compare and evaluate the conduct of firms in different market structures in terms of pricing and non-price policy, price discrimination, price leadership and in oligopoly mutual interdependence
- explain, compare and evaluate the performance of firms in different market structures in terms of output, profits, efficiency, barriers to entry, price and non-price competition and collusion
- understand why firms may pursue alternative objectives to profit maximisation, including the difficulties involved in maximising profits and the principal–agent problem
- explain the reasons firms grow in size, the methods by which they do so and why small firms continue to survive.

Exam-style questions

Essay questions

1 Assess the extent to which the law of diminishing marginal utility provides an explanation of the normal downward-sloping demand curve. [20 marks]

2 With the aid of diagrams, assess the long-run equilibrium of a firm in perfect competition compared with that of one in monopolistic competition. [20 marks]

3 Assess the view that monopoly is always against the public interest. [20 marks]

4 Assess whether healthcare can and should be provided by the free market. [20 marks]

5 Assess the different ways in which a government might approach a decision about a construction project in comparison with that used by a private firm. [20 marks]

6 Assess the extent to which insights from behavioural economics provide a more realistic explanation of actual consumer behaviour and decision making than that provided by traditional economic theory. [20 marks]

Multiple-choice questions

7 Which of the following is $\Delta TC/\Delta Q$? [1 mark]

A Average cost
B Average fixed cost
C Average variable cost
D Marginal cost

8 Which of the following is a characteristic of monopolistic competition? [1 mark]

A In the long run, firms produce at the minimum point of their average cost curve.
B In the short run, firms can make supernormal profits.
C There are barriers to entry into the industry.
D Firms produce homogeneous products.

8 Government microeconomic intervention

In this chapter you will develop your knowledge and understanding of:

- government policies to achieve efficient resource allocation and correct market failure
- equity and redistribution of income and wealth
- labour market forces and government intervention.

8.1 Government policies to achieve efficient resource allocation and correct market failure

8.1.1 *Application and effectiveness of measures to tackle different forms of market failure*

Specific and ad valorem indirect taxes

Indirect taxes were discussed in Chapter 3, section 3.2.1, in relation to the methods and effects of government interventions in markets. Specific indirect taxes were referred to there, where a specific amount of tax is required to be paid. Indirect taxes can be used to correct market failure when there is over-consumption of demerit goods.

However, another type of indirect tax is an *ad valorem* (literally "according to value") tax. An *ad valorem* tax is where the tax to be paid is a percentage of the selling price. Indirect taxes such as value added tax (VAT) and goods and services tax (GST) are examples of *ad valorem* taxes.

Key term

***Ad valorem* tax**: where the tax on the consumption of products is a percentage of the value of the product rather than a fixed amount.

Getting it right

It is important you understand that specific and *ad valorem* taxes are shown differently in a diagram. With a specific tax, the supply curve will shift to the left parallel to the original supply curve. However, with an *ad valorem* tax, the supply curve will shift to the left but the gap between the two curves will widen, i.e. the two curves diverge from each other.

Case Study

Indirect tax in Eswatini

The indirect sales tax on the consumption of goods and services in Eswatini in southern Africa (Eswatini was formerly known as Swaziland) is called value added tax (VAT). It is levied on most goods and services consumed in Eswatini at a general rate of 15 per cent. However, a higher tax rate of 20 per cent is applied to most alcohol and tobacco.

1 Explain why a country, such as Eswatini, would have an indirect tax at different rates for different products.

Link

Chapter 3, section 3.2.1 and Chapter 5, section 5.2.4 also deal with indirect taxes.

Subsidies

Subsidies were discussed in Chapter 3, section 3.2.2, in relation to the methods and effects of government interventions in markets. They can be used to achieve efficient resource allocation and to correct market failure by encouraging the consumption of certain products. For example, subsidies can be used to encourage the consumption of merit goods, such as education and health care.

Activity

Indirect taxation

Find out as much as you can about the indirect taxes in your country.

Link

Chapter 3, section 3.2.2, also deals with subsidies.

Case Study

Shaanxi History Museum, Xi'an, China

The Shaanxi History Museum in Xi'an, China, is described as "the pearl of ancient dynasties and house of Chinese precious treasures". It was opened in 1993. Xi'an is a former capital city of China and is located at the start of the famous Silk Road trade route between China and Europe.

The museum contains over 370,000 items, including a number of soldiers from the Terracotta Army and various murals, paintings, pottery and coins.

The museum can be regarded as a merit good and to encourage people to visit it, the cost of entry is subsidised to allow 6,000 free tickets to be issued every day. In 2019, it was visited by almost three million people.

1 Discuss why a museum, such as the Shaanxi Museum in Xi'an, should be subsidised.

Price controls

Price controls were covered in Chapter 3, section 3.1.3, where it was pointed out that these can come in three different forms:

- Maximum price controls: one type of market failure is that inequality in the distribution of income means that some people may not be able to afford some essential products, such as bread or rice, and so a government could establish a maximum price to enable more people to buy the product.
- Minimum price controls: another type of market failure is the possible over-consumption of demerit goods, such as alcohol and tobacco, and a government could establish a minimum price to discourage the consumption of such goods.
- Buffer stock scheme: prices may fluctuate widely in some markets, especially agricultural markets, and so a government could intervene through the operation of a buffer stock scheme to control the price over a period of time.

Activity

Subsidies

Find out as much as you can about any subsidies that have been given by the government of your country.

Link

Chapter 3, section 3.1.3, also deals with price controls.

Activity

Price controls

Find out as much as you can about any price controls that operate in your country.

Production quotas

A government could decide to set a limit to the quantity of a product that may be produced in an economy over a specific period of time. For example, if the production of a certain product is too high, lowering the market price, a quota could be used to limit production. This policy could also be used in an attempt to lower the level of pollution in a country. If a producer exceeded this quota, they could be required to pay a fine.

Key term

Production quota: a specific limit to the quantity produced of a product over a period of time.

Getting it right

A quota is often used as a form of import control, but you need to understand that it can be used in a domestic economy to limit production.

Prohibitions and licences

Another policy to achieve efficient resource allocation and to correct market failure is the use of prohibitions and licences.

A prohibition is a ban on certain products being available in an economy, i.e. a particular product is made illegal in an economy.

A licence, on the other hand, gives a government the power to have some control in an economy by granting permission to certain suppliers to produce something, but the licence will limit the freedom of the producers or suppliers in some way. For example, in many countries, it is necessary to obtain a licence before starting a new business. Obtaining a licence will then give an entrepreneur the opportunity to operate a business in a particular city or state.

Key terms

Prohibition: a situation where a certain product is banned in a country.

Licence: a situation where permission is given, often by a government, but where the permission is limited or restricted in some way.

Regulation: a rule or law that applies to firms in different circumstances.

Regulatory body: an organisation that is set up to enforce particular policies and regulations in an economy.

Regulation and deregulation

Regulation

Another way that a government could intervene in a market is through the regulation of producers.

A regulation refers to a rule or law that can be used by a government to reduce the extent of market failure in an economy. There are many examples of such regulation in different countries, such as in relation to the control of monopolies, the protection of the environment, consumer protection and transportation.

Regulation of monopolies

In some countries, a government may establish regulations to control monopolies. A government could decide to introduce a policy on mergers and acquisitions. For example, if a proposed merger was thought to be against the public interest, such as severely restricting the extent of choice for consumers, then the government could use a regulatory body to prevent the merger from taking place.

A government could use a law or a rule to insist that if a monopoly firm did exist, it would need to guarantee that a minimum quality would apply to the good or service being provided by the firm.

A government could insist that there needed to be a certain amount of competition in a particular market. For example, it could instruct a regulatory body to ensure that no one firm should control more than a specified share of a market.

Case Study

Competitive environment

Two laws have been passed in Malaysia, the Competition Act and the Price Control and Anti-Profiteering Act, which were designed to establish a more competitive environment in the country's economy. The aim is to reduce anti-competitive practices as much as possible. Consumers should be able to benefit from greater innovation, improved service and more competitive prices.

Neighbouring countries, including Indonesia and Singapore, had already established various regulations and laws to encourage competition in their economies and Malaysia, having taken fifteen years to bring these two laws into effect, was keen not to be left behind.

1 Explain the different ways in which countries, such as Malaysia, Indonesia and Singapore, could encourage competition in their economies.

Activity

Competition

Use the Internet to find out as much as you can about the ways in which Malaysia, Indonesia and Singapore have attempted to encourage competition in their economies.

Case Study

Control of monopolies in Argentina

The first anti-monopoly law in Argentina dates back to 1923. The main reason for the introduction of the law was to prevent monopolies operating against the public interest and producing very large profits. The law was further strengthened in 1946 and 1980. Fines can be imposed against firms who are found to be acting in an anti-competitive manner.

The law, however, has been criticised for limiting free market initiative in the country. Some of the firms that have been fined have argued that the large profits would be used to fund research and development into new products and into new, and more efficient, methods of production.

1 Discuss the arguments for and against the regulation of monopolies.

Protection of the environment

A government could use taxes to discourage certain forms of production, and subsidies to encourage other forms of production, but it could also use regulation to reduce the level of pollution in an economy. For example, some governments have passed laws giving the regulatory bodies the right to fine companies if they are found guilty of polluting the environment.

Case Study

Air quality regulation in the USA

The Environmental Protection Agency (EPA), the federal body in the United States responsible for oversight of environmental issues, has introduced a regulation called the Cross-State Air Pollution Rule (CSAPR). The regulation requires states to reduce emissions that contribute to pollution. For example, sulphur dioxide emissions must be no more than 27 per cent and nitrogen oxide levels must be no more than 46 per cent of what they were in 2005.

The EPA claims that CSAPR will prevent as many as 30,000 pollution-related premature deaths and yield between US$120 billion and US$280 billion per year in health and environmental benefits.

The regulation has been criticised by consumers, however, who have pointed out that the cost of implementing the regulation will be higher prices for them. It has been estimated that prices could rise by as much as 20 per cent. There is also a concern that some power plants may be forced to close, leading to a loss of jobs.

1 Discuss the possible advantages and disadvantages of introducing a regulation to limit the amount of pollution in a country, such as the USA.

Consumer protection

In some countries, the government has passed laws which give consumers certain rights. These can cover the description of products being sold, such as ensuring that the descriptions of products are accurate and honest, or the weight of something being consumed.

Case Study

Consumer protection in Sri Lanka

In Sri Lanka, the Consumer Affairs Authority (CAA) is the main government institution with the responsibility for protecting consumers against unfair trade practices and safeguarding what might be considered a fair degree of market competition in the country.

The Compliance and Enforcement Division within the CAA investigates complaints made by individual consumers or by consumer organisations. The majority of disputes are usually settled through a process of discussion and negotiation, but if an agreement cannot be reached, the dispute will need to be settled in a court.

Complaints relating to financial products can be referred to the Financial Ombudsman scheme.

1 Discuss the advantages of consumer protection to consumers, such as those in Sri Lanka.

Activity

Regulation

Find out as much as you can about the different kinds of regulation that exist in your country.

Transportation

Regulations could be put into operation to control different forms of transportation in a country. This could cover all forms of transportation, including air, rail, road and water.

Case Study

Airport regulation in the United Kingdom

In the UK, air transport is regulated by an organisation called the Civil Aviation Authority. This body has the power to regulate the take-off and landing charges at UK airports and the number of passengers each year that can use a particular airport.

One airport in the UK, Stansted, experienced quite a significant fall in the number of passengers between 2007 and 2012 and even though the number has since increased, it was only about the same in 2019 as it was in 2007.

The owners of Stansted airport have argued that if the regulations imposed by the Civil Aviation Authority were to be removed, it would be able to increase the number of passengers it can handle from 23 million to 36 million each year. The owners have stated that if the airport was to be allowed to expand, it would help to take pressure off other busy airports in the London area, such as Heathrow and Gatwick. The managing director of the airport has stressed that there should be less regulation and more competition, arguing that this would help to keep costs down for both passengers and airlines.

The Civil Aviation Authority, however, has stressed that it has important functions to perform in relation to different forms of regulation, including airspace policy, air traffic control, safety regulation and consumer protection.

1 Discuss the advantages and disadvantages of the regulation of airports, such as Stansted, to consumers.

Progress question

1 To what extent is regulation likely to reduce market failure in an economy?

Deregulation

Deregulation is where there is a reduction in the number of rules, regulations and laws that exist in an economy. The aim is to allow a greater degree of competition to take place which should lead to a situation of greater efficiency. One example of this would be the telecommunications industry in the UK.

Key term

Deregulation: the removal of legal restrictions and controls on economic activity, usually to allow a greater degree of competition in a market.

Link

The direct provision of certain goods and services by a government has been discussed in Chapter 3, section 3.2.3

Case Study

Deregulation in the UK telecommunications industry

Deregulation in the UK telecommunications industry began in 1984, removing many of the existing barriers to entry into the industry. Before then, one firm, British Telecom (BT) had a monopoly. After 1984, and especially after 1991, new firms were able to enter the industry to enhance competition.

The greater competition that then occurred led to an increase in efficiency in the industry and prices, just like prices in any other market, were determined by the forces of demand and supply. There are now many firms competing in the industry, including BT, Virgin Media, Sky and TalkTalk.

1 Discuss the advantages of greater competition in the telecommunications industry, such as in the UK.

Direct provision

Another way in which a government could attempt to achieve efficient resource allocation and to correct market failure in an economy is through the direct provision of goods and services.

The extent of market failure could be reduced in an economy if a government decides to directly provide certain goods and services. Examples of such provision, as already discussed in Chapter 3, could include education and healthcare.

> **Activity**
> **Direct provision of goods and services**
> Find out as much as you can about any goods and/or services that are directly provided by the government of your country or another country of your choice.

Pollution permits

A pollution permit (or tradeable permit) is an example of a licence that is issued by a government. The licence allows a firm to pollute, but only up to a certain level. The amount of pollution permitted by the licence will be less than what is being emitted at the moment and so in this way a government can reduce the level of pollution in an economy.

> **Key term**
> **Pollution permit**: a licence to a firm to bring about a reduction in the level of pollution over a period of time.

> **Activity**
> **Pollution permits**
> Find out as much as you can about the different kinds of pollution permits that exist in your country.

Property rights

Market failure could arise in an economy because of a lack of clear property rights. If ownership is clear, there is less likely to be a problem because of private property rights. For example, rubbish is unlikely to be dumped on a person's property because that person, in such a situation, would be likely to take legal action.

However, in certain aspects of an economy, such property rights are not so clear, such as in relation to air, water and certain open spaces. In these situations, there are common, not private, property rights.

In such situations as these, a government could pursue a policy of extending property rights to include the air, rivers and the sea. If voluntary agreements were unsuccessful, a government could decide to introduce a system of pollution permits.

> **Key terms**
> **Property rights**: a situation where owners of economic goods have a right to decide how such assets are used.
> **Nationalisation**: a process whereby private sector firms become part of the public sector of the economy, with the government or state involved in the direct provision of particular goods and/or services.

Nationalisation and privatisation

Nationalisation

Nationalisation refers to the process whereby private sector firms are transferred into public ownership and are owned and controlled in some way by the government.

The advantages and disadvantages of nationalisation are indicated in Table 8.1.

Table 8.1 The advantages and disadvantages of nationalisation

Advantages of nationalisation	Disadvantages of nationalisation
A nationalised industry can benefit from economies of scale, lowering cost and possibly price.	A nationalised industry may lack the incentive to be efficient, compared to the situation in the private sector.
If an industry is state-owned, it can avoid a wasteful duplication of resources.	Nationalised industries may lack competitive pressure, such as the pressure to be innovative.
With state ownership, it is easier to control the negative externalities and encourage the positive externalities.	It is possible that some decisions taken by a nationalised industry could be taken primarily for political, rather than economic, reasons.
A nationalised industry will prevent monopoly power being held by a private firm.	A state-owned firm may still be in a position to abuse its monopoly power.

Case Study

Mineral resources in Namibia and South Africa

African countries have a vast wealth of mineral resources. The dilemma for many of the countries, however, is whether to allow private sector companies to be responsible for the development of the resources or whether to bring this under greater state control.

In Namibia, it was decided to transfer all new mining and exploration to a state-owned company, the Epangelo Mining Company. The mineral resources would include uranium, copper, gold, zinc and coal. Mining contributes about 15 per cent of the country's gross domestic product and its export earnings contribute to more than half of Namibia's total revenue from exports. The government of Namibia announced that the state-owned company would ensure that its people would reap the benefits from the country's rich endowment of mineral resources.

In South Africa, however, which has a great deal of mineral wealth, the government has decided against such state ownership of mineral resources. It believes, instead, that it would be better to encourage private sector companies to be responsible for the exploration and mining of the resources and then to put a significant tax on the profits made by the companies. One idea is to impose a 50 per cent windfall tax on the "super profits" made by the mining companies.

1 Discuss the advantages and disadvantages of bringing companies, such as those responsible for mining, under state ownership.

Link

Chapter 7, section 7.6.1, deals with monopoly.

Link

Chapter 7, sections 7.3.1 and 7.3.2, deal with productive and allocative efficiency.

Nationalisation involves the creation of a monopoly. This is a situation where there is just one firm in an industry and this firm can control the supply of the product in the market.

If such a monopoly is in the private sector, such a market is likely to be inefficient because there will be a lack of both productive efficiency and allocative efficiency.

This inefficiency can be seen in Figure 8.1.

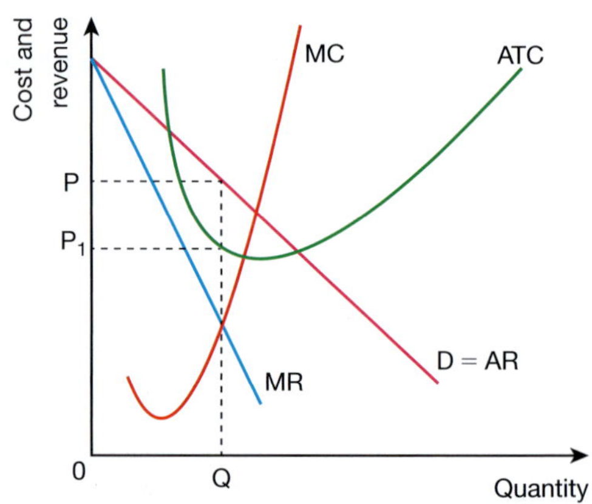

Figure 8.1 Productive and allocative inefficiency in a monopoly ▶

In a situation of perfect competition, the equilibrium would be where demand and supply intersect, i.e. where the demand or average revenue curve crosses the marginal cost curve. In this situation, the equilibrium quantity would be higher and the equilibrium price would be lower than in a situation of monopoly.

In a situation of a private sector monopoly, the firm would produce at the profit-maximising output where marginal cost and marginal revenue are equal. This can be shown in Figure 8.1 by a price of P and a quantity of Q. The effect of this is that a monopoly firm will therefore make supernormal or abnormal profits.

In this situation, there is neither productive or allocative efficiency in the market. Productive efficiency would occur at the lowest point of the average total cost curve, but it is clear in the diagram that this is not the case. Allocative efficiency would occur where price was equal to marginal cost, but it is clear in the diagram that this is not the case either. This is why a private sector monopoly is regarded as being inefficient and therefore an example of market failure.

There is an additional form of inefficiency that can occur. This is known as X-inefficiency. This can sometimes be referred to as organisational slack resulting from a firm having such a dominant position in a market. There will be a gap between the firm's average cost curve and the lowest possible cost that could be achieved. It results from the lack of competition in the market.

It is clear from the above that price and output decisions in a private sector monopoly are likely to create market failure because price will be higher, and output lower, than in perfect competition.

However, to avoid such a situation from occurring, a government can decide to run a monopoly firm as a state enterprise. This will enable price to be lower, and output to be higher, than in a private sector monopoly, but the state will need to ensure that this is indeed the case.

Case Study

The Thailand Tobacco Monopoly

The Thai government has decided to operate the tobacco industry in the country itself and has established the Thailand Tobacco Monopoly. This state enterprise has a monopoly in Thailand over the manufacture and distribution of cigarettes.

Before the establishment of this state enterprise, there had been a number of rival companies producing cigarettes in the country, but these were no longer allowed to exist. The government's argument was that such a monopoly would bring about a greater degree of efficiency. Many consumers, however, have argued that the lack of competition between producers has led to a situation of higher prices and lower quality than would have been the case if competition had been allowed to continue.

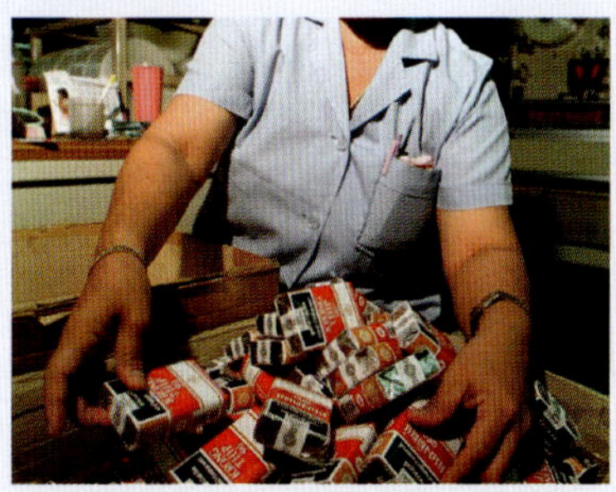

1 Explain why the establishment of TTM could be seen as an example of market failure.

A government, instead of nationalising an entire industry, could decide to control part of an industry and combine this with private sector companies. Such an arrangement is known as a joint venture.

Getting it right

Make sure that you know how to clearly distinguish between productive and allocative inefficiency in a monopoly.

Key term

X-inefficiency: the inefficiency that can occur in a monopoly when production is not at the lowest point on the average total cost curve.

Activity

X-inefficiency

Write down three examples that you can think of where a private sector monopoly could allow costs to be higher than they could be as a result of the lack of competitive pressure.

Progress question

2 Explain why a private sector monopoly firm can be regarded as inefficient.

Activity

Nationalisation

Carry out research in your own country to find out if there are any examples of nationalisation. Find out as much as you can about these examples.

Key term

Joint venture: a business arrangement between two or more organisations to work together for a particular purpose or on a particular project.

Case Study

Joint venture in Mongolia

The government of Mongolia is very keen to develop the country's infrastructure, but it has decided to co-operate in joint ventures with private sector companies in certain projects rather than provide them as a purely state-owned operation.

For example, responsibility for the building of one of the world's biggest copper mines in the middle of the desert is in the hands of a joint venture between the Mongolian government, which is providing 34 per cent of the finance, and Ivanhoe Mines of Canada, which is providing the other 66 per cent of the money.

The Mongolian government has decided to be involved in this joint venture with a private sector company because the mine will eventually become one of the five biggest copper mines in the world, producing 450,000 tonnes of copper a year.

1 Discuss the arguments for and against a government cooperating with a private sector company in a joint venture.

Key term

Privatisation: the process of transferring the ownership of assets from the public sector to the private sector, whereby public sector firms become part of the private sector of the economy, with the government or state no longer involved in the direct provision of particular goods and/or services.

Privatisation

Whereas nationalisation is the process of transferring the ownership of assets from the private sector to the public sector, privatisation refers to the transfer of ownership in the opposite direction, from the public sector to the private sector. It can also be called denationalisation.

As has already been indicated, a nationalised or state-owned firm may not be as efficient as a firm operating in the private sector, and so a decision may be taken by a government to privatise a firm or industry by transferring ownership from the public sector to the private sector.

Critics of nationalisation point out that without competition between a number of private sector firms, efficiency may be less than would otherwise be the case. This is why the process of privatisation has become so popular in many countries in the world, with competition in a market leading to greater efficiency. Therefore, a policy that could be used to try to reduce market failure is to encourage the privatisation of firms or industries. With greater competition in a market, price is likely to be lower, and output higher, than would otherwise be the case.

The advantages and disadvantages of privatisation are indicated in Table 8.2.

Table 8.2 The advantages and disadvantages of privatisation ▼

The advantages of privatisation	The disadvantages of privatisation
The reduction of government or state intervention in an economy so as to allow greater scope for the private sector to take key economic decisions. This view is based on the idea that there is a greater likelihood of economic efficiency occurring in a market that is not controlled by a government.	In some cases, a public sector monopoly could simply be replaced by a private sector monopoly. The impact of privatisation may therefore not be as great as had been predicted with one monopoly being replaced by another.
The sale of assets from the public sector to the private sector would have the effect of widening the extent of share ownership in an economy. The effect of this would be to encourage people to feel that they were part of the economic system.	Sometimes, it might be better to leave an industry in the public sector when there is a situation of natural monopoly. If a natural monopoly was privatised, the result could be a duplication of resources that is wasteful and inefficient.

The advantages of privatisation	The disadvantages of privatisation
A firm operating in the private sector would be more likely to be efficient and this would be likely to lead to an increase in quantity provided in the market and a lowering of cost. This lowering of cost could be passed on to consumers in the form of lower prices.	The greater efficiency of a private sector firm could come at a cost to the community if the number of employees was substantially reduced. This could be regarded as a negative externality resulting from the change of ownership from the public to the private sector.
The sale of assets would bring in a substantial amount of money and such revenue could play a key role in a government's fiscal policy.	The income that is brought in from the sale of shares in a former public sector company is a 'one-off' source of income and not one that will bring in revenue on a regular basis in the future.
A private sector company, being more efficient, would be able to raise capital to fund future growth rather than relying on the state to finance such expenditure.	The establishment of a private sector monopoly is likely to lead to the need to introduce a number of regulations so as to control it and ensure that consumers are not being exploited. The establishment of such regulations could severely limit the ability of the privatised firm to operate as it wishes.

The term privatisation can actually refer to a number of different government initiatives, beyond simply transferring ownership from the public to the private sector through the issuing of shares and the creation of a public limited company. These other methods can include deregulation, contracting out and franchising. These are described in Table 8.3.

Key terms

Deregulation: the removal of legal restrictions and controls on economic activity, usually to allow a greater degree of competition in a market.

Contracting out: the process whereby certain aspects of economic activity can be given to another firm, involving the transfer of responsibility for providing a particular service from the public to the private sector. This can also be known as outsourcing.

Link

Deregulation was also discussed earlier in this section.

Table 8.3 indicates the range of activities that can be included as examples of the privatisation process.

Table 8.3 The different forms of privatisation ▼

Economic activity	Meaning of activity
Sale of assets	This is where a nationalised firm or industry is sold to the private sector, a process that is often termed denationalisation. The firm therefore ceases to be state-owned and becomes a private sector company, usually a public limited company, in which shares can now be bought.
Deregulation	This process occurs when the regulations, rules, controls and laws that are imposed by the state on a firm or an industry are removed. This allows a much greater degree of competition to take place in the market.
Contracting out	This is where the extent of public sector control is reduced by allowing private sector firms to be involved in certain parts of an operation. There is also the possibility of bringing in private sector firms to provide some of the funding; some countries have specific initiatives to encourage the private sector to provide some of the funding (in the UK, two of these are PFI (Private Finance Initiative) and PPP (Public Private Partnerships)).
Franchising	This process occurs where a private sector firm may be allowed to bid for a franchise to operate a particular part of an industry.

Progress question

3 Explain the differences between the various forms of privatisation that can take place in an economy.

Progress question

4 Discuss the possible advantages and disadvantages of privatisation in an economy for (i) the consumers, (ii) the producers and (iii) the government.

Activity

Privatisation

Find out the extent to which privatisation has taken place in your country or a country of your choice.

Case Study

Privatisation in Pakistan

In recent years, a number of industries in Pakistan have been privatised, either completely or to a large extent.

One of these is the telecommunications industry. The Pakistan Telecommunication Company Ltd (PTCL), established in 1947, used to be completely run within the public sector and owned by the government of Pakistan. Since 2006, however, the firm has been partially privatised so that in 2020 38 per cent of the ownership was in private hands and 62 per cent was government owned. A total of 26 per cent of the shares are controlled by a company in the United Arab Emirates, Etisalat, and 12 per cent are controlled by the general public in Pakistan.

The consumers in Pakistan have benefited greatly from this partial change in ownership. For example, the cost of a telephone call from Karachi to Lahore is now 5 per cent of what it was before the change in ownership. The workers in the firm, however, were less pleased. They were concerned that some of them would lose their jobs and that those who kept their jobs would receive a cut in their wages. There were protests and strikes by the firm's workers against the partial privatisation.

Another industry in Pakistan that has been partially privatised is banking. In 2020, 85 per cent of banking was controlled by private banks, compared with only 10 per cent in 1990. The efficiency of the private banks is generally believed to be significantly greater than that of the former public sector banks. The country's central bank, the State Bank of Pakistan (SBP), however, remains under government control.

1 Discuss the possible advantages and disadvantages of privatisation in such industries as telecommunications and banking.

Case Study

Privatisation in Jamaica

The privatisation process began in Jamaica in the 1980s and it has carried on ever since. Over 100 businesses in a variety of industries have been privatised during this period and these have included maintenance of parks, street cleaning and garbage collection, Trans-Jamaican Airlines, public services and the Jamaica Broadcasting Corporation.

Governments in Jamaica have repeatedly stressed the importance of this process of privatisation to the greater efficiency of economic activity on the island. Creative entrepreneurship has been encouraged and it is believed that this will contribute to a higher rate of economic growth.

Jamaican governments have stressed that the process of privatisation is part of a wider strategy to liberalise the Jamaican economy, creating a more competitive and market-driven economic environment.

1 Explain how privatisation can contribute to more efficient economic activity in Jamaica.

Provision of information

A government could try to increase the availability of information to consumers in an attempt to influence their economic behaviour. If consumers are to maximise their satisfaction or utility, then they will need to have the necessary information in order to make appropriate decisions. If consumers do not have perfect information, it is unlikely that they will make the most rational decisions. Information failure is a major cause of market failure and if there is a lack of full and appropriate information in an economy, then the allocation of scarce resources in that economy is likely to be less efficient than it would otherwise be.

A government, therefore, can decide to improve the quality and accuracy of information that is made available to consumers in an economy. For example, information about the advantages of the consumption of merit goods could be improved and be made more readily available. Also, information about the disadvantages of the consumption of demerit goods could be improved and be made more readily available. A particular example of this would be in relation to the application of "nudge" theory.

> **Link**
>
> Chapter 1, sections 1.6.3 and 1.6.4 and Chapter 3, section 3.2.6, also deal with the provision of information.

Behavioural insights and "nudge" theory

Behavioural insights into the achievement of resource allocation and the correction of market failure emphasise the importance of the actual behaviour of people in an economy. This is in contrast to the traditional approach that is based on the idea that a consumer will act in a rational way.

Nudge theory is a particularly good example of this behavioural insight into economic behaviour. The theory is based on the idea that the economic behaviour of people can be "nudged" in a particular direction. The origin of the idea of nudge theory is associated with Richard Thaler, a Professor of Behavioural Science and Economics at the University of Chicago in the USA. The theory has been prominent since 2008.

> **Key term**
>
> **Nudge theory**: an attempt by a government to alter the economic behaviour of people in some way.

> **Getting it right**
>
> It is important that you can clearly recognise that a nudge is an attempt to influence economic behaviour, but it is not the same as a ban.

An example of this would be in relation to the discouragement of the consumption of demerit goods. Governments in some countries, for example, include a warning about the possible effects of consuming cigarettes. This could be in the form of a relatively mild nudge, such as when a packet of cigarettes includes on it the warning "smoking can damage your health". A stronger nudge could occur, however, if the wording was changed to "smoking can kill".

Similar examples can be found in relation to the consumption of alcohol. A government might decide to nudge consumers in a particular direction by including wording such as "drink sensibly", both on the product and in the advertising of the product. In some countries, the government will support a Drink Aware campaign where consumers of alcohol are informed about the possible dangers to their health of excessive consumption.

> **Progress question**
>
> **5** To what extent is the behaviour of individuals likely to be "nudged" in a particular direction by government intervention in an economy?

Case Study

Nudging people to use public transport in Los Angeles

Greater Los Angeles, with a population of over 20 million, is the largest city in California and the second largest city in the whole of the USA after New York. It has been described as the "car capital of the world" because of the large number of cars owned by its inhabitants. One of the most prevalent myths about Los Angeles is that it does not have any public transport and that therefore everyone must use a car to get about. However, this is not the case.

People in Los Angeles are being encouraged, or "nudged", to use public transport. This is because a reduction in the use of private cars will reduce pollution and improve air quality in the city. The city does have a comprehensive public transportation system of buses and trains. Most public transportation in the city is operated by Metro and it charges relatively low prices for its passes in an attempt to persuade people to use its services rather than private cars. These cost US$7 for a day pass and US$25 for a week pass, both with unlimited rides on trains and/or buses. The public transport system in the city has also been upgraded, with a greater frequency of services from 2020 in an attempt to make the system more efficient and therefore more attractive to consumers.

1 Discuss the possible advantages of "nudging" people in large cities, such as Los Angeles, to use public transport.

Activity

Nudge theory

Find out if the government of your country has attempted to "nudge" consumer behaviour in any particular ways.

Key term

Government failure: the failure of a government to achieve desired objectives as a result of intervention in a market.

8.1.2 *Government failure in microeconomic intervention*

Definition of government failure

Section 8.1.1 of this chapter has indicated a number of different ways in which a government can intervene to achieve efficient resource allocation and to correct market failure. However, government intervention in a market could contribute to an element of economic inefficiency that would not have existed in a free market and this is called government failure. This could come about as a result of different problems.

The causes of government failure

Problem of information

It has already been argued that there are potential advantages of a government intervening in a market to reduce or eliminate failures, but this is only likely to be successful if the government has the necessary up-to-date information to make an informed decision. The concept of information failure has been discussed in relation to the decisions of consumers, such as when consumers over-consume demerit goods and under-consume merit goods. The concept can also be applied to decision making by a government.

For example, a firm may be involved in the creation of a negative externality, such as air or noise pollution, and a government decides to intervene in the market by imposing an indirect tax on the firm. This would have the effect of increasing the cost of production to the firm, leading to a fall in the output being produced. This will have the effect of reducing the extent of the pollution. The problem with such an approach, however, is that the government may not have all the necessary information to decide on the exact amount of tax that is required as it is not easy to place a monetary value on a negative externality, such as pollution.

Problem of incentives

Another type of problem that could arise as a result of government intervention in a market is that of incentives. These can be distorted when a government decides to intervene in a market.

For example, a government may decide to reduce, or even withdraw, the benefits paid to a person if that person works longer hours and, as a result, earns a higher wage. The government could defend such a decision on the basis that the person is less in need of the benefit, but the possibility of a lowering or termination of the benefit may act as a disincentive to the person to work longer hours. This is why such a situation has been described as a poverty trap, i.e. it is often not worth working longer hours and gaining a higher income if a person receives less benefits from the state because they are no better off as a result of the extra work carried out.

Another example of government failure in relation to microeconomic intervention is where a firm or industry is nationalised and brought under state ownership. There is less incentive for a public sector firm to make a profit than a private sector firm and this could lead to inefficiency. Also, public sector workers may be paid less than equivalent workers in the private sector and this could reduce their incentive to work hard.

Problem of distribution

One of the reasons why a government might decide to intervene in a market is to create a greater degree of equity in an economy. However, it is possible that as a result of such intervention in a market, a government may actually increase the degree of inequality.

For example, a government may decide to impose a tax on energy producers because of the pollution they have caused. The effect of such a tax, however, may be to increase the prices charged to consumers. The increase in price is likely to be the same for all the consumers of the energy, but the effect of such a price rise will not be equal because some consumers will be better able to afford the price increase. The distributional effect of the tax, therefore, will be a greater degree of inequality than was the case before the tax was imposed.

There are other possible causes of government failure in relation to its microeconomic intervention, including the following:

- **Moral hazard:** a government could decide to take decisions that lead to the encouragement of risk taking, e.g. when a government decides to support financial institutions that are at risk of going out of business, but this government support encourages them to take poor decisions because they know that they will ultimately be supported by the government.

- **Unintended consequences:** a government could decide to try to reduce the extent of poverty through the provision of benefits, but a side-effect of this policy would be the creation of a situation of "welfare dependency".
- **Regulatory capture:** it has been argued that it is possible a government could become too friendly with those organisations that they are trying to regulate, making the regulation less effective than it would otherwise be.
- **Political interference:** it is possible that a government decision could be taken for short-term political gain rather than for long-term economic gain.

The consequences of government failure

There are a number of possible consequences of government failure in microeconomic intervention, including the following:

- Distortion of price signals: an advantage of a free market is that it can give out price signals which lead to an efficient allocation of resources, but government microeconomic intervention in a market could distort those signals so that the outcome could be an inefficient allocation of resources, e.g. a government could decide to support a failing industry through subsidies when a better decision might have been to allow it to fail.
- Taxation: a government could decide to use a progressive income tax to bring about a more equitable income distribution, but if the top rate of tax is very high, there may be a disincentive effect where the higher paid are less willing to work as much. Some workers may even decide to emigrate from the country and seek employment elsewhere (this is sometimes referred to as a "brain drain").
- Employment: a government could be reluctant to take a decision which leads to people being made redundant, e.g. if workers are relatively unproductive in a public sector organisation, a government might not be willing to dismiss such workers because this would lead to an increase in the rate of unemployment in the economy.
- Net welfare loss to society: it is important to contrast the consequences of government microeconomic intervention with the original problem that brought about the intervention in the first place and it may be the case that the overall effect is a net welfare loss, i.e. the consequences of the government failure have actually made the situation worse than it was before.

Progress question

6 Discuss to what extent a government is likely to be successful in its attempt to correct market failure in an economy.

8.2 Equity and redistribution of income and wealth

8.2.1 *The difference between equity and equality*

Key term

Equity: the idea of fairness or justice, such as in terms of the distribution of output.

- Equity: One reason why a government may intervene in a market to correct market failure is because of equity. Equity refers to the idea of fairness, justice or impartiality. A market may be said to be efficient in terms of the production of a maximum output from a minimum of resources, but the distribution of this output may not be equitable or fair. A government may decide to intervene in a market to bring about a fairer and more equitable distribution of income and wealth, such as through a progressive form of taxation. An alternative approach is through the use of subsidies, such as when these are used to keep down the costs, and ultimately the prices, of essential goods, e.g. certain items of food.

- Equality refers to a situation where everyone is at the same level, such as the idea of equal life chances or of everyone having the same income or wealth. It is where there is the same status, rights and responsibilities for all members of a group or society.

Key term

Equality: the idea of all members of a group or society having the same rights and responsibilities.

Getting it right

It is important that you can clearly distinguish between equity and equality.

It is important to understand the difference between equity and equality. Whereas equity is concerned with a process, equality is concerned with an outcome. With equity, differences are recognised and efforts are made to respond to situations where opportunities are unequal; with equality, the end product is a situation where all segments of society have the same opportunities. In 2021, a research report on Economics stated that inequality was the most pressing economic problem of the day.

Equity is a situation where income is distributed in such a way that it can be considered fair or just. This is not the same as an equal distribution of income. Equity is therefore possible when income is unevenly distributed, as long as this distribution is considered fair and just.

8.2.2 The difference between equity and efficiency

The concept of equity has already been referred to in section 8.2.1 in relation to the key features of fairness, justice and impartiality.

One reason why a government may intervene in a market to correct market failure is to establish a situation of economic efficiency. This has already been discussed in Chapter 7 in terms of productive, allocative and dynamic efficiency. The achievement of such efficiency would ensure that scarce resources in an economy were allocated in the best possible way, i.e. it is concerned with optimality in the allocation and use of resources. Economic efficiency occurs when an economy obtains the largest possible amount of output from its limited resources.

Key term

Efficiency: the use of scarce resources in the most economical or optimal way.

Getting it right

It is important that you can clearly distinguish between equity and efficiency.

It is important to understand the difference between equity and efficiency. The difference between them relates to how resources are distributed. Whereas equity involves giving everyone in a society the same amount of resources, efficiency involves an optimal distribution of resources, i.e. producing at the lowest possible cost.

It is possible that there could be a trade-off between equity and efficiency in an economy. This is because maximising the productive efficiency of a market could lead to a reduction in its equity, e.g. in terms of how equitably the wealth is distributed.

8.2.3 *The distinction between absolute poverty and relative poverty*

It is important to understand the distinction between absolute poverty and relative poverty.

- Absolute poverty is a type of poverty that occurs when the resources required for minimum physical health are lacking. This is defined in terms of limited access to food, clothing and shelter. The World Bank defines the international poverty line as US$1.90 a day (using purchasing power parity). It refers to a particular condition which is the same in every country and which does not change over a period of time. This condition of absolute poverty makes it possible to compare the situation in different countries over time; the figure of US$1.90 a day was last updated in 2015.
- Relative poverty is a type of poverty that means a situation of low income relative to other people in a particular country. For example, it could be stated as income that is below 50 per cent or 60 per cent of the median income of people in that country.

Key terms

Absolute poverty: a condition where household income is below a necessary level to maintain basic living standards in relation to food, shelter and housing.

Relative poverty: a condition where household income is a certain percentage below the median income of a country.

Getting it right

It is important that you can clearly distinguish between absolute poverty and relative poverty.

Progress question

7 Distinguish between absolute poverty and relative poverty.

Case Study

Poverty in Egypt and Nepal

The condition of absolute poverty in a country can be established by the number of people who are living below the international poverty line, which is an amount of money required to maintain basic living conditions. The international poverty line of US$1.90 a day, adjusted for purchasing power parity, means that poverty can therefore be compared in different countries.

In Egypt, it has been estimated that between 30 per cent and 40 per cent of the population in 2020 live below the international poverty line.

In Nepal, it has been estimated that between 15 per cent and 25 per cent of the population in 2020 live below the international poverty line.

1 Explain what is meant by absolute poverty.

8.2.4 *The poverty trap*

If a person gains more income, perhaps by working longer hours, means-tested benefits may be reduced, or even possibly withdrawn, because the person is less in need than was the case before. If this is the case, the person will be less inclined to earn more money; the means-tested benefit therefore operates as a disincentive to work longer hours and earn more money. This disincentive effect is known as the poverty trap.

It comes about because of the combined effects of the marginal rates of taxation paid on any additional income and the rate at which benefits are no longer payable. The tax threshold, at which a person starts to pay tax, may be quite low and the means-tested benefits can rapidly disappear as incomes rise. The overall effect, therefore, is that a person may possibly become worse off as a result of earning more money.

Key term

Poverty trap: a situation where a person can become worse off as a result of an increase in wages because they will lose their entitlement to certain benefits which are means-tested. This can occur when there is a low tax threshold and means-tested benefits up to a particular level of income.

Progress question

8 Explain why a person may not necessarily be any better off as a result of working more hours and gaining a higher wage.

8.2.5 *Policies towards equity and equality*

Negative income tax

It will be clear from what has already been said that a government could assist in the redistribution of income and wealth in an economy through a system of benefits and taxes. One proposal, however, has been to combine benefits and taxes in one system.

The idea of a negative income tax involves the combination of the payment of income tax and the receipt of benefits in one system. The idea was first put forward by the economist, Milton Friedman, of the University of Chicago, in 1962. The idea is that a government would determine a particular income level and all people earning above that level would pay income tax, while all people earning below that level would not pay any income tax but would receive benefits.

The advantage of this scheme is that it would bring together the income tax and the benefits systems. It would also help make the labour markets more flexible by removing the poverty trap.

Key term

Negative income tax: a system which brings together the payment of tax and the receipt of benefits.

Case Study

The idea of a negative income tax in Canada

The government of Canada has been thinking about the possibility of introducing a negative income tax in that country. It was first proposed in 1971.

The idea is that the government would determine a particular level of income. Any person falling below that "income line" would be given benefits in order to reach this "income line".

An advantage of such a scheme is that it would avoid a complicated system of benefit payments and make labour markets more flexible by eliminating the poverty trap. A disadvantage of such a scheme is that it would be difficult for a government to get everybody's agreement as to what the "income line" should be set at. One proposal is to set the line at CAN$20,000 per annum, but this would be likely to be seen as too high for some people and too low for others.

1 Explain what is meant by a negative income tax.
2 Discuss the advantages of a country, such as Canada, establishing a negative income tax.

Universal benefits and means-tested benefits

Benefits can be paid to people on low incomes in order to increase their disposable income. There are two main types of such benefits: universal benefits and means-tested benefits.

- Universal benefits are paid to every person who is entitled to such a benefit irrespective of their income or wealth. Such benefits have the advantage of providing money to people without having to ask them a lot of questions, which could be seen as an invasion of privacy, but they also have the disadvantage of providing money to people who might not really need it. They could therefore be regarded as being somewhat wasteful of public expenditure.
- An alternative form of benefit is called a means-tested benefit. This literally means that certain people are tested, by asking them questions, to see if they have sufficient means to pay for certain things; if they can prove that they need additional funds, then they can receive the benefit. Such benefits have the advantage of targeting those people who are most in need of additional funds. As has already been indicated, a disadvantage is that a lot of questions will need to be asked and people might find this very intrusive and embarrassing. Perhaps the most significant disadvantage of means-tested benefits is that they can give rise to what has been called the poverty trap.

An example of a means-tested benefit would be a tax credit. Tax credits are paid to those people who have children or who have a job that pays a very low wage.

Examples of tax credits could include a child tax credit, if a person is responsible for a child or a young person, and a working tax credit, if a person is employed but receiving a low wage. The actual payments depend on the income; the lower the income, the more tax credits a person can get.

Key terms

Universal benefit: a benefit that is paid to everybody who is entitled to it, irrespective of their income and wealth.

Means-tested benefit: a benefit that is paid to those people who are entitled to it, taking into account their income and wealth.

Tax credit: a payment from a government to an individual or a family that is dependent on income.

Getting it right

Make sure you understand that a tax credit is something that is given to a person, rather than a tax which involves taking money from a person.

Activity

Benefits

Find out as much as you can about the different benefits that are given out by the government of your country or another country of your choice.

Case Study

Tax credits in the USA

In the USA earned income credit is given to people on low income and the actual amount is dependent on the number of children that they have. Once a person earns above a certain income, the credit is phased out. It is indexed to the rate of inflation.

Other examples of tax credits in the USA include child tax credit, investment tax credit, low-income housing tax credit, retirement savings contribution tax credit, elderly and disabled tax credit and work opportunity tax credit.

1 Explain, with the use of examples from the USA, what is meant by tax credits.

Key term

Universal basic income: a payment by a government to all those entitled to it without a means test.

Universal basic income

A universal basic income is a government guarantee that each person in an economy receives a minimum income. The idea is that the basic income will provide enough money to cover the basic cost of living.

Case Study

Universal basic income in Finland

Finland is the first country to implement a universal basic income (UBI) scheme at the national level. UBI is an unconditional cash payment with the aim of reducing the extent of poverty in a country.

In Finland, UBI has been given to certain unemployed people as part of a two-year trial. They have been paid 560 euros a month (about US$620). At the moment, it has been introduced on a limited scale, but it is expected to be established more widely after 2020.

1 Explain what is meant by a universal basic income.

Case Study

Income distribution in Bangladesh

All countries in the world have, to varying degrees, an unequal distribution of income and wealth. The table below indicates the distribution of income in Bangladesh.

Division of population into five groups, each showing 20% of the population	Percentage of income held by that group of the population in 2020.
Highest 20% of the population	41%
Second-highest 20% of the population	21%
Third-highest 20% of the population	16%
Fourth-highest 20% of the population	12%
Lowest 20% of the population	9%

1 Calculate the percentage of income held by the highest 40 per cent of the population.
2 Calculate the percentage of income held by the lowest 40 per cent of the population.
3 Discuss the measures that could be adopted by the government of Bangladesh to try to bring about a more equitable distribution of income.

Key term

Derived demand: a situation in which a good or service, in this case labour, is not demanded for itself, but its demand is dependent on the demand for the product it helps to produce.

8.3 Labour market forces and government intervention

8.3.1 *The demand for labour as a derived demand*

The demand for labour is a derived demand. The demand for workers in a particular industry is necessarily dependent (derived) from the demand for the product which they help to produce. For example, teachers in a school are demanded because there is a demand from students to study their courses.

8.3.2 The factors affecting the demand for labour in a firm or an occupation

There are a number of factors that can affect the demand for labour in a firm or an occupation, including the following:

- **The demand for the product:** it has already been pointed out in section 8.3.1 that the demand for labour is a derived demand, so one influence on the demand for labour is the demand for the product that the labour is employed to produce.
- **The price of labour and other factors of production:** the demand for labour will depend, to some extent, on the price of labour, i.e. the wage or salary paid to labour, compared with the prices of the other factors of production, especially capital; there is an inverse relationship between the demand for labour and the wage or salary paid.
- **The productivity of labour and the other factors of production:** the demand for labour will depend, to some extent, on the productivity of labour relative to the productivity of the other factors of production. The demand for labour is closely linked to the marginal physical product of labour; this refers to the additional output produced if a firm increases the labour input by one unit.

Key term

Marginal physical product: the amount of extra output that is produced if a firm increases its input of labour by one unit.

8.3.3 The causes of shifts in and movements along the demand curve for labour in a firm or an occupation

Movements along a demand curve for labour

The demand curve for labour is a function of the wage or salary paid to it. The higher the wage rate, the lower the demand for labour; the lower the wage rate, the higher the demand for labour. There is therefore an inverse relationship between the demand for labour and the wage or salary paid. The demand curve for labour, therefore, slopes downwards from left to right. Other possible factors affecting the demand for labour are assumed to be constant. Therefore, if the wage rate changes, there will be a movement along the demand curve.

Higher wages will cause a movement upwards along the demand curve, leading to a fall in the quantity of labour demanded – this is known as a contraction of demand. Lower wages will cause a movement downwards along the demand curve, leading to a rise in the quantity of labour demanded – this is known as an extension of demand.

Shifts of a demand curve for labour

A shift of a demand curve for labour occurs when there is a change in a determinant of the demand for labour, apart from a change in the wage rate (see Figure 8.4). These could include the following:

- Productivity: changes in the productivity of labour; an increase in the productivity of labour will shift the demand curve for labour to the right.
- Skills: changes in the skills of labour; an improvement in the skills of labour will shift the demand curve for labour to the right.
- Price of product: changes in the price of the product that the labour is employed to produce; a rise in the price of a product will shift the demand curve for labour to the left.
- Demand for the product: changes in the demand for the product produced by the labour; a rise in consumer demand will shift the demand curve for labour to the right.
- Prices of substitutes and complements: changes in the prices of substitutes and/or complements of the product; an increase in the price of a complement will shift the demand curve for labour to the left.
- Subsidy: changes in the subsidies given to a firm; a decrease in the subsidy given to a firm will increase costs and this will shift the demand curve for labour to the left.
- Capital: changes in the cost of capital equipment (capital can be considered a substitute for labour); an increase in the cost of capital will shift the demand curve for labour to the right.

Getting it right

It is important that you can clearly distinguish between a movement along a demand curve for labour, when only the wage rate has changed, and a shift of a demand curve for labour, when other factors apart from the wage rate have changed, such as a change in the productivity of labour.

The demand curve for labour would shift inwards at a time of recession when the demand for products falls as there would be a decline in the demand for labour at each wage rate. The demand curve for labour would shift outwards in a boom when the demand for products rises as there would be a rise in the demand for labour at each wage rate.

8.3.4 *Marginal revenue product (MRP) theory*

Definition and calculation of marginal revenue product

Firms are interested not only in the extra output that is produced by employing one more unit of labour (the marginal physical product), but also in the revenue obtained from selling the additional output that has been produced. The marginal revenue product of labour is obtained by multiplying the marginal physical product of labour by the marginal revenue received by a firm.

Key term

Marginal revenue product: the extra output produced by an additional worker (the MPP) multiplied by the additional revenue earned by the firm from this output (the MR).

Derivation of an individual firm's demand for labour using marginal revenue product

A profit-maximising firm will produce at the output where MC = MR. The principle is the same for a profit-maximising employer in deciding on the demand for labour, i.e. the number of workers to employ.

The profit-maximising employer will employ workers up to the point where the extra cost of employing an additional worker (the MC of labour) is equal to the additional revenue brought in from the worker's output (the MR of labour).

The MC of labour is equal to the wage rate (W).

The MR of labour is known as the marginal revenue product (MRP) and, as has already been pointed our, is equal to the extra output produced by the additional worker (the marginal physical product or MPP) multiplied by the additional revenue earned by the firm from this output (the marginal revenue or MR):

MRP = MPP × MR

If we assume that the final product is sold in a perfectly competitive market (all units of a product are sold at the same price in perfect competition), this means that the profit-maximising employer will employ workers up to the point where the wage rate equals the marginal revenue product of labour@

W = MRP

Link

see Chapter 7, section 7.5.1, for an explanation of the law of diminishing returns.

It is now possible to derive an individual firm's demand for labour. It is assumed that the firm is operating in the short run and that labour is the only variable factor with all other factors fixed in supply. In the short run the law of diminishing returns will apply as increasing units of a variable factor are added to fixed quantities of other factors.

Consequently, as the number of workers employed is increased, the MPP of labour falls. This is illustrated in Table 8.4 and Figure 8.2.

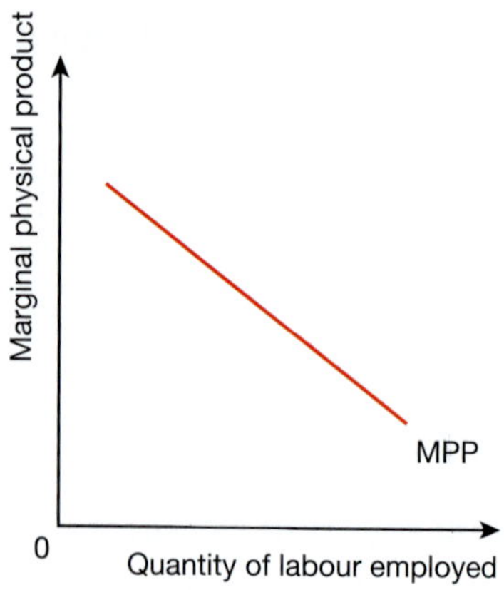

Figure 8.2 The MPP curve ▲

Table 8.4 Changes in marginal physical product ▼

Numbers employed	MPP	Price = MR ($)	MRP MPP × MR (P)	Wage rate per week
1	20	10	200	160
2	18	10	180	160
3	16	10	160	160
4	14	10	140	160
5	12	10	120	160
6	10	10	100	160

If we now assume that all output is sold at $10 per unit, it is possible to calculate the MRP (Table 8.4) and draw the MRP curve which, because all output is sold at the same price, has the same slope as the MPP curve. Figure 8.3 shows the firm's MRP curve.

We are now in a position to derive the firm's demand curve for labour. We assume that the current wage rate is $160. The profit-maximising employer will employ workers up to the point where W = MRP.

This means that if the weekly wage rate is $160, then three workers will be employed because W = MRP. The fourth worker brings in less in terms of MRP than the wage and so will not be employed.

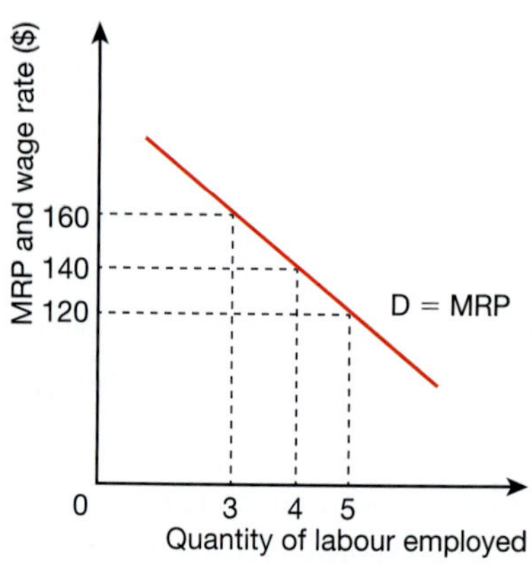

Figure 8.3 The firm's demand curve for labour ▲

If the wage falls to $140 per week this worker now brings in an MRP equal to the wage and so now will be employed. Similarly, if the wage now falls to $120 per week then the employer will again fix employment levels where W = MRP and five workers will be employed.

At each wage rate the demand for labour will be at the point where the wage rate = MRP. The MRP curve thus shows the quantity of labour employed at each wage, which is the demand curve for labour.

Therefore, **the firm's demand curve for labour is the MRP curve.**

Any change in the wage rate will bring about a movement along the firm's demand curve. A rise in wages will lead to a fall in the quantity of labour demanded and vice versa.

Figure 8.4 A shift of the demand curve for labour ▲

A shift of the demand curve for labour will be caused by a change in the MPP of labour or a change in the price of the product. For example, if labour productivity increases (increasing MPP) or the price of the final product increases then the demand curve for labour will shift to the right from D $(MRP)_1$ to D $(MRP)_2$ as shown in Figure 8.4.

The industry's demand curve for labour will be the sum of the individual firm's demand for labour at each wage.

Key term

Elasticity of demand for labour: a measure of the responsiveness of the demand for labour to a change in the wage rate.

The elasticity of demand for labour

The elasticity of demand for labour is a measure of the responsiveness of demand for labour to a change in the wage rate. If demand for labour is elastic then a given change in the wage rate will bring about a greater percentage change in the quantity of labour demanded. If the change in the wage rate leads to a smaller percentage change in the quantity of labour demanded, then the demand for labour is inelastic. This is shown in Figure 8.5.

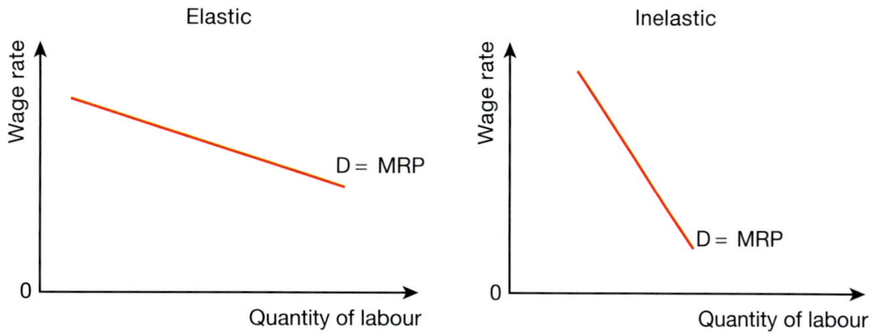

Figure 8.5 Differences in the elasticity of demand for labour ▲

The factors affecting the elasticity of demand for labour are summarised in Table 8.5.

Table 8.5 Factors affecting the elasticity of demand for labour ▼

Factor affecting elasticity of demand for labour	Impact
Proportion of labour costs to total costs	If labour costs in a firm are high relative to total costs of production, the elasticity of demand is likely to be high because any given increase in wages will have a significant impact on total costs. For example, if a firm's total costs are $1 million, of which 90 per cent or $900,000 are labour costs, then a 10 per cent increase in wages will raise costs substantially by $90,000. It may prove difficult for the firm to absorb this cost increase by reducing profits or increasing prices. In this case it will have to shed proportionately more labour. However, if labour costs constituted only 10 per cent of total costs then total costs will rise by only $1000, which the firm might find easier to pass on to consumers or absorb by making savings elsewhere.
Factor substitution	If labour can easily be replaced by other factors, particularly capital, then demand for labour is likely to be elastic. Such factor substitution is more likely if the processes involved require relatively unskilled labour.
Price elasticity of demand for the final product	If the price elasticity of demand for the final product is high then it will not be possible for wage rises to be passed on to consumers through increases in price and so the demand for labour will also be elastic. This is likely to be the case if the firm is operating in a highly competitive product market which means that consumers can easily switch to other substitutes for the firm's products.
Time	The elasticity of demand for labour is likely to increase over time as firms have longer to find substitutes for labour. It is also the case that in some countries government legislation and employment law make it difficult for firms to shed labour in very short periods of time.

8.3.5 *Factors affecting the supply of labour to a firm or to an occupation*

The factors affecting the supply of labour can be divided into two types:

- wage factors
- non-wage factors.

Wage factors

For the industry as a whole, the supply curve of labour will be upward sloping from left to right because more people will make themselves available for work when the wage is increased. A wage factor can also be described as a pecuniary advantage of work.

An increase in wages will have a substitution effect and an income effect for an individual, which taken together determine the effect on a particular individual's willingness to supply his or her labour.

The substitute for work is leisure. If an individual decides to work an additional hour then the opportunity cost is one hour of leisure forgone. If the wage rate in an occupation is increased then the opportunity cost of leisure increases as more income is given up when

Key terms

Substitution effect: if wages rise, individuals will increase the number of hours worked because leisure has now become more expensive.

Income effect: if wages rise, the individual will work fewer hours because a given income can now be achieved through less work.

not working. The substitution effect, therefore, will lead to individuals working more hours increasing.

The income effect tends to work in the opposite direction to the substitution effect, discouraging work. As a result of a pay rise an individual can now achieve a given target income by working fewer hours and may, therefore, decide to take more leisure.

The overall effect of an increase in the wage rate on an individual's supply of labour will clearly depend on the relative magnitudes of the substitution and income effects as shown in Table 8.6.

Table 8.6 Substitution and income effects of a wage increase ▼

Substitution and income effects of a wage increase	Effect on individual's labour supply
Substitution effect > Income effect	Increase
Substitution effect < Income effect	Decrease

Figure 8.6 An individual's supply curve to a particular occupation ▲

For most individuals, particularly over lower levels of income, the substitution effect of a wage increase outweighs the income effect with the result that the supply curve for labour is upward sloping as shown in Figure 8.6 with the supply increasing as the wage rate increases and vice versa.

However, it has been argued that for some individuals, at high levels of income, the income effect may outweigh the substitution effect, with the result that fewer hours are worked with each increase in the wage rate. This results in a backward sloping supply curve beyond a wage rate of W3 in Figure 8.7. This, of course can only occur if the individual is in a position to vary the number of hours worked.

The market or industry supply curve for a particular occupation is the sum of the individual supply curves for all the workers in this particular labour market and is shown in Figure 8.8.

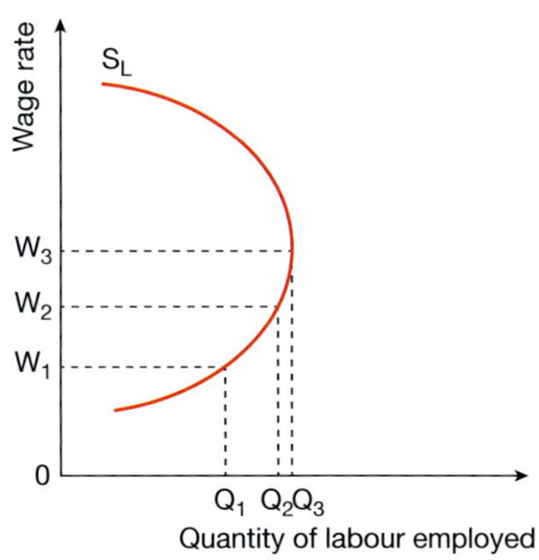

Figure 8.7 A backward sloping supply curve for labour ▲

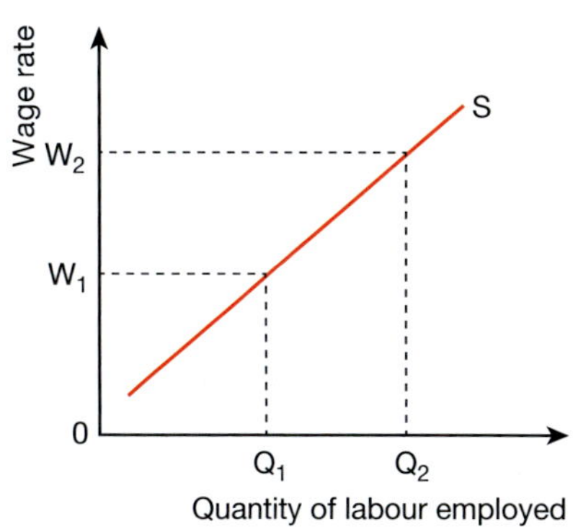

Figure 8.8 The industry supply curve for a particular occupation ▲

Non-wage factors

It has already been pointed out that the supply of labour to a firm or to an occupation is determined by non-wage factors as well as wage factors. The non-wage factors can also be described as a non-pecuniary advantage of work. These can include the following:

- Fringe benefits: benefits such as a company car and free health insurance may add to the attraction of a particular position.
- Status: a barrister may be prepared to take a reduced income for the status and prestige of becoming a High Court judge.
- Working conditions: if the work is unpleasant, dirty or dangerous such as mining, a higher wage may be paid than in other jobs requiring similar skills to compensate for this.
- Facilities available at work: some individuals may choose employment because of certain facilities provided, such as access to a fitness area.
- Flexible hours of work: individuals may be prepared to accept lower wages for the benefit of being able to work flexible hours.
- Length of holidays: these may be important for some individuals.
- Sense of vocation: some individuals may enter professions such as medicine and education because they gain job satisfaction from helping people.
- Promotion prospects: some individuals may choose a job because of the promotion prospects and career opportunities provided.
- Training/professional development: some workers may be attracted by the training and professional development offered by some employers.
- Pension: a final factor could be the pension provision offered by some employers.

Key terms

Net advantages: the overall advantages to a worker of choosing one job rather than another. These can consist of both pecuniary and non-pecuniary advantages.

Pecuniary advantage: monetary reward obtained in a particular occupation.

Non-pecuniary advantage: non-monetary reward obtained in a particular occupation.

Net advantages

Traditional wage theory argues that an individual deciding upon an occupation will look at the balance of advantages between those available and choose the one which gives the greatest net advantages overall. These advantages will be made up of pecuniary advantages and non-pecuniary advantages. As has been pointed out, the pecuniary advantages are the monetary rewards associated with the job, mainly the wage rate. The non-pecuniary aspects of a job are any non-wage factors that make it more or less attractive to an individual than other jobs offering the same wage.

Progress question

9 Distinguish, with the use of examples, between pecuniary and non-pecuniary advantages of employment.

The elasticity of supply of labour

The ease with which the supply of labour can be increased or decreased following a rise or fall in wages is determined by the elasticity of supply of labour. This is illustrated in Figure 8.9.

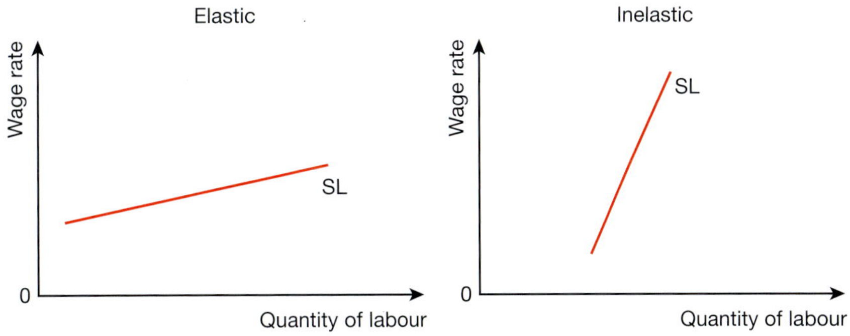

Figure 8.9 The elasticity of supply of labour ▲

A major factor influencing the elasticity of supply of labour to a particular firm or industry is the extent of the occupational and geographical mobility or immobility of labour.

If labour is highly mobile, both occupationally and geographically, then the elasticity of supply is likely to be high.

The occupational mobility of labour depends on such factors as the level of education, training and skills required by the job, together with the length of training. It requires a great deal of education and skill as well as many years of training to become a barrister or cardiac surgeon and so the supply of labour can be relatively inelastic for quite long periods of time. If the job requires little skill or training, such as stacking shelves in a supermarket, then the supply can be increased relatively quickly and is hence relatively elastic.

Geographical mobility is influenced by factors such as family ties and the nature of the housing market. In many countries, house prices are generally much higher in some areas than in others and this can act as a disincentive for individuals to take up jobs in different regions even if they are available. This tends to reduce the elasticity of supply.

Other factors which might affect the elasticity of supply to a particular occupation or industry include:

- The availability of suitable workers in other industries. It may be possible for labour to be recruited from other industries, particularly if the workers required are unskilled.
- Unemployment in the economy. If there are high levels of unemployment in an economy, then there will be a large pool of available labour and supply should be more elastic, but again mainly for industries requiring unskilled labour.

Finally, as with all elasticity concepts, the time period is important. The longer the time period, the more elastic the labour supply is likely to become. Even in professions such as law and medicine, given a

Key terms

Elasticity of supply of labour: a measure of the responsiveness of the supply of labour to a change in the wage rate.

Occupational mobility/immobility of labour: the ease or otherwise by which individuals can move between occupations.

Geographical mobility/immobility of labour: the ease or otherwise by which individuals can move between geographical areas.

sufficiently long period of time, more barristers and cardiac surgeons can be trained to the required level.

8.3.6 *Causes of shifts in and movements along the supply curve of labour to a firm or an occupation*

Movements along a supply curve of labour

Labour supply is defined as the number of workers willing and able to work, multiplied by the hours they are willing and able to work. The higher the wage rate, the more labour is supplied; the lower the wage rate, the less labour is supplied. The supply curve of labour, therefore slopes upwards from left to right. Other possible factors affecting the supply of labour are assumed to be constant. Therefore, if the wage rate changes, there will be a movement along the supply curve.

Shifts of a supply curve of labour

A shift of a supply curve of labour will occur when there is a change in a determinant of the supply of labour, apart from a change in the wage rate. These changes include the following:

- Working population: the size of the working population of a country could change, i.e. the number of people of working age who are willing and able to work and this will be affected by such factors as the school leaving age and the retirement age.
- Tax and benefit levels: changes in the taxes paid by workers and/or changes in the benefits paid to those not in work could affect the labour supply.
- Net migration: the extent of immigration into, and emigration out of, a country will affect the population size.
- Preferences for work: people's preferences for employment will reflect any possible changes in attitudes to work.
- Net advantages of work: the non-wage factors may be significant, such as enhanced job security and better working conditions.
- Information: the availability of information will affect the number of people who know about particular jobs.
- Wages in other industries: changes in the wages paid by other firms in the same industry and/or changes in the wages paid by other industries could have an impact.

8.3.7 *Wage determination in perfect markets*

Equilibrium wage rate and employment in a labour market

The conditions of a perfect labour market are similar to those of a perfectly competitive product market. The characteristics of a perfect labour market are:

- very large numbers of firms employing labour
- very large numbers of homogeneous workers who are perfectly mobile within the industry
- perfect knowledge in the market for both workers and employers.

Under these circumstances, firms and workers in the industry are unable to affect the prevailing wage rate by their own actions. They are effectively price takers in a labour market.

As a result, the wage rate will be determined by the demand for and the supply of labour in the particular market as a whole and then each individual firm will employ all the workers it requires at this wage. This effectively means that the supply curve of labour for the firm is perfectly elastic and the equilibrium employment level for the firm will be given by the intersection of this supply curve with the downward-sloping demand (MRP) curve. This is illustrated in Figure 8.10.

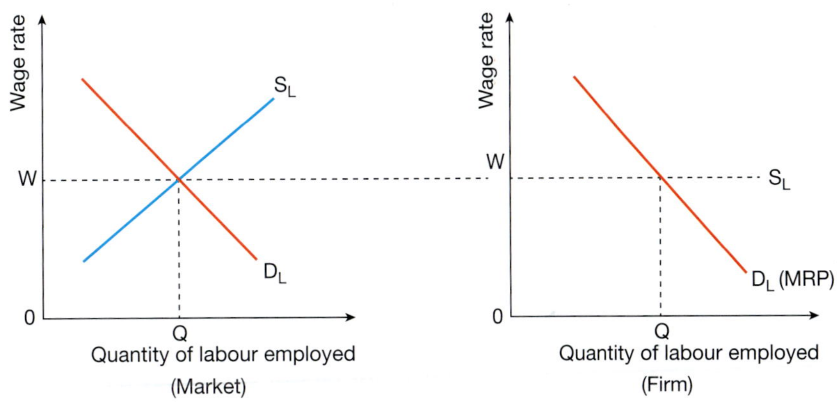

Figure 8.10 Wage determination in perfectly competitive markets

Clearly any factor which brings about a shift of the demand or supply curves for labour will bring about a change in the equilibrium wage and employment levels. This is illustrated in Figure 8.11 and the results summarised in Table 8.7.

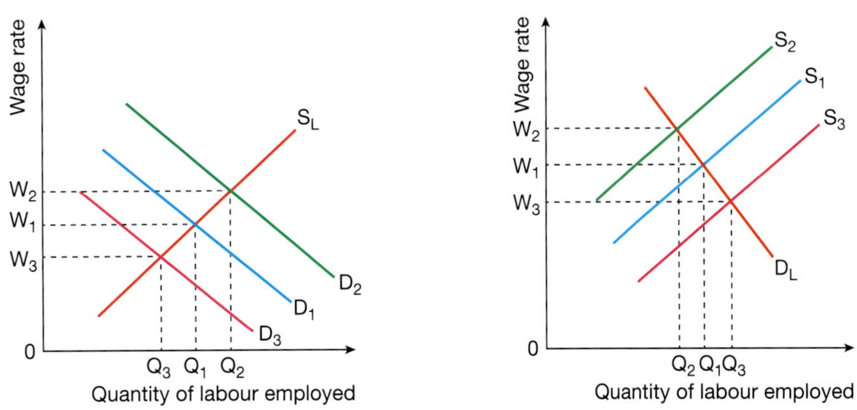

Figure 8.11 The effects of changes in the demand and supply curves for labour on wages and employment

Table 8.7 The impact on the equilibrium wage and employment of changes in demand and supply ▼

Change	Impact
Increase in demand – demand curve for labour shifts to the right	Increase in wages, increase in employment
Decrease in demand – demand curve for labour shifts to the left	Decrease in wages, decrease in employment
Increase in supply – supply curve for labour shifts to the right	Decrease in wages, increase in employment
Decrease in supply – supply curve for labour shifts to the right	Increase in wages, decrease in employment

8.3.8 *Wage determination in imperfect markets*

Key term

Trade union: an organisation of workers which is active on behalf of its members in many ways, such as in relation to increasing wages and salaries and improving working conditions.

The influence of trade unions on wage determination and employment in a labour market

A trade union may be in a position to raise wages in a number of ways, including the following:

- improving the productivity of labour
- restricting the supply of labour
- engaging in industrial action.

Improving the productivity of labour

If a trade union can raise the productivity of labour (MPP) and/or the price of the final product (MR), then it will shift the demand (MRP) curve for labour to the right, from D_1 to D_2, increasing both the wage rate (from W_1 to W_2) and the number of workers employed (from Q_1 to Q_2) as shown in Figure 8.12. It is unlikely that the trade union will have much direct influence over the price of the final product, but it might be able to increase the level of productivity and hence the MPP of the workers by agreeing to more flexible working practices or the introduction of new technology.

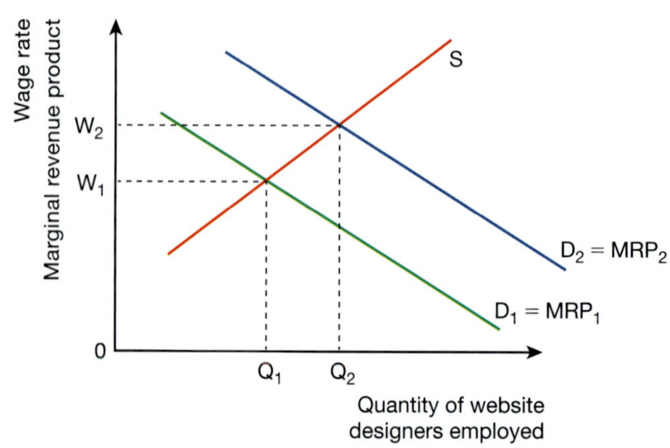

Figure 8.12 The effect of increasing the MRP of labour ▲

Restricting the supply of labour

If a trade union can somehow restrict or limit entry to a particular occupation, the supply curve for labour in the industry will shift to the left, from SL to SL_1. Professional associations such as those in law and accounting can achieve this by requiring a certain minimum level of qualifications or period of training in order to work in the profession. As Figure 8.13 shows, this will lead to an increase in wages (from W to W_1) for those in the industry, but the number of workers employed will be reduced (from Q to Q_1).

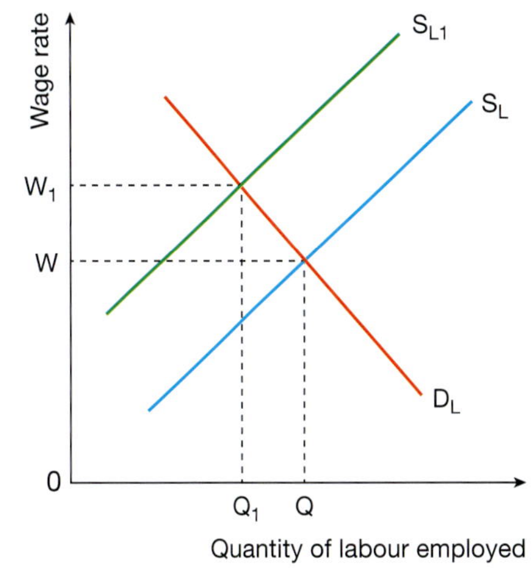

Figure 8.13 The effect of restricting the supply of labour ▶

Engaging in industrial action

Finally, a trade union may be able to push the wage rate above the equilibrium by exercising its collective bargaining strength or by threatening or taking industrial action to disrupt production. The ability of some trade unions to do this will be enhanced by the fact that they operate a closed shop and, therefore, have the backing of the entire workforce in that industry. This is illustrated in Figure 8.14. Through collective bargaining, where the union negotiates with employers on behalf of its members, the trade union has pushed the wage rate up to W2. In this case, those workers who retain their jobs in the industry will receive a higher wage, but Q1–Q2 workers are made unemployed. In addition, Q3–Q1 workers who now wish to work at the higher wage are excluded from doing so.

Key terms

Closed shop: this occurs when workers are only able to work in a particular industry if they are members of a trade union.

Collective bargaining: a process of negotiation over pay and conditions between a trade union, representing a group of workers, and employers.

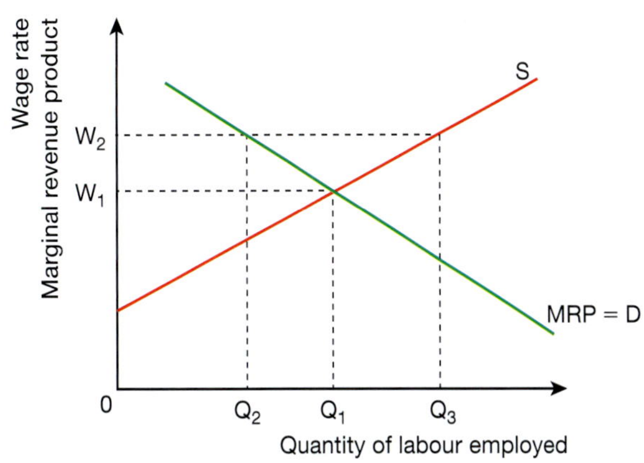

Figure 8.14 The effect of industrial action ▲

The ability of a trade union to influence the wages of its members will depend on a number of factors, including the following:

- Size of membership: the more members that a trade union has, and the higher the percentage of workers in an industry that are members of the trade union, the more influence it is likely to have
- Legal environment: the power and influence of a trade union will be influenced by the legal environment, e.g. whether closed shops are made illegal or whether there are restrictions on the ability of trade unions to engage in industrial action
- The demand for the product: it has already been pointed out in section 8.3.1 that the demand for labour is a derived demand, and so the demand for the product produced by the labour will be a factor; if the demand for the product is inelastic, a firm will be more likely to pay higher wages because it will be better able to pass the higher costs on to the consumer in the form of higher prices
- Labour costs as a percentage of total costs: if labour costs are a relatively small percentage of total costs, the effect of a wage increase will be less if labour costs are only a relatively small proportion of the total costs of production
- Profitability of the firm: if the firm is profitable, it may be more likely to pay higher wages to employees than a firm that is making a loss.

> **Activity**
>
> **Trade unions**
>
> Use the Internet to find out as much as you can about the power and influence that trade unions have in your country or another country of your choice in relation to wage determination.

The influence of government on wage determination and employment in a labour market using a national minimum wage

The most obvious way in which a government may influence wages is through the establishment of a national minimum wage. The effect of this is illustrated in Figure 8.15.

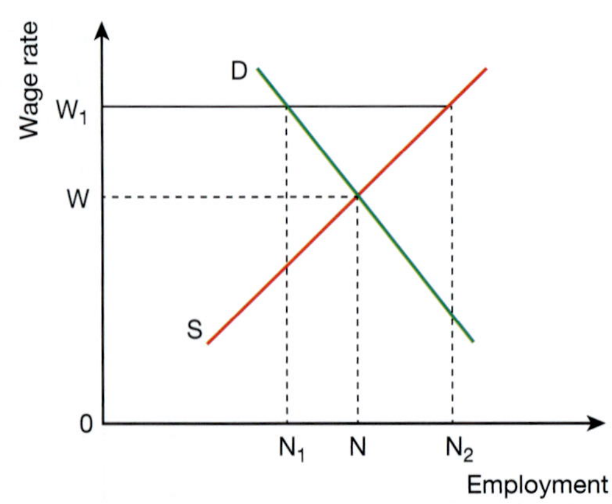

Figure 8.15 A national minimum wage ▲

The equilibrium wage is W where the demand and supply curves for a particular occupation intersect. The equilibrium level of employment is ON. If a government imposes a minimum wage above the equilibrium, this will increase firms' costs of production and reduce the demand for labour to ON_1. The effect of this is to make NN_1 workers who are currently in work unemployed. At the same time, at the higher wage more individuals in the labour force are prepared to offer themselves for work; the supply of labour increases to N_2. However, as the demand for labour is only N_1, the additional NN_2 workers will be unable to find employment. Overall, at the minimum wage, there will be an excess supply of labour equal to N_1N_2. Clearly the extent of these effects will depend on the level at which the minimum wage is set and the elasticity of demand for and supply of labour to a particular occupation.

Link

See Chapter 3, section 3.3.4, which is also concerned with a minimum wage.

Economists are divided on the merits of a national minimum wage. Opponents argue that it creates unemployment and by raising costs causes cost-push inflation, which may render an industry uncompetitive and impact negatively on the balance of payments.

Link

See section 4.6.4 of Chapter 4 on cost-push inflation and section 6.3 of Chapter 6 on the balance of payments.

Supporters of a national minimum wage argue that it is important in terms of fairness and social justice to reduce income inequality and to ensure that all workers are able to afford a minimum standard of living. They also argue that far from creating unemployment it actually creates employment because those on the lowest incomes tend to spend a higher proportion of what they earn. Moreover, they assert that a minimum wage may increase productivity. Workers may feel more valued and, therefore, work harder and at the same time, because they are paying more, employers may have the incentive to increase expenditure on training and developing their employees. All this may also reduce labour turnover, which will mean that firms can save money on the process of attracting, employing and training new workers.

Empirical evidence is mixed, but seems to reinforce the view that the level at which the minimum wage is fixed is crucial in determining the effect on employment. In the USA, the minimum wage is 35.8 per cent of the median income, in the UK it is 48.7 per cent with a lower rate for younger workers, and in France it is 62.3 per cent. In the UK, where the minimum wage is regularly reviewed and increased, and in the USA, the minimum wage appears not to have had a negative effect on employment. In France, however, rates of youth unemployment were very high at 26 per cent for 15–24 year olds in 2019, double the UK rate of 13 per cent.

Case Study

Minimum wage

A minimum wage has been introduced in the majority of countries around the world, although there are some countries that have not done so. These include Sweden, Norway, Demark, Singapore, Hong Kong and Austria. In 2020, the ten highest minimum wage rates were as follows:

1. Luxembourg: US$13.78
2. Australia: US$12.14
3. France: US$11.66
4. New Zealand: US$11.20
5. Germany: US$10.87
6. Netherlands: US$10.44
7. Belgium: US$10.38
8. United Kingdom: US$9.62
10. Republic of Ireland: US$9.52

However, another way of analysing a country's minimum wage is to consider it as the percentage of the median wage in that country. On this basis, the top ten countries in 2020 were as follows:

1. Turkey: 70.2 per cent
2. Chile: 66.2 per cent
3. France: 62.3 per cent
4. New Zealand: 59.8 per cent

   Slovenia: 59.8 per cent

6. Israel: 58.1 per cent
7. Portugal: 56.9 per cent
8. Luxembourg: 54.8 per cent
9. Australia: 53.5 per cent
10. Hungary: 52.5 per cent

1 Explain why it is important to know not only the amount of a minimum wage in a country but also the percentage that it represents of the median income in that country.

Case Study

A living wage

Many countries now have a minimum hourly wage although the level in relation to the average hourly wage differs significantly between countries. In the UK, however, economists and politicians are increasingly turning their attention to the notion of a "living wage", which is the hourly rate estimated to enable individuals to have a reasonable standard of living. In April 2020, the living wage was £8.72 per hour, the same figure as the minimum wage for those aged 25 and over. For those younger than 25, the minimum wage was less: £6.45 for those aged 18–20 and £8.20 for those aged 21–24.

1 Evaluate the likely economic effects of compelling all firms in the UK to pay the "living wage".

Activity

Minimum wage

Use the Internet to find out as much as you can about any minimum wage that exists in your country or another country of your choice.

Key term

Monopsonist: a sole buyer, in this case of labour.

Other government influences on wages

There are a number of other ways that a government can influence wages either directly or indirectly, other than through a national minimum wage. Government equal pay and anti-discrimination legislation will obviously have an impact as will direct action on pay. For example, a government could impose a pay freeze on all public sector workers for a period of time or limit pay increases to, say, 1 per cent.

The influence of monopsony employers on wage determination and employment in a labour market

A monopsonist refers to a sole buyer of labour.

It is possible to look at two monopsonist cases:

- a labour market where labour is employed by a monopsonist, but supplied competitively
- a labour market where there is a monopoly supplier of labour, in the form of a trade union, and a monopsonistic buyer of labour.

Labour is employed by a monopsonist, but supplied competitively

Table 8.8 and Figure 8.16 illustrate the situation in a labour market where there is a single buyer of labour (monopsonist), but labour is supplied competitively rather than through a trade union.

Table 8.8 ▼

Number of workers	Wage rate ($)	Total cost ($)	Average cost ($)	Marginal cost ($)
1	50	50	50	50
2	55	110	55	60
3	60	180	60	70
4	65	260	65	80
5	70	350	70	90
6	75	450	75	100

In order to attract additional labour, the monopsonist has to increase the wage rate and so the supply curve of labour is upward sloping. It is clear from the table also that the supply curve for labour is the same as the average cost of labour (ACL) curve. In order to attract additional labour, the monopsonist will have to increase the wage rate, but this higher wage will also have to be paid to all existing employees. This means that the marginal cost of labour curve (MCL) is above the ACL curve. This is shown in Figure 8.16.

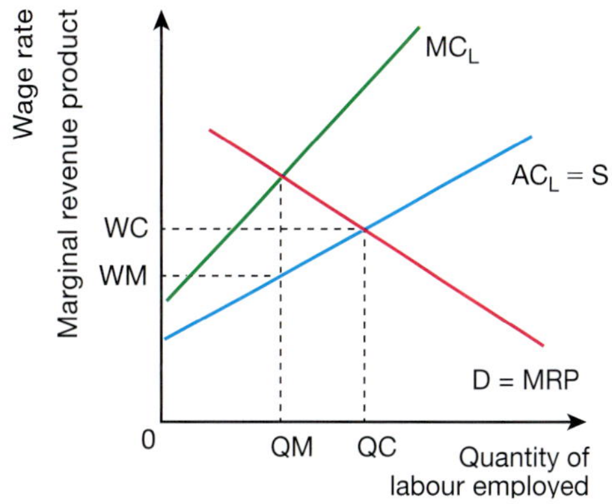

Figure 8.16 Equilibrium in a monopsonist labour market ▲

If the demand curve for labour (MRP) is then added to the diagram, then the profit-maximising monopsonist will employ workers up to the point where MCL = MRP giving an employment level of QM. The wage rate will be determined by the ACL = S curve giving a wage rate of WM.

Bilateral monopoly

This refers to a labour market in which there is a monopoly supplier, a trade union, and a monopsonistic buyer of labour. In order to illustrate the market, Figure 8.16 can again be referred to. The trade union will wish to achieve the competitive equilibrium position with a wage rate of WC and an employment level of QC. The monopsonist, however, will wish to be at the profit-maximising position, with a wage rate of WM and an employment level of QM. The wage rate and employment levels eventually agreed will depend upon the relative bargaining strengths of the trade union and the employer at the time, but there is clearly scope within this range for the trade union to achieve an increase in both the wage rate and the level of employment for its members.

Activity

Wage differentials

Identify the five highest earning occupations in your country and explain why incomes in these occupations are so high.

8.3.9 The determination of wage differentials by labour market forces

As has already been indicated, there are significant differences in the earnings of individuals within countries and between countries. Table 8.9 shows the ten occupations with the highest and lowest weekly pay in the UK in 2020.

Table 8.9 The highest-paid and lowest-paid occupations in the UK in 2020 ▼

Highest-paid occupations	Median full-time weekly pay	Lowest-paid occupations	Median full-time weekly pay
Chief executives and senior officials	£3,004.01	Bar staff	£308.75
Air traffic controllers	£1,806.83	Waiters and waitresses	£313.19
Marketing and sales directors	£1,795.62	Kitchen and catering assistants	£319.31
Legal profession	£1,745.98	Leisure and theme park attendants	£322.42
Financial planners and directors	£1,689.52	Launderers, dry cleaners and pressers	£328.65
Aircraft pilots and flight engineers	£1,657.77	Educational support assistants	£330.19
Dentist	£1,593.06	Beauticians	£330.37
Doctor	£1,534.02	Nursery nurses and assistants	£334.46
IT directors	£1,524.23	Pharmacy assistants	£338.35
Advertising and PR directors	£1,524.23	Hairdressers and barbers	£338.63

Activity

Highest and lowest paid

Table 8.9 identifies the highest and lowest paid occupations in the UK for 2020.
Explain the main factors that might account for the significant difference in the median weekly wage of those in the ten highest-paid occupations and those in the ten lowest-paid occupations.

In addition, there are individuals who earn truly huge sums of money. In sport, the four highest paid soccer players in 2019 were Lionel Messi (Barcelona) US$127 million, Cristiano Ronaldo (Juventus) US$109 million, Neymar (Paris Saint-Germain) US$105 million and Paul Pogba (Manchester United) US$33 million. The highest paid male tennis player in 2019 was Roger Federer who earned US$93 million, while the highest paid female tennis player (and the highest paid female athlete) was Serena Williams who earned US$29 million in 2019. In Formula 1 motor racing, Lewis Hamilton was the highest paid driver in 2019, earning US$57 million. In golf, the two highest earners in 2019 were Brooks Koepka (US$9 million) and Rory McIlroy (US$7 million).

Taylor Swift ▲

Actors and musicians can also earn vast sums of money. The two highest paid actors in 2019 were Dwayne Johnson (US$89 million) and Chris Hemsworth (US$76 million), while the two highest paid female actors were Scarlett Johansson (US$56 million) and Sofia Vergara (US$44 million). In music, the highest earners in 2019 were Taylor Swift (US$185 million) and Kanye West (US$150 million).

Reasons for wage differentials

Elasticity of demand and supply

Generally speaking, if the demand for labour is high and inelastic and the supply of labour low and inelastic, as in the case of a corporate manager, then the salary will be higher than if the demand for labour is low and elastic and the supply high and elastic, as in the case of a cleaner. This is illustrated in Figure 8.17.

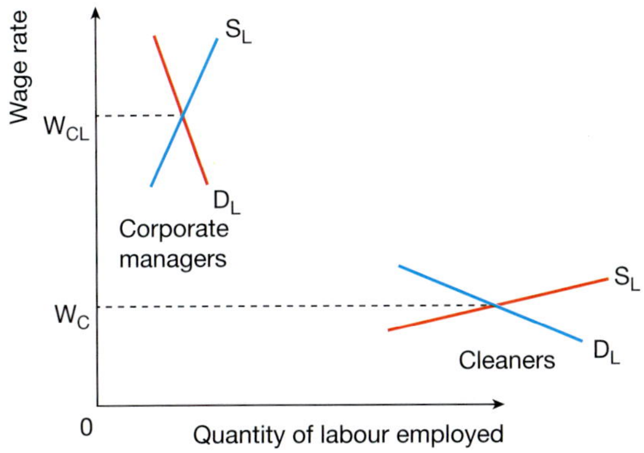

Figure 8.17 The labour market for corporate managers and cleaners ▲

The factors affecting the elasticity of demand and supply of labour have already been considered earlier in this chapter.

From the demand side, high wages and salaries are likely to be paid if labour has a high MRP and if the demand for the final product of the organisation is high and inelastic. High demand for the final product is clearly a major factor in the very high earnings of professional athletes, actors and musicians.

From the supply side, higher wages and salaries are likely to be paid if high levels of skill, expertise and qualifications are required, long periods of training are necessary or the geographical and occupational mobility of labour is low.

Hence, corporate managers are paid 17 times more than cleaners in the UK because they are perceived to have a higher MRP and they require significantly higher levels of qualifications as well as extensive periods of training compared to cleaners.

Market power

It has already been established that the market for some occupations is imperfect, with workers or employers or both having some power to influence wages. The agreed wage rate is, therefore, likely to be the result of negotiation between the two. The final result will depend on their relative bargaining strength at the time.

Gender

Even though many countries have passed equal pay legislation to ensure that men and women in the same occupation earn the same wage for performing the same job, or a job of the same value, it is still the case that women earn on average less than men. There are a number of reasons for this. Women may take time out to have children in their 20s and 30s and may thus miss out on promotion. They are also disproportionately represented in low-wage occupations and part-time work. They are also less likely to be members of a trade union.

Case Study

Equal pay legislation in the USA and the UK

Equal pay legislation has been introduced in a number of countries in the world. In the USA, the Equal Pay Act was passed in 1963. However, despite this law, in 2020 women only earned 81.6 per cent of what men earned for doing the same job or a job of the same value.

In the UK, the Equal Pay Act came into effect in 1970. However, in 2020, fifty years after the Act was passed, women in the UK only earned 90.6 per cent of what men earned for doing the same job or a job of the same value.

1 Explain why there is still a gender pay gap despite the existence of equal pay legislation.

Age

In many professional occupations, such as teaching, employees will obtain an annual increment to their salary. Hence, older workers will earn more than those new to the profession. Age may also bring with it seniority and, therefore, higher wages.

Non-pecuniary rewards

As has already been discussed in this chapter, some workers may be prepared to accept lower wages in return for non-monetary rewards such as holidays, perks or status, or they may demand higher wages to compensate them for dangerous or dirty and unpleasant work.

Part-time and full-time work

Generally, hourly wages paid to part time workers are less than those paid to permanent full-time staff.

Discrimination

Although legislation exists in most countries to counter discrimination on grounds, for example, of gender, race, disability or age, there are unfortunately complaints each year that these groups of workers are experiencing prejudice in the workplace, particularly in terms of promotion and salaries. Such discrimination normally acts on the demand side reducing the demand for certain types of labour.

A number of countries around the world are now attempting to counter aspects of negative discrimination by taking measures to actively promote positive discrimination. For example, the European Union, India and Malaysia have introduced legislation setting minimum quotas for the number of women to be on the boards of companies in excess of a certain size.

Activity

Equal pay

Use the Internet to find out as much as you can about the extent to which there is an even gender balance in relation to pay in your country or another country of your choice.

Case Study

Advancing gender equality in Malaysia

Malaysia has taken steps to address sources of gender inequality. In 2004, the government committed itself to a policy of filling at least 30 per cent of key roles in the public sector with women and, in fact, by 2017, women comprised 36 per cent of these public sector roles.

In 2015, the government stated that women should comprise at least 30 per cent of the boards of large organisations by 2020. Malaysia is a member of ASEAN (Association of Southeast Asian Nations) and it is the only one of the ten member countries to introduce such a directive.

1 Evaluate the impact that government intervention, such as that undertaken by the government in Malaysia, could have on the wages of women.

8.3.10 *Transfer earnings and economic rent*

An individual's earnings can be divided into transfer earnings and economic rent.

Definition of transfer earnings

Transfer earnings are essentially the opportunity cost of working in a particular job. If at least this amount is not earned, the individual will move into the next best-paid alternative occupation. This assumes, of course, that the individual is only concerned with the pecuniary rewards of a particular occupation.

Key terms

Transfer earnings: the earnings an individual can obtain in the next best paid occupation.

Economic rent: earnings in excess of transfer earnings.

Definition of economic rent

Economic rent is any earnings above transfer earnings. Hence if an individual is paid $2000 per month and he or she would have been prepared to work for $500 per week, then the transfer earnings are $500 and the economic rent $1500.

Factors affecting transfer earnings and economic rent in an occupation

Figure 8.18 illustrates transfer earnings and economic rent. In this case, all workers are paid a wage equal to W and Q workers are employed. However, the upward-sloping supply curve indicates that all workers except the last worker employed would have been prepared to work for less than the wage W. The area under the supply curve OBAQ represents the workers' transfer earnings. The difference between the actual wage paid W and the amount the workers would have been prepared to accept is, therefore, their economic rent and is given by the area BWA.

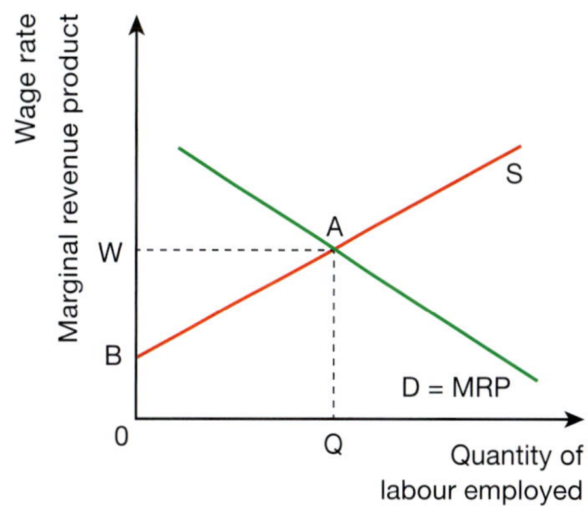

Figure 8.18 Transfer earnings and economic rent ▲

Clearly the proportion of any given wage that represents economic rent and transfer earnings depends upon the elasticity of supply. The more inelastic the supply, the greater is the proportion of any given earnings that constitute economic rent relative to transfer earnings.

The majority of the very high earnings of the athletes, musicians and actors mentioned earlier thus constitutes economic rent because they all have an extremely inelastic supply. In the extreme case of an individual having a unique talent, the supply curve would be vertical or perfectly inelastic and the whole of the individual's earnings would constitute economic rent. In this case the individual's wage would be entirely determined by the demand for their services.

Getting it right

Make sure you are able to explain the transfer earnings and economic rent components of an individual's wage and can illustrate this on a diagram

Progress question

10 An individual is currently earning $500 per week as a builder. They could earn $400 per week as a taxi driver, $450 per week as a librarian or $490 per week working in a supermarket. Explain the worker's transfer earnings and economic rent in their current occupation as a builder.

Key concepts

- **The margin and decision-making** marginal physical product (MPP) is important in indicating the amount of extra output that is produced if a firm increases its input of labour by one unit and marginal revenue (MR) is important in indicating the additional revenue brought in from selling the extra output. These two elements determine marginal revenue product (MRP) and this theory is crucial to wage determination in establishing the demand curve for labour.
- **Equilibrium and disequilibrium** these concepts are important in relation to wage determination and the establishment of equilibrium wage and equilibrium employment in a labour market.
- **Efficiency and inefficiency** the difference between efficiency and equity is important and one of the arguments in favour of privatisation is that by allowing for more competition in an industry, it is likely that there will be greater efficiency.

- **Time** the importance of time can be seen in a variety of contexts, such as the time needed to benefit from deregulation in an industry and the time needed to influence the supply of labour in an economy.
- **The role of government and the issues of equality and equity:** regulation can be used to correct market failure and the difference between equality and equity is an important distinction. Policies towards equality and equity need to be understood, such as in relation to negative income tax, universal and means-tested benefits and universal basic income.

Progress check

After completing this chapter you should be able to:

- understand the government policies to achieve efficient resource allocation and to correct market failure
- understand equity and the redistribution of income and wealth
- understand labour market forces and government intervention.

Exam-style questions

Essay questions

1 Discuss to what extent the privatisation of an industry is likely to improve efficiency in the allocation of resources. [20 marks]

2 Discuss to what extent economic efficiency can be improved if a government is involved in the regulation and provision of goods and services when there is market failure. [20 marks]

3 Discuss to what extent a government can bring about a more equal distribution of income and wealth in an economy. [20 marks]

4 To what extent is it possible for a trade union to increase both wages and the level of employment for its members? [20 marks]

5 Evaluate the economic arguments in favour of a country increasing its national minimum wage by 20 per cent. [20 marks]

6 Discuss how effective a government's microeconomic intervention in an economy is likely to be. [20 marks]

Multiple-choice questions

7 An indirect tax imposed on a product will: [1 mark]

A shift the demand curve to the left
B lead to an increase in price
C lead to an increase in quantity
D shift the supply curve to the right

8 A benefit which people are entitled to, irrespective of their income and wealth, is known as a: [1 mark]

A means-tested benefit
B universal benefit
C monopsonist benefit
D absolute benefit

9 The macroeconomy

In this chapter you will develop your knowledge and understanding of:

- the circular flow of income
- economic growth and sustainability
- employment/unemployment
- money and banking.

9.1 The circular flow of income

9.1.1 *The multiplier process*

Definition of the multiplier

The multiplier represents the number of times by which any change in injections (J) is increased or decreased to give the final change in national income. If a government, for example, increases its expenditure, this results in a greater change in national income. The multiplier effect happens all the time in an economy.

Link

See Chapter 4, section 4.2, to revise your knowledge of the circular flow of income.

Key term

Multiplier: the number of times by which a change in injections is increased, or decreased, to give the final change in national income.

Calculation of average and marginal propensities to save

Average propensity to save (APS) is the proportion of total income that is saved. It is calculated as: $\frac{\text{total savings}}{\text{total income}}$ or $\frac{S}{Y}$

If a person's income was \$100 and they saved \$20 then APS would be $S = \frac{20}{100} = 0.2$

Marginal propensity to save (MPS) is the proportion of any change in (always shown as Δ) income that is saved. It is calculated as: $\frac{\text{the change in savings}}{\text{the change in income}} = \frac{\Delta S}{\Delta Y}$

If someone had an increase in their income from \$100 to \$140 and they increased their savings from \$20 to \$30 then MPS would be $\frac{\Delta S}{\Delta Y} = \frac{10}{40} = 0.25$

Calculation of average and marginal propensities to consume

Similar to savings, above, the average propensity to consume (APC) is the proportion of total income that is consumed. It is calculated as:

$$APC = \frac{\text{total savings}}{\text{total income}} \text{ or } \frac{C}{Y}$$

If a person's income was \$100 and they consumed \$80 then APS would be $C = \frac{80}{100} = 0.8$

As individuals either consume or save APC + APS = 1.

Marginal propensity to consume (MPC) is the proportion of any change in income that is consumed. It is calculated as:

$$\frac{\text{change in consumption}}{\text{change in income}} = \frac{\Delta C}{\Delta Y}$$

Key terms

Average propensity to save (APS): the proportion of total income that is saved.

Marginal propensity to save (MPS): the proportion of any change in income that is saved.

Average propensity to consume (APC): the proportion of total income that is consumed.

Marginal propensity to consume (MPC): the proportion of any change in income that is consumed.

If someone had an increase in their income from \$100 to \$140 and they increased their consumption from \$80 to \$110 then MPC would be $\frac{\Delta C}{\Delta Y} = \frac{30}{40} = 0.75$

Similar to the above, MPC + MPS + 1.

Calculation of average and marginal propensities to import

Key terms

Average propensity to import (APM): the proportion of total income that is spent on imports.

Marginal propensity to import (MPM): the proportion of any change in income that is spent on imports.

The average propensity to import (APM) is the proportion of total income that is used to buy imports. It is calculated as:

$$\text{APC} = \frac{\text{total imports}}{\text{total income}} \text{ or } \frac{M}{Y}$$

If a person's income was \$100 and they consumed \$10 of import, then APM would be:

$$M = \frac{10}{100} = 0.1$$

Marginal propensity to import (MPM) is the proportion of any change in income that is spent on imports. It is calculated as:

$$\text{MPM} = \frac{\text{change in imports}}{\text{change in income}} = \frac{\Delta M}{\Delta Y}$$

If someone had an increase in their income from \$100 to \$140 and they increased their spending on imports from \$10 to \$15 then MPM would be: $\frac{\Delta M}{\Delta Y} = \frac{5}{40} = 0.125$

Calculation of average and marginal rates of tax

Key terms

Average rate of tax (ART): the proportion of total income that is paid in direct tax.

Marginal rate of tax (MRT): the proportion of any change in income that is paid in direct tax.

The average rate of tax (ART) is the proportion of total income that is paid in direct tax. It is calculated as:

$$\text{APC} = \frac{\text{total tax paid}}{\text{total income}} \text{ or } \frac{T}{Y}$$

If a person's income was \$100 and they paid \$10 in tax, then ART would be:

$$\frac{T}{Y} = \frac{10}{100} = 0.1$$

Marginal rate of tax (MRT) is the proportion of any change in income that is paid in direct tax. It is calculated as:

$$\frac{\text{change in imports}}{\text{change in income}} = \frac{\Delta M}{\Delta Y}$$

If someone had an increase in their income from \$100 to \$140 and their tax paid increased from \$10 to \$15 then MRT would be:

$$\frac{\Delta M}{\Delta Y} = \frac{5}{40} = 0.125$$

Formulae for and calculation of multiplier in a closed and open economy, with and without a government sector

The multiplier is always shown as 'k'. It concerns the marginal propensities to withdraw.

The multiplier is calculated by: $\dfrac{1}{\text{marginal propensity to withdraw}}$

In a closed economy with no government, the only withdrawal is savings. The multiplier, therefore, is: $k = \dfrac{1}{MPS}$

If MPS = 0.2 the value is: $k = \dfrac{1}{MPS} = \dfrac{1}{0.2} = 5$

If the government sector is now introduced then MRT must be added. If MRT is 0.1 the multiplier will become smaller as more money is withdrawn from the circular flow of income:

$$k = \frac{1}{MPS + MRT} = \frac{1}{0.2 + 0.1} = \frac{1}{0.3} = 3.33$$

In an open economy with no government, the only withdrawals are savings and imports. The multiplier, therefore, is: $k = \dfrac{1}{MPS + MPM}$

If MPS = 0.2 and MPM = 0.1 the value is: $k = \dfrac{1}{MPS + MPM} = \dfrac{1}{0.2 + 0.1} = 3.33$

If the government sector is now introduced then MRT must be added. If MRT is 0.1 the multiplier will become even smaller:

$$k = \frac{1}{MPS + MPM + MRT} = \frac{1}{0.2 + 0.1 + 0.1} = \frac{1}{0.4} = 2.5$$

National income determination using AD and income approach with the multiplier process

The effect of increasing injections is to raise AD from AD to AD_1 (Figure 9.1) and the level of national income from PY to P_1Y_1.

The multiplier allows us to calculate what the effect on national income will be following an injection. In a closed economy with no government there are

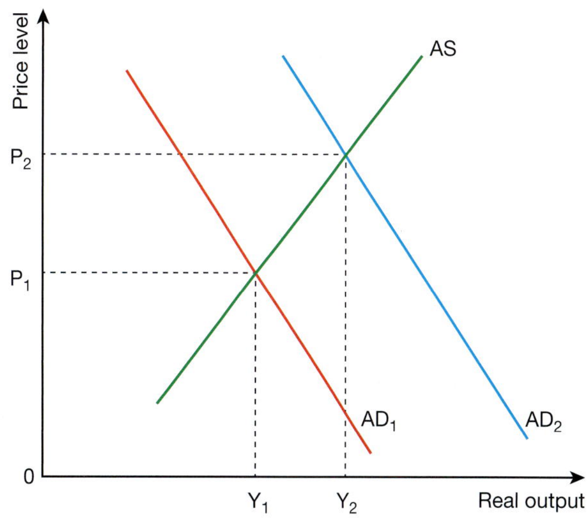

Figure 9.1 National income determination using AD ▲

> **Link**
> See Chapter 4, section 4.2.1, to revise your knowledge of the closed and open economies.

> **Link**
> See Chapter 4, section 4.2.2, for more on withdrawals.

> **Getting it right**
> In an exam keep it simple by using numbers which are easy to manipulate. Remember that as more withdrawals are added the value of the multiplier falls.

> **Activity**
> **The multiplier**
> 1 If MPC = 0.75, what is the value of k?
> 2 If MPS = 0.2; MRT =0.15, MPM = 0.15, what is the value of k?
> 3 If in an open economy with no government k = 2.5 and MPS = 0.2 what is the value of MPM?

> **Link**
> See Chapter 4 for national income, section 4.1 and section 4.3 for AD and injections, section 4.2.2.

only consumers (C) and investors (I). If investment increases by \$100 and consumers always spend 80 per cent of any increase in the incomes (MPC = 0.8) then they will, in turn, spend \$80 and save (S) \$20. This will continue until there is nothing left to spend as shown below:

$$I = \$100 + C = (80 + 64 + 51.2 + \ldots\ldots\ldots\ldots) = \$500$$

$$S = (20 + 16 + 12.8 + \ldots\ldots\ldots\ldots) = \$100$$

There are two different, but related, changes to note:

1 National income has risen by \$500 which is 5× the initial injection. This because the value of the multiplier (k) is 5. This is derived from the following equation:

$$k = \frac{1}{1-MPC} = \frac{1}{1-0.8} = \frac{1}{0.2} = 5$$

2 Savings have increased to \$100 which equals the amount invested. This is because J = W. In a simple economy Y= C + S. In this situation mps $= \frac{\Delta S}{\Delta Y}$ is equal to 1 – MPC so that MPS = 0.2

If all withdrawals are now considered, an open system with government, then the multiplier is: $k = \frac{1}{MPS + MRT + MPM}$

This means that if the marginal propensity to save is 0.2 and of imports is 0.1 while the marginal rate of tax is 0.1 then the value of the multiplier is: $k = \frac{1}{0.2 + 0.1 + 0.1} = \frac{1}{0.4} = 2.5$

If the original injection is still \$100 then national income will have increased by \$250.

Calculation of effect of changing AD on national income using the multiplier

AD = C + I + G + X. As any change in C will also affect S which as MPS is part of the multiplier, the changes in AD are equivalent to changes in injections.

If the multiplier is now put together with injections the formula is: $\Delta Y = (I + G + X)k = \Delta J \times k$

The overall effect of any changes in injections will depend on the size of the multiplier. This can be seen in the following examples:

1 If ΔJ = \$100 and k = 5, then ΔY must equal \$500.

2 If G increases from \$40 to \$50 then ΔJ = \$110 and ΔY will rise to \$550.

3 If I then increases from \$40 to \$50 and X from \$20 to \$25 then ΔJ = \$125 and ΔY = \$625.

4 If in this instance k changed from 5 to 4 due to an increase in MRT then ΔY would only rise to 500.

Getting it right

The multiplier will always be a number greater than or equal to 1.
The more withdrawals there are, the smaller the size of the multiplier.

The important factor to note is that the larger the value of the multiplier is, the greater will be the change in national income, while the smaller it is, the less will be the change.

Case Study

The multiplier in different countries

The value of the multiplier will vary between countries depending on factors such as the extent of international trade and people's behaviour regarding saving.

The following values have been calculated for four developing countries:

- Iran 2.56

Tehran

- India 3.53

Mumbai

- Indonesia 3.20

Jakarta

- Malaysia 2.54

Kuala Lumpur

1 Calculate the effect of an injection of 10 million rupiah on the Indonesian national income.

2 Explain two different effects on the countries shown of an investment of $10 million from a US company.

3 Explain one other effect that such an investment might have on your country.

9.1.2 Components of Aggregate Demand (AD) and their determinants

Consumption function: autonomous and induced consumer expenditure

The consumption function is shown by the equation C = a + bY, where 'b' is the MPC and 'a' is autonomous consumption. This is the level of consumption which does not depend on income so even if Y = 0, C can be a positive number. This is the idea that even when income is zero there will be some spending on basics, possibly funded from savings.

Induced consumption depends on the level of income. As income increases, so does induced consumption depending on the size of the MPC.

An example would be: if a = 10, b = 0.8 and Y = 100 then:
C = 10 + 0.8 × 100 = 10 + 80 = 90.

Savings function: autonomous and induced savings

The savings function is shown by the equation S = sY, where 's' is the MPS and 'a' is autonomous saving. This is the level of saving does not depend on income. As Y = C + S, if C is positive when Y = 0, then savings must be negative.

Induced savings depends on the level of income. As income increases, so does induced savings depending on the size of the MPS.

An example would be: if a = –10, s = 0.2 and Y = 100 then:

S = –10 + 0.2 × 100 = –10 + 20 = 10.

Autonomous and induced investment; the accelerator

The accelerator is based on the idea that the level of aggregate demand generates investment. If national income increases then more investment is needed to meet the higher demand. This investment that responds to changes in national income is called induced investment, whereas the investment as an injection in the multiplier is called autonomous investment.

In Table 9.1 at the start the firm has ten machines, one of which needs replacing each year, able to produce 100 units each per year. It shows how investment will respond to a change in demand. In year 4, constant demand means that there is no induced investment while the fall in demand in year 5 leads to no investment.

Key terms

Accelerator: the level of investment depends on the rate of growth of demand.
Induced investment: investment that depends on changes in national income.
Autonomous investment: investment that is not related to the level of national income. It is an injection into the circular flow and interacts with the multiplier.

Activity

National income and the multiplier

I = 10, G = 10 and X = 10
mps = 0.25, mpm = 0.1,
mrt = 0.15

1. What is the value of the national income (Y)?
2. If all of the injections doubled, but mpm rose to 0.15 and mrt to 0.3, what is the new value of Y?

Link

If you are not sure about MPC and MPS see section 9.1.1 of this chapter.

Key terms

Autonomous consumption: the level of consumption that does not depend on income. It is the level of consumption when Y = 0 .
Induced consumption: depends on the level of income.
Autonomous saving: the level of saving that does not depend on income. It is the level of saving when Y = 0.
Induced savings: depends on the level of income.

Getting it right

Make sure that you do not confuse the multiplier and the accelerator.

Link

For more on trade cycles see section 9.2.3 of this chapter. For more on capital see Chapter 1, section 1.3.1.

Key terms

Capital-output ratio: the amount of capital required to produce a defined level of output.

Yield: the return, such as interest or dividends, from an asset shown as a percentage of the investment's cost, market price or face value.

Table 9.1 Induced investment and the accelerator ▼

Year	Demand	Number of machines	New machines needed	Replacement investment	Induced investment	Total investment
1	1000	10	10	1	0	1
2	1100	10	11	1	1	2
3	1400	11	14	1	4	5
4	1400	14	14	1	0	1
5	1300	14	13	0	0	0

There are clear links between the accelerator and the multiplier. If income rises then the accelerator predicts that businesses will invest more. This through the multiplier will, in turn, lead to higher national income. In order to explain the persistence of trade cycles, investment is now seen as dependent not only on income, but also on businesses' productive capacity.

An important idea associated with the accelerator is the capital-output ratio. This is the ratio of capital used to produce a unit of output in a given time period. Where capital is cheap relative to other factor inputs, the ratio is likely to be high.

Investment is influenced, also, by the yield which is the income return on an investment such as dividends on shares divided by its price. The higher the yield, the more attractive is the investment.

Progress question

1 Explain the differences and similarities between the multiplier and the accelerator.

Government spending

Government spending (G) is spending on state-provided goods and services including public goods and merit goods as well as defence, environmental protection, etc. The size of G will change each year and is affected by how the economy is performing and the political priorities of the government. Due to the coronavirus pandemic, most governments have spent more in 2020 and 2021 than previous years.

Keynes recognized that the government budget was a major method for influencing AD. The size of government spending could both increase and reduce AD. He argued that during extreme times like deep recessions, only the government had the power and resources to stimulate AD.

In addition to times of crises such as economic recessions or pandemics, other determinants of government expenditure would include: the level and rate of economic growth; the amount of government revenue; the size and composition of the national debt; trade conditions; poverty and population.

Link

For more on AD, government spending and net exports see Chapter 4, section 4.3, Chapter 5 section 5.2.5 and section 9.1.2 of this chapter.

Link

For more on public goods and merit goods see Chapter 1, section 1.6, Chapter 3, section 3.1 and Chapter 7, section 7.4.

Net exports (exports minus imports)

As seen earlier, net exports is the difference between exports and imports.

The main determinants of net exports are shown in Table 9.2. A change in the price level causes a change in net exports that moves the economy along its aggregate demand curve.

John Maynard Keynes ▲

Link

For more on economic growth see Chapter 4, section 4.4 and section 9.2 of this chapter.

Table 9.2 The determinants of net exports ▼

Determinant	How it affects net exports
Incomes, both domestic and foreign	A country's own level of income affects its imports similar to that of consumption. If consumers' income increases, they will buy more goods and services. Because some of those goods and services are produced in other nations, imports will rise. An increase in real GDP thus boosts imports; a reduction in real GDP reduces imports. In a similar way, if incomes in other countries rise, they will be able to buy more goods and services, including foreign goods and services. Any one country's exports will increase as incomes rise in other countries and will fall as incomes drop in other countries.
Relative prices	Changes in the price level in a country will affect both exports and imports. A higher price level in, for example, Chile makes its exports more expensive leading to a fall in demand. At the same time, this higher price level makes foreign goods and services more attractive to people in Chile, increasing imports. A higher price level therefore reduces net exports. A lower price level encourages exports and reduces imports, increasing net exports.
Exchange rate	An increase in the value of, for example, the South African rand means that exports cost more in terms of other currencies. This will reduce South African exports. At the same time, a higher exchange rate means that the prices of imports fall in terms of the rand so imports will rise. An increase in the exchange rate should reduce net exports, while a fall should increase net exports.
Trade policies	Exports depend on both the trade policies of the country and those of other countries. A country could increase its exports by, for example, giving subsidies. On the other hand, if another country imposes protectionist measures then exports to that country will fall.
Preferences and technology	Consumer preferences are one determinant of the consumption of any good or service; a shift in preferences for a foreign-produced good will increase imports of that good. Changes in technology can affect the kinds of capital equipment firms will import. The move to 'green' energy will both reduce the demand for coal by importers, but also boost the exports of countries that manufacture wind turbines, solar panels, etc.

Link

Protection and free trade are covered in Chapter 6, sections 6.1 and 6.2.

Case Study

Government spending in Nigeria

In a majority of developing countries, the government is seen as an important agent of change. The size of government expenditure reveals the extent of government involvement in the economy. The shift in the role of government from traditional functions such as provision of security, administration and law and order to direct intervention in income generating activities like capital investment and distributive roles like subsidies and transfers have significantly expanded the scope of governments in many countries.

The major objective of government is therefore to promote societal welfare by means of appropriate economic, political, social and legal programmes. These programmes, however, have led to expansion in government expenditure size particularly in the developing economies like Nigeria with a weak and uncompetitive private sector.

Despite a large growth in government expenditure in Nigeria, issues such as high levels of poverty, unemployment, lack of sufficient infrastructure and insecurity in both the economy and society persist.

1. Using examples from your own country, do you agree that the main objective of a government is to promote societal welfare?
2. Explain two advantages and two disadvantages of expanding government expenditure.
3. Discuss why a large growth in government expenditure may not solve economic and social problems.

9.1.3 *Full employment level of national income and equilibrium level of national income*

The equilibrium level of national income occurs where J = W, see Figure 9.2, or when aggregate expenditure (AE) intersects the 45 ˚degree line, see Figure 9.3. This is not the same as full employment equilibrium level which is where resources are fully employed and the price level is not increasing, whereas J = W says nothing about the level of employment or the rate of inflation. The economy can be in equilibrium with millions of people unemployed or, equally, where prices are rapidly rising.

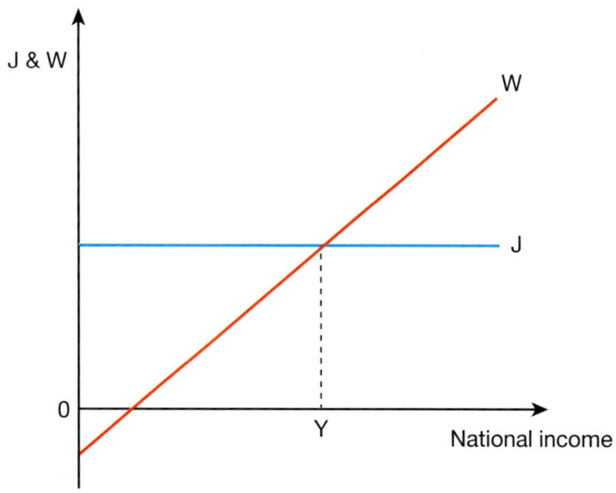

Figure 9.2 Equilibrium national income using injections and withdrawals ▲

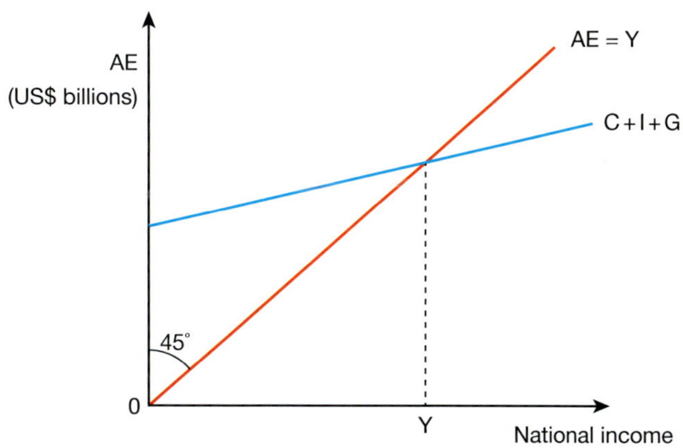

Figure 9.3 Aggregate expenditure equilibrium national income ▲

The relationship between the two methods can be seen in Figure 9.3. Both methods result in the same level of national income.

Inflationary and deflationary gaps

Inflationary and deflationary gaps (sometimes called expansionary and output gaps) refer to the relationship between real GDP and potential GDP. This can be shown using AE or AD/AS.

Key terms

Inflationary gap: where aggregate demand is greater than aggregate supply leading to inflation. It is also where real GDP exceeds potential GDP.

Deflationary gap: where aggregate demand is less than aggregate supply or real GDP is less than potential output.

Activity

Net exports

Table 9.2 gives some of the main factors affecting net exports. Discuss in groups **either** whether there are others which affect the net exports of your country **or** which of those given is the most important for your country, making clear the reasons for your decision.

Getting it right

This would be a good point in your studies to spend some time making sure you have a good grasp of AD. In doing so, do not forget to revisit the material covered in Chapter 4.

Key terms

Equilibrium level of national income: where the economy is neither growing nor shrinking J = W.

Full employment equilibrium: where all resources are fully employed.
real GDP = potential GDP

Getting it right

Be careful not to confuse equilibrium national income and full employment national income. This is a common error by candidates.

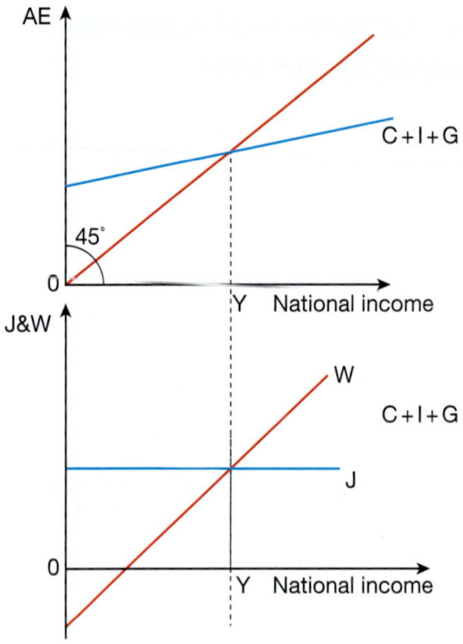

Figure 9.4 Comparison of AE and J/W methods for determining national income ▲

In the case of the inflationary gap, as actual demand exceeds that which the economy can supply the gap is filled by the price level rising i.e. inflation. Equally, in the case of a deflationary gap, actual demand is less than the economy can supply so that not all resources are employed so the price level falls (Figures 9.4 to 9.7).

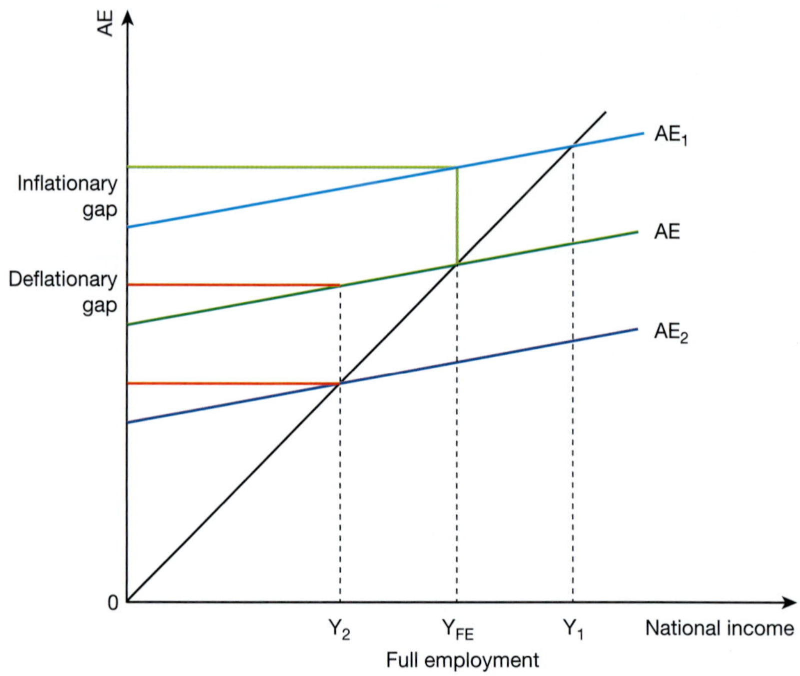

Figure 9.5 Inflationary and deflationary gaps ▲

Progress question

2 Explain what happens to i) the rate of inflation, and ii) employment when a country has either an inflationary or a deflationary gap.

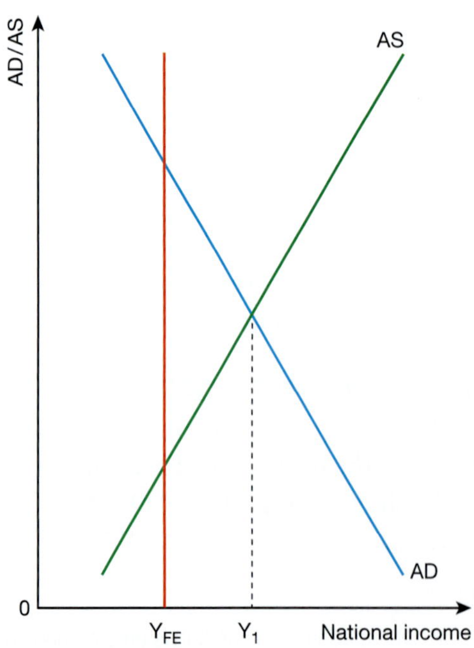

Figure 9.6 Inflationary gap ▲

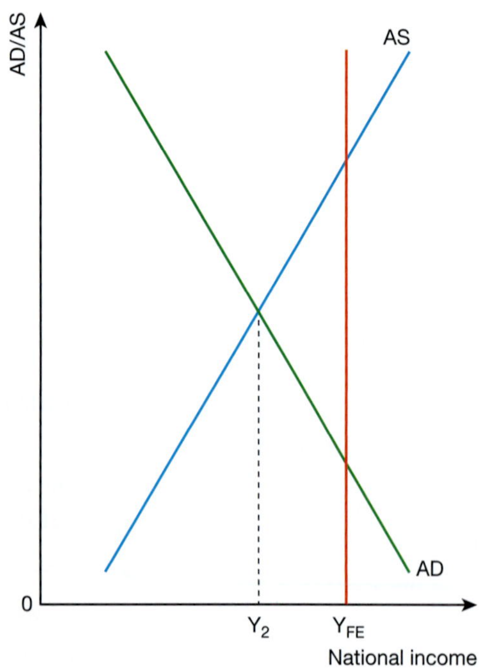

Figure 9.7 Deflationary gap ▲

9.2 Economic growth and sustainability

9.2.1 Actual growth versus potential growth in national output

Actual growth occurs when existing factors of production are utilised in a more efficient manner so as to achieve a higher level of output.

This can be shown using a production possibility curve as seen in Figure 9.8. Originally the economy is producing X amount of goods and services. If, for example, the economy was in recession, but the government used fiscal and monetary policies to increase aggregate demand then output of both could rise to Y on the current production possibility curve AB. This represents an actual increase in growth or GDP. It can also be shown by an increase in aggregate demand, see Figure 9.10. Potential growth can be shown by an increase in aggregate supply, see Figure 9.9.

Further increases in output are only possible if there is an increase in the potential growth shown by the outward shift from AB to CD. The output of goods and services could then increase to Z. In the long run, the focus of economic growth needs to be on expanding the potential capacity (potential output) of an economy.

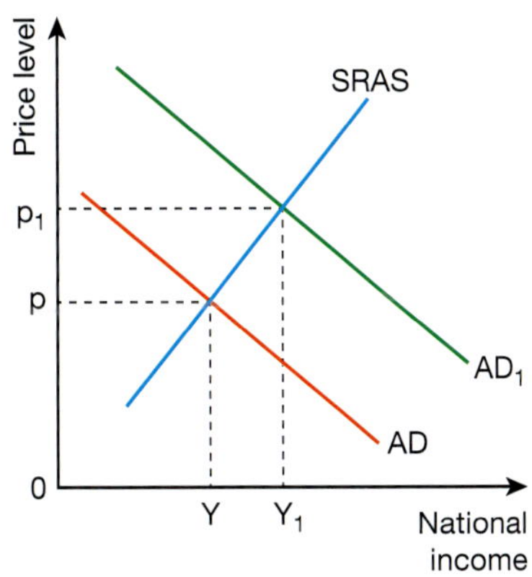

Figure 9.9 Actual economic growth ▲

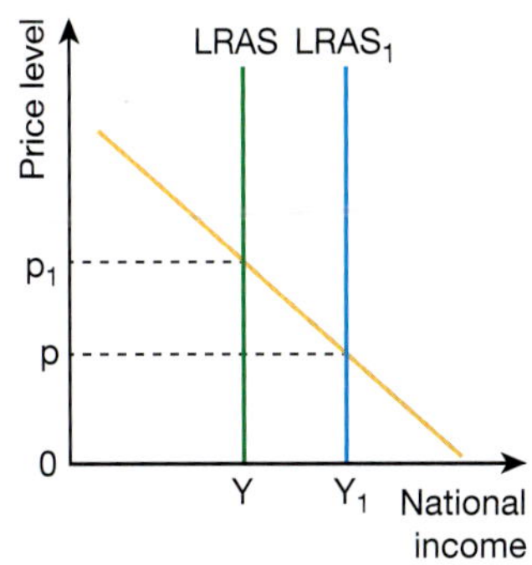

Figure 9.10 Potential economic growth ▲

9.2.2 Positive and negative output gaps

The output gap measures how close current output is to an economy's long-term potential output, i.e. the difference between the two. If actual output is less than potential output, there is a negative output gap. Some factor resources are under-utilized. There is likely to be downward pressure on inflation and higher unemployment. A positive output gap occurs when actual output is more than full-capacity output due to high aggregate demand resulting in, for example, factories and workers operating above their most efficient capacity. This will result in higher rates of inflation. In both cases the economy is performing inefficiently.

Link

Before starting this section, you may want to refer back to economic growth in Chapter 4, section 4.4.

Link

For production possibility curves see Chapter 1, section 1.5.

Key terms

Actual growth: the rate of growth in national output or the increase in output when all resources fully employed.

Potential growth: the rate at which the economy could increase.

Negative output gap: occurs when actual output is less than what an economy could produce at full capacity.

Positive output gap: occurs when actual output is more than full-capacity output.

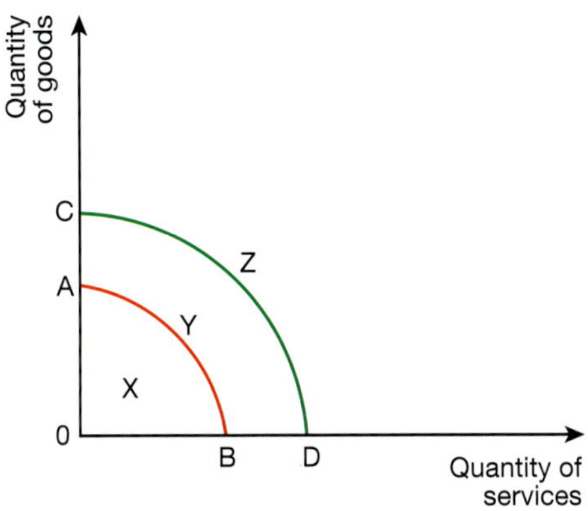

Figure 9.8 Actual and potential growth of an economy ▲

Link

For more on AD/AS see Chapter 10, sections 10.2 and 10.3.

Progress question

3 Discuss the extent to which potential growth is more important for an economy than actual growth.

Key term

Business (or trade) cycle: the way in which economic growth fluctuates over a period of time.

Activity

Output gap

Find out whether your country has a negative or a positive output gap. You must state what evidence you are using for your conclusion.

9.2.3 *Business (trade) cycle*

The business cycle is the way in which economic growth fluctuates over a period of time.

Phases of the cycle

A business (or trade or economic) cycle consists of boom, slump, recession and recovery as part of short-term changes in GDP, see Figure 9.11. The duration of the cycle varies due to different political and external events. US research shows that the recovery/boom period is of much longer duration than the slump/recession period.

Trade cycles can apply to individual countries or groups of countries or can be on a global scale.

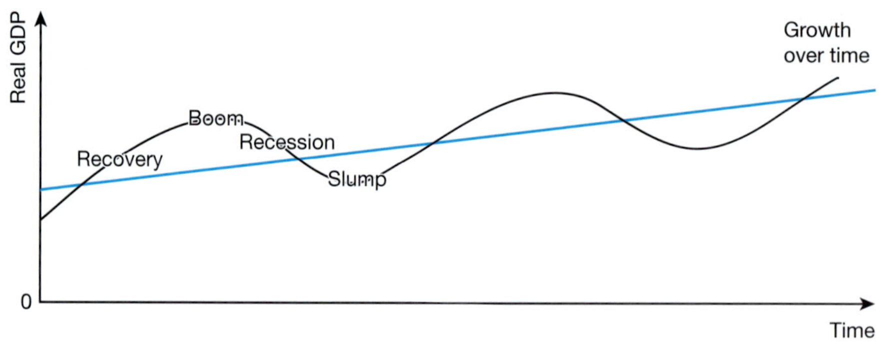

Figure 9.11 The trade cycle ▲

Activity

Business cycle

Try to draw a business cycle for your country for the past 50 years.

Causes of the cycle

There are many different causes of the business cycle. Demand side factors include interest rates and credit cycles and supply-side ones such as technological shocks. These are summarised in Table 9.3.

Table 9.3 Causes of the business cycle ▼

Cause	Explanation
Interest rates	If interest rates are cut, borrowing costs fall which can lead to higher spending and economic growth. If the Central Bank increases interest rates to reduced inflation, this will lead to reduced consumer spending and investment, leading to an economic downturn and recession.
Changes in house prices	A rise in house prices creates a positive wealth effect and leads to higher consumer spending. A fall in house prices causes lower consumer spending and bank losses.
Consumer and business confidence	People are easily influenced by external events. If there is a succession of bad economic news, this tends to discourage people from spending and investing, making a small downturn into a bigger recession. When the economy recovers, this can cause a positive bandwagon effect. Economic growth encourages consumers to borrow and banks to lend. This causes higher economic growth. Confidence is an important factor in causing the business cycle. Fall in confidence in May 2008 contributed to the deepest recession for a considerable time.

Continued . . .

Multiplier effect	The multiplier effect states that a fall in injections may cause a bigger final fall in real GDP. If a government cut public investment, there would be a fall in aggregate demand and a rise in unemployment leading to less consumption and even lower demand in the economy. Alternatively, an injection of investment could have a positive multiplier effect.
Accelerator effect	If the growth rate falls, firms will reduce investment because output is likely to rise more slowly. This theory suggests investment is quite volatile and small changes in the rate of growth have a big effect on investment levels. This contributes to a more volatile business cycle.
Credit cycle	This was the primary cause of the 2008/09 recession. A boom in credit and lending helped to promote economic growth during the 2000s. When banks became over-stretched and needed to call in loans, the financial system was short of liquidity.
Supply-side	Some economists have stressed the importance of factors such as technological shocks or changes in productivity.

Role of automatic stabilisers

Automatic stabilisers refer to how fiscal policy, such as the tax and transfer systems, will influence the rate of GDP growth and help counter swings in the business cycle without direct intervention by the government.

When the economy grows, and incomes rise, tax liabilities increase and eligibility for government benefits falls, without any change in tax rates or other legislation. Equally, when growth declines, and incomes fall, tax liabilities decrease and more families become eligible for benefits such as unemployment pay, family benefits, etc, again without any changes in fiscal policy.

9.2.4 Policies to promote economic growth and their effectiveness

These policies can be grouped under demand-side, fiscal and monetary, and supply-side.

Demand-side

- Expansionary fiscal policy involves cutting tax and increasing government spending. Lower income tax will increase disposable income and encourage consumer spending. Higher government spending will create jobs and provide a boost demand. It works well if consumption is falling and savings rising as it can increase demand without causing crowding out.

  The problem is that it leads to an increase in government borrowing. To finance this extra spending, governments borrow from the private sector. If the economy is already growing, then this can result in crowding out.

- Lower interest rates reduce the cost of borrowing, encouraging investment and consumer spending. Lower interest rates also reduce the incentive to save, making spending more attractive instead. Lower interest rates will also reduce mortgage interest payments, increasing disposable income for consumers.

  Lower interest rates may not always boost spending as consumers may lack confidence and/or banks have liquidity shortages. In

Activity

Causes of the business cycle

1 Using the business cycle you have drawn for your country, discuss as a group what has caused these cycles.
2 Try to find out more about supply-side causes. Discuss their importance for your economy.

Link

For interest rates see sections 9.4.6–9.4.8.
For the multiplier see section 9.1.1.
For the accelerator see section 9.1.2.

Key term

Automatic stabilisers: the way in which elements of fiscal policy, such as tax and transfer systems, can help counter swings in the business cycle without direct government intervention.

Link

For fiscal, monetary and supply-side policies see Chapter 5, sections 5.3 and 5.4.

Key term

Quantitative easing (QE): where a central bank buys financial assets from banks and other private sector businesses with new electronically created money.

addition, cutting interest rates very low could distort future economic activity by, for example, leading to future overheating in terms of housing and other assets.

- Quantitative easing (QE) has been introduced to try to overcome the failure of low interest rates to boost demand. This increases the money supply. The problem is that this could possibly cause inflation. Evidence from when it has been used shows that the inflationary impact was minimal and did not itself stimulate a recovery. Probably, however, without QE a recession would be deeper.

If there is spare capacity (negative output gap) then demand-side policies can help, see Figure 9.12, to increase the rate of economic growth. If, however, the economy is already close to full capacity, a further increase in AD will mainly cause inflation, see Figure 9.13. Nevertheless, managing AD to avoid boom and bust cycles can help provide longer periods of economic expansion.

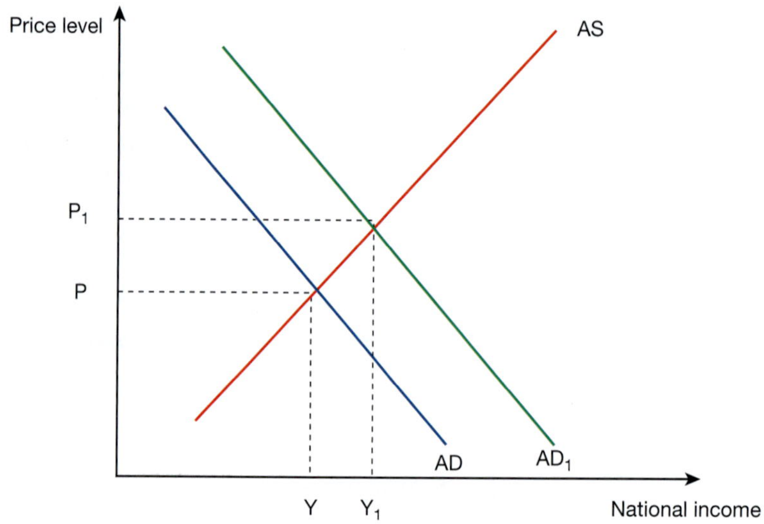

Figure 9.12 Demand-side policy with spare capacity ▲

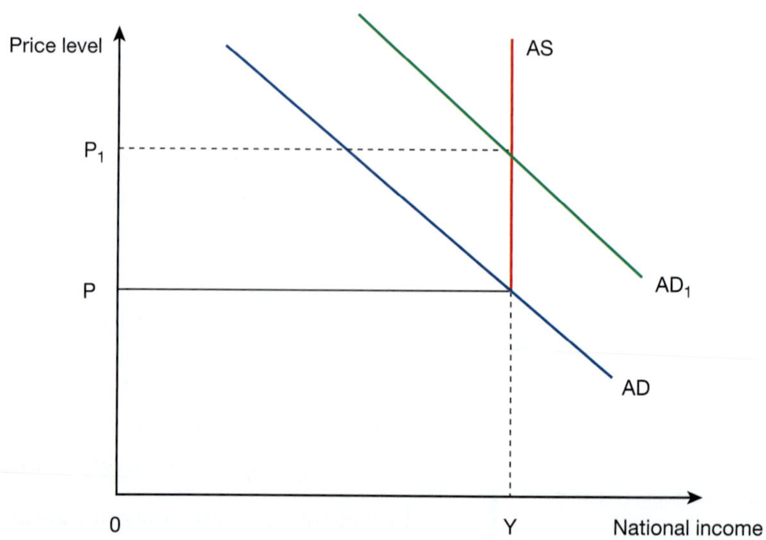

Figure 9.13 Demand-side policy with full capacity ▲

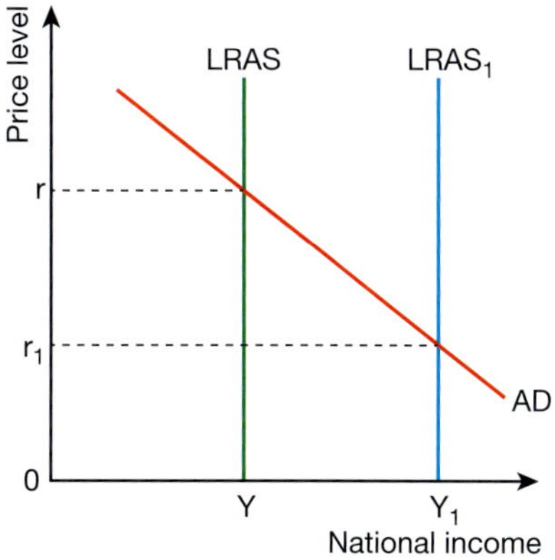

Figure 9.14 Supply-side policy ▲

> **Key term**
>
> **Inclusive economic growth**: economic growth that is distributed fairly across society and creates opportunities for all.

> **Link**
>
> For equity and equality see Chapter 8, section 8.2.1.

> **Key term**
>
> **OECD**: The Organisation for Economic Co-operation and Development is an intergovernmental economic organisation with 37 member countries, founded in 1961 to stimulate economic progress and world trade economic growth that is distributed fairly across society and creates opportunities for all.

> **Key term**
>
> **Sustainable economic growth**: a rate of growth which can be maintained over the long run without creating significant costs on future generations.

Supply-side

Supply-side policies attempt to increase productivity and efficiency of the economy. They include: privatisation, deregulation, tax cuts, education and training, and better infrastructure. These are all long-run policies. Their effect can be seen in Figure 9.14 where real output/national income increases and the price level is reduced.

Supply-side policies can take a considerable time to act in terms of growth. Investing in better education and training would take many years to give higher labour productivity. In a recession, supply-side policies are not going to solve the lack of sufficient aggregate demand. Without demand, firms will be unwilling to expand their output.

9.2.5 *Iclusive economic growth*

Definition of inclusive economic growth

Inclusive economic growth is economic growth that is distributed fairly across society and creates opportunities for all.

Impact of economic growth on equity and equality

There is no certain impact of economic growth on equity and equality. Some countries in the latter half of the twentieth century, for example, Indonesia, Malaysia and Singapore managed to achieve rapid growth and relatively low inequality. On the other hand, the majority of the members of the OECD saw inequality increase with economic growth.

The case for economic growth reducing inequality and boosting equity can be seen in the Kuznets curve, see Figure 11.5 which shows that as an economy develops, initially inequality increases, but then decreases.

Policies to promote inclusive growth

Some policies have contributed to narrower inequality by delivering stronger income gains for households at the bottom of the distribution compared with the average household. Such is the case, for instance, of reducing regulatory barriers to domestic competition, trade and inward foreign direct investment, as well as improving job-search support and programmes to increase economic activity including improved skills training.

In addition, some policies have had a positive effect on all income groups. Investment in information and communications technology, raising the average level of education in the working age population and reductions in marginal income taxes for wage earners have had this effect.

9.2.6 *Sustainable economic growth*

Definition of sustainable economic growth

Sustainable economic growth means a rate of growth which can be maintained over the long run without creating significant costs on future generations.

Sustainable growth involves both environmentally sustainable growth, by not exhausting scarce resources, and, also, growth in terms of low inflation and a balanced economy.

Using and conserving resources; and impact of economic growth on the environment and climate change

There is a trade-off between rapid economic growth today, and growth in the future. Rapid growth today may exhaust resources and create environmental problems for future generations, including the depletion of raw materials and global warming.

Economic growth today must not, therefore, use up raw materials and destroy the environment so as to reduce the quality of life available in the future. This means that there is pressure on countries to ensure that growth does not needlessly waste resources and that it improves not only living standards, but also the quality of life. There are many ways that can be tried to do this including recycling of used materials and reduction of pollution.

The International Resource Panel has stated that there is a need to break the link between economic growth and ever greater use of resources and environmental degradation. While economic growth has resulted in hundreds of millions of people being no longer in poverty, unsustainable production and consumption patterns have resulted, among other problems, in a quarter of the earth's land area being highly degraded, millions of hectares of forests lost every year, rivers and lakes drying up and widespread overfishing.

Climate change with warmer temperatures, rising sea levels and more extreme weather patterns has already affected many countries. In the future it will lead to: greater damage to property and infrastructure, decline in agriculture, forestry, fisheries and tourism; decline in productivity; negatively affecting sectors such as agriculture, forestry, fisheries and tourism; and increasing demand for energy as power generation becomes less reliable. In addition it may disrupt global trade and supply chains. It has been estimated that without major changes the GDP per capita of countries will fall, for example, the US by 10.5 per cent and China by 4.3 per cent by 2100.

Policies to mitigate the impact of economic growth on the environment and climate change

Policies roughly divide into market-based ones and regulations. The market based ones include pollution permits and emission taxes.

There are a wide range of regulatory policies that have been proposed or have started to be implemented. Some examples are shown in Table 9.4.

Table 9.4 Policies to deal with environmental damage and climate change ▼

Policy	Comment
Renewable energy sources	These include solar, wind power and hydro-electric. The adoption of these energy sources also reduces the environmental damage from coal, gas and oil extraction.
Sustainable transport	Including bus rapid transit, electric vehicles, and hydrogen-powered vehicles. These would reduce climate pollution and also use of oil. Bus rapid transit systems would encourage people to use public transport as against private cars, again reducing oil use. It would also decrease the need for more roads and thus reduce environmental degradation.

Continued . . .

Link
For Gini coefficient see Chapter 3, section 3.3.2 and Chapter 11, section 11.4.2.

Link
Kuznets curve is covered in detail in Chapter 11, section 11.3.3.

Progress question
4 Discuss whether countries should use demand-side policies to promote economic growth.

Activity
Inclusive growth

To what extent has equality and equity improved in your economy over the last 30 years? Try to find information for the Gini coefficient and/or for income share of the bottom, middle and upper quartiles of the population

Activity
Sustainable growth

1 To what extent are resources in your country being depleted?
2 What is the government of your country doing to try achieve more sustainable growth?
3 Discuss how easy your country would find it to become more sustainable.

Link
For policies to correct market failure see Chapter 8, section 8.1.

Getting it right

Pollution permits are sometimes called tradable permits. Emission taxes work just like any other tax on production of demerit goods.

Promote the benefits of sustainable agriculture and forestry	Land use changes from forestry and agriculture account for nearly 25 percent of human generated greenhouse gas emissions. More trees need to be planted: land with trees can absorb up to ten times more carbon than similar treeless land. Diversifying crops, and including cattle, can give farmers additional sources of income and reduce the risks to them of more unpredictable weather.
Use natural barriers	Especially in coastal areas where land has been drained causing environmental damage. Wetland areas including salt marshes and mangrove forests protect against storms and floods. This also allows local communities to be involved such as in Fiji and Papua New Guinea.

Case Study

Papua New Guinea and climate change

In Papua New Guinea (PNG) climate change causes gradual shifts of agricultural yields, constant increases in malaria prevalence and the bleaching of corals. Moreover, climate change increases the likelihood and potential magnitude of event-driven hazards like coastal and inland flooding as well as landslides.

If we continue to extract from primary forest we are likely to run out of commercially accessible primary forest shortly after 2030. This will be doubly devastating as we would lose both our source of family incomes as well as the bounty and protection afforded by our great forests. To do so we must: review clearance of primary forest for large-scale agricultural development; reduce damage and forest degradation via reduced logging; and increase yields in subsistence and smallholder agriculture.

Without action on our part, the total annual cost of climate-related hazards in PNG is forecast to double between 2015 and 2030 to $280–370 million.

By applying cost-effective adaptation measures, we can avert up to half of these losses.

1 Explain the environmental problems facing PNG.
2 Explain how improving efficiency in agriculture could help reduce economic problems caused by environmental degradation
3 Discuss how a country should best try to reduce future climate change effects.

Source: Papua New Guinea's Commitment to Act on Climate Change

Link

Before starting this section you may wish to refer back to Chapter 4, section 4.5 on unemployment.

Key term

Full employment: when all those who are willing and able to work at the given wage rate are either in a job or are about to take up a job.

Equilibrium unemployment: the difference between those who would like to work and those who are willing and able to take up a job offer at current wage rate.

9.3 Employment/unemployment

9.3.1 *Definition of full employment*

Full employment is one of the aims of governments. It does not mean that all those of working age are employed, as some may choose early retirement or to continue with education or to stay at home to look after children. In addition, some people at any time are between jobs. In reality, full employment is usually claimed to have been reached when somewhere between two and four per cent of the working population are not in jobs. It can be defined, therefore, as a situation where all those who are willing and able to work at the given wage rate are either in a job or are about to take up a job.

9.3.2 *Equilibrium and disequilibrium unemployment (including hysteresis)*

Equilibrium unemployment is the difference between those who would like to work and those who are willing and able to take up a job offer at current wage rate. Figure 9.15 shows that the labour market is at equilibrium as the aggregate supply of, is equal to the aggregate demand for, labour at W_1, but while jobs exist people are unwilling or unable to take them. This is shown by the distance ab. These people may not be working because their benefits

Getting it right

Be careful not to confuse full employment and full employment national income.

Key term

Disequilibrium unemployment: occurs where wages are higher than the equilibrium wage.

Link

For trade unions and the minimum wage see Chapter 8, section 8.3.8.

are more than they could earn in work or because their skills are no longer needed. It is essentially frictional and structured unemployment.

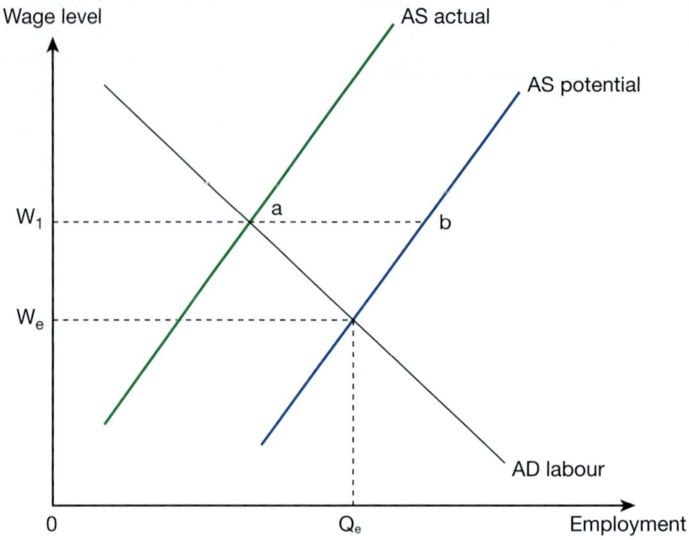

Figure 9.15 Equilibrium unemployment ▲

Disequilibrium equilibrium, shown as ab in Figure 9.16, occurs where wages are higher than the equilibrium wage, W_1 as against W_e. The labour market cannot clear because either organisations, such as trade unions, or legislation, such as minimum wage, prevents it from so doing, so supply is greater than demand.

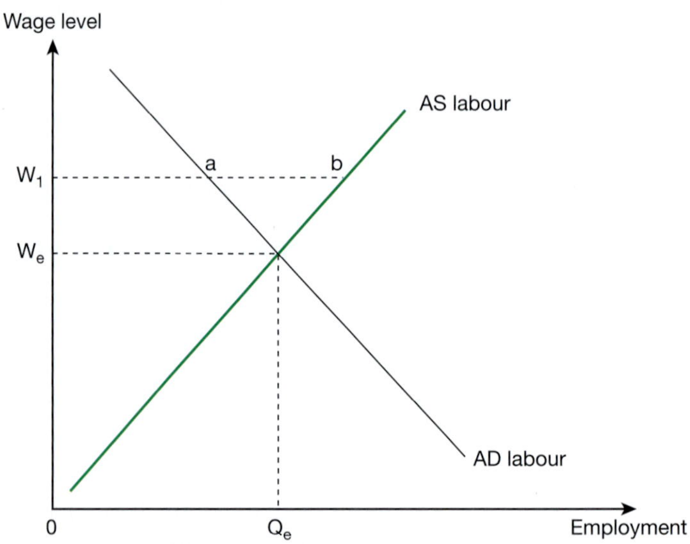

Figure 9.16 Disequilibrium unemployment ▲

Both of these types can lead to hysteresis.

Link

For hysteresis see Chapters 4 see Chapter 4, section 4.5.4 and also under 'determinants' of the natural rate later in this chapter.

9.3.3 *Voluntary and involuntary unemployment*

Voluntary unemployment occurs when someone who is able to work is not willing to do so, even though suitable work is available. Most frictional unemployment is considered voluntary because one is looking for work rather than taking any job available. Some economists claim that structural unemployment can often be voluntary as those with specific skills may not be willing to take lower-skilled work.

Key term

Voluntary unemployment: occurs when someone who is able to work is not willing to do so.

Key term

Involuntary unemployment: occurs when a worker is willing to take a job but cannot find one.

Involuntary unemployment occurs when those who are able and willing to work at the going wage rate cannot find work. The main form of this is demand deficient or cyclical unemployment which is linked to the trade cycle and the lack of aggregate demand causing the supply of workers wanting to work exceeding the demand for them. Some structural, especially technological, unemployment may also be involuntary.

9.3.4 *Natural rate of unemployment*

Definition

Key term

Natural rate of unemployment (NAIRU): the rate of unemployment when the labour market is in equilibrium.

The natural rate of unemployment is the rate of unemployment where real wages have found their free market level and where the aggregate supply of labour is equal to the aggregate demand for labour. At the natural rate, all those wanting to work at the current real wage rate are employed and there is no involuntary unemployment. Some voluntary unemployment still exists due to frictional and some structural unemployment.

Link

For types of unemployment see Chapter 4 Table 4.4.

Determinants

As the natural rate of unemployment is mainly composed of frictional and structural unemployment, factors that affect these types of unemployment will alter the natural rate.

Activity

Voluntary v involuntary unemployment

Discuss whether the unemployment in your country is mainly voluntary or involuntary.

Table 9.5 Determinants of the natural rate of unemployment ▼

Determinant	Explanation
Geographical immobility – frictional unemployment	Parts of a country may be too expensive to live in so workers cannot afford to take jobs in the area. This may also result from poor or too expensive transport links. If new industries are established in areas of old industries then this can be avoided.
Lack of relevant skills – structural unemployment versus retraining	Workers trained to work in one industry may have skills that are no longer required as new industries develop. If retraining is available then this may be avoided.
Level of unemployment, and other, benefits versus wages	If unemployment benefits are too generous compared to the wage from working then the trade-off from income and leisure is diminished. If the minimum wage is high enough, it has the opposite effect
Labour market flexibility	If the labour market becomes more flexible due to reducing trade union powers or less restrictive limits on working hours and other practices or making it easier to hire and fire workers or not setting the minimum wage too high then the natural rate may fall
Hysteresis	This is the idea that if unemployment increases (e.g. during a recession) then it is likely to remain high for some time because workers become de-motivated and deskilled whilst remaining unemployed and therefore find it difficult to get a job in the future.

Link

For NAIRU see Chapter 4, section 4.5.4.
For the Phillips curve and NAIRU Chapter 10, section 10.2.5.

Policy implications

Demand-side policies have problems as there is a need to measure aspects such as the output gap, but this has proved difficult to do. There are also issues with the Phillips curve, see Chapter 10.

Link

For supply-side policies see Chapter 5, section 5.4 and Chapter 10, section 10.3.1.

The result is that supply-side policies have usually been used to try to reduce or stabilise the natural rate. These include:

- improved education and training to reduce occupational immobility through new skills
- greater availability of different kinds of housing to make it easier for workers and firms to be relocated
- making labour markets more flexible, see Table 9.5.

9.3.5 *Patterns and trends in (un)employment*

Using Figure 9.17, a number of patterns stand out:

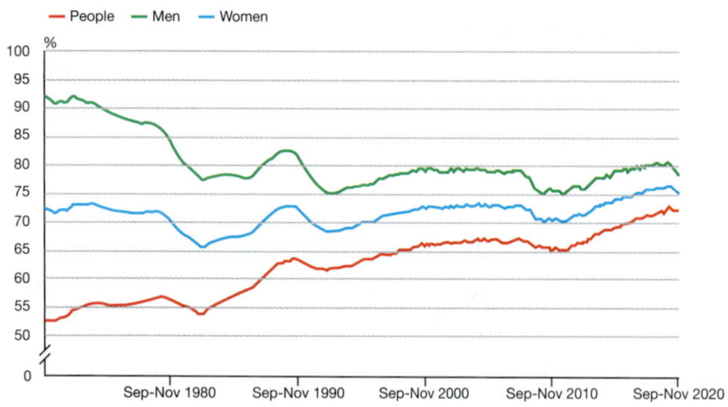

Figure 9.17 UK employment rates (aged 16 to 64 years), seasonally adjusted between January to March 1971 and September to Noivember 2020 ▲

Source: ONS

- employment rates vary over time with the rises and falls
- fluctuations correspond to the recoveries and recessions in the UK economy.

The trends that stand out are:

- an overall decline in the proportion of people employed
- the proportion of men employed fluctuates between 65 per cent and 75 per cent
- the proportion of women employed rises across the years.

Activity

Unemployment trends

1 Find out what has happened to unemployment rates in your country over the last ten years. If possible do so by: total unemployment; gender; age groups; and any other that you can find.

2. Plot the information on a graph (s) and discover the trend. You may find it useful to split these two activities between you and then to compare your findings.

3 If any interesting patterns occur, you should discuss why these are happening. You could compare your overall trend with that of another country.

Getting it right

If you are asked about trends, **do not** describe, but try to comment on the overall pattern.

Key terms

Geographical mobility of labour: the ease or otherwise with which individuals can move between geographical areas.

Occupational mobility of labour: the ease or otherwise with which individuals can move between occupations.

9.3.6 *Mobility of labour*

Forms of labour mobility: geographical and occupational

Geographical mobility of labour is the ease or otherwise with which individuals can move between geographical areas, whether these are within a country or between countries. It is affected by factors such as family ties, transport networks, transferable qualifications, common language and international relations and situations.

Occupational mobility of labour is the ease or otherwise with which individuals can move between occupations. The occupational mobility of labour depends on such factors as the level of education, training and skills required by the job, together with the length of training. It is possible to distinguish between horizontal and vertical labour mobility.

Horizontal mobility is a worker's ability to move to another job at a similar wage such as being a shop assistant in one store to being a shop assistant in another store. Vertical mobility is, however, the worker's ability to move up, and down, the employment hierarchy. A teacher, for example, could move from a being a new young recruit to being a headteacher.

Factors affecting labour mobility

Factors affecting geographical mobility include:

- The cost and availability of suitable housing, such as in countries like China and the UK, may restrict workers' ability to move area.
- Good transport determines how easy it is to move around a country. In addition, housing problems can partly be overcome if, for example, there are good rail links allowing people to live in cheaper areas, but to commute into cities for work.
- Immigration policies can both facilitate and hinder mobility. The EU allows freedom of movement thus encouraging workers to move from low pay/high unemployment areas to parts of the EU with better job prospects. Many countries, however, try to restrict immigration.
- Migration, where unrest in one country encourages people to move to another one both for better job prospects, but also for greater safety.
- Family ties often restrict geographical mobility. Many people are reluctant to move far away from their family.

Activity

Geographical mobility

Try to find out what are the main causes of geographical mobility in your country. How important is geographical mobility for your country?

Increasingly, the most important factor affecting occupational mobility is education and training. The ability to gain relevant qualifications and skills not only at the start of a career, but also throughout and the types of jobs available, determine mobility. This means both vertical mobility, but, also, moving to different types of occupation.

Both geographical and occupational mobility are affected by factors such as: labour market regulations; types of work contract – long term, short term, zero hours; the power of trade unions; etc.

Link

For fiscal and monetary policies refer to Chapter 5.

9.3.7 Policies to reduce unemployment and their effectiveness

Policies depend both on how the causes of unemployment are viewed and also on the time period.

Link

To review your knowledge of AD refer to Chapter 4, sections 4.3.1–4.3.5 and section 9.1.2 of this chapter.
The Phillips curve is covered in Chapter 10, section 10.2.5.

In the short term both fiscal and monetary policies can be used. Fiscal policy will involve: the cutting of taxes for consumers, both direct and indirect, so as to increase consumption (C); cutting of taxes on companies, such as corporation or profits tax, so as to encourage greater investment (I); and a direct increase in government expenditure (G). As C, I and G are all part of aggregate demand (AD) this will then increase leading to a rise in output, income and employment, see Figure 9.18.

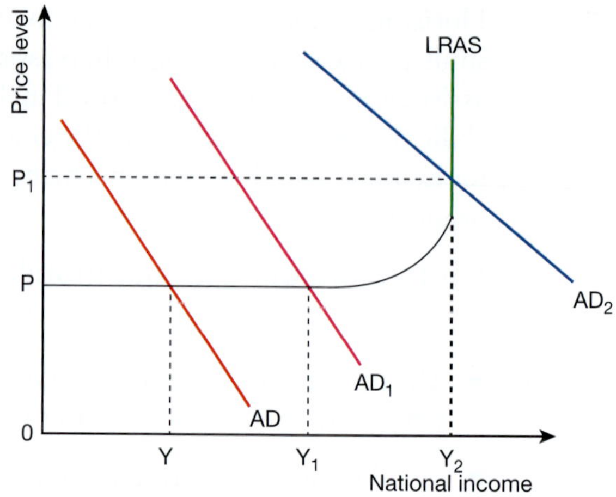

Figure 9.18 The effect of an increase in aggregate demand ▲

Figure 9.18 shows that any increase in a component of AD will shift it from AD to AD_2 leading to greater output, income and employment at Y_1. If, however, AD increases by too much to AD_2, then inflation rises from P to P_1. This could lead to the long run Phillips curve where attempts to reduce unemployment have no real effect except to increase inflation.

> **Link**
>
> Exchange rates are covered in Chapter 6, section 6.4 and Chapter 11, section 11.2.

Using monetary policy, the rate of interest can be cut or a policy such as quantitative easing used. Reducing interest rates will: encourage consumers to save less and spend more, as the opportunity cost of doing so has fallen, and to borrow more; encourage firms to invest more as the cost of borrowing has fallen; and lead to a fall in the exchange rate leading to a rise in exports. The effect on AD is shown in Figure 9.18.

In the long run, supply-side policies would be effective in improving labour productivity by (re)training and by better education and health services. Figure 9.19 shows that shifting AS to AS_1 will overcome any inflationary effects of increasing AD and at the same time increase

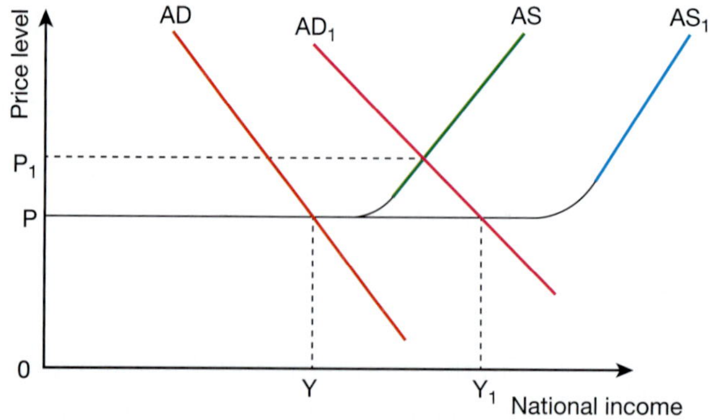

Figure 9.19 Operation of supply-side policy ▲

> **Progress question**
>
> 5 Explain the effectiveness of different policies in reducing unemployment.

Case Study

Australia starts to recover from high unemployment

In September 2020 unemployment fell as fiscal and monetary stimulus helped to boost the labour market with more than half of the jobs lost from the pandemic recovered. The jobless rate dropped to 6.8 per cent in August from 7.5 per cent a month earlier.

This fall seems to be due to the government's "JobKeeper" employment subsidy and to monetary stimulus provided by the central bank. The central bank this month announced an expansion of its lending facility for banks and signalled that it remains open to exploring additional measures to support the economy.

Much of this upswing in employment comes from self-employed workers with part-time jobs returning at twice the pace of full-time ones. It is thought that food delivery services are expected to be responsible for much of this rise.

1 With the aid of diagrams, explain what the effect of fiscal and monetary stimulus might be on unemployment.
2 Explain how schemes, such as the Jobkeeper one, could help keep unemployment under control.
3 Explain why part-time work might recover faster than full-time work.

Discuss the effectiveness of the central bank expanding its lending facilities in increasing employment.

9.4 Money and banking

9.4.1 *Definition, functions and characteristics of money*

Definition

Money can be defined as anything which is generally acceptable as a means of payment. Before the development of money, barter was used. This involves the direct exchange of goods and services without the use of any monetary mechanism.

Barter had a number of distinct disadvantages:

- It required a double coincidence of wants, i.e. one person offering a good or service needs to find someone who wants that good or service and that person also needs to be offering something in exchange that the seller wants.
- It was often difficult to compare the value of different goods and services.
- The products may be indivisible, e.g. in the case of animals.
- The products may be difficult to store while a seller is looking for an appropriate buyer.

These various disadvantages of barter meant that economies moved towards the development of money which would avoid the direct exchange of goods and services.

Key terms

Money: usually defined as anything which is universally acceptable as a means of payment for goods and services and a settlement of debt.

Barter: the direct exchange of one good or service for another.

Double coincidence of wants: the situation where, in a barter system of exchange, a seller needs to find a buyer who not only wants what the seller is selling, but also has something that the buyer wants.

Getting it right

You need to be able to explain clearly why money is preferred to barter as a means of exchange.

Progress question

6 Discuss why money is a more effective means of exchange than barter.

Key terms

Cash: the notes and coins in existence in an economy. This is the most liquid form of asset.

Legal tender: not all coins in an economy may be acceptable for all transactions; the term legal tender indicates if coins are only acceptable up to a specified amount.

Bank deposits: money that is held in accounts with a financial institution, such as a bank, building society, credit union or friendly society.

Near money: an asset that can easily and quickly be transferred into money, but is not actually money; sometimes known as "quasi money".

Liquidity: a term used to indicate when a financial asset is turned into cash. Cash is 100 per cent liquid, but a three-year bond will be less liquid than a one-year bond because there is a longer period of time to its maturity, i.e. when it can be changed into cash.

Cheque: often used as a method of payment, but a cheque is simply a written instruction to a financial institution to pay an amount of money from an account; a cheque is therefore not a form of money.

Although money has largely replaced barter, it is still necessary to establish what is, and what is not, money:

- Cash: the most obvious form of money is cash, whether in the form of notes or coins.
- Legal tender: some money may only be acceptable in transactions up to a certain amount and this is referred to as legal tender; this means that it must be accepted legally as a means of payment.
- Bank deposits: much money is in the form of money deposited in banks, building societies, credit unions and other financial institutions; these monetary deposits can be in current accounts or various forms of savings account.
- Near money: near money, or quasi money as it is sometimes called, refers to an asset that is immediately transferable into money and so can be used to settle some, but not all, debts. Near money, therefore, is able to fulfil some of the functions of money, but not all of them. For example, it cannot be used as a medium of exchange.
- Liquidity: the ability to turn an asset into cash refers to its liquidity. Cash is the most liquid form of asset. The more liquid an asset, the easier it is to convert it into money.
- Cheque: it is important to know not only what money is, but also what it is not. For example, a cheque is sometimes believed to be a form of money, but this is incorrect as a cheque is simply a means of payment and is not actually a form of money.

The functions of money

Money is said to perform four essential functions in an economy:

1. A medium of exchange. A very important function of money is that it operates effectively as a means of exchange. Money is generally accepted as a means of payment for goods and services. This is the great advantage of money over barter, i.e. it overcomes the problems associated with the need to have a double coincidence of wants between two people.
2. A measure of value or unit of account. This function of money can either be described as a measure of value or as a unit of account. This is the idea that money enables the value of different goods and services to be compared. The direct exchange of goods and services in a barter system made it very difficult to give a valuation of the different products being traded. This function of money makes it possible to compare the value of different goods and services.
3. A standard for deferred payment. Money enables people to borrow money and pay it back at a later date. This encourages the provision of credit and so acts as an incentive to trade. Buyers are able to consume goods and services immediately, but the payment can be spread over a period of time. This was a major limitation of the barter system.

Money ▲

4. A store of value or wealth. A final function of money is that it enables wealth to be stored in the form of money. Compared to the barter system, money does not physically deteriorate and it is usually not expensive to store it, although this function of money does face the problem of a possible deterioration in its value if there is a situation of inflation in an economy as inflation erodes the value or purchasing power of a given sum of money over a period of time.

The characteristics of money

Money has a number of distinctive characteristics and these are outlined in Table 9.6.

Table 9.6: The characteristics of money ▼

Characteristic	Explanation
Acceptability	Money needs to be generally acceptable in an economy if it is going to be used to facilitate the exchange of goods and services.
Divisibility	Money in an economy needs to be divided into smaller units, especially so that cheaper items can be bought and sold. This division into smaller units is explained by the term "denominations". For example, in Mauritius, the Mauritian rupee is divided into 100 cents.
Portability	Any money needs to be portable if it is going to be convenient for the users of it.
Durability	Money needs to be relatively durable if it is going to be acceptable although, of course, bank notes will eventually need to be replaced by newly printed ones.
Scarcity	Money needs to be relatively scarce; if it literally did "grow on trees", it would soon become worthless.
Stability of supply	As well as being relatively scarce, there also needs to be a stability of supply over a long period of time.
Recognisability	Money needs to be easily recognisable in an economy and this contributes to confidence in it.
Uniformity	It is necessary that each particular coin or note being used in an economy is uniform, i.e. has exactly the same value.
Stability of value	It is important that money has a reasonable degree of stability of value over a period of time, although inflation will erode the value or purchasing power of money over time.

Getting it right

Make sure that you do not get the characteristics and the functions of money confused, although, of course, the characteristics are necessary for money to function effectively in an economy.

9.4.2 *Definition of money supply*

The money supply is the total amount of money in an economy at any one time. It includes notes and coins and also any deposits, such as current accounts in banks, which can be quickly converted into cash.

Today more and more transactions are done using cheques, debit cards, credit cards and electronic bank transfers. It is usual, therefore, to distinguish between narrow money and broad money although there is no completely agreed definition of either between countries or economists. Narrow money is sometimes referred to as M0 or M1 and broad money as M3 or M4.

Key terms

Money supply: the total amount of money in an economy at any one time.

Narrow money: consist of notes, coins and usually demand deposits (sometimes called current accounts).

Broad money: consists of notes and coins and all bank deposits together with easily available money in other financial institutions.

Link

For causes of inflation see Chapter 4, section 4.6.4.

9.4.3 *Quantity theory of money (MV=PT)*

The quantity theory of money is used by monetarists to help explain the cause of inflation as they claim it shows a direct link between increases in the money supply and increases in prices.

The quantity theory (sometimes called the Fisher equation) is stated as MV = PT where:

- M is the money supply
- V the velocity of circulation or the number of times money changes hands
- P is the general price level
- T the number of transactions or output.

The equation itself is true as it says that demand equals supply or that both sides represent total expenditure. To use the equation, V and T are held to be constant over a period of time so that any increase in the money supply must lead to a similar increase in prices given a time lag of around eighteen months.

Key terms

Quantity theory of money: states that any increase in the money supply will lead to an increase in the price level after a time lag.

Commercial banks: financial institutions in which individuals and firms can save their money and obtain loans.

9.4.4 *Functions of commercial banks*

Commercial banks are financial institutions which take deposits from, and loan out money to individuals and firms.

Providing deposit accounts (demand deposit account, savings account)

The most significant and traditional function of commercial banks is accepting deposits from the public. Demand deposit, or current, accounts usually do not have interest paid on the money as it can be withdrawn at any time either through taking notes and coins out or by using cheques or through the use of bank cards. Saving accounts do attract interest because although money can normally be withdrawn from them at any time, the bank can require notice of withdrawal. This is most likely if a very large sum is required.

Key terms

Demand deposit, or current, accounts: usually do not have interest paid on the money as it can be withdrawn at any time.

Saving accounts: attract interest because although money can normally be withdrawn from them at any time, the bank can require notice of withdrawal.

Lending money (overdrafts, loans)

Banks having accepted deposits, and paid interest on some, need to lend money at higher interest rates in order to pay their depositors. They can lend money in the form of overdrafts or loans.

Overdrafts are an arrangement by which a person can borrow money they do not have through their current account. If, for example, you spend \$100 when you have only \$50 in your account then your balance is –\$50 and you are using an overdraft. An overdraft is a form of debt and is repayable on demand. Normally you will arrange an overdraft with your bank which allows you to spend up to an agreed limit. This is typically to allow you to manage your income and expenditure if you have to cover short-term expenses such as an unexpected bill. Most businesses will have these overdrafts as they cannot guarantee that their revenue will arrive before having to pay for supplies or their wages. An unarranged

Key terms

Overdraft: an arrangement by which a person can borrow money they do not have through their current account.

Loans: a sum of money given by a bank to a borrower for a set period of time where interest is paid on the whole of the loan and normally a form of security is required.

overdraft is when you spend more money than you have without having sought permission to do so. These carry a higher interest rate than arranged overdrafts.

Loans, however, are a sum of money given by a bank to a borrower for a set period of time where interest is paid on the whole of the loan. Normally the bank will ask for some form of security in exchange for the money (see below).

Activity

Deposits and loans

Ask a local bank to provide a speaker for your group or visit a local bank and arrange to speak to someone about deposits and loans.

Holding or providing cash, securities, loans, deposits, equity

- Cash is held by banks to provide depositors with the money in their account. Banks in India hold about 4 per cent of their deposits as cash.
- Most loans are secured loans, in that the borrower has to offer some way in which the bank could regain its money if the loan was not repaid. If you borrow $20,000 to buy a house, the bank may require you to give them the deeds, or legal ownership, of the house. If you fail to repay the loan the bank could then sell the house and repay itself.
- Making loans and taking deposits are the two major functions of as commercial bank (see below).
- Equity is the ownership of assets. In the case of banks, other than the banks' buildings, the main equity is the money that a bank has obtained from its shareholders and other investors and any profit that it has made and not paid out.

Key terms

The reserve ratio: the percentage of deposits which commercial banks are required, by the country's central bank, to keep as cash.
The capital ratio: the funds that a commercial bank has in reserve measured against the total value of assets which are a risk.
Asset: anything of monetary value owned by a person or business.
Liabilities: what you owe other people or businesses.
Stress test: assess how banks can cope with severe economic scenarios.
Liquidity: how easily assets can be turned into cash. The most liquid asset is cash.

Reserve ratio and capital ratio

The reserve ratio is the percentage of deposits which commercial banks are required, by the country's central bank, to keep as cash. In the UK it is 12.5 per cent. The reserve ratio is an important tool of monetary policy and plays an essential role in regulating the money supply. When the central bank wants to increase money supply in the economy, it lowers the reserve ratio. As a result, commercial banks have higher funds to disburse as loans, thereby increasing the money supply in an economy. The opposite is true when money supply needs to be reduced.

The capital ratio is the funds that a commercial bank has in reserve measured against the total value of assets which are a risk, that is might not be able to be repaid. This is an attempt to prevent banks from not being able to meet their liabilities. Since the financial crises of 2008, many central banks now run "stress tests" to check whether banks have enough capital to cope with a crisis.

Objectives of commercial banks: liquidity, security, profitability

In order to survive and to be able to pay its liabilities, mainly deposits, banks must ensure that they have sufficient liquidity. Its most liquid asset is cash, but it also involves how easily it can turn other assets

Activity

Reserve and capital ratios

Try to find out for your country:

1 What the reserve ratio is?
2 What the capital ratio is?
3 Whether the central bank runs "stress tests"?

Key terms

Security: the ability to keep the assets, deposits and information of its customers safe.

Profitability: earning more from the interest charged on loans, and other services, than the interest paid to depositors.

Credit creation: the ability of banks, and other lenders of money, to lend money to borrowers thus increasing the supply of money in circulation.

Bank credit multiplier: the number of times by which a change in bank deposits is increased, or decreased, to give the final change in total bank assets.

into cash. It is an important objective as the "stress test" will be testing it.

Security is another objective. Clearly banks need to ensure that their customers' money is kept safe. This has become increasingly important with the use of online and similar technological innovations. Cyber security is now essential as otherwise criminals can gain access to large sums of deposited money as well as private information.

The major objective, however, is probably profitability. Not only will a bank go out of business if it is not profitable, but both shareholders and depositors are likely to withdraw their money if there is any sign of problems. The objective is to make a profit by earning more from the interest charged on loans than the interest paid to depositors. Profit can also be made by providing services such as deposit security, currency trading, business advice, cheque and credit-card processing.

9.4.5 Causes of changes in the money supply in an open economy

Commercial banks as sources of credit creation and the bank credit multiplier

A major source of money supply is the commercial banks through credit creation, which is when banks, and other lenders of money, lend money to borrowers thus increasing the supply of money in circulation. This works through the bank credit multiplier which refers to the amount of any deposit that a commercial bank is required to hold in reserves. If, for example, customer A makes an initial deposit of $100 with Bank 1, and the credit ratio is 10 per cent, then the bank can lend out $90 to customer B. Customer B then uses this to buy goods from customer C who in turn deposits it with Bank 2 who lends $81 to customer D and so on. This can be seen in Table 9.7. The credit multiplier operates in a similar way to the multiplier with the formula:

$$\text{change in money supply} = \frac{\text{initial deposit}}{\text{credit ratio}} = \frac{100}{10}$$

$$= 100 \times 10 = \$1000$$

Table 9.7 Credit creation ▼

Bank	Liabilities: deposits	Assets: loans	Reserves	Total assets
Bank 1	100.00	90.00	10.00	100.00
Bank 2	90.00	81.00	9.00	90.00
Bank 3	81.00	72.90	8.10	81.00
–	–	–	–	–
–	–	–	–	–
Bank n	0.00	0.00	0.00	0.00
Total	**1000.00**	**900.00**	**100.00**	**1000.00**

Activity

Credit creation

Using Table 9.7, recalculate the credit creation process on the basis of a) a 12.5 per cent ratio, and b) an 8 per cent ratio.

Case Study

US housing crises

The collapse of the US housing market in 2008 seems to have been caused by the overlending by financial institutions of loans to buy houses. This came about because the credit worthiness of borrowers was no longer being checked so money was lent to people who could not afford to pay them back.

Once people started to default on the loans, this led to a loss of confidence and banks raised their credit ratios thus reducing the amount of money available to borrow. This meant that people could no longer find the money to buy houses. Thus demand fell and prices collapsed.

1 Explain how raising the credit ratio would lead to a fall in the money available in the economy.
2 Discuss why a loss of confidence could severely affect people's willingness to borrow and lend money.

Key term

Central bank: the issuer of notes and coins in an economy and in many countries; it sets the rate of interest.

Link

For quantitative easing see Chapter 5, section 5.3.2 and 9.4.5 of this chapter.
Rate of interest was covered in Chapter 5, section 5.3.2 and Chapter 10 section 10.3.1.
The national debt was covered in Chapter 5, section 5.2.3.

Key term

Government deficit financing: ways in which the gap between public revenue and public expenditure can be financed.

Head office of the central bank of Japan in Tokyo ▲

Role of a central bank

The central bank acts as the issuer of notes and coins in an economy and can, therefore, directly determine how many are in circulation. In many countries it also controls the rate of interest through setting the base rate. It can also determine the level of deposits that commercial banks must make with it. The larger the deposit, the smaller will be the ability of these banks to create credit. In Table 9.7, a 10 per cent deposit was assumed. If the central bank wanted to reduce the supply of money, it could raise this to, for example, 12.5 per cent, or if it wanted to increase the money supply, it could reduce the level to 8 per cent. In recent years many central banks have used quantitative easing as a way of increasing the supply of money so as to encourage consumption and investment.

Government deficit financing

The government can finance a budget deficit, government deficit financing, by two methods. Firstly, it can borrow money from the central bank or from commercial banks. If it borrows from the central bank this means that more money finds its way to the commercial banks as deposits so allowing them to expand lending. Equally, if it issues short-term government stock to the commercial banks, these act as liquid assets and can be used to back loans. Either way will increase the money supply.

Secondly, a government can sell long-term securities to the non-bank private sector. To purchase these, individuals or firms will draw money from their bank accounts leading to a fall in the money supply.

Quantitative easing

Since 2009, central banks have purchased financial assets from banks and businesses resulting in an increase in the money supply to expand economic activity.

It works by the central bank buying large amounts of government bonds which then lowers the interest rates on those bonds. This, in turn, pushes down the interest rates offered on loans because rates on government bonds tend to affect other interest rates in the economy. This makes it cheaper for individuals and businesses to borrow money, encouraging spending.

In addition, it can boost a wide range of financial asset prices. By purchasing the government bonds, other financial institutions have more money which they can invest in other financial assets such as shares increasing their price. This makes businesses and individuals holding shares wealthier, making them more likely to increase spending leading to more economic activity.

Changes in the balance of payments

The current account balance indicates whether an economy is generating enough savings to finance domestic investment. When the current account balance is equal to zero, domestic saving is equal to domestic investment. There is no effect on the money supply. When the current account is in deficit, it means that domestic savings are insufficient to meet investment needs leading to an inflow of money, increasing the money supply. On the other hand, a surplus on the current account shows that some domestic saving is going abroad to finance investment in other countries. There is a fall in the money supply.

Link

For the flow of income see Chapter 4, section 4.2.

9.4.6 *Policies to reduce inflation and their effectiveness*

Governments normally pursue a mixture of fiscal, monetary and supply-side policies. Although supply-side policies can avoid the conflicts in policy objectives which fiscal and monetary policies face, the time span in which they operate means that they cannot be used to deal with immediate problems.

Fiscal policy

In theory, fiscal policy can directly lead to lower inflation. To reduce inflation, a government should reduce government expenditure (G) and increase taxation (T). This will result in a fall in aggregate demand (AD).

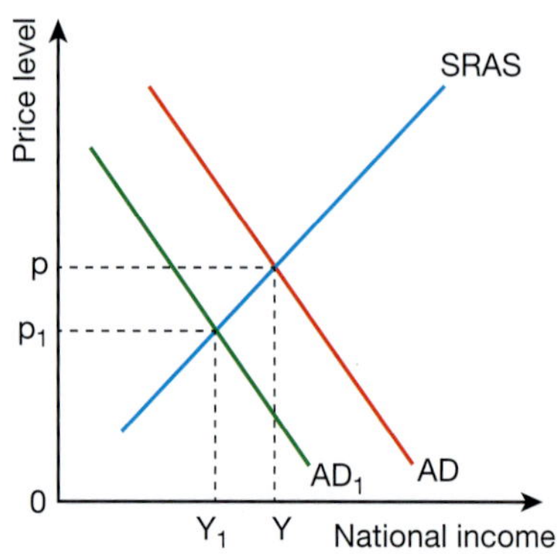

Figure 9.20 Operation of fiscal policy – control of inflation ▲

Figure 9.20 shows that if AD falls to AD_1 then inflation will fall from P to P_1. The problem is that except under extreme difficulties, such as Greece in 2013, it is very difficult to just cut G as against cutting future G so it takes time to implement. Equally, tax changes take time to work their way from announcement to implementation to having an effect.

There also appears to be a trade-off between inflation and employment. In Figure 9.20, the fall in inflation is accompanied by a fall in real output, and thus employment, from Y to Y_1.

John Maynard Keynes said that governments should be prepared to borrow money and spend it so as to get people back into work and to stimulate the economy. The problem is that this will result in a large increase in government debt. Shinzo Abe, Prime Minister of Japan 2012–2020, used fiscal policy, along with monetary policy, to try to stimulate the economy. This has been called "Abeconomics".

Link

To review inflation see Chapter 4, section 4.6.
See Chapter 5 for policies, section 5.2 for fiscal, section 5.3 for monetary and section 5.4 for supply side.

Activity

Abeconomics

Find out how successful Abeconomics has been for Japan.

1 What economic factors have affected its success?
2 Would such a policy be suitable for your country's economy. If not, why not?

Link

For more on government debt see Chapter 5, sections 5.2.2 and 5.2.3.

Link

Unemployment, see Chapter 4, section 4.5.
Economic growth, see Chapter 4, section 4.4.

Milton Friedman receiving his Nobel Prize for Economics ▲

Link

For quantitative easing see Chapter 5, section 5.3.2 and section 9.4.5 of this chapter,

Monetary policy

Inasmuch as monetary policy operates on the demand-side of the economy, it has similar effects to fiscal policy (see Figure 9.20). The main difference is that control of inflation is the main emphasis stemming from Milton Friedman's view that only by controlling inflation can sustainable economic growth, low unemployment and a more favourable balance of payments be achieved.

By bringing down inflation, interest rates can be lowered. This leads directly to more investment, assuming that investment is interest elastic. Higher investment generates more growth and employment as well as making goods and services more competitive through innovation and invention. Up to 2008, there was some evidence that this was happening, as many central banks brought inflation down while stimulating growth and employment. Governments have also set central banks' inflation targets, see Table 9.8, which they can only achieve by using their policies, which are all monetary.

Table 9.8 Selected central bank inflation targets for 2021 ▼

Country	Inflation target %
China	3
Eurozone	<2
Kenya	5, ±2
Mexico	3, ±1
Pakistan	5
UK	2

Using monetary policy to combat inflation would involve lowering interest rates and the use of quantitative easing (QE). In theory, cutting interest rates to low levels should stimulate both consumers and businesses to spend and invest thus generating demand and employment leading to an increase in AD. The Bank of England estimates that a change in interest rates takes between 18 months and two years to fully work its way through the economy. The bank rate in Japan has been at or very near 0 per cent since 1999, but this has done little to stimulate demand due to underlying economic problems. Under Abeconomics The Bank of Japan has used QE.

Supply-side policy

As previously stated, supply-side policies can avoid the trade-off between policies which tends to occur with both fiscal and monetary policies. They also reduce long-term inflation as aggregate supply increases to meet expansion in aggregate demand and provides sustainable growth as these policies increase a country's competitiveness and employment. In Figure 9.21, an increase in AD leading to inflation, p to p_1, can be offset by an increase in aggregate supply (AS) from AS to AS_1 leading to inflation being controlled while real output increases from Y to Y_1.

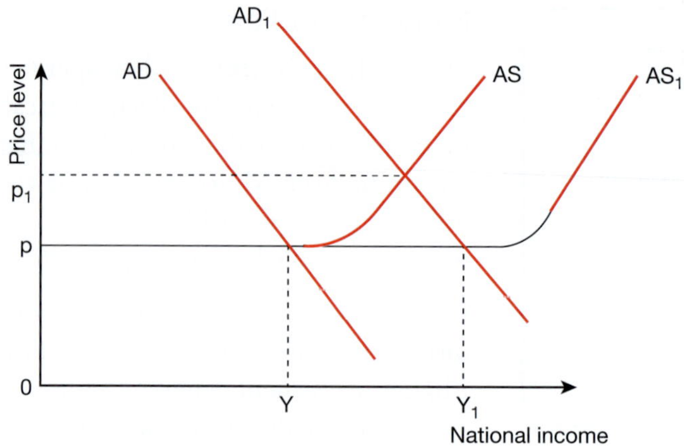

Figure 9.21 Operation of supply-side policy ▲

On the other hand, while fiscal and monetary policies can start to affect the economy relatively quickly, supply-side policies take a considerable time and are often expensive to implement e.g. the cost of education and training, while others e.g. labour market policies, may face resistance from interest groups.

Governments have in the last thirty years favoured using fiscal and/ or monetary policies to control inflation in the short term, while implementing supply-side policies to achieve lower long-term inflation. In recent years both fiscal and monetary policies have been used by governments facing deflation, but supply-side policies can be effective in dealing with the underlying structural problems such as monopoly power and lack of innovation.

> **Activity**
>
> **Economic policies**
>
> 1 What policies has your country used during the last 10 years?
>
> 2 How successful have these been?
>
> This could be done in pairs with a report back to the whole class.

9.4.7 Demand for money: liquidity preference theory

Demand for money

Keynes argued that people demand money for three reasons:

1. Transactions demand: money held for normal purchases e.g. food, transport, etc. It is not responsive to changes in the rate of interest i.e. it is interest inelastic.
2. Precautionary demand: money held over and above transactionary demand in case of unexpected needs e.g. to replace a broken kettle. It is not responsive to changes in the rate of interest i.e. it is interest inelastic.
3. Speculative demand: money held to be used to buy assets in the future. It is inversely related to the rate of interest.

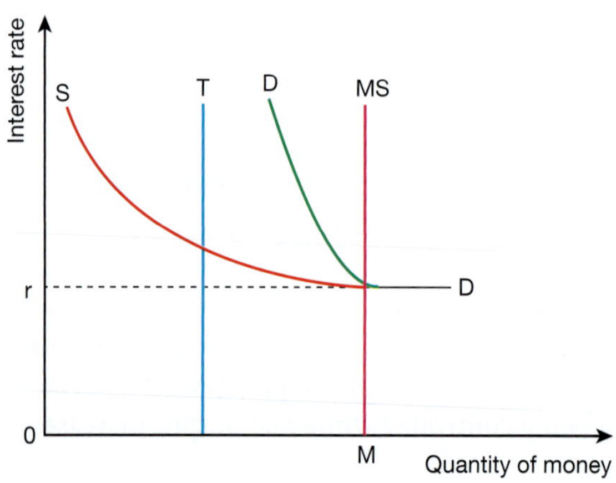

Figure 9.22 The three demands for money ▲

In Figure 9.22:

- T is the precautionary and transactionary demands together
- S is the speculative demand
- D = T + S

Progress question

7 Explain why the rate of interest does not affect the active balances of money, but does affect the idle balances.

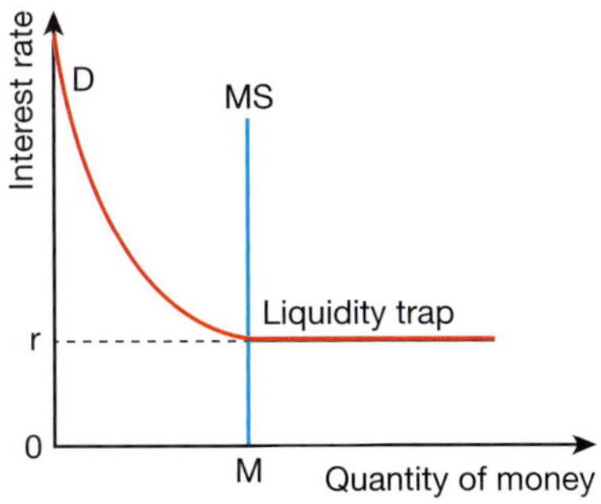

Figure 9.23 Liquidity preference curve ▲

Progress question

8 Explain how liquidity preference theory shows how interest rates are determined.

Key terms

Liquidity preference: the relationship between the quantity of money people wish to hold and the rate of interest.

Active balance: the transactionary and precautionary combined. It is not responsive to the rate of interest.

Idle balance: the speculative demand, responsive to the rate of interest.

Liquidity trap: where any addition to the supply of money results in no change in the rate of interest.

Loanable funds: the relationship between those who supply the funds (savers) and those who are demanding funds (borrowers).

Liquidity preference theory

These three demands added together give the liquidity preference curve as shown in Figure 9.23. The transactionary and speculative demands are used to make purchases and are sometimes called active balances, whereas the speculative demand is sometimes called the idle balance. The curve is completely elastic beyond point M showing that any addition to the supply of money fails to affect either interest rates or economic growth. This is the liquidity trap (see Figure 9.23).

9.4.8 *Interest rate determination: loanable funds theory and Keynesian theory*

An alternative approach to liquidity preference is that of loanable funds. This assumes that there are three major demands for loanable funds:

- households for the purchase of goods and services
- firms for investment
- governments to fund any deficit

Loanable funds bring together savers who are supplying the funds and borrowers who are demanding funds. In this case the rate of interest is determined by where the supply of funds equals the demand for funds as shown in Figure 9.24.

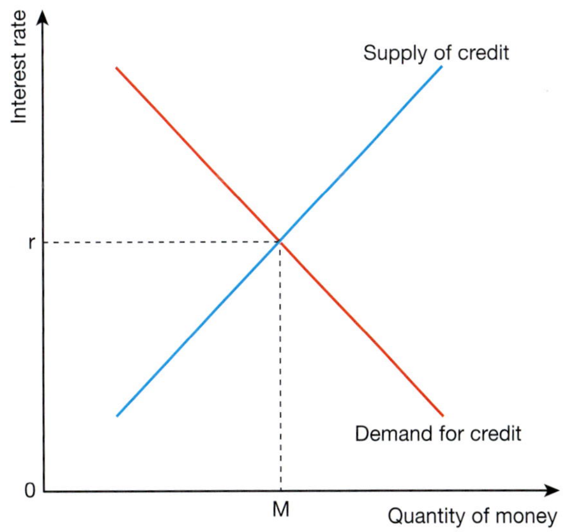

Figure 9.24 Supply and demand of loanable funds ▲

Case Study

Japan and low interest rates

In the 1990s asset prices in Japan collapsed and economic growth deteriorated. To counter this, the Bank of Japan lowered interest rates to almost zero. This did not, however, lead to the expected increase in demand. One reason for this was that the price level was negative leading to a relatively high real rate of interest.

1 What is meant by the real rate of interest?

2 What is meant by a negative price level?

3 How might knowledge of the liquidity trap help explain what happened in Japan?

Interest rates are determined by the supply of, and demand for, money.

As can be seen in Figure 9.25, the supply of money is fixed so that an increase in the demand will just lead to a rise in the rate of interest. Equally, Figure 9.26 shows that an increase in the supply of money without any corresponding rise in the demand will lead to a fall in the rate of interest.

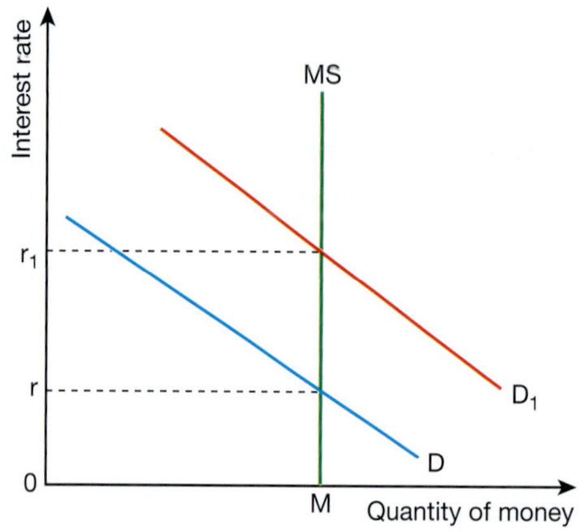

Figure 9.25 Increase in the demand for money ▲

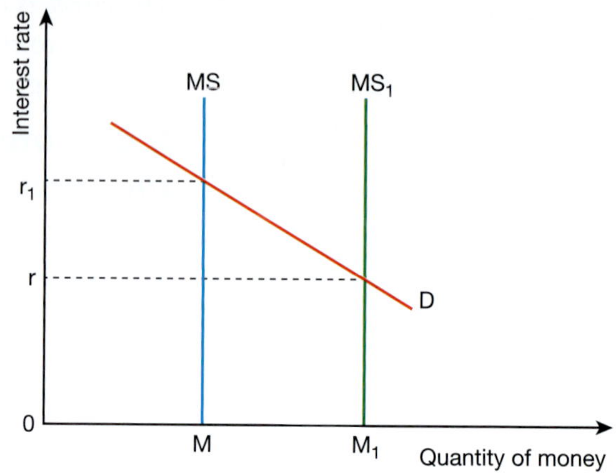

Figure 9.26 Increase in the supply of money ▲

> **Key term**
>
> **Transmission mechanism**: the way in which changes in the money supply or the interest rate can affect variables such as aggregate output and employment.

Changes in interest rates affect inflation through the monetary transmission mechanism. Any change in the central bank's interest rate will lead to other financial institutions, such as banks, changing their savings and lending rates. The change will affect, also, the price of assets such as shares and houses as well as the expectations of individuals and firms. Externally the change will lead to a movement in the exchange rate.

If the rate of interest was lowered, individuals and firms will be more confident about the future. The exchange rate, however, is likely to fall. All of this will affect aggregate demand as, in this example, consumers would be likely to spend more so AD would increase. Exports would be likely to rise and imports to fall, again increasing AD.

> **Activity**
>
> **Rate of interest**
>
> Find out what has happened to interest rates in your country and in either the US or the UK in the last 10 years.
> Discuss either in small groups or as a class why there are differences and/or similarities.
> Use your knowledge of Economics to try to explain these differences and similarities.

> **Key concepts**
>
> - **Margin and decision making** can be seen especially in the multiplier and unemployment.
> - **Equilibrium and disequilibrium** can be seen in AD, employment and interest rates.
> - **Progress and development** can be seen in economic growth, unemployment and money and banking.

Progress check

After completing this chapter you should be able to:

- explain and calculate the multiplier and its components
- explain the components of AD and their determinants
- explain inflationary and deflationary gaps

- explain actual and potential growth, output gaps and the business cycle
- explain and evaluate the policies to promote economic growth
- differentiate between and explain inclusive and sustainable growth
- define full employment
- explain equilibrium and disequilibrium and voluntary and involuntary unemployment
- define and explain the natural rate of unemployment and the patterns and trends in unemployment
- explain the forms of, and factors affecting, labour mobility
- explain and evaluate the policies to deal with unemployment
- define the functions and characteristics of money
- define the money supply and explain the quantity theory of money
- explain the functions of commercial banks
- explain the causes of changes in the money supply in an open economy
- explain and evaluate policies to reduce inflation
- explain the demand for money and interest rate determination.

Exam-style questions

Essay and data response questions

1 Evaluate whether demand-side policies are more effective than supply-side policies in promoting economic growth. [20 marks]

2 Assess how effective your country's government has been in dealing with unemployment. [20 marks]

3 Assess whether your country would be better off pursuing inclusive rather than sustainable growth. [20 marks]

4 Evaluate the effectiveness of monetary policies in keeping inflation under control. [20 marks]

5 Assess the effectiveness of government policies in mitigating climate change. [20 marks]

6 Evaluate the reasons why governments wish to increase labour mobility. [20 marks]

Multiple-choice questions

7 If the income velocity of circulation of money is constant, the rate of growth of the money supply is 5 per cent and the average price level increases by 3 per cent, what will be the approximate change in real output? [1 mark]

A −2 per cent
B +2 per cent
C +3 per cent
D +8 per cent

8 In an economy, from any addition to national income 5 per cent is saved, 15 per cent is paid in taxes and 20 per cent is spent on imports with 60 per cent consumed. What is the value of the multiplier? [1 mark]

A 1.25
B 1.66
C 2.5
D 4

10 Government macroeconomic intervention

In this chapter you will develop your knowledge and understanding of:

- government macroeconomic policy objectives
- links between macroeconomic problems and their interrelatedness
- effectiveness of policy options to meet all macroeconomic objectives.

Link

Inflation see Chapters: 4 section 4.6, 5, sections 5.2.7, 5.3.4 and 5.4.4 and 9, section 9.4.6.
Balance of payments see Chapters 6, sections 6.3 and 6.5 and 11. section 11.1.
Unemployment see Chapters: 4, section 4.5, 5 sections 5.2.7, 5.3.4 and 5.4.4 and 9, section 9.3.
Economic growth see Chapters: 4, section 4.6, 5, sections 5.2.7, 5.3.4, 5.4.4, 9, section 9.3 and 11, section 11.3.4.
Development see Chapter 11, section 11.3.
Sustainability see Chapter 9, section 9.2.
Redistribution of income and wealth see Chapters: 3, section 3.3, 5, sections 5.2.4 and 5.2.5, 11, section 11.4.2.

10.1 Government macroeconomic policy objectives

10.1.1 *Objectives in terms of inflation, balance of payments, unemployment, growth, development, sustainability and redistribution of income and wealth*

Inflation

Although inflation is seen as inevitable, and normal, all governments are concerned to try to achieve stable prices, or at least ones which only rise at a slow rate. If prices are continually rising at high rates then investors are reluctant to invest in new machinery, factories and products because they cannot calculate the outcome of their investments. Rising inflation leads to menu costs such as revising price lists. Similarly, those who are on fixed incomes, usually the economically inactive, such as those relying on state benefits, suffer as any increases lag well behind price rises.

In addition, inflation is likely to lead to other macroeconomic problems.

Activity

Worst inflation rate in history (2)

In 1946 inflation in Hungary reached a rate of 13,600,000,000,000,000 per cent per month. Prices ended up doubling every 15 hours.

In 2008 prices in Zimbabwe doubled every 24.7 hours.

Discuss as a group what could have been the causes of these very large rises in inflation.

Then, try to find out the actual causes of these inflation rates.

Balance of payments

The ideal situation is for the balance of payments to be in equilibrium i.e. the inflows of money equal the outflows across the whole account. Countries are usually concerned about their current accounts. If there is a persistent deficit then a country could face severe economic and financial problems such as depreciating exchange rate, inability to pay its debts and in extreme circumstances bankruptcy.

> **Key terms**
>
> **Monetary union**: a group of countries with a single currency, or different currencies having a fixed mutual exchange rate monitored and controlled by one central bank.
>
> **Eurozone**: those members of the European Union who have adopted the euro as their currency.

> **Activity**
>
> **Balance of payments**
>
> Look at the current account of the balance of payments for your country and one other for the last 10 years.
>
> Over the 10 years has it achieved a surplus, a deficit or nearly equilibrium?
>
> If it is a surplus, have they used this to help trading partners?
>
> If it is a deficit, how have they financed it? Look at the capital account.

> **Activity**
>
> **SDG**
>
> Find out what your government is doing about the 17 goals.
>
> Do you think they will achieve them?
>
> If you have difficulty accessing the information, the UK government has set out their plan:
>
> https://assets.publishing.service.gov.uk/government/uploads/system/uploads/attachment_data/file/603500/Agenda-2030-Report4.pdf

Equally, a continual positive balance is problematical because it causes difficulties for trading partners, especially if they are in a monetary union and cannot depreciate the exchange rate. A number of countries within the Eurozone have faced this with Germany being in credit and, for example, Greece in debt.

This does not mean that a country should balance its account every year with every country it trades with, because a country may have a positive with some countries and negative with, others. The aim should be in the long run to achieve an equilibrium level on the balance of payments.

Unemployment

Governments aim to achieve full employment. It is difficult to know what this means as not only are there different definitions of full employment, but there is no agreement on what percentage of unemployment would indicate that full employment had been reached. All governments, however, aim for this objective.

Economic growth

Governments aim to achieve sustainable economic growth. High growth rates may be very good for developing countries, but if they are achieved by depletion and exhaustion of scarce natural resources or by too much pollution, leading to climate change, then the high rates will not be sustainable.

Development

The need for development is to raise the standard of living of the country as a whole and of the poorest groups in particular. This includes: higher incomes; more jobs to reduce unemployment; better, and more, food, housing, etc; greater availability of, and higher quality, education and health facilities.

Sustainability

The idea is to develop growth which is lasting and makes a real difference to individuals. It recognises that everybody has the right to a healthy, clean and safe environment. In 2015 the United Nations passed a resolution called Agenda 2030. This set out 17 Sustainable Development Goals (SDGs), sometimes called Global Goals as a "blueprint to achieve a better and more sustainable future for all".

Table 10.1 17 Sustainable Development Goals

1. No poverty	5. Gender equality	9. Industry, innovation and infrastructure	13. Climate action	17. Partnership for the goals
2. Zero hunger	6. Clean water and sanitation	10. Reducing inequality	14. Life below water	
3. Good health and well being	7. Affordable and clean energy	11. Sustainable cities and communities	15. Life on land	
4. Quality education	8. Decent work and economic growth	12. Responsible consumption and production	16. Peace, justice and strong institutions	

Redistribution of income and wealth

Governments aim to reduce inequalities of income and wealth through taxation and expenditure. This is done by imposing taxes on the rich and spending more on the welfare of the poor. It will reduce income of the rich and raise standard of living of the poor, thus reducing inequalities in the distribution of income. Wealth can be redistributed through taxes such as capital gains, inheritance and wealth.

Inequality is much higher in developing than in advanced economies. This is often because many developing nations lack the resources and fiscal policy structures to make much difference.

> **Key terms**
>
> **Capital gains tax**: a tax on the profit when you sell an asset that has increased in value.
>
> **Inheritance tax**: a tax on the property, money and possessions of someone who has died.
>
> **Wealth tax**: a tax on the value of held assets.

> **Activity**
>
> **Income and wealth**
>
> 1 How does your government try to reduce income inequality?
> 2 What taxes do your government use to try to reduce wealth inequality?
> 3 In both case, discuss whether they should do more and how.

10.2 Links between macroeconomic problems and their interrelatedness

Economic problems such as how to achieve low inflation and full employment do not exist in isolation, but are interconnected. Any action to try to achieve one economic aim, see above, may well result in adverse effects on other aims. In a textbook it is not possible to look at all of the links between macroeconomic objectives, but below a number of the main ones are considered.

10.2.1 *Relationship between the internal value of money and the external value of money*

The internal value of money is how much a unit of money can buy i.e. its internal purchasing power or the real value of money, while the external value is the value of a currency as measured in foreign currency. A direct comparison is with purchasing power parity.

A fall in the internal value of money is a result of inflation. A country with an inflation rate higher than that of other countries will find that people lose confidence in holding its currency so its foreign exchange rate depreciates. This means that less can be bought in terms of purchasing power parity. If, however, a country has a lower rate of inflation than its main trading partners then, although the internal value of money is falling, the external value will rise. This is partly because the country's goods will appear cheaper on world markets than its competitors and partly because foreign holders of money would prefer to hold that country's currency.

> **Key terms**
>
> **Internal value of money**: what a unit of money will buy. It is the real value of money in terms of its purchasing power.
>
> **External value of money**: what a unit of currency will buy when compared to other currencies – see purchasing power parity.

10.2.2 *Relationship between the balance of payments and inflation*

To some extent, this follows on from the discussion above concerning the internal and external values of money. Inflation will mean that the internal cost of goods and services rises. Assuming that a country's inflation rate is higher than its main trading partners, the price of its exports rises while imports now appear to be cheaper. This means that the current account of the balance of payments will deteriorate assuming that the sum of the price elasticities of demand for exports and imports is greater than one, the Marshall–Lerner effect. In addition, higher inflation will deter investors leading to an outflow

> **Activity**
>
> **Internal and external values of money**
>
> Compare the inflation and exchange rates of your country with that of some of its main trading partners.
>
> What conclusions can you draw from this comparison?

Link

For both Marshall–Lerner and the J-curve effect see Chapter 11, section 11.2.5.

Activity

Price elasticity of demand for X and M

Are your exports and imports elastic or inelastic? On what have you based your decisions?

If there are several of you, this could lead to a debate, or a discussion in order to gain a class view.

Key term

Trade-off: when in order to obtain a desired economic goal it is necessary to accept an adverse effect on another goal.
This idea is closely related to opportunity cost and to production possibility curves.

of money in the capital account leading to a worsening of the whole balance of payments account. Once more, if inflation is lower than that of a country's main competitors, or if Marshall–Lerner is less than one, then the opposite effect will be true.

This relationship is complicated because of the exchange rate. If the exchange rate falls then, given the Marshall–Lerner condition, the balance of payments will improve although this may only happen in the medium term due to the 'J' curve effect.

A deterioration of the balance of payments is likely to lead to a fall in the value of the exchange rate. This may well increase inflation making exports more expensive and the balance of payments to deteriorate. Elasticities are not always simple. Singapore, for example, has an elastic demand for its exports, but an inelastic one for its imports. In addition, changes in world demand, especially for primary products, can greatly affect the balance of payments from year to year.

As can be seen above, any attempt to reduce inflation could lead to an adverse reaction in either the balance of payments or in the exchange rate. This idea that an improvement in one objective can lead to an adverse effect in another objective is called a trade-off.

These trade-offs can often be seen when considering the exchange rate and the balance of payments. A country may not want its exchange rate to appreciate because this would make its exports less competitive. It may, therefore, try to reduce its value by selling its currency. If, imports, however, are price inelastic then this would raise the amount spent on imports adversely affecting the balance of payments. In addition it would lead to higher inflation.

10.2.3 *Relationship between growth and inflation*

As can be seen in Figure 10.1 an increase in AD, from AD to AD_1, has led, in the short run, to an increase in real output indicating economic growth and more employment, from Y to Y_1, but inflation has risen from P to P_1.

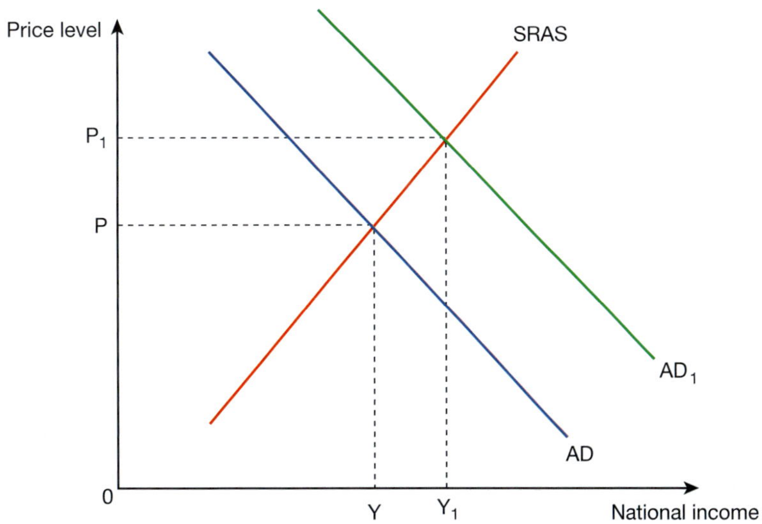

Figure 10.1 Increased economic growth with higher inflation ▲

The relationship, however, is more complex. If the government uses supply side measures in the long run then as can be seen in Figure 10.2 it is possible to have economic growth, more employment/lower unemployment and a low level of inflation.

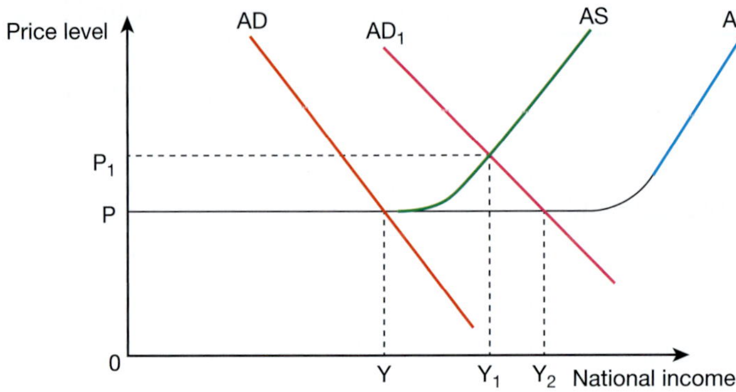

Figure 10.2 Supply-side policy effects on economic growth and inflation ▲

In Figure 10.2 the increase in AD has the same effects as in Figure 10.1, but the introduction of supply-side policies shifts the AS curve from AS to AS_1. This results in further economic growth and employment from Y_1 to Y_2, while inflation falls from P_1 to P.

> **Link**
>
> For supply side policies see Chapter 5, section 5.4.

10.2.4 Relationship between growth and the balance of payments

As an economy grows, import spending is stimulated relative to export revenue. This may result in a balance of payments deficit both because of higher prices, see Figure 10.1, but also because domestic production cannot expand fast enough to meet the extra demand. Where economic growth leads to higher real incomes, consumers may prefer 'better' foreign goods causing higher imports.

Many developing, and other countries, have used exports to generate economic growth, given that AD = C + I + G + X − M. In this case, an improvement in the balance of payments can have a positive effect on growth.

10.2.5 Relationship between inflation and unemployment

Traditional Phillips curve

One of the best known trade-offs has traditionally been between inflation and unemployment. If governments try to reduce inflation, for example by using fiscal and monetary policies, then unemployment rises. Equally, any attempt at reducing unemployment by, for example, cutting interest rates or increasing government expenditure, will result in higher inflation.

The ideal situation for an economy would be to have a low and steady rate of inflation together with a low level of unemployment. Generally this has proved to be impossible to achieve. In 1959, Professor Phillips plotted data for the UK for the period 1861 to 1957 to show an inverse relationship between inflation and unemployment (see Figure 10.3).

> **Activity**
>
> **Balance of payments and economic growth**
>
> Find out your country's balance of payments figures and its economic growth for the last 6 years.
>
> Can you discover any relationship between them (don't forget there may be time lags).
>
> What conclusions can you draw from your investigation?

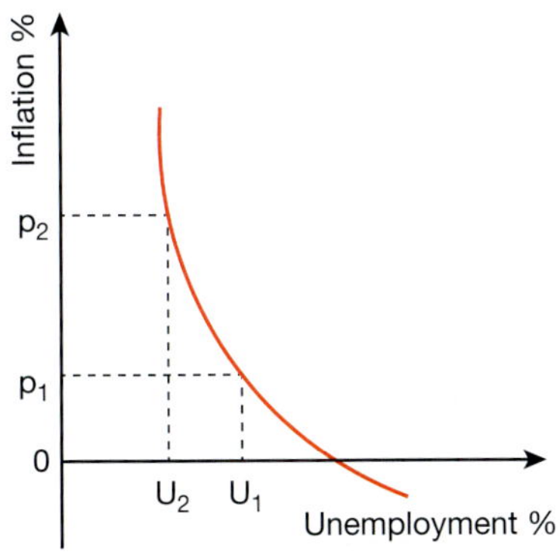

Figure 10.3 Phillips curve ▲

As can be seen, a fall in unemployment from U_1 to U_2 would lead to a rise in inflation from P_1 to P_2. This is a straightforward trade-off in that a government could choose the levels of inflation and unemployment they thought correct for their country. This relationship broke down in several countries in the 1970s when stagflation occurred.

> **Link**
>
> For more on fiscal and monetary policies see Chapter 5, sections 5.2 and 5.3.

> **Getting it right**
>
> The long-run Phillips curve and the LRAS curves are the same.

> **Key terms**
>
> **Stagflation**: exists where there are high levels of both inflation and unemployment.
>
> **NAIRU**: the non-accelerating inflation rate of unemployment i.e. when inflation is zero.

Expectations-augmented Phillips curve (short- and long-run Phillips curve)

Monetarists, however, claimed that although there might be a trade-off in the short-run this was not true in the long run. Friedman claimed that people had expectations concerning what would happen to prices and built this in to their demand for wages while firms had similar expectations for costs so adjusted prices to take this into account. In this way expectations that prices would rise would lead to higher wage demands, thus higher costs and higher prices. As a result he developed the expectations-added Phillips curve, often called the long-run Phillips curve. This curve is a vertical line based on NAIRU. In the long run any attempt to reduce unemployment by increasing demand will just lead to higher inflation. NAIRU can only be reduced by increasing aggregate supply and reducing inflation through tight monetary policy.

As can be seen in Figure 10.4, an increase in demand to reduce unemployment would take the economy along SRPC from A to B decreasing unemployment, but raising inflation from 0 to P_1. Workers then demand higher wages so that firms' costs rise leading to less employment, B to C, but no reduction in prices. Any further attempt to increase demand moves the economy along $SRPC_1$ from C to D and then E. Friedman argued that continual increases in demand could lead to the relationship changing so that higher inflation would lead to higher unemployment. He felt that the only way, therefore, to reduce unemployment permanently was to reduce inflation first. This has influenced Central Banks in their targeting of inflation.

Ibn Khaldun ▲

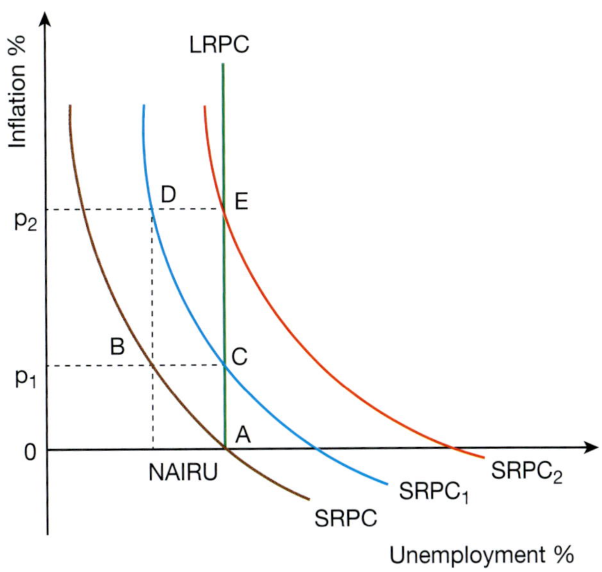

Figure 10.4 Expectations-augmented Phillips curve ▲

10.3 Effectiveness of policy options to meet all macroeconomic objectives

10.3.1 *Effectiveness of different policies in relation to different macroeconomic objectives*

Fiscal policy including Laffer curve analysis

The success of fiscal policy will depend on several factors, such as the:

- size of the multiplier. If it is large then changes in government spending will have a bigger effect on AD. In most developed economies it is, however, small.
- ability to fine tune the economy. Fiscal policy tends to try to make small changes to affect growth, employment or inflation. The existence of time lags in implementing changes and the difficulties in forecasting what will happen may result in unexpected, and unwanted, outcomes.
- state of the economy. Fiscal policy is most effective in a recession where monetary policy is insufficient to boost demand, as increased spending will not cause crowding out. It is efficient if the economy experiences a liquidity trap.
- spending is on capital items such as infrastructure then this can improve future growth and reduce unemployment. It can, also, compensate for falls in consumption and investment, that is: AD + C + I + G + (X – M).

For inflation see the Phillips curve above.

It is argued that high rates of direct tax act as a disincentive to people to work and firms to make profits. Lower rates would encourage more people to work, especially if these were linked to lower unemployment benefits thus providing a real incentive to find jobs. Equally, lower taxes on firms would lead to them trying to be more efficient as they now keep more of their profits and to use these for investment. This idea is associated with Arthur Laffer. Lower income tax will act as an incentive for unemployed workers to join the labour market, or for existing workers to work harder. Lower corporation tax provides an incentive for entrepreneurs to start and so increase national output.

As can be seen in Figure 10.5 as the tax rate increases, tax revenue at first rises, but then after some point falls.

Laffer first drew his curve in 1974 on a napkin in a Washington DC restaurant. He has pointed out that the idea was not new and goes back as far as Ibn Khaldun in 1377.

Progress question

1 Discuss the view that the use of fiscal policy will only result in higher inflation.

Activity

Phillips curve

Find the figures for unemployment and inflation for your country. Plot them against each other. What relationship(s) can you observe?

Link

For the multiplier see Chapter 9, section 9.1.1.

For liquidity trap see Chapter 9, section 9.4.7.

Key term

Fine tuning: maintaining a steady rate of economic growth by changes in government expenditure and taxation.

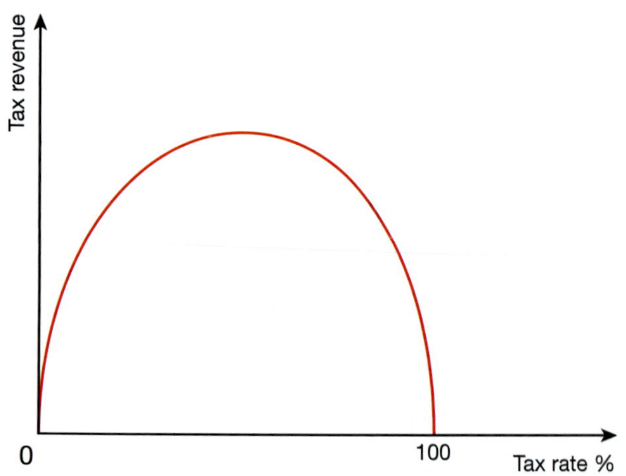

Figure 10.5 The Laffer curve ▲

Professor Arthur Laffer ▲

Link

To revise monetary policy see Chapter 5, section 5.3 and Chapter 9, section 9.4.6. Quantitative easing is covered in Chapter 9, section 9.4.6.

Activity

Seesaw and monetary policy

Using a large sheet of paper (A3), draw a seesaw. Write the advantages (positives) on one side and the disadvantages (negatives) on the other.

Make a judgement as to which side outweighs the other.

This activity could be done in small groups and then the points and the judgements shared. It could be used, also, to judge other policies.

Key terms

Market-based policies: those designed to increase competitiveness and free-market efficiency.

Interventionist policies: these involve government intervention to overcome market failure.

Monetary policy

The success of monetary policy will depend on several factors, such as the:

- rate of interest can easily be changed, unlike fiscal policy, and has a direct effect on consumption and therefore on all government objectives, see above
- state of the economy as interest rates may fall to very low levels during a recession, resulting in a liquidity trap
- clashes between sectors in that different parts of the economy may ideally need different interest rates (see below)
- time lags, as a change in interest rates can take between one and two years to have its full effect.

In addition, the money supply has proved difficult to manipulate so has generally been ignored although low interest rates have seen the rise of quantitative easing.

Supply-side policy including market-based and interventionist policies

Market-based policies are those designed to increase competitiveness and free-market efficiency. Interventionist policies involve government intervention to overcome market failure.

The main drawback to all supply-side policies is the length of time between starting to implement them and their full effect. Education reforms, for example, may take anything from ten to thirty years. This means that although the policies can be effective in helping all the macroeconomic objectives, the needs of those objectives may have changed in the intervening years. In addition, supply-side policies are unlikely to be effective in a recession where the problem is lack of demand.

Exchange rate policy

The exchange rate of an economy affects other macroeconomic objectives through its effect on export and import prices and, thus, on the prices in the economy. It can be seen as a type of monetary policy.

In general, it is a way of controlling the economy by adjusting the exchange rate to meet its macroeconomic objectives. Between 1985 and 1992 the UK government maintained a high exchange rate to control inflation and to try to force firms to become more productively efficient in order to reduce costs and be more competitive. This ended in failure and has not been repeated.

One country which has pursued an exchange rate policy is Singapore. To do so it had to give up control over domestic interest rates, and the money supply. Its effectiveness for Singapore may be because of the very open nature of the Singapore economy.

Activity

Market based and interventionist policies

Make a list of possible market-based and interventionist policies.

Make a list of market-based and internationalist policies used in your economy and discuss how effective they have been.

Link

For more on exchange rates, Marshall–Lerner and the J-curve see Chapter 11, section 11.2.5.

Link

For more on the World Bank and expenditure switching see Chapter 11, sections 11.5.7 and 11.1.3.

For free trade see Chapter 6, section 6.1 and Chapter 11, section 11.6.

For protection see Chapter 6, section 6.2.

Activity

Trade policies

Try to find out what trade policies are used by your government.

What effects have they had on the economy?

Progress question

2 Assess the effectiveness of exchange rate policies in generating economic growth.

Case Study

Singapore's exchange rate policy

The monetary policy of the Monetary Authority of Singapore (MAS) is based on managing the exchange rate with the primary objective of promoting price stability to achieve sustainable economic growth.

This has involved:

- a trade-weighted exchange rate being allowed to float between undisclosed bands
- intervention in the foreign exchange market to buy or sell the currency if it goes outside these bands
- regular reviews of this band to ensure that the exchange rate is still allowing Singapore to achieve its economic objectives
- willingness to give up control of domestic interest rates so that the latter are determined by foreign interest rates and expectations about the value of the currency.

1 What is meant by a trade-weighted exchange rate?

2 Explain the effect of the Singapore government buying its currency on:

a the value of the Singapore currency

b exports and imports

c inflation.

Table 10.2 shows some of the effects of changing exchange rates.

Table 10.2 Effects of changing exchange rates on the economy ▼

Effect	How this affects the economy
Inflation	If the exchange rate falls, imports will be more expensive. This will push up prices, especially if the demand for imports is price inelastic.
Unemployment	If the exchange rate rises, then exports are more expensive leading to a fall in demand, especially if demand for exports is elastic.
Economic growth	A fall in the exchange rate will make exports cheaper. If the Marshall-Lerner condition holds then exports will increase and imports will fall thus increasing the country's aggregate demand leading to more growth and employment.
Balance of payments	A fall in the exchange rate would make export prices cheaper and import prices more expensive. Assuming the Marshall–Lerner effect works then in the long run exports should increase and imports fall improving the current account. In the short run, however, there may be a J-curve effect leading to the opposite result.

International trade policy

Exports and imports are part of AD so affect domestic output, employment and inflation. Trade policy tends to favour either free trade or protection. The World Bank claims that countries that are open to international trade tend to grow faster, innovate, improve productivity and provide higher income and more opportunities to their people. By expanding markets for domestic firms, exports create conditions for production costs to fall as firms benefit from economies of scale. As a result, firms' productivity will increase. Many countries have relied on exports as a way of generating economic growth.

On the other hand, import tariffs and export subsidies induce expenditure-switching towards domestic goods, increasing domestic output, but also pushing up inflation.

10.3.2 *Problems and conflicts arising from the outcome of these policies*

The problems and conflicts are summarised in Table 10.3. The assumption is that these are expansionary fiscal, monetary and supply-side policies.

Table 10.3 Summary of problems and conflicts of the macroeconomic policies ▼

Policy	Problems	Conflicts
Fiscal	They take time to implement and generate change and in a democracy require the assent of parliament. If spending exceeds revenue then governments will need to borrow more money. Expansionary policy will increase C and I leading to more imports.	Rising economic growth and employment with inflation. Balance of payments deficit as more imports come in and exports may be diverted to domestic use. Inflation and this deficit are likely to lead to a fall in the exchange rate.
Monetary	Expanding too much can result in high inflation or as interest rates fall a subsequent fall in exchange rates. There is also the problem of the liquidity trap if interest rates fall too far. As above, there is also a time lag.	The conflicts are very similar to those above, but with more emphasis on growth at the expense of inflation and exchange rates. There is also the inflation-unemployment trade-off.
Supply-side	The major problem is the very long time it takes for these policies to fully work. There is also a limit to which technological change etc can be pushed to improve productivity. The fundamental problem is that in a recession these policies are largely ineffective.	Flexible labour markets may reduce unemployment, but evidence shows that they do not stimulate productivity. Cutting MRT may lead to growth and employment, but are likely to increase inequality.
Exchange rate	A floating exchange rate set by the market changes all the time. If governments try to influence the exchange rate through monetary policy, they surrender using monetary policy to control inflation, etc. Some countries have used currency manipulation, but this tends to lead to trade disputes.	Controlling exchange rates can lead to not being able to control inflation etc by using interest rates.
International trade	Protectionist policies may be contrary to WTO rules. Protection invites retaliation from other countries. Free trade can lead to current account deficits and exchange rate fluctuations.	Protection can lead to rising exchange rates while free trade may lead to falling rates. The former could lead to unemployment and the latter to unflation.

Activity

WTO

Find out more about the WTO and how your country has engaged with it.

Key terms

Currency manipulation: where a government, or central bank, acts to artificially set the foreign exchange value of its currency. This is usually by lowering the price to boost exports and discourage imports.

World Trade Organisation (WTO): exists to promote free trade and the reduction of protectionist barriers.

Case Study

Economic problems in Argentina

The Argentine economy was expected to contract by 12 per cent in 2020 worse than previous forecasts of 9.4 per cent. At the same time, inflation was expected to reach 40.7 per cent this year. The exchange rate continues to fall and is expected to reach 88 pesos per dollar in December 2020 and drop even further to 122.5 pesos per dollar in December 2021. All of this is not helped by Argentina having to resolve its $65 billion debt owed to overseas lenders.

Although, post-pandemic, the economy is expected to show some recovery, a combination of longstanding macroeconomic imbalances, high inflation, capital controls and potentially market-unfriendly policies will hinder growth.

Some of the problems can be seen in the data:

1 Explain the relationship shown between the exchange and inflation rates.

2 What has been the trend in GDP per capita?

3 Explain the relationship between GDP per capita and economic growth.

4 Assess the extent to which the problems identified in the case study may hinder economic growth in the future.

	2016	2017	2018	2019
GDP per capita (US $)	12,778	14,727	12,123	9,679
Economic growth	−2.1	2.7	−2.5	−2.2
Unemployment rate	8.4	8.4	9.2	9.8
Inflation rate (CPI)	41.0	24.8	47.6	53.8
Interest rate	19.88	23.25	49.50	40.31
Exchange rate (vs US$)	15.86	18.60	37.66	59.88
Current account balance (US$bn)	−15.1	−31.2	−27.3	−3.5

Link

For government failure and the market see Chapter 8, section 8.1.

For national minimum wage see Chapter 8, section 8.2.8.

For information failure see Chapter 3, section 3.2.6.

10.3.3 Existence of government failure in macroeconomic policies

In the same way as government failure can cause market failure, it is possible to have government failure in the macroeconomy. Free market economists argue that attempts by the government to reduce income and wealth inequalities can actually worsen incentives and productivity in the economy. They would argue against the national minimum wage because they believe that it can lead to real-wage unemployment. They would also argue against raising the higher rates of income tax because it is deemed to have a negative effect on the incentives of wealth-creators in the economy and generally acts as a disincentive to work longer hours or take a better paid job. They are critical of the government focusing welfare benefits on the poorest because they might damage the incentive to find work.

The opposite point of view is that a lack of effective government policies to reduce the scale of income and wealth inequality is also a cause of government failure since inequality can, over the longer term, create many deep-rooted problems for society once social cohesion starts to break down.

In addition, there is once more the problem of information failure. Economic data is constantly revised as more information becomes available. It can mean that policy is being implemented which is wrong for what is actually happening in the economy. This can be compounded by the fact that policies take time to work their way through the economy e.g. a change in interest rates is estimated to take around 18 months to be fully effective.

Economists cannot agree as to which policies are most effective to meet a certain objective. This, again, may lead to governments not choosing the best policy.

Key concepts

- **Scarcity and choice** can be seen throughout the chapter.
- **Margin and decision making** can be seen particularly in policy options to meet macroeconomic objectives.
- **Equilibrium and disequilibrium** can be seen especially in the context of inflation and unemployment and effectiveness of policy options.
- **Time** can be seen in relation to how the policies react to each other and in fiscal, monetary and supply-side policies.
- **Efficiency and inefficiency** can be seen particularly in policy options.
- **Progress and development** can be seen throughout this chapter.

Progress check

After completing this chapter you should be able to:

- explain government macroeconomic policy objectives
- explain the links between macroeconomic problems and their interrelatedness
- explain the relationship between inflation and unemployment and the Phillips curve
- explain the effectiveness of different policies in relation to different macroeconomic objectives
- identify the problems and conflicts arising from the outcome of these policies
- explain the existence of government failure in macroeconomic policies.

Exam-style questions

Essay and data response questions

1 Evaluate whether economic growth always leads to a balance of payments deficit. [20 marks]

2 Assess the extent to which the control of inflation can cause problems for other macro policy aims. [20 marks]

3 Evaluate the view that the best way to control unemployment is to control inflation. [20 marks]

4 Assess the effectiveness of monetary policy in achieving the government's macroeconomic objectives. [20 marks]

5 Evaluate the extent to which internal and external values of money reflect each other. [20 marks]

6 Assess the effectiveness of exchange rate policy in achieving the government's macroeconomic objectives. [20 marks]

Multiple-choice questions

7 Which of the following is a true statement? [1 mark]

A The external value of money is the amount of imports a unit of currency can buy.
B The external value of money is the value of a currency as measured in foreign currency.
C The internal value of money is established by the central bank and the government.
D The internal value of money is the standard of value of all goods and services.

8 One result of government failure in macroeconomic policies is: [1 mark]

A a worsening of the current account balance
B an increase in monopoly power
C the conflict between inflation and unemployment
D the worsening of incentives and productivity

11 International economic issues

In this chapter you will develop your knowledge and understanding of:

- policies to correct disequilibrium in the balance of payments
- exchange rates
- economic development
- characteristics of countries at different levels of development
- relationship between countries at different levels of development
- globalisation.

11.1 Policies to correct disequilibrium in the balance of payments

11.1.1 Components of the balance of payments accounts: current account, financial account and capital account

The International Monetary Fund (IMF) has a recommended method for the presentation of a nations' balance of payments accounts to enable international comparisons to be made.

In order to explain the main components of a country's balance of payments accounts, reference will be made to the UK accounts for 2019. These are summarised in Table 11.1.

Table 11.1 Summary of UK balance of payments accounts for 2019

Category	Credits	Debits	Balance
Current account			
Trade in goods	373,149	5 040,29	–129,729
Trade in services	317,674	217,296	103,824
Total trade	690,823	721,325	–25,895
Primary income	161,980	164,234	–30,342
Secondary income	18,040	45,535	–27,526
Current balance	870,843	931,094	–83,763
Capital balance	916,360	1,011,670	–801
Net financial transactions	57,798	165,274	–102,683
Net errors and omissions	–	–	–18,119

All figures in £ million
Source: ONS

Link
IMF is covered in section 11.5.6 of this chapter.

Getting it right
Make sure you are absolutely clear as to the difference between a deficit or surplus on the balance of payments and a budget surplus or deficit. These are often confused.

The balance of payments account is a systematic record of all economic transactions between a particular country and the rest of the world.

The balance of payments accounts are divided into three sections:

1. current account
2. capital account
3. financial account

Link

To review your understanding of the current account see Chapter 6, section 6.3.

In all cases, credit items bringing money into the UK are represented by a plus (+) sign and debit items taking money out of the country by a negative (−) sign.

In addition, because the balance of payments is an account it must balance i.e. the inflows of money must equal the outflows. As the figures are collected by many different government departments the account often does not balance. To correct the problem a net errors and omissions figure is included.

Key terms

Net errors and omissions: these reflect the imbalances resulting from imperfections in source data and compilation of the balance of payments accounts.

Capital account: a record of the transfers of ownership of fixed assets and of non-financial assets.

Financial account: a record of the movement of money in the form of investments by the residents of a country and the inward flow of investment.

The capital account is the part of the balance of payments which shows the changes in a country's asset ownership as a result of both public and private investment inflows and outflows. Capital transfers are those involving transfers of ownership of fixed assets, except land, and transfers of funds linked to the acquisition or disposal of fixed assets or cancellation of liabilities by creditors.

The financial account records an economy's transaction in external financial assets and liabilities, e.g. investment-owned assets such as foreign reserves, gold, etc. Assets owned by foreigners, those private and official, are also recorded in the financial account. These assets are both fixed (e.g. the opening of mines or pharmaceutical production plants in Indonesia), often referred to as foreign direct investment, and portfolio investments such as shares as well as non-financial (e.g. the buying or selling of land). It also includes short-term monetary flows, so-called "hot money", where investors move their money to where they can get the best return often because of a change in interest rates.

11.1.2 *Effect of fiscal, monetary, supply-side, protectionist and exchange rate policies on the balance of payments*

Fiscal and monetary policies

Link

For fiscal and monetary policy see Chapter 5, sections 5.2 and 5.3 and Chapter 10, section 10.3.1.
For the marginal propensity to import see Chapter 9, section 9.1.1.

Demand-side policies will directly affect the trade in goods and services. Reductions in government spending, and higher taxes, fiscal, or higher interest rates and reducing the availability of credit, monetary, could all have the effect of dampening consumer demand and reducing the demand for imports. This is an example of expenditure reduction, see next section. This process can also lead to an increase in spare productive capacity which can then be used to increase exports. It is difficult, however, to predict the precise effect of a fall in spending on imports, which requires an accurate calculation of the marginal propensity to import.

Activity

Supply-side policies and the balance of payments

Investigate what supply-side policies your government has used to try to improve the balance of payments.

Supply-side policies

Supply-side policies focus on improving the supply-side performance of the economy in order to increase competitiveness. As seen before when looking at these policies, this is inevitably a long-run solution, unlike demand-side policies. Some of these policies are set out in Table 11.2 below.

Link

For human capital see factors of production in Chapter 1, section 1.3.2.

Link

For more detail on protectionism see Chapter 6 Figures 6.3 and 6.4.
To see diagrams showing how tariffs and a quota could affect imports see Figures 6.3 and 6.4 Chapter 6.

Key terms

Brexit (British Exit): the leaving of the EU by the United Kingdom on 1 January 2021.
European Union (EU): 27 European countries that are in a free trade area with each other with a common external tariff barrier.

Progress question

1 Assess the effectiveness of protectionist policies for the balance of payments.

Link

For more on exchange rates see section 11.2 of this chapter, Chapter 6, section 6.4 and Chapter 10, section 10.3.1.
For more on Marshall–Lerner see section 11.2.5 of this chapter.

Table 11.2 Supply-side policies and the balance of payments ▼

Policy	Effect on the balance of payments
Increasing productivity	These focus on increasing innovation and investment in industries with potential to increase exports and compete with imports. This would improve the trade balance.
Education and health	Improving and increasing education and health facilities and standards would boost human capital and see more people employed in modern high-value industries such as bio-technology. This would again increase exports and possibly decrease imports of goods and services.
Infrastructure	Improving the roads, rail, airports, sea-ports, etc, of the country would allow goods to flow more freely abroad. It could also increase tourism, a service export.
New businesses	Supporting the start-up of new businesses could increase exports and/or decrease imports.

Protectionist policies

Protectionist policies are all designed to reduce imports of goods and services. This initially has a positive effect on the current account, assuming that domestic industries can provide acceptable substitutes. Other countries, however, may retaliate by imposing their own protectionist measures on the country's exports. A more subtle policy is that of "red tape". In the case of Brexit, UK exporters have complained that, although there is a free trade agreement between the UK and the European Union (EU), they find the amount of paperwork required for goods to enter the EU a real barrier.

Exchange rate policies

The exchange rate may fall either because of a current account deficit or because of other policies such as lowering interest rates, see above. Allowing it to fall should improve the balance of payments especially the trade in goods and services part of the current account. Export prices fall while import prices rise. Given a favourable Marshall–Lerner effect, the value of exports increase, while the value of imports fall.

A fall in the exchange rate has the effect of increasing the value of profits and income for a country's businesses with investments overseas and thus improving the financial account. All of this works so long as capital is not free to move from one economy to another. If an economy is growing and there is a rise in consumer expenditure then investors and speculators may buy the currency even if the current account deficit is increasing as they think that the economy is improving.

Progress question

2 Explain why an increase in the current account deficit might see a rise in the value of the currency.

11.1.3 *Difference between expenditure-switching and expenditure-reducing policies*

Expenditure-switching policies try to shift expenditure from imported to domestically produced goods. This can be done in three ways, as explained above.

Expenditure-reducing policies are aimed at trying to reduce excess demand which has led to high levels of imports (see fiscal and monetary policies above).

11.2 Exchange rates

11.2.1 *Measurement of exchange rates*

Distinction between nominal and real exchange rates

Exchange rates can be measured in terms of nominal value, real value and trade-weighted value.

The nominal exchange rate is the one which is usually quoted e.g. if you go to a bank or look at the rate on the internet then you will see this rate. The real exchange rate is what the currency will buy in terms of other currencies. This is often referred to as purchasing power parity.

Trade-weighted exchange rates

The trade-weighted exchange rate is the measurement, in terms of an index, of changes in a country's currency against a basket of other currencies. These are weighted to reflect the relative importance of trade for the country of the currencies in the basket. If, for example, the UK does five times more trade with the EU as it does with Japan then the euro will b e given five times the weight of the yen.

11.2.2 *Determination of exchange rates under fixed and managed systems*

A fixed exchange rate is one where little or no change is possible from the agreed rate. In practice, a small variation of around two per cent is usually allowed, but the central bank of the country is committed to maintain the value by buying its own currency, to prevent the price falling, or to sell its currency to stop it rising. In practice, countries often have to either revalue or devalue (see next section) their rates from time to time to allow for differences in economic growth.

Many developing countries use fixed or pegged exchange rates for their currencies (Figure 11.1). A pegged exchange rate is where a country sets a specific fixed exchange rate for its currency with a specific foreign currency, or basket of currencies. This provides these countries with more stability.

Key terms

Expenditure-switching policies: policies which lead to a fall in imports and an increase in consumption of domestically produced goods.

Expenditure reducing policies: used to correct a balance of payments disequilibrium by reducing consumer purchasing power. This is likely to involve monetary (interest rates) and fiscal (taxes) policies.

Key terms

Nominal exchange rate: the rate at which one currency exchanges for another. It is sometimes just called the foreign exchange rate.

Real exchange rate: the value of a currency in terms of what it can actually buy.

Trade-weighted exchange rate: an index calculated using weights showing the relative importance of trade between the country and its trade partners.

Purchasing power parity: a way of showing the exchange rate in terms of how much a typical basket of goods cost in one country compared to another country.

Fixed exchange rate: where the value of a country's exchange rate is determined by its government which is committed to maintain the value.

Pegged exchange rate: policy of fixing the exchange rate of the nation's currency to the currency of another country.

Link

For more on purchasing power parity see section 11.3.3 of this chapter.

Activity

Exchanging your currency

Find out the value of your exchange rate against five different currencies. If you were to visit these countries and to take with you 100 units (or 1000 units if more appropriate) of your currency, how much of these foreign currencies would you get for your 100 (1000) units?

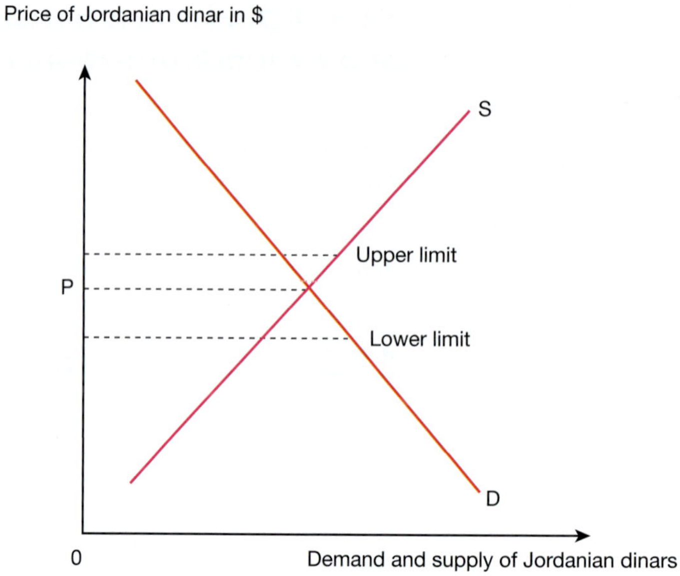

Figure 11.1 Fixed exchange rate Jordanian dinars to $ ▲

Key terms

Managed float: where a government intervenes in the foreign exchange market to try to prevent wild movements of its currency.

Speculation: where one or more people gamble on a currency rising, by buying it, or falling, by selling it.

Dirty float: where a country deliberately sets its exchange rate at a low level to gain a trade advantage.

Devaluation: when the value of a fixed exchange rate is decreased to a new lower rate.

Revaluation: when the value of a fixed exchange rate is increased to a new higher rate.

Governments can try to manage their currency by intervening in the market to influence its price. This is called a managed float. The purpose is to try to prevent wild fluctuations in the value of the currency, one cause of which is speculation. Where governments use this idea to deliberately set their currency at a lower rate than the market would under a floating system in order to gain a trading advantage, this is called a "dirty float". Japan was accused of this in the 1960s and 1970s while China has more recently faced similar accusations.

11.2.3 Distinction between revaluation and devaluation of a fixed exchange rate

Unlike floating exchange rates, fixed exchange rates can only change their value if the government decides that this is necessary. A lowering of the exchange rate, i.e. a fall in the value, is a devaluation, while a raising of the exchange rate, i.e. it goes up in value, is a revaluation. This can be seen in Figure 11.3 below.

11.2.4 Changes in the exchange rate under different exchange rate systems

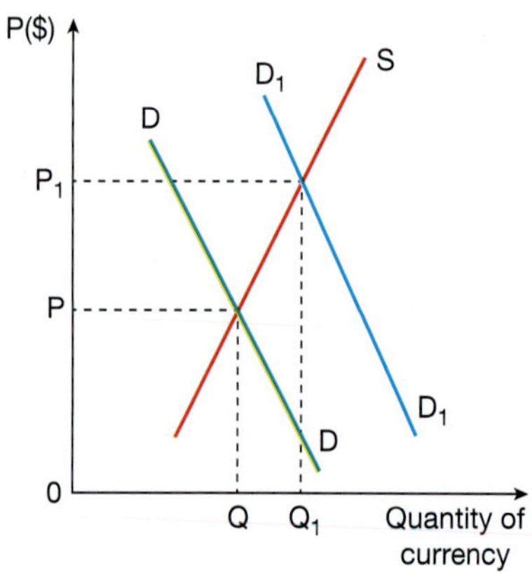

Figure 11.2 Depreciation and appreciation ▲

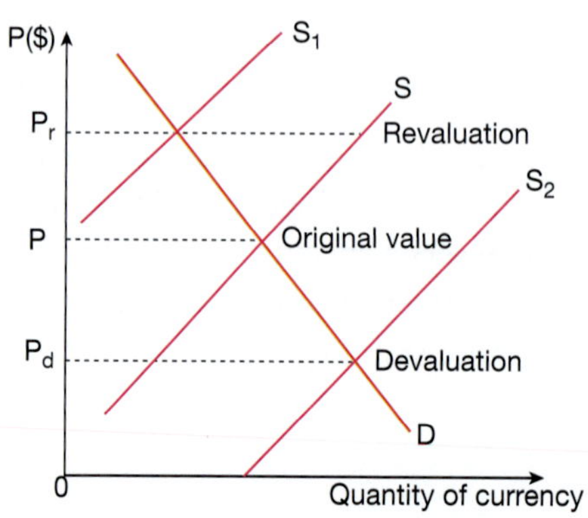

Figure 11.3 Revaluation and devaluation ▲

Floating exchange rates can either depreciate, i.e. fall in value, or appreciate, i.e. rise in value. As can be seen in Figure 11.2 an increase in demand for the currency, from DD to D_1D_1, leads to a rise in the currency's value, an appreciation, whereas a fall in demand leads to the opposite effect, a devaluation.

Figure 11.3 shows the effects of revaluation and devaluation. If the original fixed value was 'P', then a revaluation will move it to 'P_r'. Equally, a devaluation will lower the price to 'P_d'. A government can achieve this by either buying their currency, thus reducing supply from S to S_1, or by selling the currency, thus increasing supply from S to S_2.

11.2.5 *The effects of changing exchange rates on the external economy using Marshall–Lerner and J-curve analysis*

Any change in the exchange rate will affect the price and thus the quantity of exports and imports. This will in turn affect both the current account and also AD as AD = C + I + G + X – M. Marshall–Lerner shows the conditions under which a change in the exchange rate of a country's currency leads to an improvement or worsening of a country's balance of payments. If a country's exchange rate rises so that exports are more expensive and imports are cheaper then, if Marshall–Lerner holds, the volume and value of exports will fall while the volume and value of imports will rise. This results in a deterioration in the current account.

Equally, a fall in the value of a country's exchange rate will, assuming Marshall–Lerner holds, lead to an improvement in the current account, as exports rise and imports fall. This, however, may not happen immediately. Contracts have been signed at the old value and cannot be changed. It also takes time for exporters and importers to react to the change. This gives rise to the J-curve effect. The diagram shows that devaluation/depreciation leads to an immediate worsening of the current account with this only benefiting from the devaluation/depreciation in the longer run.

Link

For appreciation and depreciation see Chapter 6, section 6.4.3.

Getting it right

Make sure you are absolutely clear as to the difference between an appreciation and a revaluation and between a depreciation and a devaluation.

Progress question

3 Explain the differences between an appreciation and depreciation of a currency and the revaluation and devaluation of a currency.

Activity

Value of your country's exchange rate

Find out what has happened to the value of your country's exchange rate over the last two years. Try to discover what factors have affected its value.

Link

Marshall–Lerner and the J-curve were also referenced in Chapter 6, section 6.3.4.

Key term

Marshall–Lerner: states that the sum of the price elasticities of demand for exports and imports must be greater than one if a devaluation is to lead to an improvement in the current account.

Case Study

Exchange rates

In the current system, exchange rates among the major currencies (principally the U.S. dollar, the euro, and Japanese yen) fluctuate in response to market forces, with short-run volatility and occasional large medium-run swings. Some medium-sized industrial countries also have market-determined floating rate regimes, while others have adopted harder pegs. Developing economies have a wide variety of exchange rate arrangements, with a tendency for many but by no means all countries to move toward increased exchange rate flexibility.

One group of countries for which pegged exchange rates would seem to remain sensible are small economies with a dominant trading partner that pursues a reasonably stable monetary policy, including small Caribbean and Pacific island economies. For such countries, there is generally little point in incurring the costs of attempting to run an independent monetary policy.

1 Explain why a country such as the US would prefer a floating exchange rate system.
2 Explain why countries with a dominant trading partner might prefer a pegged exchange rate.
3 Discuss why many developing countries might be moving towards a floating exchange rate.

Source: IMF

11.3 Economic development

Economic growth and development are linked. While growth is possible without development because growth is just an increase in real GDP, development cannot take place if there is no growth.

Economic development is a far more comprehensive idea than economic growth. In addition to a rise in real output, it involves changes in the composition of this output and a consequent shift in the allocation of resources as well as the reduction of poverty, inequalities and unemployment. In addition, development can refer to the availability of education and literacy rates as well as health and life expectancy.

Amartya Sen stated that development is about creating freedom for people and removing obstacles to greater freedom. Greater freedom enables people to choose their own destiny. Obstacles to freedom, and hence to development, include poverty, lack of economic opportunities, corruption, poor governance, lack of education and lack of health.

Key term

J-curve: the short term response of the current account to a significant fall in the exchange rate.

Economic development: an increase in the economic wealth of a country so as to benefit all of its people.

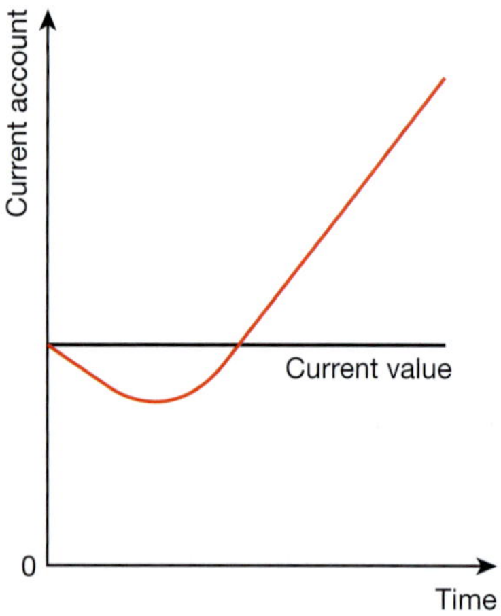

Figure 11.4 J-curve effect showing initial fall and then rise in the value of the current account▲

Link

Economic growth was covered in Chapter 4, section 4.4 and Chapter 9, section 9.2.

11.3.1 *Classification of economies in terms of their level of development*

Criteria for evaluating a country's level of development are GDP per capita, the level of industrialization, the general standard of living, and the amount of technological infrastructure.

The United Nations classifies countries into three groups:

- Developed countries are those which have a high level of economic growth and security.
- Transitional countries are those which are in a process of moving from a centrally planned economy to a mixed or free market economy.
- Developing countries are those that have a low GDP per capita and, normally, rely heavily on agriculture as the primary industry.

Key terms

Developed countries: those which have a high level of economic growth and security.

Transitional countries: those which are in a process of moving from a centrally planned economy to a mixed or free market economy.

Developing countries: those that have a low GDP per capita and, normally, rely heavily on agriculture as the primary industry.

Key term

World Bank: provides loans for developing countries. Its official goal is the reduction of poverty. According to its Articles of Agreement, all its decisions must be guided by a commitment to the promotion of foreign investment and international trade and to the facilitation of capital investment. The World Bank group consists of five agencies.

11.3.2 *Classification of economies in terms of their level of national income*

The World Bank assigns the world's economies to four income groups – low, lower-middle, upper-middle, and high-income countries. Examples of these groups for 2021 are shown in Table 11.3. This information is revised every year.

Amartya Sen ▲

Link

To review planned, mixed and free market economies see Chapter 1, section 1.4.
For World Bank see section 11.5.7 of this chapter.

Key term

Living standards: measures the material welfare of the residents of a country.

Link

To review GNI see Chapter 3, section 3.3.2.

Link

To review GDP and NNI see Chapter 4, section 4.1.2.
To review what real means and how it differs from nominal see Chapter 4, section 4.6.3.
For more on purchasing power parity see later in this section.

Getting it right

Remember that Real GNP/GNI/NNI per capita are averages and not what everybody gets. These figures may disguise great wealth and poverty.

Table 11.3 Classification of countries by GNI per capita in $ for 2021 ▼

High income >12535	Upper-middle income 4046–12535	Lower-middle income 1036–4045	Low income <1036
Austria	Argentina	Angola	Afghanistan
Bermuda	Belize	Bangladesh	Burundi
Chile	Botswana	Ghana	Ethiopia
Norway	Montenegro	Morocco	Haiti
Qatar	Peru	Pakistan	Malawi
Seychelles	Russia	Philippines	Sierra Leone
South Korea	South Africa	Ukraine	Syria
United Kingdom	Thailand	Vietnam	Yemen

Activity

Classification of countries

Either individually or in groups, answer the following:

1. How is your country classified in terms of development?
2. How is your country classified in terms of income group?
3. Do you agree with these classifications?
4. How does your country compare to neighbouring ones?

11.3.3 *Indicators of living standards and economic development*

Living standards refers to the amount and quality of material goods and services available to the population of a country. It includes many aspects such as: income; housing; employment; hours of work required to purchase necessities; education; environmental quality.

Monetary indicators including real per capita national income statistics (GDP, GNI, NNI) and purchasing power parity and issues of comparison using monetary indicators

GDP per capita is the most widely used monetary measure of living standards. IT, together with GNI and NNI, are easy to obtain and give an 'at a glance' comparison without needing further understanding. Real and per capita allow for different inflation rates and different levels of population. GDP is a production concept, but the way that it is constructed makes it equal to the total income earned in the production process. Some of this income is paid to non-residents, while residents receive some income from production in other countries. GDP can be adjusted for "net income from abroad" to arrive at the concept of gross national income, GNI, which is more relevant for the well-being of residents of a country. In turn, by deduction, capital consumption NNI can be achieved. Unfortunately, there are a number of difficulties involved in using the figures:

Progress question

4 Explain why real GNI per capita might not be a good measure of the standard of living in your country.

Activity

GDP and standard of living

Depending on the size of your class, you may want to split into smaller groups and then come back to exchange views. Would the following changes result in real GDP per capita overstating or understating the effect on the standard of living?

1. Infant mortality declines
2. The level of pollution increases
3. The quality of health services increases
4. The crime rate declines
5. Consumers are able to obtain a greater variety of products

Link

For unemployment see Chapter 4, section 4.5 and Chapter 9, section 9.3.
For equality and equity see Chapter 9, section 9.2.5.

Key term

Non-monetary indicator: anything which contributes to the standard of living or development of a country, but does have directly a value in terms of money.

- Work v leisure time: a higher per capita income ignores that one country may have shorter working hours and/or offer longer holidays to its workers.
- Shadow economy: GDP includes production that is exchanged in the market, but it does not include black market activities nor ones you may do yourself. Cleaning your own house is not counted, but hiring a cleaner to do the work is. Activities such as self-employment may not be (fully) reported or taxation figures used to calculate NI may be subject to tax evasion.
- What expenditure does or does not show: this is a question of quantity, or money spent, which is measurable, against quality. It shows what is spent on environmental protection, but not whether the air and water are cleaner. Equally, it shows how much is spent on education, but not the proportion of the population who are literate.
- Income distribution is ignored because these measurements are only averages.

Using these measures to compare standard of living between countries has the further difficulty of currency conversion, as the exchange rate may not reflect accurately what money can buy in each country. One way round this is to use purchasing power parity (PPP). This takes into account the local purchasing power of the currency, using a basket of goods, and is a better guide to actual living standards.

An example would be: if a pair of trousers cost \$40 in the US and an identical pair cost €32 in Italy and the exchange rate meant that this was equivalent to \$60 then the PPP would be $\frac{60}{40} = 1.5$. This means that for every dollar spent in US it takes £1.50 dollars to buy the same trousers in Italy using the euro.

Although there are problems with these monetary measures, they do indicate when a country is materially better or worse off in terms of jobs and incomes. In most countries, a significantly higher GDP per capita is an indicator of improvements in everyday life along with aspects such as education and health.

Non-monetary indicators

A non-monetary indicator is anything which contributes to the standard of living or development of a country, but does have directly a value in terms of money. While there is no agreement as to which factors to include, the following are often referred to:

- Unemployment rate: people may be unemployed with low, or no, incomes and unable to access goods available to the majority of society.
- Social cohesion: if society does not have the same basic goals and cultural norms then there may be lack of support for those with disadvantages. The ability of economies to work efficiently and develop effectively depends on the establishment of an environment in which legal rights, especially property and contractual rights,

> **Key terms**
>
> **Legal framework**: rules, procedural steps or tests by which judgements can be determined in any given legal case.
>
> **Corruption**: behaviour which aims to make private gains at public expense.

are enforced and protected. There is evidence which shows that countries where the law applies equally to all and have developed strong institutional and legal frameworks have performed better in terms of sustained growth and human development.

- Level of corruption: corruption is present in every country, but its effects are especially damaging in those which are still developing. The amount of corruption is negatively linked to the level of investment and economic growth, that is to say, the more corruption, the less investment and the less economic growth. And the lower the standard of living for many citizens.
- Degree of equality and equity: there are many countries where groups of people based on gender, sexual orientation, ethnicity, etc. are disadvantaged and often excluded from well-paid jobs or from taking a wider role in society.

> **Activity**
>
> **Corruption and the legal system**
>
> 1 Find out where your country ranks in terms of GDP per head.
> 2 Discuss how important corruption is in your country. Do you think it restricts development?
> 3 If you were to set up your own business, to what extent do you feel that the law would enable you to easily grow the business?

Composite indicators

Human Development Index (HDI)

> **Key term**
>
> **Human Development Index (HDI)**: a means of measuring countries' economic and social development using life expectancy, years of schooling and GNI per capita.

The problems of using GDP/GNP to compare living standards and economic development between countries over time has led to the development of other measures, the best known being the Human Development Index (HDI). This measures changes in development levels over time and compares development levels in different countries. The 2019 report includes:

- a long and healthy life: life expectancy at birth
- education index: mean years of schooling and expected years of schooling
- a decent standard of living: GNP per capita (PPP US$).

> **Activity**
>
> **HDI**
>
> Using the web link given for Table 11.4, find out where your country is located.
>
> Has this changed over the last five years? Try to explain any change or why it is still the same. How does this compare with your position in terms of GDP?

Table 11.4 Top 10 and the bottom 10 countries on the HDI ▼

Rank	Country	HDI value (2019)	Life expectancy at birth (years) SDG3	Expected years of schooling (years) SDG 4.3	Mean years of schooling (years) SDG 4.6	Gross national income (GNI) per capita (PPP $) SDG 8.5
1	Norway	0.957	83.8	16.3	13.4	69,394
2	Ireland	0.955	82.3	18.7	12.7	68,371
3	Switzerland	0.955	82.4	18.1	12.9	66,494
4	Hong Kong, China (SAR)	0.949	84.9	16.9	12.3	62,985
4	Iceland	0.949	83.0	19.1	12.8	54,682
6	Germany	0.947	81.3	17.0	14.2	55,314
7	Sweden	0.945	82.8	19.5	12.5	54,508
8	Australia	0.944	83.4	22.0	12.7	48,085
9	Netherlands	0.944	82.3	18.5	12.4	57,707
10	Denmark	0.940	80.9	18.9	12.6	58,662
180	Eritrea	0.459	66.3	5.0	3.9	2,793
181	Mozambique	0.456	60.9	10.0	3.5	1,250
182	Burkina Faso	0.452	61.6	9.3	1.6	2,133
183	Sierra Leone	0.452	54.7	10.2	3.7	1,668
184	Mali	0.434	59.3	7.5	2.4	2,269
185	Burundi	0.433	61.6	11.1	3.3	754
186	South Sudan	0.433	57.9	5.3	4.8	2,003
187	Chad	0.398	54.2	7.3	2.5	1,555
188	Central African Republic	0.397	53.3	7.6	4.3	993
189	Niger	0.394	62.4	6.5	2.1	1,201

Source: UNDP

Key terms

Measure of Economic Welfare (MEW): starts with GDP, but adds the value of leisure time and the amount of unpaid work in an economy and subtracts the value of the environment damage caused by industrial production and consumption.

Multidimensional Poverty Index (MPI): identifies multiple deprivations at the household and individual level in health, education and standard of living.

Measure of Economic Welfare (MEW)

The Measure of Economic Welfare (MEW) was the work of Nordhaus and Tobin as an alternative to just using GDP. MEW took national output as a starting point, but adjusted it to include an assessment of the value of leisure time and the amount of unpaid work in an economy. This increased the welfare value of GDP. On the other hand, the value of the environment damage caused by industrial production and consumption was also included which reduced the welfare value of GDP.

Multidimensional Poverty Index (MPI)

The Multidimensional Poverty Index (MPI) identifies multiple deprivations at the household and individual level in health, education and standard of living (Table 11.5).

Table 11.5 Multidimensional Poverty Index Dimensions of Poverty and Weightings 2020

Dimensions of Poverty	Indicator	Deprived if living in the household where…	Weight
Health	Nutrition	Any adult under 70 years of age or any child for whom there is nutritional information is undernourished.	1/6
	Child mortality	Any child under the age of 18 years has died in the family in the five-year period preceding the survey.	1/6
Education	Years of schooling	No household member aged school entrance age + six years or older has completed six years of schooling.	1/6
	School attendance	Any school-aged child is not attending school up to the age at which he/she would complete class eight.	1/6
Standard of living	Cooking Fuel	The household cooks with dung, wood, charcoal or coal.	1/18
	Sanitation	The household's sanitation facility is not improved (according to SDG guidelines) or it is improved but shared with other households.	1/18
	Drinking Water	The household does not have access to improved drinking water (according to SDG guidelines) or improved drinking water is at least a 30-minute walk from home, round trip.	1/18
	Electricity	The household has no electricity.	1/18
	Housing	At least one of the three housing materials for roof, walls and floor are inadequate: the floor is of natural materials and/or the roof and/or walls are of natural or rudimentary materials.	1/18
	Assets	The household does not own more than one of these assets: radio, television, telephone, computer, animal cart, bicycle, motorbike or refrigerator, and does not own a car or truck.	1/18

Source: UNDP

MPI uses three dimensions and ten indicators which are:

- education: years of schooling and child enrolment (1/6 weight each, total 2/6)
- health: child mortality and nutrition (1/6 weight each, total 2/6)
- standard of living: electricity, flooring, drinking water, sanitation, cooking fuel and assets (1/18 weight each, total 2/6).

A person is multidimensionally poor if they are deprived in one-third or more (means 33% or more) of the weighted indicators (out of the ten indicators). Those who are deprived in one half or more of the weighted indicators are considered living in extreme multidimensional poverty.

MPI is significant as it recognises poverty from different dimensions compared to the conventional methodology that measures poverty only from the income or monetary terms.

Case Study

Multidimensional Poverty Index (MPI)

Tamang, a 56-year-old landless woman, lives near a remote jungle in Nepal with her husband, who is living with significant disabilities, and two granddaughters, who are attending school. Her livelihood is collecting and selling wood. Waking before dawn, she feeds the chickens then walks with friends to the jungle to collect wood, often going deep inside, which is not safe due to wild animals. After chopping the wood, she carries it on her back to the market, because she does not own any means of transportation. If it sells, she buys some rice and vegetables for the family, returning home around 11 am. After cooking lunch, she returns to the jungle to fetch her own cooking fuel.

Tamang lives in a single room rudimentary hut with a dirt floor. She has no toilet and uses her neighbour's unprotected well for drinking water. She has electricity but does not own a phone, refrigerator, television or even a radio. Despite plentiful obstacles, she is happy because the family bonds of affection are strong. She observes that happiness is something that we cannot buy in the market. Tamang is poor according to the global MPI. She is deprived in 44.4 percent of weighted indicators.

1 Explain why Tamang is poor according to the MPI.

2 Discuss the extent to which the MPI is a good measure of living standards.

Source: OPHI

Link

For Gini coefficient see Chapter 1, section 1.4.2 and Chapter 3, section 3.3.2.

Key term

Kuznets curve: an inverted U curve, although variables along the axes are often mixed and matched, with inequality or the Gini coefficient on the *y*-axis and economic development, time or per-capita incomes on the *x*-axis.

Kuznets curve

The Kuznets curve is an inverted U curve, although variables along the axes are often mixed and matched, with inequality or the Gini coefficient on the *y*-axis and economic development, time or per-capita incomes on the *x*-axis.

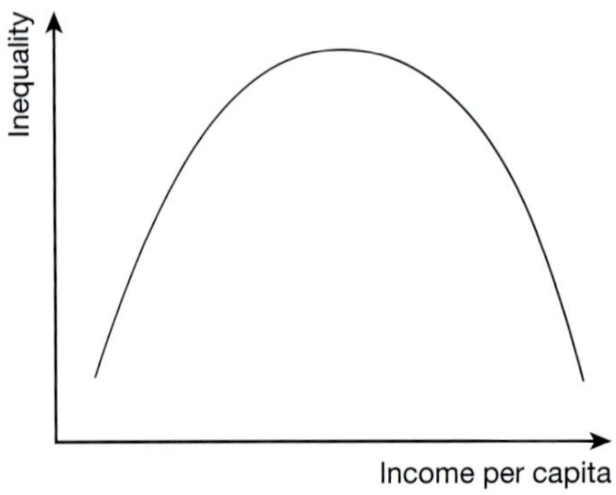

Figure 11.5 Kuznets curve

The curve claims to show that as an economy develops, initially inequality increases, but that after a certain average income is reached, inequality then decreases. This assumes that a country which is industrialising (and mechanising agricultural production) will draw people into urban areas improving their standards of living, but causing greater inequality with those still in rural areas. Only at a later stage will the benefits of growth reach these people and start to close the gap. Although this was based on historical evidence, the "East Asian miracle" showed low inequality and high output, while in some more autocratic countries there has been high inequality and low output.

Activity

Kuznets curve

As a group discuss whether your country's development can be shown using the Kuznets curve. What evidence have you used to support your conclusion?

11.3.4 Comparison of economic growth rates and living standards over time

Assuming that the cost of living has not changed by more than the growth in income, then an increase in real GDI per capita should indicate not only economic growth, but also a rise in the standard of living. Table 11.6 shows how economic growth of New Zealand has changed over the period 2015–2019 using real GDP.

Table 11.6 Economic growth in New Zealand

Year	Growth rate %
2015	4.11
2016	4.20
2017	3.80
2018	3.21
2019	2.22

Source: World Bank

Activity

Economic growth over time

Using Table 11.6:

1 Explain the trend in economic growth over the period 2015–2019

2 Discuss whether you consider real GDP to be a good indicator of i) economic growth, and ii) standard of living.

Then find out what has happened to economic growth in your country over the last five years.

Between countries

In any comparison of living standards between countries, it is important to remember that GDP/GNP/NNI per capita is an average figure. It ignores the fact that income may be very unequally distributed so that only some people have a higher standard of living than those in the other country.

Comparing growth rates can be equally problematical. Many of the problems mentioned above apply again, e.g. the black economy leading to understating of real GDP. In addition, in countries where literacy levels are low, for example Niger has one of the lowest literacy rates in the world where just over 19 per cent of adults can read and write, information provided by individuals may not exist or be unreliable. Another issue is how countries value government services which are provided free. These methods not only vary between countries, but individual countries sometimes change how they are estimated.

Key terms

BRIC: Brazil; Russia; India and China.

MINT: Mexico; Indonesia; Nigeria and Turkey.

Table 11.7 shows how difficult it can be to compare economic growth rates not only over time or between very different countries, but also between designated groups of countries. Looking at the BRIC countries, two have growth rates at least double that of the other two.

Activity

Comparing growth rates

Use Table 11.7 to answer the following.

1. To what extent is it possible to compare the developed countries with the BRICs, MINTs and developing countries? Try to update the figures to see if there have been any major changes.
2. What other information would be helpful in making the comparisons?
3. Find out the growth rates for your country, or for another country, for the period shown. How well is that country doing?
4. Find out what the growth rate was 20 years ago. Discuss the extent to which you can compare the rates.

Table 11.7 Economic growth rates for developed, BRIC, MINT and developing countries 2015–2019 ▼

Country	2015	2016	2017	2018	2019
Austria	1.0	2.0	2.4	2.6	1.4
Netherlands	2.0	2.2	2.9	2.4	1.7
Norway	2.0	1.1	2.3	1.3	1.2
United States	2.9	1.6	2.4	2.9	2.2
Brazil	–3.5	–3.3	1.3	1.3	1.1
Russia	–2.0	0.2	1.8	2.5	1.3
India	8.0	8.3	7.0	6.1	4.2
China	7.0	6.9	6.9	6.7	6.1
Mexico	3.3	2.6	2.1	2.2	–0.1
Indonesia	4.9	5.0	5.1	5.2	5.0
Nigeria	2.7	–1.6	0.8	1.9	2.2
Turkey	6.1	7.3	7.5	3.0	0.9
Chile	2.3	1.7	1.2	3.9	1.1
Mauritius	3.6	3.8	3.8	3.8	3.0
Tanzania	6.2	6.9	6.8	5.4	5.8
Vietnam	6.7	6.2	6.8	7.1	7.0

Source: World Bank

Key terms

Birth rate: number of live births per thousand population per year.

Death rate: number of deaths per thousand population per year.

Infant mortality rate: number of deaths of infants under one year old in a given year per thousand live births in the same year.

Natural increase: the difference between birth rate and death rate.

11.4 Characteristics of countries at different levels of development

11.4.1 *Population growth and structure*

Measurement and causes of changes in birth rate, death rate, infant mortality and net migration

Birth and death rates are two key factors in population growth. They are both measured per thousand of the population per year. As countries develop, health and education services improve leading to lower birth and death rates. Also important is the infant mortality rate which is again improved health care will lead to a decline. The two developed countries in Table 11.9 have much lower rates than the other countries. The greater the difference between the birth and death rates, the higher is the population growth. This difference is called the natural increase. This can be seen in Table 11.8.

Table 11.8 Birth and death rates in 2018 ▼

Status	Country	Birth rate	Death rate	Difference
Developed	Canada	10	8	2
Developed	New Zealand	12	7	5
BRIC	Brazil	14	6	8
BRIC	India	18	7	11
MINT	Mexico	18	6	12
MINT	Turkey	16	5	11
Developing	Iraq	29	5	24
Developing	Zambia	36	6	30

Source: World Bank

Table 11.9 Infant mortality rates in 2018 ▼

Status	Country	Infant mortality rate
Developed	Canada	4
Developed	New Zealand	4
BRIC	Brazil	12
BRIC	India	28
MINT	Mexico	12
MINT	Turkey	9
Developing	Iraq	22
Developing	Zambia	42

Source: World Bank

Key terms

Migration: the movement of people between countries.

Emigration: where people leave one country to go to another.

Immigration: where people come into a country from other countries.

Net migration: the difference between emigration and immigration.

In addition, migration plays a part in determining population growth. In many developing countries there is, often, a net outflow, emigration, of people seeking employment and higher standards of living in other countries, whereas in countries, such as the UK, there is a net inflow, or immigration. The difference between emigration and immigration is net migration.

Table 11.10 Some causes of changes in birth rate, death rate and infant mortality rate ▼

Birth rate	Death rate	Infant mortality rate
Female education and employment: increases lead to lower birth rate	Medical services and health care and medical advances: as these improve, death rate falls	Medical services and health care and medical advances: reduction in death at birth and from infectious diseases
Family planning services increase then birth rate falls	State of the country: abolition of internal conflicts and reduced violent crime lead to falling death rate	Education for mothers so they are more aware of factors like "sudden infant death syndrome"
Economic prosperity: increases in this result in lower birth rates; whereas with poverty children are often seen as an economic resource	Living standards: especially in relation to better nutrition, clean drinking water, improved hygiene and better quality housing all reduce the death rate	Nutrition: improvements in nutrition both for expectant mothers and for children when born reduce the rate
Social and religious beliefs can affect birth rates especially in relation to contraception and abortion	Increased income: individuals can achieve better nutrition, etc; for countries more money to spend on health etc	Increased income for families so home conditions are better and better care can be afforded

It is often assumed that migration is increasing, but the number of people living outside their country of birth has been a relatively stable percentage of the world's population for a long time, although with substantial fluctuations. Equally, although ten countries, United States, Germany, Russia, Saudi Arabia, United Kingdom, United Arab Emirates, Canada, France, Australia, and Spain dominate global migration, the majority of people from developing countries in fact go to another such country. Among the factors causing migration are:

- lack of safety, including war and crime
- crop failure, including drought and flooding
- lack of opportunities, including employment and education
- poverty.

Optimum population

The optimum population is the population size that results in the maximum income per head. Given the stock of natural resources, production methods and the capital stock of a country, there will be a definite population size corresponding to the highest per capita income.

If the population of a country is less than the optimum, there will not be enough people to fully use all of the resources. If an increase in population results in an increase in per capita income then the country is under-populated. If, however, the population is above the optimum there will be too many people to work efficiently and produce the maximum goods so the per capita income falls.

Key terms

Optimum population: the population size that results in the maximum income per head.

Urbanisation: the increase in people living in towns and cities.

Level of urbanisation

Urbanisation is the increase in the proportion of people living in towns and cities. This has become very important in developing countries.

Vila Estrutural, Brasilia ▲

Urbanisation is about a concentration of people. The majority of the world's population live in urban areas, but most people do not live in cities. The majority of global urbanisation is currently happening in small towns. This is even the case in Asia and Africa where urbanisation is increasing fastest, although the pace is slower than has been predicted.

While the growth of cities and towns can lead to economic growth and increased prosperity, it is also true that these large urban areas can result in poverty and crime.

Link

For Gini coefficient see Chapter 3, section 3.3.2.

Case Study

Future urbanisation in India

In 2011, the urban population was 31.8 per cent, but by 2036 it is forecast to increase to 38.2 per cent. In the period 2020–2036, urban growth would account for about 75 per cent of total population increase.

It is expected that 100 per cent of the population of National Capital Territory of Delhi, Chandigarh and Lakshadweep would be living in urban areas, but only 10.5 per cent of the population of Himachal Pradesh, a mountain state of northern India. Many southern Indian states such as Kerala, are expected to show steep rises in urbanisation.

1. Explain two possible causes of the rise in urban population from 2011 to 2036.
2. Explain two possible consequences of this urbanisation.
3. Discuss why some states in India are rapidly urbanising while others are not.

Source: The New Indian Express

11.4.2 *Income distribution*

The Lorenz curve is a graphical representation showing the extent of inequality in the distribution of income in an economy. The more unequal the distribution of income in an economy, the more divergent the Lorenz curve will be from the diagonal line of absolute equality.

Key term

Lorenz curve: a method of showing the degree of inequality in the distribution of income and wealth in an economy.

Calculation of Gini coefficient and Lorenz curve analysis

Figure 11.6 shows how Lorenz curves can demonstrate the distribution of income in, and between, countries, in this case countries X and Y. The 45 degree line represents a totally even distribution of income. The greater the degree of inequality, the further the Lorenz curve will be below the 45 degree line. The difference between the 45 degree line and the Lorenz curve is called the inequality gap. It is clear that this is the case with Country X, indicating that income is more unevenly distributed in Country X than in Country Y.

The Gini coefficient can be calculated using the formula: Gini Coefficient $= \frac{a}{a + b}$, where 'a' is the area above the Lorenz curve and 'b' is the area below the Lorenz curve (see Figure 11.6). The higher is the value of the Gini coefficient, the more unequal is income distributed so 0 is perfect equality and 1 is perfect inequality. Values for different countries for 2021 are shown in Table 11.11.

Table 11.11 Gini coefficient values 2021 for selected countries ▼

Country	Gini coefficient
Thailand	0.846
Saudi Arabia	0.834
Lesotho	0.805
Brunei	0.787
Jamaica	0.775
Costa Rica	0.750
Austria	0.739
Nepal	0.710
Portugal	0.692
Slovakia	0.498

Source: World Population Review

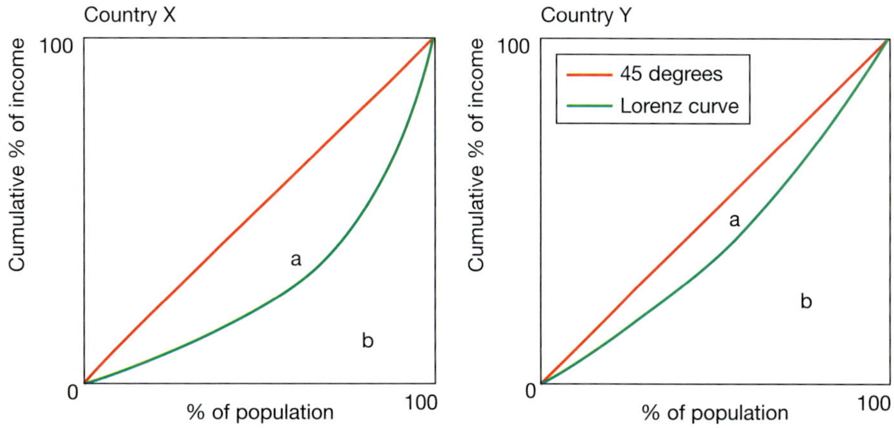

Figure 11.6 A comparison of the income equality in two countries ▲

11.4.3 *Economic structure*

The economic structure relates to the fact that any economy can be divided into a number of different sectors. There are three such sectors although one of them (the secondary sector) is often divided into two parts.

Employment composition: primary, secondary and tertiary sectors

- Primary: The primary sector is concerned with extractive activities and examples would include forestry, fishing, agriculture, mining, quarrying and oil extraction.
- Secondary: The secondary sector can be divided into two parts. Firstly, it is concerned with manufacturing activities and examples would include car production, computers and textiles. Secondly, it is concerned with construction activities and examples would include the building of roads, houses and factories.
- Tertiary: The tertiary sector is concerned with the various services that are provided in an economy, such as financial services, education and health.

Countries vary enormously in the division of their economy into these three distinct sectors. Table 11.12 shows the division of a range of countries into these three sectors on the basis of the proportion of the workforce that work in the different sectors.

Table 11.12 Economic structure of selected countries by proportion of the workforce employed in each sector in 2020 ▼

Country	Primary sector	Secondary sector	Tertiary sector
Afghanistan	42	19	39
Algeria	10	30	60
Barbados	3	18	79
Denmark	2	18	80
India	41	27	32
Mozambique	70	9	21
Peru	27	15	58
Somalia	83	4	13

Source: World Bank

Activity

Gini coeffcient

With reference to Table 11.11 find out what the Gini coefficient is for your country and any two others.
Discuss what these values tell you.

Key terms

Primary sector: refers to all activities in an economy that are concerned with extraction, such as agriculture.
Secondary sector: refers to all activities in an economy that are concerned with either manufacturing, such as the production of televisions, or construction, such as the building of an airport runway.
Tertiary sector: refers to all activities in an economy that are concerned with services, such as tourism.

The figures for the size of the primary, secondary and tertiary sectors in any particular country will not be static, but will change over a period of time as a country becomes more developed. It would be expected that the size of the primary sector would fall, the size of the secondary sector would first grow and then shrink and the size of the tertiary sector would continually grow.

Pattern of trade at different levels of development

The global economy has grown continuously since the Second World War. Global growth has been accompanied by a change in the pattern of trade, which reflects changes in the structure of the global economy. These changes include: the rise of regional trading blocs; deindustrialisation in many advanced economies; the increased participation of former communist countries; and the emergence of China and India.

Demographic change affects trade through its impact on countries' comparative advantage and on import demand. An ageing population, migration, educational improvements and women's participation in the labour force have and will continue to be important in changing trade patterns.

Traditionally the pattern of trade has been reflected by:

- developed countries having a greater share of global trade than developing countries
- developed countries usually export valuable manufactured goods such as electronics and cars and import cheaper primary products such as tea and coffee from developing countries
- the greatest volume of trade occurring between the developed, rich countries, especially between countries such as Germany, Japan, the United Kingdom and the United States.

Changing patterns are as follows:

- Developed countries have seen the comparative advantage they once had in manufacturing shift to developing countries especially to those in Asia such as China and South Korea. The developed countries are importing far more manufactured goods, but are exporting services.
- The greatest shift has been in the exporting of goods, both traditional manufactured ones and hi-tech, by China and India.
- Some countries have resources which are now in high demand for electric bar batteries, mobile phones, etc. As these are essential for modern technological equipment, countries producing them will see exports and trade increase.
- Trading agreements, especially bilateral ones, such as that between Canada and the EU, and trading blocs, such as the EU and MERCOSUR, result in trade diversion towards trade creation with its members.

Activity

Three sectors

Research your own country and find out information about:

1 the size of the three sectors
2 the change in the size of the three sectors over the last hundred years.

Progress question

5 Explain how knowledge of the economic structure of a country would help in understanding its stage of development.

Key terms

Trading blocs: a group of countries which have preferential trading arrangements with each other, leading to more trade amongst members, resulting in some *trade diversion* from non-member countries.

Deindustrialisation: involves a decrease in the relative size and importance of the industrial sector in an economy.

Key terms

Bilateral trading agreements: involve preferential trading arrangements between two countries or groups of countries.

MERCOSUR: consists of Argentina, Brazil, Paraguay, Uruguay and Venezuela.

Link

For trade diversion and trade creation see section 11.6.3 of this chapter.

11.5 Relationship between countries at different levels of development

11.5.1 *International aid*

International aid is the giving of money and/or goods by one country to another or by an organisation to another country.

Forms of aid

Aid comes in a variety of forms and classifications. One way is shown in Table 11.13.

Table 11.13 Forms of international aid ▼

Form of aid	Explanation
Economic aid	This is intended to support the economies of recipient countries. Generally this aid is provided by one country to one or more other countries. Aid of this type can be in the form of loans, grants or credits. It is sometimes tied to the recipient country spending the money in a given way.
Bilateral aid	This is a form of economic aid. It is when a single country gives aid to another.
Multilateral aid	Again this is a form of economic aid. It is when international organizations such as the World Bank, the United Nations, etc. receive funding from multiple countries and then disburse that money to countries so they can use it for improvements in many ways.
Humanitarian aid	Although governments do give humanitarian aid to other countries, it is often provided by Non-Governmental Organisations (NGOs). The primary purpose of humanitarian aid is to improve the social wellbeing and the living situations for people in the recipient country. This can take place in response to a natural disaster, in which emergency supplies like first aid, water, food and clothing go to a country in need.
Military aid	This is aid given to strengthen the security of a country. This aid may be in the form of weapons, training of military personnel; or the provision of military personnel to work with the country's own forces. This type of aid is often controversial.

Reasons for giving aid

Countries provide aid for a wide variety of reasons. Aid programmes often serve several purposes simultaneously. It is difficult, therefore, to state which might be the most important. The reasons include:

- to promote economic development, sometimes through international organisations
- to help in the reduction of poverty
- to promote a country's exports by requiring the recipient country to use the aid to purchase the donor country's products
- to relieve suffering caused by natural or man-made disasters such as earthquakes or diseases
- to try to prevent the destruction of the environment
- to help improve their own security by preventing friendly governments from falling under the influence of unfriendly ones or as payment for

Key term

International aid: the giving of money and/or goods by one country to another or by an organisation to another country.

Activity

Trade patterns

Find out how your country's trade patterns have changed during your lifetime.
You may wish to divide the work up using the following and then to exchange information.

1. What are the main goods you export and import?
2. What are the main services you export and import?
3. Which are the main countries involved in your trade in goods and services?

Key term

Non-Governmental Organisations (NGOs): a non-profit group that functions independently of any government. Examples include Medicine sans Frontiers and Oxfam.

> **Activity**
>
> **Receiving aid**
>
> If your country has received aid, try to find out why it was given. Do you think there were any other reasons?
> If your country has not received aid, then choose another country for this activity.

the right to establish or use military bases in the aid receiving country or to combat international terrorism, and other crimes

- to achieve a country's political goals including getting support for its positions in international organisations, or to increase its diplomats' access to foreign officials
- to increase the influence of its language, culture or religion.

Effects of aid

There is no agreement on whether international aid is good, bad or somewhere between. This is because the effect of aid often depends on the political situation in the country. Table 11.14 sets out some of the positive and some of the negative effects.

Table 11.14 Some positive and negative effects of aid ▼

Positive	Negative
It promotes economic growth especially in countries with good governance.	Increases aid dependency, harming domestic producers, and supports poor economic management. This can be because aid donors fail to coordinate activities or because of corruption.
It reduces poverty through the provision of jobs and by direct action such as clean drinking water supplies.	Aid tied to buying from the donor may lead to the purchase of poorer quality and/or higher priced products.
Aid is often most effective when directed at areas such as enhancing education, building rural and urban infrastructure, protecting private property, and reducing trade risks.	Government approach: in some countries aid has generally benefited the ruling elite so that instead of creating prosperity and economic development it has reduced the living standards of most of the inhabitants of the country.

> **Link**
>
> For corruption see later in this section.

> **Progress question**
>
> 6 Discuss how effective aid has been in your country, or in a country of your choice.

Importance of aid

Importance of foreign aid clearly overlaps with many of the points given in the previous sections. Table 11.15 list some of the areas of importance with a brief explanation.

Table 11.15 The importance of aid ▼

Importance	Explanation
Humanitarian help in crises	Provides quick and large-scale help in times of e.g. natural disasters until the country can take over the disaster relief effort.
Improving health	Helps to eliminate diseases in developing countries such as smallpox in 1980 and the UN project for HIV/AIDS by 2030. Includes, also, vaccinations, safe drinking water, hygiene education and basic sanitation.
Provision of infrastructure	Provides not only roads and bridges, but also communication systems, electricity, schools and health clinics, etc.
Promotes economic growth and development Better agriculture	Increasing industry results in more goods and services produced which can attract new investors leading to further development. Farmers can be taught how to utilise their land and resources, including machinery, more efficiently to produce more crops to feed more people.
Poverty relief	In 2019, just under 600 million people were in extreme poverty. By 2030, this figure is expected to fall to some 436 million. Many of the poor live in rural areas where they do not have access to adequate medical treatment and education.
World security	Aid reduces the threat of terrorism by reducing poverty and can help strengthen good governance, transparency and the economy.

11.5.2 *Trade and investment*

Foreign direct investment (FDI) has become a key element of trade between different countries. Traditionally a firm in one country would invest in either the natural resources of another country by, for example, opening a mine or would set up a factory in another country, often to get round trade barriers. Today, however, rather than businesses in one country simply trading with international partners, more and more companies are buying controlling stakes in foreign enterprises.

Global value chains (GVCs) have increased the interdependency between trade and FDI as companies combine trade with investment to organise the supply of inputs, to expand in new markets, to access knowledge, and to provide services to consumers.

In addition, whereas thirty years ago FDI was mainly from the developed countries to the developing ones, nowadays many developing countries such as China, India and the UAE have invested in other countries. This has created a more global world and a great expansion of trade.

The World Bank has said that FDI is not only about capital, but increasingly about sharing technology and intangible assets such as know-how or brands in conjunction with local capital or tangible assets of domestic investors.

Getting it right

Make sure you read the section on aid all together so as to get a full overall picture.

Activity

Importance of aid

As a group discuss how important aid has been for your country, or another of your choice.

Link

For trade see Chapter 6, section 6.1.
For globalisation see section 11.6 of this chapter.

Activity

Trade and investment

Individually try to find at least six examples of FDI in your country. Then share this information and build up a larger picture of FDI. Is there evidence of this increasing trade between your country and the one from which the FDI comes?

Key terms

Foreign direct investment (FDI): finance to provide for the building or purchase of productive assets in a country by the residents of a different country.

Global value chains (GVCs): refer to international production sharing where it is broken down into activities and tasks carried out in different countries. This is like a large-scale extension of division of labour.

Multinational corporations (MNC): firms that have their head offices in one country, but have operations in a number of other countries.

11.5.3 *Role of multinational companies (MNCs)*

Definition of MNC

Multinational corporations (MNCs) – sometimes called transnational corporations – are firms that operate in a number of different countries. They have their head offices in one country, but have operations in a number of other countries.

Activities of MNCs

MNCs indulge in a range of activities including:

- factories to manufacture the whole product
- factories to manufacture parts which are then sent to factories in other countries
- factories to assemble parts from other factories in different countries
- expanding their size through mergers and takeovers

- sponsoring relevant university courses and employing the best graduates
- FDI (see above and below)
- supporting cultural, sporting, etc. activities.

> **Key term**
> **Economic dependency**: exists when one country does not control its resources and is dependent on other countries for investment and production in major industries.

Consequences of MNCs

Among the top twenty firms are Royal Dutch Shell, Sinopec Group, Toyota and Glencore International. Royal Dutch Shell's revenue in 2019 at $344.9 billion is greater than the majority of countries.

Over a number of years the total FDI received can amount to many times a country's GDP. While FDI increases growth and employment in a country and, therefore, has a multiplier effect, it may not be entirely beneficial as profits are sent back to the home country of the MNC while they may bring with them their own skilled workforce rather than training people in the developing country. In some cases this can lead to economic dependency where one country exploits the resources of another for the former's benefit. In Nigeria the oil industry is totally dependent on the FDI received from a number of foreign firms. In addition, domestic businesses may not be able to compete with MNCs and go out of business allowing the MNC to gain a larger market share. MNCs have been accused, also, of: avoiding paying the correct amount of tax due to tax avoidance schemes; imposing their culture on the country; and not acting in socially-responsible ways.

> **Link**
> For mergers and takeovers see Chapter 7, section 7.7.3.

> **Activity**
> **Multinationals**
> 1 In which countries are the head offices of the four firms mentioned in the text?
> 2 How does your country's GDP in US $ compare with that of Royal Dutch Shell?
> 3 Find out about five other multinationals that operate in your country. What is their policy on employment?
> 4 Do they have any domestic rivals?

MNCs do, however, bring considerable benefits including:

- employment and training for the labour force, together with transfer of skills
- significant tax revenues enabling the country to spend more on, for example, education and health
- greater investment with often this providing extra income for local suppliers
- incentives to domestic firms to improve their competitiveness through the competition they provide
- greater consumer and business choice
- greater GDP through their spending and investment.

11.5.4 *Foreign Direct Investment (FDI)*

> **Link**
> For more on FDI see section 11.5 of this chapter.

Definition of FDI

UNCTAD defines FDI as "investment made to acquire lasting interest in enterprises operating outside of the economy of the investor". It is investment in the form of a controlling ownership in a business in one country by an individual or organisation based in another country. It involves the idea of direct control as against just an investment.

> **Key term**
> **UNCTAD**: United Nations Conference for Trade and Development

Consequences of FDI

Some of the main consequences, both positive and negative, are set out in Table 11.16.

Table 11.16 Consequences of FDI ▼

Positive	Negative
Economic growth – allows countries to obtain higher economic growth by opening the economy up to new markets, as seen in many developing countries.	Long-term capital movement – in some cases once the investment becomes profitable, capital begins to flow out of the host country and to the investor's country.
Job creation and employment – often creates new businesses in the country leading to both job creation and, also, higher wages.	Local industry – in some circumstances it may cause problems for local firms by taking away some of their market and by attracting the best workers.
Technology transfer – FDI brings with it new modern technology and technical expertise.	Foreign exchange rate – the inflow of capital will increase exchange rate and could make exports less competitive.
Terms of trade – an increase in the exchange rate due to the inflow of capital will lead to an improvement in the terms of trade.	

11.5.5 *External debt*

External debt consists of the part of the total debt of a country that is owed to people, firms, banks, international financial organisations which are external to the country together with foreign governments.

Causes of debt

The main causes of external debt in recent years have been:

- persistent trade deficits leading to borrowing money to pay for the goods and services and to support the exchange rate
- high internal debts caused by consistently spending more than revenue
- high inflation leading to having to borrow with high interest rates which make repayment ever more difficult; Argentina has defaulted on its debts on a number of occasions, the last being in 2020
- misuse of funds: funds are often used to boost consumption rather than for capital investment; in other cases corruption plays a part
- over lending by foreign banks.

Consequences of debt

External debt in itself is not a problem. Indeed, economic theory suggests that a reasonable level of debt should help both developing and developed countries enhance their economic growth. This is true especially if the debt is a result of investment in areas such as infrastructure, new production methods, etc.

The negative consequences come about because the debt is too large. Among these consequences are:

- decline in economic growth as the servicing of the debt of the country causes large outflows of money
- decline in economic development as repaying the debt will mean less money for education, infrastructure, health care, etc.

Key term

External debt: the part of the total debt of a country that is owed to people, firms, banks international financial organisations which are external to the country together with foreign governments.

Link

For corruption see Table 11.14.

Key term

Debt servicing: the money required to cover the repayment of interest and principal on a debt for a particular period.

- loss of confidence as lenders worry about whether they will lose their money and are hesitant to lend more. This often leads to high interest rates on future loans
- fall in the external and internal values of the currency to the point where the currency may become unusable in terms of buying imports or even buying these imports in shops.

Case Study

External debt in sub-Saharan Africa

Developing countries rely on external borrowing both because excessive domestic borrowing can lead to financial instability and also because developing countries often need to borrow externally because of inadequate domestic capital for investment.

External debt has had two main effects on countries in sub-Saharan Africa.

In the first place FDI has enhanced economic growth through investment in industry and in infrastructure including education, health facilities, sanitation and water supplies.

On the other hand, debt servicing has had a very negative effect. GDP growth decreases as total debt service increases. Payments crowd out internal investment while often requiring governments to cut their budgets to service the debt.

One way forward is to adopt policies that create incentives for domestic investment, including FDI, and can increase export earnings, thus reducing dependence on external debt for economic development.

1 Explain how FDI can enhance economic growth "through investment in industry and in infrastructure".
2 Explain how debt servicing can have a negative effect on growth.
3 Discuss the extent to which the policies suggested would lead to economic development.

11.5.6 *Role of the International Monetary Fund (IMF)*

The International Monetary Fund (IMF) is one of the agencies that keep track of the country's external debt.

It aims to offer:

- policy advice to governments and central banks based on analysis of economic trends and cross-country experiences
- research, statistics, forecasts, and analysis based on tracking of global, regional, and individual economies and markets
- loans to help countries overcome economic difficulties
- concessional loans to help fight poverty in developing countries
- technical assistance and training to help countries improve the management of their economies.

Key terms

International Monetary Fund (IMF): an overarching international organisation which, amongst other tasks, offers advice to governments and central banks and makes loans to countries with severe economic difficulties.

World Bank: provides loans for developing countries. Its official goal is the reduction of poverty. According to its Articles of Agreement, all its decisions must be guided by a commitment to the promotion of foreign investment and international trade and to the facilitation of capital investment. The World Bank group consists of five agencies.

11.5.7 *Role of the World Bank*

The World Bank group consists of five agencies:

- The International Bank for Reconstruction and Development (IBRD) lends to governments of middle-income and creditworthy low-income countries.
- The International Development Association (IDA) provides interest-free loans, called credits, and grants to governments of the poorest countries.

- The International Finance Corporation (IFC) provides loans, equity and technical assistance to stimulate private sector investment in developing countries.
- The Multilateral Investment Guarantee Agency (MIGA) provides guarantees against losses caused by non-commercial risks to investors in developing countries.
- The International Centre for Settlement of Investment Disputes (ICSID) provides international facilities for conciliation and arbitration of investment disputes.

Both the IMF and the World Bank aim to try to help countries with debt problems to overcome them through a mixture of advice and aid.

11.6 Globalisation

11.6.1 *Meaning of globalisation and its causes and consequences*

Globalisation is the spread of products, technology, information and jobs across national borders and cultures. In economic terms, it describes an interdependence of nations around the globe fostered through free trade.

There are lots of possible causes of globalisation, but the main ones are shown in Table 11.17.

Key term

Globalisation: the expansion of world trade in goods and services, together with capital flows, leading to greater international interdependence.

Table 11.17 Causes of globalisation ▼

Cause	Explanation
Improved transport	Allows for greater movement of people and goods across the globe.
Containerisation	The lower unit cost of shipping products helps to bring prices in the country of manufacture closer to those in export markets, and it makes markets more contestable globally.
Communications	The growth of the internet makes it easier to communicate and share information. Where a business is and where its products are being made are much closer together. This may overcome managerial diseconomies of scale. Equally, consumers are able to order online.
Reduction in trade barriers	There has, in general, been a decline in trade barriers.
MNCs	Prepared to move wherever they can gain the greatest advantages. This has also increased the mobility of capital and labour.
Economies of scale	If the minimum efficient scale associated with an industry is rising, a domestic market may be regarded as too small to satisfy the selling needs of these industries.

Link

For free trade see section 11.6.2 of this chapter and Chapter 6, section 6.1.
For deindustrialisation see section 11.4.3 of this chapter.
For MNCs see section 11.5.3 of this chapter.
Trade cycles are covered in Chapter 9, section 9.2.3.

The consequences of globalisation include:

- economic growth: adopting a more open trade policy allows a country to profit from international trade and FDI leading to the introduction of new technologies and a higher competitiveness. MNCs provide new jobs and skills
- consumers enjoy a greater choice of goods and services at lower prices
- global trade cycle: as countries are increasingly interconnected, a crises in one country may cause problems in other countries. This can be true for changes in the business cycle and financial crashes

Activity

Globalisation

Find out as much as possible about how globalisation has affected your country. Discuss whether the benefits have outweighed the costs.

Progress question

7 Explain two major causes of globalisation.

Key terms

Free trade area: a group of countries that have few or no price controls in the form of tariffs or quotas between each other.

Customs union: a group of countries that have free trade between members, but common external barriers.

Monetary union: a group of countries with a single currency, or different currencies having a fixed mutual exchange rate monitored and controlled by one central bank.

Full economic union: a customs union which also co-ordinates a range of other economic policies, including social, fiscal and monetary, among its members.

Link

For protection and tariffs see Chapter 6, section 6.2.

Link

For monetary policy see Chapter 5, section 5.3.

- tax competition: to attract MNCs, many countries have engaged in tax competition both in terms of taxes on profits, thus gaining more FDI, and to attract foreign workers
- MNCs may drive local companies out of business
- deindustrialisation in developed countries.

11.6.2 *Distinction between a free trade area, a customs union, a monetary union and full economic union*

Free trade area

In recent years a number of trading blocs have been formed, each of which practises free trade between members.

Table 11.18 Some examples of trading blocs

Trading Bloc	Membership
European Union (EU)	27 members, 18 of whom are members of the single currency (Euro)
Association of Southeast Asian Nations (ASEAN)	10 members
North American Free Trade Association (NAFTA)	Canada, Mexico and USA
Union of South American Nations (USAM)	12 members (including MERCOSUR, the Andean Community of Nations, Chile, Guyana and Surinam)

A free trade area consists of countries which have removed barriers to trade between themselves, but maintain their own individual barriers against non-member countries. Free trade areas include: European Free Trade Area - EFTA (EEA), NAFTA and South Asian Free Trade Area –SAFTA.

Customs union

In contrast, a customs union has free trade between its members, but common external tariff barriers against all non-members. An example of a common market is the Caribbean Community (CARICOM).

Monetary union

In the case of a monetary union, the members adopt the same currency. This implies a common central bank which controls the quantity of money and the rate of interest and by so doing seeks to influence the rate of inflation in the member countries.

18 members of the EU have formed a monetary union with the euro (€) as its currency. It is called the Eurozone. Although each member has kept its own central bank, the Eurozone is managed by the European Central Bank which sets monetary policy.

Full economic union

Economic Union is the highest form of integration encompassing the features of a common market, but going further to develop some harmonisation of economic policies. The EU, for example, has developed a range of policies in such areas as competition, agriculture and social policies. The Common Agricultural Policy (CAP) is one such example. CARICOM has also moved in this direction by creating the CARICOM Single Market and Economy (CMSE).

CMSE members have adopted measures to converge and coordinate their macroeconomic policies, harmonise foreign investment decisions and facilitate technology transfer. In monetary and fiscal policy there are measures to coordinate exchange rate and interest rate policy as well as coordinate indirect taxes and national budget deficits.

In some ways economic integration into regional trading blocs can be regarded as a "second best solution" in that it enables members to enjoy the benefits of comparative advantage, but involves protectionist policies against non members and consequently stops short of allowing all nations in the world to benefit from free trade.

11.6.3 *Trade creation and trade diversion*

Trade creation and trade diversion

A feature of customs unions and higher forms of economic integration is that member nations experience both trade creation and trade diversion.

Key terms

Trade creation: transfer of consumption from high to low cost producers.

Trade diversion: transfer of consumption from low to high cost producers.

As a result of trade barriers being removed when a country enters a customs union, it can now buy goods at a lower price. For example, before joining the EU, if Malta wished to buy pasta from Italy it would have to pay a tariff thereby raising the price in Malta. Now Malta is a member of the EU, the tariff has been abolished and consumers can now purchase the pasta at a lower price, increasing their welfare. This shifting of consumption from high to low cost producer is known as trade creation.

However, membership of a customs union may lead to trade diversion. For example, before joining the EU, Ireland could buy cheap food from the lowest cost producer. However, now that Ireland is a member of the EU, she is required to impose the EU Common External Tariff on goods from non-EU members. As a result, this cheap food has become more expensive than the same food products produced by other members of the EU. As a result, although Irish consumers may be purchasing from the cheapest nation in the EU, they are paying more than previously. This is trade diversion, the transfer of consumption from low to high cost producers.

Trade creation

Trade creation occurs when the removal of tariff barriers results in an increase in consumer welfare. In Figure 11.7, DH and SH represent the domestic demand for and supply of tomatoes in Ireland. Assuming that:

- Ireland imports tomatoes from Spain
- the supply of tomatoes from Spain is perfectly elastic, so that the supply curve is S_S
- Ireland imposes a tariff on Spanish tomatoes equal to P_2P_1.

The effective supply curve for tomatoes from Spain is, therefore, Ss + Tariff.

Originally, the quantity of tomatoes in Ireland will be Q_1 of which OQ_2 is produced in the UK and Q_2Q_1 is imported. The price will be P_1. At this price Irish citizens' consumer surplus is given by the areas 1 + 2.

If Ireland and Spain enter into a customs union the tariff will be removed and the price of Spanish tomatoes falls to P_2. Consumption of tomatoes in Ireland increases to OQ_3 of which OQ_4 is supplied by Irish producers and Q_4Q_3 imported. Trade creation has resulted as there has been a movement away from high cost production to low cost production. Irish consumer surplus has now been increased by:

1 + 2 + 3 + 4

The overall welfare gain is, however, only areas 2 + 4 since area 1 represents a redistribution of producer surplus to consumers and area 3 a redistribution from the government to consumers (lost tariff revenue).

In this case there has been a net gain in welfare for Ireland.

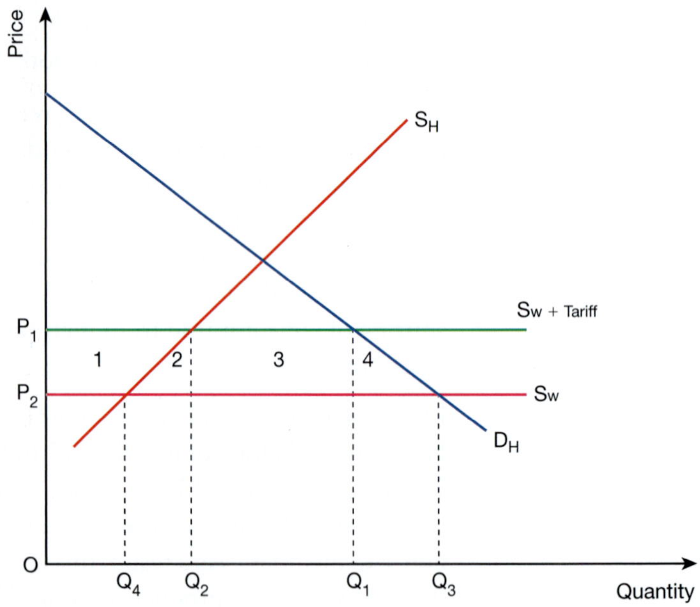

Figure 11.7 Trade creation ▲

Link

For consumer and producer surplus see Chapter 2, section 2.5.

Trade diversion

Trade diversion is when a tariff is imposed so that consumers can no longer benefit from low cost supply. Assume that before the creation of the customs union the UK is importing tomatoes from the cheapest world producers. In Figure 11.8, D_H and S_H again represent the UK domestic demand for and supply of tomatoes and Sw represents the world supply curve. Before the customs union, there were no tariffs on tomatoes. OQ_3 tomatoes would be consumed with OQ_4 produced in the UK and Q_2Q_3 imported.

If now the UK and Spain become part of a customs union, then a tariff is imposed on imported tomatoes from outside the customs union meaning it is cheaper for the UK to purchase tomatoes from less efficient producers such as Spain. The price rises to Sw + tariff. The demand falls to Q_1, but UK production increases to Q_2 with Q_2Q_1 being imported from Spain. The results will be:

- consumer welfare falls by 1 + 2 + 3 + 4
- government revenue rises shown by 3
- producer surplus rises by 1
- deadweight loss (lost by consumers, but not gained by government/producer) 2 + 4

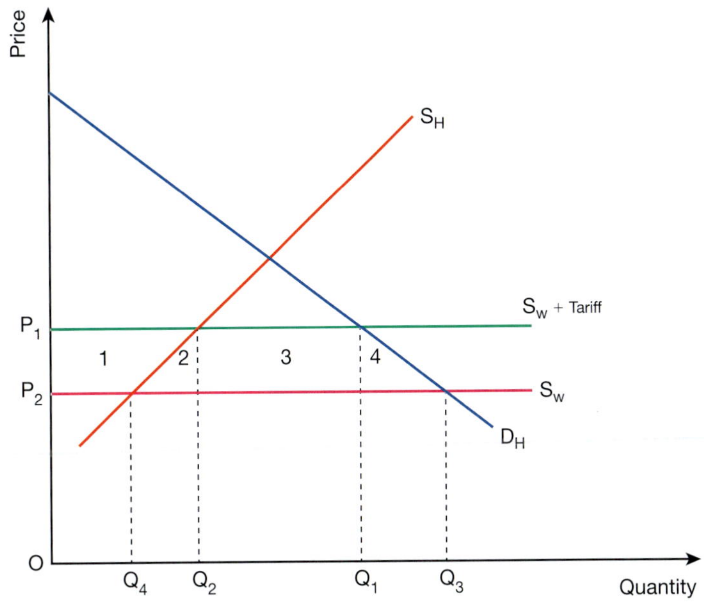

Figure 11.8 Trade diversion ▲

Progress question

8 What factors are likely to determine whether joining a customs union will lead to trade creation or trade diversion for a country?

Activity

Economic integration

Conduct a class investigation to discover:

1. whether your country is a member of a regional trading bloc and if so which one
2. the type of trading bloc
3. the other members of the trading bloc
4. the advantages and disadvantages to your country of being a member of this trading bloc
5. whether membership of the trading bloc has resulted in trade creation or trade diversion; if so give an example.

Key concepts

- **Scarcity and choice** can be seen throughout the chapter.
- **Time** can be seen throughout the chapter.
- **Progress and development** can be seen in economic development and globalisation.

Progress check

After completing this chapter you should be able to:

- explain the components of the balance of payments
- explain the policies to correct disequilibrium in the balance of payments
- explain how exchange rates are measured
- explain fixed and managed exchange rates including revaluation and devaluation
- explain how exchange rates can change and assess the effect of change on the external economy
- outline the classification of economies in relation to development
- explain the indicators of living standards and economic development
- compare economic growth and living standards
- explain the characteristics of countries at different levels of development
- explain the relationship between countries at different levels of development
- explain the meaning of globalisation along with its causes and consequences
- explain differences between free trade areas, custom unions, monetary unions and full economic unions
- analyse trade creation and trade diversion.

Exam-style questions

Essay and data response questions

1 Discuss whether fiscal policies would be the best way of dealing with a deficit on the balance of payments. [20 marks]

2 Assess the effects of a rising exchange rate on the external economy of a country. [20 marks]

3 Evaluate the statement that the multidimensional poverty index [MDI] is the best way of measuring living standards in developing economies. [20 marks]

4 Discuss whether the presence of multinational corporations [MNCs] is beneficial for developing countries. [20 marks]

5 Evaluate the extent to which a developing country should encourage foreign direct investment. [20 marks]

6 Assess the problems involved in comparing living standards between two countries. [20 marks]

Multiple-choice questions

1 The capital account of the balance of payments is concerned with: [1mark]

A changes in a country's asset ownership

B transactions in external financial assets and liabilities

C balancing items to reflect imperfections in source data

D movements of money due to changes in interest rates

2 Which of the following could be described as: ‘it involves changes in the composition of real output and a consequent shift in the allocation of resources as well as the reduction of poverty, inequalities and unemployment’. [1 mark]

A Economic growth
B Economic development
C International aid
D Living standards

A LEVEL ECONOMICS SYLLABUS MATCHING GRID

Topic number in this book	Topic title	Syllabus section
1.1.1	The fundamental economic problem of scarcity	1.1.1
1.1.2	The need to make choices at all levels	1.1.2
1.1.3	The nature and definition of opportunity cost	1.1.3
1.1.4	The basic questions of resource allocation	1.1.4
1.2.1	Economics as a social science	1.2.1
1.2.2	Positive and normative statements	1.2.2
1.2.3	The meaning of the term "ceteris paribus"	1.2.3
1.2.4	The importance of the time period	1.2.4
1.3.1	The nature and definition of the factors of production	1.3.1
1.3.2	The difference between human capital and physical capital	1.3.2
1.3.3	The rewards to the factors of production	1.3.3
1.3.4	Division of labour and specialisation	1.3.4
1.3.5	The role of the entrepreneur in contemporary economies	1.3.5
1.4.1 & 1.4.2	Decision-making in market, planned and mixed economies	1.4.1 & 1.4.2
1.5.1	The nature and meaning of a production possibility curve (PPC)	1.5.1
1.5.2	The shape of the PPC: constant and increasing costs	1.5.2
1.5.3	The causes and consequences of shifts in a PPC	1.5.3
1.5.4	The significance of a position within a PPC	1.5.4
1.6.1	The nature and definition of free goods and private goods (economic goods)	1.6.1
1.6.2	The nature and definition of public goods	1.6.2
1.6.3	The nature and definition of merit goods	1.6.3
1.6.4	The nature and definition of demerit goods	1.6.4
2.1.1	Effective demand	2.1.1
2.1.2	Individual and market demand and supply	2.1.2
2.1.3	Determinants of demand	2.1.3
2.1.4	Determinants of supply	2.1.4
2.1.5	Causes of a shift in the demand curve (D)	2.1.5
2.1.6	Causes of a shift in the supply curve (S)	2.1.6
2.1.7	Distinction between the shift in the demand or supply curve and the movement along these curves	2.1.7
2.2.1	Definition of price elasticity, income elasticity and cross elasticity of demand	2.2.1
2.2.2	Formulae for and calculation of price elasticity, income elasticity and cross elasticity of demand	2.2.2
2.2.3	Significance of relative percentage changes, the size and sign of the coefficient of price, income and cross elasticity of demand	2.2.3
2.2.4	Descriptions of elasticity values: perfectly elastic, (highly) elastic, unitary elasticity, (highly) inelastic, perfectly inelastic	2.2.4
2.2.5	Variation in price elasticity of demand along the length of a straight-line demand curve	2.2.5
2.2.6	Factors affecting price, income and cross elasticity of demand	2.2.6
2.2.7	Relationship between price elasticity of demand and total expenditure on a product	2.2.7

2.2.8	Implications for decision-making of price elasticity, income elasticity and cross elasticity of demand	2.2.8
2.3.1	Definition of price elasticity of supply (PES)	2.3.1
2.3.2	Formula for and calculation of price elasticity of supply	2.3.2
2.3.3	Significance of relative percentage changes, the size and sign of the coefficient of price elasticity of supply	2.3.3
2.3.4	Factors affecting price elasticity of supply	2.3.4
2.3.5	Implications for speed and ease with which firms react to changed market conditions	2.3.5
2.4.1	Definition of market equilibrium and disequilibrium	2.4.1
2.4.2	Effects of shifts in demand and supply curves on equilibrium price and quantity	2.4.2
2.4.3	Relationships between different markets: joint demand (complements), alternative demand (substitutes), derived demand and joint supply	2.4.3
2.4.4	Functions of price in resource allocation: rationing, signalling (transmission of preferences) and incentivising	2.4.4
2.5.1	Meaning and significance of consumer surplus	2.5.1
2.5.2	Meaning and significance of producer surplus	2.5.2
2.5.3	Causes of changes in consumer and producer surplus	2.5.3
2.5.4	Significance of price elasticity of demand and of supply in determining the extent of these changes	2.5.4
3.1.1	Addressing the non-provision of public goods	3.1.1
3.1.2	Addressing the under-consumption of merit goods and the over-consumption of demerit goods	3.1.2
3.1.3	Controlling prices in markets	3.1.3
3.2.1	The impact and incidence of specific indirect taxes	3.2.1
3.2.2	The impact and incidence of subsidies	3.2.2
3.2.3	The direct provision of goods and services	3.2.3
3.2.4	Maximum and minimum prices	3.2.4
3.2.5	Buffer stock schemes	3.2.5
3.2.6	The provision of information	3.2.6
3.3.1	The difference between income as a flow concept and wealth as a stock concept	3.3.1
3.3.2	Measuring income and wealth inequality; the Gini coefficient	3.3.2
3.3.3	Economic reasons for inequality of income and wealth	3.3.3
3.3.4	Policies to redistribute income and wealth: minimum wage, transfer payments, progressive income taxes, inheritance and capital taxes and state provision of essential goods and services	3.3.4
4.1.1	Meaning of national income	4.1.1
4.1.2	Measurement of national income: GDP, GNI and NNI	4.1.2
4.1.3	Adjustment of measures from market prices to basic prices	4.1.3
4.1.4	Adjustment of measures from gross values to net values	4.1.4
4.2.1	The circular flow of income in a closed economy and an open economy	4.2.1
4.2.2	Injections and leakages	4.2.2
4.2.3	Equilibrium and disequilibrium	4.2.3
4.3.1	Definition of Aggregate Demand (AD)	4.3.1
4.3.2	Components of AD and their meanings: AD=C+I+G+(X-M)	4.3.2

4.3.3	Determinants of AD	4.3.3
4.3.4	Shape of the AD curve	4.3.4
4.3.5	Causes of a shift in the AD curve	4.3.5
4.3.6	Definition of Aggregate Supply (AS)	4.3.6
4.3.7	Determinants of AS	4.3.7
4.3.8	Shape of the AS curve in the short run	4.3.8
4.3.9	Causes of a shift in the AS curve in the short run and in the long run	4.3.9
4.3.10	Distinction between a movement along and a shift in AD and AS	4.3.10
4.3.11	Establishment of equilibrium in the AD/AS model and the determination of real output, the price level and employment	4.3.11
4.3.12	Effects of shifts in the AD curve and the AS curve on the level of real output, the price level and employment	4.3.12
4.4.1	Meaning of economic growth	4.4.1
4.4.2	Measurement of economic growth	4.4.2
4.4.3	Distinction between growth in nominal GDP and real GDP	4.4.3
4.4.4	Causes of economic growth	4.4.4
4.4.5	Consequences of economic growth	4.4.5
4.5.1	Meaning of unemployment	4.5.1
4.5.2	Measures of unemployment, with reference to possible difficulties in measurement	4.5.2
4.5.3	Causes and types of unemployment: frictional, structural, cyclical, seasonal and technological	4.5.3
4.5.4	Consequences of unemployment	4.5.4
4.6.1	Definition of inflation, deflation and disinflation	4.6.1
4.6.2	Measurement of changes in the price level: consumer price index (CPI) and possible difficulties in measurement	4.6.2
4.6.3	Distinction between money values (nominal) and real data	4.6.3
4.6.4	Causes of inflation: cost-push and demand-pull inflation	4.6.4
4.6.5	Consequences of inflation	4.6.5
5.1.1	Use of government policy to achieve macroeconomic objectives: price stability, low unemployment and economic growth	5.1.1
5.2.1	Meaning of government budget	5.2.1
5.2.2	Distinction between a government budget deficit and a government budget surplus	5.2.2
5.2.3	Meaning and significance of the national debt	5.2.3
5.2.4	Taxation: types of taxes, rates of tax and reasons for taxation	5.2.4
5.2.5	Government spending: types of spending and reasons for government spending	5.2.5
5.2.6	Distinction between expansionary and fiscal policy	5.2.6
5.2.7	AD/AS analysis of the impact of expansionary and contractionary fiscal policy on the equilibrium level of national income and the level of real output, the price level and employment	5.2.7
5.3.1	Definition of monetary policy	5.3.1
5.3.2	Tools of monetary policy: interest rates, money supply and credit regulations	5.3.2
5.3.3	Distinction between expansionary and contractionary monetary policy	5.3.3

5.3.4	AD/AS analysis of the impact of expansionary and contractionary monetary policy on the equilibrium national income and the level of real output, the price level and employment	5.3.4
5.4.1	Meaning of supply-side policy, in terms of its effect on LRAS curves	5.4.1
5.4.2	Objectives of supply-side policy: increasing productivity and productive capacity	5.4.2
5.4.3	Tools of supply-side policy, for example training, infrastructure development and support for technological improvement	5.4.3
5.4.4	AD/AS analysis of the impact of supply-side policy on the equilibrium national income and the level of real output, the price level and employment	5.4.4
6.1.1	Distinction between absolute and comparative advantage	6.1.1
6.1.2	Benefits of specialisation and free trade (trade liberalisation), including the trading possibility curve	6.1.2
6.1.3	Exports, imports and the terms of trade: measurement of the terms of trade, causes of changes in the terms of trade and the impact of changes in the terms of trade	6.1.3
6.1.4	Limitations of the theories of absolute and comparative advantage	6.1.4
6.2.1	Meaning of protectionism in the context of international trade	6.2.1
6.2.2	Different tools of protection and their impact: tariffs, import quotas, export subsidies, embargoes and excessive administrative burdens ('red tape')	6.2.2
6.2.3	Arguments for and against protectionism	6.2.3
6.3.1	Components of the current account of the balance of payments: current account (trade in goods, trade in services, primary income and secondary income); definition of balance and imbalances (deficit and surplus) in the current account of the balance of payments	6.3.1
6.3.2	Calculation of balance of trade in goods, balance of trade in services, balance of trade in goods and services and current account balance (CAB)	6.3.2
6.3.3	Causes of imbalances in the current account of the balance of payments	6.3.3
6.3.4	Consequences of imbalances in the current account of the balance of payments for the domestic and external economy	6.3.4
6.4.1	Definition of exchange rate	6.4.1
6.4.2	Determination of a floating exchange rate	6.4.2
6.4.3	Distinction between depreciation and appreciation of a floating exchange rate	6.4.3
6.4.4	Causes of changes in a floating exchange rate: demand and supply of the currency	6.4.4
6.4.5	AD/AS analysis of the impact of exchange rate changes on the domestic economy's equilibrium national income and the level of real output, the price level and employment	6.4.5
6.5.1	Government policy objective of stability of the current account	6.5.1
6.5.2	Effect of fiscal, monetary, supply-side and protectionist policies on the current account	6.5.2
7.1.1	Definition and calculation of total utility and marginal utility	7.1.1
7.1.2	Diminishing marginal utility	7.1.2
7.1.3	Equi-marginal principle	7.1.3
7.1.4	Derivation of an individual demand curve	7.1.4
7.1.5	Limitations of marginal utility theory and its assumptions of rational behaviour	7.1.5
7.2.1	Meaning of an indifference curve and a budget line	7.2.1

7.2.2	Causes of a shift in the budget line	7.2.2
7.2.3	Income, substitution and price effects for normal, inferior and Giffen goods	7.2.3
7.2.4	Limitations of the model of indifference curves	7.2.4
7.3.1	Definitions of productive efficiency and allocative efficiency	7.3.1
7.3.2	Conditions for productive efficiency and allocative efficiency	7.3.2
7.3.3	Pareto optimality	7.3.3
7.3.4	Definition of dynamic efficiency	7.3.4
7.3.5	Definition of market failure	7.3.5
7.3.6	Reasons for market failure	7.3.6
7.4.1	Definition and calculation of social costs (SC) as the sum of private costs (PC) and external costs (EC), including marginal social costs (MSC), marginal private costs (MPC) and marginal external costs (MEC)	7.4.1
7.4.2	Definition and calculation of social benefits (SB) as the sum of private benefits (PB) and external benefits (EB), including marginal social benefits (MSB), marginal private benefits (MPB) and marginal external benefits (MEB)	7.4.2
7.4.3	Definition of positive externality and negative externality	7.4.3
7.4.4	Positive and negative externalities of both consumption and production	7.4.4
7.4.5	Deadweight welfare loss arising from positive and negative externalities	7.4.5
7.4.6	Asymmetric information and moral hazard	7.4.6
7.4.7	Use of costs and benefits in analysing decisions	7.4.7
7.5.1	Short-run production function: fixed and variable factors of production; definition and calculation of total product, average product and marginal product; law of diminishing returns (law of variable proportions)	7.5.1
7.5.2	Short-run cost function: definition and calculation of fixed costs (FC) and variable costs (VC); definition and calculation of total, average and marginal costs (TC, AC, MC), including average total cost (ATC), total and average fixed costs (TFC, AFC) and total and variable costs (TVC, AVC); explanation of shape of short-run average cost and marginal cost curves	7.5.2
7.5.3	Long-run production function: no fixed factors of production; returns to scale	7.5.3
7.5.4	Long-run cost function: explanation of shape of long-run average cost curve; concept of minimum efficient scale	7.5.4
7.5.5	Relationship between economies of scale and decreasing average costs	7.5.5
7.5.6	Internal and external economies of scale	7.5.6
7.5.7	Internal and external diseconomies of scale	7.5.7
7.5.8	Definition and calculation of revenue: total, average and marginal revenue (TR, AR, MR)	7.5.8
7.5.9	Definition of normal, subnormal and supernormal profit	7.5.9
7.5.10	Calculation of supernormal and subnormal profit	7.5.10
7.6.1	Perfect competition and imperfect competition: monopoly, monopolistic competition, oligopoly, natural monopoly	7.6.1
7.6.2	Structure of the listed markets as explained by the number of buyers and sellers, product differentiation, degree of freedom of entry and availability of information	7.6.2
7.6.3	Barriers to entry and exit: legal barriers, market barriers, cost barriers and physical barriers	7.6.3

7.6.4	Performance of firms in different market structures: revenues and revenue curves, output in the short run and the long run, profits in the short run and the long run, shutdown price in the short run and the long run, derivation of a firm's supply curve in a perfectly competitive market, efficiency and X-inefficiency in the short run and the long run, contestable markets (features and implications), price competition and non-price competition, collusion and the Prisoner's Dilemma in oligopolistic markets, including a two-player pay-off matrix	7.6.4
7.6.5	Definition and calculation of the concentration ratio	7.6.6
7.7.1	Reasons for different sizes of firms	7.7.1
7.7.2	Internal growth of firms: organic growth and diversification	7.7.2
7.7.3	External growth of firms: integration (mergers and takeovers); methods of integration (horizontal, vertical (forwards and backwards) and conglomerate; reasons for integration; consequences of integration	7.7.3
7.7.4	Cartels: conditions for an effective cartel; consequences of a cartel	7.7.4
7.7.5	Principal-agent problem arising from differing objectives of shareholders/ owners and managers	7.7.5
7.8.1	Traditional profit-maximising objective of firms	7.8.1
7.8.2	An understanding of other objectives of firms: survival, profit satisficing, sales maximisation, revenue maximisation	7.8.2
7.8.3	Price discrimination (first, second and third degree): conditions for effective price discrimination; consequences of price discrimination	7.8.3
7.8.4	Other pricing policies: limit pricing, predatory pricing, price leadership	7.8.4
7.8.5	Relationship between price elasticity of demand and a firm's revenue: in a normal downward sloping demand curve; in a kinked demand curve	7.8.5
8.1.1	Application and effectiveness of measures to tackle different forms of market failure: specific and ad valorem indirect taxes, subsidies, price controls, production quotas, prohibitions and licences, regulation and deregulation, direct provision, pollution permits, property rights, nationalisation and privatisation, provision of information, behavioural insights and 'nudge' theory	8.1.1
8.1.2	Government failure in microeconomic intervention: definition of government failure; the causes of government failure; the consequences of government failure	8.1.2
8.2.1	The difference between equity and equality	8.2.1
8.2.2	The difference between equity and efficiency	8.2.2
8.2.3	The distinction between absolute poverty and relative poverty	8.2.3
8.2.4	The poverty trap	8.2.4
8.2.5	Policies towards equity and equality: negative income tax; universal benefits and means-tested benefits; universal basic income	8.2.5
8.3.1	The demand for labour as a derived demand	8.3.1
8.3.2	The factors affecting the demand for labour in a firm or an occupation	8.3.2
8.3.3	The causes of shifts in and movements along the demand curve for labour in a firm or an occupation	8.3.3
8.3.4	Marginal revenue product (MRP) theory: definition and calculation of marginal revenue product; derivation of an individual firm's demand for labour using marginal revenue product	8.3.4
8.3.5	Factors affecting the supply of labour to a firm or to an occupation: wage and non-wage factors	8.3.5
8.3.6	Causes of shifts in and movements along the supply curve of labour to a firm or an occupation	8.3.6

8.3.7	Wage determination in perfect markets: equilibrium wage rate and employment in a labour market	8.3.7
8.3.8	Wage determination in imperfect markets: influence of trade unions on wage determination and employment in a labour market; influence of government on wage determination and employment in a labour market using a national minimum wage; influence of monopsony employers on wage determination and employment in a labour market	8.3.8
8.3.9	The determination of wage differentials by labour market forces	8.3.9
8.3.10	Transfer earnings and economic rent: definition of transfer earnings; definition of economic rent; factors affecting transfer earnings and economic rent in an occupation	8.3.10
9.1.1	The multiplier process: definition of the multiplier; formulae for and calculation of the multiplier in a closed and open economy, with and without a government sector; calculation of average and marginal propensities to save (APS and MPS), average and marginal propensities to consume (APC and MPC), average and marginal propensities to import (APM and MPM) and average and marginal rates of tax (ART and MRT); national income determination using AD and income approach with the multiplier process; calculation of the effect of changing AD on national income using the multiplier	9.1.1
9.1.2	The components of Aggregate Demand (AD) and their determinants: consumption function (autonomous and induced consumer expenditure); savings function (autonomous and induced savings); autonomous and induced investment; the accelerator; government spending; net exports (exports minus imports)	9.1.2
9.1.3	Full employment level of national income and equilibrium level of national income: inflationary and deflationary gaps	9.1.3
9.2.1	Actual growth versus potential growth in national output	9.2.1
9.2.2	Positive and negative output gaps	9.2.2
9.2.3	The business (trade) cycle: phases of the cycle; causes of the cycle; the role of automatic stabilisers	9.2.3
9.2.4	Policies to promote economic growth and their effectiveness	9.2.4
9.2.5	Inclusive economic growth: definition of inclusive economic growth; impact of economic growth on equity and equality; policies to promote inclusive economic growth	9.2.5
9.2.6	Sustainable economic growth: definition of sustainable economic growth; using and conserving resources; the impact of economic growth on the environment and climate change; policies to mitigate the impact of economic growth on the environment and climate change	9.2.6
9.3.1	Definition of full employment	9.3.1
9.3.2	Equilibrium and disequilibrium unemployment (including hysteresis)	9.3.2
9.3.3	Voluntary and involuntary unemployment	9.3.3
9.3.4	The natural rate of unemployment: definition; determinants; policy implications	9.3.4
9.3.5	Patterns and trends in (un)employment	9.3.5
9.3.6	Mobility of labour: forms of labour mobility (geographical and occupational); factors affecting labour mobility	9.3.6
9.3.7	Policies to reduce unemployment and their effectiveness	9.3.7
9.4.1	Definition, functions and characteristics of money	9.4.1
9.4.2	Definition of the money supply	9.4.2
9.4.3	The quantity theory of money (MV=PT)	9.4.3

9.4.4	Functions of commercial banks: providing deposit accounts (demand deposit account, savings account); lending money (overdrafts, loans); holding or providing cash, securities, loans, deposits, equity; reserve ratio and capital ratio; objectives of commercial banks (liquidity, security and profitability)	9.4.4
9.4.5	Causes of changes in the money supply in an open economy: commercial banks as sources of credit creation and the bank credit multiplier; the role of a central bank; government deficit financing; quantitative easing; changes in the balance of payments	9.4.5
9.4.6	Policies to reduce inflation and their effectiveness	9.4.6
9.4.7	The demand for money: liquidity preference theory	9.4.7
9.4.8	Interest rate determination: loanable funds theory and Keynesian theory	9.4.8
10.1.1	Government macroeconomic policy objectives in terms of inflation, balance of payments, unemployment, growth, development, sustainability and the redistribution of income and wealth	10.1.1
10.2.1	The relationship between the internal value of money and the external value of money	10.2.1
10.2.2	The relationship between the balance of payments and inflation	10.2.2
10.2.3	The relationship between economic growth and inflation	10.2.3
10.2.4	The relationship between economic growth and the balance of payments	10.2.4
10.2.5	The relationship between inflation and unemployment: the traditional Phillips curve; the expectations-augmented Phillips curve (short- and long-run Phillips curve)	10.2.5
10.3.1	The effectiveness of different policies in relation to different macroeconomic objectives: fiscal policy (including Laffer curve analysis); monetary policy; supply-side policy (including market-based and interventionist policies); exchange rate policy; international trade policy	10.3.1
10.3.2	Problems and conflicts arising from the outcome of these policies	10.3.2
10.3.3	The existence of government failure in macroeconomic policies	10.3.3
11.1.1	Components of the balance of payments accounts: current account, financial account and capital account	11.1.1
11.1.2	The effect of fiscal, monetary, supply-side, protectionist and exchange rate policies on the balance of payments	11.1.2
11.1.3	The difference between expenditure-switching and expenditure-reducing policies	11.1.3
11.2.1	Measurement of exchange rates: the distinction between nominal and real exchange rates; trade-weighted exchange rates	11.2.1
11.2.2	The determination of exchange rates under fixed and managed systems	11.2.2
11.2.3	The distinction between revaluation and devaluation of a fixed exchange rate	11.2.3
11.2.4	Changes in the exchange rate under different exchange rate systems	11.2.4
11.2.5	The effects of changing exchange rates on the external economy using Marshall-Lerner and J curve analysis	11.2.5
11.3.1	Classification of economies in terms of their level of development	11.3.1
11.3.2	Classification of economies in terms of their level of national income	11.3.2
11.3.3	Indicators of living standards and economic development: monetary indicators (including real per capita national income statistics (GDP, GNI, NNI) and purchasing power parity); issues of comparison using monetary indicators; non-monetary indicators; composite indicators (Human Development Index (HDI), Measure of Economic Welfare (MEW) and Multidimensional Poverty Index (MPI)); the Kuznets curve	11.3.3

11.3.4	Comparison of economic growth rates and living standards: over time; between countries	11.3.4
11.4.1	Population growth and structure: measurement and causes of change in birth rate, death rate, infant mortality and net migration; optimum population; level of urbanisation	11.4.1
11.4.2	Income distribution: calculation of Gini coefficient and Lorenz curve analysis	11.4.2
11.4.3	Economic structure: employment composition (primary, secondary and tertiary sectors); pattern of trade at different levels of development	11.4.3
11.5.1	International aid: forms of aid; reasons for giving aid; effects of aid; importance of aid	11.5.1
11.5.2	Trade and investment	11.5.2
11.5.3	The role of multinational companies (MNCs): definition of an MNC; activities of MNCs; consequences of MNCs	11.5.3
11.5.4	Foreign direct investment (FDI): definition of FDI; consequences of FDI	11.5.4
11.5.5	External debt: causes of external debt; consequences of external debt	11.5.5
11.5.6	The role of the International Monetary Fund (IMF)	11.5.6
11.5.7	The role of the World Bank	11.5.7
11.6.1	The meaning of globalisation and its causes and consequences	11.6.1
11.6.2	The distinction between a free trade area, a customs union, a monetary union and full economic union	11.6.2
11.6.3	Trade creation and trade diversion	11.6.3

Index